D0996473

THE
# CONSTITUTION
## OF THE
## COMMONWEALTH
### OF
## AUSTRALIA
# ANNOTATED

# THE
# CONSTITUTION
## OF THE
# COMMONWEALTH
## OF
# AUSTRALIA
# ANNOTATED

*by*

**R D LUMB, LLM (Melb) D Phil (Oxon)**
Barrister and Solicitor of the High Court of Australia
Reader in Law, University of Queensland

*and*

**K W RYAN, BA LLB (Qld) Ph D (Cantab)**
Barrister-at-Law (Queensland)
Professor of Law, University of Queensland

# BUTTERWORTHS
Sydney — Melbourne — Brisbane
1974

AUSTRALIA:
BUTTERWORTHS PTY LIMITED
586 Pacific Highway, Chatswood 2067
343 Little Collins Street, Melbourne 3000
240 Queen Street, Brisbane 4000

NEW ZEALAND:
BUTTERWORTHS OF NEW ZEALAND LIMITED
New Zealand Law Society Building,
26-28 Waring Taylor Street, Wellington 1

ENGLAND:
BUTTERWORTH & CO (PUBLISHERS) LTD
88 Kingsway, London, WC2B 6AB

CANADA:
BUTTERWORTH & CO (CANADA) LTD
14 Curity Avenue, Toronto 374, Ontario

SOUTH AFRICA:
BUTTERWORTH & CO (SA) (PTY) LTD
152-154 Gale Street, Durban

National Library of Australia
Cataloguing-in-Publication entry

---

**Lumb, Richard Darrell**
The Constitution of the Commonwealth of Australia,
annotated/ by R. D. Lumb and K. W. Ryan.—Sydney:
Butterworths, 1974.
Index.
ISBN 0 409 37880 1.
ISBN 0 409 37881 X (Paperback).
1. Australia—Constitution. 2. Australia—Constitutional Law.
I. Ryan, Kevin William, joint author. II. Title.
342.94023.

---

Registered in Australia for transmission by post as a book.

Wholly set up and printed in Australia by
Hogbin, Poole (Printers) Pty. Ltd., Sydney
for the publishers Butterworths Pty. Limited

# PREFACE

A need has long been felt for a comprehensive text which will elucidate the Constitution section by section, one which would aid not only practitioners and law students, but also students in related disciplines, as well as those who are associated with the processes of government at all levels.

Quick and Garran's *Annotated Constitution* published in 1901 is, of course, the classic early text which even to-day provides understanding of many of the sections of the Constitution which have not received judicial exegesis. However, the course of judicial interpretation of the Constitution by the High Court, and the activities of the Federal Parliament in the last seventy years or so, have given a meaning to many sections of the Constitution which those learned authors could not have foreseen, restricted as they were to the sources of the raw material of the Convention Debates, and comparative constitutional material such as the United States Constitution and the decisions of the United States Supreme Court.

In this work we have attempted to produce a concise commentary on the constitutional text as it stands in 1973 with due deference to the demands of space and relevance. It is no longer possible in the compass of one book to give an exhaustive statement of the law on all the matters which are covered by the Constitution. In this respect, the book, while drawing assistance from many of the insights of Quick and Garran, does not deal with the material of the Convention Debates with which they deal and which has recently been treated in La Nauze's work, *The Making of the Australian Constitution*. Nor is there to be found in the work a comparison with the United States text and interpretation. With the passing of time the justices of the High Court have constructed an "indigenous" jurisprudence which departs in many respects from the United States framework. This is as much a matter of a different judicial technique as of a different text.

We feel that no commentary on the present state of the Constitution is complete without references to the provisions of statutes enacted under the authority of a particular head of power, or which relate to matters within the scope of particular sections of the Constitution, although it has not been our task to provide a comprehensive statement of the content of these enactments. Space has not permitted us to refer to all such statutes nor to all judicial decisions, but the footnotes contain sufficient citations to give a representative picture of judicial opinions on all the sections.

In a number of areas we have detailed the changes in interpretation of a particular provision through the various High Court decisions; in other areas early trends, which have at a later stage been rejected by the Court, are dealt with in a more perfunctory fashion.

In 1973 certain bills of constitutional significance were introduced by the Federal Parliament. These bills at the time of writing have not yet passed through both Houses. They are dealt with in Appendix 1.

Our thanks are due to the research assistants who have, over the years, helped in the preparation of the text, in particular to Mr A Heyworth-Smith BA LLB of the Queensland Bar, and to Messrs K G Berry BA, M J Kenny B Com, D J Lewis BA, G L Mann BA and G L Redlich BA. Our thanks are also due to the typing staff in particular, Mrs B Rogan, and the members of the publishers' staff, who have seen the manuscript through to completion.

Acknowledgement is made of a research grant received from the Australian Research Grants Committee which has greatly facilitated the preparation and production of the book.

R D LUMB

K W RYAN

*June 1973*

I was invited by Dr Lumb to become a co-author of this book at a stage when work on it was already well advanced. My contribution is limited to writing a commentary on the sections of the Constitution concerned with trade and taxation, and to offering suggestions on the text prepared by Dr Lumb. Credit for initiating work on the text, and for its final production, is due almost entirely to Dr Lumb

K W RYAN

# CONTENTS

Also by R D Lumb:

*The Constitution of the Australian States* (3rd ed) 1972, University of Queensland Press

*The Law of the Sea and Australian Off-shore Areas* 1966, University of Queensland Press

Also by K W Ryan:

*Manual of the Law of Income Tax in Australia* (3rd ed) 1972, The Law Book Company Limited

*An Introduction to the Civil Law* 1962, The Law Book Company Limited

# ABBREVIATIONS OF MAJOR WORKS CITED

Quick and Garran

> Quick J, and Garran R R, *The Annotated Constitution of the Australian Commonwealth* (Angus and Robertson, Sydney, 1901)

Wynes

> Wynes W A, *Legislative Executive and Judicial Powers in Australia* (Law Book Co Ltd, Sydney, 4th ed, 1970)

Howard

> Howard C, *Australian Federal Constitutional Law* (Law Book Co Ltd, Sydney, 2nd ed, 1972)

Lane

> Lane P H, *The Australian Federal System with United States Analogues* (Law Book Co Ltd, Sydney, 1972)

Essays

> Else-Mitchell R (Ed), *Essays on the Australian Constitution* (Law Book Co Ltd, Sydney, 2nd ed, 1961)

Nicholas

> Nicholas H S, *The Australian Constitution* (Law Book Co Ltd, Sydney, 2nd ed, 1952)

# TABLE OF CASES

# TABLE OF CASES

# TABLE OF STATUTES

## IMPERIAL

## COMMONWEALTH

# TABLE OF STATUTES

## NEW SOUTH WALES

## VICTORIA

# INTRODUCTION

(i) **Federation.**[1] The first steps towards a federation of the Australian colonies were taken as far back as 1849, at a time when discussions were taking place on the granting of responsible government to them. The Committee for Trade and Plantations (a sub-committee of the Privy Council), to which the Secretary of State for the Colonies, Earl Grey, had referred the question of the future government of the colonies, had, in its report, recommended that an intercolonial uniform tariff be established. The tariff would be subject to amendment by a general assembly which would be representative of the colonies. The assembly, in addition to its power over customs, would also have the power to deal with matters affecting relations between the colonies, such as posts, lighthouses, weights and measures, harbour dues. It would also have the power of creating an Australian Supreme Court as well as appropriating revenue in relation to the powers conferred upon it.

The Constitution Bill of 1850 which provided for the separation of New South Wales and Victoria included provisions along these lines, but because of opposition in England and Australia the provisions were dropped from the Bill. The first attempt to create a federal system had failed.

Nevertheless, an initiative was taken to introduce some co-ordination of executive powers when the Governor of New South Wales was appointed as Governor-General of all the Australian colonies (the Governors of the other colonies becoming Lieutenant-Governors). The scheme did not last for long and the title was discontinued in 1861.

Within the colonies themselves, various moves were made to promote the federal cause, for example, by the appointment of select committees in the two major colonies, New South Wales and Victoria, to consider the matter. However, intercolonial jealousies and opposition rendered these moves nugatory.

In one vital area—tariffs—some attempt had to be made to co-ordinate the policies of the colonies. As early as 1855 certain "free trade" arrangements had been made with respect to goods crossing the Murray, although these arrangements were not to last. There was, however, a legal fetter which prevented the colonies from granting concessions to one another which were denied to goods imported from abroad: the existence of Imperial legislation which prohibited differential tariffs. The *Australian Colonies Duties Act* which was passed in 1873 opened the way for such preferential arrangements. The trade policies of Victoria and New South Wales were, however, in conflict, with protectionism flourishing in Victoria, and, therefore, the possibility of a customs union or free trade area permitted by the Imperial Act was not realized.

In the 1870's external affairs and defence were issues which took root in the Australian consciousness: European colonization in the Pacific Islands near the Australian coastline had raised fears in Australian politicians. In 1883,

---

1 Quick and Garran, 79-261. Moore, *The Constitution of the Commonwealth of Australia* (2nd ed 1910), 17-64. La Nauze, *The Making of the Australian Constitution* (1972). Bennett, *The Making of the Commonwealth* (1971).

1

Queensland purported to annex New Guinea only to find its action to be overridden by the Imperial authorities at a later stage. A Victorian Royal Commission stressed the need for a united defence policy to deal with the dangers from military involvement in the region.

During the period there were a number of conferences of representatives of the colonies to consider the matters on which uniform Imperial legislation might be requested but with little result. As Moore points out, such conferences had no corporate legal status and the dissent of one colony prevented Australia from speaking with one voice to the Home Government.[2]

In 1883 a convention of the colonies was held in Sydney. On its agenda was the question of the federation of the Australasian colonies. From this convention came a recommendation for a limited federal authority which would have powers in relation to certain matters of common concern. In the following year the Australasian colonies (with the vital exception of New South Wales but including Fiji) requested the Imperial authorities to adopt the recommendation, and in 1885 the *Federal Council of Australasia Act* was enacted.

The Act constituted a Council consisting of representatives nominated by the colonies. It was to meet at least once every two years. When not in sesssion, a Standing Committee was to carry out executive functions on its behalf. The limited legislative powers of the Council comprised the following matters:

(a)  Relations of Australia with the Islands of the Pacific.
(b)  Prevention of the influx of criminals.
(c)  Fisheries in Australian waters beyond territorial limits.
(d)  Service and execution of process beyond a colony.
(e)  Enforcement of intercolonial judgments.
(f)  Extradition and criminal process beyond the confines of a colony.
(g)  Custody of offenders on board colonial ships outside territorial limits.
(h)  Matters referred to it by the Queen on the request of the colonies.
(i)  Matters referred to it at the request of two or more of the colonial legislatures.

The importance of the Act was to be seen in its provision for a legislature to legislate with regard to matters of common concern. Its defects included a lack of provision for an executive body (cabinet) or a court. A major defect was that membership was voluntary and in fact New South Wales never became a member. Hence it could be described as a confederal rather than a federal institution. It was not surprising, therefore, that as time went on other forms of intercolonial co-operation (eg, Premiers' Conference) overshadowed the work of the Council. In all, only nine Acts were passed by the Council.

One other important event to note was the passage of the *Imperial Defence Act* in 1888. The Act ratified an agreement reached between the Australian colonies and the Imperial Government whereby a contribution was to be made by the colonies towards the formation of an Australasian squadron. The basis for a common defence system was, therefore, established.

The time was now ripe for pushing ahead with the more ambitious plans for federation. Parkes, the New South Wales Premier, gave his support to the federal cause. In 1890 a conference of the seven colonies (including New Zealand) was held and a recommendation was made for the holding of a

---

2  Moore, op cit, 35-6.

national Australasian convention. The convention opened in Sydney on 2 March 1891. It consisted of seven representatives from each of the Australian colonies (appointed pursuant to resolutions passed by the Houses of Parliament of each colony).

It approved resolutions embodying the following principles:

(1) That the powers and privileges and territorial rights of the existing colonies should remain intact except in respect of such surrender as may be agreed upon as necessary and incidental to the power and authority of the new federal Government.

(2) No new State shall be formed by separation from another State, nor shall any State be formed by the junction of two or more States or parts of States without the consent of the legislatures of the States concerned as well as of the federal Parliament.

(3) That trade and intercourse between the federated colonies, whether by land carriage or coastal navigation, shall be absolutely free.

(4) That the power and authority to impose customs duties and duties of excise upon goods the subject of customs duties and to offer bounties shall be exclusively lodged in the federal Government and Parliament, subject to such disposal of the revenues thence derived as shall be agreed upon.

(5) That the naval and military defence of Australia shall be entrusted to federal forces under one command.

(6) That provision be made in the federal Constitution which will enable each State to make such amendments in its Constitution as may be necessary for the purposes of the federation.[3]

The convention approved the framing of a federal Constitution establishing

(1) A Parliament which shall consist of a Senate and a House of Representatives, the former consisting of an equal number of members for each colony, to be elected by a system which shall provide for the periodical retirement of one third of the members, so securing to the body itself a perpetual existence combined with definite responsibility to the electors, the latter to be elected by districts formed on a population basis and to possess the sole power of originating all Bills, appropriating revenue or imposing taxation.

(2) A judiciary consisting of a federal Supreme Court which shall constitute a High Court of Appeal for Australia.

(3) An executive consisting of a Governor-General and such persons as from time to time may be appointed as his advisors.[4]

Three committees were established to frame a Constitution containing these principles: one dealing with constitutional functions, the second with finance and the third with the judiciary. A drafting committee consisting of Griffith as chairman, Inglis Clark (who had presented an initial draft of a federal Constitution), Barton and Kingston prepared a draft incorporating the work of those committees. The draft Bill was then considered in full committee and then reported to the convention where it was adopted. Quick and Garran comment that:

in the first draft of 1891 the whole foundation and framework of the present Constitution was contained. Its general characteristics, as compared with the Constitution as it now stands, may be summed up in a few words. In the first place—as is natural in a first draft—it followed more closely in substance and in language, the literary models—American, Canadian and Australian—which were available to

---

3   Quick and Garran, 125.
4   Ibid.

the Convention. In the next place, it was in some few respects less essentially democratic in its basis—a circumstance which is also natural, in view both of the continuous development of democratic ideas, and of the more completely popular impulses of the later stages of the federal movement. And lastly, it was less definite and less elaborate in its treatment of some of the vexed problems—problems which had not yet been the subject of exhaustive discussions, and some of which had only been mooted in vague and general terms. The peculiarities of our railway development, the unique characteristics of our river system, the special difficulties arising out of our tariff policies and requirements, had not yet been adequately studied.[5]

The learned authors go on to point out also that "the problem of reconciling the representation of State interests with British principles of legislation and finance and of bringing in harmony the conflicting elements of State rights and national rights—in short of securing responsible government, legislative finality, the general predominance of the House of Representatives without killing federalism, was as yet incompletely solved."[6]

Before concluding its session the convention recommended that the Parliaments of the colonies make provision for the adoption by the people of the colonies of the draft Constitution and for subsequent approval by the Imperial Government.

The Bill was, however, "shelved". The Parkes Ministry went out of office in New South Wales, and the other colonies dealt with the Bill in a dilatory fashion. It was clear that there was a need to arouse the citizens of the colonies in favour of the federal cause.

The opportunity for doing this arose with the holding of a conference promoted by an influential body, the Australian Natives Association, at Corowa in 1893. On the motion of Dr. Quick a plan was adopted for popular election of delegates to a new convention. The conference produced a "groundswell" in favour of the federal movement. In 1895 a Premiers' Conference supported the proposal for a new convention. According to the programme approved, the convention was to consist of 10 delegates from each colony directly chosen by the electors. The draft Bill emanating from the convention was to be submitted to the electors at a referendum; if adopted in three or more colonies it was to be submitted to the Imperial Government for ratification.

An enabling Bill along these lines was drafted. This Bill in its essential features was passed by four colonial legislatures (New South Wales, Victoria, South Australia and Tasmania). In Western Australia, however, there was a substantial departure from the scheme; in place of popular election, the delegates were to be selected by both Houses sitting together. In Queensland the Bill was lost due to a lack of consensus between the northern, central and southern regions of the colony.

The elections for the convention were duly held and the delegates took their seats at the first session of the convention which commenced in Adelaide in March 1897, with Kingston being elected president and Barton (who had received more votes than another candidate) becoming leader of the convention.

Initially it was necessary to decide whether to adopt the 1891 Bill as the basis for discussion or to start afresh on a new draft. It was decided that in so far as the delegates had been chosen by the people to frame a constitution it would be better to start afresh. However, the draft Bill in Moore's words "was by common consent taken as the foundation of the work of the Convention.[7]

5   Ibid, 135-6.
6   Ibid, 136.
7   Op cit, 47.

As with the first convention, three committees were appointed. Their work was to be submitted to a drafting committee consisting of Barton, O'Connor and Downer. The draft was duly completed and submitted to the convention in April 1897. After discussion, the convention was adjourned to allow the colonial legislatures to consider the Bill. The legislatures sat and a number of amendments were suggested. The second session of the convention was held in Sydney in September and some amendments were made. The third session was held in Melbourne, commencing in January 1898.

At this session, compromises were reached on the vexed question of financial relations between the Commonwealth and States with the introduction of the Braddon clause providing for payment to the States of a certain proportion of the revenue from customs and excise duties, and also on a deadlock clause for resolving disputes between the House of Representatives and the Senate. The Bill was revised by the drafting committee and adopted by the convention in March 1898.

Under the terms of the enabling legislation, the Bill was to be submitted now to the electors in each colony.

Referenda were held in four colonies (Queensland not having been represented and Western Australia taking no steps at this stage to hold a referendum). In New South Wales significant opposition was encountered, this being directed particularly against the clauses providing for equality of representation in the Senate, and the financial clauses which were thought to favour the smaller States. There was also concern about the location of the seat of government.

The Bill was approved by majorities in Victoria, Tasmania and South Australia but failed to secure the minimum number of votes required by New South Wales legislation.

In the light of the agreement of the Premiers' Conference in 1895 that approval by three of the colonies was sufficient it was theoretically possible to submit the Bill to an Imperial Government. But the absence of approval from the largest State had clearly jeopardized the scheme and it would have not been practicable to have gone ahead at this stage. After a parliamentary election in that colony, certain modifications to the draft Bill were suggested by the Legislative Assembly. A Premiers' Conference (in which all six colonies participated) was held in Melbourne in January 1899, and agreement was reached on several amendments to the draft Bill. A further referendum was, therefore, necessary.

In June 1899 New South Wales, Victoria, South Australia and Tasmania approved the terms of the revised Bill and in September, Queensland finally came in to give its approval. No action was taken in Western Australia which hoped for concessions in favour of its special interests.

The next step was that the five colonial legislatures adopted addresses requesting its enactment by the Imperial Parliament. Delegates from the colonies went to England to confer on the Bill with the Law Officers and the Colonial Office. Minor amendments were made by the Imperial authorities to the covering clauses. The substantial matter in dispute was the question of appeals to the Privy Council. Under the original clause the jurisdiction of the Privy Council in relation to appeals from the High Court was limited to questions involving the public interest affecting another part of Her Majesty's Dominions.[8] This clause was not acceptable to the Imperial authorities:

---

8 Earlier versions of s 74 are to be found in La Nauze, *The Making of the Australian Constitution*, Appendix 6, 303-4.

ultimately a compromise was reached and the present wording of s 74 was agreed upon.

The Bill received the Royal assent on 9 July 1900. It was to come into force on a proclamation being made by the Queen. A referendum was held in Western Australia and a majority of the electors in that colony accepted the Bill, following which the Western Australian Parliament requested that it be included as an original State. Although provision was made for New Zealand to become an original State, that country did not do so.

The Commonwealth of Australia was proclaimed to come into existence on 1 January 1901, the proclamation being issued on 17 September 1900.

(ii) **Structure of the Constitution.** *The Commonwealth of Australia Constitution Act* consists of nine sections which are referred to as the covering clauses of the Constitution and which are mainly of a formal nature, although cl 5 (and possibly cl 8) have some continuing substantive effect.

The Constitution itself is contained in cl 9 of the Act. It is divided into eight chapters originally consisting of 128 sections but section 127, which provided that "In reckoning the numbers of the people of the Commonwealth, or of a State or other part of the Commonwealth, aboriginal natives shall not be counted", was deleted pursuant to a constitutional referendum held in 1967.[9]

Chapter I of the Constitution is headed "The Parliament" and consists of five parts. Part I is of a general nature and deals, *inter alia,* with the term of the Parliament, while Parts II and III contain provisions relating to the Senate and House of Representatives respectively: matters such as method of election, terms, and voting procedure are to be found in these Parts. Part IV consists of provisions which relate to both Houses (eg qualifications and disqualifications of members and parliamentary privilege).

The most important part is Part V, s 51 of which consists of 39 paragraphs or placita[10] relating to Commonwealth heads of power most of which are concurrent powers. The following section, s 52, contains a small list of powers which are expressly designated to be exclusive powers of the Commonwealth Parliament. Other sections in Part V deal with the relationship between the Houses and assent to Bills.

Chapter II of the Constitution (ss 61-70) deals with "the Executive Government". In this chapter are to be found provisions relating to the appointment of Ministers of the Crown and other matters relating to the administration of the affairs of the Commonwealth.

Chapter III is entitled "The Judicature" and consists of 10 sections: the size of the chapter does not, however, give a true indication of its importance. This part is the foundation for the elaborate structure of judicial review by the courts, for the strict separation of judicial power from the other powers and for the paramount role of the High Court both as a court of appeal from State Supreme Courts and other courts exercising federal jurisdiction, and as a tribunal of original jurisdiction in constitutional and various federal matters. But the role of the State courts in these matters is recognized by s 77 which empowers the federal Parliament to invest these courts with federal jurisdiction.

---

9   *Constitution Alteration (Aboriginals) Act,* No 55 of 1967.

10  On the use of this word to describe the paragraphs of s 51, see Dixon, *Jesting Pilate and Other Essays* (1965) 133.

"Finance and Trade" is the heading of Chapter IV, comprising ss 81-105. While a number of these sections were of a temporary nature expiring within a short period of federation, there is in this chapter a dominant limitation on both Commonwealth and State powers in s 92 which protects freedom of trade between the States. Also in this chapter is the power given to the Commonwealth to make grants to the States (s 96) which has turned out to be a vital basis for Commonwealth financial control.

Chapter V is entitled "The States" and contains certain important sections relating to State Constitutions and legislative power as well as an assertion of Commonwealth paramountcy where there is a conflict between Commonwealth and State legislative power (s 109). In this chapter are also to be found a small number of provisions protecting individual freedoms (ss 116, 117). These sections together with a few others (eg, s 80) are the only sections dealing with individual freedoms: there is no comprehensive Bill of Rights such as is to be found in the United States Constitution.

The remaining Chapters VI, VII and VIII contain only a small number of sections. Chapter VI entitled "New States" provides for the method of establishing new States, for the government of Territories, and for the alteration of boundaries. Chapter VII is a miscellaneous chapter of little importance except that it establishes the location of the seat of government. Chapter VIII consists of one section detailing the manner in which the Constitution may be amended.

(iii) **Imperial connexions.** The monarchical principle is recognized in a number of sections of the Constitution. The Queen is at the apex of the legislative structure (s 1). She is also the Chief Executive (s 61). In both cases, however, her powers are exerciseable by the Governor-General (ss 2, 61). Consequently in respect of the duties associated with the governmental structure, the Governor-General, acting on the advice of the Executive Council in most cases (see ss 62, 64), is the repository of federal executive authority.

There are other connexions between the Commonwealth and the United Kingdom. It was recognized in 1900, although not without some doubts,[11] that the Commonwealth of Australia—the union of federated States—would still continue to have the status of a "self-governing" colony although proposals to incorporate this status formally in the covering clauses were not proceeded with.[12] The consequence of this status was to subject the Commonwealth Parliament to the provisions of the *Colonial Laws Validity Act* and, therefore, to the paramountcy of Imperial legislation. This "colonial" status was also embodied in the doctrine of extraterritorial legislative incompetence which was applied to the Commonwealth in several early cases.[13]

Conventional practice after the First World War, recognized in the Balfour Declaration of 1926, gave birth to the doctrine of equality between members of the British Commonwealth. *Inter alia*, this conventional practice recognized that the Imperial Parliament would not enact legislation for a dominion without the latter's request and consent.[14] The *Statute of West-*

---

11  See O'Connell and Riordan, *Opinions on Imperial Constitutional Law* (1971) 398.
12  Quick and Garran, 347-52.
13  See, for example, *Union Steamship Co of New Zealand v Commonwealth* (1925) 36 CLR 130.
14  This was recognized in 1936, at the time of the abdication crisis, in relation to the royal succession: see Sawer, *Australian Federal Politics and Law,* vol 2 at 93.

*minster* 1931 gave statutory effect to this principle. It removed the extra-territorial and repugnancy limitations. The Commonwealth legislation adopting the Statute was not however passed until 1942, the adoption dating back to the commencement of the Second World War in 1939.

The Balfour Declaration had recognized the Crown as the "symbol of association" of the member countries: this implied a common citizenship and a duty of allegiance to the Monarch. With the admission into the Common-wealth of Nations of the new members, some with republican constitutions, after the Second World War, the symbol and its implications were modified—henceforth the Queen became Head of the Commonwealth with the option being open to each member in accordance with its constitution to adopt a monarchical or republican form of government.[15]

The passage of the *Royal Style and Titles Act* in 1953 was designed to regularize this position in Australia. According to the preamble to that Act, it was passed to give effect to the recommendations of a Prime Ministers' Conference that a new style for the Monarch be adopted reflecting the special position of the Sovereign as Head of the Commonwealth, and that each country adopt a royal style which was suitable to its particular circumstances but retained a substantial element common to all. The Royal style and titles set out in the Schedule to that Act are as follows: "Elizabeth the Second, by the Grace of God of the United Kingdom, Australia and Her other Realms and Territories Queen, and Head of the Commonwealth." So far as Australia is concerned, therefore, the Queen occupies a dual role as Head of the Common-wealth (of Nations) and Head of State of the Commonwealth of Australia, her relationship with the latter being the only one of constitutional significance (in relation to the exercise of executive powers by the Governor-General, her representative).[16]

The monarchical principle is also recognized in the oath of allegiance taken by public-office holders and in the duty of allegiance owed by all Australian citizens to the Monarch. The concept of allegiance to the Crown is an ancient one, and although it has emotional significance its precise legal significance is not easy to determine: it is most commonly associated with the crimes of treason and other offences against the state.[17]

Until 1948 the status of a British subject was the basic element in our nationality and citizenship legislation. But pursuant to recommendations of a Commonwealth Conference after the Second World War the concept of a "member country citizenship" was superadded to that of a British subject. The *Nationality and Citizenship Act* of 1948 recognized this when it provided for an Australian citizenship which automatically entailed being a British subject. A more radical "separateness" was effected by the *Citizenship Act* of 1969 which seems to attribute paramountcy to the concept of Australian citizen-ship.[18] An Australian citizen under this Act is now deemed to have the *status* of a British subject and not to be a British subject. This separateness may be further extended as a consequence of the *Immigration Act* 1971 of the United Kingdom which restricts the entry of Commonwealth citizens, and by the accession of the United Kingdom to the Treaty of Rome which confers distinct privileges on citizens of countries making up the European Economic Com-

---

15  See Wheare, *The Constitutional Structure of the Commonwealth* (1960), ch V.
16  It seems difficult, in the light of these changes, to retain the traditional concept of the "indivisibility" of the Crown.
17  See *Crimes Act* 1960 (Com).
18  *Citizenship Act* 1969 s 6.

munity in comparison with those held by other countries (including Commonwealth countries).

In the judicial sphere a connexion with the United Kingdom system is constitutionally entrenched in s 74 of the Constitution which recognizes the Judicial Committee of the Privy Council as the ultimate tribunal in the Australian hierarchy, although the *Privy Council (Limitation of Appeals) Act* of 1968, which was passed pursuant to the final paragraph of that section, has made the High Court the ultimate arbiter in constitutional (apart from *inter se*) matters and also other federal matters. Appeals are still available from State courts in matters of State jurisdiction under the *Judicial Committee Acts* of 1833 and 1844.

In April 1973 the Prime Minister (Mr Whitlam) after consultations with the Queen and the British Government announced that a change in the Australian Royal style and titles had been approved under which the phrases "Defender of the Faith" and the "United Kingdom" would be deleted. He also announced that legislation would be prepared "requesting and consenting to" the enactment of United Kingdom legislation abolishing appeals from State courts to the Privy Council. This has raised the question as to what restrictions cl 9 of the Statute of Westminster imposes on Commonwealth legislation enacted under cl 4 of the Statute.

(iv) **Federal nature.** The federal nature of the Constitution is proclaimed in the first paragraph of the preamble which refers to the agreement on the part of the people of the colonies to unite in "one indissoluble Federal Commonwealth under the Crown of the United Kingdom of Great Britain and Ireland, and under the Constitution hereby established.[19] In terms of the political structure, it is supported by the establishment of a bicameral legislature, one house of which—the Senate—is composed of persons directly chosen by the electors of each State. It is also supported by the requirement that the original States shall have equal representation, and by the prohibition of a dissolution of the Senate except under the conditions laid down in s 57.

As to legislative powers, the federal principle is worked out in detail in terms of the specification of Commonwealth legislative powers in ss 51 and 52, in terms of the preservation of the State Constitutions (s 106) and powers (ss 107, 108), and of the paramountcy of Commonwealth legislation (s 109). In a recent case Windeyer J pointed out that the theory of Australian federalism was, in particular, based on these last three sections.[20]

The federal structure also extends to the executive power (the general rule being that executive power follows legislative power)[21] and to the judicial power in respect of which an elaborate jurisprudence has been constructed to distinguish that power which can only be exercised by federal courts (or State courts invested with federal jurisdiction under s 77) and other categories of power (administrative, legislative) which must be exercised by organs of government separate from the courts.[22]

*Financial and trade relations.* Federalism not only implies a distribution of power between national and State organs of authority. It also implies some

---

19   As to whether the federal nature of the Constitution can be abolished, see discussion of s 128.
20   *R v Phillips* (1970) 44 ALJR 497 at 506; [1971] ALR 161 at 175.
21   See discussion of s 61.
22   See discussion of s 71.

control on legislative and executive practices discriminating between the States which might adversely affect the concept of basic equality which is the foundation of the federal system. This means, in particular, that the finance and trade powers of the Commonwealth must be strictly controlled to prevent any discrimination or preference between States which would distort the federal relationship. One of the main objects in federating was to eliminate the economic rivalry between the Australian colonies which was hampering the development of the Continent, and to ensure that it would not be reborn by a combination of State interests pushing discriminatory legislation through the federal Parliament. Consequently, the prohibitions attached to the financial and revenue clauses are designed to ensure that this does not occur. Thus the Commonwealth may not in any taxation law discriminate between States or parts of States (s 51 (ii)). Duties on the production or importation of goods must observe the norm of uniformity (ss 80, 90). No trade or revenue measure may give preference to one State or part thereof over another State or part thereof (s 99). Dominating the finance and trade chapter of the Constitution is s 92 which protects free trade between the States.

Financial relations between the Commonwealth and States during the early period of Federation were regulated by elaborate provisions relating to the distribution of revenue. The Braddon clause (s 87) provided for the return to the States of a proportion of the revenue which the Commonwealth raised from excise and customs duties, while s 94 provided for the payment to the States of the surplus revenue of the Commonwealth. The inadequacy of this latter section was demonstrated when the *Surplus Revenue Act* was passed and upheld in a subsequent judicial challenge.[23] The effect of this Act was to "debit" Commonwealth expenditure in relation to social services and coastal defence by appropriation to trust accounts of moneys required for these purposes, thus ensuring that there was no constitutional excess to be distributed.

In 1910, when the Braddon clause expired, a per capita system of State grants was established and this continued until 1927 when the Financial Agreement was made. Under this agreement a Loan Council was created to co-ordinate governmental borrowing. A concomitant aspect of the scheme was the taking over by the Commonwealth of State debts with a contribution by the Commonwealth towards their repayment as well as towards the redemption of future debts.[24] The Commonwealth had, besides making *per capita* grants to the States under s 96, also assisted States in special difficulties. In 1933 this assistance was placed on a more formal basis with the establishment of the Commonwealth Grants Commission to assess the so-called "claimant" States' needs.[25]

In 1942 the *Uniform Tax Case*[26] was decided. In upholding the power of the Commonwealth to make grants to the States on the condition that they abstained from levying their own income taxes the High Court had sanctioned the dominant power of the Commonwealth in the area of Commonwealth-State relations. Having lost de facto power to levy such tax, the States became dependant on annual Commonwealth grants (which until 1959 were described as reimbursement grants) for a large proportion of their revenue. A new basis

---

23    *New South Wales v Commonwealth* (1908) 7 CLR 179.
24    See s 105A.
25    *Commonwealth Grants Commission Act* 1933. See Hannan, ch IX, "Essays on the Australian Constitution", 247 at 256 *et seq.*
26    65 CLR 373.

for allocating the grants was agreed upon in 1959 and the general revenue grants of the Commonwealth to the States under s 96 became known as financial assistance grants, which have increased in amount from year to year. The last decade has also seen a vast increase in the special purpose or "tied" grants made by the Commonwealth to the States.[27]

As contrasted with the prohibitions attaching to the trade and taxation powers, there is nothing in s 96 to prevent the Commonwealth from giving special assistance to one or more States which is not given to all the States. The absence of a prohibition in s 96 against discrimination does of course in reality promote the federal principle in that it enables the Commonwealth to equalize the geographical, economic and other disabilities of the various States when special assistance is required.[28]

Financing of projects and other activities which do not fall directly within Commonwealth power is also possible under a liberal application of the appropriation power (s 81). The *Pharmaceutical Benefits Case*[29] did not express a concluded opinion on the meaning of the term "purposes of the Commonwealth", but the Commonwealth has on a number of occasions acted on the basis that the appropriation power is not tied to specific legislative powers. Rather it has adopted a wider view of its powers including the incidental power in promoting development work in the States (for example through the Snowy Mountains Engineering Corporation)[30] and in financing research activities, for example the Institute of Criminology[31] and in education and health matters. Legislative power over these matters is primarily within the legislative power of the States. The Territories power (s 122) provides a total basis for regulating these matters within the area of the territories.

*Legislative co-operation.* While it is often maintained that the federal division of power leads to legalistic interpretations which fetter the powers of the national Parliament over the Australian continent, it is often forgotten that certain national purposes which cannot be attained by the Commonwealth under its present legislative powers may yet be promoted through Common-wealth-State co-operation in the legislative, administrative or judicial spheres.[32]

The Constitution itself requires certain forms of co-operation (e g in the area of railway construction, borrowing of moneys, imprisonment of offenders against Commonwealth laws).

There is also s 51 (xxxvii) which empowers the Commonwealth Par-liament to make laws with respect to matters which are referred to it by the legislatures of one or more States. References have been made very sparingly, except in time of war.[33]

A common form of legislative co-operation is to be seen in the "pooling" or joint exercise of legislative powers. This has occurred particularly in the field of the marketing of primary products where it is desired to achieve price stabilization for a particular commodity. One example is the wheat stabilization scheme where the States have legislated with respect to the production and

---

27  See discussion of s 96.
28  See Hannan, op cit, 257.
29  *Attorney-General (Vic) ex rel Dale v Commonwealth* (1946) 71 CLR 237. See later discussion of s 81.
30  *Snowy Mountains Engineering Corporation Act* 1970.
31  *Criminology Research Act* 1971.
32  See generally *Report of the Senate Select Committee on Off-Shore Petroleum Resources* (1971), Appendix C, 739 *et seq.*
33  See s 51 (xxxvii).

sale of the commodity (intrastate commerce) while the Commonwealth has used its power under s 51 (i) to regulate the "overseas" incidents of the scheme.[34] Another example is the poultry industry stabilization legislation. The feature of this scheme is the control of marketing arrangements (and thereby price levels) by State authorities in co-ordination with Commonwealth taxing policy.[35]

Another interesting form of Commonwealth-State co-operation is to be seen in the coal industry legislation of the Commonwealth and the State of New South Wales the purpose of which is to ensure that sufficient coal is produced to meet the needs of New South Wales and the export trade and to promote friendly industrial relations (without the requirement of invoking the procedure specified in s 51 (xxxv)). Here the respective powers which have been utilized are the intrastate trade and industrial powers (State) and s 51 (i).[36]

Control of certain border rivers is vested in a Commission by the *River Murray Waters Act* 1915-1970. This legislation was passed to give effect to an agreement between the Commonwealth and the States of New South Wales, Victoria and South Australia. The Commission has the duty of supervising the utilization of the waters for irrigation and navigation purposes.[37]

"National development" is promoted within the territorial areas of the States by the Snowy Mountains Engineering Corporation, the successor to the Snowy Mountains Hydro-electricity Authority. The functions of the Corporation, which are set out in s 17 of the *Snowy Mountains Engineering Corporation Act* 1970, are to carry out investigations in relation to water resources, to design engineering works (in Australia or elsewhere), to supervise the construction of engineering works (in Australia or elsewhere) and to construct engineering works (*outside* Australia). Public works of this nature are recognized as generally falling within the legislative power of the States. Consequently, s 17 of the Act provides that a function of the Corporation is exercisable in relation to any matter with respect to which Parliament has power to make laws or in relation to a Territory. This amounts to heavy reliance on the incidental power. The omission of a reference to the specific head of power to which the work of the Corporation is related does raise the question of "sufficient nexus". Nevertheless it is open to any State which would require the assistance of the Corporation on any developmental work within its own territorial area to enact legislation giving approval to activities of the Corporation within that territory.[38]

Perhaps the most significant form of co-operative federalism practised in recent years is embodied in the *Petroleum (Submerged Lands) Act* 1967-1968 of the Commonwealth and the States. These Acts contain a common mining code which is applied to the maritime areas from low-water mark (but excluding internal waters) to the outer limits of the Continental Shelf. The

---

34   See the *Wheat Industry Stabilization Acts* 1968 (Com Aust States).

35   See *Poultry Industry Levy Act* 1965-1966, *Poultry Industry Levy Collection Act* 1965-1966, *Poultry Industry Assistance Act* 1965-1966 (Com). The State controls are exercised through various marketing Acts.

36   See *Coal Industry Act* 1946-1966 (Com); *Coal Industry Act* 1946-1965 (NSW).

37   See also *Dartmouth Reservoir Agreement Act* 1970.

38   See, for example, *Snowy Mountains Engineering Corporation (Queensland) Act* 1971 s 4.

law applicable to the area is the law in force in the adjacent State (including any federal legislation).[39]

*Administrative co-operation.* There are also various administrative arrangements between the Commonwealth and the States which involve co-ordination of policies. We have already noted the Loan Council established by the Financial Agreement. This body determines the amount and distribution of moneys to be raised by way of borrowing by both Commonwealth and States.

Another important body (but one which lacks a statutory charter and corporate structure) is the Standing Committee of Attorneys-General which examines the need for uniform legislation by the States and the Commonwealth (either in its capacity as a national legislature or as the exclusive legislative body for the Territories).

Other bodies which involve regular meetings of Commonwealth and State officials include the Premiers' Conference, the Agricultural Council, the Transport Advisory Council, and the Australian Minerals Council. Unlike the Loan Council, however, these bodies of Ministers are merely consultative bodies and have no power to reach binding decisions.

On the public service level there is also co-operation in a number of areas, for example, the use of common rolls for Commonwealth and State elections (provided for in the *Commonwealth Electoral Act* 1918-1973), the supervision of fishing activities (under the Commonwealth *Fisheries Act* 1952-1970), and the exchange of statistics under the *Statistics (Arrangements with States) Act* 1956-1958.

We have already mentioned the grants-in-aid schemes of the Commonwealth which enable the Commonwealth to contribute to the financing of many functions which fall within State responsibility. But in one sense these are not true forms of co-operation as a State must forego a grant made for specific purpose if it is not prepared to accept the conditions attached to the grant.

*Co-operation in the judicial sphere.* The Constitution itself specifically provides for the investment of State courts with federal jurisdiction. The *Judiciary Act* 1903-1969 is the pivotal Commonwealth Act which defines the conditions under which the jurisdiction may be exercised.[40]

*Intergovernmental immunities.* The federal Constitution contains a few provisions which define the powers of the Commonwealth and State Parliaments to legislate in a manner which affects the activities of each other. The most notable prohibition in this respect is s 114 which prohibits the Commonwealth and the States from taxing each other's property.

Nevertheless, it is clear that in order for the federal principle to work, some regulation of the powers of the legislatures in their relations *inter se* is necessary. The scope of intergovernmental immunities has become a matter for juristic construction worked out on the basis of a doctrine of federal implications which have been radically altered over the years.[41]

The early doctrine adopted by the High Court in *D'Emden v Pedder*[42] reflecting a contractual view of federation (and, therefore, inclined to uphold-

---

39   See Lumb, "The Off-Shore Petroleum Agreement Legislation" (1966) 41 ALJ 453.

40   See discussion of s 77.

41   See discussion of ss 51 (Introductory) and 106.

42   (1904) 1 CLR 91.

ing a wide doctrine of intergovernmental immunity) was rejected by the Court in the *Engineers Case*.[43]

But certain reservations were made in that case as to the ability of the Commonwealth to affect the States in certain ways. It was not until the *State Banking Case*[44] that the Court was given the opportunity to reaffirm that certain federal implications prevented the Commonwealth from enacting legislation discriminating against the States. Some doubt existed, however, as to whether the federal principle had a wider operation extending to Commonwealth laws of general application. In the *Pay-roll Tax Case*[45] several members of the Court conceded that the principle did have such a wider operation, but nevertheless they rejected the view that a taxation law of general operation could not be applied to the States. It would seem that only a Commonwealth law of general operation which struck at basic State functions or which discriminated against the States would fall foul of this principle.

As to Commonwealth immunity from State legislation, the area of immunity is much wider. The *Cigamatic Case*[46] is the major authority here. It suggests that a State cannot interfere with Commonwealth fiscal rights and probably all Commonwealth governmental functions as such. But it would seem that the general law in force in a State would still regulate activities of the Commonwealth (in the absence of any Commonwealth legislation affecting the situation) where the Commonwealth is engaging in ordinary transactions and activities, as, for example, by entering into a contract for the sale of goods.

(v) **Separation of powers.** The doctrine of the separation of powers has a long history in the British constitutional tradition. It is not, however, a strict doctrine involving the allocation of specific powers to defined functionaries. Rather it constitutes a general framework within which it is appropriate that general powers of legislating should be exercised by the legislature, administration of the law and affairs of State by the Executive, and interpretation of the law by the courts which should have an independent status.

As to the relationship between the legislature and the Executive, the development of the doctrine of responsible government in the eighteenth and nineteenth centuries involved a "fusion" of personnel whereby the members of the Government were required to hold seats in either House, with primary responsibility being to the popularly elected House. This in turn meant that delegation of law-making power to the Executive was not regarded as in breach of the doctrine, provided that the general authority of the legislature was not compromised, ie provided that there was no abdication of power as such, or delegation on matters of substance. In this respect the concept of the rule of law provides an important conventional basis for determining the types of activity appropriate to the Parliament and the Executive.[47]

The absence of a written constitution did allow for flexibility in terms of various aspects of the relationship, and it is in this respect that we find a fundamental difference between the British position and the position under the federal Constitution.

As to the federal Constitution, a general separation of powers is affected by the structure of, and specific sections of the Constitution. Thus legislative

43 (1920) 28 CLR 129.
44 *City of Melbourne v Commonwealth* (1947) 74 CLR 31.
45 *Victoria v Commonwealth* (1971) 122 CLR 353; [1971] ALR 449.
46 *Commonwealth v Cigamatic Pty Ltd* (1962) 108 CLR 372; [1963] ALR 304.
47 See Dicey, *Law of the Constitution* (9th ed 1939), 183-205.

power is by s 1 vested in the Parliament, executive power is by s 61 vested in the Queen and is exercisable by the Governor-General, and judicial power is by s 71 vested in the courts. We, therefore, have a written constitution which allocates "governmental" power between these organs.

To what extent does this distribution require that a particular part of a power (whether it be legislative, executive or judicial) be exercised *only* by the organ in which the general power is vested? It has, of course, always been recognized that the doctrine of incidental powers enables a body to exercise ancillary powers which though not partaking of the qualities of the main power, are nevertheless attracted to it for the purpose of assisting its exercise.[48] Among examples often cited are the power of the courts to make rules of court, the power of the legislature to punish for contempt of Parliament, and the power of the Executive to use quasi-judicial methods in the performance of its executive functions. Section 51 (xxxix) implicitly recognizes the validity of such "associations" of power.

Apart from this question, it is necessary to determine whether a particular organ can in any circumstances exercise the broad power which is allocated to another organ. In *Dignan's Case*[49] the High Court was called upon to determine the validity of the *Transport Workers Act* 1928-1929 which by s 3 empowered the Governor-General to make regulations with respect to the employment of transport workers, that phrase being defined to include waterside workers working on ships engaged in interstate and overseas trade. Various regulations had been made under the Act. The Act was challenged on the ground that it infringed the doctrine of separation of powers as incorporated in the Constitution.

Previous discussions of the High Court had upheld the right of the legislature to delegate to the Executive a broad law-making authority in particular areas.[50] But the effect of s 3 of the *Transport Workers Act* was even greater. In the words of Dixon J "it gives the Governor-General in Council a complete, although of course, a subordinate power over a large and by no means unimportant subject in the exercise of which he is free to determine from time to time the ends to be achieved and the policy to be pursued as well as the means to be adopted. Within the limits of the subject matter, his will is unregulated and his discretion unguarded. Moreover, the power may be exercised in disregard of other existing statutes, the provisions of which concerning the same subject-matter may be overridden".[51]

However, Dixon J was not prepared to hold that even this wide grant of power infringed the doctrine of separation. A statute, which conferred upon the Executive a power to legislate on some matter contained within one of the heads of legislative power conferred upon the federal Parliament, was to be characterized as a law with respect to that subject-matter. The distribution of legislative, executive and judicial powers did not prevent the Parliament from enacting such a law.[52]

Evatt J pointed out that the doctrine of responsible government qualified the doctrine of the separation of powers. The close relationship between the

---

48  See discussion of s 51 (xxxix).
49  *Victorian Stevedoring and General Contracting Co v Dignan* (1931) 46 CLR 73.
50  *Baxter v Ah Way* (1909) 8 CLR 626.
51  46 CLR 73 at 100.
52  Ibid, 101.

legislature and the Executive had to be borne in mind on any examination of the power of the legislature to delegate. If it were recognized that the legislature had no power to vest in the Executive a rule-making power, effective government would be impossible.[53]

The question arises as to whether there are any limits on the power of the Parliament to delegate. Dixon J considered that an invalid delegation might occur where there was "such a width or such an uncertainty of the subject-matter to be handed over that the enactment attempting it is not a law with respect to any particular head or heads of legislative power".[54] Evatt J found a limitation in the principle that it was not competent for the Parliament to abdicate its powers. A law passed by the Parliament "must answer the description of a law upon one or more of the subject-matters stated in the Constitution. A law by which Parliament gave all its law-making authority to another body would be bad merely because it would fail to pass this test".[55]

In the last resort, therefore, there is no ultimate conflict between the delegation of legislative power and the doctrine of the separation of powers. The reason is that, in Howard's words, ". . . Parliament retains ultimate control. The enabling Act may be repealed at any time. If it is repealed the Executive loses its subordinate legislative power . . . . Even while it remains unrepealed the Executive must keep within its terms. Regulations going beyond the scope of the enabling Act are invalid".[56] Moreover, wherever an Act confers power on the Executive to make regulations, then, unless a contrary intention appears, such regulations must be laid before both Houses which have a power of disallowance.[57]

*Judicial power.* When we turn to the place of the judicial power in the constitutional scheme we find that the doctrine of the separation of powers operates in full vigour, namely, as requiring a strict separation between that power, on the one hand, and the legislative and executive powers, on the other hand.

It has been consistently held by the High Court that the judicial power of the Commonwealth is exercisable only by the courts mentioned in s 71, namely, the High Court, other federal courts and State courts invested with federal jurisdiction. The result is that there is an asymmetry between the interpretation of the legislative and executive powers as compared with the judicial power—a fact which was recognized by Dixon J in *Dignan's Case*.[58]

The stated justification for this strict separation of the judicial power was explained by the Privy Council in the *Boilermakers Case*[59] as being based on the ground that "in a federal system, the absolute independence of the judiciary is the bulwark of the Constitution against encroachments whether by the legislature or by the Executive".[60]

---

53  Ibid, 117.
54  Ibid, 101.
55  Ibid, 121.
56  *Australian Federal Constitutional Law*, at 140. See also *Crowe v Commonwealth* (1935) 54 CLR 69; *Radio Corporation Pty Ltd v Commonwealth* (1938) 59 CLR 170; *Giris Pty Ltd v Commissioner of Taxation* (1969) 119 CLR 365; [1969] ALR 369.
57  *Acts Interpretation Act* 1901-1966 s 48.
58  46 CLR at 101.
59  *Attorney-General (Commonwealth) v R; Ex parte Boilermakers Society of Australia* (1957) 95 CLR 529.
60  Ibid at 540.

The two most common situations in which it has been found necessary to draw a distinction between judicial and non-judicial power are:

(a) Where some authority appointed otherwise than in accordance with the requirements of Chapter III is empowered by the Parliament to exercise judicial power,

(b) Where the federal Parliament confers a power on a State court.

As to (a) it has been held that the combined effect of ss 71 and 72 is that judicial power can only be vested in bodies which must be either federal courts, the personnel of which are appointed for life[61] or State courts exercising federal jurisdiction. Judicial power itself involves the exercise of an interpretative function by a tribunal which has the power of reaching a conclusive decision (which will usually mean that the tribunal can enforce its decision).[62] (On the other hand, quasi-judicial power can be exercised by bodies, the personnel of which are not appointed for life.) Furthermore, the decision in the *Boilermakers Case* permits no mingling of judicial and administrative power.[63] A federal court cannot, therefore, be invested with any power other than judicial, except to the extent that the other power is incidental to the exercise of its judicial power.[64]

As to (b), it has been held that the federal Parliament can only invest State courts with federal jurisdiction under ss 71 and 77. Federal jurisdiction has been equated with the exercise of the judicial power of the Commonwealth and, therefore, it is not competent to invest State courts with any non-judicial power.[65]

(vi) **The High Court and judicial review.** The High Court is invested with further jurisdiction by federal Parliament. Under various provisions of the *Judiciary Act* and also under particular statutes the High Court has received a statutory jurisdiction under s 76 in addition to its constitutionally vested jurisdiction under s 75. Pursuant to its power to make the jurisdiction of the High Court exclusive of that of the State courts, the federal Parliament has also stipulated in the *Judiciary Act* those matters which are within the exclusive jurisdiction of the High Court, and also the conditions under which the State courts may exercise federal jurisdiction in the non-exclusive matters.[66]

The High Court has also an appellate jurisdiction under s 73 from State Supreme Courts, federal courts and State courts invested with federal jurisdiction.

The judicial style of the High Court has been adverted to by many writers who stress the comparison between it and the judicial philosophy of the United States Supreme Court where broad considerations of policy often obtrude, particularly in the case of the interpretation of the Bill of Rights, the content of which is value-oriented.[67] In contrast, there are only a small number

---

61  *Waterside Workers' Federation of Australia v Alexander* (1918) 25 CLR 434.
62  See discussion of s 71.
63  See discussion of s 71.
64  A court may, however, be invested with jurisdiction to review an administrative decision provided that the grounds on which the review may take place are justiciable: see *Report of the Commonwealth Administrative Review Committee* (1971), ch 4.
65  *Queen Victoria Memorial Hospital v Thornton* (1953) 87 CLR 144.
66  See discussion of s 77.
67  The best study is Sawer, *Australian Federalism in the Courts* (1967). See, in particular, ch V, 52 *et seq.*

of individual rights enshrined in the Commonwealth Constitution and the interpretation given to these rights by the High Court has generally accorded with its approach to other sections of the Constitution: textually related, structurally controlled, with a tendency to avoid discussions of policies and social goals. In so far as it is a national court of appeal dealing with day-to-day civil issues more often than constitutional issues, it is natural that it has not constructed a judicial philosophy of government, or indeed of civil liberties, which can be traced through the cases. This is not to say that political or social assumptions are not to be found in High Court decisions. They lie, however, beneath the surface, and the legal techniques of interpretation which are used tend to prevent their overt formulation.[68]

The High Court's approach is probably best illustrated by its handling of what has been called the "characterization" question. This involves the approach which the Court takes to the question whether a Commonwealth or State law breaches the distribution of powers imposed by the Constitution, particularly to the question whether a Commonwealth Act is within a power conferred by s 51.

It can be said that the High Court has always been keenly aware of its vital role as the interpreter of the Constitution, and also aware of the inherent rigidity of a written constitution. While recognizing it as a statutory instrument and applying to it the canons of statutory interpretation, the Court has been concerned to make it work as an instrument of government. In the *Union Label Case*[69] Higgins J put it in this way: "We are interpreting a Constitution, a mechanism under which laws are made, and not a mere Act which declares what the law is to be." And in the *Bank Nationalization Case*[70] Starke J said: "The Constitution must not, therefore, be cut down by a narrow and technical construction, but must be given a large and liberal interpretation."

The need to give a broad and liberal construction to the provision conferring legislative power on the Commonwealth was strongly affirmed in the *Engineers Case*[71] (where the doctrine of implied prohibitions recognized in the early cases was rejected) and has generally been recognized by the High Court since. In the *Bank Nationalization Case*[72] Dixon J quoted with approval the following passage: "Where the question is whether the Constitution has used an expression in the wider or the narrower sense, the Court should, in my opinion, always lean to the broader interpretation unless there is something in the context or in the rest of the Constitution to indicate that the narrower interpretation will best carry out its object and purpose." However, different judges are likely to have different views as to how far the liberal approach should be pressed in particular cases. A good illustration is to be found in the case just cited in the judgments of Dixon J on the one hand, and Rich and Williams JJ on the other hand.[73]

Isaacs J used the phrase "the organic law of the Constitution" to describe the process whereby the Court was able to take cognizance of developments in thought, and new discoveries in the realm of science, in interpreting a word

---

68    Sawer, *op cit* at 57.
69    *Attorney-General (NSW) v Brewery Employés' Union of NSW* (1908) 6 CLR 469 at 612.
70    *Bank of New South Wales v Commonwealth* (1948) 76 CLR 1 at 298.
71    (1920) 28 CLR 129.
72    76 CLR at 332, citing O'Connor J in *Jumbunna Coal Mine v Victoria Coal Miners' Association* (1908) 6 CLR 309 at 367-8.
73    76 CLR at 256-8, 333-4.

or phrase in the Constitution.[74] But again the need to preserve fidelity to the written text may require the Court to desist from taking a "broad" step. One may contrast the decisions in the *Union Label Case*[75] and the recent case of *King v Jones*[76] with *Brislan's Case*.[77]

Hovering in the background is the federal principle which at least inhibits the Court from pushing to extremes a particular legislative power which would make a mockery of the distribution of powers effected by the Constitution.

One common method of formulating a test of invalidity for the exercise of legislative power is to ask whether the Act is "in pith and substance" a law with respect to a particular head of power conferred on the Commonwealth Parliament by the Constitution. But this is but one way of expressing the need for the Court to determine the characteristics of the Act and to see whether the head of power covers those characteristics. Other ways of expressing the question are: what is the primary subject-matter dealt with by the Act? What is its true nature?

In determining what is the "pith and substance" of the Act, the primary subject of the Court's examination is, of course, the text of the Act itself. But as with any question of statutory interpretation, the Court is entitled to look at the object to which the Act is directed. This requires some examination of the circumstances which gave rise to the Act and its "social" setting. Of course this immediately creates a tension between the historical-textual approach and the "developing concept" or organic approach mentioned earlier.

The Court has not, however, allowed the use of material such as the convention debates to directly determine the meaning of a phrase or concept.[78] Likewise, it has, apart from a few exceptional cases, not allowed the presentation of evidence to back up a constitutional argument,[79] although under the *Judiciary Act* this is possible. It is true that many of the heads of power contained in the Constitution present no great difficulty of interpretation or characterization, eg, copyright, bankruptcy. They represent fairly well-recognized commercial or legal categories, though, as can be seen in several cases, there may be a doubt as to the "penumbra" or borderline areas covered by the particular category.

But several powers, in particular defence, raise more difficult questions. This is because the Court must look not only at the terms of the legislation but also at its purpose in advancing the defence of the country, and that purpose may vary in the light of the changing circumstances in which the

---

74  The application of this principle of interpretation is to be found, *inter alia*, in his dissenting judgment in the *Union Label Case* (1908) 6 CLR 469 at 553 *et seq*.

75  (1908) 6 CLR 469.

76  (1972) 46 ALJR 524: the word "adult" in s 41 of the Constitution is to be construed in the light of the meaning which it had in 1901.

77  *R v Brislan; Ex parte Williams* (1935) 54 CLR 262.

78  See Brazil, "Legislative History and the Interpretation of Statutes", (1961) 4 UQLJ 1 at 16 *et seq*.

79  See *Breen v Snedden* (1961) 106 CLR 406 at 412; [1962] ALR 340 at 343 (Dixon CJ); *Sloan v Pollard* (1947) 75 CLR 445; *Jenkins v Commonwealth* (1947) 74 CLR 400. See also Holmes, "Evidence in Constitution Cases" (1949) 23 ALJ 235; Brazil, "The Ascertainment of Facts in Constitutional Cases" (1970) 4 Fed LR 65.

Commonwealth may find itself.[80] Defence in time of war is quite different from defence in time of peace.

It is not only the defence power which is seen to encompass an expanding or potential area of operation which may be adapted to the needs of the times. The history of the arbitration power shows how the Court has fashioned that power to become a potent source for the settlement of industrial disputes, particularly in relation to the extended meaning given to the words "dispute" and "interstate" which are requisite elements to the operation of the Commonwealth power.[81]

Although "taxation" is a well-recognized type of governmental action, it raises special difficulties in the constitutional sphere because of the many ways in which it may be imposed and of the many indirect results which it may be used to produce. For example, business activity may be directly affected by company taxation (s 51 (ii)) or excise duties (s 90).[82] Customs and excise duties may be designed not merely to raise revenue but to protect local industries from overseas competition.

Although the Court will disregard indirect effects in characterizing a law enacted under this head, it will nevertheless be prepared to examine the substance of the Act to determine whether it is in reality a law with respect to taxation.[83] Although the majority judgment in the *Barger Case* was coloured by a particular doctrine of Commonwealth-State relations which was later rejected in the *Engineers Case*[84] the actual decision on the taxation power has never been overruled.[85]

Two other powers which, in particular, offer room for differing interpretations are the external affairs[86] and corporations[87] powers.

With regard to the individual rights and liberties guaranteed by the Constitution, the tendency has been for the Court not to adopt the same liberal attitude to their construction as has been adopted towards affirmative grants of power. This can be seen in the interpretation of s 92 under which matters which are incidental or conducive to interstate trade and commerce have been held not to be within the scope of the immunity accorded by that section.[88] The protection of the right of trial by jury has turned out to be nugatory[89] and the protection against discrimination on the basis of State residence has remained ineffective under early High Court interpretations.[90]

On the other hand, the protection of certain categories of professional people from civil conscription has been interpreted in a generous way by the High Court.[91]

---

80  See the judgment of Dixon J in *Stenhouse v Coleman* (1944) 69 CLR 457 at 471.
81  See discussion of s 51 (vi).
82  The concept of excise, too, has been greatly expanded in the *Receipt Duties Case*. See discussion of s 90.
83  *R v Barger* (1908) 6 CLR 41.
84  (1920) 28 CLR 129.
85  But see *Fairfax v Commissioner of Taxation* (1965) 114 CLR 1; [1966] ALR 1073.
86  See discussion of s 51 (xxix).
87  See discussion of s 51 (xx).
88  See discussion of s 92.
89  See discussion of s 80.
90  See discussion of s 117.
91  See discussion of s 51 (xxiiiA).

*Locus standi.* In so far as many challenges to the constitutionality of legislation occurring in the original jurisdiction of the High Court are actions for a declaration that the impugned legislation is invalid it is necessary to establish what interest is required in order for a party to institute proceedings.

It is established that the Attorney-General of a State (in relation to an action against the Commonwealth) or the Attorney-General of the Commonwealth (in relation to an action against a State) has a sufficient interest for the purposes of instituting proceedings on behalf of the political community which he represents. Thus in the *Pharmaceutical Benefits Case* it was said: "It is the traditional duty of the Attorney-General to protect public rights and to complain of excesses of power bestowed by law and in our Federal system the result has been to give the Attorney-General of a State a locus standi to sue for a declaration wherever his public is or may be affected by what he says is an *ultra vires* act on the part of the Commonwealth or of another State".[92]

The basis for the suit is that the Attorney-General is protecting the rights of the general public, or is intervening to protect the rights of the State or Commonwealth Crown as the case may be.[93]

The action may be instituted by the Attorney-General in his own name (after obtaining the consent of the Cabinet) or it may be an *ex relatione* action at the request of a member or members of the public. There is, however, no compulsion on the Attorney-General to give his fiat at the request of a member of the public.

If a member of the public wishes to challenge the constitutionality of legislation he must show that a private interest of his own has been infringed or will be infringed by the legislation. General "taxpayer" actions are, therefore, not sustainable without the fiat of the Attorney-General.[94]

*Effect of judicial review.* A judicial declaration that a statute is *ultra vires* is, in effect, a declaration that it is not a law. It follows, therefore, that any action taken in pursuance of it or in reliance on it is not, to that extent, authorized by law. Although the making, or the administration of, an invalid "law" does not *in itself* give rise to a cause of action at law on the part of any person who claims to be adversely affected, it is clear that, in so far as action taken in reliance on the law constitutes a legal wrong for which a remedy is available in the absence of lawful justification, then the invalidity of the "law" destroys the defence open to the person acting according to it.[95]

However, any money paid in pursuance of legislation accepted as valid at the time the payment was made is not recoverable, in the event of the legislation being subsequently held invalid, under a general common law principle that money paid under a *mistake of law* is irrecoverable, except in cases where it is paid under compulsion.[96]

*Severance.* When part only of a statute or other instrument is held invalid, the question arises whether the remainder of the instrument can be severed from the invalid portions and continue to operate. The question arises in two distinct types of cases: (i) where a provision expressed in general terms is

---

92 (1945) 71 CLR 237 at 272.
93 Wynes, 420.
94 See *Anderson v Commonwealth* (1932) 47 CLR 50; *Pye v Renshaw* (1951) 84 CLR 58. Cf, *Crouch v Commonwealth* (1948) 77 CLR 339.
95 See *James v Commonwealth (No 2)* (1939) 62 CLR 339.
96 *Mason v State of New South Wales* (1959) 102 CLR 108.

invalid as including within its operation subject-matters or areas or persons, etc., which are beyond the power of the legislature in question, but would be valid if limited to a subject-matter or area or class of persons, etc., within the power of the legislature; (ii) where a provision is *ultra vires* whether read as applying generally or only to particular matters, areas or persons, etc. The problem of severability in the first type of case is: can the provision be read down so as to confine its operation within the powers of the legislature? For example, in the case of a State law applying in terms extraterritorially as well as within the State itself, can it be read down so as to give it a territorial application only and so to make it valid? The problem in the second type of case is: can the invalid provisions (whether they are parts, divisions, sections, subsections, or merely words or phrases) be separated from the remainder of the law so as to make the remainder a valid law?

The general presumption is that a legislative instrument is intended to have effect *as a whole* so that if part of it is held to be invalid, the whole is invalid.

This presumption, however, must give way to the intention of the legislature as expressed in the particular legislation in question. The general presumption against severability is, in fact, reversed in practically all cases in Australia today by virtue of severability clauses.[97]

However, severability clauses themselves only raise a presumption of the independence and severability of the provisions of a legislative instrument, rebuttable if "some positive indication of interdependence appears from the text, context, content or subject-matter of the provisions".[98] In particular, the valid provisions, when severed, must constitute a complete intelligible law capable of execution as it stands; otherwise the whole must fail. Furthermore, the whole must fail if the effect of severance would be to make a *substantially different law* from that which was enacted. Or, as Rich, Starke and Dixon JJ said in the *ARU Case*, "the court cannot separate the woof from the warp and manufacture a new web".[99]

(vii) **Amendment of the Constitution.** Under s 128 the procedure laid down for admendment of the Constitution involves the initiation of the amending Bill by Parliament and then ratification at referendum in all the States. For a proposal to become law it must be approved by a majority of all the electors voting and also by a majority of the electors voting in four States.

Unlike the United States Constitution, there is no alternative procedure for holding a constitutional convention to propose amendments.

Nevertheless, a convention does seem to be an important forum for arriving at a consensus on major reforms to the Constitution. In 1972 the Committee of Commonwealth and State Attorneys-General took the initial steps for convening a convention.[1] It is clear that any resolutions issuing from such a convention would have no legally binding force, but they would have a

---

97    See *Acts Interpretation Act* 1901-1966 ss 15A, 46 (b).

98    *Australian National Airways Pty Ltd v Commonwealth* (1946) 71 CLR 29 at 92 (Dixon J).

99    *Australasian Railways Union v Victorian Railways Commissioner* (1930) 44 CLR 319 at 386. See also *Pidoto v State of Victoria* (1943) 68 CLR 87 at 107-11 (Latham CJ); *R v Poole* (1939) 61 CLR 634 at 651-2 (Dixon J); *Huddart Parker Ltd v Commonwealth* (1931) 44 CLR 492 (Dixon J); *Strickland v Rocla Concrete Pipes Ltd* (1971) 45 ALJR 485.

1    The convention, however, is not of the statutory type providing for elected representatives as was the 1897-8 convention.

powerful persuasive effect so far as the Commonwealth (the initiating body under s 128) is concerned.

In the past there have been two major reviews of the Constitution, one by a Royal Commission (consisting mainly of parliamentarians) in 1929,[2] the other by an all-party committee of the federal Parliament in 1959.[3] The 1929 review was rather an inconclusive affair although it did contain a commitment to the preservation of the federal system. The 1959 review recommended an increase in Commonwealth powers over a number of areas—corporations, restrictive trade practices, scientific research, nuclear energy and a number of other economic areas (including capital issues). However, it made no attempt to deal with the vexed question of federal-State financial relations. The committee merely noted its belief that a conference of the political leaders of the Commonwealth and States was necessary to discover whether any substantial adjustment should be made to these relations.[4]

Proposals for constitutional reform which are the subject-matter of disagreement between the major parties have great difficulty in securing the necessary approval under s 128. A study of the referenda shows that the majority of proposals have been rejected, most of these involving recommendations for increased Commonwealth powers. Only six proposals have secured the necessary majorities.[5]

---

2  *Report of the Royal Commission on the Constitution* (1929).
3  *Report of the Joint Parliamentary Committee on Constitutional Review* (1959).
4  Ibid, 21.
5  See discussion of s 128. As to the areas in which constitutional revision might be appropriate, see Durack and Wilson, "Do we Need a New Constitution for the Commonwealth?", (1967-8) 41 ALJ 231.

# COMMONWEALTH OF AUSTRALIA CONSTITUTION ACT

## (63 & 64 VICTORIA, CHAPTER 12)

*An Act to constitute the Commonwealth of Australia*

[*9th July 1900*]

PREAMBLE

WHEREAS *the people of New South Wales, Victoria, South Australia, Queensland, and Tasmania, humbly relying on the blessing of Almighty God, have agreed to unite in one indissoluble Federal Commonwealth under the Crown of the United Kingdom of Great Britain and Ireland, and under the Constitution hereby established:*

*And whereas it is expedient to provide for the admission into the Commonwealth of other Australasian Colonies and possessions of the Queen:*

The rule is that the preamble is not part of the Act and can only be used as an aid in interpretation in resolving ambiguities in the text.

The preamble of the Constitution Act refers to the popular referenda held in five of the six original colonies which led to the agreement on the part of the people of these colonies to accept the new federal Constitution. The reference to an "indissoluble Federal Commonwealth" raises the question, to be discussed later,[1] whether an amendment to the Constitution, purporting to abolish its federal nature, would be valid.

ENACTING WORDS

*Be it therefore enacted by the Queen's most Excellent Majesty, by and with the advice and consent of the Lords Spiritual and Temporal, and Commons, in this present Parliament assembled, and by the authority of the same, as follows:—*

SHORT TITLE

**1.** *This Act may be cited as the Commonwealth of Australia Constitution Act.*

The Imperial Act establishing the Constitution consists of nine clauses called the covering clauses, the ninth of which contains the Constitution itself.[2] The description of the new political organism established by the Act as the "Commonwealth of Australia" prevailed over alternative titles suggested, such as "United Australia", "Federated Australia", "the Australian Dominion", "Federated States of Australia". It is a general political term which, as Quick and Garran point out, became associated with the terms "State", "realm", "community", "republic", "nation". They add: "Some authorities have described

---

1 See discussion of s 128. The question of the secession of a State is also discussed.
2 The question whether s 128 permits the amendment of the first eight clauses is discussed under s 128.

it as synonymous with league, alliance, coalition, confederacy, and confederation".[3] Applied to Australia it describes "the new political community created by the union of the people and of the colonies of Australia".[4]

ACT TO EXTEND TO THE QUEEN'S SUCCESSORS

**2.** *The provisions of this Act referring to the Queen shall extend to Her Majesty's heirs and successors in the sovereignty of the United Kingdom.*

This is a purely formal section which gives recognition to the constitutional practice that the Crown is a corporation sole and, therefore, that the provisions referring to the Monarch of the time (Queen Victoria) apply to her heirs and successors (whether male or female).

PROCLAMATION OF COMMONWEALTH

**3.** *It shall be lawful for the Queen, with the advice of the Privy Council, to declare by proclamation that, on and after a day therein appointed, not being later than one year after the passing of this Act, the people of New South Wales, Victoria, South Australia, Queensland, and Tasmania, and also, if Her Majesty is satisfied that the people of Western Australia have agreed thereto, of Western Australia, shall be united in a Federal Commonwealth under the name of the Commonwealth of Australia. But the Queen may, at any time after the proclamation, appoint a Governor-General for the Commonwealth.*

The force of this section is now spent. Western Australia approved the new Constitution and with the other five States were united in the federal Commonwealth on 1 January 1901, the day appointed by Royal proclamation.

COMMENCEMENT OF ACT

**4.** *The Commonwealth shall be established, and the Constitution of the Commonwealth shall take effect, on and after the day so appointed. But the Parliaments of the several colonies may at any time after the passing of this Act make any such laws, to come into operation on the day so appointed, as they might have made if the Constitution had taken effect at the passing of this Act.*

The Commonwealth was established on the date appointed and the Constitution took effect at the same time.

OPERATION OF THE CONSTITUTION AND LAWS

**5.** *This Act, and all laws made by the Parliament of the Commonwealth under the Constitution, shall be binding on the courts, judges, and people of every State and of every part of the Commonwealth, notwithstanding anything in the laws of any State; and the laws of the Commonwealth shall be in force on all British ships, the Queen's ships of war excepted, whose first port of clearance and whose port of destination are in the Commonwealth.*

**"This Act, and all laws made by the Parliament of the Commonwealth under the Constitution, shall be binding on the courts, judges, and people of every State and of every part of the Commonwealth, notwithstanding anything in the laws of any State"**

This part of cl 5 affirms the supremacy of the Constitution and laws made under it throughout the Commonwealth (States and Territories). In association with other sections (eg, s 109) it embodies the doctrine that State Constitu-

---

3   *Annotated Constitution*, 311-2.
4   Ibid, 312.

tions and State laws are, to the extent to which they are inconsistent with the Commonwealth Constitution and laws made under it, inoperative.[5] The duty of obedience is cast on the citizens and officials throughout the Commonwealth, and State courts (not only federal courts) are invested with the jurisdiction to declare unconstitutional any legislation (from whatever source) which contravenes the Constitution.[6]

**"and the laws of the Commonwealth shall be in force on all British ships, the Queen's ships of war excepted, whose first port of clearance and whose port of destination are in the Commonwealth"**

Initially the power vested in the Commonwealth under ss 51 (i) and 98 of the Constitution to make laws relating to navigation and shipping was, according to Quick and Garran, restricted to "making laws applicable to the Commonwealth and operative within the three-mile limit all around the ocean boundary of the Commonwealth".[7] This, of course, was in accordance with the doctrine that the laws of a colony did not have an extraterritorial operation.[8] Clause 5 was, therefore, intended to extend the power of the Commonwealth to affect matters, events and persons associated with, occurring or being on British ships engaged in a voyage of the nature specified outside territorial waters.

In several early cases it fell to the High Court to interpret the meaning of cl 5. In *Merchant Service Guild v Currie & Co*[9] it was held that a ship trading between Australia, Calcutta and South Africa did not have a first port of clearance and a port of destination in Australia. Likewise in *Clarke v Union Steamship Co*[10] a ship registered outside the Commonwealth but engaged in regular trading between Sydney and San Francisco was held to fall outside the clause. The ship was engaged in taking freight and passengers to the United States from where it returned to Sydney with fresh cargo and new passengers.

However, in *Merchant Service Guild v Steamships' Owners' Association*[11] the High Court was prepared to accept that a "round" voyage involving journeys to ports outside Australia could come under cl 5. In this case the ships concerned were engaged in carrying cargo to Pacific Island and New Zealand ports, returning either with ballast or new cargo to Australia after intermediate trips between those ports.[12]

The view of Isaacs J, which was accepted by the majority of the Court, was that the words "first port of clearance and port of destination" indicated the beginning and end of an actual voyage which was in fact intended at the time of the commencement of the voyage, and that the ship's papers were not

---

5   See *Attorney-General for Queensland v Attorney-General for the Commonwealth* (1915) 20 CLR 148 at 172; *Clyde Engineering Co v Cowburn* (1926) 37 CLR 466 at 488, 497.
6   See *Baxter v Commissioner of Taxation* (NSW) (1907) 4 CLR 1087 at 1125, 1136.
7   *Annotated Constitution*, 361.
8   See below discussion of s 51. See also *Australian Steamships Pty Ltd v Malcolm* (1915) 19 CLR 298 at 324.
9   (1908) 5 CLR 737.
10  (1914) 18 CLR 142.
11  (1913) 16 CLR 664.
12  See also on this question *Merchant Service Guild v Commonwealth Steamship Owners' Association* (1906) 1 CAR 1.

conclusive as to what the voyage was.[13] Isaacs J pointed out that the word
"clearance" could denote either the authorization for a departure or a document (such as a customs certificate) evidencing that authority.[14] As to the
meaning of the phrase "port of destination", the ship's port of destination was
not mentioned in her official papers for the purpose of authorizing the voyage,
but for the purpose of recording what the master asserted was his intention at
the beginning of the voyage.[15] In both cases, therefore, a court was not precluded by the documents from examining the real and bona fide intention of
the master.

The vessels to which cl 5 is directed are British vessels (apart from navy
vessels). The word "British" is to be given a wide meaning as indicating ownership by British subjects[16] and not merely registration in the British registry.
Royal Navy vessels are, of course, subject to the exclusive jurisdiction of Her
Majesty's Government.

With the passage of the *Statute of Westminster* and the abolition of the
extraterritorial limitations on the Commonwealth Parliament, the question
arises as to the operative effect today of this part of cl 5. In *R v Foster;
Ex parte Eastern & Australian Steamship Co*[17] it was held that s 51 (xxxv)
conferred power to make awards with respect to conditions on vessels trading
between Australia and foreign ports even though they did not have a final
port of clearance and port of destination in Australia. The courts, therefore,
will examine the nature of the power conferred by a particular paragraph of
s 51 or other sections of the Constitution without regard to the old doctrine of
extraterritorial limitation; and provided that the legislation is intended to
operate extraterritorially, whether on ships or elsewhere, it will be upheld as
a valid exercise of Commonwealth power. Therefore, legislation may affect the
working conditions of Australian seamen on vessels trading between Australian
and foreign ports.[18] In *Foster's Case* Windeyer J expressed the view that the
only effect of cl 5 after the *Statute of Westminster* is to aid in the interpretation
of Commonwealth legislation.[19]

## DEFINITIONS

**6.** *"The Commonwealth" shall mean the Commonwealth of Australia as
established under this Act.*

*"The States" shall mean such of the colonies of New South Wales, New
Zealand, Queensland, Tasmania, Victoria, Western Australia, and South
Australia, including the northern territory of South Australia, as for the time
being are parts of the Commonwealth, and such colonies or territories as may
be admitted into or established by the Commonwealth as States; and each of
such parts of the Commonwealth shall be called "a State."*

*"Original States" shall mean such States as are parts of the Commonwealth
at its establishment.*

---

13 16 CLR at 695 *et seq.* Cf Barton J in the same case at 684-5, who considered
that the port of destination was the port for which the ship was bound as stated
in the entry outwards, shipping bill or manifest.
14 Ibid, 696.
15 Ibid, 696-7.
16 Ibid, 693.
17 (1959) 103 CLR 256.
18 Of course, from the point of view of international law no jurisdiction can
(subject to certain limited exceptions) be exercised over a foreign vessel exercising the freedom of the high seas.
19 103 CLR at 309. See also discussion of s 98.

The effect of this clause is self-explanatory. It distinguishes a class of political entities of the Federation, called "States", from others which have received the name of "Territories".[20] Secondly, it has the effect of distinguishing original States from those which may, at some future time, be admitted to the Federation as States.

## Repeal of Federal Council Act

**7.** *The Federal Council of Australasia Act, 1885, is hereby repealed, but so as not to affect any laws passed by the Federal Council of Australasia and in force at the establishment of the Commonwealth.*

*Any such law may be repealed as to any State by the Parliament of the Commonwealth, or as to any colony not being a State by the Parliament thereof.*

The Acts passed by the Federal Council were nine in all. All of these have become inoperative by lapse of time, have been superseded by inconsistent Commonwealth legislation or have been expressly repealed.[21]

## Application of Colonial Boundaries Act

**8.** *After the passing of this Act the Colonial Boundaries Act, 1895, shall not apply to any colony which becomes a State of the Commonwealth; but the Commonwealth shall be taken to be a self-governing colony for the purposes of that Act.*

The *Colonial Boundaries Act* provides:—

(1) Where the boundaries of a colony have, either before or after the passing of this Act, been altered by the Queen by Order-in-Council or letters-patent, the boundaries so altered shall be, and be deemed to have been from the date of the alteration, the boundaries of the colony.

(2) Provided that the consent of a self-governing colony shall be required for the alteration of the boundaries thereof.

(3) In this Act "self-governing" colony means any of the colonies specified in the Schedule to this Act.

### Schedule
#### Self-governing colonies

| | | |
|---|---|---|
| Canada | South Australia | New Zealand |
| Newfoundland | Queensland | Cape of Good Hope |
| New South Wales | Western Australia | Natal |
| Victoria | Tasmania | |

Quick and Garran comment that the effect of this clause is to make the *Colonial Boundaries Act* apply not to the separate States of the Commonwealth,

---

20  See s 122. The following *external* Territories of the Commonwealth were acquired after Federation: Papua, Norfolk Island, Cocos Island, Christmas Island, Ashmore and Cartier Islands, Coral Sea Islands. New Guinea was acquired as a mandated and later a Trust Territory as was Nauru (administered jointly by Australia, Britain and New Zealand until it gained independence). The following *internal* Territories were acquired: Northern Territory (by separation from South Australia), Australian Capital Territory (by separation from New South Wales).

21  The last repeal was effected in 1952 when the *Pearl-Shell Fisheries* (*Extra-territorial*) *Acts* (51 Vict No 1 of 1888; 52 Vict No 1 of 1889) were repealed by the *Pearl Fisheries Act* 1952-1953. This Act has now been repealed by the *Continental Shelf* (*Living Natural Resources*) *Act* 1968.

but to the Commonwealth as a whole—just as it applied, say, to Canada as a whole. In other words, the colonies which became Australian States are in effect struck out of the Schedule and the Commonwealth substituted for them.[22]

It would seem that the purpose of the Act is to allow the Queen by executive act to alter boundaries with the consent of the legislature of the colony affected without the need for Imperial legislation.

However, the question arises as to what operation the Act has at the present time. Even in 1900, as Quick and Garran mention, much of the ground of boundary alteration was covered by certain sections of the Commonwealth Constitution, eg s 121 (admission of new States), s 122 (admission and government of Territories), s 123 (alteration of boundaries of States) and also s 51 (xxix) (external affairs). Indeed it is difficult to imagine a boundary alteration which would not be affected by these sections. It is possible that cl 8 was intended to preserve an Imperial initiative in boundary alterations which would be available as an alternative to the methods set out in these sections.

Even if this were the case, it is difficult to accept that the Act could be applied after the adoption of the *Statute of Westminster* which in effect removed the Commonwealth from the status of a "self-governing colony".

If it were still in operation, then its effect would be restricted to the alteration of boundaries of Commonwealth Territories, although it will seem that s 122 of the Constitution would also be a basis for altering the boundaries of such Territories.[23]

CONSTITUTION

**9.** *The Constitution of the Commonwealth shall be as follows:*—

## THE CONSTITUTION

*This Constitution is divided as follows:*—

---

22   *Annotated Constitution*, 378-9.
23   See discussion of s 122.

# CHAPTER I

# THE PARLIAMENT

## PART I—GENERAL

LEGISLATIVE POWER

**1.** *The legislative power of the Commonwealth shall be vested in a Federal Parliament, which shall consist of the Queen, a Senate, and a House of Representatives, and which is herein-after called "The Parliament," or "The Parliament of the Commonwealth."*[1]

The first six sections of the Constitution deal with general matters relating to the Legislature and the Executive. This section deals appropriately with the legislative power. This power is to be exercised by a bicameral legislature which is defined as consisting of the Queen, the House of Representatives and the Senate.

In accordance with British and colonial constitutional practice it is specifically recognized that the Queen is a constituent part of Parliament. Of course the Queen's participation in legislation is purely formal. Her powers are exercised by the Governor-General (ss 2, 61) who assents in Her name to Bills passed by both Houses (or, in the case of a deadlock, follows the procedure laid down in s 57). Such assent of course is, in the light of the doctrine of responsible government, given on the advice of the Ministry (see s 64). One type of Bill must be reserved for the Royal assent (see ss 74, 58, 60) but this is a purely formal requirement. The Queen may disallow a Bill assented to by the Governor-General (s 59), but despite suggestions to the contrary in an early case[2] this power must be regarded as moribund today.[3]

The conferment of legislative power on the Parliament does not prevent that body from delegating part of its power to the executive or to a subordinate law-making body. This was recognized in *Victorian Stevedoring and Contracting Co Pty Ltd v Dignan*[4] and in the *Boilermakers Case.*[5]

The conferment of wide law-making powers on the executive, provided that it does not amount to an abdication of power[6] is justified in the light of the operation of the doctrine of responsible government: those who exercise the power will be held answerable to the House of Parliament for any abuse of such power. Consequently, as has been pointed out in the Introduction[7] the doctrine of separation of powers has a practical operation only in respect of the separation of judicial from legislative and executive power.

---

1 Quick and Garran, 384-7.
2 *Commissioner of Taxation (NSW) v Baxter* (1907) 4 CLR 1087 at 1097.
3 See discussion of s 59.
4 (1931) 46 CLR 73.
5 (1957) 95 CLR 529. See discussion of s 71; *Baxter v Ah Way* (1909) 8 CLR 626; *Crowe v Commonwealth* (1935) 54 CLR 69.
6 *Dignan's Case* (1931) 46 CLR 73 at 121 (Evatt J).
7 *Ante,* 14 et seq.

GOVERNOR-GENERAL

**2.** *A Governor-General appointed by the Queen shall be Her Majesty's representative in the Commonwealth, and shall have and may exercise in the Commonwealth during the Queen's pleasure, but subject to this Constitution, such powers and functions of the Queen as Her Majesty may be pleased to assign to him.*[8]

This section must be read in conjunction with s 61 which provides that the executive power vested in the Queen is exercisable by the Governor-General, and also with other sections which confer executive power upon the Governor-General.

The appointment of the Governor-General is usually for a period of five years (although he may be re-called at any time by the Queen on the advice of the federal Ministry).[9] Reappointment may occur, usually for a more limited period. In accordance with the doctrine of responsible government the appointment is made on the advice of responsible Ministers. Initially this was the advice of British Ministers, but after 1930 on the advice of Australian Ministers. This change reflected the growth in dominion status occurring after the First World War which was recognized by the Imperial Conference in 1930.[10]

The Governor-General's powers are derived from three sources: those vested in him by the Constitution, those deriving from the common law which are commonly described as prerogative powers (and which may be regulated by Royal Commission and Letters Patent), and those derived from statute. We are not concerned with the last category, except to indicate that there are numerous statutory sources of both legislative and executive power which the Governor-General (or Governor-General in Council) exercises.

As to constitutional sources, the Governor-General has the formal powers, *inter alia*, of fixing the times for holding parliamentary sessions and for proroguing the House of Representatives (s 4), of dissolving both Houses in the event of a deadlock (s 57) and of assenting to Bills (s 58). The executive power of the Commonwealth is exercisable by him (s 61). He appoints Ministers (s 64) and is Commander-in-Chief of the military forces of the Commonwealth (s 68). He is also responsible for other matters which, in accordance with the federal division of power, were transferred from the Governors of the colonies on Federation (s 70). Judges of federal courts are appointed by him (s 72). In some cases the power is conferred on the Governor-General, in other cases on the Governor-General in Council. The difference is merely one of terminology: the Governor-General must act on the advice of the Ministry.[11]

As to the prerogative powers,[12] some of these ancient powers which were

---

8   Quick and Garran, 387-400.
9   Crisp, *Australian National Government* (1971 ed), 400.
10   Ibid, 397. As to the controversy surrounding the appointment of Sir Isaac Isaacs as Governor-General in the 30's, see Crisp, 411.
11   Quick and Garran, 406. As to the existence of any reserve powers, see discussion of ss 5, 62.
12   In *Federal Commissioner of Taxation v E O Farley Ltd* (1940) 63 CLR 278 at 320-1 Evatt J distinguished three classes of prerogative rights: 1. those relating to foreign relations (making peace, declaring war); 2. common law prerogatives which conferred superior rights on the Crown *vis-à-vis* the subject (eg certain privileges in litigation, the right to priority in payment of debts in a winding up); 3. prerogative rights of a proprietary nature (the right to wrecks, royal metals).

derived from the common law must now be regarded as vested in the Governor-General by virtue of ss 61 and 51 (xxxix) of the Constitution. Others have been absorbed by statutory enactment[13] made under various heads of Commonwealth legislative power (eg, the right to unclaimed wrecks)[14] while others (immunity from suit) have been overridden by constitutional interpretation or statutory enactment.[15]

The relationship between the Monarch and the Governor-General is regulated by the Letters Patent,[16] constituting the office of Governor-General, and by the Governor-General's Commission and Royal Instructions.[17] Some of the matters covered by these instruments are dealt with in the Constitution and in this respect may be regarded as superfluous.[18] Others are of a ministerial nature with little constitutional significance (e g the keeping of the Great Seal).[19]

The question arises as to whether there are certain prerogative powers which are still inherent in the Monarch and which have not been conferred on the Governor-General either by delegation under s 2 or by implication under s 61. An affirmative answer to this question is probably required,[20] although much would depend on the interpretation given the phrase "the executive power of the Commonwealth" in s 61. The right of legation (the power of approving the credentials of diplomatic representatives)[21] and the prerogative of honours are still exercised by the Monarch.

A further question which arises is whether under s 2 a full delegation of royal powers placing the Governor-General in the position of a Viceroy over the whole of Australia is possible. If all royal prerogatives were conferred on the Governor-General, this would enable him to deal with matters affecting the State constitutional system (e g appointment of State Governors, award of honours for service to the States, incorporation of companies by Royal charter). It would appear that such complete powers cannot be delegated. The phrase "subject to this Constitution" appears in s 2. A basic section protecting the State constitutional structure is s 106. Consequently, the Monarch would appear to be obliged to recognize the constitutional procedure under which the State Government through their Governors have a separate right of access and the right to give advice on these matters which are not of federal significance.[22]

SALARY OF GOVERNOR-GENERAL

**3.** *There shall be payable to the Queen out of the Consolidated Revenue fund of the Commonwealth, for the salary of the Governor-General, an annual sum which, until the Parliament otherwise provides, shall be ten thousand pounds.*

---

13   For the effect of a statute on the prerogative, see the statement of Lord Atkinson in *Attorney-General v De Keyser's Estates Ltd* [1920] AC 508 at 539-40.
14   *Navigation Act* 1912-1972 s 308.
15   See Wynes, 427 *et seq.*
16   These are set out in Moore, *Constitution of the Commonwealth of Australia* (2nd ed 1910), 670-4.
17   Ibid, 674-81.
18   For example, for the power of appointing judges, see Moore, op cit, 162.
19   Ibid, 165.
20   See the *Wooltops Case* (1922) 31 CLR 421 at 453-4 (Higgins J).
21   See Wynes, 85.
22   See Lumb, *The Constitutions of the Australian States* (3rd ed 1972), 70-80.

*The salary of a Governor-General shall not be altered during his continuance in office.*[23]

The independence of the Governor-General is supported by the requirement in the last paragraph that his salary shall not be altered during his continuance in office. It is significant that the word "altered" is used (as compared with the word "diminished" in relation to the salary of a federal judge: see s 72). This means in the first place that the salary of a Governor-General cannot be increased during his term of office: in terms of the concepts of political morality prevailing at the time of Federation, it was considered that the prospect of an increased salary should not be open to a Governor-General once he had taken up office. Secondly, the salary cannot be diminished; such a possibility would undermine the independence attaching to this office.

The salary, therefore, can only be altered following on the retirement of one Governor-General and prior to the time when the new incumbent takes up office or if it was altered during the term of one Governor-General, can only take effect after his retirement.

Expenses and allowances for the upkeep of the Governor-General's residence and for other purposes are provided for under annual appropriations made by Parliament, and, therefore, can be altered.

PROVISIONS RELATING TO GOVERNOR-GENERAL

**4.** *The provisions of this Constitution relating to the Governor-General extend and apply to the Governor-General for the time being, or such person as the Queen may appoint to administer the Government of the Commonwealth; but no such person shall be entitled to receive any salary from the Commonwealth in respect of any other office during his administration of the Government of the Commonwealth.*[24]

This section envisages the appointment of a federal administrator under Royal Commission who would exercise the full powers of the Governor-General during his absence or incapacity (unless a deputy is appointed under s 126). Such a person cannot receive the salary attaching to any other Commonwealth office, thus fettering the power to select a Commonwealth judge or officer to act as administrator.

The practice has been for a State Governor to be appointed as administrator during the Governor-General's absence.

SESSIONS OF PARLIAMENT: PROROGATION AND DISSOLUTION

**5.** *The Governor-General may appoint such times for holding the sessions of the Parliament as he thinks fit, and may also from time to time, by Proclamation or otherwise, prorogue the Parliament, and may in like manner dissolve the House of Representatives.*

SUMMONING PARLIAMENT

*After any general election the Parliament shall be summoned to meet not later than thirty days after the day appointed for the return of the writs.*

FIRST SESSION

*The Parliament shall be summoned to meet not later than six months after the establishment of the Commonwealth.*[25]

---

23    Quick and Garran, 400-2.
24    Ibid, 402-3.
25    Ibid, 404-10.

The powers of the Governor-General in relation to Parliament are set out in this section. Acting on the advice of the Ministry he fixes the time for holding the sessions of Parliament. Under s 6 one session must be held in each year of the Parliament's life (which is restricted to three years: s 27). The session is usually divided into two sittings, the first commencing in February or March, the second in August when the Budget is presented.

The one restriction on the power of fixing the time of opening of Parliament is found in the second paragraph. After a general election (ie, after an election for all the members of the House of Representatives and the Senate) the Parliament shall be summoned to meet not later than 30 days after the return of the writs. In so far as s 32 provides that writs for the election of members shall be issued within 10 days from the expiry of a House or proclamation of its dissolution, an inordinate period of time cannot elapse between the end of one House and the beginning of the new Parliament.[26]

The section also empowers the Governor-General to prorogue Parliament, that is, to adjourn Parliament at the end of a session[27] and to dissolve the House of Representatives. (The only way in which the Senate can be dissolved is under s 57.)

*Reserve power in relation to requests for dissolution.* The question has been canvassed as to what extent the Governor-General has any reserve power to refuse a request for dissolution from a Government defeated on the floor of the House on a vote of confidence or on a critical issue. Is the Governor-General entitled to assess the parliamentary situation to determine whether an alternative Government may be formed?

During the first 10 years of Federation there were three instances of refusal of dissolution advised by the Prime Minister of the day.[28] At the Imperial Conference in 1926 it was recognized that the Governor-General of a dominion held in all essential respects the same position in relation to the administration of public affairs in the dominion as held by the Monarch in England.[29] This declaration was buttressed by a further declaration at the 1930 Conference to the effect that the doctrine of ministerial responsibility was likewise applicable to the Governor-General.[30]

No request for a dissolution has been refused by the Monarch in modern times. In Australia in 1929 a request of the Prime Minister of the day (Bruce) who had been defeated on the floor of the House during the first year of Parliament was granted,[31] and in 1931 a dissolution was granted to the Prime Minister (Scullin) whose Government had been defeated, Parliament having run two years.[32]

The declarations of the Imperial Conferences and the passage of the *Statute of Westminster* in 1931 all point to the development of the doctrine of equality and independence (further recognized by post-World War II develop-

---

26  Under s 141 of the *Commonwealth Electoral Act* 1918-1973 the electoral officer must return the writs as soon as is convenient after the result of the election has been ascertained. Under s 65 of the Act the date of return cannot be more than 90 days after the date of issue.
27  Adjournment during a session is in the hands of the particular House.
28  See Evatt, *The King and His Dominion Governors* (1967), 50-4; Crisp, *Australian National Government,* 401-2.
29  Evatt, *The King and His Dominion Governors,* 192.
30  Ibid.
31  Ibid, 234-5.
32  Ibid, 235-7.

ments[33] and, consequently, an equality in relation to the exercise of powers by the Chief Executive Officer of the Commonwealth country concerned. In the light of the Australian precedents of 1929 and 1931, particularly the former, it can be stated that convention would seem to require the Governor-General to accede to a request for a dissolution from the Prime Minister.[34]

### YEARLY SESSION OF PARLIAMENT

**6.** *There shall be a session of the Parliament once at least in every year, so that twelve months shall not intervene between the last sitting of the Parliament in one session and its first sitting in the next session.*[35]

The guarantee of an annual session of Parliament, which is entrenched in English and colonial constitutional law, is essential for the appropriation of revenue for the public service as well as providing a regular forum for the "redress of grievances", that is, for allowing members to effectively represent the electorates.[36]


### PART II—THE SENATE

### THE SENATE

**7.** *The Senate shall be composed of senators for each State, directly chosen by the people of the State, voting, until the Parliament otherwise provides, as one electorate.*

*But until the Parliament of the Commonwealth otherwise provides, the Parliament of the State of Queensland, if that State be an Original State, may make laws dividing the State into divisions and determining the number of senators to be chosen for each division, and in the absence of such provision the State shall be one electorate.*

*Until the Parliament otherwise provides there shall be six senators for each Original State. The Parliament may make laws increasing or diminishing the number of senators for each State, but so that equal representation of the several Original States shall be maintained and that no Original State shall have less than six senators.*

*The senators shall be chosen for a term of six years, and the names of the senators chosen for each State shall be certified by the Governor to the Governor-General.*[1]

---

33   See Wheare, *The Constitutional Structure of the Commonwealth* (1961), ch 2.

34   This does not prevent a Prime Minister (defeated on the floor of the House) from advising the Governor-General to call for the Leader of the Opposition to form a Government. This actually occurred during the Second World War when Prime Minister Fadden was defeated, and advised the Governor-General to call for Curtin: see Crisp, 403-4. Clearly in a time of war or national emergency the holding of elections might prove damaging to the effective prosecution of the war. As to the position of State Governors, see Lumb, *The Constitutions of the Australian States* (3rd ed 1972), 77-9.

35   Quick and Garran, 410-1.

36   Where there is a continuous session of Parliament which extends beyond one calendar year the constitutional requirement is fulfilled in respect of two years. In other words, s 6 would seem to require not that there should be a distinct session in every year, but that a calendar year should not pass without there having been a sitting of Parliament: see Sawer, *Australian Federal Politics and Law, 1901-1929*, 179.

1   Quick and Garran, 411-23.

This section provides for the basic constitution of the Senate. Under its provisions the Senate is to be chosen by popular election with the people of the State voting, until the Parliament otherwise provides, as one electorate. The number of the members of the Senate may be increased or diminished subject to compliance with the requirement of a minimum of six senators for each original State, as well as maintaining equal representation for these States. The term of a senator is six years.

**"The Senate shall be composed of senators for each State, directly chosen by the people of the State, voting, until the Parliament otherwise provides, as one electorate"**

Quick and Garran summarize the effect of this paragraph as follows:
The Senate is one of the most conspicuous, and unquestionably the most important, of all the federal features of the Constitution, using the word federal in the sense of linking together and uniting a number of co-equal political communities, under a common system of government. The Senate is not merely a branch of a bicameral Parliament, it is not merely a second chamber of revision and review representing the sober second thought of the nation such as the House of Lords is supposed to be; it is that, but something more than that. It is the chamber in which the States, considered as separate entities, and corporate parts of the Commonwealth, are represented."[2]

It is not our purpose to determine whether the Senate has lived up to this role. We may note that there are some who think that the development of the party system has militated against the conception of the Senate as a States' House.[3] Certainly as a house of revision and review it has in recent years established itself as a powerful body in the parliamentary system, and the development of a system of committees highlights this role.[4]

The provision for voting as one State electorate was intended to diminish local and parochial influences in the election of senators for a State: the principle of local representation was adequately catered for by the electoral system applicable to the House of Representatives.[5]

The requirement of direct election by the people[6] is explicable in the light of the attitude of the convention delegates to the composition of Upper Houses. The hereditary principle, of course, was antiquated and applicable only to British conditions. The system of nomination by the Government of the day was rejected on the ground that a body composed of nominees would be "an infirm and comparatively ineffective legislative body".[7] While there was some value in the view that senators should be elected by State legislatures, this would be contrary to the democratic principle which appealed to the majority of the delegates. Moreover, as Quick and Garran point out, two of the colonial Upper Houses (Queensland and New South Wales) were structured on the nominee principle.[8] If the Senate were to be elected by State legislatures, there would be a lack of uniformity as between the different States.[9]

---

2   Ibid, 414.
3   Crisp, *Australian National Government*, 327 *et seq*.
4   See *Report on Committees of the Australian Senate* (*Parliamentary Papers* 1971).
5   Quick and Garran, 420.
6   Described by Griffith CJ in *Vardon v O'Loghlin* (1907) 5 CLR 201 at 206 as the dominant requirement of Part II of Chapter I of the Constitution.
7   Quick and Garran, 418.
8   Ibid, 419.
9   Ibid, 421.

"But until the Parliament of the Commonwealth otherwise provides, the Parliament of the State of Queensland, if that State be an Original State, may make laws dividing the State into divisions and determining the number of senators to be chosen for each division, and in the absence of such provision the State shall be one electorate"

In the case of Queensland, particular concern was expressed as to the requirement for people of that State to vote as one electorate. It was provided that if that State became an original State (which it did) the Parliament of Queensland could, until the federal Parliament otherwise provided, make provision for dividing the State into divisions which could be represented by different senators. This was designed to assuage the feelings of separateness prevalent in the northern and central areas of the State, feelings which had adversely affected Queensland's participation in the convention activities.

No legislation was passed pursuant to this section.

"Until the Parliament otherwise provides there shall be six senators for each Original State. The Parliament may make laws increasing or diminishing the number of senators for each State, but so that equal representation of the several Original States shall be maintained and that no Original State shall have less than six senators"

The effect of this paragraph is to establish the principle of equality of representation for the original States and thus to emphasize State representation in the Senate as compared with population representation in the House of Representatives. The number of such members can be changed subject to this limitation and the requirement of a minimum of six senators for each original State. The *Representation Act* 1948-1949 increased the number of senators from six to ten for each State.

It must be noted that the section does not require equality of representation for subsequently admitted States and thus if a federal Territory with a small population were admitted as a State (see s 121), the federal Parliament could fix a lower number of senators to represent that new State.

"The senators shall be chosen for a term of six years, and the names of the senators chosen for each State shall be certified by the Governor to the Governor-General."

The term for each senator is six years taking account of the rotation principle laid down in s 13. The method of electing senators lies with the federal Parliament (s 9). The certification of the result rests with the Governors of the States.

QUALIFICATION OF ELECTORS

8. *The qualification of electors of senators shall be in each State that which is prescribed by this Constitution, or by the Parliament, as the qualification for electors of members of the House of Representatives; but in the choosing of senators each elector shall vote only once.*[10]

The effect of this section is to ensure that the qualifications of electors for the Senate be the same as for the House. Those qualifications are dealt with in s 30 and will be discussed under that section. The latter part of the section was designed to prevent plural voting.

---

10    Quick and Garran, 425-7.

METHOD OF ELECTION OF SENATORS

9. *The Parliament of the Commonwealth may make laws prescribing the method of choosing senators, but so that the method shall be uniform for all the States. Subject to any such law, the Parliament of each State may make laws prescribing the method of choosing the senators for that State.*

TIMES AND PLACES

*The Parliament of a State may make laws for determining the times and places of elections of senators for the State.*[11]

It is within the power of the federal Parliament to prescribe the method of choosing senators, but that method cannot vary between the States. A State Parliament also has the power, subject to the overriding power of the federal Parliament, to deal with this matter. A State Parliament may also make laws for determining the times (subject to s 13) and places of elections of senators for the State.

The "method of choosing senators" includes matters usually found in an Electoral Act, including the issue and return of electoral writs, nomination of candidates, electoral rolls, qualifications of electors, the mode of voting and the mode of counting votes (the "scrutiny").[12] These matters[13] are dealt with in the *Commonwealth Electoral Act* 1918-1973 and the *Senate Elections Act* 1903-1966.

There are also in existence some State Acts dealing not only with the times and places of holding elections but also with times to be observed in relation to the issue of writs.[14] These are uniform in nature prescribing times (polling to take place on a Saturday between the hours of 8 am and 8 pm) and places (which are fixed according to those prescribed under Commonwealth legislation). There are identical provisions in the *Commonwealth Electoral Act* dealing with these matters.[15] While the latter paragraph of s 9 seems to give exclusive power to the State Parliaments to determine times and places, it is difficult to give these matters an independent position in electoral arrangements separate from the "method" of choosing senators. The *Commonwealth Electoral Act,* in prescribing procedures to be followed with regard to writs (which must indicate time of issue, nomination and return) and polling, is, therefore, to be sustained under the first paragraph of s 9, even though it deals with times and places.

If, however, a State Parliament passed legislation on the specific matters of time and place which differed from Commonwealth legislation,[16] it could be argued that the State legislation would be sustained under the second paragraph. However the following section (s 10) gives to the Commonwealth Parliament a much wider power than s 9 and, consequently, it would be

---

11  Quick and Garran, 425-7.
12  Ibid, 426. In *Judd v McKeon* (1926) 38 CLR 380 a provision penalizing electors for failure to vote was upheld under s 9.
13  It may be noted that the method of counting votes is by a complex system of proportional representation laid down in s 135 of the *Commonwealth Electoral Act* 1918-1973.
14  NSW *Senators' Elections Act* 1903, *Senators' Elections (Amendment) Act* 1912; Vic *Senate Elections Act* 1958; Qld *Senate Elections Act* 1960; SA *Election of Senators' Act* 1903; WA *Election of Senators' Act* 1903, *Election of Senators' (Amendment) Act* 1912; Tas *Senate Elections Act* 1935.
15  See in particular Part X of the Act.
16  See later discussion of s 109.

possible under this section for the Commonwealth Parliament to "cover the field" in all matters relating to Senate elections.[17]

### APPLICATION OF STATE LAWS

**10.** *Until the Parliament otherwise provides, but subject to this Constitution, the laws in force in each State, for the time being, relating to elections for the more numerous House of the Parliament of the State shall, as nearly as practicable, apply to elections of senators for the State.*[18]

The second part of this section was intended to operate until the federal Parliament enacted legislation relating to the election of senators. In this interim period the laws of a State relating to the election of its more numerous House of Parliament (the Lower House) were to apply to senatorial elections in the State.

The first part of this section gives the Commonwealth a much wider power than the power conferred by s 9. The power conferred by this section extends to "elections", not merely the method of choosing senators. Matters within this section include matters within the preceding section but also other matters pertaining to the conduct of an election.[19] These matters are dealt with in the *Commonwealth Electoral Act* 1918-1973 and the *Senate Elections Act* 1903-1948. A law requiring the signing of articles on election issues at the time of elections is such a law.[20] Also included would be provisions regulating broadcasting of electoral matter,[21] and electioneering practices.[22]

### FAILURE TO CHOOSE SENATORS

**11.** *The Senate may proceed to the despatch of business notwithstanding the failure of any State to provide for its representation in the Senate.*[23]

This section must be read in conjunction with s 22 which provides that the presence of one-third of the whole number of the senators shall be necessary to constitute a meeting of the Senate for the exercise of its powers.

The section is designed to ensure the prompt return of senators of the States.[24]

It is difficult to see how any State could fail to provide for its representation on the Senate in so far as the *Commonwealth Electoral Act* and the *Senate Elections Act* regulate procedural steps to be taken in the election of senators. Presumably this might occur if the Governor of a State failed to certify the successful candidates under s 7, but it would be difficult to envisage such an eventuality.

---

17   See Quick and Garran, 428.
18   Quick and Garran, 427-8.
19   See *R v Brisbane Licensing Court ex parte Daniell* (1920) 28 CLR 23: a provision prohibiting the holding of a State election on the same day as a Commonwealth election was upheld under this power.
20   *Smith v Oldham* (1912) 15 CLR 355.
21   *Commonwealth Electoral Act* s 164A.
22   Sections 154-63.
23   Quick and Garran, 428-9.
24   Ibid, 429. However, in the light of ss 9 and 10, Quick and Garran seem to be in error in saying that "the whole carriage of Senate elections is vested in the State authority; the federal Government can exercise no control or supervision over them". In the light of the Commonwealth legislation, the Commonwealth has primary control over them.

ISSUE OF WRITS

**12.** *The Governor of any State may cause writs to be issued for elections of senators for the State. In case of the dissolution of the Senate the writs shall be issued within ten days from the proclamation of such dissolution.*[25]

The power to issue the writs for the Senate is vested in the Governor of the State. The form of the writ is prescribed in Schedules to the *Commonwealth Electoral Act* and *Senate Elections Act*. The former Act regulates the times to be observed in relation to the writ. Under Part X the writ shall fix the dates for nomination of candidates, for polling, and for the return of the writ.[26] The date fixed for the nomination shall be not less than seven nor more than 21 days after the date of the writ.[27] The date for the polling shall not be less than seven nor more than 30 days after the date of nomination[28] and the date for the return of the writ shall not be more than 90 days after the issue of the writ.[29]

No time is fixed for the issue of the writs except in the case of a dissolution of the Senate under s 57 when they must be issued within 10 days from the proclamation of the dissolution. In *Vardon v O'Loghlin*[30] it was said that s 12 empowers the Governor of a State to issue writs whenever a vacancy occurs.[31] In the case of a periodical election this would be governed by the time at which the terms of the retiring senators were due to expire (see s 13 which provides that the election shall occur within one year before the places are to become vacant).

The issue of the writ by a State Governor[32] in the form laid down in the Commonwealth legislation would be an act taken on the advice of the federal Ministry, which would therefore determine the time of polling.

ROTATION OF SENATORS

**13.** *As soon as may be after the Senate first meets, and after each first meeting of the Senate following a dissolution thereof, the Senate shall divide the senators chosen for each State into two classes, as nearly equal in number as practicable; and the places of the senators of the first class shall become vacant at the expiration of three years, and the places of those of the second class at the expiration of six years, from the beginning of their term of service; and afterwards the places of senators shall become vacant at the expiration of six years from the beginning of their term of service.*

*The election to fill vacant places shall be made within one year before the places are to become vacant.*

*For the purposes of this section the term of service of a senator shall be taken to begin on the first day of July following the day of his election, except in the cases of the first election and of the election next after any dissolution of the Senate, when it shall be taken to begin on the first day of July preceding the day of his election.*[33]

---

25   Quick and Garran, 429-30.
26   *Commonwealth Electoral Act* s 59.
27   Section 62.
28   Section 63. It must be a Saturday: s 64.
29   Section 65.
30   (1907) 5 CLR 201.
31   Ibid, 209.
32   In *R v Governor of South Australia* (1907) 4 CLR 1497 it was held that no process would lie against the Governor of a State to compel him to issue a writ.
33   Quick and Garran, 430-4.

This section gives effect to the principle that the Senate is a continuous body the members of which, although they have a term of six years (viz twice that of a member of the House), must submit themselves for re-election at periodic intervals. To this end, the section institutes a system of rotation under which the seats of one-half of the number of senators are vacated at three-yearly intervals.

The first paragraph, therefore, provides for the initial division of the Senate into two classes, the first class retiring at the end of the third year from the beginning of their term of service, the second group retiring at the end of the sixth year. In 1901 the Senate effectuated this division by providing that the class which received the smaller number of votes was to retire at the end of three years.[34]

The term of a senator will commence on 1 July following the date of his election. If, therefore, the election is held near the end of the previous year (as has been usual in recent years) the senators elected will not take their seats until 1 July of the following year, the vacancies actually occurring on 30 June.

The one exception is the case of a double dissolution when the term of service of a senator elected subsequent to such dissolution is deemed to commence on 1 July *preceding* the day of his election. When such a dissolution occurs, the Senate must divide the senators so elected (i e all the members of the Senate) into two classes in order to preserve the rotation principle laid down in the first paragraph. The term of the senators in one class will, therefore, expire three years from 1 July preceding the date of election consequential on the double dissolution.

Periodical elections must be held to fill the vacancies occurring at three-yearly intervals, the requirement under the second paragraph being that they shall be held within one year before the places are to become vacant. This allows some leeway to the Ministry in fixing the actual date of a Senate election. It can take place at any time between 1 July preceding the time when the places of the senators are to become vacant and a date prior to 30 June of the following year. The actual date chosen must allow for the prescribed electoral procedures in relation to the return of writs and the certification of the successful candidates to be complied with.[35]

FURTHER PROVISION FOR ROTATION

**14.** *Whenever the number of senators for a State is increased or diminished, the Parliament of the Commonwealth may make such provision for the vacating of the places of senators for the State as it deems necessary to maintain regularity in the rotation.*[36]

When the number of senators for each State was increased from six to ten by the *Representation Act* 1948-1949, provisions of that Act dealt with the manner in which seats would be vacated to maintain the rotation principle.[37]

---

34    See Moore, *The Constitution of the Commonwealth* (2nd ed 1910), 113. The original terminology in s 13 was amended in 1907 pursuant to a constitutional referendum: *Constitution Alteration (Senate Elections) Act* 1907 (No 1) s 2.

35    When a by-election is held because the seat of a senator elected at a periodical election has become vacant as a result of a decision of a Court of Disputed Returns, the senator elected at that by-election merely takes the term attaching to the original vacancy: *Vardon v O'Loghlin* (1907) 5 CLR 201 at 210.

36    Quick and Garran, 434.

37    See s 5 of the Act.

It must be noted, however, that the requirement of a division into two classes
(s 13) does not apply in this situation.

CASUAL VACANCIES

   **15.** *If the place of a senator becomes vacant before the expiration of
his term of service, the Houses of Parliament of the State for which he was
chosen shall, sitting and voting together, choose a person to hold the place
until the expiration of the term, or until the election of a successor as herein-
after provided, whichever first happens. But if the Houses of Parliament of
the State are not in session at the time when the vacancy is notified,
the Governor of the State, with the advice of the Executive Council thereof,
may appoint a person to hold the place until the expiration of fourteen days
after the beginning of the next session of the Parliament of the State, or until
the election of a successor, whichever first happens.*

   *At the next general election of members of the House of Representatives,
or at the next election of senators for the State, whichever first happens, a
successor shall, if the term has not then expired, be chosen to hold the place
from the date of his election until the expiration of the term.*

   *The name of any senator so chosen or appointed shall be certified by the
Governor of the State to the Governor-General.*[38]

   This section makes provision for the filling of casual vacancies in the
Senate. These are vacancies occurring because of the death or retirement of a
member, or because of the vacation of his seat in other ways provided for by
the Constitution (e g absence under s 20). Its purpose is to save the time and
expense in holding a State-wide election for the vacancy. This section allows
the vacancy to be filled by a vote of both Houses[39] of the Parliament of the
State in which the vacancy occurs (the Houses sitting together). If the
Houses are not in session then the right of selection is conferred on the
Governor of the State acting with the advice of the (State) Executive Council
(i e the State Cabinet). It must be noted that a person so chosen or appointed
does not have a fixed term.[40] He must submit himself for election at the next
House of Representatives or periodical Senate election (whichever first
occurs). The person elected at this election holds his place only until the
six-year term attaching to the "original" seat (i e before the casual vacancy
occurred) expires.[41]

   In *Vardon v O'Loghlin*[42] it was held that a popular election was required
to fill a vacancy occurring when a seat of a senator was declared vacant
because of irregularities in the election. In this case a Court of Disputed
Returns had found an election for senators in the State of South Australia to
be void,[43] and the Houses of Parliament of that State had purported to fill

---

38   Quick and Garran, 434-8.
39   Or one House in the case of Queensland.
40   "In that event the State Parliament or the State Governor in Council as the case
     may be does not elect a successor—there is created no new place and no new
     term; there is merely the nomination of a temporary occupant in the place
     already granted for the constitutional term by the people to the late Senator
     and the new occupant so chosen holds the place not as a successor, but rather
     as a substitute and for no definite period.": per Isaacs J in *Vardon v O'Loghlin*
     (1907) 5 CLR 201 at 215-6.
41   Unless of course that term has expired at the election (if it is a periodical
     election of senators).
42   (1907) 5 CLR 201.
43   *Blundell v Vardon* (1907) 4 CLR 1463.

the vacancy under s 15. It was held that this action was a nullity and that s 15 did not apply to a vacancy occurring when an election was found to be void. In such a case a by-election must be held.[44]

The question arises as to what criteria are to guide the Houses of Parliament of a State or the State Cabinet in choosing a person to fill a casual vacancy under s 15. Recent precedents suggest the growth of a convention that a person belonging to the same political party as that to which the late senator belonged should be chosen. This would give expression to the popular will expressed at the periodical election at which the late senator was elected, until the electorate is called upon again to give its verdict at the next periodical election of senators, or general election of members of the House of Representatives.

## QUALIFICATIONS OF SENATOR

**16.** *The qualifications of a senator shall be the same as those of a member of the House of Representatives.*[45]

This section prevents the federal Parliament from differentiating between the qualifications of a senator and those of a member of the House of Representatives.

The qualifications of a member of the House of Representatives are dealt with in s 34. Initially these were: minimum age of 21 years; residence for three years within the Commonwealth; British nationality[46] (either natural-born or naturalized for a period of five years) and possession of the electoral qualifications for voting at House of Representatives elections.

These requirements are subject to amendment by federal Parliament. The *Commonwealth Electoral Act* s 69 repeats these qualifications with the exception that it does not require a period of naturalization: the naturalized British subject is qualified from the time of naturalization provided the other criteria are complied with. Under an amendment to the Act in 1973 the minimum age has been reduced to 18.

## ELECTION OF PRESIDENT

**17.** *The Senate shall, before proceeding to the despatch of any other business, choose a senator to be the President of the Senate; and as often as the office of President becomes vacant the Senate shall again choose a senator to be the President.*

*The President shall cease to hold his office if he ceases to be a senator. He may be removed from office by a vote of the Senate, or he may resign his office or his seat by writing addressed to the Governor-General.*[47]

Under this section the Senate has the power of selecting its President.[48] He must be an existing member. The President may be removed by vote of the Senate, and he may resign his office in the prescribed manner.

---

44   For a discussion of the events leading up to this case, see Sawer, *Australian Federal Politics and Law, 1901-1929*, 80-2. *Essays*, ch 2 (Beasley), 49 at 52-4.
45   Quick and Garran, 439-40.
46   Under the *Citizenship Act* 1969 s 21 it is provided that a reference in a law of the Commonwealth to a British subject shall be read as including a reference to an Australian citizen and to any other person who, under the Act, has the status of a British subject or has the status of a British subject without citizenship. See later discussion of s 51 (xix).
47   Quick and Garran, 440-1.
48   See the *Parliamentary Presiding Officers Act* 1965.

ABSENCE OF PRESIDENT

**18.** *Before or during any absence of the President, the Senate may choose a senator to perform his duties in his absence.*[49]

The section is self-explanatory.

RESIGNATION OF SENATOR

**19.** *A senator may, by writing addressed to the President, or to the Governor-General if there is no President or if the President is absent from the Commonwealth, resign his place, which thereupon shall become vacant.*[50]

A person is not constitutionally obliged to remain as a senator for the period for which he is elected. He may, therefore, resign in the manner laid down by this section.

VACANCY BY ABSENCE

**20.** *The place of a senator shall become vacant if for two consecutive months of any session of the Parliament he, without the permission of the Senate fails to attend the Senate.*[51]

This is one of the ways in which the seat of a senator can become vacant —absence for two consecutive months in the one session (unless he has obtained the permission of the Senate).

VACANCY TO BE NOTIFIED

**21.** *Whenever a vacancy happens in the Senate, the President, or if there is no President or if the President is absent from the Commonwealth the Governor-General, shall notify the same to the Governor of the State in the representation of which the vacancy has happened.*[52]

The procedure for notifying vacancies occurring in the Senate is laid down by this section. In so far as the Governor of the State issues the writs for a new election, the duty is imposed on the President (or in his absence the Governor-General) to notify the Governor of the vacancy. Such a vacancy may occur as a result of death, retirement, absence without leave, disqualification or as a result of a void election.[53]

QUORUM

**22.** *Until the Parliament otherwise provides, the presence of at least one-third of the whole number of the senators shall be necessary to constitute a meeting of the Senate for the exercise of its powers.*[54]

The quorum is, by this section (and subject to parliamentary amendment), set at one-third of the whole number of the senators.

VOTING IN SENATE

**23.** *Questions arising in the Senate shall be determined by a majority of votes, and each senator shall have one vote. The President shall in all cases be*

---

49   Quick and Garran, 441-2.
50   Ibid, 442.
51   Ibid, 442-3.
52   Ibid, 443.
53   See *R v Governor of South Australia* (1907) 4 CLR 1497 at 1509.
54   Quick and Garran, 443.

*entitled to a vote; and when the votes are equal the question shall pass in the negative.*[55]

The method of voting is determined by a simple majority of members present and voting. The President is entitled to an ordinary vote but has no casting vote. As Quick and Garran point out, the object of giving the President, unlike the Speaker, an ordinary vote is to ensure that the State which he represents shall not "be deprived of its benefit of the constitutional privilege of equal representation. He is not given a casting vote as well, because that would give his State more than equal representation."[56]

The Constitution prescribes a particular method of voting in relation to Bills amending the Constitution. These must be passed by an absolute majority of the whole number of members of the Senate (as well as the House).[57]

Standing Orders of the Senate which are made under s 50 of the Constitution stipulate types of majority on certain questions. For example, an absolute majority is required for a motion without notice suspending Standing Orders. In so far as the Senate can regulate its own procedure under s 50, these requirements would be valid.[58]

## PART III—THE HOUSE OF REPRESENTATIVES

### CONSTITUTION OF HOUSE OF REPRESENTATIVES

**24.** *The House of Representatives shall be composed of members directly chosen by the people of the Commonwealth, and the number of such members shall be, as nearly as practicable, twice the number of the senators.*

*The number of members chosen in the several States shall be in proportion to the respective numbers of their people, and shall, until the Parliament otherwise provides, be determined, whenever necessary, in the following manner:*

(i) *A quota shall be ascertained by dividing the number of the people of the Commonwealth, as shown by the latest statistics of the Commonwealth, by twice the number of the senators:*

(ii) *The number of members to be chosen in each State shall be determined by dividing the number of the people of the State, as shown by the latest statistics of the Commonwealth, by the quota; and if on such division there is a remainder greater than one-half of the quota, one more member shall be chosen in the State.*

*But notwithstanding anything in this section, five members at least shall be chosen in each Original State.*[1]

This section determines the composition of the House of Representatives. It enshrines the principle that the House is both a national and democratic chamber in stipulating that it shall consist of members directly chosen by the people of the Commonwealth. But a balance or nexus between the members of the House and the Senate is preserved by the requirement that the

---

55 Quick and Garran, 444.
56 Ibid.
57 See discussion of s 128.
58 Odgers, *Australian Senate Practice*, 187-9.
 1 Quick and Garran, 445-55.

number of members of the House shall be, as nearly as practicable, twice the number of the senators.

This condition was inserted to prevent disproportionate increases in the membership of the House. This two to one ratio was, in the words of Quick and Garran,

adopted after due consideration and for weighty reasons. It was considered that, as it was desirable, in a Constitution of this kind, to define and fix the relative powers of the two Houses, it was also but fair and reasonable to define their relative proportions, in numerical strength, to each other so as to give that protection and vital force by which the proper exercise of those powers could be legally secured. It was considered extremely necessary to prevent an automatic or arbitrary increase in the number of members of the House of Representatives, by which there could be a continually growing disparity between the number of members of that House and the Senate; and to give some security for maintaining its numerical strength, as well as the constitutional power, of the Senate.[2]

The words "as nearly as practicable" allow some leeway to the federal Parliament in selecting the upper limit of the membership of the House.[3] The original constitutional requirement of 75 members of the House as against 36 senators reflected this leeway. At the present time there are 125 members of the House and 60 senators. The absence of an exact arithmetical ratio takes account of the fact that there are two members representing the Territories (the Australian Capital Territory and the Northern Territory)[4] which do not have Senatorial representation. An addition to the number of the seats was also made after the last redistribution to comply with the provisions of the *Representation Act* enacted under the second paragraph of s 24, which requires the number of members chosen in each State to be in proportion to its population and establishes a procedure for working out the number.

There is a minimum constitutional requirement of five members for each original State.[5]

The second paragraph of s 24, as we have said, contains a constitutional requirement that the number of members chosen in the several States shall be in respect of the numbers of their people. This, of course, is designed to ensure that there shall be a relationship between State population and State representation. It does not, however, require that individual electorates within a State be based on the "one man, one vote, one value" principle, that is to say, consist of the same number of electors.[6]

The remainder of s 24 deals with the manner in which the number of members for each State is to be determined. This part is subject to parliamentary amendment. The *Representation Act* 1905-1964, which has been enacted pursuant to this section, follows the original pattern set out in the section, subject to only minor amendments. Under the Act the procedure for determining the number of members of each State is as follows: (a) a quota is ascertained by dividing the number of people of the Commonwealth, as

---

2   Ibid, 452.
3   See Sawer, *Australian Federal Politics and Law, 1901-1929,* 215.
4   *Australian Capital Territory Representation Act* 1948-1973, *Northern Territory Representation Act* 1922-1968. Originally the members representing the Territories only had a vote on matters affecting their respective Territories. Now they have a full vote.
5   This is an exception to the principle that the States should be represented in proportion to population.
6   See Lane, "Commonwealth Electors' Rights", (1968) 42 ALJ 139. See also Paterson "Federal Electorates and Proportionate Distribution," ibid, 127.

shown by the latest statistics of the Commonwealth, by twice the number of senators; (b) the number of people of the State is divided by the quota.[7] If in such a division there is a remainder greater than one-half of the quota, one more member shall be chosen for the State.

However, in so far as redistribution of electorates is a matter for the Government (see later under s 29 of the Constitution), this latter provision will not have operative effect until the machinery provided for in the *Commonwealth Electoral Act* is set in train.

The *Commonwealth Electoral Act* provides that a quota of electors for *an electoral division* is determined by dividing the whole number of electors of a State by the number of members to be chosen for that State.[8] However, in making a distribution of a State into divisions, Distribution Commissioners may adopt a margin of allowance of 20 per cent on either side of the quota. Factors to be taken into account by the Commissioners include (a) community or diversity of interest; (b) means of communication; (c) physical features; (d) existing boundaries of divisions and subdivisions; (e) State electoral boundaries.[9] Variations in the number of electors in divisions within a State based on these criteria are not prohibited by s 24 and are sustainable under s 29 of the Constitution.

PROVISION AS TO RACES DISQUALIFIED FROM VOTING

**25.** *For the purposes of the last section, if by the law of any State all persons of any race are disqualified from voting at elections for the more numerous House of the Parliament of the State, then, in reckoning the number of the people of the State or of the Commonwealth, persons of that race resident in that State shall not be counted.*[10]

This section, which is based on the 14th Amendment to the U.S. Constitution,[11] was designed to penalize any State (in respect of its federal representation) which prevented the persons of any race from participating in State elections for the more numerous House (the Lower House). It provides that for the purpose of determining the population of that State (which affects the number of members to be chosen for the State under s 24), the people of the "excluded" race shall not be counted. Early State discriminatory laws (as well as s 127 which constituted a constitutional discrimination against the aboriginal race)[12] have now been repealed. Consequently, this section has no practical operation at the present time.

REPRESENTATIVES IN FIRST PARLIAMENT

**26.** *Notwithstanding anything in section twenty-four, the number of members to be chosen in each State at the first election shall be as follows:*

| | |
|---|---|
| New South Wales | twenty-three; |
| Victoria | twenty; |
| Queensland | eight; |
| South Australia | six; |
| Tasmania | five; |

---

7   Section 10. The certificate as to population is issued by the Commonwealth Electoral Officer.
8   Section 18. As to the times at which redistribution may occur, see later discussion of s 29 of the Constitution.
9   Section 19.
10   Quick and Garran, 455-6.
11   Ibid, 456.
12   Deleted from the Constitution pursuant to a constitutional referendum in 1967.

*Provided that if Western Australia is an Original State, the numbers shall be as follows:*

| | |
|---|---|
| New South Wales | twenty-six; |
| Victoria | twenty-three; |
| Queensland | nine; |
| South Australia | seven; |
| Western Australia | five; |
| Tasmania | five.[13] |

These numbers were based on statistics agreed upon at a conference of statisticians held early in 1900 to determine the population of Australia as at the end of 1899.[14] The section also enabled Western Australia to come in as an original State with a fixed representation in the House of Representatives.[15]

ALTERATION OF NUMBER OF MEMBERS

**27.** *Subject to this Constitution, the Parliament may make laws for increasing or diminishing the number of the members of the House of Representatives.*[16]

The federal Parliament has power to increase or diminish the number of members of the House subject to the Constitutional requirements.

Under s 24 an increase in the number of members of the House must be in the ratio of two to every one senator. Consequently, any increase in the number of members of the House must be accompanied by an increase in the number of senators in this ratio. Moreover, s 7 imposes equality of representation for the six original States. Therefore, apart from the case where new States are admitted, an increase in the membership of the House must be twelve (twice the number of the original States) or a multiple of twelve (with the leeway allowed by the words "as nearly as practicable").

With the rapid increase in population after the Second World War the size of both Houses was increased in 1948 in accordance with the constitutional formula.[17] The present number of members of the House is 125 and the number of senators 60.

DURATION OF HOUSE OF REPRESENTATIVES

**28.** *Every House of Representatives shall continue for three years from the first meeting of the House, and no longer, but may be sooner dissolved by the Governor-General.*[18]

The House of Representatives has a limited existence which is determined by this section. This is based on the triennial rule. The House, therefore, cannot continue more than three years from its first meeting. If it has not been dissolved by the Governor-General at this time (under s 5) it expires by effluxion of time. In accordance with the requirements of s 5, the first meeting after a general election shall be not later than 30 days after the day appointed for the return of the writs.

---

13   Quick and Garran, 456-60.
14   Ibid, 457.
15   See Introduction, *ante.*
16   Quick and Garran, 460. *Essays,* Ch 11.
17   See *Representation Act* 1905-1964. *Representation Act* 1948-1949. See *Essays,* at 62.
18   Quick and Garran, 461-4.

The later words of the section specifically recognize that the House may be dissolved before the three-year period has expired. In so far as the doctrine of responsible government applies to this as to other powers of the Governor-General, the decision on a dissolution (and the time of the subsequent election) rests with the Prime Minister and his Cabinet.[19]

ELECTORAL DIVISIONS

**29.** *Until the Parliament of the Commonwealth otherwise provides, the Parliament of any State may make laws for determining the divisions in each State for which members of the House of Representatives may be chosen, and the number of members to be chosen for each division. A division shall not be formed out of parts of different States.*

*In the absence of other provision, each State shall be one electorate.*[20]

This is a grant of power by virtue of the initial words of the section to divide the States into electoral divisions for the purpose of House of Representatives elections, although State legislative power was continued until the Commonwealth enacted its own legislation.[21] The section enables the federal Parliament to determine the divisions, subject to the limitation that a division cannot be formed out of parts of different States. The power to choose the number of members for a division implies a power to create multi-member divisions, as well as, of course, single member electorates.

Part III of the *Commonwealth Electoral Act* 1918-1973 is an exercise of the power conferred by s 29. One member only can be elected for each division. It has already been indicated that for the purposes of re-distribution a quota is determined by the Chief Electoral Officer and that the commissioners in drawing the boundaries are enjoined to give consideration to various matters, but may adopt a variation of 20 per cent on either side of the quota.[22] A re-distribution of any State into divisions may be directed by the Governor-General[23] by proclamation

(a) whenever an alteration is made in the number of members of the House of Representatives to be elected for the State; and

(b) whenever in one-fourth of the divisions of the State, the number of electors differs from a quota ascertained in the manner provided in this Part to a greater extent than one-fifth more or one-fifth less; and

(c) at such other times as the Governor-General thinks fit.[24]

It has already been stated that there is no requirement of "one man, one vote one value". The *Commonwealth Electoral Act* allows a substantial variation

---

19    It has already been suggested that the Governor-General would act on such advice even if the Government had been defeated on the floor of the House. See under s 5 below.

20    Quick and Garran, 465-6.

21    The State acts were superseded when the Commonwealth enacted its first electoral act in 1902.

22    See above under s 24 of the Constitution.

23    On the advice of Cabinet. See below under s 62.

24    *Electoral Act,* s 25. Note that under s 24 (ii) of the Act it is provided that "if either House of the Parliament passes a resolution disapproving of any proposed distribution, or negatives a motion for the approval of any proposed distribution, the minister (responsible for the administration of the Act) may direct the distribution commissioners to propose a fresh distribution of the State into divisions."

from the quota. Because of the discretion granted in the section quoted, a re-distribution may occur well after the 20 per cent margin has been passed, particularly in times of population growth and mobility.

## QUALIFICATION OF ELECTORS

**30.** *Until the Parliament otherwise provides, the qualification of electors of members of the House of Representatives shall be in each State that which is prescribed by the law of the State as the qualification of electors of the more numerous House of Parliament of the State; but in the choosing of members each elector shall vote only once.*[25]

This section enables the Parliament to determine the qualifications of electors of members of the House (which apply also to the Senate: s 16) subject to any limitations arising from s 41.

Until the federal Parliament enacted its first electoral law in 1902,[26] the qualifications for House of Representatives elections in a particular State were those applying to elections for the Lower House in that State.

The present electoral qualifications are that a person must be (a) a British subject,[27] (b) of the age of 18 years or over, (c) who has resided in Australia continuously for a period of six months.[28]

Plural votes are prohibited by the final paragraph of s 30.

## APPLICATION OF STATE LAWS

**31.** *Until the Parliament otherwise provides, but subject to this Con-stitution, the laws in force in each State for the time being relating to elections for the more numerous House of the Parliament of the State shall, as nearly as practicable, apply to elections in the State of members of the House of Representatives.*[29]

This section empowers the federal Parliament to regulate the method of electing members of the House. Pending such regulation, State laws were to operate.

The power carries provisions relating to elections including preparation of electoral rolls, enrolment of voters, writs for elections, nomination, polling, scrutiny (counting of votes), return of writs and ancillary matters.[30]

All these matters are dealt with by the *Commonwealth Electoral Act*.[31]

---

25  Quick and Garran, 467-70. *Essays*, Ch 12 (Beasley).
26  *Commonwealth Franchise Act*, No 8, 1902.
27  See now *Citizenship Act* 1948-1969, s 51: a reference to British subject includes a person who is an Australian citizen.
28  *Commonwealth Electoral Act*, s 39 (1). Under s 39 (3) an elector is not entitled to vote as an elector of the division in respect of which he is enrolled unless his real place of living was at some time within three months im-mediately preceding polling day within that division. Disqualifications are set out in s 39 (4): insanity, conviction for treason, conviction and under sentence for an offence punishable by imprisonment for one year or more. See also s 41 of the Constitution.
29  Quick and Garran, 471-2. *Essays* Ch 2.
30  Section 181AA of the *Commonwealth Electoral Act*, which requires the signing of articles on election issues in newspapers, is within this power: *Smith v Oldham* (1912) 15 CLR 355. See also *Fabre v Ley* (1972) 46 ALJR 718.
31  Two aspects of the Act which deserve mention are the provision for compulsory voting and the method of counting votes which is based on the preferential principle.

## WRITS FOR GENERAL ELECTION

**32.** *The Governor-General in Council may cause writs to be issued for general elections of members of the House of Representatives.*

*After the first general election, the writs shall be issued within ten days from the expiry of a House of Representatives or from the proclamation of a dissolution thereof.*[32]

The writ is the direction of the Governor-General issued (on the advice of the ministry) to the electoral officer commanding him to take steps for the election of a member to represent the particular division. Its form is regulated by Part X of the *Commonwealth Electoral Act*. Three dates must be inserted in the writ: (a) the date of nomination of the candidates, (b) the polling date and (c) the date for the return of the writ.[33] The date fixed for nomination shall be not less than seven nor more than 21 days after the issue of the writ;[34] for the polling not less than seven nor more than 30 days after the date of nomination;[35] for the return, not more than 90 days after the issue of the writ.[36]

The postponement of an election after the House has come to an end (by dissolution, or effluxion of time) is prevented by the requirement in the second paragraph of s 32 that the writs be issued within ten days of that event.

## WRITS FOR VACANCIES

**33.** *Whenever a vacancy happens in the House of Representatives, the Speaker shall issue his writ for the election of a new member, or if there is no Speaker or if he is absent from the Commonwealth the Governor-General in Council may issue the writ.*[37]

The procedure for issuing a writ when a casual vacancy occurs (e g, by death or retirement) is laid down in this section. In this case it is the Speaker who has the duty of issuing the writ although, if he is absent from Australia, the Governor-General in Council takes the necessary steps.

## QUALIFICATIONS OF MEMBERS

**34.** *Until the Parliament otherwise provides, the qualifications of a member of the House of Representatives shall be as follows:*

> (i) *He must be of the full age of twenty-one years, and must be an elector entitled to vote at the election of members of the House of Representatives, or a person qualified to become such elector, and must have been for three years at the least a resident within the limits of the Commonwealth as existing at the time when he is chosen:*

> (ii) *He must be a subject of the Queen, either natural-born or for at least five years naturalized under a law of the United Kingdom, or of a Colony which has become or becomes a State, or of the Commonwealth, or of a State.*[38]

---

32   Quick and Garran, 472-3.
33   *Commonwealth Electoral Act* s 59.
34   Section 62.
35   Section 63. It shall be a Saturday (s 64).
36   Section 65. Under s 142, the writ must be returned by the electoral officer as soon as is convenient after the result of the election has been ascertained.
37   Quick and Garran, 473.
38   Ibid, 474-6.

The qualifications of a member at the present time are laid down in the *Commonwealth Electoral Act*.[39] He must be aged at least 18 years, a British subject, having three years residence within Australia, and being an elector entitled to vote at House of Representatives elections (or having the qualifications to become an elector).[40]

### ELECTION OF SPEAKER

**35.** *The House of Representatives shall, before proceeding to the despatch of any other business, choose a member to be the Speaker of the House, and as often as the office of Speaker becomes vacant the House shall again choose a member to be the Speaker.*

*The Speaker shall cease to hold his office if he ceases to be a member. He may be removed from office by a vote of the House, or he may resign his office or his seat by writing addressed to the Governor-General.*[41]

This section provides for the appointment of the presiding officer of the House who will supervise the activities of the House and enforce the Standing Orders. The Speaker must be appointed at the commencement of the life of the House before any other business is transacted. If, during the life of the House, the office becomes vacant, the election of a successor would take precedence over other business.

The Speaker shall cease to hold office if he ceases to be a member (by death, retirement, or disqualification). He may resign his office and he may be removed by vote of the House.[42]

### ABSENCE OF SPEAKER

**36.** *Before or during any absence of the Speaker, the House of Representatives may choose a member to perform his duties in his absence.*[43]

To allow for occasions when the Speaker is ill or absent (e g, because of the need to perform other duties), and to allow him some respite from continuously presiding over the House, particularly when its sittings are extended over a large part of the day, a deputy may be chosen to perform his duties. The deputy Speaker can exercise the full powers of the Speaker while presiding in the House.

### RESIGNATION OF MEMBER

**37.** *A member may by writing addressed to the Speaker, or to the Governor-General if there is no Speaker or if the Speaker is absent from the Commonwealth, resign his place, which thereupon shall become vacant.*[44]

Under an older principle of English parliamentary law, a sitting member of the House of Commons could not resign his seat during the life of the Parliament: the only method whereby he could escape the duties of representation cast upon him by his election was by accepting an office of profit under the Crown (the Chiltern Hundreds).

This section makes it clear that resignation is open to a member of the

---

39    Under general principles of interpretation, the pronoun "he" would include the feminine.
40    Section 69. As to disqualifications see under s 44 of the Constitution.
41    Quick and Garran, 479-80.
42    See also the *Parliamentary Presiding Officers Act* 1965.
43    Quick and Garran, 480.
44    Ibid, 481.

House of Representatives by the simple method of notification in writing to the Speaker (or, in his absence, to the Governor-General).

## VACANCY BY ABSENCE

**38.** *The place of a member shall become vacant if for two consecutive months of any session of the Parliament he, without the permission of the House, fails to attend the House.*[45]

This is one of the ways in which the place of a member of the House is vacated: absence for two consecutive months during any Parliamentary session, without the consent of the House.

## QUORUM

**39.** *Until the Parliament otherwise provides, the presence of at least one-third of the whole number of the members of the House of Representatives shall be necessary to constitute a meeting of the House for the exercise of its powers.*[46]

The quorum of the House is by this section set at one-third of the whole number of members of the House. The Parliament alone is given power to amend this requirement, and Standing Orders must conform to it.[47]

## VOTING IN HOUSE OF REPRESENTATIVES

**40.** *Questions arising in the House of Representatives shall be determined by a majority of votes other than that of the Speaker. The Speaker shall not vote unless the numbers are equal, and then he shall have a casting vote.*[48]

Unlike the President of the Senate, the Speaker does not have a deliberative but only a casting vote (i e, when the numbers are equal).

It would seem, however, that this section refers only to voting at full sessions of the House. There is indeed a precedent which accepts the position that the Speaker has a deliberative vote in committee.[49] Sawer comments that "the section was drafted with a full knowledge of British and Colonial parliamentary procedure, in which the Speaker had always been regarded as occupying that office only in relation to full sessions of the House, and not in relation to the proceedings of the House when in committee."[50]

A majority of votes in this context means a simple majority of members present and voting. However, an absolute majority of the whole number of members is required for constitutional amendment Bills under s 128.[51] Moreover, pursuant to its power to make standing orders regulating its procedure under s 50 the House may require certain types of majorities for determining the passage of certain motions.[52]

---

45    Quick and Garran, 481-2.
46    Ibid, 482-3.
47    Sawer, *Australian Federal Politics and Law 1901-1929*, 54, 249.
48    Quick and Garran, 483.
49    *Australian Federal Politics and Law 1901-1929*, 125.
50    Ibid.
51    It was suggested at the Convention Debates that the Speaker should have a deliberative vote on this type of question, but the suggestion was rejected.
52    See previously under s 23 of the Constitution. A requirement of an absolute majority for a motion without notice suspending standing orders would be of this nature: See Odgers, *Australian Senate Practice*, 187-9.

## PART IV—BOTH HOUSES OF THE PARLIAMENT

### Right of electors of States

**41.** *No adult person who has or acquires a right to vote at elections for the more numerous House of the Parliament of a State shall, while the right continues, be prevented by any law of the Commonwealth from voting at elections for either House of the Parliament of the Commonwealth.*[1]

This section was recently "resurrected" as the basis for an argument that the reduction by some of the States of the age for voting in State elections from 21 years to 18 years obliged the Commonwealth to recognise that reduction for federal elections in those States. Involved in the determination of this question is the meaning of the word "adult".

The major issue is to what extent this section imposes a limitation on the power of the federal Parliament to determine the qualifications of electors under s 30.

The Convention Debates indicate that one reason for including this section was to ensure that women who had recently gained the right to vote in South Australian elections should not, when the Commonwealth Parliament enacted its own franchise law, be deprived of the right to vote at federal elections in that State.[2] In its original form the word "elector" rather than the word "adult" was used, but when some of the delegates pointed out that this might entitle "minors" to be enfranchised, the word was changed to "adult".[3]

The initial question, as Quick and Garran suggest, is to determine whether the section has the effect of preserving the rights of individual adults who have under the law of a State acquired the right to vote for the Lower House in that State, or whether it has a more sweeping operation and requires recognition by the Commonwealth Parliament of State franchises when framing its own electoral law.[4] They are surely right in asserting that this interpretation is incorrect. Section 30 would seem to be the dominant section and, in so far as it authorizes the Commonwealth Parliament to determine electoral qualifications, there would seem to be no obligation on the Parliament to frame those qualifications in terms of State qualifications.

If, then, we regard s 41 as preserving the rights of adults to vote in federal elections in their own States, we must next ask what is the effect of the section. Quick and Garran suggest three possible interpretations:

(a) The right may be acquired at any time under a State law passed at any time;

(b) The right may be acquired at any time, but only under a State law passed before the federal franchise was determined (which occurred in 1902);

(c) The right must be acquired by the adult persons concerned before the federal franchise was determined.[5]

The latter two interpretations are narrow ones and would mean that s 41 has only a historical significance. Nevertheless they do seem to accord

---

1   Quick and Garran, 483-7.
2   Ibid at 483-4.
3   Ibid at 484.
4   Ibid at 484-5.
5   Ibid at 486.

with the scope of s 30. It seems contrary to the intention of that section to uphold the power of a State Parliament to modify the federal parliamentary franchise once that franchise had been determined by the Federal Parliament, thereby conferring a right to vote on additional categories of persons.[6]

The preservation of the right to vote would therefore seem to rest on a choice between the second and third interpretations. The literal interpretation of the section supports the third interpretation, viz, that the individual himself (or herself) must be enfranchised before the first Commonwealth electoral law is passed, that right being preserved until death or other event which would omit him (or her) from the electoral roll.[7] Whether this or the second interpretation is adopted is of no current importance. In either case the effect of s 41 is of historical interest only.[8]

If, however, the more sweeping interpretation—the first one—is adopted that the section confers a right to vote on adults who have acquired a right to vote under a State law passed at any time, it would then be necessary to determine whether a State law enfranchising persons under the age of 21 years for State elections could enable that age group to vote in federal elections in that particular State.

Here the word "adult" is the pivotal term. Is it to be interpreted in the light of conceptions of adulthood and civil responsibility held by the community in 1901 (which must limit the meaning to those persons aged 21 or more) or are changing conceptions of adulthood (which have not as yet crystallized in the sense of being emphatically accepted throughout Australia) to be taken into account?

The question arose for determination in 1972 in *King v Jones*[9] where it was argued that s 41 (which was reproduced in s 39B of the *Commonwealth Electoral Act*) conferred a federal vote on persons resident in South Australia under the age of 21 years who had acquired a right to vote in Lower House elections in that State. In support of this contention it was said that the word "adult" was not to be given any fixed meaning which it may have had in 1901, viz, as applying to persons, whether male or female, of a minimum age of 21 years, but was a term which could be interpreted in the light of changing concepts of "maturity". On this basis, it was said, modern attitudes to maturity recognized that a person between the ages of 18 and 21 could be characterized as "adult".

The court unanimously rejected this contention. It was stated emphatically that the word "adult" was to be given the meaning which it had in 1901 and this did not include persons under the age of 21. It was a matter for the federal Parliament acting under s 30 to determine whether the voting age should be reduced below 21 years.

---

6   For a discussion of these interpretations see *King v Jones* (1972) 46 ALJR 525 at 538-9 (Gibbs J). No member of the court found it necessary to determine the question.

7   For an unusual case in which a person enrolled for a State election but disqualified from voting for these elections was held not entitled to be enrolled for federal elections under s 41 see *Muramats v Commonwealth Electoral Officer for Western Australia* (1923) 32 CLR 500.

8   It is interesting to note that some British subjects, natives of enemy countries, who were enfranchised in their States, were disqualified from voting in Commonwealth elections in 1917, but the matter was not brought before any court.

9   (1972) 46 ALJR 525.

OATH OR AFFIRMATION OF ALLEGIANCE

**42.** *Every senator and every member of the House of Representatives shall before taking his seat make and subscribe before the Governor-General, or some person authorised by him, an oath or affirmation of allegiance in the form set forth in the schedule to this Constitution.*[10]

The Oath is in the following form:

"I ................... do swear that I will be faithful and bear true allegiance to Her Majesty, Queen Elizabeth II, Her Heirs and Successors according to law. So help me God!"

This follows the form laid down in the *Promissory Oaths Act* (U.K.) of 1868.

The affirmation is as follows:

"I ................... do solemnly and sincerely affirm and declare that I will be faithful and bear true allegiance to Her Majesty, Queen Elizabeth II, Her Heirs and Successors according to law."

This is based on the English Act of 1888 which enabled members of the House of Commons who had conscientious objections to taking the oath to make a solemn affirmation in lieu thereof.[11]

MEMBER OF ONE HOUSE INELIGIBLE FOR OTHER

**43.** *A member of either House of the Parliament shall be incapable of being chosen or of sitting as a member of the other House.*[12]

This section is self-explanatory. It prevents both a Senator and a Member of the House from being elected to or sitting in the other House. Consequently, a Senator who becomes a candidate for an election to the House of Representatives must resign his seat before the day of election.[13]

DISQUALIFICATION

**44.** *Any person who—*

   (i) *Is under any acknowledgment of allegiance, obedience, or adherence to a foreign power, or is a subject or a citizen or entitled to the rights or privileges of a subject or a citizen of a foreign power: or*

  (ii) *Is attainted of treason, or has been convicted and is under sentence, or subject to be sentenced, for any offence punishable under the law of the Commonwealth or of a State by imprisonment for one year or longer: or*

 (iii) *Is an undischarged bankrupt or insolvent: or*

 (iv) *Holds any office of profit under the Crown, or any pension payable during the pleasure of the Crown out of any of the revenues of the Commonwealth: or*

---

10  Quick and Garran, 487-8.
11  The Act was passed after the furore involving Charles Bradlaugh, the free thinker. See *Attorney-General v Bradlaugh* (1885) 14 QBD 667.
12  Quick and Garran, 488.
13  Section 70 of the *Commonwealth Electoral Act* provides that a member of a State Parliament cannot be *nominated* as a candidate for a federal election, ie, such a person must resign his seat before the day of nomination.

(v) *Has any direct or indirect pecuniary interest in any agreement with the Public Service of the Commonwealth otherwise than as a member and in common with the other members of an incorporated company consisting of more than twenty-five persons:*

*shall be incapable of being chosen or of sitting as a senator or a member of the House of Representatives.*

*But sub-section iv does not apply to the office of any of the Queen's Ministers of State for the Commonwealth, or of any of the Queen's Ministers for a State, or to the receipt of pay, half pay, or a pension, by any person as an officer or member of the Queen's navy or army, or to the receipt of pay as an officer or member of the naval or military forces of the Commonwealth by any person whose services are not wholly employed by the Commonwealth.*[14]

The five categories of disqualification for membership of Parliament are set out in this section which imposes an absolute prohibition of a person falling within any one of them from being chosen or sitting in either House. Consequently, if a candidate is subject to any of these disqualifications at the date of his election and he is "elected" to a seat, his election is null and void and the House make take the appropriate action to have the election set aside and the vacancy filled (see later under s 47). The "common informer's" action is also available under s 46.

**"(i) Is under any acknowledgment of allegiance, obedience, or adherence to a foreign power, or is a subject or a citizen or entitled to the rights or privileges of a subject or a citizen of a foreign power"**

This ground of disqualification would disqualify a person who, although formally an Australian citizen, has transferred his loyalty to a foreign country. This would usually be attested to by the fact that the person has taken on foreign citizenship, but there would be cases where de facto allegiance is given without taking on formal citizenship of that country, for example by accepting a foreign passport[15] or serving in the armed forces of the foreign country. The act must be one which clearly establishes allegiance to the foreign country. To act as an "honorary" consul would not be of this nature nor would acceptance of a foreign award or honour.

The second part of this paragraph covers cases where an Australian citizen formally takes on foreign citizenship (even without renouncing his own citizenship), or where an Australian naturalized citizen voluntarily retains the privileges or rights attaching to his former citizenship.

**"(ii) Is attainted of treason, or has been convicted and is under sentence, or subject to be sentenced, for any offence punishable under the law of the Commonwealth or of a State by imprisonment for one year or longer"**

Conviction for treason is the major crime which would disqualify an Australian citizen for membership of Parliament. As to other crimes, it is provided that a convicted person who is *still under sentence or subject to be sentenced* for a crime punishable under Commonwealth or State law by imprisonment for one year or longer is incapable of being chosen or sitting

---

14    Quick and Garran, 489-94.
15    Cf. *Joyce v Director of Public Prosecutions* [1946] AC 347.

as a member of Parliament.[16] If such a person has served his sentence, the disqualification is at an end.[17]

**"(iii) Is an undischarged bankrupt or insolvent"**

A person who has not received his discharge after being declared bankrupt is disqualified from membership of Parliament.[18]

**"(iv) Holds any office of profit under the Crown, or any pension payable during the pleasure of the Crown out of any of the revenues of the Commonwealth"**

**"But sub-section iv does not apply to the office of any of the Queen's Ministers of State for the Commonwealth, or of any of the Queen's Ministers for a State, or to the receipt of pay, half pay, or a pension, by any person as an officer or member of the Queen's navy or army, or to the receipt of pay as an officer or member of the naval or military forces of the Commonwealth by any person whose services are not wholly employed by the Commonwealth"**

The holding of an office of profit under the Crown is a traditional form of disqualification for membership of Houses of Parliament established on the British pattern. Employment by the Crown or in the public service was regarded as affecting the independence of the member. However, there is an exception in the case of ministers of the Crown. In so far as the doctrine of responsible government by necessity requires them to be members of Parliament, they are entitled to receive the emoluments attaching to ministerial office.[19] It is to be noted that incapacity also attaches to persons who receive a Commonwealth pension payable during the pleasure of the Crown.

But the disqualification does not attach to the receipt of either pay or pension as an officer or member of the Queen's army or navy. This would enable present or past members of the British armed forces (if they were qualified under the *Commonwealth Electoral Act*, e g, on grounds of residence) to become members of the Australian Parliament. This seems to effect a discrimination between these persons and members of the Australian naval or military forces who are only exempted from the disqualification if their services are *not* wholly employed by the Commonwealth.

**"(v) Has any direct or indirect pecuniary interest in any agreement with the Public Service of the Commonwealth otherwise than as a member and in**

---

16   But note s 211 of the *Commonwealth Electoral Act*: "Any person who (a) is convicted of bribery or undue influence, or of attempted bribery or undue influence, at an election; or (b) is found by a Court of Disputed Returns to have committed or attempted to commit bribery or undue influence when a candidate shall, during a period of two years from the date of the conviction or finding, be incapable of being chosen or of sitting as a member of either House of Parliament."

17   In some States persons who have been convicted of crimes are disqualified even though they have served their sentence. See *Re Walsh* [1971] VR 33.

18   For the procedure applicable to obtaining a discharge see *Bankruptcy Act, 1966-1970*, Part VII.

19   On the question of the receipt by a Minister of expenses associated with another position, see Sawer, *Australian Federal Politics and Law 1929-1949*, 65. The positions of President of the Senate and Speaker of the House of Representatives are not offices of profit under the Crown.

common with the other members of an incorporated company consisting of
more than twenty-five persons"

This section was based on the traditional English prohibition which was
designed to diminish the power of the Crown to exert corrupt influence over
Parliament.

Government contractors, i e, persons who deal with the public service
by providing goods or services are disqualified. However, the phrase
"pecuniary interest" implies that the agreement between the member and
the Crown or public service (whether it be government department or instrumentality) must be for valuable consideration.[20] Performance of services
gratis is not covered.

The paragraph does not apply to the situation where a member of
Parliament indirectly benefits from a government grant, e g, as a member of
an agricultural body which receives government assistance.[21]

If the parliamentary member is a member of a company (consisting of
more than 25 persons) which deals with the public service, then he is not
disqualified. The requirement of 25 persons would be aimed at the "one-man
company" which could be used by an intending candidate as a "front" for
carrying on his business activities with the public service after being elected.

VACANCY ON HAPPENING OF DISQUALIFICATION

**45.** *If a senator or member of the House of Representatives—*

    (i) *Becomes subject to any of the disabilities mentioned in the last
preceding section: or*

    (ii) *Takes the benefit, whether by assignment, composition, or other-
wise, of any law relating to bankrupt or insolvent debtors: or*

    (iii) *Directly or indirectly takes or agrees to take any fee or honor-
arium for services rendered to the Commonwealth, or for
services rendered in the Parliament to any person or State:*

*his place shall thereupon become vacant.*[22]

This section deals with members who, while qualified at the time of
election, subsequently become subject to disqualification. When the disqualifying event occurs, the place of the member becomes vacant.

The categories of what might be called supervening disqualification are
those set out in the preceding section together with the addition of two
further categories:

    (a) taking the benefit whether by assignment composition or otherwise
of any law relating to bankrupt or insolvent debtors,

    (b) receiving payment by way of fee or honorarium for services rendered
to the Commonwealth *or* for services rendered in the Parliament to any person
or State.

The first category covers the case where the member is not made bankrupt
for his inability to pay his debts but takes advantage of the alternative procedure to sequestration laid down in the *Bankruptcy Act* 1966-1970 by
entering into an arrangement with his creditors.[23]

The second category covers cases where a member receives fees for

---

20   In *Hobler v Jones* [1959] StRQd 609, it was held that a similar disqualification
     in the Queensland Constitution Act did not prevent a member of Parliament
     from holding a Crown leasehold.
21   See Sawer, *Australian Federal Politics and Law 1901-1929*, 249.
22   Quick and Garran, 494-5.
23   See Part X of the Act.

services rendered to the Commonwealth Government, although this does not prevent a member from receiving allowances for services rendered to the Parliament or its committees.[24] The category also prevents a member from receiving payments for "lobbying" in Parliament on behalf of any person or on behalf of a State.

It does not prevent a member of Parliament from receiving a gift of moneys raised by public subscription for "public services".[25]

## Penalty for sitting when disqualified

**46.** *Until the Parliament otherwise provides, any person declared by this Constitution to be incapable of sitting as a senator or as a member of the House of Representatives shall, for every day on which he so sits, be liable to pay the sum of one hundred pounds to any person who sues for it in any court of competent jurisdiction.*[26]

This section preserves the "common informer" suit whereby a private individual may sue the disqualified member who continues to sit for the penalty laid down, i e, two hundred dollars for each day during which the member sits subsequently to the occurrence of the disqualification.

A court of competent jurisdiction would be a State court invested with federal jurisdiction under s 39 of the *Judiciary Act*.[27]

If, however, the matter is being dealt with by the House or has been referred to a Court of Disputed Returns, the common informer's suit would be excluded.[28]

## Disputed elections

**47.** *Until the Parliament otherwise provides, any question respecting the qualification of a senator or of a member of the House of Representatives, or respecting a vacancy in either House of the Parliament, and any question of a disputed election to either House, shall be determined by the House in which the question arises.*[29]

Under the *lex et consuetudo parliamenti* each House has control over its members and may decide questions as to their qualifications, elections, and other matters affecting the proceedings of Parliament.[30] However, s 47 allows the Parliament to adopt a different procedure for determining these questions.

Under Part XVIII of the *Commonwealth Electoral Act,* a Court of Disputed Returns is established.[31] This court shall be either the High Court, or the Supreme Court of the State (in which the election is held) if the matter is referred to it by the High Court. The Court of Disputed Returns has the jurisdiction to decide the validity of an election or return.[32] It has various powers, including the power to compel attendance of witnesses, to declare an election void, and to declare any person duly elected who was not returned as

---

24 Sawer, *Australian Federal Politics and Law 1901-1929,* 151.
25 Ibid 215.
26 Quick and Garran, 495.
27 See later under s 77.
28 See under the next section, s 47.
29 Quick and Garran, 495-8.
30 *Bradlaugh v Gossett* (1884) 12 QBD 271.
31 Section 183. The validity of any election "may be disputed by petition addressed to the court and not otherwise."
32 Section 184.

elected.[33] A copy of the order of the court is sent to the House concerned.[34] Section 201 would seem to make the court's decision mandatory, for it provides:

Effect shall be given to any decision of the Court as follows:

(i) If any person returned is declared not to have been duly elected he shall cease to be a Senator or Member of the House.
(ii) If any person not returned is declared to have been duly returned, he may take his seat accordingly.
(iii) If any election is declared absolutely void, a new election shall be held.

As to other questions, viz, questions concerning vacancies or qualifications of members (i e, which do not involve the validity of an election or a return), the House in which the question arises *may* refer the matter to the Court of Disputed Returns.[35] This means that in these matters each House retains the power to decide whether to deal with the matter itself or to refer it to the court. However, as these are essentially legal questions it is to be expected that they will be referred to the court. The court has similar powers to those which may be exercised by it when determining a disputed election, and in addition, the power to declare that any person was not capable of being chosen on sitting as a Senator or member of the House, and to declare that a vacancy exists.[36]

### ALLOWANCE TO MEMBERS

**48.** *Until the Parliament otherwise provides, each senator and each member of the House of Representatives shall receive an allowance of four hundred pounds a year, to be reckoned from the day on which he takes his seat.*[37]

The allowances have been otherwise provided for by the federal Parliament and are set out in the *Parliamentary Allowances Act* 1952-1973[38] while their pensions are set out in the *Parliamentary Retiring Allowances Act* 1948-1968. The salaries of Ministers are set out in the *Ministers of State Act* 1952-1971.

Although the latter words of s 48 provide that the allowance is to be reckoned from the day in which the member takes his seat, the Parliament has "otherwise" provided under the intial words of the section: payment is to be "reckoned" from the date of the member's election in the case of a member of the House of Representatives.[39] In the case of a Senator taking his place on the 1st July after a periodical election, it is determined from that date.[40]

### PRIVILEGES ETC OF HOUSES

**49.** *The powers, privileges, and immunities of the Senate and of the House of Representatives, and of the members and the committees of each House, shall be such as are declared by the Parliament, and until declared*

---

33    Section 189.
34    Section 196.
35    Section 203.
36    Section 206.
37    Quick and Garran, 498-500.
38    They consist of a basic allowance and additional allowances in respect of expenses.
39    *Parliamentary Allowances Act*, s 5.
40    *Parliamentary Allowances Act*, s 4.

*shall be those of the Commons House of Parliament of the United Kingdom, and of its members and committees, at the establishment of the Commonwealth.*[41]

The effect of this section is to empower the federal Parliament to define the powers, privileges and immunities attaching to the Senate and the House of Representatives, their committees and members. In the absence of such definition, the privileges etc shall be those of the House of Commons and of its members and committees as at 1 January 1901 (the date of the establishment of the Commonwealth).

The federal Parliament has not enacted a comprehensive code relating to parliamentary privilege but has merely dealt with two aspects thereof by legislation pursuant to s 49: publication of parliamentary papers (*Parliamentary Papers Act* 1908-1963) and broadcasting of Parliamentary proceedings (*Parliamentary Proceedings Broadcasting Act* 1946-1960). The consequence is that the major source of the law of parliamentary privilege is that applying to the House of Commons in 1901. As it was recognized as long ago as 1704 that the House of Commons could create no new privilege, the law is based on ancient practice (the *lex et consuetudo parliamenti*) as interpreted by the courts and supplemented by English legislation passed before 1 January 1901.[42]

It is usual to classify parliamentary privileges into two groups according as to whether they are inherent in the House themselves—corporate privileges—or are primarily held by the members themselves—individual privileges—although this distinction is not a hard-and-fast one as the privileges held by the members are related to the fact that they are members of a corporate body. We will examine the major categories.

*Corporate privileges.* (i) CONTROL OF INTERNAL PROCEEDINGS. Each House has full control over its proceedings. This is recognized by s 50 of the Constitution which enables each House to make standing orders for the conduct of its business. These standing orders made by the House to regulate their proceedings embody some, but by no means all, of the law relating to parliamentary privilege. The courts will not question the regularity of the application of standing orders or of any ad hoc resolution of the House dealing with internal proceedings,[43] except to the extent to which the Constitution or legislation of the Commonwealth otherwise provides.

(ii) CONTROL OF MEMBERS. The House of Commons traditionally maintained the right to inquire into and determine the validity of elections of its members. The Australian Constitution expressly authorizes the federal Parliament to deal with such matters (s 47). Reference has already been made to the legislation establishing the jurisdiction of the Court of Disputed Returns in relation to such matters.

Each House of the federal Parliament has the right to suspend a member from the service of the House for disorderly conduct on his being "named" by the Speaker or President of the Senate. The suspension power is exercised to punish persistent interjectors or for refusal to withdraw an offensive remark

---

41 Quick and Garran, 500-6. Campbell, *Parliamentary Privilege in Australia* (1966). *May's Parliamentary Practice* (18th ed, Cocks, 1971).
42 *May's Parliamentary Practice*, 69.
43 *Bradlaugh v Gossett* (1884) 12 QBD 271. *Chubb v Salomons* 3 Car and Kir Dignan v Australian Steamship Pty Ltd (1931) 45 CLR 188 at 205.

made of another member after a request to do so by the presiding officer. In extreme cases a member may be expelled.[44]

(iii) INQUISITORIAL POWER. Each House has the right to summon non-members (as well as members) to attend upon it or any of its committees to give evidence or to produce documents.[45]

(iv) PUBLICATION OF DEBATES AND DOCUMENTS. Each House has complete control over the publication of its proceedings and over the admission of non-members to the House. The publication of reports and proceedings is a privilege: representatives of the press can be excluded as has happened during time of war when a debate has been held or a report has been made to the Parliament by the Government in secret.

The authorized Hansard reports of proceedings (as well as reports, documents etc published by authority of the House) are the subject of absolute privilege so far as the law of defamation is concerned. Broadcast and re-broadcast of parliamentary proceedings is regulated by the *Parliamentary Proceedings Broadcasting Act* 1946-1960. Conversely, *unofficial* proceedings are not the subject of absolute privilege but only qualified privilege: they must be fair and accurate reports published in good faith.

(v) PUNISHMENT FOR CONTEMPT OR BREACH OF PRIVILEGE. Each House has the right to punish any person for disobedience to its lawful orders, or for interference with it in the course of its business, or with members in the performance of their duties, or for contempt of the House generally. The form of punishment may be admonition by the Speaker or President, reprimand or committal to custody. The practice of imposing fines was discontinued by the House of Commons at an earlier stage and is obsolete. An offence is usually purged by apology to the House. Committal to custody must terminate at the latest at the prorogation of Parliament (or dissolution). A determination by the House as to a breach of privilege is usually preceded by an enquiry conducted by a Committee on Privileges.

In *R v Richards ex parte Fitzpatrick and Browne*[46] two journalists were sentenced to gaol for three months or earlier prorogation or dissolution of the House of Representatives for conduct found by the House to be a breach of privilege.[47] It is to be noted that committal in this case was by means of a general warrant for contempt of the House and did not, therefore, specify the actual conduct which was regarded as constituting the breach of privilege. A court in such cases cannot enquire into the grounds for committal.

This punitive power has been criticized, and suggestions have been made

---

44   In 1920, Hugh Mahon, Federal member for Kalgoorlie was expelled from the House of Representatives on the motion of the Prime Minister, W M Hughes, for making a "blistering" public speech against British rule in Ireland. Crisp comments: "This would appear to be a precedent which would, however, be well forgotten: it represents almost certainly the Commonwealth Parliament's worst lapse into illiberalism." (*Australian National Government*, 288).

45   As to the power of a House to enquire into matters relating to the amendment of the Constitution, see *Colonial Sugar Refining Co Ltd v Attorney-General for the Commonwealth* (1912) 15 CLR 182 at 217 (Isaacs J).

46   (1955) 92 CLR 157. See 29 ALJ 97.

47   The conduct concerned alleged intimidation of a member arising from a newspaper article to the effect that he was implicated in an immigration racket concerning the obtaining of entry permits for aliens.

that it is appropriate for the matter to be determined by a court and not by the House affected, which is acting as a judge in its own case.[48]

In recent years, committees have been set up to enquire into a particular type of breach of privilege, viz, alleged misreporting of proceedings or of a member's speech.[49]

*Individual privileges.* (i) FREEDOM OF SPEECH. The absolute privilege which attaches to official reports of parliamentary proceedings also attaches to the speeches of members themselves, the idea being that only if members are immune from the possibility of suit for defamation for their speeches and statements in Parliament, will they be able to speak their minds freely on the affairs of the country.

This principle was established by Article 9 of the *Bill of Rights* 1689.[50] It is not, of course, limited to defamation proceedings as the terms of the article indicate. It covers judicial proceedings and enquiries of any kind which involve the questioning of an MP or senator as to statements made by him in the House. An interesting illustration of the extent of the privilege is provided by the refusal of Mr Ward, Minister for Labour and National Service, to submit himself for questioning before a Royal Commission appointed in 1943 to enquire into certain matters arising out of statements made by Mr Ward in the House of Representatives concerning the "Brisbane Line". The Commissioner, Lowe J's ruling on Mr Ward's claim of privilege illustrates both the wide interpretation given by the courts to this privilege and also its limits. He held that he had no power to require Mr Ward to attend before him, but that he did have power to enquire into the matters submitted to him in his commission so far as his enquiries could be directed to persons outside Parliament.[51]

It is clear that an MP is not bound to give evidence before a court or a Royal Commission of enquiry as to anything said in the House without the leave of the House. Whether he is bound if the House gives leave does not seem to have been definitely determined. It would then become a question of the extent to which the individual member's privilege is to be regarded as merely ancillary to the corporate privilege of the House. The question was left open by Townley J in his decision on the liability of Senator Wood to give evidence before the Queensland Royal Commission into Crown Lease-holds in respect of allegations of corruption made by him in the Senate.[52]

(ii) FREEDOM FROM ARREST. Members of the House of Commons were traditionally privileged from arrest in civil proceedings while the House was in session and for a period of 40 days before and after a session.[53] No protection was given from arrest on a criminal charge for an indictable offence, and it seems generally agreed that members have no protection from arrest

---

48  See Pearce, "Contempt of Parliament", 3 Federal Law Review (1969) 241, Campbell, *Parliamentary Privilege in Australia*, 123; cf, Odgers, *Australian Senate Practice*, 463.

49  Odgers, 467-8.

50  "The freedom of speech and debate or proceedings in Parliament might not to be impeached or questioned in any court or place out of Parliament."

51  See "Privilege of Parliament" (1944) 18 ALJ 70, at 74-6.

52  *Royal Commission into Certain Crown Leaseholds* [1956] StRQd 225 at 232. The better view is that, he would not be obliged.

53  This period was designed to insure that the representatives of remote con-stituencies were not prevented from attending sessions of Parliament.

in respect of non-indictable offences,[54] nor from arrest for contempt of court of a criminal nature.[55]

As arrest in civil proceedings is now rare, though still permissible in case of non-payment of judgment debts, this particular privilege is no longer of importance. Furthermore, the *Bankruptcy Act* specifically applies to members of Parliament,[56] and so they are not privileged from arrest in bankruptcy proceedings where arrest is authorized by the Act.

There is some doubt as to whether a member is entitled to refuse to comply with a subpoena to attend as a witness in court proceedings (unrelated to a proceeding in the House). May states that the privilege has been asserted by the House on the basis that it is entitled to the attendance and service of its members.[57] It would seem, therefore, that a member could be entitled to resist a subpoena while the House (or one of the committees of which he is a member) is sitting.

RULES AND ORDERS

**50.** *Each House of the Parliament may make rules and orders with respect to—*

    (i) *The mode in which its powers, privileges, and immunities may be exercised and upheld:*

    (ii) *The order and conduct of its business and proceedings either separately or jointly with the other House.*[58]

The first part of this section enables each House to deal with procedural matters relating to its privileges (e g, formalities to be observed in summoning members or non-members to the House and its committees, procedure for determining breach of privilege).

The second part enables each House to make rules and orders regulating the conduct of its business. These rules may be either standing orders or by way of ad hoc resolutions. They concern, inter alia, matters relating to the sitting of the House, the conduct of its business including the procedures for debating Bills and other matters, and the establishment of committees.[59]

---

54    For an analysis of a recent matter coming before the House of Representatives Committee of Privileges, see *Report relating to the commitment to prison of Mr T Uren.* Parliamentary Paper No 40, 1971. It concerned commitment to prison of a member of the House for non-payment of costs awarded against the member in an unsuccessful prosecution brought by him in a criminal matter. The committee's opinion was that this committal was technically a breach of parliamentary privilege. See Sawer, "The Privilege of Ministers of Parliament from Detention", 7 UQLJ (1971) 226.

55    A distinction is made between civil and criminal contempt. The former involving mere non-compliance with a court order made for the benefit of another party cannot be a ground for arresting a member. See *Stourton v Stourton* [1963] 1 All ER 606; Campbell, op cit at 63.

56    Section 7.

57    Op cit at 99.

58    Quick and Garran, 507-8.

59    In recent years the Senate has established an elaborate committee system. See *Report on Committees of the Australian Senate* (Parliamentary Papers, 1971). A discussion of the Senate's procedure is to be found in Odgers, *Australian Senate Practice.*

## PART V—POWERS OF THE PARLIAMENT

### Legislative powers of the Parliament

**51.** *The Parliament shall, subject to this Constitution, have power to make laws for the peace, order, and good government of the Commonwealth with respect to:*[1]

The main grant of legislative power to the federal Parliament is to be found in the various paragraphs of s 51. Section 51 does not distinguish between exclusive and concurrent powers, although s 52 and certain other sections of the Constitution make particular Commonwealth powers exclusive to the federal Parliament. However, there are some matters covered by s 51 which by their nature are exclusive to the federal Parliament, e g, s 51 (iv), (xxiv), (xxv), (xxx), (xxxi), (xxxiii), (xxxvi), and (xxxviii).[2] But apart from these matters the powers conferred on the federal Parliament are not exclusive of State powers: they are concurrent with continuing powers of the States over the same matters. However, if there is any inconsistency between a (valid) exercise of power by the Commonwealth and an exercise of power by the States, the Commonwealth exercise of power prevails under s 109 of the Constitution.

**"The Parliament shall ... have power to make laws for the peace, order, and good government of the Commonwealth with respect to ..."**

Before the adoption of the *Statute of Westminster* the extraterritorial limitation applying to the Australian States also applied in some measure to the Commonwealth Parliament except to the extent to which a particular power by its very nature was intended to have an extraterritorial operation. Consequently the Commonwealth found itself to be without legislative power in certain matters and, therefore, it was necessary for the Imperial Parliament to confer extraterritorial power on the Commonwealth Parliament in relation to those matters.[3] The *Statute of Westminster* was adopted in Australia by the *Statute of Westminster Adoption Act* of 1942 which had effect from 3 September 1939 (the date on which war was declared on Germany). From this time legislation could be passed by the federal Parliament without any doubt as to its validity on grounds of extraterritorial operation. Although s 3 of the Statute provides that the Parliament of a dominion has full power to make laws having extraterritorial operation, it must be remembered that ss 51 and 52 of the Constitution confer power to make laws for the peace, order and good government of the Commonwealth. It is, of course, clear that no court can substitute its own idea of peace and good government for that of the Government, but at least this introductory phrase means that prima facie the various paragraphs following in s 51 are tied to law-making for the Commonwealth as distinct, for example, for some foreign country.[4] However, there is a

---

1   Quick and Garran, 508-15. Wynes, Ch IV.
2   A full list is to be found in the discussion of s 107.
3   See *Whaling Industry (Regulation) Act* 1934 s 15; *Geneva Convention Act* 1937 s 2; *Emergency Powers (Defence) Act* 1939 s 5; *Army and Air Force (Annual) Act* 1940 s 3.
4   However, where the nature of a power is such that it is clear that it may affect persons living outside, or events occurring outside, Australia, the courts will give effect to such extraterritorial operation: *R v Foster; Ex parte Eastern & Australian Steamship Co* (1959) 103 CLR 256; Wynes, 64-9.

*presumption* that a statute is to be construed as limited in its operation either to territory or to the nationals of the State which enacted it.[5]

The *Statute of Westminster* s 2 also removed the limitation (deriving from the *Colonial Laws Validity Act* 1865) that Commonwealth legislation could be invalidated on the ground of repugnancy to Imperial legislation.[6]

It is also clear that the power to make laws for the peace, order and good government of the Commonwealth is plenary in the sense that the federal Parliament may delegate to a subordinate law-making body.[7] Moreover, laws passed under s 51 may have a retrospective operation, there being no prohibition against passing *ex post facto* laws.[8]

### "... subject to this Constitution ..."

It is necessary when one is determining the nature and content of a head of power conferred by s 51 to ascertain whether there is any prohibition contained in another part of the Constitution which operates to cut down or interfere with Commonwealth legislation passed under a specific head of power. To take one clear example, any legislation passed under s 51 (i) is subject to the prohibition contained in s 92.

One question which has been before the High Court in a number of notable cases, including the *Engineers Case,* is to what extent the Commonwealth may, by legislating under a head of power contained in s 51, interfere with the powers of a State or a State instrumentality.[9]

In the early cases[10] the High Court had espoused the doctrine of immunity of instrumentalities. This was a doctrine which operates reciprocally to protect Commonwealth and State instrumentalities from control or interference by one another. In *D'Emden v Pedder*[11] and the cases which followed it involved the question whether a State could impose duty on receipt of (or tax) payment of salary received from the Commonwealth by a Commonwealth officer. The decision of the Court denied to the States that right, the rationale being expressed by the Court in this way: "When a State attempts to give to its legislative or executive authority an operation which, if valid, would fetter, control or interfere with the free exercise of the legislative or executive power of the Commonwealth the attempt unless expressly authorized by the Constitution, is to that extent invalid and inoperative".[12] Despite a Privy Council decision to the contrary,[13] the High Court adhered to the doctrine, but the particular issue of taxation of salaries became moribund when, in 1907, the

---

5    See *Meyer Heine Pty Ltd v China Navigation Co Ltd* (1966) 39 ALJR 448.
6    See also s 4 of the Statute and *Copyright Owners Reproduction Society Ltd v EMI (Aust) Pty Ltd* (1958) 100 CLR 597; Wynes, 69 *et seq.*
7    *Victorian Stevedoring & General Contracting Co Ltd v Dignan* (1931) 46 CLR 73; *Huddart Parker Ltd v Commonwealth* (1931) 44 CLR 492; *Crowe v Commonwealth* (1935) 54 CLR 69; *Roche v Kronheimer* (1921) 29 CLR 329; *Baxter v Ah Way* (1909) 8 CLR 626; Wynes, 117-21.
8    *R v Kidman* (1915) 20 CLR 425; *Colonial Sugar Refining Co v Irving* [1906] AC 360; Wynes, 121-2.
9    See Howard, ch 2; Wynes, ch 2; Essays, ch 1 (Latham); Lane, 763-812. A recent discussion is Sackville, "The Doctrine of Immunity of Instrumentalities in the United States and Australia", (1969) 7 MULR 15.
10   These are examined by Howard, op cit 47-63.
11   (1904) 1 CLR 9.
12   Ibid at 111.
13   *Webb v Outrim* (1906) 4 CLR 356.

*Commonwealth Salaries Act* was passed rendering Commonwealth salaries subject to non-discriminatory State income tax.[14]

The doctrine was applied reciprocally in the *Railway Servants Case*[15] where it was decided that employees of the NSW State Railways could not be registered as an organization under the *Commonwealth Conciliation and Arbitration Act*, the Court pointing out that the doctrine was not limited to taxing statutes. In later cases, however, a qualification to the doctrine was recognized to the effect that the doctrine must give way where it was necessary for the effective exercise of the Commonwealth power for it to apply to State functions.[16]

Associated with the doctrine of immunity of instrumentalities was a doctrine which became known as the doctrine of implied prohibitions under which the High Court took a narrow view of Commonwealth power in order to preserve what it considered to be State residuary power under s 107 of the Constitution. This doctrine was exemplified in cases such as *Peterswald v Bartley*,[17] *Huddart Parker and Co Pty Ltd v Moorehead*[18] and the *Union Label Case*.[19]

The *Engineers Case*[20] spelt the demise of these doctrines. The actual decision in that case was that a Commonwealth award could bind State instrumentalities. The *Railway Servants Case* was overruled but *D'Emden v Pedder* was sustained on the rather specious ground that inconsistency under s 109 existed between the State and Commonwealth legislation.[21] As to the doctrine of implied prohibitions, it was pointed out that s 107 could not be regarded as "reserving any power from the Commonwealth that falls fairly within the explicit terms of an express grant in s 51, as that grant is reasonably construed, unless that reservation is as explicitly stated".[22] The trends in interpretation set in train by this decision can be seen in the construction of the various placita of s 51.

But the question of the extent to which an intergovernmental immunity doctrine still remained part of the constitutional framework was one which was attended by some uncertainty. As was stated in the *Engineers Case*, "if in any future case regarding the prerogative in the broader sense, or arising under some other Commonwealth power—for instance taxation—the extent of that power should come under consideration . . . the special nature of the power may have to be taken into account".[23]

Subsequent cases suggest the following limitations on the power of the Commonwealth Parliament to bind the States by legislation enacted under s 51:

---

14   The statute was held to be within Commonwealth power in *Chaplin v Commissioner of Taxes (SA)* (1911) 12 CLR 375.

15   *Federated Amalgamated Government Railway v NSW Railway Traffic Employés Association* (1906) 4 CLR 488.

16   *Attorney-General for NSW v Collector of Customs for NSW* (1908) 5 CLR 818 (*Steel Rails Case*). Later cases such as the *Engine Drivers Case (No 1)* (1911) 12 CLR 398, the *Municipalities Case* (1919) 26 CLR 508 and the *Wheat Lumpers' Case* (1919) 26 CLR 460 revolved around the question whether the functions being carried on by the State or its instrumentalities were governmental or non-governmental.

17   (1904) 1 CLR 497. See later discussion of s 90.

18   (1909) 8 CLR 330.

19   (1908) 6 CLR 469.

20   (1920) 28 CLR 129.

21   Ibid at 156.

22   Ibid at 154.

23   Ibid at 143-4.

1. *Constitutions of the States.* The Commonwealth Parliament cannot impair the Constitution of a State. In the *ARU Case*[24] it was pointed out that while an award could be made under the *Arbitration Act* which bound a State, enforcement of that award was a different question. It was a constitutional power of State Parliaments to appropriate the moneys required to satisfy the financial obligations imposed by the award. (This is subject to the exception recognized in the *Garnishee Case*.[25])

2. *Prerogative and governmental rights.* In *Federal Commissioner of Taxation v E O Farley Ltd*[26] Dixon J stated that debts due to the Crown in right of a State or the Commonwealth were co-existing debts—as between them there was no priority. If either the Commonwealth or a State attempted to impair the prerogative of the other, this would be invalid. He went on to state that the special position of these prerogatives was a consequence of the federal system. Although they were not rights created by the Constitution they depended upon the concept of separate governmental entities retaining the rights appropriate to their governmental status.[27] The immunity was, however, subject to the qualification that where the Commonwealth Constitution made an affirmative grant of power to the Commonwealth which by its nature included power over the subject-matter of a State prerogative, then the Commonwealth Parliament would have a power to regulate that prerogative. An example would be the bankruptcy power (s 51 (xvii)) which by its nature covered the ranking of debts.[28]

However, the taxation power was in a different category. It was not incidental to the Commonwealth taxation power to subordinate a State's claim (to payment of a tax debt due under a State Act) to that of the Commonwealth. Incidental powers could not be "stretched" as to authorize the Commonwealth to interfere with the fiscal rights of a State.[29]

The refusal by Dixon J to allow the Commonwealth to disturb the relationship between the taxpaying (as distinct from bankrupt) citizen and his own State Government received the support of the Court in the *Second Uniform Tax Case*[30] where the issue was squarely raised. The Court invalidated a provision in the Commonwealth Act giving priority in collecting of Commonwealth tax over State tax.

3. *Discriminatory legislation.* In *West v Commissioner of Taxation (NSW)*[31] a distinction was drawn between taxation laws of general application and taxation laws which discriminated against federal servants. According to Latham CJ such discriminatory legislation would probably be invalid for two reasons: (a) as encroaching on the exclusive power of the Commonwealth to make laws for the departments of the public service transferred to the Commonwealth under s 52 (ii) "because it would be legislation specifically

---

24   *Australian Railways Union v Victorian Railways Commissioners* (1930) 44 CLR 319. See later discussion of s 106.
25   *NSW v Commonwealth (No 1)* (1932) 46 CLR 155. See later discussion of s 105A.
26   (1940) 63 CLR 278.
27   Ibid at 312. For a discussion of the views of Dixon J, see Zines, "Sir Owen Dixon's Theory of Federalism" (1965) 1 Fed LR 221.
28   63 CLR at 313-4.
29   Ibid at 315-6.
30   *Victoria v Commonwealth* (1957) 99 C.L.R. 575. See discussion of s 96.
31   (1937) 56 CLR 657.

dealing with matters relating to the government of the Commonwealth, with which the State Parliament has no concern, and not relating to the government of the State."[32]; (b) on the basis of principle of characterization. In the view of Latham CJ the law could be characterized not as a law with respect to taxation but as a law with respect to the exercise of Commonwealth power, namely, the power to regulate the income of Commonwealth servants.[33]

Dixon J, however, considered that it was the discriminatory element which spelt invalidity: "Surely", he said, "it is implicit in the power given to the executive Government of the Commonwealth that the incidents and consequences of its exercise shall not be made the subject of special liabilities or burdens under State law".[34] This formulation foreshadowed the approach he was to take to discriminatory Commonwealth laws in the *State Banking Case*.[35] It also pointed to the fact that the *Engineers Case* did not rule out the use of federal implications in determining the powers of a State Parliament or the federal Parliament to bind one another.

This viewpoint was developed by Dixon J in the following significant passage:

The principle is that whenever the Constitution confers a power to make laws in respect of a specific subject-matter, prima facie it is to be understood as enabling the Parliament to make laws affecting the operations of the States and their agencies. The prima facie meaning may be displaced by considerations based on the nature or the subject matter of the power or the language in which it is conferred or on some other provision in the Constitution. But, unless the contrary thus appears, then, subject to two reservations, the power must be construed as extending to the States. The first reservation is that in the *Engineers Case* the question was left open whether the principle would warrant legislation affecting the exercise of a prerogative of the Crown in right of the States. The second is that the decision does not appear to deal with or affect the question whether the Parliament is authorized to enact legislation discriminating against the States or these agencies.[36]

In *Essendon Corporation v Criterion Theatres Ltd*[37] Dixon J adverted to a third reservation—the power of the Commonwealth Parliament to tax a State (and vice versa). Latham CJ also considered that taxation by one government of the other was invalid except within certain carefully-defined limits.[38]

In the *State Banking Case*[39] the Commonwealth had attempted by legislation to deprive the States of the freedom of choosing banking institutions with which to bank. All the judges (except McTiernan J) held this legislation to be invalid as involving a serious interference with the constitutional powers of the States. Latham CJ applied the characterization test and considered the legislation to be legislation with respect to State government powers and, therefore, not within any head of power in s 51.[40] Dixon J based his decision on the

---

32 Ibid at 668.
33 Ibid at 669.
34 Ibid at 681.
35 *Melbourne Corporation v Commonwealth* (1947) 74 CLR 31.
36 56 CLR at 682.
37 (1947) 74 CLR 1 at 23.
38 Ibid at 14.
39 (1947) 74 CLR 31. This case is discussed by Holmes, "Back to Dual Sovereignty" (1947) 21 ALJ 162; Sawer "Implications and the Constitution", (1948-9) 4 *Res Judicatae* 15, 85.
40 74 CLR at 61.

ground that the legislation discriminated against the States. Following the theory of intergovernmental immunities which he had outlined in the earlier cases he said:

The efficacy of the system logically demands that unless a given legislative power appears from its content, context or subject-matter so to intend, it should not be understood as authorizing the Commonwealth to make a law aimed at the restriction or control of a state in the exercise of its executive authority. In whatever way it may be expressed, an intention of this sort is, in my opinion, to be plainly seen in the very frame of the Constitution.[41]

Both Rich and Starke JJ considered that the law interfered with essential functions of government. They were of the opinion that even a non-discriminatory law would fall foul of the constitutional limitations.[42] Starke J referred to the proposition that "neither federal nor State Governments may destroy the other nor curtail in any substantial manner the exercise of its powers or obviously interfere with another's operations".[43]

There the matter rested until 1971, the uncertainty lying in the questions whether a State was immune from Commonwealth taxation laws and whether the federal principle operated to invalidate non-discriminatory legislation interfering with the functions of a State Government.

In 1971 the *Pay-roll Tax Case*[44] was decided. The Court was concerned with the *Pay-roll Tax Act* 1941-1969 which made the Crown in right of a State liable to pay tax in respect of wages paid to employees of government departments. It was held unanimously that s 51 (ii) of the Constitution was a sufficient basis for the legislation. The Act did not single out the States as entities liable to pay pay-roll tax: it applied to private employers as well.

Barwick CJ[45] (with whom Owen J agreed)[46] interpreted the authorities as supporting the proposition that a discriminatory Act directed against the States could not be upheld as an exercise of power under a specific head of power contained in s 51 (the characterization test), and rejected the doctrine that there was any implied federal principle governing the matter.

A majority of the judges, however, approached the question differently. They were agreed that there was no principle which exempted the States from taxation laws of the Commonwealth.[47] In this respect they rejected the supposed third reservation to the *Engineers Case* which had been put forward by Dixon J and Latham CJ in earlier cases.

They were in agreement, however, with the view of Dixon J that a law which discriminated against the States would be invalid as being contrary to a fundamental federal premise.[48] Several expressed the view that this federal premise extended beyond the realm of discriminatory laws. A law of general application could infringe the principle.[49] Although the formulation of the principle was vague, it would seem that a Commonwealth law of general application which interfered in some substantial or basic manner with the

---

41  Ibid at 83.
42  Ibid at 66 (Rich J), 74 (Starke J).
43  Ibid at 74.
44  *Victoria v Commonwealth* (1971) 45 ALJR 251; [1971] ALR 449.
45  45 ALJR at 256.
46  Ibid at 269.
47  See, for example, the judgment of Walsh J at 272.
48  45 ALJR at 262 (Menzies J), 268 (Windeyer J), 272 (Walsh J), 275 (Gibbs J).
49  Ibid at 264 (Menzies J), 272 (Walsh J), 277-8 (Gibbs J).

functions of a State Government might infringe this principle. The pay-roll tax did not, however, have this effect.

What, then, are the implied federal or intergovernmental rules which affect the power of the Commonwealth to enact legislation affecting the States. They may be framed in this way: (1) a Commonwealth Act which discriminates against the States is invalid. (2) a Commonwealth Act which unduly burdens the States in carrying out their constitutional functions or their essential governmental activities (or at least one which would prevent them from continuing to exist or function as such) is invalid.

It should be noted that the question of the prerogative does not receive a separate treatment under this classification. This is because this question can be subsumed under one or other head. If the Commonwealth Act is directed against a fiscal or governmental right of the State (as in the *Second Uniform Tax Case*) then the first rule could operate to invalidate the Commonwealth Act.

If the law is of general application it may affect State government rights and functions if it falls within an enumerated Commonwealth head of power (e g as in the case of the bankruptcy power) provided that it does not amount to such a burden on the States as to be invalid under the criterion stated in (2) above. The delineation of what is such a burden is a matter for determination by the Court where in any specific case in the future it is argued by a State that the federal principle has been infringed.

4. *Indivisibility of the Crown.* Reference must be made to one other aspect of the matter: the doctrine of the indivisibility of the Crown.[50] While the judgment in the *Engineers Case*[51] proclaimed the view that the Crown was one and indivisible (although acting in different jurisdictions and on the advice of different Ministers), the course of judicial interpretation demonstrates the separate structure of the Commonwealth and the States. Nevertheless, the doctrine continues to have some significance in relation to the question of the interpretation of statutes.

The Commonwealth Parliament may grant immunity to the Commonwealth Crown from the operation of its own legislation while binding the State Crown. Likewise legislation establishing a Commonwealth instrumentality may exempt that instrumentality from State laws affecting its operations. Section 109 here comes into operation to render inoperative the State legislation in its application to the instrumentality.[52]

It is a recognized principle that the Crown is not bound by a statute unless named therein or bound by necessary implication.[53] How is the principle to be applied in the federal system? We have already said that the Commonwealth Parliament may subject the State Crown to the operation of its legislation. The question must be asked whether the State Crown is bound where the Act is silent or where the Act is merely expressed to bind the "Crown".

---

50  See Hogg, "The Crown and Statutes in the Australian Federation" (1969) 1 ACLR 22; Cuppaidge, "The Divisibility of the Crown" (1954) 27 ALJ 594; Wynes, 369-71.
51  (1920) 28 CLR 129 at 152.
52  *Australian Coastal Shipping Commission v O'Reilly* (1962) 107 CLR 46; [1962] ALR 502.
53  See Benjafield & Whitmore, *Principles of Australian Administrative Law* (3rd ed 1966) 259-66.

Two views have been put forward. The first, "the executive authority" test, proceeds on the basis that the rule of interpretation mentioned above applies only to the Crown and its instrumentalities which have executive authority in the area to which the Act extends.

In the case in which this formulation was expressed—the *Wire Netting Case*[54]—the question was whether the *Customs Act* (Com) applied to the NSW Government so as to make goods imported by that Government liable to duty. The Court considered that the only Executive concerned with implementing and administering the *Customs Act* was the federal Crown, and it was only in relation to that Crown that the rule that the Crown is not bound by a Statute unless named therein (or bound by necessary implication) had any meaning. The NSW Crown had nothing whatever to do with enforcing the *Customs Act* so that the rule had no application to it. The result was that it was bound just like any ordinary citizen.[55]

Support for the view is able to be found in the judgments of Latham CJ and McTiernan J in *Minister for Works (WA) v Gulson.*[56]

The second view rests on the orthodox theory expressed in the *Engineers Case* that the Crown is one and indivisible. Hence unless the Act itself makes some kind of division (e g by referring to "the Crown in right of the Commonwealth"), it is necessary to treat the aggregate of federal and State Crowns alike. Thus if a federal Act does not refer to the "Crown" either expressly or by necessary implication it binds neither Commonwealth nor States. If, however, it is expressed to bind the Crown (or binds by necessary implication) then it binds both Commonwealth and State Crowns.

In *Gulson's Case* the question was whether the *National Security (Landlord and Tenant) Regulations* (Com), which did not mention the Crown, bound the Crown in right of the State of Western Australia. It was held by the majority that the State Crown was not bound. Rich and Williams JJ extended the presumption beyond the "enacting" Crown (i e the Commonwealth) in holding that the Western Australian Crown was not affected.[57]

The second view is one which does seem to preserve a certain equality between the Commonwealth and the States. It is one which preserves the governmental status of the States by refusing to treat them as entities to be subjected to the operation of Commonwealth statutes in the same way as residents of the States are treated. But, as Wynes points out, it does not seem to have commanded the support of a majority of the judges of the High Court who have expressed an opinion on the question.[58]

(i) *Trade and commerce with other countries, and among the States*:[59]

The power accorded to the Commonwealth Parliament by this placitum,

---

54    *R v Sutton* (1908) 5 CLR 789.
55    This view was also taken by Rich and Williams JJ in *Minister of Works (WA) v Gulson* (1944) 69 CLR 338 at 355-6, 365-7.
56    Ibid at 348-50, 359.
57    Starke J agreed that on the construction of the regulations they did not apply to the State Crown. Latham CJ and McTiernan J, as we have seen, took the view that the presumption did *not* extend beyond the "enacting" Government (ie the Commonwealth). See also *Commonwealth v Bogle* (1953) 89 CLR 229 at 259; *Re Young's Horsham Garage* [1969] VR 977 at 978-9. (References to the "Crown" mean the Crown in right of the "enacting" State.)
58    *Legislative, Executive and Judicial Powers in Australia*, 371.
59    Quick and Garran, 515-48, 847-57; Wynes, 218-45; Howard, 203-305; *Essays* pp 34-35, 129-155.

like all powers accorded by s 51 of the Constitution, is made "subject to this constitution". In the case of the second limb of s 51 (i) this limitation has a particular significance, since s 92 provides that trade and commerce among the States shall be absolutely free. The apparent anomaly of the co-existence in the Constitution of a provision conceding power to the Commonwealth to make laws with respect to trade and commerce among the States, and a further provision guaranteeing absolute freedom of trade and commerce among the States, was resolved in *McArthur's Case*[60] by holding that s 92 did not apply to the Commonwealth. When this decision was reversed by the Privy Council in *James v Commonwealth*[61] it emphasized that the application of s 92 to the Commonwealth would not nullify s 51 (i), since although trade and commerce meant the same thing in s 92 as in s 51 (i), they did not cover the same area because s 92 was limited to a narrower context by the word "free".

Section 51 (i) operates to confer legislative power on the Commonwealth Parliament; s 92 operates to confer immunity from that power. If the extent of the immunity were the same as that of the grant of power, there would obviously be a complete nullification of the grant of power by the immunity from the power. The courts have avoided this result in two ways. On the one hand, they have held that Commonwealth legislative or executive acts will infringe s 92 only if they go beyond the regulation of interstate trade and commerce, and involve prohibition or interference with it. At the same time, they have stressed that different principles govern the interpretation of grants of power and immunities from power. The High Court has said that "a legislative power with respect to a subject-matter carries with it power to make laws governing or affecting many matters that are incidental or ancillary to the subject-matter; but it was fallacious to say that because freedom of trade, commerce and intercourse among the States was assured by the Constitution, all ancillary or incidental matters were also protected from interference or control".[62]

*Trade and Commerce.* In *McArthur's Case*[63] the High Court rejected an argument that trade and commerce among the States was confined to the act of transportation of goods across a State border. It stated:

Trade and commerce between different countries . . . has never been confined to the mere act of transportation of merchandise over the frontier. That the words include that act is, of course, a truism. But that they go beyond it is a fact quite as undoubted. All the commercial arrangements of which transportation is the direct and necessary result form part of trade and commerce. The mutual communings, the negotiations, verbal and by correspondence, the bargain, the transport and the delivery are all, but not exclusively, parts of that class of relations between mankind which the world calls trade and commerce.[64]

In *McArthur's Case* the court was concerned to emphasise that trade and commerce was not limited to inter-State transportation, but included also commercial transactions by way of the sale, purchase or exchange of commodities between persons in different States. In *Australian National Airways*

---

60   *W & A McArthur Ltd v Queensland* (1920) 28 CLR 530.
61   (1936) 55 CLR 1.
62   *Grannall v Marrickville Margarine Pty Ltd* (1955) 93 CLR 55 at 77.
63   (1920) 28 CLR 530.
64   28 CLR at pp 546-7.

*Pty Ltd v Commonwealth* (the Airlines Case)[65] it was faced with the contrary argument that inter-State transportation was not itself included within the category of inter-State trade and commerce. This contention was based on certain High Court decisions which had drawn a distinction between trade and the instruments of trade for the purpose of determining the applicability of s 92 to transport legislation, and which seemed to suggest that transportation and trade and commerce were different subjects. But in that case the court, particularly in the judgments of Latham CJ and Dixon J, made it clear that all inter-State transportation, at least when conducted for reward, fell within the concept of inter-State trade and commerce.[66]

There were two basic issues relevant to the scope of the concept of inter-State trade and commerce which were raised in the *Airlines Case*. One was whether inter-State transportation was covered by the protection afforded by s 92; it was held that it was. The other was whether the Commonwealth was competent to create a corporation with power to conduct inter-State air transport services. It was argued that the power of the Commonwealth was only to regulate such activities, and not to undertake them. The High Court rejected this suggested limitation. As Dixon J said, "a law authorising the government to conduct a transport service for inter-State trade, whether as a monopoly or not, appears to me to answer the description, a law with respect to trade and commerce amongst the States. It is only by importing a limitation into the descriptive words of the power that such a law can be excluded."[67]

The High Court has, on several occasions, considered the question whether legislation regulating the persons who might engage in inter-State or overseas trade and commerce was justified by s 51 (i). In the *Railway Servants Case*[68] the court stated that s 51 (i) did not embrace matters the effect of which upon inter-State trade and commerce was not direct, substantial and proximate, and that the general conditions of employment were not of this character. However in *Huddart Parker Ltd v Commonwealth*,[69] it was held that as the power authorised full control of the operation of the movement of commodities between states or overseas, it justified legislation relating to the employment of transport workers directly engaged in inter-State or overseas trade, including the persons to whom preference might be given in such trade.[70] Moreover, the power to make laws with respect to trade and commerce includes by virtue of s 98 of the Constitution a power to make laws with respect to navigation and shipping as ancillary to such trade and commerce. "It (s 98) authorises Parliament to make laws with respect to shipping, and

---

65　(1945) 71 CLR 29.

66　In *Hughes and Vale Pty Ltd v NSW (No 1)* (1954) 93 CLR 1 at p 23, the Privy Council stated: "There are tendencies in the *Transport Cases* to thrust the carriage of goods and persons towards the circumference of the conception of commerce, but in the *Airlines Case* it was shown that it must be at or near the centre."

67　(1945) 71 CLR 29 at p 81. The power of the Commonwealth to establish a government shipping line for the purpose of inter-State and overseas trade and commerce is confirmed by *Australian Coastal Shipping Commission v O'Reilly* (1962) 107 CLR 46, [1962] ALR 502.

68　(1904) 4 CLR 488, p 545.

69　(1931) 44 CLR 492. In *Australian Steamships Ltd v Malcolm* (1915) 19 CLR 298, the High Court held that the *Seamen's Compensation Act* 1911 was valid, since s 51 (i) and s 98 conferred power on the Commonwealth to regulate the rights and obligations of those engaged in inter-State and overseas shipping.

70　See also *Dignan v Australian Steamships Pty Ltd* (1931) 45 CLR 188 at p 198.

the conduct and management of ships as instrumentalities of trade and commerce, and to regulate the relations and reciprocal rights and obligations of those conducting the navigation of ships in the course of such commerce, both among themselves and in relation to their employers on whose behalf the navigation is conducted."[71]

In *R v Foster, ex parte Eastern and Australian Steamship Co Ltd*[72] Windeyer J expressed the view that by virtue of the trade and commerce power Parliament could regulate the conditions of work of persons engaged in inter-State or overseas trade and commerce.[73] This opinion would seem justified in particular by *R v Wright, ex parte Waterside Workers' Federation of Australia*[74] which upheld the validity of a section of the *Stevedoring Industry Act* 1949 which enabled the Court of Conciliation and Arbitration to prescribe conditions of employment in the stevedoring industry, pursuant to the trade and commerce power.

The *Bank Nationalisation Case*[75] raised a further important issue as to the scope of the concept of inter-State trade and commerce, namely whether banking is trade or commerce. Latham CJ held that it was not, since in the business of a bank there were no goods passing into or out of the State, and inter-State trade and commerce was concerned with the movement of goods. But a different view was expressed by other members of the court, who held that the term "trade and commerce" covered intangibles as well as the movement of goods. The majority opinion was upheld on appeal to the Privy Council.[76]

*With other countries.* The power given by s 51 (i) clearly authorises prohibition of the export of any commodity, or prohibition except upon compliance with prescribed conditions.[77] But in *O'Sullivan v Noarlunga Meat Ltd*[78] the power of the Commonwealth to control exports was held to be much wider. It embraces "all matters which may affect beneficially or adversely the export trade of Australia in any commodity produced or manufactured in Australia. . . Such matters include not only grade and quality of goods but packing, get-up, description, labelling, handling, and anything at all that may reasonably be considered likely to affect an export market by developing it[79] or impairing it . . . the power of the Commonwealth extended to the supervision and control of all acts or processes which can be identified as being done or carried out for export."[80] Hence in that case it was held that the Commonwealth had power to authorise legislation regulating and controlling the slaughter of meat for export.

---

71  *Australian Steamships Ltd v Malcolm* (1915) 19 CLR 298 at p 335 (Gavan Duffy and Rich JJ).
72  (1959) 103 CLR 256.
73  Taylor J, however, was not prepared to accept the proposition that it was permissible under the trade and commerce power to prescribe conditions of employment generally with respect to all ships, foreign or otherwise, which carry goods or passengers to or from the Commonwealth.
74  (1955) 93 CLR 528.
75  *Bank of NSW v Commonwealth* (1948) 76 CLR 1.
76  See (1949) 79 CLR at p 632.
77  *Crowe v Commonwealth* (1935) 54 CLR 69, at p 96.
78  (1954) 92 CLR 565.
79  Thus in *Logan Downs Pty Ltd v FCT* (1965) 112 CLR 117; [1965] ALR 954, it was held that laws for the promotion of Australia's international trade were authorised by the trade and commerce power.
80  92 CLR at p 598.

Though the decision in *O'Sullivan v Noarlunga Meat Ltd* related to the scope of the trade and commerce power in relation to overseas trade, the basic principle of constitutional interpretation upon which that decision is founded is equally applicable to inter-State trade and commerce. That principle is that an express grant of a power includes every power the denial of which would render the grant itself ineffective. In some circumstances the effective regulation of inter-State or overseas trade may justify legislation controlling activities prior to the stage when commodities are put into the course of inter-State or overseas trade and commerce; as the court said, it may be necessary "even to enter the factory or the field or the mine".[81] But the court declined to lay down any rule as to how far back the Commonwealth might go, beyond saying that it "must in any case depend on the particular circumstances attending the production or manufacture of particular commodities". In *O'Sullivan v Noarlunga Meat Ltd*, the particular circumstance was that the "slaughter for export" of meat involved a whole process of preparation of the meat from killing to packing which was distinct from the process in slaughter for home consumption.[82]

Section 51 (i) also clearly authorises the prohibition of imports, or their prohibition except upon specified conditions.[83]

*And among the States.* Dixon CJ has emphasised that "the distinction which is drawn between inter-State trade and the domestic trade of a State for the purpose of the power conferred upon the Parliament by s 51 (i) to make laws with respect to trade and commerce with other countries and among the States may well be considered artificial and unsuitable to modern times. But it is a distinction adopted by the Constitution and it must be observed however much inter-dependence may now exist between the two divisions of trade and commerce which the Constitution thus distinguishes."[84]

In *Redfern v Dunlop Rubber Australia Ltd*,[85] one question before the Court was whether s 4 (1) (a) of the *Australian Industries Preservation Act* 1906-1950 was valid. This provided that any person who entered into a contract, or was or continued to be a member of or engaged in any combination, in relation to trade or commerce among the States in restraint of trade or with the intention to restrain trade or commerce was guilty of an offence. One argument adduced against the validity of this provision was that it was not limited to contracts or combinations in restraint of trade which related only to inter-State or overseas trade, but extended to those which related also to intra-State trade. In rejecting this argument, Menzies J stated that while "it is, of course, clear that Commonwealth power over trade and commerce can only extend to such intra-State trade and commerce as is inseparably connected with inter-State trade and commerce, full acceptance of this limitation is quite consistent with according to the Commonwealth power to prohibit or regulate acts which relate to intra-State trade and commerce if they relate to inter-State

---

81    92 CLR at p 598.
82    In *Grannall v Marrickville Margarine Pty Ltd* (1955) 93 CLR 58 at p 78, the court observed that "whether activities which insure production may be the subject of valid legislation under s 51 (i) must depend on the nature of the business or trade and upon the character of the legislation".
83    *Baxter v Ah Way* (1909) 8 CLR 626; *Burton v Honan* (1952) 86 CLR 169.
84    *Wragg v NSW* (1953) 88 CLR 353 at pp 385-6.
85    (1964) 110 CLR 194; [1964] ALR 618.

or overseas trade and commerce as well ... It is true that the constitutional distinction between overseas and inter-State trade and other trade would enable a person engaged in trade to make arrangements relating to his intra-State trade free from control under Commonwealth legislation, but it does not enable such a person, by making arrangements relating to trade generally, to put these arrangements beyond Commonwealth control if they do relate to inter-State or overseas trade."[86]

However, the High Court has refused to accept the proposition that where inter-State or overseas trade and commerce and intra-State trade and commerce are intermingled, the Commonwealth has power under s 51 (i) to deal with intra-State trade and commerce. "The express limitation of the subject matter of the power to commerce with other countries and among the States compels a distinction however artificial it may appear and whatever interdependence may be discovered between the branches into which the Constitution divides trade and commerce. This express limitation must be maintained no less steadily in determining what is incidental to the power than in defining its main purpose".[87] Accordingly in *R v Burgess, ex parte Henry*[88] a claim by the Commonwealth that its power to legislate with respect to inter-State trade extended to all aircraft engaged solely in intra-State trade because of the "commingling" of intra-State and inter-State air traffic was rejected. The claim was rejected again in *Airlines of NSW Pty Ltd v NSW (No 2)*.[89] But in both these cases the point was emphasised that while the Commonwealth did not by virtue of the commingling of inter-State and intra-State trade obtain any power to make laws with respect to any aspects of intra-State trade and commerce, there could be occasions when a Commonwealth law might validly include intra-State activities as part of its regulation of inter-State trade.[90] In particular, a Commonwealth law with respect to inter-State and overseas air navigation may validly extend to air navigation within a State, since "inter-State and overseas air navigation can only be effectively regulated if all aircraft using the air in Australia are subject to the same code of rules".[91]

*Legislation with Respect to Trade and Commerce*: (a) IMPORTS AND EXPORTS. The power of the Commonwealth to control imports and exports has been exercised mainly through the *Customs Act* 1901-1971. This provides, in s 50, that no prohibited imports shall be imported. Section 52 sets out a list of prohibited imports, which includes "all goods the importation of which may be prohibited by regulation". By s 56, the power of prohibiting importation of goods authorises prohibition subject to any specified condition or restriction, and goods imported contrary to any such condition or restriction are prohibited imports.

In *Baxter v Ah Way*,[92] the High Court considered the predecessor of s 50, which referred to "all goods the importation of which shall be prohibited by proclamation", and held that it was not invalid as a delegation of legislative power. In 1934 the section was recast in its present form, and regulations termed *Customs (Prohibited Imports) Regulations* were made under it. An

---

86 110 CLR at p 221.
87 *R v Burgess, Ex parte Henry* (1936) 55 CLR 608 at p 672 (per Dixon J).
88 (1936) 55 CLR 608.
89 (1965) 113 CLR 54; [1965] ALR 984.
90 See 55 CLR at p 677, and 113 CLR at p 78.
91 113 CLR at p 151. (per Windeyer J).
92 (1909) 8 CLR 626.

unsuccessful attack was made in *Radio Corporation Pty Ltd v Commonwealth*[93] on the validity of a regulation which provided for the prohibition of importation of specified goods unless the consent in writing of the Minister to the importation of the goods had first been obtained, the main ground of attack once again being that it amounted to an unconstitutional delegation of legislative power.

Section 111 of the *Customs Act* provides that no prohibited exports shall be exported. By virtue of s 112, the Governor-General may, by regulation, prohibit the exportation of any goods in the circumstances set out in the section. The power extends to authorize the prohibition of the exportation of goods generally, or to any specified place, and either absolutely or so as to allow of the exportation of the goods subject to any condition or restriction. The power has been exercised principally through the *Customs (Prohibited Exports) Regulations*.

(b) COMMONWEALTH TRADING CORPORATIONS. The Commonwealth Parliament has passed several Acts in pursuance of its power to create corporations with authority to conduct inter-State or overseas trading operations. In *Australian National Airways v Commonwealth*[94] the High Court upheld the validity of s 19 of the *Australian National Airlines Act* 1945, which gives to the Australian National Airlines Commission, a body corporate established by that Act, power to establish maintain and operate airline services for the transport for reward of passengers and goods between States, between Territories and other places in Australia, and within any Territory. Similarly the *Australian Coastal Shipping Commission Act* 1956-1969 constitutes a body corporate with power to establish and maintain shipping services not only in Australian coastal waters, but also international services between any place in the Commonwealth or a Territory and a place in another country.

The *Export Payments Insurance Corporation Act* 1956-1973 establishes a corporation to encourage export trade by protecting exporters against risks of non-payment not normally insured by commercial insurers. It also insures Australian overseas investment against certain types of non-commercial risks.

The *Australian Industry Development Corporation Act* 1970 establishes a body corporate, the functions of which are to assist in the provision of financial resources required by Australian companies engaging in industries in Australia concerned with the manufacture, processing or treatment of goods, or with the recovery of minerals, for the purpose of facilitating and encouraging the establishment, development and advancement of those industries. The link with constitutional heads of power is to be found in the provision that the Corporation is to perform its function in such manner as will (a) promote trade and commerce between Australia and places outside Australia; (b) promote trade and commerce among the States, between the States and Territories and within the Territories; (c) promote the economic development of the Territories; and (d) further the development of Australian resources necessary for the defence of the Commonwealth.

(c) MARKETING LEGISLATION. Commonwealth legislation for the marketing of primary products has assumed a number of forms. The main kinds are as follows:—

---

93   (1938) 59 CLR 170; 44 ALR 146.
94   (1945) 71 CLR 29.

(i) *Trading boards.* These have been constituted for wheat (*Wheat Industry Stabilization Acts* 1946-1970), for dairy produce (*Dairy Produce Export Control Act* 1924-1972), and eggs (*Egg Export Control Act* 1947-1966). The Australian Wheat Board, constituted under the Commonwealth *Wheat Industry Stabilisation Acts* and complementary State legislation, is the sole constituted authority for the marketing of wheat within Australia and for the marketing of wheat and flour for export from Australia. The Australian Dairy Produce Board was established to control the sale and disposal of Australian butter and cheese in the United Kingdom and to determine minimum terms and conditions for exports to other markets. The Australian Egg Board was established to control the export and distribution after export of eggs.

(ii) *Regulatory boards.* These boards have considerably more restricted powers and functions than the trading boards.

In general, they do not themselves trade in the product, but make recommendations to a Minister relating to the export of the product, including recommendations as to export quotas, the regulation of shipments, the licensing of exporters, and export promotional activities. They have been constituted for canned fruits (*Canned Fruits Export Marketing Act* 1963-1970, which constitutes the Australian Canned Fruits Board and regulates the export and distribution after export of canned fruits); for apples and pears (*Apple and Pear Organization Act* 1938-1966, which constitutes the Australian Apple and Pear Board to regulate the export of apples and pears from Australia and to engage in sales promotion overseas); for dried fruits (*Dried Fruits Export Control Act* 1924-1966, which constitutes the Australian Dried Fruits Control Board to control the export and sale and distribution after export of dried currants, sultanas and raisins); for honey (the Australian Honey Board was set up under the *Honey Industry Act* 1962 to control exports and promote the sale of honey in Australia and overseas); for meat (the Australian Meat Board was reconstituted in 1964 under the *Meat Industry Act* 1964 to regulate the export of meat and meat products) and for wine (the Australian Wine Board was constituted under the *Wine Overseas Marketing Act* 1929-1966 to promote the sale of Australian wine and brandy in Australia and overseas and to control the export of those products).

The power of the Commonwealth to enact the legislation creating the trading and regulatory bodies referred to above, and giving them authority (even exclusive authority) to conduct overseas trade in particular commodities, is clearly justified by s 51 (i) of the Constitution. The position is more complex in the third common kind of marketing legislation, viz:

(iii) *Stabilisation schemes.* These are in operation in relation to wheat, dairy produce, dried vine fruits, eggs and tobacco. The schemes are complex, and depend upon Commonwealth-State co-operation. For example, the current (fifth) Wheat Industry Stabilisation Plan is based upon three factors: the constitution of the Australian Wheat Board as the sole marketing authority for Australian wheat; a Commonwealth guarantee equal to cost of production on exports of wheat up to a certain quantity; and the fixing of a home-consumption price on a uniform basis by the States at cost of production. When export prices are above the guaranteed price, growers pay an amount into the stabilisation fund. If they fall below the guaranteed price, payments are made out of the fund. Stabilisation of growers' incomes depends on preserving a relation between the home-consumption price and the guaranteed export price so that if one falls, the other is increased. The Commonwealth

*Wheat Industry Stabilization Act* 1968 empowers the Australian Wheat Board to require any person in possession of wheat in the Australian Capital Territory to deliver that wheat to the board. The wheat thereupon becomes the absolute property of the board, which is required to pay a price determined in accordance with s 21 of the Act. The State Acts empower the Australian Wheat Board to require any person to deliver to the board wheat in his possession, and contain provisions corresponding to those in the Commonwealth Act about the determination of the price payable. The Constitutional efficacy of these schemes must depend in particular upon the success with which their draftsmen have "exorcised the uncertain but threatening form of s 92".[95] This question is considered in some detail in the discussion of s 92.

(d) RESTRICTIVE TRADE PRACTICES. The first legislative attempt by the Commonwealth Parliament to control restrictive trade practices, the *Australian Industries Preservation Act* 1906, followed (with significant variations) the *Sherman Act* of the United States. Reliance was placed on the trade and commerce power in s 4 of the Act, which made it an offence for a person to enter into a contract or engage in any combination in relation to trade or commerce with other countries or among the States with intent to restrain trade or commerce to the detriment of the public. It was also made an offence in s 7 to monopolise or attempt to monopolise or combine with any other person to monopolise any part of the trade or commerce with other countries or among the States with the intention of controlling, to the public detriment; the supply or price of any service, merchandise or commodity.

No attack was made on the constitutional validity of these sections until 1964, when in *Redfern v Dunlop Rubber Australia Ltd*[96] s 4 of the Act was held to be a valid exercise of the trade and commerce power.

The *Trade Practices Act* 1965, which superseded the *Australian Industries Preservation Act,* was likewise based in part upon the trade and commerce power. It was declared unconstitutional in *Strickland v Rocla Concrete Pipes Ltd,*[97] but no doubt was cast on the power of Parliament to make a law forbidding restrictive trade practices in relation to trade or commerce with other countries or among the States. The subsequent legislation, the *Restrictive Trade Practices Act* 1971, was based exclusively on the corporation power.

(e) SHIPPING. The *Navigation Act* 1912-1972 is a lengthy Act relating to a host of matters concerned with navigation and shipping. The Act does not apply to any Australian trade ship or its crew unless the ship is engaged in trade or commerce with other countries or among the States or with or among Commonwealth Territories, or is on the high seas, or in waters which are used by ships engaged in trade or commerce with other countries or among the States, or is in the territorial waters of a Commonwealth Territory.

The *Sea Carriage of Goods Act* 1924 was designed to give effect to the Hague Rules of 1922 on bills of lading, which are set out in the schedule. They have effect in relation to the carriage of goods by sea in ships carrying goods from any port in the Commonwealth to any other port whether in or outside the Commonwealth. However, they do not apply to the carriage of goods by sea from a port in any State to any other port in the same State.

---

95   *Nelungaloo Pty Ltd v Commonwealth* (1948) 75 CLR 495 at p 559 (per Dixon J).
96   (1964) 110 CLR 194; [1964] ALR 618.
97   (1971) 45 ALJR 485.

(f) AVIATION. The *Civil Aviation (Carriers' Liability) Act* 1959-1966 was enacted to give effect to the Warsaw Convention of 1929 on international carriage by air, and the Hague Protocol of 1955 amending the Warsaw Convention. The convention and protocol are inserted in schedules to the Act. The provisions of the convention and protocol have the force of law in Australia in relation to any carriage by air to which the convention applies, irrespective of the nationality of the aircraft performing that carriage. The Act also applies to carriage of passengers between a place in a State and a place in another State; between a place in a Territory of the Commonwealth and a place in Australia outside that Territory; between a place in a Territory and another place in that Territory; and between a place in Australia and a place outside Australia. The Act limits the liability of a carrier for a death or injury to a passenger or in respect to baggage at a specified sum or such higher sum as is specified in the contract of carriage.

The *Air Navigation Act* 1920-1971 gives effect to the Chicago Conventions on International Civil Aviation as amended by various protocols. The question of the authority of the Commonwealth to regulate air navigation under the trade and commerce power was considered in *R v Burgess, ex parte Henry*[98] and *Airlines of NSW Pty Ltd v NSW (No 2)*[99] to which reference is made above.

The crime of air piracy and other offences in the air are proscribed by the *Crimes (Aircraft) Act* 1963. The Act applies to any aircraft engaged in a flight between two States in the course of trade and commerce with other countries or among the States, or a flight within a Territory, between two Territories or between a State and a Territory, or outside Australia while engaged in a flight that commenced in Australia, or while engaged in a flight between a part of Australia and a country or place outside Australia.

(ii) *Taxation; but so as not to discriminate between States or parts of States:*[1]

The grant to the Commonwealth of a power to tax, though expressed in a completely general form, is subject to certain express qualifications. The first of these is expressed in s 51 (ii) itself: laws with respect to taxation must not discriminate between States or parts of States. Cognate limitations are contained in s 99, which provides that the Commowealth shall not, by any law or regulation of trade, commerce or revenue, give preference to one State or any part thereof over another State or any part thereof, and in s 88, which requires that duties of customs shall be uniform. Section 114 prohibits the imposition by the Commonwealth of any tax on property of any kind belonging to a State. Sections 53-55 contain provisions about the manner in which tax laws may be enacted.

The Commonwealth and the States have concurrent powers of taxation.[2] The exception to this is that the power of the Commonwealth Parliament to impose duties of customs and of excise is made exclusive by s 90.

*Taxation.* The cases which have raised the issue of the definition of taxation have arisen mainly from challenges to the validity of State Acts on the

---

98  (1936) 55 CLR 608.
99  (1965) 113 CLR 54; [1965] ALR 984.
1   Quick and Garran, 549-56; Wynes, 168-84, 372-85; Howard, 306-25; *Essays*, 247-73.
2   More strictly, they are separate powers, as McTiernan J observed in the *First Uniform Tax Case* (1942) 65 CLR at p 452.

ground that they imposed duties of excise. A measure imposing excise duties must necessarily be a tax: and the States have frequently contended that the Acts being challenged did not impose taxes. In *Crothers v Sheil*,[3] a scheme for the compulsory acquisition of milk and payment of compensation from the proceeds arising from its resale by a statutory marketing board was held not to be a scheme for taxation merely because the proceeds were subject to the deduction of expenses of administration, contributions to a sinking fund, and interest on advances or loans. On the other hand, in *Matthews v The Chicory Marketing Board (Victoria)*[4] a levy imposed by a statutory marketing board on producers of chicory was held to be taxation. It was, said Latham CJ, "a compulsory exaction of money by a public authority for public purposes, enforceable by law, and not a payment for services rendered". In the former case, no pecuniary payment was exacted from the producers; in the latter case, it was.[5]

In *Attorney-General (NSW) v Homebush Flour Mills Ltd*,[6] the court held that legislation which expropriated flour at a "fair and reasonable price", and revested it at a higher "standard price", imposed a tax on producers of flour, since it amounted to an exaction of money by a government in obedience to what was really a compulsive demand.

*The scope of the taxation power.* A Commonwealth law will be supported under the taxation power only if it is a law "with respect to" taxation. The critical question in *R v Barger*[7] was whether the *Excise Tariff* 1906 should be characterised as an Act imposing taxation, or whether the subject matter of the enactment was with respect to a matter beyond Commonwealth power, namely the regulation of conditions of employment in an industry. The Act imposed duties of excise on agricultural implements, but excepted goods manufactured under certain conditions as to remuneration of labour. The majority of the court[8] held that the Act was not an Act imposing duties of excise, but was one to regulate the condition of manufacture of agricultural implements and was accordingly beyond power.

*Barger's Case* was heavily relied upon by the appellants in *Fairfax v FCT*[9] who challenged the validity of a section of the *Income Tax Assessment Act* on the ground that it was not a law with respect to taxation, but was one with respect to investment in public securities. The challenge was unsuccessful. Three members of the court[10] simply asserted that a law relating to exemption from income tax did not lose its character as a law with respect to taxation simply by reason of its likely consequences upon the investing of the assets of superannuation funds or because of the

---

3   (1933) 49 CLR 399.
4   (1938) 60 CLR 263.
5   Similarly, a compulsory levy on milk distributors was held to be taxation in *Parton v Milk Board (Victoria)* (1949) 80 CLR 229. Levies imposed by way of contributions towards administrative expenses of a statutory body were held in *Hartley v Walsh* (1937) 57 CLR 372 to be payments for services rendered and not taxation. In *Parton v Milk Board*, Rich and Williams JJ expressed the view that *Hartley v Walsh* was inconsistent with *Matthews v The Chicory Marketing Board*, and stated their preference for the latter decision.
6   (1937) 56 CLR 390.
7   (1908) 6 CLR 41.
8   Griffith CJ, Barton and O'Connor JJ, with Isaacs and Higgins JJ dissenting.
9   (1965) 114 CLR 1.
10  Barwick CJ, Menzies and Windeyer JJ.

motives of the Legislature in enacting it. At the same time, they conceded that there might be laws ostensibly imposing tax which were not to be truly characterised as laws with respect to taxation. None of these judgments commented upon *Barger's Case*. The other two members[11] emphasised two points in particular: that the decision of the majority in *Barger's Case* was based in large measure upon the exploded doctrine of reserved powers of the States; and that the challenged Act imposed no duties or liabilities upon trustees of superannuation funds other than to pay income tax in certain events.[12]

The judgments in which the scope of the taxation power was most fully examined were delivered in the two *Uniform Tax Cases*. In the *First Uniform Tax Case*,[13] the Commonwealth relied on the taxation power to support two out of the four Acts enacted to give effect to the scheme. All members of the court[14] held that the *Income Tax Act* 1942 was a valid exercise of the power. And all except McTiernan J held that the section of the *Income Tax Assessment Act* which gave priority to the liability to pay Commonwealth taxation over the liability to pay State taxation on the income of any year was within the taxation power.[15] Starke J observed in this regard that "the taxing power gives the Commonwealth authority to make its taxation effective and to secure to it the full benefit thereof. In my opinion, there is no distinction in principle between the Commonwealth giving itself priority in the administration of assets in bankruptcy and in giving itself priority in payment of the personal obligations imposed by an income tax".[16]

There were, however, dicta in earlier cases which were to the contrary effect. In particular, Dixon J in *FCT v Official Liquidator of E O Farley Ltd*[17] had stated that "neither in the nature nor in the form of the taxation power is there anything to suggest that the relations of the two governments *inter se* or any rights of the States are involved". In the *Second Uniform Tax Case*[18] Dixon CJ, McTiernan and Kitto JJ decided that on the priorities point the *First Uniform Tax Case* should not be followed. The relevant provision in the *Income Tax Assessment Act* provided that "a taxpayer shall not pay any tax imposed by or under any State Act on the income of any year of income in respect of which tax is imposed by or under any Act with which this Act is incorporated until he has paid that last-mentioned tax or has received from the Commissioner a certificate notifying him that the tax is no longer payable". To support this provision, said Dixon CJ, "it must be said to be incidental to the federal power of taxation to forbid the subjects of a state to pay the tax imposed by the State until that imposed upon them by the Commonwealth is paid, and, moreover, to do that as a measure assisting to exclude the States from the same field of taxation. This appears to me to go beyond any true conception of what is incidental to a legislative power . . .". On the other

---

11 Kitto and Taylor JJ.
12 In *Osborne v Commonwealth* (1911) 12 CLR 321, an "Act to impose a progressive land tax on unimproved values" was unsuccessfully challenged as being in substance an attempt to regulate the holding of land in the Commonwealth and not an exercise of the Commonwealth's taxing powers.
13 (1942) 65 CLR 373.
14 Latham CJ, Rich, Starke, McTiernan and Williams JJ.
15 McTiernan J found it unnecessary to decide whether the section was within the taxation power, as he held it justified by the defence power. See 65 CLR at p 453.
16 65 CLR, at p 441.
17 (1940) 63 CLR 278 at p 316.
18 (1957) 99 CLR 575.

hand, Williams, Webb and Fullagar JJ considered that the decision in the *First Uniform Tax Case* was right and should be followed. Taylor J took a different line, holding that the issue was distinguishable from that which arose in the *First Uniform Tax Case*. His Honour observed that the earlier case was concerned with a temporary measure designed to deal with a very special war-time situation; in the later case, what was in issue was a permanent measure which applied to every taxpayer whatever his financial circumstances might be, and which failed "to specify as a condition of its operation the existence of any circumstance relevant to the exercise by the Commonwealth of a legislative power to protect its revenue".[19]

*Commonwealth taxation and the operations of the States.* The *Engineers' Case*[20] laid down the "prima facie rule that a power to legislate with respect to a given subject enables the Parliament to make laws which, upon that subject, affect the operation of the States and their agencies".[21] But in the *Engineers' Case* the court inserted a warning which could be interpreted as meaning that the prima facie rule might be displaced by virtue of the special nature of the Commonwealth power involved, and it mentioned as an instance the taxation power. In a series of decisions, Dixon J emphasised that the prima facie rule might be displaced by considerations based on the nature or subject matter of the power or the terms in which it was expressed, or from some other provision of the Constitution, and that it was subject to two reservations: one relating to the validity of legislation affecting the exercise of a prerogative of the Crown in right of the States, and the other relating to the validity of legislation discriminating against the States or their agencies.[22] His decision in the *State Banking Case* was based essentially on the view that a section of a Commonwealth Act in respect to banking was void because it discriminated against the States in the use of banks for the conduct of their banking business. In relation to the taxation power, he quoted with approval the opinion of the Supreme Court of the United States that a State cannot be singled out for taxation or for a special burden of taxation in respect of acts or things when others are not taxed or are not so burdened in respect of the same act or things, in other words, that a taxing law discriminating against a State is unconstitutional and void.

The question whether the Commonwealth Parliament may include the Crown in right of a State in the operation of a law imposing tax was answered in the affirmative by the whole court in *State of Victoria v Commonwealth*.[23] But there was disagreement within the court on two points in particular, namely whether the taxation power authorised the imposition of a tax upon any essentially governmental activity of a State, and whether the fact that a Commonwealth tax Act discriminated against the States made it unconstitutional. Barwick CJ, with whom Owen J agreed, held that undue interference by Commonwealth legislation with the performance of what were clearly functions of government was not a ground for invalidity, and that the discriminatory character of legislation was only relevant in determining whether it was

19   99 CLR at p 660.
20   (1920) 28 CLR 129.
21   Per Dixon J in the *State Banking Case* (1947) 74 CLR 31 at p 78.
22   See in particular the *ARU Case* (1930) 44 CLR 319 at p 390, and *West's Case* (1937) 56 CLR 657 at p 682.
23   (1971) 122 CLR 353; [1971] ALR 449. The question had been answered in the same way in *R v Sutton* (1907) 5 CLR 789, and *Attorney-General (NSW) v Collector of Customs (NSW)* (1908) 5 CLR 818.

with respect to a head of Commonwealth power. On the other hand, Menzies J recognised that a law which interfered with the performance by the States of their functions of government might be invalid, though he held that the requirement to pay pay-roll tax was not an interference of the kind which could result in invalidity. He also considered that a law which discriminated against States was invalid, even though it was a law with respect to a subject matter within Commonwealth legislative power. The judgments by Walsh and Gibbs JJ agreed substantially with that of Menzies J.[24] Windeyer J thought that "a law, although it be with respect to a designated subject matter, cannot be for the peace, order and good government of the Commonwealth if it be directed to the States to prevent them carrying out their functions as parts of the Commonwealth".

*Discrimination between States or parts of States.* In *Barger's Case*,[25] the court had to consider the validity of a proviso to a section of the *Excise Tariff* 1906 which exempted from taxation goods manufactured by any person in any part of the Commonwealth under certain conditions as to the remuneration of labour. These conditions could vary according to locality. This fact was considered by Griffith CJ, Barton and O'Connor JJ to invalidate the Act, on the ground that it discriminated between States or parts of States. In the judgment of Griffith CJ,[26]

The words "States or parts of States" must be read as synonymous with "parts of the Commonwealth" or "different localities within the Commonwealth". The existing limits of the States are arbitrary, and it would be a strange thing if the Commonwealth Parliament could discriminate in a taxing Act between one locality and another merely because such localities were not coterminous with States or with parts of the same State.

An opposing view in which a narrower construction was given to the constitutional prohibition was expressed by Isaacs J:[27]

The treatment that is forbidden, discrimination or preference, is in relation to the localities considered as parts of States, and not as mere Australian localities or parts of the Commonwealth considered as a single country ... the pervading idea is the preference of locality merely because it is locality, and because it is a particular part of a particular State.

This statement by Isaacs J was quoted with approval in *Cameron v Deputy Federal Commissioner of Taxation*[28] and by the Privy Council in *Moran's Case*.[29] It was also accepted as correct by Latham CJ in *Elliott v Commonwealth*[30] but in that case Evatt J agreed with the conclusion of the majority in *Barger's Case*.[31] Subsequently, in *FCT v Clyne*[32] Dixon CJ stated

---

24  Gibbs J considered that "a general law of the Commonwealth which would prevent a State from continuing to exist and function as such would be invalid".
25  (1908) 6 CLR 41.
26  6 CLR at p 78.
27  6 CLR at pp 107-8.
28  (1923) 32 CLR 68. In that case, a regulation under which the value of live stock was determined by reference to whether it was in one State or another was held to infringe the proviso to s 51 (ii).
29  63 CLR 338 at p 348.
30  (1936) 54 CLR 657 at p 673.
31  54 CLR at p 690.
32  (1958) 100 CLR 246. The principal point decided in that case was that the system of provisional tax is within the taxation power.

that he had the greatest difficulty in grasping what exactly was the requirement that the selection of an area should be as part of the State, and confessed
that he found himself "unable to appreciate the distinction between the selection by an enactment of an area in fact forming part of a State for the bestowal
of a preference upon the area and the selection of the same area for the same
purpose as part of the State."[33]

A law with respect to taxation does not discriminate contrary to the terms
of s 51 (ii) if its operation is general throughout the Commonwealth even
though, by reason of circumstances existing in one or other States, it may
not operate uniformly.[34]

In *Conroy v Carter*,[35] Barwick CJ McTiernan and Menzies JJ considered
that a section of the *Poultry Industry Levy Collection Act* 1965-1966 (Com)
amounted to an unlawful discrimination.[36] This authorised (in the case where
the Commonwealth had made an arrangement with a State for the collection of
the levy in that State by its egg board) retention by a State egg board of an
amount owing by it to a taxpayer not exceeding the amount of any levy a
a person was liable to pay. They considered that this made a person in a State
with which the Commonwealth had made an arrangement liable to a particular
disadvantage to which a person in a State with which no such arrangement
was made was not exposed.

In some cases it has been argued that the injunction against discrimination
in taxation has been breached through a legislative scheme which brought
about discrimination, though not through the machinery of a taxing Act. In
*Deputy Federal Commissioner of Taxation v W R Moran Pty Ltd*,[37] Commonwealth and State legislation was enacted to give effect to a scheme under
which (a) a uniform federal excise duty was imposed upon flour; (b) the
revenue received by the Commonwealth was then paid by it in grants to the
States upon condition that they apply it to the assistance and relief of wheat
growers, but (c) in the case of Tasmania, the grant was made without conditions, but on the understanding that it would be applied by the Government
of Tasmania in paying back to Tasmanian millers the flour tax paid by them.
The High Court held (with Evatt J dissenting) that the legislation did not
infringe the prohibition in s 51 (ii). The federal Taxation Acts did not discriminate between States, and the special treatment accorded to Tasmania
did not arise from discrimination in a law with respect to taxation.[38] The
Privy Council affirmed the decision, but it warned that a grant under s 96 of
the Constitution might be used for the purpose of effecting discrimination in
regard to taxation under the guise or pretence of assisting a State with money.
However, in the *First Uniform Tax Case*, where the issue was raised again,
Latham CJ said of this warning that "it will not be easy to find a case where it
can properly be held that an appropriation Act making grants to States is
invalid because it involves an infringement of the provision that *Acts with*

---

33   100 CLR, at p 266. These observations were made in relation to an attack on
     the validity of s 79A of the *Income Tax Assessment Act* (deduction for residents
     of isolated areas).
34   *Conroy v Carter* (1968) 118 CLR 90 at p 101 (per Taylor J), and *Colonial
     Sugar Refinery Co v Irving* [1906] AC 360.
35   (1968) 118 CLR 90.
36   Kitto, Taylor and Windeyer JJ dissented.
37   (1939) 61 CLR 735; (1941) 63 CLR 338 (PC).
38   Per Latham CJ at p 757. Evatt J dissented substantially on the ground that the
     scheme created an exemption from tax in favour of Tasmania.

*respect to taxation* shall not discriminate between States or parts of States".[39]

*Legislation.* The principal types of tax levied by the Commonwealth are income tax, customs, excise, sales tax, pay-roll tax (until 1971), estate duty, and gift duty. The legislation relating to customs and excise is noted in the commentary on s 90 of the Constitution. A brief reference to the other forms of tax is given here.

The assessment of income tax is dealt with by the *Income Tax Assessment Act* 1936-1973. Section 17 of this Act provides that income tax and social services contribution at the rates declared by Parliament shall be levied and paid upon the taxable income derived during the year of income by any person, whether a resident or a non-resident. The rates are declared and tax is imposed in the (annual) *Income Tax Act.*[40] The taxable income is defined as the amount remaining after deducting from the assessable income all allowable deductions. The assessable income of a tax-payer includes, where the taxpayer is a resident, the gross income derived directly or indirectly from all sources whether in or out of Australia; and where the taxpayer is a non-resident, the gross income derived directly or indirectly from all sources in Australia which is not exempt income.

A number of sections in the Assessment Act provide for the inclusion of certain amounts in the assessable income, though some of these would not be receipts of an income nature on ordinary concepts.

In calculating the taxable income of a taxpayer, the total assessable income derived by him during the year of income is taken as a basis, and from it there are deducted all allowable deductions. These include not only deductions related to the gaining of the assessable income (general deductions) but also deductions related to the personal circumstances of the taxpayer (concessional deductions).

The fact that the Act includes certain gains of a capital nature in a tax-payer's assessable income has been held not to constitute an infringement of s 55 of the Constitution.[41] Provisions permitting the collection of provisional tax in advance of assessment have been upheld as laws with respect to taxation within the meaning of s 51 (ii) of the Constitution.[42]

In *Giris Pty Ltd v FCT*[43] the High Court held that a provision in the *Income Tax and Social Services Contribution Assessment Act* which gave a discretion to the Taxation Commissioner to assess tax under one section (s 99A) unless he was of the opinion that it would be unreasonable that that section should apply was not deprived of the character of a law with respect to taxation as prescribing no rules at all or as constituting a delegation of legislative power so complete as not to constitute a law at all.

The assessment of sales tax is regulated by the *Sales Tax Assessment Acts* 1930-1966. The tax is levied on nine different classes of sales and hence nine Acts were enacted. Act No 1 is the principal Act, in which provision is made for administration, liability to taxation, collection of the tax, and offences against the Act. It applies to goods manufactured in Australia and sold by the

39  65 CLR 373 at p 428.
40  See also the *Income Tax (Non-Resident Dividends and Interest) Act* 1967, the *Income Tax (Drought Bonds) Act* 1969, the *Income Tax (Bearer Debentures) Act* 1971, and the *Income Tax (Withholding Tax Recoupment) Act* 1971.
41  *Harding v FCT* (1917) 23 CLR 119, and *Resch v FCT* (1942) 66 CLR 198.
42  *Moore v Commonwealth* (1951) 82 CLR 547; *FCT v Clyne* (1958) 100 CLR 246.
43  (1969) 43 ALJR 99; 119 CLR 365; [1969] ALR 369.

manufacturer. Acts Nos 2-4 deal with goods manufactured in Australia and sold by a purchaser from the manufacturer or by another person, or applied by the purchaser to his own use. Acts Nos 5-8 deal with goods imported into Australia. Act No 9 deals with goods in Australia dealt with by lease. In each case, the tax is imposed by a taxing Act.

In *Re Dymond*[44] it was argued that a provision in the *Sales Tax Assessment Act* imposing additional tax following a default assessment was a law imposing taxation, and that as the other provisions dealt with matters other than the imposition of taxation, s 55 of the Constitution was infringed. The argument was rejected, on the ground that additional tax was a penalty imposed by the Act, and not a tax.

The *Pay-roll Tax Assessment Act* 1941-1969 provided for the payment of tax on wages and salaries—subject to certain deductions and exceptions. In *State of Victoria v Commonwealth*[45] it was held that the Commonwealth Parliament could validly include the Crown in right of a State within the operation of this Act. In 1971, an agreement between the Commonwealth and the States provided for the transfer of pay-roll tax to the States.[46]

By the *Estate Duty Assessment Act* 1914-1972, estate duty is assessed on the net value of the estate. This comprises the deceased's real property in Australia, his personal property wherever situate if the deceased was domiciled in Australia at the time of his death, and his personal property in Australia if at the time of his death he had a foreign domicile. The Act extends the definition to include various kinds of notional estate. It was decided in *National Trustees Executors and Agency Co of Australasia Ltd v FCT*[47] that this did not invalidate the Act on the ground that it dealt with more than one subject of taxation contrary to s 55 of the Constitution.

By the *Gift Duty Assessment Act* 1941-1972, gift duty is payable in respect of every gift made by a person domiciled or incorporated in Australia of any property wherever situated or by any other person of any property situated in Australia at the time when the gift is made. The Act contains a number of exemptions from duty. No duty is payable under the *Gift Duty Act* 1941-1972 where the value of the gift together with the total value of gifts made by the donor during the preceding eighteen months does not exceed $10,000.

(iii) *Bounties on the production or export of goods, but so that such bounties shall be uniform throughout the Commonwealth:*[48]

The power of the Commonwealth Parliament to grant bounties on the production or export of goods is exclusive: s 90. To this there is an exception. Nothing in the Constitution prohibits a State from granting any aid to or bounty on mining for gold, silver or other metals, nor from granting, with the consent of both Houses of the Parliament of the Commonwealth expressed by resolution, any aid to or bounty on the production or export of goods.

It is essential to the conception of a bounty that a grant or allowance

44  (1959) 101 CLR 11.
45  (1971) 122 CLR 353; [1971] ALR 449.
46  Tax imposed by the *Pay-roll Tax Act* 1941-1966 was terminated by the *Pay-roll Tax (Termination of Commonwealth Tax) Act* 1971. Certain Commonwealth authorities are made liable to State pay-roll tax by the *Pay-roll Tax (State Taxation of Commonwealth Authorities) Act* 1971.
47  (1916) 22 CLR 367.
48  Quick and Garran 556-8. Wynes 354-5. Howard 77, 203, 307-9. *Essays* 131-2.

is made for or on behalf of a State or an authority under a State.[49] In *Moran's Case* it was argued that provisions in the *Wheat Industry Assistance Act* 1938 involved a bounty on the production or export of goods which was not uniform throughout the Commonwealth. The contention was rejected on the ground that the provisions granted no bounties, but were grants of financial assistance to the States upon condition that the amount granted was distributed to wheat growers in the specified manner.[50]

In *Barger's Case*[51] the majority of the High Court treated the qualification to s 51 (iii), viz, "but so that such bounty shall be uniform throughout the Commonwealth", as equivalent to that in s 51 (ii), viz, "but so as not to discriminate between States or parts of States". In both cases, they stated "Parliament was precluded from attempting to equalise the conditions which nature had made unequal."

*Legislation.* The list of Acts relating to the granting of bounties by the Commonwealth is extensive. In some instances bounties are paid as part of a primary industry stabilisation scheme; in other cases they are paid independently of such schemes.

An instance of the former kind is the bounty paid under the Dairy Industry Stabilisation Plan. Under the provisions of the *Dairying Industry Act* 1962-1972, a bounty on the production of butter at butter factories and on the production of cheese at cheese factories is payable to the proprietor of the factory at which the butter or cheese was produced. Amounts received by the proprietor of the factory as bounty are to be used only to make payments to producers of milk or cream in respect of milk or cream supplied by them to the factory. The subsidies are distributed by the Commonwealth Dairy Produce Equalisation Committee Ltd. The bounty to producers paid under the *Raw Cotton Bounty Act* 1963-1969 on raw cotton produced and sold for use in Australia is an instance of a bounty paid independently of a stabilisation scheme.

The *Phosphate Fertilizers Bounty Act* 1963-1971 provides for payment of a bounty for superphosphate and ammonium phosphate produced at registered premises, and sold for use in Australia as a fertilizer or used by the producer in the production in Australia of a fertilizer mixture for use in Australia. The *Nitrogenous Fertilizers Subsidy Act* 1966-1972 similarly provides for a subsidy on the production of a manufactured nitrogenous substance. This Act also provided for a subsidy in respect of the importation into Australia of a manufactured introgenous substance in certain circumstances. The terms of s 51 (iii) are not wide enough to cover a subsidy on importation, but s 51 (i) presumably justifies that part of the legislation.

Under the *Book Bounty Act* 1969-1970 provision is made for a bounty to be payable outside the agricultural sphere. A bounty of one-quarter of the total cost of production is payable on Australian books produced during the period to which the Act applies.

It should be observed that the General Agreement on Tariffs and Trade

---

49  *Vacuum Oil Co Pty Ltd v Queensland* (1934) 51 CLR 108; *A C Munro and Sons Ltd v Sheehy* [1934] QSR 251.
50  In the *Second Uniform Tax Case*, Dixon J commented that the provisions could not be justified under s 51 (iii) because the basis of the distribution of the moneys was not the production but the sale of wheat (99 CLR at p 607).
51  (1908) 6 CLR 41 at p 70; 14 ALR 304.

(GATT) to which Australia is a party contains provisions restricting the rights of contracting parties to grant bounties and subsidies.

### (iv) *Borrowing money on the public credit of the Commonwealth:*[52]

The scope of this power was discussed in *Commonwealth v Queensland*.[53] Section 52B of the *Commonwealth Inscribed Stock Act* 1911 provided that the interest derived from stock or treasury bonds should not be liable to income tax under any law of the Commonwealth or a State unless the interest was declared to be so liable by the prospectus relating to the loan on which the interest was payable. The High Court held that this provision was justified by s 51 (iv). The power to make laws with respect to Commonwealth borrowing, said Isaacs and Rich JJ, included "the power to fix the terms of the bargain between the Commonwealth and the lenders, and to ensure by appropriate and paramount legislation that the terms it provides shall be enforced".[54]

Section 105A of the Constitution, which was inserted in 1929 to give effect to the financial agreement made in 1927 between the Commonwealth and the States, empowers the Commonwealth to make agreements with the States with respect to the public debts of the States, including the borrowing of money by the Commonwealth. Every such agreement is binding upon the Commonwealth notwithstanding anything in the Commonwealth Constitution. The financial agreement contains provisions for the control of future borrowing by the States and the Commonwealth, and of the conversion, renewal, redemption and consolidation of the public debts of the Commonwealth and of the States. The powers accorded to the Commonwealth by s 51 (iv) of the Constitution are accordingly subject to the provisions of the financial agreement or any variation thereof.

The *Commonwealth Inscribed Stock Act* 1911-1966 authorises the Governor-General to create capital stock for the purpose of raising by way of loan any money authority to borrow which is granted by any Act; for converting any loan raised by the Commonwealth into any other loan so raised; and for paying any expenses of carrying the Act into effect. The principal moneys secured by any stock and the interest thereon are a charge on and payable out of the consolidated revenue fund. All moneys raised by the sale of stock are placed to the credit of the loan fund. Power is also given to issue treasury bonds for the same purposes.

Authority to borrow money is given by a series of loan Acts. The purposes for which the proceeds of a loan raised may be applied are stated in the Act or more commonly in the schedule thereto. For example, the *Loan Act* 1950 authorised the raising and expenditure of money for war service homes and war service land settlement. The *Loan (Housing) Act* 1949 authorised the raising of moneys to be advanced to the States for the purposes of housing. The *Loan (International Bank for Reconstruction and Development) Act* 1950 authorised the raising of a loan from the World Bank.

The *Loans Redemption and Conversion Act* 1921-1950 authorises the paying off, repurchasing, redeeming and converting of loans. The *Loans Securities Act* 1919-1968 provides that when authority is given to borrow money, the Treasurer may be authorised to borrow it on such terms and conditions and issue such securities in such form as the Governor-General approves.

---

52　Quick and Garran 558-9. Wynes 344-5. *Essays* 255.
53　(1920) 29 CLR 1.
54　29 CLR at p 21.

Other Acts relating to the borrowing of money are noted in the commentary on s 105A of the Constitution.

(v) *Postal, telegraphic, telephonic, and other like services:*[55]

Under this head of power the Commonwealth Parliament has power to control communications of the nature specified both within Australia and between Australia and other countries. These services were one of the departments of the public service which were transferred to the Commonwealth after federation.[56]

In *R v Brislan ex parte Williams*[57] an owner of a broadcasting reception appliance challenged provisions of the *Wireless Telegraphy Act* 1905-1919 requiring her to hold a licence for an appliance on the ground that the constitutional power did not sanction such a requirement. In the course of their judgments, which upheld the validity of the legislation, the members of the High Court examined the meaning of the words used in placitum(v). Much of the discussion was centred around the genus constituted by the words "postal, telegraphic and telephonic" services and in particular whether these words extended far enough to enable the federal Parliament to control programmes which were broadcast for general entertainment as well as covering messages and communications of an inter-individual nature. While Dixon J in dissent from the other members of the court was prepared to accept a narrow view of the genus as being based on individual inter-communication,[58] the other members of the courts adopted a wider view. Latham CJ considered that the common characteristics of postal, telegraphic and telephonic services were to be found in the services which they perform: "they are each of them communication services. If a new form of communication should be discovered, it too could be made the subject of legislation as a 'like' service."[59] Rejecting the notion that the paragraph was restricted to services providing inter-individual communication, Rich and Evatt JJ went on to describe broadcasting by a wireless as telephonic in nature. From the point of view of the listener it was a public service designed not only to provide sounds in the form of words but also musical and other forms which might entertain as well as instruct.[60]

In the more recent case of *Jones v Commonwealth*[61] the High Court was called upon to decide the validity of provisions of the *Broadcasting and Television Act* 1942-1962 which permitted land to be acquired for the National Broadcasting and Television Service, i e, the ABC, under procedures laid down in the *Lands Acquisition Act* 1955-1966. In this case it was argued for the plaintiff that the land could not be validly acquired as some of the functions of the Australian Broadcasting Commission were not within the constitutional head of power, i e, in respect of the transmission of television programmes in particular, control over which had been conferred on the Commission with the advent of television in Australia in the 1950s. Television, it was argued, was a completely new form of communication unknown to the drafters of the Constitution and outside the area of scientific and technological knowledge in

---

55    Quick and Garran, 559-60. Wynes, 131-3.
56    Under s 69.
57    (1935) 54 CLR 262 reviewed in 9 ALJ 348.
58    Ibid at 292-3.
59    Ibid at 280.
60    Ibid at 282-3.
61    (1964-5) 112 CLR 206, [1965] ALR 706.

1900: therefore, it was beyond the genus to be derived from the words used in section 51 (v). Here again an overwhelming majority of the court upheld the validity of the legislation and the purposes of the commission as set out in the amendments to the Act. Barwick CJ considered that the basic characteristic of the services was to be founded in the "organized communication of messages from a distance, as well as the communication of messages by an organized means from a distance." The power covered the provision of programmes as well as the means of conveying those programmes to a listening or viewing audience physically separated from the point of origin of the programmes.[62] While Barwick CJ considered that television was a "telephonic" service, McTiernan J took the view that it was a "like service."[63] The result is the same whether one treats the form of communication as being within the specific part of the genus or within the genus itself. Menzies J, who dissented, said he was inclined to adopt the view of Dixon J in *Brislan's Case.*[64]

Under the *Wireless Telegraphy Act* 1905-1967, authority is given to the Minister for Posts and Telegraphs to regulate the establishment and maintenance of appliances used for transmitting messages by wireless telegraphy as well as for licensing broadcasting reception appliances. This power now extends to the establishment of broadcasting appliances on vessels in waters adjacent to Australia and thus what has become known as "pirate broadcasting" is prohibited.[65] The *Broadcasting and Television Act* 1942-1972 has established a Broadcasting Control Board with wide powers including the supervision of the standards of programmes of both the National Broadcasting Commission (the Australian Broadcasting Commission) and commercial stations, as well as technical powers of determining frequencies and locations of stations. This Act also establishes the Australian Broadcasting Commission to provide wireless and television programmes of an adequate standard. The Commission, inter alia, is given power to subsidise concerts and to publish material relating to broadcasting. The granting of licences to set up broadcasting or television stations is a matter for the final decision of the Minister after an inquiry has been conducted by the Broadcasting Control Board. It is to be noted that there are sections in the Act which prohibit the concentration of shareholding in companies controlling stations in a few hands. From one point of view these provisions could be characterized as legislation with respect to the ownership of property, and therefore outside Commonwealth power; however, the more persuasive way of characterizing them is as legislation incidental to the control of broadcasting, i e, it could be shown that it is in the interest of the effective control of broadcasting that limitations should be imposed on the ownership or "control" rights of individuals and groups so that monopolies are not created.[66]

So far as postal services (communications by *missive* as Dixon J put it in *Brislan's Case*) are concerned, it would seem that it would be within the power conferred by s 51 (v) to impose controls not only on the means of communication but also the content of communications which are sent. The Post Office

---

62   112 CLR at 219.
63   Ibid at 222.
64   Ibid at 229-31.
65   *Wireless Telegraphy Act,* No 59 of 1967.
66   In *Herald and Weekly Times Ltd v Commonwealth* (1966) 115 CLR 418 that part of the Act which imposes conditions upon the holding of commercial television station licences and prohibits certain conduct in relation to such licences was held to be validly enacted under s 51 (v).

may, for example, refuse to receive or transmit a telegram containing indecent or offensive matter.[67] Another Act to be noted is the *Telephonic Communications (Interception) Act* 1960 which prohibits telephones from being "tapped" except under authority given to the ASIO.[68]

In recent years international communications have grown. Satellites are now being used to assist the speedy transmission of pictures and sounds from one country to another. Telecommunications with other countries falls within s 51 (v) as well as being within s 51 (xxix), the External Affairs power, Australia being a party to a number of agreements on this matter.[69]

(vi) *The naval and military defence of the Commonwealth and of the several States, and the control of the forces to execute and maintain the laws of the Commonwealth:*[70]

The powers and duties of the Commonwealth in relation to defence are derived not only from s 51 (vi) but also from other sections of the Constitution, e g, ss 68, 52 (ii), 69, 70, 114 and 119. Defence in its basic connotation has been understood as meaning defence against hostile warlike action (actual or potential) from some external source. In the light of modern concepts of the relationships between States it may be extended to cover reaction to foreign policies of other States in the diplomatic and even psychological areas of "contest".[71]

There is also an internal security aspect of defence which is derived partially from s 51 (vi) but is usually held to reside primarily in s 61 (the Executive power) and s 51 (xxix) (the incidental power).[72]

In earlier years it had been thought that the defence power was exclusive to the Commonwealth. In *Joseph v Colonial Treasurer*[73] which involved proceedings against a NSW minister for acts affecting contracts of the plaintiff, the war prerogative was pleaded by the State in justification.[74] A majority of the court held that the defence power was exclusively assigned to the Commonwealth. "It is a matter of common knowledge that the necessity of a single authority for the defence of Australia was one of the urgent, perhaps the most urgent of all the needs for the establishment of the Constitution. That power now rests in the one hand so far as Australian authority extends."[75] In *Australian Workers' Union v Adelaide Milling Company*[76] Higgins J stated

---

67    *Post and Telegraph Act* 1901-1971, s 96. See also s 121 of the Act (offensive material) and s 124 (defamatory material on radio or TV) discussed in 4 U Tas LR (1972) 70.

68    For a discussion of this legislation see Barry, "An End to Privacy", (1960) 2 MULR 443. Comment "Eavesdropping—Four Legal Aspects", (1962) 3 MULR 364.

69    The *Overseas Telecommunications Act* 1946-1971 establishes a statutory corporation to carry on communications with other countries.

70    On this placitum see Quick and Garran, 561-5. Wynes, 188-218. Nicholas, 110-33. Essays, 157-92. Lane, 71-97. Howard, 422-41.

71    For a discussion of the fluctuating nature of the defence power in relationship to the facts which call it forth, see *Stenhouse v Coleman* (1944) 69 CLR 457 at 471-2 (Dixon J).

72    See below.

73    (1918) 25 CLR 32.

74    The action of the State was taken pursuant to a scheme agreed upon by the Commonwealth and States which involved the pooling of wheat produced in Australia in order to assist the Imperial war effort.

75    25 CLR at 46.

76    (1919) 26 CLR 460.

that the State of Victoria did not have the "war power".[77] However, the question was re-examined in *Carter v Egg and Egg Pulp Marketing Board*.[78] The case concerned a challenge to Victorian marketing legislation established to control the sale of eggs during wartime. It was argued that the legislation was in effect legislation with respect to defence and did not fall within the ordinary powers of a State parliament. The majority of the court (Latham CJ, Starke and McTiernan JJ) were of the opinion that the power was not exclusive. Latham CJ said "Section 51 (vi) is not exclusive in terms. It confers a power affirmatively upon the Commonwealth Parliament but it contains no words which can be used in support of an argument that the States are completely or in any degree excluded from dealing with the subject of defence. There is no reason arising from the nature of the subject matter why a State should not, subject to such control as the Commonwealth Parliament may think proper to be exercised, assist the Commonwealth to the maximum in the defence of the country."[79] On the other hand, Williams J (with whom Rich J agreed) considered that the Commonwealth could legislate on matters which related exclusively to defence while the States only had a concurrent power to deal with the economic aspects of wartime organisation arising from the war. "Legislation on these subjects is legislation with regard to matters upon which the States are entitled to legislate not to defend themselves, but to carry out their civil policy, and to do so in times of war as well as in times of peace."[80] It would appear that Williams J differs from the majority in being prepared to treat legislation of this nature as legislation not with respect to defence but with respect to civil organisation.

It may be that the difference between the two approaches is merely one of emphasis. In terms of some parts of the defence power the Commonwealth power is by its nature exclusive or has been made so by other sections of the Constitution: e g, the raising of armed forces (s 114), the control of the armed forces and the defence department (s 69, 52 (ii)) and in an executive sense, the royal prerogative[81] of making war and peace must also be regarded as exclusive to the Commonwealth. On the other hand, it is only necessary to characterise the State law as being for the peace, welfare and good government of the State and as not intruding on the exclusive aspects of Commonwealth power and not being inconsistent with Commonwealth legislation.[82] There may be other modes of defence which can be undertaken in time of war

---

77    Ibid at 475.
78    (1943) 66 CLR 557.
79    Ibid at 571.
80    Ibid at 596.
81    Of course where a statutory enactment covering the matter is in existence, the royal prerogative is to that extent superseded: *Attorney-General v De Keyser's Royal Hotel* [1920] AC 508. Derham, in *Essays* (at 191) states: "To the extent that the States do have a legislative defence power, some of the remarks in *Joseph v Colonial Treasurer* may seem now to be wrong; but insofar as the prerogative provides powers to the Executive for defence purposes, that decision may still be regarded as correct, since executively the defence power is in a real sense made exclusive to the Commonwealth by the joint action of ss 52 (ii), 68, 69, 70 and 114 of the Constitution.
82    See Wynes at 190, who views *Carter's Case* as primarily raising the question of inconsistency. On the other hand, Isaacs J in *Pirrie v Macfarlane* (1929) 36 CLR 170 at 199-200 considered the defence power to be exclusive to the Commonwealth. The view of Isaacs J on this point has been criticized by Sawer, "Implication and the Constitution" 4 Res Judicatae at 85-6.

which concern Australia as a whole and, therefore, only to be undertaken by the Commonwealth Parliament which is responsible for the defence of the Australian nation as a whole. However, the economic aspects or conditions arising from war-control of prices, housing and the like (the matters which Williams J refers to as the economic organisation of the war) are within the legislative power of States as well as, of course, of the Commonwealth.

*Elastic nature of the defence power and problems of judicial review.* In *Farey v Burvett*[83] the High Court held that the word "naval and military" as used in s 51 (vi) were words of extension and not of limitation, that is, that they were merely illustrative of the purposes for which the defence power could be used and did not exhaust its content. Consequently the defence power extended to matters beyond the merely physical methods of defence by armies and navies. In this case regulations made under a First World War statute—the *War Precautions Act* of 1914—fixing the price of a basic commodity, were upheld.[84] Thus, at an early stage the argument that the power of the Commonwealth was to be restricted to the raising and maintaining of forces was laid to rest.

Dixon J pointed out in *Stenhouse v Coleman*[85] that the defence power could be defined only in terms of purpose.[86] In this respect it differed from other powers which depended on characterisation of subject matter. This means that a court when considering the validity of any measure from the point of view of defence, is inevitably required to look at the purpose of the measure and to determine whether it could be considered to help in the defence of the Commonwealth. On the other hand this does not mean that the court sits in judgment on legislative policy. It has been repeatedly emphasized by the High Court that its function is not to decide whether any measure is or is not appropriate for the purposes of the defence of the Commonwealth. That, it has been said is entirely a matter for the Parliament and the government. But the court must be satisfied that there is some connection, or real connection, to use an expression commonly used, between the law in question and the defence of Australia. In *Dawson v The Commonwealth*[87] Latham CJ stated,

It is not the duty or the function of the court itself to consider whether in its opinion such regulations are "necessary" for defence purposes. Questions of legislative policy are determined by the Legislature, not by the courts. If it can reasonably be considered that there is a real connection between the subject matter of the legislation and defence, the court should hold that the legislation is authorized by the power to make laws with respect to defence.[88]

In spite of this attitude adopted by the High Court, it is obvious that the enquiry whether there is a real connection between a law and the subject matter of defence cannot ignore altogether questions of governmental policy. If the defence plan is simple, probably little difficulty will be encountered,

---

83   (1916) 21 CLR 433.
84   For a discussion of the case see Derham in *Essays* at 159-60. It must be noted that *Farey v Burvett* and other early decisions regarded Australian defence as a component part of Imperial defence. The full development of the defence power could not take place until after this concept had been discarded.
85   (1944) 69 CLR 457.
86   Ibid at 471.
87   (1946) 73 CLR 157.
88   Ibid at 173.

but an elaborate plan of defence will necessarily entail the enactment of many laws which taken by themselves may not seem to accomplish much in the way of increasing the efficiency of armed forces or in the defence of the Commonwealth generally. The Government may take the view, quite genuinely, that as a policy every such law is essential or important to the whole plan. But this would not be conclusive on the court, which may hold that it can see no real connection between some particular law and defence.

The extent of the defence power varies accordingly as the Commonwealth is at war or at peace, or more accurately speaking, according to the degree and nature of the danger of external aggression at a given period of time. In a period of stable and amicable international relations the extent of the power is small; there could be no reasonable justification for interference by the Commonwealth with most ordinary civil activities. But at a period of international discord the danger of the Commonwealth becoming involved in war may be great and additional measures (i e, measures indicating an increase in the range of subjects of legislative action otherwise beyond the constitutional power of the Commonwealth Parliament) to prepare for such an eventuality would be justified. Nevertheless, here also matters of policy may be involved, because there may be genuine and fundamental differences of opinion as to the imminence of the danger or as to the direction in which it lies. In its search for a real connection between a law and defence, the court is bound to come to some conclusion on these matters, and its conclusion will not necessarily be the same as that of the government.[89]

It is obvious that in determining whether a law is or is not within the defence power, judges are required to have a very wide knowledge of human affairs outside the narrow confines of the law. As economics are a vital factor in war and defence today they must have a broad knowledge of economic matters. In so far as the defence of Australia may be vitally linked with the defence of the United Kingdom, the Commonwealth, Asian countries and Pacific countries, they may be required to have some knowledge of broad international defence strategy. And they must necessarily have some knowledge of international affairs generally. These are all matters on which genuine differences of opinion are possible, matters which, in a unitary State, are essentially problems for the executive and legislative authorities to decide.

The question arises then as from what source the judges are to obtain their wide and, in some cases, precise knowledge of these matters. Traditionally they have relied simply on general knowledge. The doctrine of *judicial notice,* whereby the courts require no evidence of matters which are so notorious that evidence of their existence is deemed unnecessary, has been very broadly applied. In *Farey v Burvett*[90] Griffith CJ took judicial notice of the fact that the previous season's wheat harvest was abundant, that a great surplus was waiting export, and that shipping for that purpose was scarce. This, therefore,

---

89    This type of question gives rise to questions similar to those which have arisen recently in the courts in which a Government claims privilege from disclosure of documents on the ground of prejudice to the public good, eg, *Conway v Rimmer* [1968] AC 910. The tendency of the courts has been to reject the conclusiveness of the governmental claim of privilege.

     It is true of course that there was a minority viewpoint first proposed by Isaacs J and later developed by Williams and McTiernan JJ that was more deferential to Government policy. See Sawer, "The Defence Power of the Commonwealth in Time of War" (1946) 20 ALJ 295 at 297.

90    (1916) 21 CLR 433.

justified Commonwealth control over the disposition of and pricing and other matters associated with basic food resources.[91]

Because of the vagueness and imprecision associated with the doctrine of judicial notice, some commentators have claimed that evidence should be admitted in order to support a claim of constitutionality.[92] In actual fact in certain cases the High Court has admitted evidence to show the requisite degree of connection between the needs of defence and the concrete provisions of a particular act. In *Jenkins v Commonwealth*[93] the validity of a statutory instrument preventing the sale of mica, a mineral used in the production of armaments, was upheld on the basis of evidence relating to the use of the mineral and its availability on the world market.[94] In *Sloan v Pollard*[95] post-war controls on the sale of cream were upheld on the basis of the adduction of evidence showing that arrangements between Australia and the United Kingdom for the supply of butter necessitated controls on the sale of cream within Australia in the "winding-up" period.[96]

The *Communist Party Case*[97] (to be discussed in detail later) also emphasized the doctrine of judicial notice as assisting the court in determining whether the basis for the exercise of the "secondary" aspect of the defence power existed.

*The power in peace time.* One has to distinguish between times of profound peace and times of international uncertainty. While in early periods of Australian history there may well have been periods of profound peace, events since the Second World War have indicated that the international situation is never likely to become so stabilized that one could refer to a long period of profound peace; Australia has been involved in the Korean War and more recently in the war in Vietnam and in military action in Malaysia and Borneo. These are facts which a court must take judicial notice of and, to the extent to which judicial notice is applied, Commonwealth measures in peace time may receive more favourable consideration than they would have if the international situation were ignored. However, it is also true that the nature of the threat or hostilities will qualify the nature of the controls which may be imposed. When the reaction is merely to a "threat", the scope for judicial notice will be narrower.

In the *Commonwealth v Australian Commonwealth Shipping Board*[98] it was held that a Commonwealth Shipping Authority could not constitutionally enter into an agreement with a local council to sell certain machinery, viz,

---

91  Ibid at 442-3. See also *Australian Textiles Pty Ltd v Commonwealth* (1946) 71 CLR 161. *Crouch v Commonwealth* (1948) 77 CLR 339. *Hume v Higgins* (1949) 78 CLR 116.
92  See Holmes "Evidence in Constitutional Cases" (1949) 23 ALJ 235.
93  (1947) 74 CLR 400.
94  This case was heard before a single justice, thus allowing for a trial of facts which cannot occur in a full court determining a matter on demurrer (unless the case is remitted for trial before a single judge).
95  (1947) 75 CLR 445.
96  See also *Wilcox Mofflin v New South Wales* 85 CLR 488. *Boland v Sneddon* (1959) 102 CLR 280 at 292, per *Dixon CJ*: "All that is necessary is to make the point that if a criterion of constitutional validity consists in a matter of fact, that fact must be ascertained by the court as best it can, when the court is called upon to pronounce upon validity."
97  (1951) 83 CLR 1.
98  (1926) 39 CLR 1.

steam turbo-alternators. This period, 1926, was a period which one might say was a period of total peace, and the court was not prepared to accept any argument that the defence power allowed the establishment of governmental businesses for ordinary trade purposes. However, this case may be contrasted with *Attorney General for Victoria v Commonwealth*.[99] It is accepted that the Commonwealth can establish factories for the manufacture of service equipment and uniforms; in effect this may be regarded as part of the primary defence power, that is naval and military defence, and the organization of the armed forces. In the nineteen thirties it had entered into agreements with various State authorities and also certain private firms to sell clothing (not military clothing) to these bodies. It was argued that this "outside" trade was necessary in order to keep the Commonwealth factories in operation and in a state of preparation for a time when war broke out. It was held by the High Court that this was a valid exercise of the defence power. The difference between the *Shipping Board Case* and the *Clothing Case* may be said to be that in the first case the activity did not have imprinted on it a direct relationship with defence while in the second case a direct relationship with defence was apparent. Perhaps the circumstances of the nineteen thirties, with warlike threats emanating from Germany and Japan, was an important background factor in the latter case.

The Commonwealth established the Snowy Mountains Hydro-electric Scheme after the Second World War to provide hydro-electricity in the South-Eastern part of Australia, and one of the bases for the exercise of this power is the defence power, i e, to satisfy the need for supplies of electricity for defence works and undertakings and to provide for the immediate availability of increased supplies of electricity in the event of war.[1] It would seem, therefore, that such economic control, that is, direct involvement of the Commonwealth in economic and national development projects, is justifiable from a defence point of view, and this is what might be called an example of the secondary aspect of the defence power; one cannot make a strict separation between war and peace in so far as preparations for war or rather preparations for self-defence are very necessary. Of course, this does not mean that the Commonwealth can enter generally into the field of civilian life.[2]

*Preparation for war.* Since the range of matters which can be brought within the scope of the defence power expands and contracts according to the degree of apprehension of danger of external aggression, it follows that legislation may be justified under the power at a time of imminent danger of war or disturbed international conditions which would not be justified under ordinary conditions of peace. Two particular questions arise in this connection: (1) Can the defence power be as wide in such a case as in time of actual war? (2) How is the existence of the imminent danger of war to be determined? These questions were considered by the High Court in the *Communist Party Case*.[3]

The *Communist Party Dissolution Act* 1950 was an attempt by the Federal Parliament to arrogate to itself *conclusive* power to determine the

99 (1935) 52 CLR 533.
1 See Derham in *Essays* at 171 n 58. In the *Tennessee Valley Authority Case*, the United States Supreme Court upheld the establishment of a governmental authority to generate electricity and perform other developmental tasks.
2 See below under heading of the defence power in time to war.
3 83 CLR 1, discussed by Anderson, 1 UQLJ 34.

justification for legislation in the interests of defence and internal security. There was a long preamble containing a legislative indictment of the Australian Communist Party and also Communists, seeking to provide the necessary connection between the Act and defence.[4] The High Court by a majority of 6-1 (Latham CJ dissenting) held that Parliament could not take away from the courts the power to determine whether that necessary nexus existed, in accordance with the principles laid down in earlier decisions on the defence power. As Fullagar J put it, Parliament could not "recite itself into a field which was closed to it".[5] The court held that, at any rate in time of peace, legislation must provide scope for the court to test it against the Constitution: the operation of the law must be made to depend on the *objective existence of some fact or course of conduct*, for example, by forbidding certain descriptions of conduct or establishing objective standards or tests of liability. Those objective facts or standards could then be examined by the courts to see if they provided the necessary connection between the law and the defence power or some other head of power in the Constitution, and the execution of the law would be kept within the constitutional power by the fact that every application of it could be tested against the objective facts or standards laid down as the condition of its operation. Therefore, Parliament could not assume the power to determine conclusively the existence of the facts necessary to support the banning of the Communist Party as an exercise of the defence power. And it was held that the Parliament could not confer on the executive any similar power of dissolving organizations and forfeiting their property as well as depriving their members of civil liberties without some opportunity being given for judicial control in the interests of constitutional validity.[6] In the absence of such judicial control, the court pointed out, the government could invoke the Act against a person who, though a "communist" was not in fact engaged or likely to be engaged in activities prejudicial to the defence of the Commonwealth; that is to say, the government could apply the Act in a way which would be beyond its constitutional powers. The decision in the *Communist Party Case* thus marks an unequivocal rejection by the High Court of any *general* policy of judicial restraint in respect of the defence power, i e, of a policy of bowing to Parliament's determination of the needs of defence.

However, all the majority judges, with the apparent exception of Kitto J, indicated that they were prepared to adopt such a policy in time of actual war as, in effect, the High Court had done (though not without exceptions) during World War II. Indeed, what Fullagar J referred to as the "secondary aspect" of the defence power, under which there is a presumption of validity[7] in favour of legislation in the name of defence, would authorise in time of war such an Act as the *Communist Party Dissolution Act*, directly proscribing organisations and individuals, or conferring discretion on the executive to do so,[8] or to do other things the pursuance of which the Parliament or the

---

4    The provisions of the Act are set out in the (dissenting) judgment of Latham CJ at 129 et seq.

5    83 CLR at 264.

6    Cf, *Jehovah's Witnesses Case* (1943) 67 CLR 116 discussed below.

7    This presumption is a rule of evidence arising from the common experience of man: "The greater the threat, the more absolute the power to meet it must be".

8    In *Wishart v Fraser* (1941) 64 CLR 470 delegation of a power to make orders detaining persons in order to protect the security of the nation was upheld. For a discussion of the exercise of discretionary power in time of war see *Little v Commonwealth* (1940) 75 CLR 94, Wynes 210-4.

Executive considered to be in the interests of defence.[9] But even here, as can be seen from the *Jehovah's Witnesses Case*,[10] a connection must be shown between the acts of the organisation proscribed and the defence power, in other words it must be apparent that the organisation is engaged in activities directly prejudicial to the defence of the Commonwealth.[11]

Of the six judges who supported this secondary aspect of the defence power in time of war, all except Williams J were prepared to concede that its operation was not limited to time of actual war and that it would apply in times of imminent danger of war in order to allow the government to make what preparations it deemed fit. However, the court was satisfied in this case that there was no such imminent danger of war as to justify the Act.

If, then, the secondary aspect of the defence power may come into operation in times of imminent danger, it is necessary to answer the question, how is the existence of such an imminent danger to be determined? The majority of the court were quite definite that the decision must rest ultimately with the court itself; and normally (although Fullagar J said "always") a decision must depend on the court being able to take judicial notice of the fact.[12]

It might have been thought, on the basis of the *Communist Party Case*, that the High Court was adopting an attitude to the defence power which would have seriously inhibited the Commonwealth's power to organize the country in preparation for war. Such a view, however, was dispelled by a case in the following year: *Marcus Clark and Company Ltd v Commonwealth* (the *Capital Issues Case*).[13] The legislation impugned (the *Defence Preparations Act* 1951) and regulations made thereunder (the *Capital Issues Regulations*) allowed the Treasurer to prohibit, inter alia, new share issues in companies. The court, in upholding the validity of the Act and the Regulations, distinguished the *Communist Party Case* on the ground that the Act and Regulations provided objective standards on which the legislative and executive action, as the case might be, was made to depend, and in which the necessary connection with defence could be seen. But it must be noted that the objective standards were nothing more than "defence preparations" as very widely described in the preamble to the legislation. However, the court took judicial notice of the fact that such economic controls were the normal practice for a country going on a war footing. Moreover, 1952 was a year when Australia had committed forces to the Korean war. And indeed, the discretion conferred on the Treasurer by regulations made under the legislation had to be supported by facts showing that a refusal to issue approval in a particular case was related to defence purposes.[14]

---

9   See 83 CLR at 253 et seq (per Fullagar J) for a discussion of the secondary aspect of the defence power.

10   (1943) 67 CLR 116.

11   The defence power like all other powers is conferred "subject to the Constitution". Consequently a law must not infringe any prohibition contained in the Constitution. See *Gratwick v Johnson* (1945) 70 CLR 1.

12   For a strong criticism of this view and of the limitations of judicial notice and legal evidence in this connection see the dissenting judgment of Latham CJ 83 CLR at 163-4.

13   (1952) 87 CLR 177, discussed by Masterman in 1 Sydney Law Review 266. The Act is examined by Ellicott in (1951) 25 ALJ 162.

14   See Derham in *Essays* at 184-5.

*Defence power in time of war.* Although the general test of validity remains the same in war as in peace, the courts are more ready to uphold defence legislation in time of war. In war time it is easier to see a real connection between defence and laws which regulate ordinary civil activity. Also there is a recognition by the courts that reasons of security may prevent them in war time from being fully informed of the facts on which the legislation is based. During World War I, Isaacs J in various judgments, took a view which would have made Commonwealth powers virtually unlimited. For example in *Welsbach Light Company of Australasia v Commonwealth*[15] he stated: "defence includes every act which in the opinion of the proper authority is conducive to the public security."[16] And in *Farey v Burvett*[17] he said that in time of war the limits of the defence power were bounded only by the requirements of self-preservation.[18] However, Griffith CJ in the same case adopted a more sober test: whether the measures in question were conducive to the efficiency of the forces of the Empire.[19]

Although, during the Second World War, hardly an aspect of commercial or social life remained untouched by Commonwealth legislation, the High Court on a few occasions, by striking down legislation, made it clear that the existence of war did not mean that the Commonwealth had unlimited powers.

At the beginning of the war, the Commonwealth Parliament enacted the *National Security Act* under which myriads of regulations were made. During the course of the war there were a number of challenges to Commonwealth legislative and executive action.[20] In the early part of the war, the *Uniform Tax Case (South Australia v The Commonwealth)*[21] was decided. That case which was to have such profound effect on future constitutional Commonwealth-State relations, upheld the right of the Commonwealth to take over State taxation offices and personnel under the *Income Tax (War-Time Arrangements) Act* 1942, as having sufficient connection with the defence of the Commonwealth.

The great number of challenges came in the years 1942 and 1943, thus indicating that as the threat to the Australian mainland from the Japanese forces subsided, so there increased a tendency on the part of Australian citizens and companies to challenge defence legislation on the grounds that such legislation was not related to the defence of the Commonwealth. In *Victoria v Commonwealth*,[22] the *National Security (Supplementary) Regulations*, which brought under control the holidays and remuneration of members of the Public Service in the State of Victoria who were not engaged in war work, were declared invalid. In *Silk Brothers v State Electricity Commission of Victoria*,[23] the principal contention was that legislation controlling the price of rented houses was invalid. It was sought to show that the regulations, applying throughout the length and breadth of Australia without any regard

---

15   (1916) 22 CLR 268.
16   Ibid at 280.
17   (1916) 21 CLR 433.
18   Ibid at 453.
19   Ibid at 441.
20   The full list of cases is set out in Wynes, 194-7. See also Sugerman and Dignan, "The Defence Power and Total War" 17 ALJ 207.
21   (1942) 65 CLR 373.
22   (1942) 66 CLR 488.
23   (1943) 67 CLR 1.

to the varying conditions in that area, were in substance regulations for the social control of the relations of landlord and tenant with respect to rent, having no connection with defence. It was held, however, that the control of housing was a matter which was associated with the prosecution of the war.

In *Drummond's Case*[24] the *National Security (Universities) Regulations* controlling admission to Universities were invalidated by a three/two majority. In the words of Starke J:

In truth, in taking power to determine the total number of students who may be enrolled in any faculty or course of study in the universities of Australia, the Commonwealth is seeking to control education in the universities of Australia, which is wholly beyond its powers.[25]

In the *Industrial Lighting Case*,[26] regulations establishing the standards of lighting equipment to be used in industrial premises were invalidated. Latham CJ drew a distinction between the general relation which all matters affecting the well being of the community at war might have with the defence power, and the specific relation which such matters must have to come within the power. In this latter respect the regulations failed to measure up to the required connection.[27] In the *Prices Regulations Case*,[28] provisions controlling the prices of goods sold in Australia were upheld. As was pithily put in that case, "in modern times, all countries in time of war have found it necessary to deal with profiteering and inflation."[29]

In the *Womens Employment Regulations Case*,[30] counsel sought to counter the argument which had succeeded with the Commonwealth in the *Prices Regulations Case,* by arguing that the regulation of women's employment was not one of those things which "automatically" fell within the defence power once the nation was at war. However, in upholding the validity of the regulations Latham CJ stressed the concept of the "war-created problem". Legislation dealing with war-created problems fell within the defence power. The dislocation of normal women's employment patterns was such a problem; therefore the legislation was valid.[31] Starke J dissented, holding that the regulations were for the purpose of controlling the employment of all women in certain categories regardless of the question whether the work to be performed related or did not relate to defence.[32] The difference in approaches is obvious. The majority took what could be called a broad view; once women's employment could be called a war-created problem, any legislation which could fairly be said to regulate that problem, was legislation with respect to defence. Starke J required a more stringent test: the legislation must not only deal with a war-time problem; the substance and effect of it must be examined to show that the regulation of the problem was one stemming from the requirements of defence.

---

24   *R v University of Sydney ex parte Drummond* (1943) 67 CLR 95.
25   Ibid at 109.
26   *Victorian Chamber of Manufacturers v Commonwealth* (1943) 67 CLR 413.
27   Ibid at 417.
28   *Victorian Chamber of Manufacturers v Commonwealth* (1943) 67 CLR 335.
29   Ibid at 339.
30   *Victorian Chamber of Manufacturers v Commonwealth* (1943) 67 CLR 347.
31   Ibid at 357-8.
32   Ibid at 379 et seq.

In the *Jehovah's Witnesses Case*[33] there were two principal issues: firstly, whether the *National Security (Subversive Organizations) Regulations* infringed s 116 in their application to the Jehovah's Witnesses. Secondly, whether the operation of certain of the regulations exceeded the defence power of the Commonwealth. The scheme of the regulations was that the Governor-General could declare unlawful any body which, in his opinion, was, by its existence, prejudicial to the war effort. Other regulations set out the consequences of such declaration, one providing that the property of the declared body should become the property of the Commonwealth and permitting the Commonwealth to enter into possession of the premises of the declared organisation and to seize the property found therein. A further regulation prohibited the publication of unlawful doctrines, unlawful doctrines being defined to include any doctrine advocated by declared bodies.

It was recognized that Parliament had the right to protect the nation against subversion. But a number of the regulations were held invalid as being in excess of the defence power. In particular, fault was found with the provision that the Commonwealth could enter into occupation of the premises of a declared organization, as long as there remained in those premises property of the organization. That is to say the criterion on which the Commonwealth's right to occupy the premises depended was the presence of the property of the organization—it did not depend on unlawful user. It therefore fell outside the defence power.[34] The provision prohibiting the publication of unlawful doctrines was also invalid. As Latham CJ pointed out, such doctrines could include the ten commandments. The criterion of illegality was that, ipso facto, the doctrines were being advanced by a declared body, not that they were inherently prejudicial to the defence of the Commonwealth.[35]

The *Jehovah's Witness Case* must be set aside from the other cases discussed. In those cases where war-time regulations failed, they failed because there was no real connection between the matter regulated and the defence power, but in this case, there was no doubt that the Commonwealth could suppress subversion; the fault was that the methods sought to be used, however effective in suppressing subversion, went a great deal further. They went far beyond defence requirements.[36]

*The defence power after the conclusion of hostilities.* The Commonwealth, as an aspect of or as incidental to the defence power, is able to legislate for the orderly transition from hostilities to peace. How long does this transition

---

33   *Adelaide Company of Jehovah's Witnesses Incorporated v Commonwealth* (1943) 67 CLR 116.
34   Ibid at 141.
35   Ibid at 144.
36   Two other cases in which Commonwealth controls were held to be beyond constitutional powers were *R v Commonwealth Court of Conciliation and Arbitration ex parte Victoria* (1944) 68 CLR 485 (regulations affecting the employment of women in purely governmental activities of a State) and *Wertheim v Commonwealth* (1945) 69 CLR 601 (subordinate legislation affecting the manufacture and disposal of fly-spray). Cases in which the exercise of Commonwealth power was upheld include *Pidoto v Victoria* (1943) 68 CLR 87 (control of holidays of persons in industrial employment). *Reid v Siderberry* (1944) 68 CLR 504 (control of manpower). *Gozwa v Commonwealth* (1944) 68 CLR 469 (regulation of practice of medicine by aliens).

period last? The answer depends on the nature of the legislation in question.[37] Legislation in respect of certain matters, e g for the provision of war service homes, might well be a valid exercise of the defence power for an indefinitely prolonged period after the war. The Commonwealth cannot legislate for *every* matter merely because in has been affected by the war, since the result would be virtually to give the Commonwealth unlimited power. For most purposes, the winding up process was brought to an end in 1949 by three cases in which a single consolidated judgment was delivered, reported under the name of the first case: *R v Foster.*[38]

In its judgment in *Foster's Case*, the court said:

The Constitution does not confer upon the Commonwealth Parliament any power in express terms to deal with the consequences of war, but there are some consequences which undeniably fall within the scope of the legislative power with respect to defence. Repatriation and rehabilitation of soldiers is an obvious case. Rebuilding of a city which has been destroyed or damaged by bombing would be another case. Laws relating to such matters would however, be valid not merely because they dealt with the consequences of a war, but because such laws can fairly be regarded as involved incidentally in a full exercise of a power to make laws with respect to defence. The effects of the past war will continue for centuries. The war has produced or contributed to the changes in nearly every circumstance which affects the lives of civilized people. If it were held that the defence power would justify any legislation at any time which dealt with any matter the character of which had been changed by the war, or with any problem which had been created or aggravated by the war, then the result would be that the Commonwealth Parliament would have a general power of making laws for the peace, order and good government of Australia with respect to almost every subject . . .[39]

In these post-war cases it was held that petrol rationing, the control of premises under the *National Security (War Service Moratorium) Regulations* and certain women's employment regulations were no longer within the defence power in that they were no longer incidental to a winding up process but were problems associated with the general effects of war and outside the power of the Commonwealth under s 51 (vi). But provisions relating to the re-establishment in civilian life of ex-servicemen might continue much longer. Indeed, it was not until 1959, in the case of *Illawarra District County Council v Wickham,*[40] that the High Court held that legislation conferring preference in employment on Second World War ex-servicemen was no longer valid under the defence power. Repatriation provisions relating to war-caused injuries continue indefinitely.

## LEGISLATION

*Defence Act* 1903-1970. This is one of the notable Acts in which the Commonwealth has made clear use of a defined head of power. Part II of the

---

37　See Sawer, "The Transitional Defence Power of the Commonwealth" 23 ALJ 255. Connolly, "The Defence Power of the Commonwealth at the end of the Second World War", 1 UQLJ 60.

38　*R v Foster and Others ex parte Rural Bank of New South Wales, Wagner v Gall, Collins v Hunter and Others,* (1949) 79 CLR 43.

39　Ibid at 83. As to the First World War see *Jerger v Pearce* (1920) 28 CLR 588, *Attorney-General for the Commonwealth v Balding* (1920) 27 CLR 395.

40　(1959) 101 CLR 467.

Act sets up the administrative structure under which defence is carried on. Part III determines the structure of the defence forces, including the constitution of the defence force, the raising of the defence force, the enlistment and discharge of members and service in the forces. Part IV provides for liability of citizens to serve in the citizen forces in time of war. This part is based on the concept that a sovereign State has the power to levy its citizens for the defence of the country. Part VI goes some distance away from the simple concept of defence in that it gives to the Commonwealth special powers in relation thereto. Although much of the content of this section is obsolescent (e g, the establishment and maintenance of horse depots) certain powers, for example powers of impressment of vehicles (s 67), could be utilized in time of national emergency. Part VII of the Act, dealing with offences, contains material incidental to the exercise of the defence power and is best referable to s 51 (xxxix). Part VIII (courts-martial) is referable to s 51 (vi): it is part of the connotation of defence that the administrators of the forces should have the power to administer justice to their members in respect of matters within their jurisdiction.[41] In the case of the military forces, a huge body of legal rules is set out in the Australian Military Regulations and Orders contained in the Army Law Manual, which are plainly designed to secure a compromise between the requirements of justice, and the need to conduct an army as an army. Reference may also be made to s 100 of the Act which provides that no court-martial is subject to a writ or certiorari. Part X of the Act contains a staggering array of miscellaneous matters, all variously incidental to the exercise of the defence power while Part XI deals with the matters upon which regulations may be made.

*Defence (Visiting Forces) Act* 1963. The purpose of this Act is to regulate relations between Australian and visiting forces in relation to the civilian legal system. If it is accepted that the very concept of defence includes the concept of alliances, and this involves the presence of foreign forces on Australian soil, then legislation regulating the legal status of the members of those forces is legislation incidental to the exercise of the defence power valid under s 51 (xxxix).

*National Service Act* 1951-1971. The Act defines national service as service in the military forces of the Commonwealth. Consequently the requirement of national service which extended to twenty year old males was firmly attached to the defence power. The term "national servicemen" is defined to include one who is engaged to serve either in the regular army reserve or supplement. It is clear that the whole purpose of the Act was to secure or to ensure an adequacy of man power for the military forces (as opposed to naval or air forces) of the Commonwealth.

The Act established an elaborate system of registration and selection for service. But if the basic scheme is accepted as constitutional, which would seem to be beyond doubt, then the manner of its working out is a matter for Parliament: there is no prohibition in the Constitution affecting the manner of selection of national servicemen.[42]

Section 29 (a) deals with exemption on ground of conscientious belief. Power to conscript must obviously include a power to select and exempt unless it is expressly qualified as are some other powers in the Constitution, e g, the taxation power.

---

41   See *R v Cox* (1945) 71 CLR 1; *R v Bevan* (1942) 66 CLR 452.
42   See *Giltinan v Lynch* (1971) 45 ALJR 372; [1971] ALR 697.

At the end of 1972 the first Whitlam administration terminated the "call-up" and granted a deferment of indefinite duration to all persons obliged to render national service.[43] The Act was subsequently repealed.

*Australian Security Intelligence Organization Act* 1956. This short Act puts on a statutory basis the security organization which had been formed by Prime Ministerial directive in March 1949. The functions of the organization are set out in s 5 (i) (a) and (b) and are certainly a proper exercise of the internal security power conferred by ss 61, 51 (xxxix) and (vi).

*Crimes Act* 1914-1966. The Crimes Act is the principal Act by which the Commonwealth has made use of its power of self-protection. Part I does no more than establish incidentally to that power a system for the administration of criminal justice.

Substantive offences created by the Act include treason (s 24), treachery (s 24A (a)), sabotage (s 24A (b)), sedition (s 24 (a)) and espionage.

The definition of seditious intention in s 24 (a) is very widely worded but it must be read subject to s 24 (f) which makes certain Acts done in good faith not unlawful. Section 24 (f) (ii) (b) has an obvious reference to s 51 (vi) of the Constitution; sub-paragraphs (c) and (d) a less obvious one, as they depend wholly upon s 24A (a).

Under s 24A (a) a person is deemed to be guilty of treachery if he *inter alia* assists by any means a group of persons proclaimed by the Governor-General to be opposed to part of the defence force which is on or is proceeding to service outside the Commonwealth. It may well be that this part of the provision is supportable by a combination of ss 61 and 51 (xxxix) rather than by s 51 (vi), in that it is concerned with the power of self-protection. Of course, if s 51 (vi) were relied upon, then a court would take note of the international situation and might well decide that the concept of a proclaimed country in the context is a proper step for the defence of Australia.

*The Atomic Energy Act* 1953-1966. The scheme of this Act is to establish the Australian Atomic Energy Commission, the functions of which are set out in Part II, Division (ii), to deal with the control of fissionable materials (Part III) and, to provide security for the Commission's activities (Part IV). Part V deals with offences under the Act. The following sections may be noted: s 3—for the purposes of this Act a reference to the defence of Australia shall be read as including a reference to the defence of countries associated with Australia in resisting or preparing to resist international aggression; ss 17-18—these sections set out the functions of powers of the Commission. They are widely worded and in some cases would have to be construed in the light of the *Acts Interpretation Act* as referable to activities on which is imprinted a defence character. Section 17 (e), for example, permits the Commission to construct and operate plant and equipment for the liberation of atomic energy and its conversion into other forms of energy, while s 17 (f) permits the Commission to sell or otherwise dispose of materials or energy produced as a result of the operations of the commission. These sections would seem to raise all the difficulties of the *Clothing Factory Case* and the *Shipping Board Case*. However, it would seem that there is no great difference between selling atomic electricity under the defence power in terms of this Act and selling hydro-electricity under the terms of the *Snowy Mountains Hydro-Electric Power Act* of 1949. It would seem, therefore, that

---

43   Under s 31 of the Act.

the *Clothing Factory* principle would be applied if these sections were ever judicially attacked.

*Supply and Development Act* 1939-1966. The Act creates a Department of Supply with the functions of *inter alia* supplying war material. There is also provision made for the entry into arrangements for the establishment or extension of industries for purposes of defence. Here again the establishment of Commonwealth factories engaged in armament production and ancillary activities would seem to be justifiable under the *Clothing Factory* principle.

### (vii) *Lighthouses, lightships, beacons and buoys:*[44]

It is a truism that maritime travel, when it involves navigating near to a coast, is extremely difficult without assistance from navigation aids. It was realised in pre-federation discussions that the erection and maintenance of these aids could be more easily carried out on a federal basis rather than by the individual colonies (particularly the smaller ones) lacking the resources as they did for these purposes.[45] It was provided in s 69 of the Constitution that on a date to be proclaimed by the Governor-General certain departments of the public service including lighthouses, lightships, beacons and buoys should be transferred to the Commonwealth. However, there was no specific department of State of the Colonies with this title, these matters falling within the general administration of marine and navigation departments. Therefore, as Wynes points out, the Commonwealth power under s 51 (vii) is not exclusive.[46]

In 1915 the Commonwealth under its acquisition power (s 51 (xxxi)) took over control of all State navigation aids outside harbours and ports. All inner lighthouses and other marine marks, e g, those marking the port channels, harbours and rivers remained under the control of the various States and local port authorities.[47]

The *Lighthouses Act* 1911-1972 invests the responsible Commonwealth minister with extensive powers for the lighting and marking of the coast. It empowers the Commonwealth to acquire by negotiation, or (in the event of failure to reach agreement) by compulsory acquisition, lighthouses or marine marks owned by a State. It also provides for the imposition and collection of light dues, such dues to be payable not only by owners or masters of coastal trade vessels but also owners or masters of foreign vessels in respect of voyages made in Australian coastal waters.

### (viii) *Astronomical and meteorological observations:*[48]

*Astronomical observations.* Observation of the stars and heavenly bodies for the purposes of the acquisition of scientific knowledge and the provision of funds for these purposes are matters which are more appropriately regulated by Commonwealth than State law, particularly because of the huge expenses associated with the manufacture of radio telescopes and the dissemination of the research findings arising from such studies. Nevertheless, the power is a concurrent and not exclusive power. The Commonwealth has legislated to

---

44   Quick and Garran, 565-6. Wynes, 133.
45   Quick and Garran, 565-6.
46   *Legislative, Executive and Judicial Powers in Australia,* 133.
47   See *Report of the Royal Commission on the Constitution,* 157-8.
48   Quick and Garran, 566. Wynes, 133.

establish observatories in the Australian Capital Territory.[49] There have also been arrangements made with the United States to establish tracking stations in Australia for satellites.

*Meteorological observations.* Weather forecasting again is a matter which is pre-eminently the responsibility of the federal government. Under the *Meteorology Act* 1955, a Bureau of Meteorology was set up with the functions of making meteorological observations, forecasting of weather and supply of information on these subjects. Power was also given to establish meteorological offices and observation stations. It is to be noted that these stations are on Commonwealth property and, therefore, entitled to the various immunities attaching to such property arising from other sections of the Constitution.

Although the observations defined are meteorological, i e covering the atmosphere and its phenomena, it is clear that the Commonwealth has, under other heads of power, authority to conduct observations of the sea and land, e g, for defence purposes.

### (ix) *Quarantine:*[50]

Quarantine is defined by s 4 of the *Quarantine Act* 1908-1969, as follows: "Quarantine has relation to measures for the inspection, exclusion, detention, observation, segregation, isolation, protection, treatment, sanitary regulation and disinfection of vessels, persons, goods, things, animals or plants, and having as their object the prevention of the introduction or spread of diseases or pests affecting man, animals or plants."

While in the traditional Australian context, it has been directed against the entry into Australia by sea or air of persons or animals or goods subject to infection or at least suspected of being subject to infection or disease, the definition is wide enough to encompass control of the movement of persons or goods within Australian territory. The power of course is a concurrent one although so far as the States are concerned there is a much wider control vested in them over health matters generally and they are not restricted to passing laws that fall within the narrower category of quarantine.

The Commonwealth has legislated in the *Quarantine Act* and regulations made thereunder to control the introduction of diseases on vessels and by air. It has also enacted other pieces of legislation which are partially dependent on the quarantine power: the *Therapeutic Goods Act* 1966 imposes quality controls for the preparation, packing and labelling of therapeutic substances imported into Australia or which have become the subject matter of trade and commerce among the States. Reference may also be made to the *Commonwealth Serum Laboratories Act* 1961-1970, under which a Commonwealth laboratory has been established to produce and sell biological products used for therapeutic purposes.

Two provisions of the *Quarantine Act* which deserve mention are s 2A which empowers the Governor-General to issue a proclamation declaring that State quarantine measures are for a period superseded by Commonwealth measures, and s 2B which enables the Governor-General to impose quarantine measures in any part of the Commonwealth on being satisfied that an epidemic caused by a quarantinable disease or danger of such an epidemic exists in any part of the Commonwealth.

---

49　*Mount Stromlo Observatory Act* 1956.
50　Quick and Garran, 566-8. Wynes, 133-4. Nicholas, 228-9.

In *Ex parte Nelson* (*No* 1)[51] it was argued that stock control measures introduced by New South Wales under the *Stock Act* of 1901 were invalid on the ground that they encroached on Commonwealth power. It was held by the High Court that the quarantine measures were validly imposed by the State, quarantine being a concurrent power, and that there was no inconsistency with Commonwealth legislation or regulations.[52]

Diseases are defined in the *Quarantine Act* in respect of persons and animals to which may be added diseases so proclaimed by the Governor-General. In respect of plants, specification of diseases is by virtue of executive action (s 5). Part IV of the Act deals with the quarantine of vessels, persons and goods while Part V deals with the quarantine of animals and plants.[53]

### (x) *Fisheries in Australian waters beyond territorial limits:*[54]

Before federation, the Australian Colonies exercised control over fishing in waters within three miles of the coastline which were considered to be the limits of territorial waters.[55] Outside the three-mile limit the Imperial Parliament and, after 1885 the Federal Council, exercised a certain fisheries jurisdiction.[56]

The meaning of the phrase "territorial limits" has, however, been the subject of fierce controversy. Much of the speculation starts with the case of *R v Keyn*[57] decided in 1876. One of the central issues is whether the *ratio* of this case is restricted to the exercise of jurisdiction over criminal acts committed by foreigners in territorial waters or whether it had a wider range and established the proposition that the limits of the British realm (and its colonies) ended at the low-water mark.

In Australia the case of *Bonser v La Macchia*[58] took up the discussion of this issue but with inconclusive results. The effect of the question on the federal division of power may be stated in this way. If the territory of the Colonies in 1900 ended at the low-water mark (and not at the three-mile limit) then territorial waters were from 1900 not within the territory of the newly established States of the Commonwealth. Consequently, any power which they had over the adjacent seas was an extra territorial power liable to be defeated by an exercise of paramount power either by the Imperial Parliament or by the Commonwealth Parliament. Associated with this interpretation of State competence is the view that at some time after the passage of the *Statute of Westminster* the Commonwealth as a political entity acquired

---

51  (1928) 42 CLR 209.
52  See also *Dooley v Haselby* (decision of WA Supreme Court 19 March 1958 unreported) where provisions of a State *Native Welfare Act* restricting the movements of Aboriginals within the State to prevent the spread of leprosy were upheld as not being inconsistent with the Commonwealth Act.
53  See also under s 112.
54  Quick and Garran, 568-74. Wynes, 139-40.
55  The three-mile limit is derived from custom and practice as distinct from being proclaimed formally by statutory enactment. International negotiations are at present taking place on questions of maritime jurisdiction, one proposal being to ratify by international treaty the extension of the three-mile limit to 12 miles (an extension already affected by unilateral action in the case of a number of countries).
56  Quick and Garran, 569-572.
57  (1876) 2 Ex D 63. The *Territorial Waters Jurisdiction Act* 1878 reversed the decision on the question of jurisdiction.
58  (1969) 43 ALJR 275, [1969] ALR 741, discussed by O'Connell, 44 ALJ 192.

sovereignty over the territorial waters (including the sea bed), and that
therefore the only permissible exercise of State power is one which does not
infringe on this sovereignty or which is not inconsistent with Commonwealth
legislation having paramount force by virtue of s 109 of the Constitution.
In *Bonser v La Macchia* two judges, Barwick CJ and Windeyer J took this
view of Commonwealth power.[59] Two other judges who discussed the question
(Kitto and Menzies JJ) seem to have accepted the view that the States territorial competence extended to the three-mile limit which involved the
recognition of an intrinsic connection between colonial and State practice
and legislative competence.[60] On this view territorial limits were not the low-
water mark (i e, the coastline) but the three-mile limit of territorial waters.

The *Fisheries Acts* of the States regulate the acts of fishing for, and
taking, fish within territorial limits, while the Commonwealth *Fisheries Act*
1952-1970 controls such acts occurring outside territorial limits. This Act,
amended several times since 1952, contains a distinction between a 12-mile
exclusive fisheries zone in which foreign fishermen are not permitted to fish
unless licensed[61] and the zone outside (which is demarcated by boundaries
in proclamations made under the Act)[62] within which controls operate only
on Australia fishermen or boats. In *Bonser's Case* all judges were agreed that
the fisheries power was not exceeded by the making of a proclamation which
defined proclaimed waters by limits which (except in the case of the Northern
coastline where a median line was adopted to demarcate Australian and
Indonesian jurisdiction) extended about 200 miles from the coastline.

On the precise meaning of s 51 (x) two members of the court[63] were
agreed that the Commonwealth fisheries power commenced at the three-mile
limit. Barwick CJ, also while accepting that the Commonwealth had acquired
sovereignty over the territorial sea from the Imperial Crown at some time
after the *Statute of Westminster,* took the view that (Imperial) territorial
limits in 1900 extended to the three-mile limit and that the Commonwealth
fisheries power must therefore be taken to operate outside that limit.[64] Only
Windeyer J considered that the fisheries power covered the waters within the
three-mile limit.[65]

---

59  43 ALJR at 278 et seq [1969] ALR at 744 et seq (Barwick CJ); 43 ALJR at
    290 et seq, [1969] ALR at 764 et seq (Windeyer J). Both judges were agreed
    that the Imperial Crown had sovereignty over the three-mile limit prior to
    Commonwealth acquisition of this sovereignty. Their views are in line with
    those of the judges of the Canadian Supreme Court on the relationship of
    Dominion-provincial power in Canada expressed in *Reference re Ownership of
    Off-shore Mineral Rights* (1968) 65 DLR (2d) 353. But see Lumb, *The Law
    of the Sea and Australian Off-shore Areas* (1966). O'Connell, "Problems of
    Australian Coastal Jurisdiction", in *International Law in Australia* (1966), Ch
    XI. Campbell, "Regulation of Australian Coastal Fisheries" (1960), 1 Tasmanian
    University Law Review 405. (1968) Harders, "Australia's Offshore Petroleum
    Legislation: A Survey of its Constitutional Background and its Federal Features",
    6 MULR 415.
60  43 ALJR at 285 et seq, [1969] ALR at 756 et seq (Kitto J); 43 ALJR 288 et
    seq, [1969] ALR at 761 et seq (Menzies J). See also articles cited in the previous
    footnote.
61  See s 4 as amended by Act No 116 of 1967, s 3.
62  See s 7.
63  Kitto and Menzies JJ.
64  (1969) 43 ALJR at 280-2; [1969] ALR at 748-50.
65  (1969) 43 ALJR at 295-7; [1969] ALR at 774-7.

*Continental shelf.* The Commonwealth has enacted a *Continental Shelf* (*Living Natural Resources*) *Act*[66] which controls the taking of sedentary organisms of marine life. This operates from the three-mile limit to the edge of the continental shelf (defined in the Convention on the Continental Shelf as the 200 metre line or beyond that depth to where the resources admit of exploitation) and applies both to Australian *and* foreign fishermen and boats. This Act would seem to rest on both the fisheries and external affairs powers.[67] The *Whaling Act* 1960 is also partially dependent on the external affairs power (there being an international convention on whaling). An interesting feature of this Act is that it may be applied to the territorial waters of a State pursuant to a proclamation made by the Governor-General.[68] In the light of *Bonser's Case* this particular provision could not be supported by the fisheries power but would have to derive its validity from the external affairs power.[69]

*Territorial and internal waters.* The demarcation of territorial and internal waters is affected by an international convention, the Convention on the Territorial Sea and the Contiguous Zone. This convention provides that ordinarily the baseline (which also marks the *outer* limit of internal waters) from which territorial waters are measured must follow the configuration of the coastline. However, where a coastline is deeply indented, or where there is a fringe of islands in its immediate vicinity, a straight baseline system may be adopted. The straight baseline system is also adopted to enclose bays and gulfs provided that any particular line of this nature does not exceed 24 miles in length (subject to an exception, however, in the case of historic bays).[70]

(xi) *Census and statistics*:[71]

The Oxford Dictionary defines the census as "an official enumeration of the population of a country or district with various statistics relating to them". Statistics are numerical facts systematically collected.

Under the *Census and Statistics Act* 1905-1966, provision is made for a census to be taken every tenth year (or such other time as is prescribed). In s 16 of the Act there is a list of matters on which the statistician may collect statistics: they range from population and employment figures to land owner-ship and industrial activities. Sections 17 and 18 create enforceable duties to fill in forms and to answer questions.[72] Section 19 grants to Commonwealth officials powers of entry and inspection. The Commonwealth Statistician who is appointed by the Governor-General may delegate powers to State officials

---

66  No 149 of 1968. The classes of marine organisms proclaimed under the Act are set out in (1970) Commonwealth of Australia Gazette, 2315.
67  See Helmore, "The Continental Shelf" (1954) 27 ALJ 732. Lumb, *The Law of the Sea and Australian Off-shore Areas* (1966). Harders, *op cit* n 59.
68  s 8.
69  See also the *Beaches, Fishing Grounds and Sea Routes Protection Act* 1932 which is expressed to depend on a number of paragraphs of s 51. Other maritime legislation depending on the external affairs power includes the *Pollution of the Sea by Oil Act* 1960-1972 and the *Petroleum* (*Submerged Lands*) *Act* 1967-1968. See later under external affairs.
70  Article 7.
71  Quick and Garran, 572. Wynes, 134.
72  Section 21 creates an interesting exception in favour of answers to questions as to religious discrimination: refusal to answer such questions cannot be punished.

and there is also provision for arrangements to be made with the States for the execution of duties by State officers. Under the *Statistics (Arrangements with States) Act* 1956-1958, State officials may be appointed to the Commonwealth public service to carry out Commonwealth duties and the Commonwealth may supply statistics to the various State departments. This leads to an administrative form of co-operative federalism in which duplication of duties is avoided as far as possible and the information gathered is used for the benefit of State as well as Commonwealth services.

(xii) *Currency, coinage, and legal tender:*[73]

The Commonwealth has power to make money both by the process of converting metal into money and the issue of paper money. Once this money is in existence it may be transferred from person to person. "Currency" connotes such circulation. Closely associated with the concept of "currency" is legal tender. This concept means that paper money as well as coins may be used for the payment of debts and the fulfilment of other financial obligations.

Under s 115 of the Constitution the States are prohibited from coining money and from making anything but gold and silver legal tender. However, the basic metals of gold and silver are no longer, under the *Currency Act* 1965, a major part of Australian coinage.[74] Under the *Crimes Act* 1914-1966 counterfeiting of coin or paper money is a criminal offence.[75]

The *Currency Act* provides for a monetary unit of a dollar and designates the denominations of money in the currency of Australia to be dollars and cents. The Act establishes the standard composition and weight of the coins: these coins are to be made under the direction of and issued by the Treasurer. There are also provisions to the extent to which a number of coins are legal tender.

With respect to paper money (bank notes) the *Reserve Bank Act* 1959-1966, empowers the Reserve Bank of Australia (designated as the Central Bank of Australia for these purposes) to issue and cancel Australian notes. The various denominations are set out and such notes are legal tender throughout Australia.

The *Banking Act* 1959-1967, also contains provisions relating to the protection of the currency and the public credit of the Commonwealth. Reference may be made to Part II Division 3 relating to obligations of banks to hold specified statutory reserve deposits, and Division 4 relating to mobilization of foreign currency held by banks, and Part III relating to foreign exchange control. Part IV of the Act contains provisions controlling dealings in gold under s 41 a person cannot take or send gold outside Australia without the consent of the Reserve Bank. The *Banking Act* is founded on a combination of the banking and currency powers.

(xiii) *Banking, other than State banking; also State banking extending beyond the limits of the State concerned, the incorporation of banks, and the issue of paper money:*[76]

The power conferred by s 51 (xiii) is a power over business activities described as banking as well as over the institutions which carry on such

---

73   Quick and Garran, 572-6. Wynes, 140-1. Nicholas, 187-90.
74   On the relationship of Australian currency to sterling see articles in 8 ALJ 42, 10 ALJ 264, 22 ALJ 428 and 27 ALJ 566.
75   See Part IV. See also *R v Bradley* 54 CLR 12.
76   Quick and Garran, 576-82. Wynes, 141-6. Nicholas, 191-207.

activities. The essential characteristics of the business of banking are described in *Permewan's Case*[77] as being the collection of money by receiving deposits upon loan, repayable when and as expressly agreed upon, and the utilization of the money so collected by lending it again in such sums as are required. It was held in this case that the fact that a bank did not as part of its services provide a cheque service did not prevent it from carrying on the business of banking. A bank could be merely a "savings bank" providing for payment of depositor's funds by presentation of a bank book. Moreover it also appears that the creation of credit is not the essential feature of banking as compared with other financial activities. Indeed the growth of other types of financial institutions such as hire-purchase companies has witnessed an increase in the volume of lending from these bodies.

In the *Bank Nationalization Case*[78] an attack was made on legislation of the Commonwealth (the *Banking Act* of 1947) on the ground that, in purporting to create a federal government monopoly of banking (apart from State banking) and excluding the private banking bodies from continuing to carry on such transactions by forced expropriation of their assets, the Commonwealth had exceeded its legislative power. It was argued for the plaintiffs that the words "State banking extending beyond the limits" of any one State coloured the other words of the paragraph. They denoted, it was said, that at least a minimum requirement of the power was the continuance of banking. Prohibition or abolition of banking was outside the limits. The majority held that such a restriction could not be read into the characterization of the power. Dixon J stated ". . . . . I am unable to accept the view that the word 'banking' should have ascribed to it anything but the wide meaning and flexible application of a general expression designating, as a subject of legislative power, a matter forming part of the commercial, economic and social organization of the community. I see no sufficient reason for importing into it any of the three limitations suggested, viz, (1) confining the power to laws for the governance of a continuing activity, to something that does not go beyond regulation, (2) the limitation of the conception of banking to transactions entirely consensual, and (3) to transactions between subject and subject".[79] In rejecting these interpretations Dixon J considered that the power enabled the Commonwealth to control generally banking activities and in this regard to influence monetary policies throughout the Commonwealth. It thus went well beyond the sphere of the banker-client relationship.[80] Two judges, Rich and Williams JJ, adopted a narrow view of the power in taking the view that it was confined to laws with respect to the conduct of business carried on by banks, i e, it did not extend to their winding up or expropriation.[81]

---

77  *The Commissioner for the State Savings Bank of Victoria v Permewan Wright and Co Ltd* (1914) 19 CLR 457.
78  *Bank of New South Wales v Commonwealth* (1948) 76 CLR 1 (High Court). (1949) 79 CLR 497 (Privy Council) discussed in 23 ALJ 213.
79  (1948) 76 CLR 1, at 334.
80  Sir Robert Menzies (*Central Power in the Australian Commonwealth*, at 136) points out that the management of monetary conditions through the operations of the Reserve Bank has had a large influence on the availability of money for public works and also upon taxation. This has been achieved under various provisions of the *Banking Act* allowing the Reserve Bank to control certain banking activities of the private banks (requirements of compulsory reserve deposits, controls of interest rates and foreign exchange).
81  76 CLR at 255-9.

A previous attempt by the Commonwealth to bring about a Commonwealth-controlled system of banking, by prohibiting private banks from conducting any business for a State or a State authority, was invalidated by the High Court in the *State Banking Case*.[82] The legislation was invalid because it was directed against the States and interfered with a basic function of government —the right of a State to select its banker. However, this decision reflects a more general doctrine of the prohibition of legislation which discriminates against another governmental unit in the federal system.[83]

*State banking.* Banks which have been established as State instrumentalities are, subject to the qualifications noted below, excepted from the Commonwealth power over banking and they remain therefore subject to the legislative control of the States which have created them. In the *State Banking Case* a majority of the court rejected the argument that State banking meant the banking of State moneys (i e, by private banks). It meant banking business carried on by a State as banker and not as customer.[84] In most of the States there are State savings banks which receive money on deposit. However, where such State banking extends beyond the limits of any one State, the Commonwealth power of regulation comes into operation.[85]

*Incorporation of banks.* Under this paragraph, the Commonwealth is given the power to create its own statutory corporation to carry on the business of banking as well as the power of imposing conditions for the incorporation of private banks. The Commonwealth has under the *Banking Act* 1959-1967 exercised power over bodies wishing to engage in the business of banking by requiring them to obtain authority from the Governor-General for this purpose.[86] It has empowered the Commonwealth Reserve Bank (the central bank) to oversee the general operations of the private banks and has imposed various conditions for the protection of depositors.

It has also established under the *Commonwealth Banks Act* 1959-1973 a statutory corporation called the Commonwealth Banking Corporation controlled by a board which determines the policy of the corporation. The corporation consists of three separate banking bodies: the Commonwealth Trading Bank, the Commonwealth Savings Bank, and the Commonwealth Development Bank.[87]

---

82  (1947) 74 CLR 31 (discussed in 21 ALJ 162).
83  See Introduction.
84  See in particular the judgment of Latham CJ at 51-2.
85  See *Lamshed v Lake* (1957) 99 CLR 132 at 143 per Dixon CJ.
86  See also the *Banks (Shareholdings) Act* of 1972 which controls the number of shares which persons may have in a bank.
87  In *Heiner v Scott* (1914) 19 CLR 381, it was held that a State Act imposing stamp duty on bills of exchange was enforceable against a private citizen who drew a cheque on the Commonwealth Bank (the predecessor of the Commonwealth Trading Bank). Griffith CJ considered that the carrying on of *ordinary* banking business was not a function of the executive government of the Commonwealth and therefore that, in this respect, the bank was not entitled to immunity from State legislation. The other judges also considered that the Commonwealth Bank was not an agent of the Commonwealth for these purposes. Since that time, the Commonwealth Bank has been "split" into the three Corporations mentioned above with the Trading Bank carrying on "ordinary business". However, in *Inglis v Commonwealth of Australia* (1969) 119 CLR 334; [1970] ALR 241, the trading bank was held to be an emanation of the Commonwealth—an instrument by which, together with the savings and development banks, the Commonwealth participated in the business of banking.

The Commonwealth Banking Corporation is separate and distinct from the Reserve Bank of Australia, the structure and powers of which are regulated by the *Reserve Bank Act* 1959-1966.

The Reserve Bank is both the central bank of Australia and the banker and financial agent of the Commonwealth (in so far as it is required to act in this latter capacity). It has power to issue Australian notes. Its business is subject to the direction of the Reserve Bank board which has an obligation to inform the Government of the monetary and banking policy of the bank, and its decisions are subject to review by the Treasurer.

*The issue of paper money.* Part V of the *Reserve Bank Act* deals with the note issue. Division 1 sets up and defines the duties of the note issue department of the bank, and s 34 gives the bank authority to issue, re-issue or cancel notes. Section 36 makes Australian notes legal tender throughout Australia.

(xiv) *Insurance, other than State insurance; also State insurance extending beyond the limits of the State concerned:*[88]

Insurance may be defined as the act of providing against loss or damage caused by a contingent event. Legislative power under this head could extend to all types of insurance apart from *intra-state* insurance activities carried on by States or State governmental instrumentalities.[89] Included within the scope of the power is not only the act of insurance itself but also incidental matters such as the limitation of risk and dividends.

Wynes states that "legislation under the power would extend to and include provisions relating to dividends, publication of accounts, value of policies, standards of policies, prescribing investment, requiring deposits in money or in bonds, confining the business to corporations, preventing rate discrimination, limitation of risks and any and all other regulative conditions".[90]

In actual fact the Commonwealth has in the *Insurance Act* 1932-1966, and the *Life Insurance Act* 1945-1965, dealt with many of these matters. The effective provisions of the *Insurance Act* are ss 10 (2) and 11 which compel persons carrying on insurance business (as defined) to lodge with the Treasurer certain deposits in money in approved securities.[91] Other sections of the Act set up the machinery for controlling and ensuring proper valuation of these deposits. The *Insurance Act*, 1973 has redefined many of the conditions for carrying on the business of insurance and the office of Insurance Commissioners has been established.

The *Life Insurance Act* is a detailed Act controlling life insurance, covering matters such as the registration of private insurers and prescribed standards relating to policies.[92]

---

88  Quick and Garran, 582-4. Wynes, 146-7.
89  See *Lamshed v Lake* (1958) 99 CLR 132 at 143, per Dixon J.
90  *Legislative, Executive and Judicial Powers in Australia*, 146.
91  Note, however, s 15, which gives a wide power of exemption to superannuation insurance schemes.
92  See *Associated Dominions Assurance Society Pty Ltd v Balmford* (1951) 84 CLR 249. *Insurance Commissioner v Associated Dominions Assurance Society Pty Ltd* (1953) 89 CLR 78 (where opinions were expressed to the effect that provisions relating to the control of private insurance companies were within constitutional power). See also Sawer, "Administrative Control of Companies—the Life Insurance Example" (1970) 44 ALJ 303.

The Commonwealth has also legislated with respect to marine insurance in the *Marine Insurance Act* 1909-1966.

More recently, new forms of insurance have been created by Commonwealth legislation. The *Export Payments Insurance Corporation Act* 1956-1973 establishes an "export payments insurance corporation" to provide insurance against certain risks arising out of trade with other countries which are not normally insured with commercial insurers. This legislation is based both on the trade and commerce power and on the insurance power. The *Housing Loans Insurance Act* 1965 provides insurance for lending institutions advancing loans for home purchasers. These Acts are also partially dependent on other heads of power. Other powers of insurance may also fall within specific heads of power of s 51 as being incidental to the exercise of such powers.[93]

There is no doubt that on the analogy of the banking power, the Commonwealth itself could, under the insurance power, set up a Commonwealth Insurance instrumentality to engage in all fields of insurance.[94]

(xv) *Weights and measures*:[95]

Under this head of power, the Commonwealth may prescribe national standards of weights and measures. *The Weights and Measures (National Standards) Act* 1960-1966, makes provision for the adoption of national units of measurement by regulations made under the Act.

The Act does not cover the whole field of weights and measures and indeed expressly provides that certain categories of State legislation are to continue (i e, those relating to improper practices in connection with weights and measures and providing for the verification of means of measurement other than Commonwealth standards).[96] Section 16 continues the existence of the National Standards Commission set up under earlier legislation. The scientific regulation of standards is committed to CSIRO.

Legislation relating to fair trading practices and requiring manufacturers to observe standards in the packaging of goods would of course fall within State residuary power, although no doubt the Commonwealth could, under the trade and commerce power, control the packaging of goods dispatched across a State border or imported from overseas.

(xvi) *Bills of exchange and promissory notes*:[97]

*The Bills of Exchange Act* 1909-1971 defines a bill of exchange as "an unconditional order in writing, addressed by one person to another signed by the person receiving it, requiring the person to whom it is addressed to pay on demand, or at a fixed or determinable future time, a certain sum of money to or to the order of a specified person, or to bearer".[98] A cheque is a "bill of

---

93　As with seamen's compensation which depends on ss 51 (i) and 98. See *Australian Steamships Pty Ltd v Malcolm* (1915) 19 CLR 298.

94　However, a system of compulsory national insurance (involving limitations on the rights to sue under State law) would not be within the insurance power. See discussion in 2 ALJ 219 and Wynes, at 147. See also Sawer, *Australian Federal Politics and Law* 1929-1949, 120. As Wynes points out (at 147 n 55) the question has been partially resolved by the introduction of the social services paragraph (xxiiiA) in 1946. This enables the Commonwealth to utilize moneys from consolidated revenue to support a wide range of social services.

95　Quick and Garran, 585. Wynes, 147.

96　Note, however, s 7: "(1) The regulations may prescribe units of measurement of any physical quantity. (2) The prescribed units of measurement of a physical quantity are the sole legal units of measurement of that physical quantity."

97　Quick and Garran, 585-6. Wynes, 147-8.

98　Section 8 (1).

exchange drawn on a banker payable on demand".[99] A promissory note is "an unconditional promise in writing made by one person to another, signed by the maker, engaging to pay on demand or at a fixed or determinable future time, a sum certain in money to or to the order of a specified person or to bearer."[1]

The various rules relating to negotiability are to be found in the above-mentioned Act. As being incidental to the exercise of this power, the Commonwealth Parliament has modified some general principles of the law of contract in so far as they affect these documents.[2] In the light of the decision in the *Union Label Case*[3] it would appear that "bills of exchange" have the meaning which they had in 1900.[4] Therefore, new categories of negotiable instruments would be outside this particular head of Commonwealth power although they may possibly come within the banking power.

In *Stock Motors Ploughs Ltd v Forsyth*[5] the validity of certain sections of a New South Wales *Moratorium Act* were in issue in their application to promissory notes given as collateral security for instalments payable under hire-purchase agreements. The *Moratorium Act* had the effect of requiring curial consent before any proceedings could be commenced for the recovery of an instalment under a hire-purchase agreement. It was argued that this was inconsistent with provisions of the *Bills of Exchange Act* providing for payment of promissory notes on the due date. Gavan Duffy CJ stated: "The federal Act prescribes the form of a promissory note, and the obligations which arise between the parties when that form is adopted, but it leaves it open to the parties to alter these obligations by agreement between themselves and it leaves it open to the State legislatures to determine the circumstances in which, and the extent to which, negotiable instruments shall have effect in matters under the control of those legislatures. Such a legislature may direct that a promissory note given to secure a payment unenforceable under the State law shall itself be unenforceable, or it may impose a condition precedent to its enforcement."[6]

It is clear therefore that the Commonwealth legislation provides only the machinery for the more efficacious payment of contractual and other types of debts and for the transfer of money without consideration. The general contractual relations between the maker and payee arising outside the documents are therefore the subject of State legislation.[7]

### (xvii) *Bankruptcy and insolvency*:[8]

The underlying rationale of bankruptcy and insolvency laws involves a State-supervised appropriation of the assets of the debtor, a distribution of them among his creditors and a discharge of the debtor from any future

---

99 Section 78 (1).
1 Section 89 (1).
2 For example, the doctrine of consideration. See Division 3 of the Act.
3 *Attorney-General for New South Wales v Brewery Employees' Union of New South Wales* (1908) 6 CLR 469.
4 See, however, the dissenting judgment of Higgins J 6 CLR at 610.
5 (1932) 48 CLR 128.
6 Ibid at 133.
7 See the judgment of Starke J at 134 and the judgment of Evatt J at 141. The *Bills of Exchange Act* First Schedule, specifies the State legislation rendered inoperative by the Act in relation to bills of exchange.
8 Quick and Garran, 586-93. Wynes, 148-51.

liability in respect of his then existing debts. Perhaps one of the best definitions is that of the Privy Council in a Canadian case:[9]

In a general sense, insolvency means inability to meet one's debts or obligations; in a technical sense, it means the condition or standard of inability to meet debts or obligations, upon the occurrence of which the statutory law enables a creditor to intervene with the assistance of a court, to stop individual action by creditors and to secure administration of the debtor's assets in the general interest of creditors. The law also generally allows the debtor to apply for the same administration. The justification for such proceeding by a creditor generally consists in an act of bankruptcy by the debtor, the conditions of which are defined and prescribed by the statute law.[10]

The Commonwealth *Bankruptcy Act* 1966-1970[11] sets out the rules and procedures governing bankruptcy proceedings. It covers matters such as acts of bankruptcy (Part IV Division 1) creditors' and debtors' petitions (Part IV Division 2 and 3) effect of bankruptcy on property and legal proceedings (Part IV Division 4), meetings of creditors (Part IV Division 5) and arrangements with creditors (Part IV Division 6).

Part V of the Act deals with control over person and property of debtors and bankrupts, Part VI with the administration of the bankrupt's property and Part VII with the discharge of bankrupts.

Various other incidental matters are covered by the legislation, e g, the requirement of keeping books of account. This type of provision was upheld in *R v Federal Court of Bankruptcy ex parte Loewenstein*[12] Latham CJ pointed out that since failure to keep books was a common cause of bankruptcy it came within the head of power;[13] while Starke J considered that this was a matter traditionally included within bankruptcy legislation, and therefore within the power by definition.[14]

Of course, in the light of the generic interpretation adopted with regard to other descriptive heads of power (e g, trade marks) the Commonwealth could not extend the category of acts of bankruptcy beyond its accepted meaning as in 1900, for example, by creating a general system of forfeitures.[15] This is not to say that there may be no development in the rules governing the status of the bankrupt in the light of modern needs.

While the Commonwealth Act operates as a general code in the area of bankruptcy, s 9 (1) provides that State laws relating to matters not dealt with expressly or by necessary implication in the Act are not affected. It is also to be noted that the winding up of companies which are unable to pay their debts is a matter dealt with by State companies Acts. These Acts have incorporated some basic principles of the bankruptcy legislation.[16]

---

9   *Attorney-General for British Columbia v Attorney-General for Canada* [1937] AC 391.

10  Ibid at 402.

11  There is a useful description of the Commonwealth Act in Hayek, *Principles of Bankruptcy Law*, Ch 1.

12  (1938) 59 CLR 556.

13  Ibid at 571.

14  Ibid at 574.

15  See Wynes, at 150.

16  See, for example, s 291 of the *Companies Act* (Qld). There is, however, judicial opinion to the effect that the bankruptcy power may extend to the liquidation of the assets of insolvent trading companies (*State of Victoria v Commonwealth* 99 CLR 575 at 612 per Dixon J). There are provisions of other Commonwealth Acts dealing with the effect of bankruptcy on specific statutory debts. In *State*
*continues*

(xviii) *Copyrights, patents of inventions and designs, and trade marks*:[17]

*Copyrights.* The *Copyright Act* 1968[18] defines the nature of copyright in original works as encompassing an exclusive right (a) in the case of literary, dramatic or musical works to do a number of acts which include reproduction, publication, adaptation, performance, broadcasting and the like and (b) in the case of artistic works to do similar acts as well as including the work in television programmes or in programmes to be transmitted to subscribers to a diffusion service. (s 31). Copyright subsists in an original unpublished work if the author was a qualified person (i e, an Australian citizen or a person resident in Australia) and in a published work (but only if the first publication took place in Australia). It also extends to original artistic works (including buildings or parts thereof). The period of duration of copyright is fifty years after the death of the author. There are various provisions relating to infringement as well as to acts that do not constitute infringement, for example, fair dealing with a work. It is to be noted that copying of works by or on behalf of a librarian is permitted if the copies are used inter alia by students for their own private studies. There are specific provisions relating to copyright in recordings of musical works and the copyright in subject matter other than literary works, for example, sound recordings, (see ss 85 et seq).

*Patents of Invention.* A patent has been defined as "a legal privilege granted by the Crown to an individual, and conveying to him the sole right to make, use, or dispose of some invention of a new and useful mechanism, appliance, or process in science, art, or industry for a specified period of time".[19]

The *Patents Act* 1952-1969[20] makes provision for a Register of Patents to be kept and the procedure to be followed in having a patent registered. The system of examination is provided for to determine the nature of the invention and the priority date of the claim and other matters. In the light of the restrictive interpretation adopted with respect to trademarks, "patents" must be given a similar interpretation. The Commonwealth could not legislate for the recognition of a patent irrespective of novelty etc. On the other hand there is no reason why the Commonwealth would not legislate to grant patents with respect to new forms of material unknown in 1900, e g, "plant" patents. This would accord with the interpretation adopted in *Brislan's Case* and *Jones' Case* (See discussion of s 51 (v)).

*Designs.* The *Designs Act* 1906-1968 defines a design as an industrial design applicable, in any way or by any means, to the purpose of the

---

16    *continued*
      of *Victoria v Commonwealth* provisions of the *Income Tax and Social Services Contribution Act* 1936-1956 dealing with the order of priority in which federal income tax was to be paid by a trustee in bankruptcy administering the estate of a bankrupt were upheld as an exercise of both the bankruptcy and the taxation powers (see Dixon J at 611-2, McTiernan J at 642, Fullagar J at 658). However one specific provision of the Act which forbade a person to pay State tax in priority to Commonwealth tax was invalidated on the ground of interference with State power. See *ante* 70.
17    Quick and Garran, 593-9. Wynes, 151-2. Nicholas, 243-6.
18    See Sawer "The Copyright Act, 1968" (1969) 43 ALJ 8.
19    Quick and Garran, 596.
20    Noted (1953) 27 ALJ 2.

ornamentation, or pattern or shape, or configuration, of an article, or to any two or more of these purposes. The Act provides for copyright in such design which confers an exclusive right to apply the design, or authorise another person to apply the design, to the articles in respect of which it is registered. (s 12)

*Trademarks.* A trademark has been defined as "some name, symbol, or device, consisting in general of a picture, label, word, or words, which is applied or attached to a trader's goods so as to distinguish them from the similar goods of other traders, and to identify them as his goods, in the business in which they are produced or put forward for sale".[21] It may be held either by the proprietor of the mark or by a registered user.

The *Trade Marks Act* 1955-1966[22] contains provisions relating to the registration of trademarks, one of the conditions being that the mark must be distinctive (s 26) and not one likely to be confused with one already registered (s 28). There are also provisions relating to the lapsing of registration in the event of non-use.

In the *Union Label Case*[23] it was held by a majority that the term "trademark" must be interpreted in the light of its meaning in 1900. In this case a so-called workers trademark, i e, a mark indicating that goods had been manufactured by union labour, was held not to be within the genus so understood.[24]

There is a special category of trademarks called certification marks dealt with by the *Trade Marks Act* which are registrable in a separate part of the register (s 83). The opinion of one commentator is that the dissimilarity between certification marks and workers marks are such that the former could be upheld as within the constitutional genus, particularly as there was English legislation pre-dating 1900 which provided for what were, in substance, certification marks.[25]

It is to be noted that certain actions, e g, passing off involving trade mark infringements are controlled by State law.

### (xix) *Naturalization and aliens:*[26]

*Naturalization.* The power given to the federal Parliament with respect to naturalization is a power to regulate the process by which an alien becomes an Australian national.

At the end of the Second World War a conference of British Commonwealth officials was held in London to consider questions of status and citizenship in member countries of the Commonwealth. The essential feature of the scheme agreed upon at the conference was that each of the countries

---

21  Quick and Garran, 590.
22  See Handley, "The Trade Marks Act 1955" 2 Sydney Law Review, 509.
23  *Attorney-General for New South Wales v Brewery Employees' Union* (1908) 6 CLR 469.
24  Isaacs and Higgins JJ, who dissented, considered that a workers' trade mark contained all the essential characteristics of a trade mark as understood at the time of the passage of the *Constitution Act*. Higgins J went on to say that even if the expression "trade mark" as understood in 1900 was not wide enough to include a worker's mark, it was nevertheless within the power of the federal Parliament under s 51 (xxviii) to include such a mark within the category of trade marks. (6 CLR at 610).
25  See Handley, op cit, at 529.
26  Quick and Garran, 599-604. Wynes, 286-8. Nicholas, 21-3.

should by its legislation determine who were its citizens, should declare those citizens to be British subjects, and should recognize as British subjects those who had this status under the laws of any other Commonwealth country.[27]

Section 7 of the *Nationality and Citizenship Act* 1948 (passed to give effect to this arrangement) provided "a person who under this Act is an Australian citizen or, by enactment for the time being in force in a country to which this section applies is a citizen of that country, shall, by virtue of that citizenship, be a British subject". This section then specifies a number of Commonwealth countries to which it applies. (see s 7 (ii) ). The section has been amended in later years to provide for the deletion of some of these countries and for the addition of others (dependent on whether countries have come into or left the Commonwealth). In 1969 an important change was made with the passage of the *Citizenship Act*[28] which provides that an Australian citizen shall merely have the status of a British subject (and not be deemed to be a British subject). Primary significance is attached by this Act to Australian citizenship.

It is, of course, a matter for Australia to determine whether British subjects shall be given Australian citizenship. Under s 12 of the *Citizenship Act* 1948-1969 Australian citizenship may be granted by registration to a citizen of another Commonwealth country on certain conditions being fulfilled including a period of residence (one year) within Australia. However, there is an alternative procedure whereby under the Act a citizen of a Commonwealth country may become an Australian citizen as of right, when, having completed five years residence in Australia, he gives notice of his intention to become an Australian citizen (ss 11A, 11B, 11C).

The normal method of obtaining citizenship is by birth in Australia and s 10 of the *Citizenship Act* recognizes this, subject to certain qualifications. The other method is by descent, i e, birth of a person outside Australia of a father or mother who has Australian citizenship. Such a person only becomes an Australian citizen if the birth is registered at an Australian consulate within five years after its occurrence, although this period may be extended for special reasons (s 11).

Apart from birth and descent the major method by which the citizenship of another country is acquired is by naturalization. This is the particular process referred to in s 51 (xix). Naturalization is granted under certain conditions, including a specified period of residence, which are set out in the Act. The period is five years, but may be reduced to three years (see ss 14, 15). The *Citizenship Act* provides that citizenship may be lost by virtue of the voluntary acquisition of another citizenship (s 17), by renunciation (s 18) or by service in the armed forces of an enemy country (s 19). In addition, an Australian citizen who is such by registration or naturalization may lose Australian citizenship by residence outside Australia for a continuous period of seven years, unless he fulfils the conditions set out in the section. The minister may, subject to the right of appeal of a person who may have a hearing before a board, deprive an Australian citizen who is such by registration or naturalization of his citizenship for conduct or speech which shows disloyalty or disaffection towards the monarch, or assists the enemy in time of war, or where the registration was obtained by means of fraud or concealment of particular relevant facts, or where the person at the time of registration

---

27   See Nicholas, 21. Parry, *Nationality and Citizenship Laws of the Commonwealth* (1957) Ch 3.

28   No 22 of 1969. See now amendments made in 1973 set out in Appendix 1.

or naturalization was not of good character or had been convicted within five years of that date of a crime for which the imprisonment was for a term of twelve months or more.[29]

*Aliens.* An alien is defined in the *Citizenship Act* (s 5) as a person who is not a British subject, an Irish citizen or a protected person (the latter including a citizen of the Trust Territory of New Guinea). In *Robtelmes v Brenan*[30] Griffith CJ said "The power to make such laws as Parliament may think fit with respect to aliens must surely, if it includes anything, include the power to determine the conditions under which aliens may be admitted to the country, the conditions under which they may be permitted to remain in the country, and the conditions under which they may be deported from it." It is clear, therefore, that the aliens power could be used in conjunction with, or alternatively to, the immigration power in order to exclude aliens from the country, to prescribe the condition under which they may enter the country and to deport them.[31] It has not been judicially determined whether s 51 (xix) gives to the Commonwealth power to prescribe the consequences of alienage (for example, by prescribing that no aliens shall own land). In this respect reference should be made to the (conflicting) Privy Council decisions in relation to the Canadian aliens power in *Cunningham v Tomey Homma*[32] and *Union Colliery Company of British Columbia v Bryden*.[33] Ryan states that the dictum of Griffiths CJ in *Robtelmes' Case* is consistent with the view that the Commonwealth power does extend to the consequences of alienage and that it is further supported by the generous interpretation which, has been accorded to the enumerated powers of the Commonwealth.[34] There are State laws on the subject of the consequences of an alienage which are not excluded by Commonwealth law, this being a concurrent power of the Commonwealth. Such laws are laws which regulate land owning or entry into a profession and other matters.[35]

The *Aliens Act* 1947-1966 provides for the registration of aliens, and for a certain control over their movements. It makes no attempt however to regulate the legal status of aliens.

Part II Division 2 of the *Migration Act* 1958-1973 contains provisions for

---

29  In *Meyer v Poynton* (1926) 27 C.L.R. 436 it was held that the power given by the (old) *Nationality Act* to revoke a naturalization certificate was constitutional.
30  (1906) 4 CLR 395 at 404.
31  Quite apart from the aliens power, the power to exclude aliens would be regarded as an attribute of sovereignty. See *Robtelmes v Brenan supra, Ah Yin v Christie* (1907) 4 CLR 1428, *Ferrando v Pearce* (1918) 25 CLR 241. See also *Koon Wing Lau v Calwell* (1950) 80 CLR 534 where the *War-Time Refugees Removal Act* 1949 was upheld as an exercise of both the defence and aliens powers.
32  [1903] AC 151.
33  [1899] AC 580.
34  "Immigration, Aliens and Naturalization in Australian Law", Ch XVIII of *International Law in Australia* (ed O'Connell) 465 at 485.
35  Ibid at 485-489. Some of these Acts have now been repealed by State legislation, eg the *Aliens Act* 1965 (Qld) repealed earlier provisions imposing certain restrictions on aliens.

deportation of immigrants: there is a differentiation between alien and non-alien immigrants.[36]

In *Polites v Commonwealth*,[37] Latham CJ adverted to the fact that the Commonwealth Parliament could legislate with respect to aliens even though such legislation might contravene international law.[38] In this case the court upheld the validity of s 13A of the *National Security Act* 1939-1946 which permitted aliens to be conscripted into the armed forces (while coming to no firm conclusion on the international law position). This exercise of power was referable to the defence power (as were a number of the deportation cases during the war).

(xx) *Foreign corporations, and trading or financial corporations formed within the limits of the Commonwealth*:[39]

The ambit of this legislative power was first discussed in the case of *Huddart Parker and Company Pty Ltd v Moorehead*.[40] In this case certain sections of the *Australian Industries Preservation Act* of 1906 were challenged. The sections in question were sections which prohibited combinations in restraint of trade and the formation of trade monopolies in relation to all trade and commerce within the Commonwealth by foreign corporations and trading and financial corporations formed within the Commonwealth. The attack on the legislation was based on the ground that it was not referable to paragraph (xx): it was in effect designed to control trade activities (whether intrastate or interstate) engaged in by corporations of the nature specified and therefore, in relation to intrastate trade, was outside the legislative power of the Commonwealth. A majority of the court upheld this argument. It is quite clear that their judgment was to a large extent based on the doctrine of state reserved powers which was to be rejected later by the High Court in the *Engineers Case*.

The members of the majority however differed amongst themselves as to the reasons for interpreting paragraph (xx) in the way that they did. Griffith CJ (with whom Barton J agreed in substance) considered that s 51 (xx) empowered the Commonwealth to prohibit the corporations specified from entering into a field of operation, but did not empower the Commonwealth to control the operations of the corporation once it had lawfully entered upon them.[41] Moreover, it did not enable the Commonwealth to establish such corporations:

I am of the opinion that the words in question do not on their face purport to deal with the creation of corporations. In the case of foreign corporations it is obvious that Parliament cannot create them. The formation and regulation of corporations in

---

36    See below. In *Ex parte Walsh and Johnson* (1925) 37 CLR 36 at 88 Isaacs J compared naturalization (the passing from a state of alienage across the dividing frontier to a state of British nationality) with immigration (the passing across the frontier of Australia from another country).
37    (1945) 70 CLR 60.
38    Ibid at 69.
39    Quick and Garran, 604-8. Wynes, 152-6. Lane, 99-118. Howard, 412-21.
40    (1908) 8 CLR 330.
41    Ibid at 353-4.

general is one of the matters left to the States, and in my judgment, the words 'formed within the limits of the Commonwealth' mean 'formed under State laws'.

The Commonwealth was, therefore, obliged to take such corporations "as it finds them, and may make such laws with respect to their operations as are otherwise within its competence".[42]

O'Connor J examined the historical basis for the section. He pointed out that before federation a corporation formed under the laws of a colony was not automatically entitled to recognition in the courts of another colony: "in that respect each of them was a foreign country to the other".[43] Only the British Parliament could confer a right on a corporation formed under one colony's laws to trade in the territory of another. It was therefore necessary to give to the newly formed Commonwealth Parliament a similar power—a power of making a uniform law for regulating the conditions under which foreign corporations, and trading or financial corporations created under the laws of any State, would be recognised as legal entities throughout Australia. O'Connor J continued:

Recognition of a corporation as a legal entity involves recognition of its right to exercise throughout Australia its corporate functions in accordance with the law of its being, that is, the law by which the foreign or State law gave its existence as a legal body. Recognition may be absolute or on conditions. It is unnecessary here, even if it were possible, to make comprehensive statements of the matters which might be the subject of such conditions, but it may be stated generally that Parliament is empowered to enact any laws its deems necessary for regulating the recognition throughout Australia of the corporations described in the section, and may, as part of such law, impose any conditions it thinks fit, so long as those laws and the conditions embodied in them have relation only to the circumstances under which the corporation will be granted recognition as a legal entity in Australia. It may for example prohibit altogether the recognition of a corporation whose constitution does not provide certain safeguards and security for payment of their creditors. It may impose conditions on recognition to attain the same end. As a preliminary to recognition it may insist upon a compliance with any conditions it deems expedient for safeguarding those dealing with a corporation. In the effecting of objects within these limits, it must have a right to encroach on State powers to such an extent as it may deem necessary.[44]

Higgins J adopted a similar view. He said: "The federal Parliament controls as it were the entrance gates, the tickets of admission, the right to do business and continue to do business; the State parliaments dictate what acts may be done, or may not be done, within the enclosure, prescribe laws with respect to the contracts and business within the scope of the permitted powers ... the Federal Parliament has no power, in regulating the actors, to regulate, in whole or in part, transactions which do not belong to interstate or foreign trade."[45] He pointed out that it was well established that a country had the right to prevent foreign corporations from carrying on business within its limits either absolutely or subject to conditions.

Isaacs J who dissented took a wider view of Commonwealth power. The Commonwealth could legislate with respect to corporations in their dealings with outsiders. But he agreed with the members of the majority that the power

---

42    Ibid at 348.
43    Ibid at 372.
44    Ibid at 373-4.
45    Ibid at 413.

did not enable the Commonwealth to deal with the incorporation of companies.[46]

In the *Banking Case* there was a discussion of the corporations power in the judgments of Rich, Williams, JJ and Latham CJ. Rich and Williams JJ considered that it did not extend to the prohibition of corporations from carrying on business at all but merely authorized the Commonwealth to impose conditions appropriate to the carrying on of specific operations.[47] Latham CJ stated that "the existence and powers and capacities of any corporation to which s 51 (xx) applies depend upon some law other than a law under that provision".[48] The judges were all agreed that the power was neither one of creation nor of prohibition.

The power conferred by s 51 (xx) was re-examined recently by the High Court in *Strickland v Rocla Concrete Pipes Ltd*[49] involving the *Trade Practices Act* 1965-1967 which had replaced the *Australian Industries Preservation Act*. This Act, which prohibited certain types of restrictive trade practices was drafted in a way to provide two alternative constitutional bases for the legislation: the trade and commerce power (s 51 (i)), and the corporations power. A majority of the court held that several sections of the Act extended beyond the ambit of the power conferred by these placita and that the Act as drafted was therefore invalid.[50] All the judges, however, disagreed with the *Huddart Parker* interpretation of the power on the basis that, in refusing to allow the corporations power its full operation in relation to intrastate trade practices, the majority in the earlier case were applying a doctrine which had been decisively rejected by the High Court in the *Engineers Case*.

In the *Concrete Pipes Case* there was not much discussion of the full ambit of the power and the effect of the case must be restricted to the upholding of the power of the Commonwealth under s 51 (xx) to make laws with respect to the restrictive trade practices of corporations. However, it is clear that the power has a wider operation and may affect the activities of corporations *qua* corporations.

There is some doubt as to whether s 51 (xx) would be extensive enough to empower prohibition of foreign companies from entering into Australian business fields or areas. Certainly a prohibition on financial or trading corporations formed within the limits of the Commonwealth from engaging in activities would ordinarily fall foul of other sections of the Constitution, e g, s 92. The majority of the court in the *Banking Case* considered that the corporations power did not allow the Commonwealth to prohibit corporations from carrying on business but merely authorized the prescription of conditions. This view would seem to have been applicable both to trading and commercial and financial corporations formed within the Commonwealth and also to foreign corporations. On the other hand there does seem to be a greater reason for recognizing Commonwealth power over activities of foreign cor-

---

46   Ibid at 394 et seq Cf, Sawer, *Australian Constitutional Cases* at 445: "If history is disregarded, the purely semantic considerations would support a conclusion that par (xx) does extend to general Commonwealth laws for the incorporation of these corporations. The words 'formed within the Commonwealth' would have been treated as merely contrasted with 'foreign'. . . ."

47   (1948) 76 CLR 1 at 255.

48   Ibid at 202.

49   (1971) 45 ALJR 485.

50   The Act has been re-drafted to take account of the High Court decision: See the *Restrictive Trade Practices Act* No 138 of 1971.

porations compared with those corporations that have a local origin. Higgins and O'Connor JJ in *Huddart Parker* took the view that there was a power to prohibit foreign corporations from carrying on business in Australia.[51]

It is quite clear from *Huddart Parker's Case* that the power is wide enough to affect foreign corporations and trading or financial corporations formed within the limits of the Commonwealth by way of regulating the capacities of these corporations and prescribing the conditions under which they may carry on business in Australia. Thus it would be possible for the Commonwealth to require in the case of a foreign corporation that a certain share capital be held by Australian residents; it may require that certain documents be lodged with a central stock exchange by all corporations trading in Australia. There may well be some over-lapping between these conditions and the conditions prescribed under State companies legislation. To the extent to which there was any inconsistency, the Commonwealth legislation would prevail. It is also clear that the power would allow the Commonwealth to control mergers and takeovers of Australian companies by foreign companies, for example by providing that a foreign company, or even a financial company or trading company formed in Australia, should not acquire the whole or any part of the stock or other share capital of another Australian company without the approval of the Treasurer.[52]

To what extent does the power enable the Commonwealth to introduce a general companies Act? Certainly the whole range of companies is not subject to Commonwealth legislative power. In *Huddart Parker's Case* Isaacs J pointed out that companies which were excluded from the designation of financial and trading corporations were "all those domestic corporations, for instance, which are constituted for municipal, mining, manufacturing, religious, charitable, scientific, and literary purposes, and possibly others more nearly approximating a character of trading."[53] He also considered that a purely manufacturing company was not included[54] although, as has been noted on many occasions, it is difficult to imagine a manufacturing company which does not also trade.

A more important limitation on the power of the Commonwealth Parliament to enact a general companies Act is to be found in the opinion of the judges in *Huddart Parker* that s 51 (xx) did not permit the creation of companies: it presupposed their existence under State law.[55] If this view is upheld it would fetter the Parliament powers in matters of internal organization and management of companies.[56]

The view has already been expressed that the power is wide enough to cover mergers and takeovers by foreign corporations and that certain regulatory conditions may be imposed on all corporations of the nature specified as a condition for carrying on business. The full scope of the power must be left to be determined by the future course of judicial exegesis.

---

51  On analogy with the aliens power, it could be said that there is an inherent right to exclude an alien corporation.
52  See Peden, "The Control of Mergers in Australia" 8 Western Australian Law Review (1968) 476 at 478-83.
53  (1908) 8 CLR 330 at 393.
54  Ibid.
55  See, for example, the judgment of Isaacs J, ibid; Lane, 46 ALJ 407. See, however, the view of Barwick CJ in *Strickland v Rocla Concrete Pipes Ltd* (1971) 45 ALJR 485 at 489.
56  For a criticism of this limitation see Taylor, "The Corporations Power: Theory and Practice", (1972) 46 ALJ 5 at 9.

*Restrictive Trade Practices Act 1971.*[57] The Act establishes a Trade Practices Tribunal with power to determine whether certain practices and agreements engaged in by corporations of the type specified in s 51 (xx) are contrary to the public interest. The various kinds of examinable agreements (which are subject to registration with the Commissioner of Trade Practices) are set out in s 35 of the Act. Examinable practices are set out in ss 36 and 37.

Part VII of the Act deals with resale price maintenance. Section 66 (i) makes it unlawful for a corporation or other person to engage in the practice of resale price maintenance unless the tribunal has exempted goods to be supplied from the operation of the Act.

Part X of the Act prohibits the practices of collusive tendering and collusive bidding. Several sections of the Act are drafted in a manner so as to regulate not only the situation in which the practices are engaged in by a corporation but also where the corporation is a victim, so to speak, of practices engaged in by a non-corporate person (see ss 36 (1) (b) (d) and (f) and 66 (3).)

*Companies (Foreign Take-overs) Act 1972.* This Act applies to attempted takeovers of bodies corporate described as trading or financial corporations formed within the limits of the Commonwealth or under the law of a Territory, other than Papua-New Guinea (s 5). It affects activities of foreign persons or foreign corporate bodies (as defined in s 4) directed to the acquisition of shares in Australian corporations of the nature specified. The main power conferred is the power of the responsible minister (the Treasurer) to prohibit takeover attempts involving the acquisition of shares (s 13). He may also limit the beneficial ownership of shares (s 14).

*Prices Justification Act 1973.* In 1973 the federal Parliament passed legislation to establish a Prices Justification Tribunal to enquire into prices charged by companies the turnover of which reached a certain level. While the decisions of the board are not enforceable, certain compulsory powers including the power to require production of documents are vested in the board.

This Act would seem to put to the test to what extent s 51 (xx) permits legislation affecting the internal organisation of companies.

(xxi) *Marriage:*[58]

The traditional definition of marriage is that given by Lord Penzance in *Hyde v Hyde*[59] as being "a voluntary union for life of one man and one woman to the exclusion of all others"[60] (thus reflecting the earlier Canon law doctrine although, even in the nineteenth century, certain in-roads into this doctrine were introduced with the passage of divorce legislation which made provision for the dissolution of a marriage under certain circumstances). The Commonwealth *Marriage Act* 1961-1966, s. 46 (1), in setting out the words to be used by authorised celebrants, leaves no doubt that the Act looks to the concept of marriage as defined by Lord Penzance.

One question which has been discussed is whether the Commonwealth may legislate in a manner which departs substantially from the common

---

57 Discussed Lane, "The New Trade Practices Act", 46 ALJ (1972) 170, Taylor, "The Corporations Power: Theory and Practice" 46 ALJ 5 at 11-12.
58 Quick and Garran, 608-9. Wynes, 156-9.
59 (1866) LR 1 P & D 120.
60 Ibid at 133.

law definition. Wynes expresses the view that "it is clear that, in accordance with the rule that the Constitution is to be interpreted with reference to its meaning as in 1900, the Commonwealth would be unable to legalize any form of union as marriage which does not accord with the principles of this definition, e g, it could not legalize polygamy".[61] However, it would be within the Commonwealth Parliament's power to at least regulate the recognition of polygamous marriages of aliens entered into outside Australia where the parties have subsequently settled in Australia.[62]

In the *Marriage Act* the Commonwealth has enacted a general code with respect to marriage thus superseding pre-existing State laws.[63] The Act contains provisions as to marriageable age (18 for males, 16 for females), provisions relating to solemnization of marriage in Australia and abroad, provisions relating to legitimation as well as provisions containing a code of offences against marriage the most important of which is bigamy.

The constitutional validity of the legitimation and bigamy sections of the Act were challenged in the High Court in the *Marriage Act Case*.[64]

The major legitimation provisions (s 89, 90) provided for the legitimation of a child whose parents were not married to each other at the time of birth but who had subsequently married each other (legitimation *per subsequens matrimonium*).[65] A 4-3 majority of the court[66] was of the opinion that these provisions were within Commonwealth legislative power as being incidental to the subject matter of marriage legislation. Kitto J said " ... a law which makes the legitimation of a child—perhaps one might more appropriately say the legitimation of the parent as such—an inevitable legal consequence of the intermarrying of the parents seems to me to be a law directly and squarely upon the subject of what marriage amounts to in law, and therefore upon the subject of marriage."[67] The objections of the Attorney General for Victoria that the upholding of such provisions would affect the class of persons succeeding to property under State succession legislation were answered by Kitto J in this way: "A State law which refers to 'children', for example, might be amended so as to limit the class to children born or conceived during marriage. That would suffice to create, between such children on the one hand and legitimate children generally on the other hand, just such a distinction as the common law has made familiar by distinguishing for the purpose of succession to realty between children born in lawful wedlock on the one hand and all

---

61　Op cit at 156-7.
62　This could also be regarded as within the aliens power. A marriage entered into by an *Australian citizen* abroad is regulated by the *Marriage Act*.

　　　Of course the Commonwealth can regulate various *incidentalia*, eg, the degrees of consanguinity and affinity. See *Union Label Case* (1906) 6 CLR 469 at 601-2 (per Higgins).
63　Prior to 1961 the Commonwealth Parliament had enacted legislation only with respect to certain types of overseas marriages (the *Marriage (Overseas) Acts* of 1955 and 1958).
64　*Attorney-General for Victoria v Commonwealth* (1961-2) 107 CLR 529; [1962] ALR 673, discussed in 36 ALJ 239.
65　Another provision, s 91, provided for legitimation of children of putative marriages.
66　Kitto, Taylor, Menzies and Owen JJ, Dixon CJ, McTiernan and Windeyer JJ dissenting.
67　107 CLR at 554.

legitimate children (including those whose legitimation *per subsequens matrimonium* under the law of another country is recognized in England) on the other".[68] That did not mean, of course, that all legitimation provisions would be valid. For example, the Commonwealth could not make laws on legitimacy generally which took as the basis for legitimation some fact other than marriage. It is to be noted, however, that only three of the majority judges (Kitto, Taylor and Menzies JJ) expressed their opinion on the effect of Commonwealth legitimation provisions on State law in this way. Owen J did not discuss the question whether a State could deprive a child legitimated under s 89 of rights in inheritance matters.

The minority viewpoint[69] expressed in the judgment of Dixon CJ was that the major legitimation provision (s 89) had its immediate and primary effect in relation to matters governed by State law—in matters of inheritance. In this regard the "substance" and the "incidence" of the legislation could not be distinguished, and, therefore, this provision fell outside the marriage power.[70]

The court as a whole sustained the validity of the provisions prohibiting bigamy as a matter intrinsically related to the validity of a marriage.

It would seem from the above reasoning that legislation on matters of property law associated with marriage, e g, married women's property legislation would not fall within the legislative power of the Commonwealth,[71] although it must be pointed out that under the matrimonial causes legislation enacted under s 51 (xxii) a court may dispose of property by way of an order of relief in relation to petitions arising under the Act.

(xxii) *Divorce and matrimonial causes; and in relation thereto, parental rights, and the custody and guardianship of infants:*[72]

Under this head of power the Commonwealth has authority over the granting of relief in petitions for dissolution of marriage and other actions associated with marriage, e g, petitions for judicial separation, restitution of conjugal rights, and also custody and guardianship matters associated with marital proceedings. The *Matrimonial Causes Act* 1959-1966 contains provisions in relation to void and voidable marriages, grounds for dissolution of marriages and other judicial remedies, provisions relating to maintenance, custody and settlements, and also provisions relating to recognition of decrees of divorce throughout the Commonwealth.[73]

While the *Matrimonial Causes Act* was passed, primarily in pursuance of the power granted by s 51 (xxii), a few of the provisions depend on s 51 (xxi).

Section 86 of the *Matrimonial Causes Act* empowers courts exercising

---

68   Ibid at 553.
69   Dixon CJ, McTiernan and Windeyer JJ. But McTiernan and Windeyer JJ held that s 91 (legitimation by putative marriage) was valid.
70   107 CLR at 542 et seq.
71   Wynes, op cit, at 158. He regards such matters as falling within the wider category of family law. Cf Cowen (36 ALJ 239) who suggests that if the Commonwealth can legislate with respect to the property of bankrupts under the bankruptcy power, then by analogy it should be able to legislate with respect to the property of married persons under its marriage power.
72   Quick and Garran, 609-12. Wynes, 159.
73   For a discussion of the legislation see Cowen and De Costa, *Matrimonial Causes Jurisdiction*, Introductory Chapter; articles in 34 ALJ 247, 279; 3 Sydney Law Review, 409.

federal jurisdiction in proceedings under the Act to require a party to make a property settlement for the benefit of a spouse or children which it considers just and equitable. In *Lansell v Lansell*[74] it was argued that the remedy lay outside Commonwealth power, as the matrimonial causes existing in 1900 did not encompass such a wide discretionary remedy.

However, it was pointed out by the court that while the meaning of constitutional terms did not change, their "denotation" might be extended as new concepts developed. It did not follow, therefore, that because at the time of federation, courts exercising jurisdiction in matrimonial causes had only a limited jurisdiction to direct property settlements, that a limit was, therefore, set to the concept of a "matrimonial cause".[75] Section 86 did not in effect authorize the institution of a matrimonial cause; it provided for ancillary relief in substantive proceedings either pending or completed.

But it is to be noted that while the Act entirely covers the matrimonial causes field and therefore supersedes inconsistent State legislation, the laws of the States on maintenance and custody are not affected unless a matrimonial cause has been instituted. This is because the subsidiary portion of s 51 is dependent on the primary portion. A deserted wife therefore, in the absence of a matrimonial cause, would be entitled to maintenance benefits arising under State legislation. There is still, however, some doubt as to the inter-relationship between federal relief granted under s 86 of the Act and remedies still available to a spouse in relation to property settlements under State marriage Acts unrelated to divorce proceedings.[76]

(xxiii) *Invalid and old-age pensions:*[77]

The two traditional forms of social service benefits in existence at the time of federation were assistance to those who were ill and assistance to those who were in a state of advanced age. Consequently it was understandable that the founders would consider that the federal Parliament should be given power to make laws with respect to these types of social services. This does not prevent a State from granting similar benefits. The power is a concurrent one. The Commonwealth has legislated to provide benefits of this nature under the *Social Services Act* 1947-1973, and the *National Health Act* 1953-1973, and also to provide special benefits under a number of other Acts.[78]

(xxiiiA) *The provision of maternity allowances, widows' pensions, child endowment, unemployment, pharmaceutical, sickness and hospital benefits, medical and dental services (but not so as to authorize any form of civil conscription), benefits to students and family allowances:*[79]

---

74   (1964) 110 CLR 353; [1965] ALR 153.
75   See Windeyer J 110 CLR at 370.
76   See *Johnson v Krakowski* (1965) 113 CLR 552; [1966] ALR 357. *Re Gilmore* [1968] 3 NSWR 675. *Denniston v Denniston* (1970) 15 FLR 430, [1970] ALR 707 (discussed in 44 ALJ 329). See also Howard and Sackville, "The Constitutional Power the Commonwealth to Regulate Family Relationships" (1970) Fed L R, 30. Sackville, "The Emerging Australian Law of Matrimonial Property". 7 MULR 353. Bissett-Johnson, "The Interaction of State and Federal Provisions in Matrimonial Property Disputes", 1 ACLR 143.
77   Quick and Garran, 612-3. Wynes, 134.
78   For example, *Disabled Persons Accommodation Act* 1963, *Broadcasting and Television Act* 1942-1972 (providing for reduced licence fees for recipients of pensions), *Defence (Re-establishment) Act* 1965-1968.
79   Wynes, 134-9.

Pursuant to a constitutional amendment approved by the electorate in 1945 and inserted into the Constitution by Act No 31 of 1946, the Commonwealth was given power to provide a great number of other social services besides those listed in s 51 (xxiii). Section 51 (xxiiiA) was in part due to the constitutional doubts as to the validity of an appropriation of monies for the purposes of a pharmaceutical benefits scheme embodied in the *Pharmaceutical Benefits Act* of 1944, which was the subject matter of judicial challenge in the *Pharmaceutical Benefits Case*.[80] In that case the High Court held that the provisions of that Act which provided benefits to residents of the Commonwealth on the basis of a prescription signed by a qualified medical practitioner were beyond Commonwealth power. Williams J pointed out that the Act contained provisions affecting the relationship under the laws of the States of medical practitioners and patients, of customers and chemists, and many other provisions which could only be described as legislation upon the subject matter of public health—a matter not (apart from quarantine) within Commonwealth power.[81]

The provisions inserted by the 1946 Amendment enabled the Commonwealth to legislate with respect to pharmaceutical benefits and also on a number of other benefits and systems. The following types of allowances are provided in s 51 (xxiiiA): (1) maternity allowances, (2) widows' pensions, (3) child endowment, (4) unemployment, pharmaceutical, sickness and hospital benefits, (5) medical and dental services (but not so as to authorize any form of civil conscription), (6) benefits to students, (7) family allowances.

The Commonwealth has legislated under all heads apart from the provision of dental services. Thus, there are provisions for maternity allowances, widows' pensions, child endowment, unemployment payments, pharmaceutical, sickness and hospital benefits, schemes which involve contributions from the Commonwealth and also for voluntary health schemes to which the person taking the benefit pays some contribution, as well as services of a medical nature.[82] For many years Commonwealth scholarships have been provided to university students and, in the last decade, a secondary school scholarship scheme has been in operation.[83] Family allowances have been provided in the form of Commonwealth subsidies to young married couples for purchasing a home, where the persons involved can show a specified sum saved for this purpose.[84]

Section 51 (xxiiiA) was considered by the High Court in the *British Medical Association v Commonwealth*.[85] A section of the *Pharmaceutical Benefits Act* of 1946 which required medical practitioners to use a particular formulary in writing out a prescription in order to entitle their patients to free pharmaceutical benefits was held invalid by a majority of the High Court as amounting to a form of civil conscription. Latham CJ, Williams, Rich and Webb JJ (Dixon and McTiernan JJ dissenting) held that the prohibition

---

80  *Attorney-General for Victoria ex rel Dale v Commonwealth* (1946) 71 CLR 237.
81  Ibid at 280. There was also a discussion of the appropriation power (s 81) in this case. See below. The Court rejected the argument that the Act could be characterized simply as an appropriation Act, nor could the incidental power be invoked to assist the Commonwealth.
82  These benefits are provided by the *Social Services Act* 1947-1973 and the *National Health Act* 1953-1973.
83  *Scholarships Act*, 1969.
84  *Homes Savings Grant Act* 1964-1972.
85  (1949) 79 CLR 201.

contained in the words in the brackets in s 51 (xxxiiiA)—"so as not to authorise any form of civil conscription"—had been contravened. As Latham CJ pointed out, civil conscription applied not only to legal compulsion to engage in particular conduct but also to a duty to perform work in a particular way. Section 7 (a) of the Act gave the doctor no option, as, if he did not use the formulary which was a prerequisite to the payment of pharmaceutical benefits to his patients, he would soon lose the majority of his patients.[86]

Webb J pointed out that the writing of a prescription was part of the physician's function.[87] Dixon J, however, considered that there was a difference between a regulation of the manner in which a medical service was carried out and the regulation of the service itself: the former did not amount to conscription.[88] McTiernan J thought that the law was not a law with respect to medical services but a law with respect to pharmaceutical benefits and that the civil conscription principle did not apply to this area. He considered that conscription implied a conscription of a person into the service of the Commonwealth.[89]

One final point to be made is that these particular heads refer to money payments, whether lump sum or periodical, while other parts of the list refer to the provisions of benefits.[90] This means that some benefits will include both monetary payments and the supply of things, e g, equipment and food as well as the performance of services while others referring to allowances will merely apply to financial assistance.

*Aid to students and schools.* One of the categories listed is "benefits to students". This may be achieved by a direct pecuniary grant to the student or his parents or by a grant to the school to cover the student's fees.[91] If, however, it is decided to assist a school by means of a capital grant, then this can be done by direct grants to the States under s 96 of the Constitution with the required conditions attached. The Commonwealth has, in effect, in its science laboratory and libraries schemes, assisted both State and non-State schools in this way.[92]

(xxiv) *The service and execution throughout the Commonwealth of the civil and criminal process and the judgments of the courts of the States:*[93]

This paragraph enables the Commonwealth to legislate to provide that State court processes (whether initiating or executing) and judgments have an Australia-wide operation.

Wynes states that s 51 (xxiv) confers on the Commonwealth great and important powers; certainly this is a useful placitum, borne of American experience.[94] In direct reliance upon this power, the Commonwealth Parlia-

---

86   Ibid at 251-3. Latham CJ also pointed out that the power conferred by s 51 (xxxiiiA) was limited to the provision of these benefits by the Commonwealth. It did not encompass legislation generally on these benefits (Ibid at 242-3).
87   Ibid at 293-4.
88   Ibid at 277-8.
89   Ibid at 283.
90   See Dixon J at 256-60.
91   See Lane, "Commonwealth Reimbursements for Fees at Non-State Schools" (1964) 38 ALJ 130.
92   *State Grants (Science Laboratories) Act* 1968-1971 *State Grants (Secondary School Libraries) Act* 1968-1971 *State Grants (Schools) Act* 1972.
93   Quick and Garran, 613-20. Wynes, 165-7.
94   Op cit at 165.

ment has enacted the *Service and Execution of Process Act* 1901-1968 to provide for the service of process, the execution of warrants and the enforcement of judgments and fines of the courts of one State in other States. Problems have arisen, and have been discussed in a number of cases, concerning the inter-relation of the provisions of this Act with the provisions made in the rules of various State courts for the service of civil process beyond the boundaries of the respective States.

State courts have within their rules provisions analogous to Order XI of the Rules of the Supreme Court of Victoria to the effect that service out of the (territorial) jurisdiction of the court may be allowed by the court or a Judge in certain specified cases. Once service has been achieved the defendant must enter an appearance, either conditional (i e, subject to a challenge to the court's jurisdiction) or unqualified. If he ignores the process served upon him, he risks a default judgment.

The Commonwealth Act appears to duplicate in large measure these State provisions. Section 4 states that "a writ of summons issued out of or requiring the defendant to appear at any court of record of a State or part of the Commonwealth may be served on the defendant in any other State or part of the Commonwealth". After service has been thus effected, if the defendant fails to appear, the plaintiff may obtain liberty to proceed if he persuades the court that the action falls within the classes enumerated in s 11—which are broadly analogous to the Order XI provisions. A writ of summons to be served under the Commonwealth Act must be indorsed in accordance with s 5 thereof.

It might seem that this is an example of paramount Commonwealth legislation: that is to say, the Commonwealth having legislated with respect to the service and execution of process, the pre-existing State rules should be pro-tanto invalid. But this is not the case. Philp J discussed the relation of the two sets of rules in *Dowd v Dowd*.[95]

The federal Act introduced an alternative method for valid service out of the jurisdiction, but for service only in Australia. By s 4 of that Act any writ issued out of a court of record of one State may be served in any other State. If the defendant appears to the writ, no matter what its subject matter, he subjects himself to the jurisdiction of the issuing court, and proof that the subject matter is within s 11 is required only when there is no appearance and leave to proceed is necessary. (*Luke v Mayoh* (1921) 29 CLR 435 at 439). That case also decides that any writ issued without leave may be served under the federal Act although a State law requires leave before a writ can be issued for service out of the State.

In my opinion, that case sufficiently indicates that the federal Act and the relevant State law form separate codes in relation to service of a writ issued in one State upon a person in another State and to the circumstances in which the issuing court has jurisdiction in default of appearance. If one of these codes be complied with, the rights and jurisdiction provided by that code arise and there is no need to comply with the requirements of the other code. This view is supported by the decisions in *Kuhndt v Kuhndt* [1927] SASR 426 and *Jones and Co v Gardner Brothers* (1927) 23 WALR 23.[96]

The possibility of inconsistency was raised directly in *K W Thomas (Melbourne) Pty Ltd v Groves*[97] where O'Bryan J set out the relationship of the federal and State Acts in this way:

---

95   1946 St R Qd 16.
96   Ibid at 17-18.
97   1958 VR 189 O'Bryan J.

With the establishment of federal government, it became possible for the Common-wealth Parliament to provide for a simpler and more expeditious procedure for service within the Commonwealth, of process issued out of any of the State courts. There is, in my opinion, nothing either in the terms, nature or subject matter of the *Service and Execution of Process Act* to suggest that the Commonwealth Parliament intended to cover the field in relation to the service of process of one State outside that State but within Australia, or to abrogate the existing State legislation whereby process might be served outside the State. Barton J in *Renton v Renton* 25 CLR 291 at 298 said, 'I can see nothing in the federal *Service and Execution of Process Act* to show anything that might be done under the Act in question here would be in conflict with the former Act.'

I can find nothing in Order XI which, if valid, would alter, impair or detract from the operation of the Commonwealth statute. The Commonwealth statute is wholly enabling and gives complementary or additional facilities to those already existing under State law.[98]

The High Court, in both *Luke v Mayoh*[99] and in *Tallerman and Co Pty Ltd v Nathan's Merchandise Victoria Pty Ltd*[1] acted on the assumption of the continuing validity of analogous State provisions.[2]

The Commonwealth Act does not in any way increase the jurisdiction of the State courts. Nor does it give the State courts an extra-territorial jurisdic-tion. It merely facilitates service and execution of process. The "judgment" provisions (s 20 et seq) clearly refer to all judgments, not only those obtained pursuant to process issued under the Act; this is clear from the definition of "judgment" in s 3 of the Act.

*McGlew v NSW Malting Co Ltd*[3] produced an interesting challenge to s 10 of the Act, which empowers the issuing court to order a plaintiff to give security for costs upon application for leave to issue a writ for service in another State. The section was held valid, as incidental to the purpose of the Act.

In relation to the question of execution of process, it must also be remembered that the States have legislation based on the reciprocity provisions of the *Administration of Justice Act* 1920 (Imp) which allow registration of judgments in courts in other parts of Her Majesty's dominions and consequent execution.

*Criminal process.* Criminal process is dealt with in ss 18-19 of the Com-monwealth Act which permit the execution of warrants of arrest beyond the issuing State. The validity of these provisions was challenged in *Aston v Irvine*[4] on the basis that, by authorising the manner in which the officers of one State should handle criminal process issuing from another, it constituted an interference with the executive government of the former State. However, it was held that the power given to the officers of the assisting State was an

---

98  Ibid at 197.
99  (1921) 29 CLR 435.
1  (1957) 98 CLR 93.
2  See also *Renton v Renton* 25 CLR 291 at 298 per Barton J: "Section 51 (xxiv) and (xxv) cannot be relied upon for a general displacement of State legislation by federal legislation on the matters there mentioned. These powers are given as concurrent with the powers of the States. They are intended to be of assistance in obtaining as well as enforcing judgments of the State courts".
3  (1918) 25 CLR 416.
4  (1955) 92 CLR 353. Aston, a South Australian policeman, had sought extra-dition from Victoria of persons accused of offences under South Australian law. See also *Ammann v Wegener* (1972) 46 ALJR 638 (summons to witness to attend preliminary hearing).

independent power in aid of the issuing State. Section 51 (xxiv) was recognized as the basis of extradition as between the States.

It was also argued that s 18 of the Act involved the discharge of functions which were part of the executive power of the Commonwealth. The appointment of officers to discharge these functions should be governed by s 67 of the Constitution. The argument in relation to s 18 (6) went one stage further in that it was argued that this section involved the exercise of the judicial power of the Commonwealth not in accordance with Chapter III, as it should have been vested in a State court under s 77 (iii). Section 19, it was submitted, would have to fall with s 18 from which it was not severable; and apart from that, it involved conferral of non-judicial power on the Supreme Court on the one hand, or executive power not in accordance with s 67 on any other State court.

In their joint judgment, the court explained the operation of s 18:

The sub-section is expressed to allow the making in another State or part of the Commonwealth of an indorsement on the warrant authorising its execution in that State or part of the Commonwealth and of bringing up the person apprehended before the person indorsing the warrant or before some justice of the peace. The conditions to be fulfilled are that the person mentioned in the warrant should be or should be supposed to be in or on his way to that State or part of the Commonwealth, and that the person making the indorsement should be satisfied that the warrant was issued as required by the subsection, proof of the signature to the warrant being given.[5]

The critical act in the scheme, therefore, was the indorsement of the warrant by the magistrate or justice of the peace of the State in which it is executed.

The court proceeded to explain the nature of the power in question:

It is a legislative power given to the central legislature for the very purpose of securing the enforcement of the civil and criminal process of each State in every other State. It is given to the central legislature because before Federation it had been found that territorial limitations on Colonial power made the effective reciprocal action of the colonies in this field difficult, to the point of impossibility.[6]

In this respect, reference was made to the early Victorian case of *Raye v McMackin.*[7]

Referring to the power to issue warrants, the court said:

The magistrates, justices of the peace, and other officers mentioned by 18 (1) as having power to issue warrants for apprehension of persons under the law of the State, exercise that power under the authority of the law which reposes it directly in them. They are not agents exercising an authority vicariously derived from the executive government of the State as a principal. To give them the power in question involves no interference with the functions of the executive government of the State.[8]

This meant that the magistrates were conforming with Commonwealth law, exercising a purely ministerial function vested in them by the exercise of Commonwealth legislative power under s 51 (xxiv).

In answer to the contention that this constituted an exercise of the executive power of the Commonwealth, contrary to s 67 of the Constitution, the court said:

---

5 92 CLR at 363.
6 Ibid at 364.
7 (1875) 1 VLR (L) 278.
8 92 CLR at 364.

It is enough to say that s 18 confers specific legal powers upon the magistrates, justices of the peace, and officers authorised by s 18 to issue warrants of apprehension. The use of these powers involves an *independent responsibility*, and does not involve the executive power of the Commonwealth.[9]

A further claim was made that s 18 (3) and (6) together involved the judicial power of the Commonwealth, and if so, that there would be invalidity in so far as the power was conferred not upon a "State court" but upon the magistrate, justice of the peace as *personae designatae*; in this capacity, these persons were not strictly speaking a court, although they might, under the law of some States constitute courts of petty sessions etc. The court conceded that it was arguable that here was judicial authority. But they answered the contention by saying:

But the scheme of ss 18-19 seems to be to treat the magistrate or justice as exercising a preliminary discretion so to speak, to grant process ministerially, and then to submit for *judicial* review by a judge of the Supreme Court the whole question of the liability of the person apprehended to be returned to the State originating the proceeding.[10]

Section 10 of the Act allows the accused person, or the complainant where the accused has been discharged under s 18 (6), to bring the matter before a judge of the Supreme Court for review, whereupon the judge may confirm or quash the order of the magistrate, and exercise other incidental powers. At first sight, this appears to be a similar power to that exercised by the magistrate; at least, the result is the same. And the magistrate's power had been described as ministerial. If this were so, then there would be grounds of invalidity, since non-judicial authority had been conferred on the Supreme Court,[11] but the High Court held that this was not the case; once the matter was referred to the Supreme Court, it was necessary for that court to treat the question as a matter arising under Federal law within the federal jurisdiction conferred upon it by the *Judiciary Act* in accordance with s 77 (iii) of the Constitution.[12]

All in all, then, the constitutional validity of the *Service and Execution of Process Act*, both in its criminal and in its civil aspects, has survived challenge. But *Aston v Irvine* illustrates how carefully Commonwealth legislation must be drawn to avoid the pitfalls of the doctrine of separation. One final point is that the juristic basis of the system of this Act, in its criminal aspect, is not dissimilar from that contained in the income tax legislation which was validated in the *Shell Case*.[13]

The *Service and Execution of Process Act* speaks of "States or parts of the Commonwealth". Questions have arisen as to how this legislative power interrelates with the power given by s 122, and they were adverted to in *Lamshed v Lake*.[14] Dixon CJ said:

I am disposed to think that the provisions of the *Service and Execution of Process Act* 1901-50 relating to the process of the Territories must be justified under s 122. At all events s 51 (xxiv) does not extend to the service in the States of process issuing from the Territories.[15]

---

9    Ibid at 365.
10    Ibid.
11    See *Le Mesurier v Connor* discussed below under s 77.
12    92 CLR at 366.
13    See below.
14    99 CLR 132.
15    Ibid at 145-6.

Williams J said:

There is no reason in my opinion why the Northern Territory should not like the States be subject to federal law which the Commonwealth Parliament is empowered to make for the government of the whole area of the Commonwealth. For instance, to laws made under paragraphs s 51 (vi), (xxii) or (xxiv) of the Constitution.[16]

Section 51 (xxiv) has also received comment from State courts and one case which should be noted is *Ex Parte Iskra*[17] where one of the matters in issue was the extra-territoriality of the operation of State transport legislation and the jurisdiction of a State court over persons alleged to have committed offences against it and who were resident outside the State. Amongst the arguments advanced was that the result of the *Service and Execution of Process Act* was to bring within the jurisdiction of the State court persons not resident within the State. Brereton J said:

In all the discussion which has ensued, there seems to me with deference, to be some confusion between ability to effect service outside the territorial jurisdiction of the court concerned or outside the State, and the jurisdiction over persons who may thus be served. No doubt when the legislature provides, as in the *Common Law Procedure Act,* for service of process outside the State, it is an almost conclusive indication that persons outside the State thus served are intended to be amenable to the jurisdiction of the court, though it by no means follows that every person who may be thus served is necessarily so amenable. Conversely, *Ashbury v Ellis* [1893] AC 339 is clear authority for the proposition that a person may be subjected to the jurisdiction of a court even though he cannot be served with its process. The fields of jurisdiction, *qua* persons, and of service of process are not necessarily co-extensive. As a result of the *Service and Execution of Process Act* service could be effected where hitherto it could not; but this afforded no material for construing a State enactment or for holding that, as a result, every person who could now be served with a court's process became subject to the jurisdiction of that court.[18]

It would seem to be accepted, therefore, that the *Service and Execution of Process Act* has not affected the territorial limitations on State legislation, nor has it had any effect on the common law rules of private international law.

(xxv) *The recognition throughout the Commonwealth of the laws, the public Acts and records, and the judicial proceedings of the States:*[19]

This section looks to inter-State recognition of the legislation, records and curial processes of each State.

The Commonwealth has legislated to provide for the recognition throughout the Commonwealth of both State and Territorial laws and records and judicial proceedings.[20] Section 18 of the *State and Territorial Laws and Records Recognition Act* 1901-1964 provides: "All public acts, records, and judicial proceedings of any State or Territory, if proved or authenticated as required by this Act, shall have such force and credit given to them in every court and public office as they have by law or usage in the courts and public offices of the State or Territory from which they are taken." Under this provision, therefore, public statutes and records, e g, registrations of births,

---

16 Ibid at 151.
17 (1964) 80 WN (NSW) 923.
18 Ibid at 934-5.
19 Quick and Garran, 620-1. Wynes, 162-5.
20 The power nevertheless is a concurrent one. See *Renton v Renton* (1918) 25 CLR 291 at 298, per Barton J.

deaths and marriages as well as judicial proceedings are entitled to the stipulated recognition.

There has been a great amount of academic discussion as to whether this provision is substantive in effect or merely evidentiary. In other words does it compel substantive recognition of laws, records and judgments without regard to the conflictual rules of the forum (which might permit rejection on grounds of public policy), or is it merely evidentiary in effect, that is, as requiring formal recognition to be given to those public documents of another State as are duly executed, but leaving it to the courts of the forum to decide whether, on substantive grounds, recognition should be given? In this connection reference must be made to s 118 of the Constitution —the "full faith and credit clause"—under which heading the matter will be further examined.

(xxvi) *The people of any race for whom it is deemed necessary to make special laws:*[21]

Under this head of power the Commonwealth can legislate with regard to specific classes of people who fall within the category of a race. It seems to be accepted that its particular purpose was to give the Commonwealth power to deal with problems associated with the influx of people from the Pacific Islands, although it is true to say that most legislation dealing with people of a particular race might also be validated under the immigration, aliens or external affairs power.[22]

Until 1966, the Aboriginal race was specifically excluded from the paragraph but pursuant to a constitutional amendment approved at a referendum in that year the Commonwealth now has power to make laws for the Aboriginal race. This amendment has ended any doubts which may have existed as to the power of the Commonwealth to enact laws for the benefit of the Aboriginals, for example by providing a special system of Aboriginal social services or bringing in resettlement and land-owning schemes for the Aboriginal populations of the States.[23]

(xxvii) *Immigration and emigration:*[24]

The term immigration has often been associated with the entry by a person into a country for the purpose of settling in that country. However, the legal interpretation given to the term immigration by the courts has tended to separate to a large extent the concept of entry from that of settlement, so that the immigration power is regarded as extending to those who have entered into Australia even though they have not been accepted as settlers. This was pointed out by Cussen J in the Victorian case of *Ah Sheung*

---

21    Quick and Garran, 622-3. Wynes, 288.

22    For a discussion of the section see Sawer, "The Australian Constitution and the Australian Aboriginal" (1966-7) 2 Federal Law Review 17 especially at 18-25. See also *Robtelmes v Brenan* 4 CLR 395 at 414-5.

23    Of course, the power could be exercised to impose burdens on a race. Joske: *Australian Federal Government* (1967) at 225 "The assumption that legislation with respect to the people of a particular race would be to give them benefits may well be erroneous since the historical reason for including a provision in the Constitution was to give the Commonwealth authority to deal with the problem of Chinese and Kanaka labour, the restriction of which was one of the motivating causes of federation".

24    Quick and Garran, 623-9. Wynes, 288-95. Lane, 119-133. Nicholas, 208-11.

*v Lindberg.*[25] Cussen J, having stated that "in its ordinary meaning immigration implies leaving an old home in one country to settle in a new home in another country with a more or less defined intention of staying there permanently or for a considerable time", pointed out that its meaning had been extended in the Australian context to cover the influx of persons for temporary purposes (e g, work) but who did not have the intention of settling.[26] The pre-federation practice of the colonies was to treat these categories of non-Australians as having an immigrant status and therefore subject to exclusion under colonial law.[27] This view was accepted in *Ghia Gee v Martin*[28] where it was held that a person may be an immigrant although it could not be proved that he intended to remain in Australia for any definite period. On the other hand, as we shall see later, immigration is not to be regarded in all cases as synonymous with entry.[29]

From an early period, the question arose as to how far the power would permit legislation bearing upon the incidence of the status of "immigrants", not as persons taking part in the physical act of immigration, but as persons who having done so, had been to a greater or lesser extent absorbed into the Australian community. The widest view of the power is that stated by Isaacs J, aphoristically, in the *Irish Envoys Case.*[30] "Once an immigrant always an immigrant".[31] This view implied that the Commonwealth power was an extensive one with a more or less permanent attachment to persons who, having left their home, had "settled" in Australia. On the other hand, the more restrictive view of the immigration power, accepted by some judges in later cases to be discussed, was that it did not permit the Commonwealth to legislate with regard to persons who had settled in Australia and had been absorbed into the community.

In the early case of *Potter v Minahan*[32] it was held that the immigration power did not extend to the defendant Minahan, the illegitimate son of a Victorian woman who had been taken by his father, a Chinese, at the age of five, to China where he remained for a period of twenty-six years after which he returned to Australia. Griffith CJ considered that the fact of birth in Australia set up a presumption that Australia was "home" and that the facts associated with the respondent's conduct were consistent with his continuing to regard Australia as home. He regarded Minahan's return from China as not amounting to immigration, and so Minahan was outside the scope of the immigration power.[33]

---

25   [1906] VLR 323.
26   Ibid at 332-333.
27   Indeed the power of deportation has often been the central issue in cases arising under the immigration power. See Ex parte *De Braic* (1971) 45 ALJR 284 [1971] ALR 605; Ex parte *Kwok Kwan Lee* (1971) 45 ALJR 312; [1971] ALR 715.
28   (1906) 3 CLR 649.
29   However, the *Migration Act* does make entry of non-Australians a *factum* leading to restrictions specified in the Act. See also Harrison Moore ((1928) 2 ALJ 5) who interprets the early cases as deciding that all persons entering into Australia other than those whose home is in Australia are subject to the immigration power.
30   *R v Macfarlane, ex parte O'Flanagan and O'Kelly* (1923) 32 CLR 518.
31   Ibid at 555.
32   (1908) 7 CLR 277.
33   Ibid at 289-90.

However, in *Donohoe v Wong Sau*,[34] a different view was taken. The respondent here was born in New South Wales in 1883 of Chinese parents. The family returned to China in 1889 where the father died in 1902. In 1924 Wong Sau arrived back in Australia and was treated by the immigration authorities as a prohibited immigrant. On challenging her restriction in the High Court, it was held that she was not returning to Australia as her home. She was, therefore, subject to the immigration power.

Wynes finds an inconsistency between *Potter's Case* and *Donohoe's Case* and considers that the later decision contains a better view of the law.[35] On the other hand, the two cases could be reconciled in terms of legal principle but distinguished in terms of the evidence before the courts, in that Minahan's greater attachment to Australia could be demonstrated by the lesser period of time which he spent in China compared with Wong Sau's longer sojourn in that country.

It is clear, therefore, that birth within Australia is not decisive in determining the immigrant status of a person entering from abroad. Likewise it has been held that domicile[36] and the possession of British nationality[37] do not prevent a person from having immigrant status. In *R v McFarlane*[38] it was held that the power extended to deport persons who had entered Australia from overseas to support a particular political cause even though those persons did not intend to settle in the country.

In *Ex parte Walsh and Johnson*[39] the question to be determined was the validity of the detention in custody pending deportation of two persons of British nationality who had entered Australia from abroad, under a provision of the *Immigration Act* which permitted deportation on grounds which could generally be described as grounds of national security. The provision in question provided that where the Governor-General had made a proclamation that serious industrial disturbance threatened, the Minister of Immigration could call upon persons who in his opinion were fomenting such trouble, not being persons who were Australian-born, to show cause before a Board why they should not be deported. Walsh, the first party, was born outside Australia but had migrated here in 1893; Johnson, the second party, was born outside Australia but had migrated here in 1910. It was held by the High Court that the detention of both parties was invalid. In the case of Walsh the central fact was that he had been admitted to Australia prior to federation and therefore was outside the scope of the immigration power.

However, the case of Johnson was more difficult. On the basis that the immigration power extended to persons arriving in Australia after federation the question to be determined was whether the power could be exercised over persons who had been "absorbed" into the community. The view of the majority was that the provisions impugned were not laws with respect to immigration but applied to immigrants who had completed the process of immigration and therefore were beyond the operation of the legal power conferred by the section.

The absorption test was stated by Starke J in *Ex parte Walsh v Johnson* in this way: "Those who originally associated themselves together to form the

---

34   (1925) 36 CLR 404.
35   Loc cit at 290-1.
36   *Ah Yin v Christie* (1907) 4 CLR 1428.
37   *R v Macfarlane* (1923) 32 CLR 518.
38   Ibid.
39   (1925) 37 CLR 36.

Commonwealth and those who are afterwards admitted to membership cannot thereafter, upon entering, or crossing the boundary of, Australia from abroad, be regarded as immigrating into it unless in the meantime they have abandoned their membership. They have never been within, or else have passed beyond, the range of the power. It has never operated, "or else has become exhausted". He added: "Of course, conditions may be attached to persons immigrating into Australia upon entry, and so long as they remain within the range of the power".[40] Higgins J took a similar view to that of Starke J.[41] Isaacs and Rich JJ however adopted the wider interpretation (once an immigrant always an immigrant) and therefore considered that the immigration power extended to persons who had settled in Australia for a long period after federation. It was therefore quite permissible for the Commonwealth to revoke permission to an immigrant to remain in Australia or to attach conditions to an immigrant's entry which, having been broken, justified deportation.[42] It can be seen, therefore, that the difference between the majority and minority centered on whether those persons who had been unconditionally absorbed could be brought back within the power by retrospective operation.

A similar difference of viewpoint occurred in *Koon Wing Lau v Calwell*[43] which related to the revocation of permission to stay granted to non-Australians who had been brought to Australia during the war. Latham CJ McTiernan and Webb JJ adopted the wider interpretation while Williams and Rich JJ, departing from his earlier view, adopted the narrow interpretation. The view of the minority in that case was concisely put by Williams J who said "A law with respect to immigrants cannot apply to persons who are no longer immigrants, and persons are no longer immigrants who have entered and completed their settlement in accordance with the immigration law enforced prior to this completion".[44] Latham CJ followed the view he had taken in the earlier case of *O'Keefe v Calwell*[45] where he said: "Immigrants include persons who are intending settlers in a country other than their own and seek to enter (or do enter) that country and remain in it for the purpose of making a permanent home there, or who, having entered another country without any original intention to settle there, do in fact endeavour to remain in that country as members of the community. Control of immigration involves control of the admission of such persons and determining whether such admission is to be allowed to be permanent or only temporary. Such control is the means of determining the composition of the country in respect of the admission of external elements. Admission of any person not already a member of the community may, under a power to make laws with respect to immigration, be allowed either completely or partially and subject to conditions as Parliament thinks proper."[46] Latham CJ went on to point out that immigration involved two objects, that of entry into the community and that of absorption

---

40   Ibid at 137.
41   Ibid at 109-11.
42   Ibid at 80 et seq (Isaacs), 127-8 (Rich J).
43   (1949) 80 CLR 533.
44   Ibid at 589.
45   (1949) 77 CLR 261. This case concerned a person who was repatriated to Australia under military orders during the Japanese occupation of the Phillipines in the Second World War. Of course the (transitional) defence power was also a basis for the imposition of restrictions on such persons.
46   Ibid at 276-7.

therein, and both of these elements could be controlled under the immigration power. The power of deportation, therefore, could be exercised over an immigrant until that person had been accepted into the community. He recalled the earlier statement of Barton J in *Robtelmes v Brenan*[47]: "The right to deport is the complement of the right to exclude, the right to exclude a complement of the right to regulate immigration. The right to prescribe the conditions upon which persons may remain and reside within the Commonwealth is included in the power to regulate immigration by statute."[48]

The view of Dixon J in both *O'Keefe v Calwell* and *Koon Wing Lau v Calwell* is interesting. In both cases he seems to have regarded as acknowledged that with respect to persons who belong to the Australian community a law preventing them from entering into the Commonwealth or authorising expulsion is not a law with respect to immigration. However, he stated that the test of absorption or belonging was a vague one and did not prevent the Commonwealth from attaching conditions to a permit to enter into the country or to remain therein.[49] The views of Scholl J of the Supreme Court of Victoria *R v The Governor of the Metropolitan Gaol ex parte Molinari*[50] and Maguire J in *Re Moroney*[51] interpret the views of Dixon J as being in conformity with the narrower view of the power. Both judges expressed the view that the wider interpretation would not now be upheld. However, until we have a definitive view from the High Court, this expression of view may be rather premature.

The consensus in the cases has been expressed by a commentator in this way: ". . . . Whereas the Commonwealth Parliament may impose conditions on an immigrant at the moment of his entrance into the Commonwealth or any time before he has completed the process of being absorbed into the community for breach of which he may be deported, it is not within its competence to deport for breach of conditions imposed after a person has become a member of the community."[52]

As Ryan points out, the concept of absorption is vague—nationality, domicile and residence are merely evidentiary facts. Lapse of time and long-term acceptance as a member of the community are also other factors to be considered. Of course the practical result of the decisions that have been discussed is that a temporary entry permit given to a non-Australian might operate in such a way as to prevent the holder from being absorbed until the conditions attached to the permit had been changed, i e, until he had been given a permanent residential permit.[53]

The *Migration Act* 1958-1973 is the act under which the Commonwealth controls the entry of non-Australians into Australia and, therefore, their eventual absorption. Under this Act the Commonwealth has legislated to

---

47   (1906) 4 CLR 395.

48   Ibid at 415. The cases are discussed by Malor, "Deportation under the Immigration Power", (1950) 24 ALJ 3.

49   77 CLR at 287 et seq; 80 CLR at 576 et seq.

50   (1961) 2 FLR 477 at 496.

51   (1965) 83 WN (NSW) 45 at 53.

52   Ryan, "Immigration Aliens and Naturalization in Australian Law", in *International Law in Australia*, Ch 18 at 471. See also Lane, "The Immigration Power" (1966) 39 ALJ 302. Finlay, "The Immigration Power Applied" (1966) 40 ALJ 120.

53   See *R v Green ex parte Cheung Cheuk To* (1965) 113 CLR 506; [1965] ALR 1153. *Ex parte Kwok Kwan Lee* (1971) 45 ALJR 312, [1971] ALR 715.

empower the Minister of Immigration to issue entry permits for an immigrant to enter (transient entry) or remain in Australia (permanent or indefinite entry) or both (s 6 (3)). The entry permit may be a temporary one and may be issued before the person has entered Australia. Such a permit may be cancelled by the Minister at any time (s 7 (1)). It can be seen, therefore, that Parliament has in its legislation exercised the immigration power to the fullest so that it extends to the point at which a person entering the country comes within the Act by virtue of that entry.

The Act permits the deportation of an immigrant who has been convicted of certain crimes or has been an inmate of a mental hospital or public charitable institution within five years after his entry (s 13). The Act also permits the deportation at any time of an alien who has been convicted in Australia of crimes of violence or has been sentenced for an offence involving imprisonment for more than one year.[54] It can be seen therefore, that the immigrant who is a British subject has greater protection from deportation than has an alien.[55] It is clear that the provisions of the Act accord with both the wider and narrower views of the immigration power.

*Emigration.* Under this power the Commonwealth Parliament may regulate the act of voluntarily leaving the Commonwealth to take up a permanent home in another country. As such the term would not include deportation which is comprehended under the "immigration" section of this power and also the aliens and the defence powers.[56] It would seem that the Commonwealth can attach conditions to the departure of persons resident in Australia who are leaving Australia for a temporary period abroad by issuing passports and visas prescribing conditions under which the person may travel abroad. This power would be supported by the overseas trade and commerce power (movement of persons abroad) and the external affairs power (official certification of status to travel to foreign countries)[57] and the incidental power might also be invoked to support such controls.

(xxxviii) *The influx of criminals:*[58]

The nature of this power deserves little comment. It is within the jurisdiction of any government to prevent the entry, for temporary purposes or permanently, of persons who are criminals, that is to say, who have committed offences abroad and who if absorbed into the community might "corrupt" it. In terms of the issue of entry permits under the *Migration Act* 1958-1973 such matters as the past criminal record of an intending migrant are taken into account, and, therefore, there does not seem to be any need for any general laws relating to criminals as a class, although if such laws are ever needed they would certainly be justified under this head of power.

(xxix) *External affairs:*[59]

Blackstone points out that under English law the Crown acts as the

---

54    This provision is also supported by the aliens power.
55    Reference should also be made to the provisions of the *Citizenship Act* 1948-1969 which permit non-British subjects to be naturalized after a specified period of residence in Australia. Naturalization would seem prima facie to be regarded as evidence of absorption, although under certain conditions the naturalization certificate may be revoked.
56    See Wynes, op cit at 295.
57    See the *Passports Act* 1938-1966.
58    Quick and Garran, 629-31. Wynes, 295.
59    Quick and Garran, 631-7. Wynes, 281-5. Howard, 441-60. Lane, 135-54. Nicholas, 99-109. *Essays,* 343-74.

representative of the nation in the conduct of foreign affairs, and what is done in such matters by Royal authority is the act of the whole nation.[60] In the United Kingdom this prerogative power is exercised by the Sovereign, subject only to the constitutional conventions whereby Her Majesty accepts the advice of the Cabinet or the Foreign Secretary. *Mutatis mutandis,* the situation is the same with the Australian nation, wherein the Governor-General, representing the Crown in right of the Commonwealth of Australia, exercises the executive power of the Commonwealth in relation to the making of treaties with other countries, subject to the same constitutional conventions.

But it is vitally important to distinguish at the outset this prerogative power from the legislative power vested in the federal Parliament under s 51 (xxix). The latter is a power to legislate for the good government etc, of Australia with respect to matters falling within the connotation of the term "external affairs". Without s 51 (xxix), the prerogative right of the Crown would not be any different; but the curious situation would exist that wherever foreign relations demanded a change in the internal order, this would have to be achieved by the States acting in concert.

Although in the nature of things, the Australian States cannot possess international personality, and for this reason s 51 (xxix) like s 51 (vi) looks to a dominant Commonwealth legislature, it must be remembered that neither s 51 (xxix) nor s 51 (vi) are so expressed as to give the Commonwealth exclusive power. Indeed, the Commonwealth has adopted the practice that where a treaty requires consequential legislation in a field in which the States alone have power, then that legislation ought to be passed by the State legislatures.[61]

This question of legislative power must be distingushed from the question whether the Crown in right of the States has retained a concurrent prerogative power. It has been suggested that before federation the Crown in right of the colonies possessed a nascent, if seldom used, treaty power.[62] Today the States retain Agents-General in London; they also have representatives in other countries. And those representatives negotiate with foreign governments in a wide range of matters within State power. Certainly much of that negotiation is commercial and contractual rather than "governmental". But within the limitations on their power, the State governments, as governments may possess some international personality. The basis of these limitations is that the Crown in right of the States does not represent the nation in the sense of the term as used by Blackstone. Although Sawer has suggested that the States could in theory claim an external affairs power, he admits that "no State ever claimed an independent voice in matters of high international policy, such as defence, peace or war, and it is unlikely that any such claim would now be made."[63]

---

60  *Commentaries on the Laws of England,* Vol 1, 252.
61  For recent discussions of the external affairs power and associated matters, see Sawer, "Australian Constitutional Law in relation to International Relations and International Law," in *International Law in Australia* (ed O'Connell, 1966), Ch 11, pp 35 et seq. O'Connell, "The Evolution of Australia's International Personality", Ibid, Ch 1, pp 1 et seq. Lane, "The External Affairs Power", (1966) 40 ALJ 257. Howard, "The External Affairs Power", (1971) 8 MULR 193. Connell, "International Agreements and the Australian Treaty Power", (1968-9), Australian Year Book of International Law, 83.
62  Sawer, op cit, 36-8. See also O'Connell, op cit, 2-7.
63  Op cit at 38. See also his outline of the Vondel Incident in *Australian Federal Politics and Law,* 1902-1929 31-2.

With respect to the implementation of treaties, the constitutional doctrine is that treaties which affect private rights of citizens or involve any modification of the common or statute law, which require the vesting of additional powers in the Crown, or which impose additional financial obligations on the Crown, must be incorporated into the legal system by Act of Parliament.[64] It is to this legislative incorporation that s 51 (xxix) is particularly directed. So-called "political" treaties, particularly treaties involving military obligations in respect of Australia's relations with other countries, do not need to be implemented by legislative action if appropriation of money is not involved, or if rights of the Australian citizens are not directly affected. Nevertheless, it has been the practice for these major political treaties to be brought before Parliament for legislative ratification. This has been the case with the United Nations Charter, the ANZUS Treaty, the SEATO Treaty, as well as the Australian-American agreement relating to the North-West communication station.[65] Other treaties are merely tabled for noting by Parliament. The position in the United States is quite different. In that country, a self-executing treaty is regarded as part of the law of the land, i e, it does not need congressional implementation. Of course, part of the legislature in that country— the Senate—participates in the treaty making process.

As to the external affairs power in Australia, it seems to have been recognized in earlier times that the power did at least give to the Commonwealth Parliament some legislative authority over matters occurring extra-territorially or affecting Australia's relations with other countries.[66] However, in respect of matters associated with the internal order of Australia it seems to have been recognized that the Commonwealth would only legislate under s 51 (xxix) with respect to the subject matter of a treaty which was otherwise covered by another paragraph of s 51.[67] This view was influenced, not only by the pre-Engineers philosophy, but more particularly by the awareness of the limited international personality of the Commonwealth which did not mature until after the *Statute of Westminster*.[68] Much implemental legislation would concern matters such as defence, foreign trade and migration, matters already within other heads of s 51. But there are numerous instances of treaties entered into by the Commonwealth which deal with matters not included in any other head of Commonwealth power, matters which fall within the residuary power of the States under the Constitution, the most notable being ILO conventions dealing with labour matters which, apart from the area covered by s 51 (xxxv), are the preserve of State legislative power.[69]

Therefore critical issues will only arise in cases where legislative implementation of foreign affairs matters requires changes in the internal

---

64   Starke, *An Introduction to International Law* (6th ed) 82.
65   *Charter of the United Nations Act* 1945. *Security Treaty (Australia, New Zealand and the United States of America) Act* 1952. *South-East Asia Collective Defence Treaty Act* 1954. *United States Naval Communication Station Agreement Act* 1963.
66   See *McKelvey v Meagher* (1907) 4 CLR 265, a case dealing with fugitive offenders.
67   Bailey, "Fifty Years of the Constitution" (1951) 25 ALJ 314 at 321-2.
68   See Menzies, *Central Power in the Australian Commonwealth* (1967) p 117; Sawer, *op cit*, at 38, who points out that the Australian Founders did not expect the Commonwealth to proceed to the appointment of diplomatic representatives.
69   See generally Starke "Australia and the International Labour Organization" in *International Law in Australia* Ch VI pp 115 et seq.

order which it would be incompetent for the Parliament to achieve under any other legislative power granted to it by the Constitution. In such a case the desired changes could be brought about by the States, acting individually or in concert, by virtue of s 107. And their power requires no reference to a specific font.[70]

But despite the fact that Commonwealth governments have made it a practice in relation to some conventions not to use s 51 (xxix) to create intrusions into fields of State legislative authority,[71] and have looked to the States to pass implemental legislative measures, it would seem clear that if s 51 (xxix) is to have any meaning whatsoever as an independent head of power, then it does give the Commonwealth at least some power to intrude into "State" fields, so far as this is necessary for the implementation of its foreign affairs commitments. It would be curious if the Constitution envisaged a foreign policy restricted to the subject matter of the other paragraphs of s 51.

In the *Burgess' Case*[72] the High Court discussed the nature and scope of the external affairs power in great detail, and rejected the view that s 51 (xxix) was limited to the external aspects of matters covered by other paragraphs of s 51. The particular issue was the validity of air navigation regulations made under the *Air Navigation Act* 1920 which in its turn was passed for the purposes of giving effect to an international convention dealing with matters of this nature (air navigation is not of course a head of Commonwealth power). In their discussions of the external affairs power the members of the court adopted different approaches. Latham CJ, rejecting the proposition that s 51 (xxix) should be restricted to a power to make laws only with respect to the external aspects of the other subjects mentioned in s 51, stated:

The regulation of relations between Australia and other countries including other countries within the Empire is the substantial matter of external affairs. Such regulation includes negotiations which may lead to an agreement by the Commonwealth in relation to other countries, the actual making of such agreement in a treaty or convention or in some other form, and the carrying out of such an agreement.[73]

In his view it was "impossible to say *a priori* that any subject is necessarily such that it could never properly be dealt with by international agreement."[74]

---

70  In so far as they have power to make laws for the peace, welfare and good government of the territory under their jurisdiction they may embody the content of a convention in their own legal systems.

71  Sawer (op cit at 47) has made the following pungent criticism of Australian hesitancy to use the external affairs power as a basis for legislation. "Australian governments sometimes use the Federal difficulty as an alibi for not committing the country to agreements when the government dislikes the agreement on policy grounds but does not want to say this, whether for external or internal political reasons. If an Australian Federal government strongly approves an international commitment in an area not normally the subject of Commonwealth action, and can justify to the people any additional cost which Federal administration or resulting obligations may entail, it should take its constitutional courage in its hands and ratify it without Federal reservations, relying on s 51 par 29 and the *Goya Henry Case*. It would still be appropriate to persuade the States that they should take any necessary action perhaps providing Federal financial help to the purpose, but in the last resort the government should perform the obligation itself."

72  *R v Burgess ex parte Goya Henry* (1936) 55 CLR 608.

73  Ibid, at 643.

74  Ibid, at 641.

Dixon J said:

If a treaty were made which bound the Commonwealth in reference to some matter *indisputably international in character,* a law might be made to secure observance of its obligations if they were of a nature affecting the conduct of Australian citizens. On the other hand, it seems an extreme view that merely because the Executive Government undertakes with some other country that the conduct of persons in Australia should be regulated in a particular way, the legislature thereby obtains a power to enact that regulation although it relates to a matter of internal concern which, apart from the obligation undertaken by the Executive, could not be considered as a matter of external affairs.[75]

Starke J found value in the suggestion of an American jurist[76] that the power was limited to cases where the matter was of sufficient international interest to make it a legitimate subject for international co-operation and agreement.[77]

Evatt and McTiernan JJ took, however, a much wider view. They said:

In truth, the King's power to enter into international conventions cannot be limited in advance of the international situation which may arise from time to time. In our view the fact of an international agreement having been duly made about a subject brings that subject within the field of international relations so far as such a subject is dealt with by the agreement.[78]

All the members of the court were in agreement that the Commonwealth Parliament could give effect to a treaty the implementation of which would require legislation affecting the domestic order of the Commonwealth. The treaty in question dealt with controls of aerial navigation, safety procedures and similar matters having effect within Australian air space and at Australian airports. While the actual decision in *Burgess' Case* was that the regulations had departed from the strict terms of the treaty and were therefore invalid, the enlargement of the power in that case has had a general influence on later interpretations of the external affairs power. After the decision in this case, the regulations were changed, and in the case of *R v Poole ex parte Henry*[79] the court held that the changes brought about the result that the regulations were now in conformity with the treaty. In *Poole's Case,* moreover, there was a shift of ground and it was accepted that legislation giving *substantial* effect to a treaty might be upheld even though there was not exact compliance with the treaty in matters of detail.

In the more recent case *Airlines of New South Wales Pty Ltd v The State of New South Wales*[80] a number of the members of the court were prepared to uphold provisions of legislation of the Commonwealth giving effect to the Chicago Air Convention of 1944 on the basis both of the trade and commerce power and the external affairs power. It was held in this case that provisions of air navigation regulations designed to give effect to safety procedures laid down in the Chicago convention and annexes attached to it could be validly applied to intra-State air navigation, although the Commonwealth could not exclude the operation of State licensing legislation in respect of the carriage of persons and goods by aircraft between one point in a State and another. It could, however, control the activity of intra-State transporta-

---

75   Ibid, at 669.
76   Willoughby, *The Constitutional Law of the United States,* (2nd ed 1929) 519.
77   55 CLR at 658-9.
78   Ibid, at 681
79   (1939) 61 CLR 634.
80   (1965) 113 CLR 54, [1965] ALR 984, discussed in (1965) 39 ALJ 17. See also Richardson, "Aviation Law in Australia", 1 Fed LR 242 at 251 et seq.

tion by air to the extent to which the safety rules applied to international and interstate air navigation impinged directly on intra-State air navigation. There is little thorough discussion in this case of the extent of the external affairs power, although Barwick CJ said that he was not prepared to accept the view that the mere fact that the Commonwealth had signed a convention would give it power to effectuate by legislative action the provisions of that convention.[81] Menzies J said "Under s 51 (xxix) the Commonwealth has power to make laws to carry out its international obligations under a convention with other nations concerning external affairs."[82] These views then seem to be based on the more restrictive view adopted in the earlier case by Dixon and Starke JJ and to involve a rejection of the Evatt-McTiernan view.[83]

The question now must be put: What are the precise limitations on the Federal power? In the first place it may be pointed out that all powers conferred on the Commonwealth Parliament by s 51 are exercisable subject to the Constitution. This means that the legislative power of implementing a treaty cannot be exercised in such a way as to escape or evade the prohibitions of the Constitution, for example ss 92, 113, and 116. In *Burgess's Case*, Latham CJ, Evatt[84] and McTiernan JJ all suggested that the power would not authorize the Commonwealth to give effect to a treaty entered into for the sole purpose of enabling the Federal Parliament to deal with the matter otherwise exclusively within the powers of the States. Bad faith of this kind, however, might be very difficult to establish. Of course, it is clear that in any case the power only authorizes the Federal Parliament to give effect to a treaty by legislation substantially in conformity with the treaty.[85]

Starke and Dixon JJ, as we have seen, appear to favour more extensive restrictions based on a view of matters which properly belong to external affairs as distinct from matters in respect of which there is lacking any nexus with external relations such as would bring them within the ambit of the power.

There are, of course, certain difficulties in determining whether matters are per se matters of international concern. Human rights are of course prima facie to be characterized as matters affecting the peace, welfare and good government of the States, in particular, the area of criminal law. However, in the international sphere a consensus has developed, starting with the Nuremberg Trials after the Second World War, one of the latest development being the 1966 *Covenants on Civil and Political, and Economic, Social and Cultural Rights* of 1967, that human rights are matters which affect the friendly relations between nations. Another example is the international concern about the distribution of narcotic drugs. This matter has been the subject matter of a convention, and in 1967 the Commonwealth Parliament enacted the *Narcotic*

---

81   113 CLR at 85, [1965] ALR at 994-5.
82   113 CLR, at 136, [1965] ALR at 1031.
83   Four members of a Court of seven considered that the Commonwealth regulations could be supported by the external affairs power.
84   In *Ffrost v Stevenson* (1937) 58 CLR 528 at 598 et seq, Evatt J repeated his views. See also Menzies, *Central Power in the Australian Commonwealth*, 115.
85   In *Fishwick v Cleland* (1960) 106 CLR 186, [1961] ALR 147, the High Court rejected the argument that the *Papua and New Guinea Act* 1949 was invalid as being contrary to the United Nations Charter. However, the court held that the source of legislative power for the Territory was to be found in s 51 (xxix) (Contra Evatt J in *Ffrost v Stevenson*, supra.) See also Sharwood, "Treaties in Constitutional Law—A Comment on Fishwick v Cleland", (1965) 1 Federal Law Review 306.

*Drugs Act*[86] to give effect to the provisions of the convention relating inter alia to the manufacture of narcotic drugs, a matter which is also within the legislative power of the States.

It is clear that cases will arise where, in implementing external engagements, the Commonwealth finds itself with no head of power on to which to base its legislation other than the external affairs power. In such cases it must decide whether to legislate unilaterally for the whole Commonwealth, relying on this power (and risking challenge) or whether to call upon the States to use their powers (which would generally be beyond challenge) to bring about the desired results. It could be said, therefore, that while in practice the adherence to the view that the exercise of power in the fields of human rights and labour relations only by way of State cooperation promotes the federal principle, it cannot be used to deny power to the Commonwealth to legislate unilaterally with regard to a matter where that matter has become a matter of international concern today even though some years ago it may have not had the significance it has at present.

Another matter of some importance is the extent to which legislation can be enacted with regard to external affairs which is not dependent on a treaty, e g, which is merely dependent on the promotion of friendly relations between nations. In *R v Sharkey*[87] it was held that certain sections of the Commonwealth Crimes Act relating to sedition were valid under s 51 (xxix). This is an interesting decision as it shows that Commonwealth legislation designed to strengthen relations with other countries may be valid even though such legislation is not enacted in pursuance of any specific treaty commitments. Most of the judges limited their remarks on the subject to relations with other members of the British Commonwealth—as s 24 (a) of the *Crimes Act* was limited. While the British Commonwealth is, of course, a very special institution, and the mutual relations between the member countries (whether realms or republics) are of a special kind, the same argument would seem to apply to relations between Australia and other countries and indeed another section of the Crimes Act section 24A (a) (which defines the crime of treachery) seems to involve the exercise of the external affairs power in so far as it punishes offences directed at undermining Australia's military position in foreign countries.

It is possible that in 1900, the reigning concept of external affairs did not extend beyond the fulfilment of formal treaty obligations between sovereign powers. Today, the external relations of nations involve a complex pattern of contacts in the economic, cultural and military fields, by no means all of which are the subject for formal treaties. It might be suggested that, by the canons of generic interpretation, relations which may be rather vaguely subsumed beneath the principle "promotion of friendly relations between nations", could come within the ambit of the external affairs power. The dangers of this view are referred to below.

Allied with this question is another one whether the external affairs power enables Australia by legislation to give effect to *rights* as well as to *obligations* created by treaties. In the light of the decisions in *Sharkey's Case* just discussed it could be said that rights as well as obligations are a matter of legislative concern. In *Burgess's Case*, Latham CJ stated that the Commonwealth Parliament had power under s 51 (xxix) "to give effect to international obligations binding the Commonwealth or to protect national rights

---

86   Act No 53 of 1967.
87   (1949) 79 CLR 121.

internationally obtained by the Commonwealth whenever legislation was necessary or deemed to be desirable for this purpose."[88] Indeed it could be said that when the Commonwealth ratifies the treaty it binds itself to observe the rights granted by the convention to other parties. There are a number of conventions which grant to the signatory States various rights. For example, reference may be made to international conventions dealing with resources of the sea bed. The Commonwealth has enacted legislation (in conjunction with the States) claiming the rights conferred by various maritime conventions to explore and exploit the resources of the sea bed adjacent to the Australian coastline.[89]

However, there is a danger which may lead one to reassess the phrase "friendly relations between nations". One could ask the question: is the Commonwealth to be tied to a rule that it is only with respect to treaties that its legislative power operates, or might a very vaguely-worded resolution of the United Nations Assembly be regarded as sufficient authority?[90]

The United Nations Charter prevents the UN Organisation from interfering in matters which are essentially within domestic jurisdiction. This must be kept in mind in determining whether the Commonwealth has legislative authority to give effect to resolutions of United Nations General Assembly.

The question as to the power of the Commonwealth Parliament to give effect to matters arising under customary international law must be considered in this context. There are many rights as well as obligations arising under international customary law which have not as yet been incorporated into international treaties. It would seem that the Commonwealth ought to have the power of giving effect to matters falling within customary international law.[91]

A recent exercise of Commonwealth legislative power in relation to international law is the enactment of extradition legislation which provides for the extradition of criminals to and from foreign countries and also member countries of the (British) Commonwealth.[92]

In the judicial sphere, there are certain "Acts of State" which will be

---

88   55 CLR 608 at 644.
89   See Lumb, "The Off-Shore Petroleum Agreement and Legislation" (1968) 41 ALJ 453. Harders "Australia's Off-Shore Petroleum Legislation" (1968) 6 MULR 415.
90   In *Burgess' Case* (1936) 55 CLR 608 at 687, Evatt and McTiernan JJ commented: ". . . The Parliament may well be deemed competent to legislate for the carrying out of 'recommendations' as well as the 'draft international conventions' resolved upon by the International Labour Organization or of other international recommendations or requests upon other subject matters of concern to Australia as a member of the family of nations."
91   The Commonwealth Parliament has acted on this basis. See *Public Order (Protection of Persons and Property) Act* 1971, s 14. The traditional doctrine is that customary international law is part of the law of Australia. Some writers, however, interpret this as meaning part of the law of Australia when "incorporated" by statute or judicial fiat; others would treat international law, provided that it was not in conflict with rules of Statute of common law, as automatically part of the law to be recognized as such by the courts when a question concerning international law comes before them. See Sawer, *op cit*, at pp 50-1; *Chow Hung Ching v R* (1948) 77 CLR 449. *Polites v Commonwealth* (1945) 70 CLR 60.
92   *Extradition (Commonwealth Countries) Act* 1966-1972. *Extradition (Foreign States) Act* 1966-1972. See *McKelvey v Meagher* (1906) 4 CLR 265, Shearer, "Recent Development in the Law of Extradition" (1967-8) 6 MULR 186.

taken cognizance of by the courts. These are matters which are dealt with by the Commonwealth Executive by way of a presentation to the court of a certificate usually under the hand of, or by authority of, the Minister for Foreign Affairs, stating that Australia has adopted a certain position as a matter of policy. Such matters include questions whether a government is recognized and whether a person has diplomatic immunity. Here the executive power of the Commonwealth in asserting the existence of such matters would be regarded usually as binding and authorative by a court and would be taken into account in determining legal rights and obligations involved in litigation in which such questions arise.[93]

*Legislation relating to external affairs.* The many statutes enacted under s 51 (xxix) fall into a number of categories. There are those such as the *South-East Asia Collective Defence Treaty Act* 1954 which formally ratify a treaty, and consist of little more than the ratifying clauses, with the treaty appended as a schedule to the Act. Others such as the *Geneva Conventions Act* 1957 not merely ratify the Conventions, but *uno flatu*, provide for consequential alterations of the internal order of the Commonwealth. From both classes must be differentiated those Statutes which do not spring directly from any treaty or note or even less formal engagement with a foreign policy but nevertheless are based on "relations". The major examples are provisions of the *Crimes Act* 1914-1966. Of course, where provisions are demonstrably intended to foster the security of the Commonwealth, the fact that they refer to external areas does not deprive them of the assistance of s 61/s 51 (xxxix), or when they bear upon defence, of s 51 (vi).

Some important pieces of legislation giving effect to multilateral international treaties are the *Diplomatic Privileges and Immunities Act* 1967-1972 (Vienna Treaty on Diplomatic Relations), *Consular Privileges and Immunities Act* 1972 (Vienna Convention on Consular Relations), *Geneva Convention Act* 1957 (Geneva Convention on the Laws of War), *Pollution of the Sea by Oil Act* 1960-1972 (Convention on the Pollution of the Sea by Oil), *Whaling Act* 1960 (International Whaling Agreements), *Air Navigation Act* 1920-1971 (Chicago Convention on Aerial Navigation), *Charter of the United Nations Act* 1945 (UN Charter).

(xxx) *The relations of the Commonwealth with the islands of the Pacific:*[94]

As Wynes points out, this power could seem to form part of the external affairs power. Therefore, laws passed under the external affairs power would, if so desired, cover the Pacific Islands as well as other geographical areas of the world. On the other hand, Wynes does suggest that the external affairs power might be limited to the relations of the Commonwealth with civilized sovereign or part-sovereign states, and at the time of Federation many of the Pacific Islands, were uncivilized States having protectorate status or under some form of colonial administration.[95] Today, of course, the power would be a basis, additional to the external affairs power, for legislation specifically applying to the islands of the Pacific Ocean.

---

93 See Sawer, *op cit*, at 49-50, and authorities discussed therein. However, in one case, *Bonser v La Macchia* (1969) 43 ALJR 275, [1969] ALR 741 at 750-1, a certificate was not regarded as conclusive. See also Brazil, "The Ascertainment of Facts in Constitutional Cases", (1970) 4 Federal Law Review, 65 at 84-5.
94 Quick and Garran, 637-40. Wynes, 285-6.
95 Op cit, at 286.

(xxxi) *The acquisition of property on just terms from any State or person for any purpose in respect of which the Parliament has power to make laws:*[96]

Under this head of power the Commonwealth Parliament may legislate to acquire property (whether real or personal) from either a State of the Commonwealth or a private person. The acquisition must, however, be related to Commonwealth purposes (derived from other sections of the Constitution) and must provide just terms to the dispossessed.

### "The acquisition of property"

In *Minister of Army v Dalziel*,[97] the Minister took possession of land of the defendant under *National Security (General) Regulations*. The defendant was a tenant from week to week of the land. The question to be determined was whether the acquisition of a leasehold interest amounted to an acquisition of property and therefore came within the operation of s 51 (xxxi). The majority of members of the court answered this question in the affirmative. In their opinion, the word "property" signified any tangible or intangible thing which the law protected under the name of property.[98] As one member of the court pointed out "it would be wholly inconsistent with the language of the placitum to hold that while preventing the Legislature from authorizing the acquisition of a citizen's full title except upon just terms, it leaves it open to the Legislature to seize possession and enjoy the full fruits of possession, indefinitely, on any terms it chooses, or upon no terms at all".[99]

If the effect of the instrument authorizing "acquisition" is not directly to vest a right of ownership or possession in the Commonwealth but to require a person to deliver goods at a specified price either to the Commonwealth or to persons authorized by the Commonwealth to receive the goods, such a transaction which is known as a "forced sale" would amount to an acquisition of property.[1] In *McClintock v Commonwealth*[2] growers of pineapples were directed by orders made under the *National Security (General) Regulations* to deliver part of their crop to a committee acting as agent for a department of the Commonwealth. The payment for pineapples so received was determined by another committee associated with the scheme. In the view of Starke J this transaction amounted to an acquisition of property by the "purchaser" as agent for the Commonwealth.[3]

It can be seen, therefore, that the phrase "acquisition of property" extends to the expropriation of both real and personal property for a temporary, indefinite or permanent period of time, effective control of the property passing to the acquirer.[4] Such expropriation may take the form of direct transfer of title (resumption), or rights of control and use (requisition) or it may take the form of a compulsory purchase for a money consideration,

---

96   Quick and Garran, 640-2. Wynes, 324-34. Howard, 394-412. Nicholas, 285-99.
     Lane, 155-78. *Essays*, 193-220.
97   (1944) 68 CLR 261.
98   68 CLR at 295, per McTiernan J. In respect of land, it refers to a freehold estate
     and a leasehold or possessory estate.
99   68 CLR at 286.
 1   In other words, the owner is deprived of his property by compulsion of law.
 2   (1947) 75 CLR 1.
 3   75 CLR at 24.
 4   It does not, however, cover application of enemy assets taken over in wartime
     towards war reparations. See *Re Dohnert Muller Schmidt and Co* (1961) 105
     CLR 361.

where the Commonwealth or an agent acting on its behalf receives the goods by compulsion of law for a money consideration.

### "On just terms"

Section 51 (xxxi) requires that any acquisition of property from a person or State for the purposes of the Commonwealth must be accompanied by just terms. At the outset this requirement may be said to involve the payment of fair compensation to the expropriated owner. But the interpretation of this phrase in relation to the exercise by the Commonwealth in war-time of its acquisition powers for defence purposes shows that the courts are faced with great difficulties in deciding what fair compensation is in a particular case. In so far as the general economy in time of war undergoes a profound transformation, the determination of a precise value of property must take account of a number of fluctuating and contingent factors.

Under the *National Security (General) Regulations*[5] which affected the taking of land, provision was made for compensation to be determined, in the event of disagreement between the Minister and the owner, by a board, the decision of which could be reviewed at the option of either party by a court of competent jurisdiction. With respect to other National Security Regulations pertaining to acquisitions of particular commodities[6] the compensation payable was determined by the Minister acting on the recommendation of the particular board constituted under the regulations but no reference was made to review of the determination by a court.

In *Minister of Army v Dalziel*[7] the High Court declared r 60H of the *National Security (General) Regulations* invalid on the ground that it did not provide just terms. Regulation 60H had empowered the minister to make "basis of compensation" orders which were to bind both board and court. An order was made which precluded compensation for loss of profits or occupation in respect of a taking of possession by the Commonwealth. A majority of the court held that this did not provide just terms. Regulation 60H was invalid as it was based on the assumption that a taking of possession did not have to comply with the constitutional standard.[8] However, the invalidity of r 60H did not bring down the other regulations, and in so far as r 60G empowered a court to determine compensation, such a court could work out compensation which was payable on generally established principles.[9]

The antipathy of the court to any conclusive assessment of compensation by ministerial or board decision is exemplified in *Tonking's Case*.[10] In that case the regulation under review stipulated that a grower whose produce had been acquired by the board administering the scheme should be paid such compensation as was determined by the Minister acting on the recommendation of the board. In the opinion of the court, this provision did not provide the only method by which compensation could be assessed: if, in fact, it had been intended to be exhaustive, it would not have provided just terms. Williams J emphasized the fact that in this case no provision was made for the owner to put his case before the board. In his view it was "a fundamental principle of law that claimants should have a fair opportunity of putting their

---

5  of 1941.
6  e g, *Apple and Pear Acquisition Regulations*.
7  68 CLR 261.
8  In fact it seemed that the basis of compensation order preceded on this assumption in excluding consideration of loss of occupation or profits.
9  68 CLR at 296, per McTiernan J.
10  (1942) 66 CLR 77.

case before their claims are determined ... If the Minister is the sole arbiter of the amount of compensation payable, the regulations provide no express means whereby claimants have any right to put their case before him or the Board orally or otherwise or to obtain such information which would be indispensable if it was desired to examine the fairness of the Minister's determination."[11] The court was, therefore, entitled to start afresh and determine the compensation on general principles even though the regulations had not made provision for the review of the ministerial decision.[12] However, as Dixon J pointed out in *Andrews v Howell*[13] the determination of compensation by ministerial decision does not *ipso facto* deny just terms to the claimant: the exercise of ministerial discretion was not to be regarded as an arbitrary act.[14] In *Andrews v Howell*, the regulations did not make provision for the claimant to put his case before the board, but the absence of this provision was not a sufficient basis on which to stigmatize the procedure as unjust. The better view, therefore, would seem to be that the mere absence of the right of the claimant to appear or state his case before a Minister or board does not invalidate a regulation providing for assessment by this method.[15] As long as it appears on the face of the regulations that the Minister or board will act impartially in assessing compensation the regulations will not be struck down. On the other hand, such a method of determining compensation cannot be made exclusive: it is always subject to a review by a judicial body whether the regulations make provision for judicial review or not. Where a particular procedure is invalidated, the court will assess compensation on the basis of general principles.

What, then, are the principles on the basis of which a court will determine the justice or injustice of the terms of a particular acquisition? In *Johnston, Fear and Kingham v Commonwealth*[16] Latham CJ stated that just terms was not necessarily the same thing as the price or money value of the property. In his opinion, it might be necessary to take into account any special loss suffered by the owner as the result of the compulsory taking.[17] In this case, a printing press had been acquired under the *National Security (Supply of Goods) Regulations* which provided that the remuneration for the loss of goods was to be determined in default of agreement by arbitration but was not in any case to exceed the maximum price for such goods fixed by the Commonwealth Prices Commissioner. It was held by the court that this method did not provide just terms. While as a general rule the money price, if it were related to the characteristics of the property and its market value, would be fair compensation, there were occasionally also special circumstances which ought to be taken into account, for instance, the possibility of replacing the goods. In the present case the property was not easily replaceable. The regulations, therefore, in ignoring this factor could not be said to provide just terms.[18]

As far as land is concerned, it can be said that the court will take into account not only the value of the land as such, but any loss or damage that follows as a direct and natural consequence from the expropriation of the

---

11　Ibid, at 86.
12　For a discussion of these general principles see below.
13　(1941) 65 CLR 255.
14　Ibid, at 283-4.
15　*Essays*, 193 at 209.
16　(1943) 67 CLR 314.
17　Ibid, at 322.
18　Ibid, at 323.

land, as distinct from that which affects the owner personally or indirectly in his business operations on the land. In *Grace Brothers v Minister of State for the Army*[19] a section of land which has been used as a petrol station and also for accommodation of vehicles was acquired under the *National Security (General) Regulations.* Applying the principle as to direct loss, the court allowed as an item of compensation the cost of fencing involved in separating the part retained by the owner from that acquired by the Commonwealth in order that the owner might continue to use his premises as before.[20]

As Latham CJ put it in *Minister of the Army v Parbury Henry*[21] compensation for the taking of possession of land under the *National Security Regulations* was not limited to the mere saleable value of the land. It might also include compensation for loss of business or goodwill, costs of removal, and value of fixtures, although these matters theoretically were to be taken into account to determine the value of the land to the owner. However, to be excluded from consideration was the manner of trading after dispossession as this was an indirect effect of the acquisition.[22]

There is some doubt as to what extent loss of profits or business forms part of the compensation to which the dispossessed owner is entitled under s 51 (xxxi). In *Chandler v Commonwealth*[23] the Supreme Court of Queensland held that, where acquisition had interfered with a business, compensation was not to be assessed on the basis of the profits which the owner had expected to make therefrom. In *Re Fish Steam Laundry*[24] where the Commonwealth had acquired a laundry to which valuable machinery was attached, the dispossessed owner was held entitled to a sum which took account of the diminution of his power to earn profits, the machinery being of such a kind which could not be obtained elsewhere. It seems that what the court must do is to take into account the individual circumstances of the case in order to ascertain the special value to the owner of the land on which a business is being carried on: if the owner cannot readily acquire similar property for carrying on the same business elsewhere, then the loss of business or profits may be regarded as a direct consequence of the acquisition of the land and, therefore, a factor to be taken into account in determining compensation.

Some techniques of arriving at the assessment of compensation for the acquisition of items of property (such as ships) which are of special value during times of war and for which there is no specific market value have been discussed by Dixon J in *Minister of State for the Navy v Rae.*[25] The general starting point is that the court should take into account alternative methods of assessing compensation in order to determine what is the just method in the circumstances. In the case of the requisition of a ship the following courses might be adopted: (1) to ascertain the items of capital expenditure incurred by the owner depreciated according to the physical condition of the vessel, keeping in mind that the ship constitutes a going concern used in the earning of profits; (2) to ascertain the cost of replacement or reinstatement taking into account war condition; (3) to determine the pre-war value to which is added an appropriate percentage to represent the increase in the cost of

---

19   (1945) 45 SR (NSW) 206.
20   Ibid, at 208-9, 214-5.
21   (1945) 70 CLR 459.
22   Ibid, at 492.
23   [1944] St R Qd 195.
24   [1945] St R Qd 96.
25   (1945) 70 CLR 339.

production and generally the value of the craft.[26] Such methods, of course, would also be appropriate *mutatis mutandis* to other types of property used for the production or distribution of goods to which attaches a peculiar or unusual value in times of war.

*Pooling.* Under the defence power during the war, the Commonwealth established a number of marketing schemes which involved the compulsory pooling of goods, the compensation payable to the owner being determined generally on the basis of the dividends received for the sale of the goods less administration expenses. If the sale of the goods under a pooling scheme is looked at in isolation from the surrounding circumstances such as the administrative policies of the government and the economic state of the country, it would seem that the proceeds received by the grower or producer would not amount to just terms in that he would not be getting the money equivalent of his goods. However, it seems that the court will take into account matters referred to above in determining the question of just terms.

In *Nelungaloo v Commonwealth*[27] the facts were that r 14 of the *National Security (Wheat Acquisition) Regulations* provided that the Minister might by order acquire wheat. Compensation payable to the owner was to be determined by the Minister (acting on the recommendation of a board). The basis of compensation was to be the rates per bushel arrived at by reference to the surplus proceeds from the disposal of the wheat, subject to deductions for administration and transport expenses. While the court did not express any final view of the constitutionality of pooling schemes, there are dicta which suggest that at least certain types of pooling schemes fulfil the constitutional requirement of just terms.[28] The case is also notable for the attempts made by members of the court to define the concepts of just terms. A judgment on whether such a scheme involves just terms, said Dixon J,

rests on the somewhat general and indefinable conception of just terms, which appears to refer to what is fair and just between the community and the owner of the thing taken. Importing this conception into the purposes of the board's powers, the result seems to be that the disposal of the wheat, whether for the uses of the Commonwealth or for domestic consumption, must be in return for a recompense to the pool which is honestly fixed or estimated as a fair and reasonable value. The difficulties of such a judgment in war time are great and the criticisms which may be made at any time of such a test are only too manifest. But the standards of duty supplied by the law as a result of general considerations can never be precise. When the question is one of fairness in any community, the standard must depend upon the life and experience of that community rather than upon the changing fortunes of other countries. Unlike "compensation", which connotes full money equivalence, "just terms" are concerned with fairness.[29]

From this statement, it is clear that Dixon J was willing to take into account the effect of an acquisition scheme not merely on the expropriated owners but also on the community as a whole, and the distinction which he makes between just terms and compensation implies that the proceeds returnable to the grower in accordance with the constitutional requirement need not necessarily amount to money equivalence. However, in so far as in the present case the owner had disputed the amount of compensation payable to him under the scheme, it was necessary in accordance with previous authority to work out compensation on general principles. Applying these general

---

26   Ibid, at 344-7.
27   (1948) 75 CLR 495.
28   Ibid, at 566-9.
29   Ibid, at 569.

principles, Dixon J considered that the task of the court was to recompense the owner for his loss, and therefore it was necessary to determine the value of the wheat to the owner. Such value could not be less than the money value to which he might have converted his property had the law not deprived him of it.[30] Latham CJ also felt himself obliged to assess compensation on general principles. This meant that "the assessing tribunal should endeavour to ascertain the price which a willing purchaser would give to a not unwilling vendor of the property in question, neither being under any compulsion, the price to be assessed at the value to the owner".[31] However, in assessing compensation the court could take into account the interests of the community embodied in relevant legislation and administrative acts such as the need for satisfying local needs before exporting the surplus of the commodity. In the present case, the fixing of a price for bread was a factor to be taken into account in assessing the value of the wheat to the owner.[32] Only one of the judges, Starke J, who held that the owner was entitled to the pecuniary equivalent of his goods, seemed prepared to accept the proposition that such a scheme did not measure up to the constitutional requirement.[33] However, in a later case Dixon J set out alternatives which would face a court called upon to give a decision on the validity of a pooling scheme, and it is clear that he at least has left open the question whether s 51 (xxxi) requires the pecuniary equivalent of the goods, or sanctions the pooling of goods under which owners receive proportionate shares in the moneys received from the sale of goods which are taken into the pooling scheme.[34]

One of the latest judicial authorities on this question is *Poulton v Commonwealth*[35] where the question arose as to whether the *National Security (Wool) Regulations* were valid. These regulations provided for the compulsory acquisition of wool according to a scheme whereby values were determined according to appraisals made by skilled appraisers, to which was added a proportionate share of the returns derived from the disposal of the wool on the overseas market without identification of the sale price of each lot in that market. It was held that the regulations provided just terms. Fullagar J referred to dicta in previous cases that the terms prescribed for an acquisition are not unjust merely because they depart from established principles relating to the acquisition of property. The scheme on its face was quite reasonable in that the determination of the appraised price was in the hands of impartial and skilled experts; and provision was made for the addition of a sum which was gauged on the basis of the volume of sales of the commodity in the overseas market.[36]

It would seem, therefore, that the answer to the question whether a pooling scheme provides just terms as required by s 51 (xxxi) rests on the actual terms of the scheme. Although some schemes may provide for a return

---

30    Ibid, at 571.
31    Ibid, at 540.
32    Ibid, at 541-2.
33    Ibid, at 547-8.
34    *Nelungaloo v The Commonwealth* (1952) 85 CLR 545 at 569.
35    (1953) 89 CLR 540.
36    Ibid, at 574. It may be, as Latham CJ pointed out in *Tonking's Case* that the provisions of the scheme are such that a subsidy will have to be found by the Government. In that case the owner would be entitled to compensation even though a part of the goods taken into the pool is not sold. Circumstances such as a glut in the market or diminished sales of the goods would not, it seems, be taken into account: 66 CLR at 102.

to the owner of an amount which virtually amounts to the money equivalent of the property acquired, even if this involves subsidization by the government, it is submitted that those schemes which do not involve money equivalence are not necessarily invalid. As Latham CJ pointed out in the *Nelungaloo Case* the justice referred to in s 51 (xxxi) involves justice to the community as well as to the individual.[37] Judicial cognizance of economic and administrative acts and policies in determining the constitutional validity of a pooling scheme is to be preferred to a procedure whereby the value of the goods is determined in isolation from these factors.

*Interest.* The question as to what extent interest must be allowed as part of the compensation required by s 51 (xxxi) has been examined by the High Court in a number of cases dealing with war-time acquisitions of property. The principles to be deduced from these cases seems to be that, while the paragraph does not in all cases require the awarding of interest from the date of acquisition of the property until the date of payment of the compensation, the court has a discretion as to whether to allow interest on the sum payable. In *James Patrick and Co v Minister of the Navy*[38] and *Australian Apple and Pear Marketing Board v Tonking*[39] interest was allowed. However, in *Commonwealth v Huon Transport Pty Ltd*[40] the majority of the Court held that a company, one of whose ships had been requisitioned, was not entitled as part of its compensation to interest from the date of acquisition on the balance for the time being unpaid. The members of the court referred to the English case of *Swift & Co v Board of Trade*[41] in holding that, for the requisition of goods, interest was not payable from the date of requisition, on the ground that to hold otherwise would be to give compensation not for the goods themselves but for the time occupied in ascertaining their value.[42] On the other hand, in *Marine Board of Launceston v Minister for the Navy*[43] where a ship was requisitioned under r 57 of the *National Security (General) Regulations*, it was held that the court had power to award interest on the amount of compensation from the date of acquisition to the date of the payment of compensation. Regulation 60J of these regulations empowered the Minister to award interest from a period commencing three months after the date of acquisition until the date of payment. It was held that this clause did not exclude the right of the court at its discretion to grant interest in the manner in which it thought fit. In this case it would seem that the court applied to goods the equitable principle that a person should not have the benefit of the possession of property which he has acquired, as well as the income derived from it from the date of acquisition to the date of payment of compensation.[44]

The differing views on this question of interest are summed up in two separate judgments of Latham CJ and Rich J. The view of Latham CJ was that the dispossessed owner is only entitled to compensation for the losses directly flowing from the acquisition: the award of interest for the lapse of time between acquisition and payment is not compensation for the acquisition

---

37   75 CLR at 541.
38   (1944) ALJ 126.
39   (1942) 66 CLR 77.
40   (1945) 70 CLR 293.
41   [1923] AC 520.
42   Ibid, at 533.
43   (1945) 70 CLR 518.
44   A principle that has been applied to land but not to personal property.

of property but compensation for delay in payment.[45] The view of Rich J, however, was that just terms require the payment of interest in money to which the expropriated owner is entitled for the time during which it is withheld from him.[46]

The better view, it is submitted, is that s 51 (xxxi) does not automatically require the payment of interest but that the court has (in the absence of any statutory direction) a discretion as to whether or not to award it. Dixon J considered that such an award would constitute an exceptional case.[47] It might be suggested that where there is some deliberate or unjustifiable delay in payment by the acquiring authority or where the dispossessed owner is gravely prejudiced by the delay, s 51 (xxxi) would require the award of interest to the owner.

*Acquisition of land in peace-time. The Lands Acquisition Act*[48] vests in the Commonwealth the power to acquire land for public purposes by agreement with the owner or by compulsory purchase. Acquisition is not to take place unless a notice has been served on the owner inviting him to treat for the sale of the land.[49] After a period of 28 days has elapsed from the service of the notice to treat, the Minister may recommend to the Governor-General that the land be compulsorily acquired, and the Governor-General may authorize such acquisition.[50] At this stage the interest of the owner in the land is converted into a right to compensation under the Act.[51] Courts are invested with jurisdiction to determine claims for compensation and also to formulate the basis on which such compensation is to be assessed.[52] However, certain matters must be taken into account by the courts in assessing compensation: the value of the land at the time of acquisition including damage caused to adjoining land from which the acquired land is severed, or the enhancement or depreciation caused to adjoining land by the carrying out of the public purpose for which it was acquired.[53] No regard, however, is to be had to any increase in the value of the land acquired which arises from the proposal to carry out the public purpose for which it was acquired.[54] If compensation is not determined by the Minister within three months, the claimant is entitled to sue for it in a court of competent jurisdiction.[55] In assessing compensation, the court is required to make such order as is necessary to ensure that the acquisition is made on just terms.[56]

The Act also provides that compensation is to bear interest at the rate of three per cent from the date of acquisition until the date of payment if that period does not exceed two years, or at four and one half per cent if that period exceeds two years.[57]

The general approach taken by the High Court to the *Lands Acquisition*

---

45   (1945) 70 CLR 518 at 525-6.
46   70 CLR 293 at 307.
47   70 CLR 518 at 534.
48   1955-1966.
49   s 9 (1).
50   s 10.
51   s 11.
52   s 13.
53   s 23 (1).
54   s 23 (2).
55   s 28.
56   s 31.
57   s 36.

*Act* is summed up in words of Latham CJ in *Grace Brothers v Common-wealth*:[58] "I do not think that the terms of s 51 (xxxi) entitle the court to declare a statute providing a general method for the acquisition of property invalid because in particular cases it was possible to device a more just scheme. The court should not, in my opinion, hold such legislation to be invalid unless it is such that a reasonable man would not regard the terms of the acquisition as being just."[59] Latham CJ went on to reiterate a point which he had made in the *Nelungaloo Case* to the effect that just terms must be interpreted in the light of what was just to the community as well as to the individual. He recognised that the Commonwealth was entitled to exclude from consideration of the tribunal assessing compensation the enhancement which could occur to the acquired property from the carrying out of the public purposes for which the land was acquired. In assessing compensation the task of the court was to examine the physical state of the land including its actual and potential uses.[60] Both Latham CJ and Dixon J considered that the question of interest was one for legislative determination.[61] In *Common-wealth v Arklay*[62] the principle was adopted that the court was not bound by the price which the land would fetch in the market when government price controls were in operation. It could look forward to see what the land would bring in a free market when controls had been lifted. It was pointed out that, in this respect, there was a difference between compensation for the acquisition of land and compensation for the acquisition of goods. In the latter case the property was usually intended for immediate sale or consumption so that the fixed price might well provide fair compensation (regard being had to the costs of production and the margin of profit allowed). Perishable goods especially would have no retention value to their owners. But land was in a different position: it was a permanent asset which survived temporary financial vicissitudes.[63]

The general test propounded by Australian courts as to the basis for determining compensation for the acquisition of land is the price which a willing purchaser would pay to a vendor not unwilling but not anxious to sell.[64] In determining this value, the court should consider the most advantageous purpose for which the land is adapted but ought to disregard the special value which it might have to the acquirer of the property.[65] Good-will which is of a local and not a personal nature may be included as part of the compensation, as this is loss or damage which flows directly from the expropriation, as distinct from that loss which affects the owner personally.[66]

*Acquisition of personal property in peace-time.* The case of *Bank of NSW v Commonwealth*[67] is the major authority on the power of the Commonwealth to acquire personal property in peacetime. By the *Banking Act* of 1947, the

---

58   (1946) 72 CLR 269.
59   Ibid, at 279-80.
60   Ibid, at 280-1.
61   Ibid, at 282-3, 293.
62   (1952) 87 CLR 159.
63   Ibid, at 174.
64   *Spencer v Commonwealth* (1907) 5 CLR 418.
65   *Minister of State for Home Affairs v Rostron* (1914) 18 CLR 634. *In Re Smith and Minister for Home Affairs and Territories* (1920-1) 28 CLR 513. Cf, *Anthony v Commonwealth* (1973) 47 ALJR 83 at 94 (Walsh J).
66   *Commonwealth v Reeve* (1949) 78 CLR 410.
67   (1948) 76 CLR 1 (discussed in 22 ALJ 213).

Commonwealth had provided for the taking over by the Commonwealth Bank, a Commonwealth instrumentality, of the shares and businesses of privately owned banks. Part II Division 2 of the Act empowered the Commonwealth Bank to acquire shares in private banks, either by purchasing or by compulsory acquisition. Part II Division 3 empowered the Commonwealth Bank to appoint directors of the private banks with power to dispose of their businesses. Part IV Division 4 empowered the Commonwealth Bank to take over the businesses of the private banks including both their assets and liabilities. Claims for compensation for the acquisition of shares or businesses were to be determined by a Federal Court of Claims.[68]

In its judgment on the validity of these sections the majority of the High Court were of the opinion that s 51 (xxxi) extended to the acquisition of any type of property, tangible or intangible, including the acquisition of a business as a going concern, although it did not necessarily entail the modification of the rights pertaining to that property which were derived from the laws of the States, nor did it necessarily entail novation of the debts of the acquired bodies.[69] As Latham CJ pointed out, the Commonwealth may acquire a factory or machinery but it "has no power, because it acquires a man's factory or machinery, to provide that he shall be released from his trade or other debts".[70] A power to acquire property from one person did not include a power to modify the rights of the creditors of that person unless this was justified under another head of Commonwealth power.[71]

The view of the majority was that the acquisition of the property of the private banks was for a purpose in respect of which the Commonwealth had power to make laws—banking—a power vested in the Commonwealth by s 51 (xiii). In their view the banking power was wide enough to include the selection of persons to engage in banking and the prevention of other persons from engaging in that activity.[72]

However, the legislation foundered on the just terms requirement of s 51 (xxxi). In the first place, the members of the court considered that the provisions relating to the taking over of the management of the banks by Commonwealth-appointed directors who had the power of disposing of the businesses of the banks, did not provide just terms for, in effect, the nominees of the acquiring authority were vested with a discretion as to what amount would be demanded for the sale of the businesses. In such a case, the body determining the compensation was the representative of one party only.[73] The decision of the court on this ground shows that an acquisition of property takes place not only where rights of ownership are transferred to the acquiring authority but also where the management of the property is altered so as to vest in the new management power to sell the property.

Although the Banking Act provided that fair and reasonable compensation was to be provided by the Commonwealth for the acquisition of the shares and businesses of the private banks, it was held by the High Court that the conferment of an exclusive jurisdiction on a Federal Court of Claims to determine claims for compensation had invalidly ousted the jurisdiction of

---

68   Banking Act, Part VI.
69   See the judgment of Latham CJ 76 CLR at 204-16.
70   Ibid, at 214.
71   In the instant case Latham CJ considered that such modification was justified by the banking power. Ibid, at 214-6.
72   See 76 CLR at 330-4 (Dixon J).
73   See 76 CLR at 216-8 (Latham CJ).

the High Court to determine suits which involved the Commonwealth as a party.[74] It is clear, however, that if this method of determination had not been made exclusive and if other grounds of invalidity had not been present,[75] the High Court would have worked out the compensation payable on general principles as it had done in other cases. There was no general agreement, however, on the question whether just terms required the payment of interest on compensation: the court was divided evenly on this issue.[76] It was also the view of the majority of the court that just terms are provided even though the machinery for providing compensation might create inflation in the economy.[77] When property such as a large banking business is acquired, it is quite likely that the amount needed to recompense the owners can only be found by the issue of government money or bonds, a factor that may conduce to inflation. However, Dixon J pointed out that if the terms of an acquisition necessarily involved the valuation of assets in terms of money which would lose its value as a result of the very transaction involved in compensating the owners, the constitutional requirement would not be fulfilled, but it would be necessary to prove by legal, factual and economic evidence that the very transaction involved a substantial depreciation of the money in which compensation was to be expressed.[78]

### "from any State or person"

The Commonwealth has power to acquire property from either a State or an individual. In *New South Wales v Commonwealth*[79] it was held that an acquisition of land from the State of New South Wales carried with it the rights to Royal metals and other minerals therein, and that an acquisition of *alienated* State land was freed from any rights royalties or obligations owed to the State.[80] No stamp duty is payable on a memorandum of transfer of land so acquired by the Commonwealth.[81] It is otherwise where the Commonwealth is transferring land *to* a private individual.[82]

### "for any purpose in respect of which the Parliament has power to make laws"

The Constitution permits the Commonwealth to acquire property "for any purpose in respect of which the Commonwealth has power to make laws". The Commonwealth can, therefore, acquire land in order to carry out these executive functions which under the Constitution are associated with a head of legislative power.[83] During the war the Commonwealth acquired a

---

74 A jurisdiction conferred by s 75 (iii) of the Constitution.
75 The Act was also held invalid on the ground that it contravened s 92. See later.
76 Starke, Rich and Williams JJ holding that it did; Latham CJ, Dixon and McTiernan JJ contra.
77 See the judgment of Latham CJ 76 CLR at 221.
78 76 CLR at 340-1.
79 (1923) 33 CLR 1.
80 However, a section of the old *Lands Acquisition Act* which imposed an obligation on a State Registrar of Titles to register a Commonwealth title in a manner which did not comply with a State *Real Property Act* was invalidated. See now *Lands Acquisition Act* 1955-1966, s 15. Note also the restriction (in relation to railways acquisition) embodied in s 51 (xxxii) of the Constitution.
81 *Commonwealth v New South Wales* (1906) 3 CLR 807.
82 *Commonwealth v New South Wales* (1918) 25 CLR 325.
83 The purpose may be framed in a general manner. See *Jones v Commonwealth* (1965) 112 CLR 206, [1965] ALR 706. *W H Blakeley and Co Pty Ltd v Commonwealth* (1953) 87 CLR 501.

number of freehold and leasehold properties for the purpose of providing accommodation for troops and administrative personnel, and also requisitioned personal property for the use of its armed forces. But the cases decided by the courts also establish that the power is not limited during war-time to what might be termed direct military purposes. Various national security regulations provided for acquisition of agricultural products and manufactured goods which were designed to ensure that the civilian population would be adequately supplied with goods and services at reasonable prices which otherwise would have been inflated owing to war conditions.

Although there is a dictum of Dixon J in *Andrews v Howell* that s 51 (xxxi) contemplates the acquisition of real and personal property which the Commonwealth proposes to use for the purposes of the Executive government and that it is doubtful whether it applies to acquisition of personal property intended for immediate consumption which takes place under marketing schemes,[84] there is stronger authority for the proposition that a phrase "Commonwealth purposes" must be given a wider meaning so as to extend to any purpose which may benefit the Commonwealth as a nation, provided, of course, that such purpose is related to a Commonwealth head of power (such as defence). In *Australian Apple and Pear Marketing v Tonking*[85] the court considered that s 51 (xxxi) applied to a marketing scheme requiring the delivery of pears to a government board, and in *Jenkins v Commonwealth*[86] it was considered applicable to regulations under which mineral prospectors (when requested by the government) were required to hand over, at a fixed price, their supplies of the mineral to industries which required it for defence purposes.

(xxxii) *The control of railways with respect to transport for the naval and military purposes of the Commonwealth:*[87]

Under this power the Commonwealth may assume control[88] of State railways for defence transportation purposes.[89] *The Defence Act* 1903-1970 contains provisions allowing the Governor-General to assume such control, and there are also other provisions in the Act which impose obligations on State railway officials to provide transportation for military personnel and goods (see ss 64, 65, 80 and 124). It is to be noted, too, that s 51 (i) of the Constitution, which confers power over interstate trade and commerce, would permit legislation affecting the carriage of goods or persons by rail between two or more States.[90]

---

84   (1941) 65 CLR 255 at 282.
85   (1942) 66 CLR 77.
86   (1947) 74 CLR 400. See also *Poulton v Commonwealth* (1953) 89 CLR 540.
87   Quick and Garran, 642-3. Wynes, 159-60.
88   "The word 'control' as used in Section 51 (xxxii) cannot, we think, be limited to manual or physical control. It is the widest possible term, and is at least co-extensive with the asserted general power to regulate." *Federated Amalgamated Government Railway and Tramway Service Association v New South Wales Railway Traffic Employees Association* (1906) 4 CLR 488 at 545. See also *Australian Railways Union v Victorian Railways Commissioners* (1930) 44 CLR 319 at 349 (Isaacs J).
89   "Section 51 (xxxii) ... adds to the powers of naval and military defence the power of controlling railways with respect to transport for the naval and military purposes of the Commonwealth": *Farey v Burvett* (1916) 21 CLR 433 at 464.
90   See also the Constitution, s 98, discussed below.

(xxxiii) *The acquisition, with the consent of a State, of any railways of the State on terms arranged between the Commonwealth and the State:*[91]

The Commonwealth can, under this power, acquire ownership of State railways pursuant to any arrangements made either with a particular State or with all States. To this extent this paragraph qualifies the general acquisition power contained in s 51 (xxxi). Such an arrangement could provide for the compensation to be payable to a State or States in respect of the acquisition.

(xxxiv) *Railway construction and extension in any State with the consent of that State:*[92]

Under this power the Commonwealth may assist the States in the construction and extension of their railway systems. The Commonwealth has exercised this power by providing for the construction of railway systems within various States, for example, the Trans-Continental Railway across South Australia and Western Australia and also the railway between South Australia and the Northern Territory.[93] It has also provided by arrangement with the States concerned for the construction of standard gauge railways (e g, the standard gauge between Sydney and Melbourne) to augment existing State systems.

In *Australian National Airways Pty Ltd v Commonwealth*[94] Latham CJ explained the section in this way:

In the United States it has been held that Congress can, under the commerce power, provide for the incorporation of a bridge company to build a bridge between two States or to construct railways across two States . . . . Such decisions were doubtless responsible for the grant of power to the Commonwealth Parliament to make laws with respect to the acquisition and construction of railways by the Commonwealth but subject to an express limitation requiring the consent of the State concerned: see ss 51 (xxiii) and (xxxiv). If this limitation had not been introduced, the Commonwealth Parliament would have been able to create corporations to construct or operate inter-State railways in Australia as it thought proper.

(xxxv) *Conciliation and arbitration for the prevention and settlement of industrial disputes extending beyond the limits of any one State:*[95]

The industrial power, often called the arbitration power, has been particularly remarkable for the expansive interpretation which has been accorded to it.[96] While it was probably intended by the framers of the Con-

---

91　Quick and Garran, 643-4. Wynes, 159-60.
92　Quick and Garran, 645. Wynes, 159-60.
93　See the *Commonwealth Railways Act* 1917-1968.
94　(1945) 71 CLR 29 at 59.
95　Quick & Garran, 646-7. Wynes, 295-324. *Essays,* 221-46. Nicholas, 212-26. Lane, 179-223. Sykes & Glasbeek, *Labour Law in Australia* (1972), 381 et seq.
96　For the background to the inclusion of s 51 (xxxv) in the Constitution, see Sykes, "Labour Arbitration in Australia" in *Australian Labour Relations Readings* (ed. Isaac & Ford) at 287: "The first compulsory arbitration statutes were enacted by the States but with the coming of federation in 1901, a momentous clause was written into the Constitution whereby the national Parliament was given power to enact laws dealing with labour arbitration. That power was implemented by legislation in 1904 which established that Commonwealth Court of Conciliation and Arbitration, a tribunal which under an apparently very limited constitutional mandate has yet firmly established the
*continues*

stitution only to authorize a federal arbitration tribunal to intervene when some Australia-wide situation of national emergency arose, it has resulted in a national wage fixing system which in most States is more extensive than the State machinery. However, the limits laid down in the grant of the Constitutional power in section 51 (xxxv) have made the arbitration system of the Commonwealth, considered purely as a system of determining industrial disputes, a very legalistic system.[97]

Since the power is stated to be conciliation and arbitration for the prevention and settlement of certain types of industrial disputes it cannot authorize legislation laying down general or particular rules to regulate industrial relations at large.

However, it must be pointed out that other sections of the Constitution can be used as a basis for Commonwealth legislation over industrial matters e g, s 51 (i). Although the trade and commerce power has not, in Australia, been relied upon to support labour legislation to the extent that the analogous power has been relied upon in the United States, that power will permit legislation on labour conditions when employment is connected with an inter-state transaction, e g, interstate shipping or stevedoring for inter-State shipping.[98] The Commonwealth Parliament can also regulate the conditions of officers in the Commonwealth public service under section 52, and also labour conditions generally in the territories under s 122.

### "Conciliation and arbitration"

As has been said, the Commonwealth power is restricted to the passing of laws setting up machinery for the settlement of industrial disputes by conciliation and arbitration. As the federal Parliament itself could not, from a practical point of view, perform these functions, the creation of a specialized body or tribunal was necessary. The body established in 1904 which was originally the Commonwealth Court of Conciliation and Arbitration, is now called the Commonwealth Conciliation and Arbitration Commission. The history of the legal attacks on jurisdiction and functions of the body is more appropriately dealt with in other sections of this work. At this stage it is

---

96   *continued*
     federal complex as furnishing the dominant pattern in Australian labour relations." See also Brennan, *Interpreting the Constitution* (1935) 22-25. A useful analysis of the Commonwealth and State systems may be found in *An Outline of Industrial Law* (1955) 13. See also McGarvie, "Principle and Practice in Commonwealth Industrial Arbitration After 60 Years", (1964-5) 1 Federal Law Review 47. Dunphy and Wright, "The Jubilee of Industrial Arbitration in Australia", 27 ALJ 360. Frequent proposals have been made to amend s 51 (xxxv). The Royal Commission on the Constitution (1929) advocated that the whole industrial power should be returned to the States, while the Joint Committee on Constitutional Review (1959) considered that the Commonwealth should be given the power to regulate industrial conditions generally.

97   For a survey of recent decisions see Maher and Sexton, "The High Court and Industrial Relations", (1972) 46 ALJ 109.

98   See *Huddart Parker v The Commonwealth* (1931) 44 CLR 492; *R v Wright, ex parte Waterside Workers' Federation of Australia* (1955) 93 CLR 520; *R v Foster, ex parte Eastern and Australian Steamship Co.* (1959) 103 CLR 256. For a discussion of s 51 (i) in relation to labour relations see O'Dea, *Industrial Relations in Australia*, 8-13; Foenander, *Studies in Australian Labour Law and Relations*, 1-42. Sections 30J and 30K of the *Crimes Act* which relate to industrial disputes would seem to depend on the trade and commerce power.

sufficient to note that the decisions in the *Boilermakers Case*[99] forced a division of the court's function[1] whereby the arbitral function was committed to the Commonwealth Conciliation and Arbitration Commission, and the judicial function was to be shared between the Commonwealth Industrial Court and State courts in the exercise of federal jurisdiction.

Arbitration may be defined as an impartial adjudication by an independent third party of a dispute between two persons or groups, in this case usually between an employing and an employee group.[2] Conciliation is the process whereby a third party offers his services in order to bring about an agreement or resolution of a dispute by a discussion between the two parties; in other words the conciliation process is one designed to bring about agreement. The process of conciliation is more appropriate to the prevention of industrial disputes, while that of arbitration is more appropriate to the settlement of a dispute which has occurred. However, there is no doubt that both processes may be used in relation to any type of dispute and often arbitration is used for the dispute which is about to boil over, while conciliation is used for the dispute that has occurred. In the *ARU Case*[3] it was decided that a decision arrived at by a body after private discussion was not conciliation or arbitration because the body performing the function was not separate from the contending parties.[4]

### "Disputes"

In the light of the myriad number of industrial activities being carried on throughout Australia in different factories and areas, it could not have been practicable for the Arbitration Commission to have proceeded by the method of solving particular factory disputes as they arose. The recognition of the existence of organizations representing employers and employees stemming from the *Jumbunna Case*[5] has allowed the commission to make awards binding on the members of these organizations through Australia. Indeed, s 61 of the Act specifies that an award shall be binding on all members of the organizations which are bound by it. In the light of the procedure of issuing logs of claims which may be served on any number of organizations, it is now quite simple to bring in most organizations which may be affected.

To satisfy the requirements of s 51, a party seeking to invoke the Commonwealth power must show that a dispute exists with respect to an industrial matter, as between itself and the respondent party or parties. This is a most important limitation on Commonwealth power, in that it negates the making of a common rule, i e, the general regulation of industrial matters made antecedently to any dispute, and binding on all who participate in the in-

---

99  (1956) 94 CLR 254, [1957] AC 288.
 1  However, the court itself was not dismantled: see Sykes and Glazbeek, op cit at 507.
 2  In *R v Commonwealth Court of Conciliation ex parte Whybrow* (1910) 11 CLR 1, it was held that s 51 (xxxv) empowered the Commonwealth to make arbitration compulsory.
 3  *Australian Railways Union v Victorian Railways Commissioners* (1930) 44 CLR 319.
 4  But see s 44 (3)(c) of the Act (Reference to local board).
 5  *Jumbunna Coal Mine N L v Victorian Coal Miners' Association* (1908) 6 CLR 309. The effect of this decision was described by Fullagar J in *Williams v Hursey* (1959) 103 CLR 30, as allowing the Commonwealth not only to create organisations but also to regulate their powers.

dustrial relation so regulated. In *Whybrow's Case*[6] the High Court held that where an award had been made against certain employers in the boot industry, it was beyond the power of the Arbitration Court to order that the award be made a common rule for the industry binding on all employers in the industry, whether or not these had been parties to the proceedings. It is to be noted that one is bound by being a party to the proceedings; this may be a wider or narrower class than the parties to the actual dispute. Griffith CJ said:

I adhere to the opinion which I expressed in the *Woodworkers' Case* (8 CLR at p 488) that the term dispute connotes the existence of parties taking opposite sides, to which I would add that the word arbitration connotes the same idea. . . . If therefore the state of things is such that there are no ascertainable parties between whom an ascertainable difference capable of being composed exists, the basis of arbitration is wanting.[7]

Despite this decision, the Act continued to contain a provision conferring the right to make a common rule (s 38 (f) to 1947, and thereafter, s 41 (1) until 1956). The term still appears in s 49, which permits the commission to make a common rule in respect of any Territory of the Commonwealth, which section does not depend on s 51 (xxxv). But the decision in *Whybrow's Case* was upheld in *R v Kelly ex parte the State of Victoria*[8] where the 1947 amendment was asserted to be a basis for the power to make a common rule. The following comment was made in *Kelly's Case*.

It was clearly recognised (in *Whybrow's Case*) by both Isaacs J and by Higgins J that it might (to use the words of s 41) be "necessary or expedient for the purpose of settling an industrial dispute" to make a common rule. But each, like the other members of the court, rejected the contention that this afforded any reason for saying that a specific function essentially different from conciliation and arbitration was incidental to conciliation or arbitration.[9]

In practice, however, as we shall see later, this basic limitation has been overcome by the utilization of procedural devices.

The notions of "dispute" and "parties to the dispute" are closely related. Expansive interpretation of both has allowed awards to be made which are, in effect, common rules for whole industries. Yet the attitude of the early justices of the High Court was not encouraging. In *R v Commonwealth Court of Arbitration ex parte The Merchant Service Guild*[10] the Guild advanced the proposition that every industrial claim gave rise to an industrial dispute, and therefore, providing the inter-State element was present, the requirements of s 51 (xxxv) were satisfied. Griffith CJ described the argument as fallacious. His Honour's reason for not accepting the proposition was that a claim could not lead to a dispute until the other party had rejected it.[11] This is undeniable, and other cases have held that a dispute connotes a demand, and a refusal of that demand. However, Isaacs J (dissenting) was able to read into the employers' conduct a refusal of the claim.

The concept itself is simple. Whenever a demand is made by one party, single or numerous, engaged in industry, upon another party, single or numerous, so engaged,

---

6   *Australian Boot Trade Employees Federation v Whybrow* (1910) 11 CLR 311.
7   Ibid, at 317-8.
8   (1950) 81 CLR 64.
9   Ibid, at 80.
10   (1912) 15 CLR 586.
11   Ibid, at 594 et seq.

and persisted in as an industrial right, for some alteration in the existing condition of their mutual working relations, and that demand is met with a refusal persisted in by the party on whom the demand is made, the right claimed being necessarily, expressly, or virtually denied, there then exists between them an industrial dispute.[12]

Griffith CJ (who with Barton J formed the majority) had taken a much narrower view; he felt that such a dispute could arise only after an impasse had been reached in discussions between the actual parties involved therein. The dissenting view of Isaacs J has prevailed:

The manner and motive of the demand is as irrelevant as the manner or motive of the resistance: the one jurisdictional fact, if it may be so termed, is the actual existence of the industrial dispute over the necessary area.[13]

Two years later, a similar fact situation produced an opposite result, in *R v Commonwealth Court of Conciliation and Arbitration ex parte The Builders' Labourers' Federation*.[14] The majority in this case adopted the reasoning of Isaacs J in the earlier case, in holding that a demand refused satisfied the requirement of the section. But in this case, the respondents admitted that the demand had been absolutely refused, which made the task of the court easier. And Isaacs J carefully pointed out:

It must never be supposed that this is a decision which asserts that a mere demand and refusal in all cases constitutes an industrial dispute, which is a very different thing from saying that a regular and formal demand for altered conditions and a distinct refusal is prima facie evidence of such a dispute.[15]

Following this reasoning, the courts have found in proper cases, that paper disputes have been shams and have not been constitutional disputes.[16] A frequent situation in the past in which this has occurred, has been that in which unions, to gain a point in a demarcation dispute with other unions, have sought to obtain a favourable award by putting up a non-existent dispute with one or more employers. In such a circumstance, the employer may attack the plaint on three successive grounds. Firstly, on the ground that there is no dispute between himself and the union; secondly, if he fails on the first, on the ground that the dispute is not an industrial dispute; thirdly, if he fails on the second, on the ground that it is not an industrial dispute extending beyond the limits of any one state. But it can be taken as settled law, that the refusal of a demand made with respect to some aspect of an industrial relation between the parties is *prima facie* evidence of the existence of an industrial dispute between them.

Another line of development from the early cases concerns the notion of "parties to the dispute". The arbitral principle is based on the concept of organizations representing individual employers and employees. Part VIII of the present Act is devoted to their regulation. The associations or persons

---

12   Ibid, at 609.
13   Ibid, at 609.
14   (1914) 18 CLR 224.
15   Ibid, at 246.
16   See *Re Wool Workers' Association* (1945) 58 CAR 120. *APMEU v APM Ltd* (1944) 53 CAR 5. *R v Gough ex parte BP Refineries Pty Ltd* (1967) 40 ALJR 43. Note too that the terms of the demand must be precise enough to indicate to the addressee what the claim is about: *R v Commonwealth Court of Conciliation and Arbitration ex parte The Melbourne Tramways Board* (1965) 113 CLR 228, [1966] ALR 722.

who may, on compliance with the prescribed conditions, be registered as organizations are set out in s 132 (1) of the Act.

At an early stage, the question arose whether an employer could be said to have a dispute with a union, when his employees, albeit they were members of the union, said that they had no dispute with him. This was answered in the negative in *Holyman's Case*.[17] This view denies the union the status of disputant in its own right. Not surprisingly, the issue has been since decided the other way. In *AWU v Federal Pastoralists Council*[18] Higgins J held that a union, as a party to a dispute, could secure an award binding on employers, irrespective of the attitude of their own employees. Eight years later, in *Burwood Cinema Ltd v Australian Theatrical Employees Association*[19] where logs of claims had been served by the union on numerous employers in the theatrical industry, an objection was taken in the High Court to the jurisdiction of the Arbitration Court on the ground that there could be no dispute where the individual members of the union were, in fact, content. The court rejected this reasoning based on *Holyman's Case*, and the employers were held to be in a disputant relationship with the union. The error in *Holyman's Case* was that a contractual relationship was being sought instead of an industrial relationship. Starke J said:

An organisation registered under the Arbitration Act is not a mere agent of its members: it stands in their place and acts on their account and is a representative of the class associated together in the organisation.[20]

As a corollary to this reasoning, it was also held in the *Burwood Case* that a dispute may exist between a union and an employer who employs non-unionists. This came directly in issue in 1935: the *Metal Trades Case*.[21] An award binding on an employer of non-union labour could effectively regulate the working conditions of such employees, even though they could neither enforce, nor be bound by, the award.[22]

Five devices have been utilized to overcome the bar on a common rule:

(1) By the joinder of all possible parties on both sides.

(2) By the binding of employers of non-union labour as in the 1935 *Metal Trades Case*.

(3) By the formation of associations of employers, the members of which (including those who join after the award is made) are bound where the association has been made to a party to the dispute. (*AEU v Metal Trades Employers' Association*.)[23]

---

17  (1914) 18 CLR 273.
18  (1917) 23 CLR 22.
19  (1925) 35 CLR 528.
20  Ibid, at 551.
21  *Metal Trades Employers' Association v Amalgamated Engineering Union* (1935) 54 CLR 387.
22  For the converse situation, where employers raise a dispute with unions concerning the conditions of non-unionists, see *R v United Graziers' Association ex parte Australian Workers' Union* (1956) 96 CLR 317, where it was held that a demand made by employers that a union should be bound, in respect of employees who were not members of the union, by terms as to minimum rates of pay and conditions, could not, simply on the ground that the union did not accede to it, give rise to an industrial dispute. See also, *R v Australian Conciliation and Arbitration Commission ex parte Boot Trades Employees' Federation* (1966) 114 CLR 548.
23  *Amalgamated Engineers' Union v Metal Trades Employers' Association* (1931) 30 CAR 724.

(4) By the decision in *Geo Hudson Ltd v Australian Timber Workers' Union*[24] that awards bind the employers' successors in business.

(5) By the inclusion of "sub-contract" clauses in awards.

An important limitation on the commission's power to make an award is that the terms of the award must fall within the ambit of the dispute, as must the terms of any subsequent variation of the award. This is well illustrated by *Australian Insurance Staffs' Federation v Atlas Assurance Co*[25] wherein the logs served by the employers and by the employees had claimed (for the seventh year of service) £265 p a and £220 p a respectively. The parties agreed to a rate of £225, and this was included in the award. Subsequently, in the economic depression, the employers sought a variation, and the Arbitration Court reduced this sum by 10 per cent to £202. It was held not to be competent for it to do so, since this sum was outside the area of the original dispute.

The question of compulsory unionism has turned upon this point. In *R v Findlay ex parte Victorian Chamber of Manufacturers*[26] the union claimed that no employer in the clothing trade should employ any employee who was not a member of the Clothing and Allied Trades Union. The commission refused to accede to the claim for compulsory unionism. Instead it included in the award an elaborate scheme to provide preference for unionists. The scheme was invalidated by the High Court. The High Court's attitude to this situation was put thus by Latham CJ:

A person upon whom the log was served would not, I venture to say, have any conception that by not taking part in the arbitration proceedings he exposed himself to an award in anything like the terms of Cl 61. Apart from what has already been said ... a preference to unionists is different in kind from a monopoly of employment for unionists.[27]

The claim for compulsory unionism contained in the log could not be relied upon to support an award for preference to unionists.

The earlier part of Latham CJ's statement points to a strong practical reason for maintaining the "ambit" rule. But the actual decision in this case was based no less on the point that a demand for compulsory unionism was not an industrial matter within the Act. And it would seem from *Findlay's Case* and other similar cases, that the definition of industrial matter in the Act has so filled out the constitutional limitations, that no room is left for the draftsman to add "compulsory unionism" to the category of industrial matters.[28]

Finally it must be pointed out that the *Conciliation and Arbitration Act* allows jurisdiction to be exercised in relation to "threatened, impending or probable disputes." Arbitration as well as conciliation may be used in relation to such disputes.[29]

---

24  (1922) 32 CLR 413.
25  (1931) 45 CLR 409.
26  (1950) 81 CLR 537.
27  Ibid, at 545-46.
28  See *Australian Workers' Union v United Graziers' Association of New South Wales* (1932) 47 CLR 422; *Federated Gas Employees' Union v Metropolitan Gas Company* (1919) 27 CLR 72; *R v Commonwealth Court of Conciliation and Arbitration ex parte Kirsch* (1938) 60 CLR 507; *R v Wallis ex parte Employers Association of Wool Selling Brokers* (1949) 78 CLR 529. See also Hall, "Compulsory Unionism Returns" (1971) 45 ALJ 415.
29  *Merchant Shipping Guild of Australasia Ltd v Newcastle and Hunter Steamship Co* (1913) 16 CLR 591.

"industrial"

Not only must there be a dispute; it must be an industrial dispute. Yet it must not be forgotten that the court measures jurisdictional objections not only against the Constitution, but against the definition of industrial matter in the Act; which as suggested above may have little practical consequence if the definitions are nearly synonymous. Without necessarily suggesting that the court has given a restrictive definition to "industrial", it would be true to say that it has stopped short of holding that all employment relations are industrial relations.

Isaacs and Rich JJ, in the *Federated Municipal Employees Union v Melbourne Corporation*,[30] attempted to define the issue:

Industrial disputes occur when, in relation to operations in which capital and labour are contributed in co-operation for the satisfaction of human wants or desires, those engaged in co-operation dispute as to the basis to be observed, by the parties engaged, respecting either a share of the product or any other terms and conditions of their co-operation.[31]

In the following year, an attempt to bring the newly formed Government Service Women's Federation under a Commonwealth award failed, being "an attempt to register persons under the Act who are not engaged in any industry and also persons over whom the court can have no jurisdiction."[32] Since this time, a wide variety of relationships has been admitted to be industrial, the best known cases being: municipal employees (*Federated Municipal and Shire Council Employees' Union of Australia v Melbourne Corporation*),[33] journalists (*Proprietors of the Daily News Ltd v Australian Journalists Association*),[34] and insurance staff (*Accident Insurance Staffs' Federation v The Accident Underwriters' Association*).[35] It is clear, therefore, that the categories of workers who are engaged in industry extend beyond "manual" labour. The most hotly debated case is that of the schoolteachers: *Federated State School Teachers' Association of Australia v State of Victoria*,[36] where it is held that State school teachers were not engaged in an industrial activity. In the opinion of the majority the educational activities of the States bore "no resemblance whatever to an ordinary trade, business or activity. They are not connected directly with, or attendant upon, the production or distribution of wealth; and there is no co-operation of capital and labour in any relevant sense, for a great public scheme of education is forced upon the communities of the States by law."[37] It would seem also that teachers engaged in non-State schools are not engaged in an industrial pursuit so as to come within s 51 (xxxv).[38]

---

30   (1919) 26 CLR 508.
31   Ibid, at 554.
32   Per Starke J (as deputy President) in *Commonwealth Public Service Commissioner v Government Service Women's Federation* (1920) 14 CAR 794.
33   (1919) 26 CLR 508. Cf *Pitfield v Franki* (1970) 44 ALJR 391, [1971] ALR 45 (persons employed by fire-fighting authorities not engaged in an industrial pursuit).
34   (1920) 27 CLR 532.
35   (1923) 33 CLR 517.
36   (1928) 41 CLR 569.
37   Ibid, at 575.
38   Unless the school is conducted for profit. See the *Professional Engineers' Case* (1959) 107 CLR 208 at 237 (Dixon CJ).

The principles of this case were examined in the *Professional Engineers' Association Case*,[39] particularly in the judgments of Dixon CJ and Windeyer J which contain an exposition both of the general question of what are industrial matters, and the particular problem of the State governmental employee. The association served a large number of employers of persons with certain qualifications, who were engaged in work described as "professional engineering". Amongst those served were State governments and their agencies. The ruling by the commission that it had jurisdiction in respect of employees of some departments, but not of others, was challenged both by the Association and by the State of NSW by writ of mandamus, and the matter came before the High Court. Neither side challenged the validity of the principle of the *Engineer's Case* that the legislative powers of the Commonwealth could bind the States so far as their operations fell within the subject of the power.

But the States argued that the nature of their operations could never be described as industrial, pointing to the decision of Starke J in the *Government Service Women's Federation Case* in which it was made clear that there were government employees, such as Lands Office Clerks, who were not in an industrial situation. But the Chief Justice saw this as an attempt to go back to pre-*Engineers' Case* reasoning. "That which is naturally within s 51 (xxxv) cannot cease to be so because it is 'governmental' "[40] (i e, the States were looking to the function of the department, but s 51 (xxxv) looks to the duties of the man). It was conceded that *some* engineers, those concerned with policy matters, might not stand in an industrial relation; but this was no bar to the making of an award for the benefit of those who did so stand.

It is clear of course that the connotation of the word "industrial" would preclude the making of an award in relation to the purely "regal" functions performed by State government employees eg, police.[41]

"Industrial" refers to and necessarily involves the employer/employee relationship and cannot extend to the regulation of shop trading hours.[42] Moreover, not all issues between employers and employees are industrial in character.[43] Certain cases as we have seen, suggest that a claim for compulsory unionism is not an industrial matter.[44] Such cases, it is true, involve the interpretation of "industrial matters" in the Arbitration Act, but it seems their principle may be applicable to the word "industrial" in s 51 (xxxv). It is uncertain, however, just to what extent this principle extends; for example,

---

39　(1959) 107 CLR 208, discussed 34 ALJ 35.

40　107 CLR at 234.

41　Or in relation to persons employed by fire-fighting authorities in the States: *Pitfield v Franki* (1970) 44 ALJR 391.

42　See *Clancy v Butchers' Shop Employees' Union* (1904) 1 CLR 181.

43　In *R v Commonwealth Industrial Court ex parte Cocks* (1968) 43 ALJR 32, [1969] ALR 161, it was held that a dispute relating to the employment of independent contractors was not an industrial dispute. See also *Australian Federation of Air Pilots and Others v Flight Officers Industrial Tribunal* (1968) 119 CLR 16, [1968] ALR 483. *R v Austin ex parte Farmers' and Graziers' Co-operative Company Ltd* (1964) 112 CLR 619, [1965] ALR 599.

44　eg, *R v Findlay ex parte Victorian Chamber of Manufacturers* (1950) 81 CLR 537. See n 28 ante. An award demarcating areas of work for different unions is an industrial matter if the employer is a party to the dispute: *R v The Commonwealth Conciliation and Arbitration Commission ex parte Transport Workers' Union of Australia* (1969) 43 ALJR 438, [1970] ALR 3.

is a dispute about housing conditions for members of a union in a remote area an industrial dispute?[45]

### "extending beyond the limits of any one State"

It was natural enough in 1900 that the arbitration power granted to the newly-born Commonwealth should be framed in a way as not to interfere with the management by the States of industrial matters arising solely within their boundaries. The Constitution envisages that the dispute must involve more than one State. This limitation has, however, not had the same restrictive effect as the other limitations because of the development of federally-organized industrial organizations representing employers and employees which serve logs of claims on each other. It was at an early stage emphasized that it was the dispute which had to be situate in more than one State as distinct from the industry. It is, therefore, not necessary that any one of the employers have a business which extends to more than one State. Nor is it a disqualifying factor that the industry is one determined by local State conditions in which interstate competition in its products does not exist.[46] Local limitations of the *union* do not prevent a dispute in which it is engaged from being an inter-state dispute. In *The Jumbunna Case*[47] it was held that a union could be engaged in an industrial dispute, even though it was a purely State union with a field of operations limited to the State, by co-operating with a union in other States to create an opposition in a dispute which could be extended over both States, subject to the qualification that the dispute must not be a "sham".

The *Merchant Service Guild Case (No 2)*[48] saw the court approve the "paper dispute", as a legitimate means of bringing grievances before the court. Provided that the dispute exists with respect to conditions in more than one State, the interstate criterion will be satisfied. However, it is also possible for a dispute to arise locally—in one pit, or in one shop—and thence to spread not only throughout the Commonwealth in that industry or calling, but to spread to other industries as well. This raises the point posed by Isaacs J in *The Builders' Labourers' Case*:[49]

They [disputes] may erupt in one part or several parts of the Commonwealth, just as a physical eruption may originate in one or several portions of the body and

---

45    It may well depend on the association of the housing matter with employment conditions. The problem of characterization is a difficult one. Compare, for example, *R v Commonwealth Conciliation and Arbitration Commission ex parte Melbourne and Metropolitan Tramways' Board* (1966) 115 CLR 443, [1966] ALR 122, with *Melbourne and Metropolitan Tramways' Board v Horan* (1967) 117 CLR 78, [1967] ALR 289. Another useful comparison is between *Australian Tramway Employees Association v Prahran and Malvern Tramway Trust* (1913) 17 CLR 680 (dispute about wearing a union badge industrial) and *Re Portus ex parte ANZ Banking Group* (1972) 46 ALJR 623 (dispute about deduction of union fees from wages by employer not industrial).

46    *Builders Labourers' Case* (1914) 18 CLR 224 at 243 per Isaacs J: "If a given industrial dispute answers the requisite geographical character, it is *ex vi termini* not a 'State' dispute. It is, when considered in its integrity neither a single nor a multiple State dispute, nor a *fasciculus* of separate State disputes. It is an *Australian dispute*, and cognizable as such by the Commonwealth authority."

47    (1908) 6 CLR 309.

48    (1913) 16 CLR 705.

49    (1914) 18 CLR 224 at 243.

spread, or they may originate—as in the present case—by a synchronous growth all over the area affected.

The analogy with physiological disease is a powerful one. When is the dispute/disease still able to be discerned as present in itself alone; when do the symptoms and sequelae reach such proportions as to take on separate identities?

To illustrate this, one must turn to the *Caledonian Collieries Case*.[50] As a result of attempts by employers to have wages reduced upon the northern NSW collieries, bitter unrest broke out, which culminated in the closing of the mines in mid-1929. The economic consequences forced the NSW government to re-open one of the mines with non-union labour accepting reduced rates. On the same day (16 December 1929) Beeby J, Chief Judge of the Commonwealth court summoned a compulsory conference.

As at that date, Queensland and Victorian miners were involved to a certain extent. Since the selling price of NSW coal affected that of Queensland and Victorian coal, a reduction in the price of the former, it was suggested, would affect the latter; a consequent reduction of wages in NSW would be followed by immediate demands for reduction in Queensland and Victoria. The union, through its federal organization, had arranged that its members in the rest of NSW and in Queensland and in Victoria should contribute 12½ per cent of their wages to support the out-of-work miners. One other important fact was later urged to import the necessary interstate quality to the dispute; on 16 December, telegrams were sent to miners at Wonthaggi (Victoria) and in Queensland to strike in sympathy; which they did. Beeby CJ assumed jurisdiction, and made an interim award on 19 December. The matter came before the High Court three weeks later, when Beeby CJ's jurisdiction was challenged.

The judgment of the majority (Gavan, Duffy, Rich, Starke, and Dixon JJ) depends on a distinction drawn between a dispute proper ("a disagreement between people or groups of people who stand in some industrial relation upon some matter which affects or rises out of the relationship") and the sequelae of the dispute. The dispute between the northern NSW men and their employers certainly existed—it was a dispute about the reduction of wages. But there was no such dispute between Victorian miners and Victorian coal owners, nor amongst their Queensland counterparts. Indeed, so long as the NSW mines remained closed, all others would benefit, and no reduction was remotely likely. That is to say, the dispute was in NSW, and the strikes in Victoria and Queensland did not in any way enlarge the dispute proper. The consequence was that the dispute did not fall within s 51 (xxxv).[51]

One of the difficult points is where an award has been made in settlement of a dispute which was interstate in character and some point of contention involving purely local or intrastate considerations and not dealt with by the award later occurs. If the point is within the ambit of the original dispute, it can proceed to arbitration; if not, it seems that there would be no jurisdiction.[52]

---

50  *Caledonian Collieries Ltd v Australasian Coal and Shale Employees' Federation (No 1)* (1930) 42 CLR 527.
51  Ibid, at 552-3.
52  See *R v Gough ex parte BP Refinery Pty Ltd* (1966) 114 CLR 384; *R v Commonwealth Conciliation and Arbitration Commission ex parte Melbourne and Metropolitan Tramways' Board* (1965) 113 CLR 228; [1966] ALR 722. *R v continues*

The question whether an award is constitutionally valid (or, more correctly, whether the *Conciliation and Arbitration Act* 1904-1972, in so far as it authorises the award, is constitutionally valid) is a matter usually determined by an application for a writ of prohibition under s 75 (v) of the Constitution, being a matter for the original jurisdiction of the High Court which has been made exclusive to the High Court by the *Judiciary Act*. In such a proceeding the High Court can review all the questions on which the jurisdiction of the commission constitutionally depends, e g, the factual question whether the dispute was in fact of an interstate character.[53]

*Nature of the arbitral function and the exercise of judicial power.* The arbitral function, in the sense that it creates new rights, is legislative, although the High Court in *Alexanders Case*[54] has taken the view that it is not the arbitrator who legislates but Parliament.

Though the power is legislative or at least ancillary to the legislative function, the arbitral tribunal is under a duty to proceed judicially: it is on this ground that the prerogative writ of prohibition lies.

The power to make laws for the enforcement of awards results from a combination of ss 51 (xxxv) and 51 (xxxix). In itself the enforcement process is a judicial function and so cannot be exercised by any body other than a court.[55] Since the decision in *The Boilermakers' Case*,[56] such a court cannot be constituted to perform arbitral functions as well.

The power of arbitrating therefore is exclusively vested in the Commonwealth Arbitration Commission while the power of performing various judicial functions under the *Conciliation and Arbitration Act*, including the power of committing for contempt and the power of enforcing awards, has been conferred on the Industrial Court.[57]

The *Conciliation and Arbitration Act* also contains various provisions, for example, allowing the Industrial Court to adjudicate on disputed union elections and allowing it to take control of the elections, and other matters which are dependent for their legislative validity on s 51 (xxxix)—the incidental power[58]

Once a Commonwealth award has been validly made, it displaces all State industrial awards which are inconsistent with it or, even when they are not technically inconsistent, where the federal award evinces an intention

---

52   *continued*
     *Commonwealth Conciliation and Arbitration Commission ex parte Australian Workers' Union* (1957) 99 CLR 505. Section 51 (xxxv) also applies to a dispute relating to conditions of work outside the Commonwealth (ie, on vessels): *R v Foster ex parte Eastern and Australian Steamship Co* (1959) 103 CLR 256.

53   See *R v The Commonwealth Conciliation and Arbitration Commission ex parte Melbourne and Metropolitan Tramways' Board* (1962) 108 CLR 166; [1962] ALR 646.

54   (1918) 25 CLR 434.

55   *Alexander's Case.* See also *R v Gough ex parte Meat and Allied Trades Federation* (1970) 44 ALJR 48, [1970] ALR 343, (power to order re-instatement judicial and therefore cannot be exercised by the Commission).

56   (1956) 94 CLR 254, [1957] AC 288.

57   See later discussion under Judicature chapter.

58   See Part IX of the Act.

to cover the field.[59] But it must be shown that the Commonwealth award does cover the field. In *Robinson and Sons Pty Ltd v Haylor*[60] it was held that a State law giving long service leave to employees could still validly operate even though there was an award covering conditions of work and benefits generally in that area of employment. It was held that the award had not specifically dealt with long service leave, and the doctrine of "covering the field" could not be applied so as to exclude the State law.

LEGISLATION

*Conciliation and Arbitration Act* 1904-1972. The Act is entitled "an Act relating to conciliation and arbitration for the prevention and settlement of industrial disputes extending beyond the limits of any one State, and for other purposes." It thereby implies in its title that it contains provisions for the constitutional support of which one may have to look beyond ss 51 (xxxv) and 51 (xxxix). Few Acts have been so frequently or so drastically amended as this; in all about fifty times. Many of the amendments have been parliamentary responses to constitutional challenges. While this is the principal legislative provision on which the massive Commonwealth industrial power has been built, it must be remembered that there is a miscellany of Acts relating to specific industries, which have "built-in" arbitral provisions. The *Northern Territory (Administration) Act* 1910-1973 is particularly interesting, in that it contains industrial provisions unfettered by any constitutional limitation.

Turning now to the principal Act, it must be first noted that it is less complex in its provisions than its State analogues, which because of their wider operation, include much detailed regulation of such things as long service leave and trading hours.

The introductory part (ss 1-5) contains the definition section, and the definitions of "industrial dispute" and "industrial matter" are of critical importance. It would seem that the content of the latter definition allows the Commission to proceed to the very boundaries of constitutional power. Section 5, which makes it an offence to prejudice a man in his employment because of union activities, is a case in point. If this provision depends on s 51 (xxxv) alone, then at first sight it seems to run across the general interpretation of the power, which limits it to the prevention and settlement of actual disputes; but s 5 certainly is an attempt to remove a potential industrial danger area and therefore can be related to the prevention of industrial dispute.

There are three vital components of the arbitration structure: the Conciliation and Arbitration Commission, the Industrial Court, and the Industrial Registry.

The commission consists of Presidential members (who must have the qualifications set out in s 7) and commissioners who are designated either as conciliation or arbitration commissioners by the Governor-General (s 6). The Industrial Court (ss 98-118) the members of which are appointed for life, exercises judicial power under the Act. The allocation of arbitral (quasi-legislative) and enforcement (judicial) powers to the commission and court respectively is a consequence of the interpretation of ss 71 and 72 of the Constitution in the *Boilermakers Case*.

The functions of the commission are set out in Part III of the Act. The

---

59   *Clyde Engineering Company v Cowburn* (1926) 37 CLR 466. See also Healey, *Paramountcy of Commonwealth Industrial Awards over State Awards* (1951) 24 ALJ 242. See discussion of s 109.

60   (1957) 97 CLR 177.

commission has the power to prevent or settle disputes by conciliation or arbitration (s 18). The powers of the commission are exercisable either on its own motion or on the application of a party (s 21). In most cases the functions of conciliation are only exercisable by a conciliation commissioner while the arbitral functions are exercisable only by a Presidential member or an arbitration commissioner (s 22). Provision is made for panels of members of the commission to be assigned to particular industries or groups of industries (s 23).

When a dispute occurs, a conciliation commissioner has the function of arranging conferences between the parties (s 26). He also has the power of calling a compulsory conference (s 27). Section 28 provides that if, before a dispute proceeds to arbitration, the parties reach agreement they may apply to have the terms of the agreement certified by the commissioner or for him to make a consent award. The commissioner may however (on certain grounds including the ground of public interest: s 28) refuse to certify the agreement or hand down an award. If a dispute is not settled the commission proceeds to deal with it by arbitration (s 30). Some matters including national wage and standard hours matters must come before a full bench consisting of not less than three Presidential members (s 31). A member of the commission may refer a matter to a full bench (s 34) and an appeal is available from a member of the commission to the full bench if the bench deems the matter to be of "such importance that, in the public interest an appeal should lie" (s 35). An important provision is s 39 which enables the commission in certain cases (e g, national wage, standard hours cases) to take into account the public interest, in particular "the state of the national economy and the likely effects on that economy of any award that might be made in the proceedings."

Section 60 provides that awards made by the commission shall be final and conclusive; but the privative clause contained therein cannot surmount the constitutional guarantee of prohibition in s 75 (v) and it is by this means that most of the cases which the High Court has decided upon the interpretation of s 51 (xxxv) and upon the Act have come before it.

The Act contains various provisions adverting to the existence of the State arbitral systems. But ss 65, 66 represent a legislative statement of the overriding power of Commonwealth awards conferred by s 109 of the Constitution as interpreted by the High Court. In fact, these provisions have seldom been invoked. But there is a procedural provision in s 108, whereby an interested party can obtain from the Industrial Court a "declaration" as to the validity of a State law dealing with an "industrial matter." This provision was challenged (inter alia) in Seamen's Union of Australia v Matthews[61] wherein the whole post-Boilermakers' Case reorganisation was challenged. It was held to be a proper conferment of federal jurisdiction upon a federal court. Section 67 empowers the commission to confer with State industrial authorities.

Part V deals with the Commonwealth Industrial Court. Whereas the old Commonwealth Court of Conciliation and Arbitration held a united arbitral and judicial function, that of the Commonwealth Industrial Court is entirely judicial, apart from those administrative functions which have been held to be properly incidental to the judicial function. Its role is one of interpretation and enforcement. The court is a superior court of record, and appeals to the High Court are severely limited by s 114 of the Act.

---

61  (1957) 96 CLR 529.

The penal jurisdiction of the court has passed through three phases. Until the 1930 amendments, the Act directly prohibited strikes and lockouts. Thence, until 1947, awards could be enforced, but there was no prohibition of direct action as such. But since 1947 the court has possessed a contempt jurisdiction which appears as s 111 of the present Act. Prior to that date, it could punish contempt only *coram iudice*. But once the court was made a Superior court of record in 1947, it had power to punish a party for failure to perform its orders.[62] Thus, where an award was being breached, the other party could seek an order to restrain the breach (e g, in the case where there was a clause in the award banning a strike). Armed with this, the party could then draw the court's attention to continuance of the breach so that it might attract the harsher sanction of s 111 (contempt). In 1970, amendments were made which greatly restricted this procedure.[63]

Less frequently invoked penalties exist under s 138 (incitement to boycott awards), s 146 (interference with secret ballots) and s 160 (interference with an inquiry into a ballot) and the power under s 143, by which the court is given power to cancel the registration of an organisation which has wilfully ignored an order. A full list of the penal clauses is set out in O'Dea.[64] In the same context, one should remember s 30J of the *Crimes Act* 1914-1960, which depends overtly on s 51 (i)—a relation which can be satisfied by the opinion of the Governor-General—and contains a potentially enormous power of industrial compulsion.

Beyond the penal powers the court has powers to disallow union rules (s 140) and to interpret awards. Section 112 provides that the registrar may refer to the court questions of law arising before him. The court also has an appellate jurisdiction from decisions (including sentences) of State courts other than Supreme Courts in matters arising under the Act (s 113), and such jurisdiction is exclusive of that of State courts. It is also the final court of appeal in such matters.[65] But an appeal to the High Court is guaranteed as of right by s 73 of the Constitution in all matters arising in the 'original' jurisdiction of the Industrial Court. (cf, the 'internal appeals' within the Commission: s 35).[66]

Part VII deals with the third of the elements of the system, the registry. The registrar exercises entirely administrative functions, incidental to the arbitral and judicial powers. But in practice they are of immense importance. One of his most important functions is to maintain the register of registered organizations and their rules, in respect of which he has considerable powers (cf, s 139 and s 142). He has an important right under s 143 to apply to the court for deregistration of a recalcitrant organization.

Part VIIIA contains elaborate provisions relating to the approval of union amalgamations including provision for ballots of members of the affected unions if the registrar so directs. Part IX is a complete set of regulations as to the conduct of union elections; but before it can be invoked, the elections must be "disputed". Finally, Part XI contains miscellaneous provisions of

---

62  See *R v Metal Trades Employers' Association ex parte Amalgamated Engineering Union* (1951) 82 CLR 208; *R v Taylor ex parte Roach* (1951) 82 CLR 587.
63  Act No 53, s 4.
64  Op cit, at 43. The power of the Commonwealth Parliament to prohibit incitements to commit breaches of the Act was upheld in *Graziers' Association of New South Wales v Labor Daily Ltd* (1930) 44 CLR 1.
65  *Cockle v Isaksen* (1957) 99 CLR 155.
66  Subject to any exceptions determined by the Federal Parliament. See discussion of s 73.

which ss 182-4 are of interest, if only as an admission that the industrial tribunals must, of necessity, work in a turbulent, and sometimes violent atmosphere.

(xxxvi) *Matters in respect of which this Constitution makes provision until the Parliament otherwise provides:*[67]

In the Constitution there are a number of sections which provide for a temporary *modus vivendi* or temporary regulation of a matter "until the Parliament otherwise provides".

Under this power the Parliament may at any time regulate the subject matter so covered. Reference may be made to s 3 of the Constitution (matters relating to the salary of the Governor-General), s 7 (election of senators), s 24 (election of members of the House of Representatives), s 29 (electoral matters), s 34 (qualifications of members) and s 46 (disqualifications of members).[68] Section 51 (xxxvi) is to be regarded as a blanket provision conferring on the Commonwealth legislative power with regard to matters listed in these and other sections of the Constitution. Most of these matters relate to the parliamentary and executive structure. The Parliament has enacted legislation in relation to most of these matters thereby "otherwise providing" and so modifying the original constitutional scheme.[69]

(xxxvii) *Matters referred to the Parliament of the Commonwealth by the Parliament or Parliaments of any State or States, but so that the law shall extend only to States by whose Parliaments the matter is referred, or which afterwards adopt the law:*[70]

The first question to be discussed is the nature of the reference which forms the subject-matter of this power.[71] A view has been expressed that the reference should be quite precise in its terms; so precise indeed that the States must agree upon a draft Bill, which by s 51 (xxxvii), the Commonwealth might then exact.[72] This view presumably had its origins in ideas current during the period of the Federal Council, the constituting Act of which contained a similarly worded provision. However, it seems clear that the use of the word "matters" allows the subject of the references to be expressed in general terms.[73] The phrase "which afterwards adopt the law" specifically permits another method of accomplishing the end result viz, by State legislation adopting the Commonwealth enactment.

---

67 Quick and Garran, 647-8. Wynes, 160.
68 See Quick and Garran, op cit, for the complete list.
69 For references to the power see *Smith v Oldham* (1914) 15 CLR 355; *R v Brisbane Licensing Court ex parte Daniell* (1920) 28 CLR 23; *State of Victoria v Commonwealth* (1957) 99 CLR 575 at 604-605 (Dixon CJ). The incidental power can also be invoked to support legislation of this nature.
70 Quick and Garran, 648-9. Wynes, 160-2.
71 An excellent discussion is to be found in Anderson, "Reference of Powers by the States to the Commonwealth", 2 Western Australian Annual Law Review (1951) 1.
72 Opinion of Sir E F Mitchell before the Royal Commission discussed in Anderson, op cit, at 4.
73 See *R v Public Vehicles Licensing Appeal Tribunal ex parte Australian National Airways Pty Ltd* (1965) 113 CLR 207 at 225 [1964] ALR 918 at 924 (per curiam): "It seems absurd that the only matter which could be referred was conversion of a specific Bill for a law into a law."

In the second place, the question arises as to whether a State parliament retains any power to legislate on any power to legislate on a particular subject matter once the reference has been made to the Federal Parliament. The answer to this question would seem to be that the Commonwealth Parliament may cover the field, and consequently, by virtue of s 109, exclude inconsistent State legislation; until it does so, however, State legislation would continue to operate. In *Graham v Paterson*[74] a baker was prosecuted under the *Profiteering Prevention Act* of Queensland, 1948, for having sold bread above a fixed price. By the *Commonwealth Powers Act*[75] of 1943, the Parliament of Queensland had referred to the Commonwealth, inter alia, "the matter of profiteering and prices" for a period lasting five years after the end of the war. Latham CJ said, "s 51 (37) does not provide that any power of the Parliament of a Colony which becomes a State should become exclusively vested in the Commonwealth Parliament or be withdrawn from the parliament of a State. It is s 52, and not s 51 which gives exclusive power to the Commonwealth Parliament. Therefore, the powers of the State parliament are not diminished when an Act is passed to refer a matter under s 51 (37)."[76] The *Profiteering Prevention Act* was, therefore, still in operation.

The most important question is whether reference is revocable i e, whether the State legislature, once having legislated, may take back its control over the subject matter. Wynes has expressed the view that "a reference once made would clearly be revocable until acted upon by the Commonwealth, but not afterwards, since an Act passed in accordance with this paragraph becomes binding in respect of the referring or adopting State as a law of the Commonwealth to which supremacy and binding force are attached by s 109 and cl 5 of the covering clauses of the Constitution."[77] One must distinguish however certain types of reference. The reference may be unqualified as to time or scope. On the other hand, it may be expressed as being for a limited period. At the far extreme, it may be expressed to be irrevocable, or its demise may be contingent upon the occurrence of some event. In *Graham v Paterson*, Latham CJ stated:

"It has sometimes been suggested that a reference under s 51 (xxxvii) must be an irrevocable reference for all time; that while a matter referred must necessarily be described by reference to its attributes or its qualities, yet the reference cannot be limited by a reference to a quality or attribute of a temporal character. Such a contention would involve the proposition that a State parliament can pass an unrepealable statute, or at least that any attempt to repeal an Act referring a matter under s 51 (xxxvii) would necessarily produce no result. The result of the adoption of such a suggestion would be that one State parliament could bind subsequent parliaments of that State by referring powers to the Commonwealth Parliament."[78]

Latham CJ did not find it necessary to express an opinion on this suggestion. In *R v Public Vehicles Licensing Appeal Tribunal*[79] legislation referring power over air navigation to the Commonwealth Parliament for an indefinite period, withdrawable at the will of the State parliament, was upheld.

It is clear, therefore, that a State parliament may refer a matter to the

---

74    (1950) 81 CLR 1.
75    This Act was passed pursuant to agreement reached at a Constitutional Convention of Commonwealth and States in 1942. See (1943) 16 ALJ 323.
76    81 CLR at 19.
77    *Legislative, Executive and Judicial Powers in Australia*, 161.
78    81 CLR at 18.
79    113 CLR 207.

Federal Parliament for a fixed period, or for an indefinite period of time or without any period of time specified. There is grave doubt, however, as to whether the reference may be in terms specifically irrevocable as this would constitute an infringement of a basic constitutional principle that a State parliament cannot bind its successor.[80] Taking the matter further one might also venture the opinion that a reference of power made in unqualified terms (i e for an indefinite period) may be repealed by a State parliament at any time. In this situation the Commonwealth would enact legislation upon such a foundation at its own peril. Once the basis for the reference of power has ceased, there can be no valid legislation to which the Commonwealth Act may refer. Of course, some control over the State power of repealing a reference statute can be achieved by virtue of manner and form limitations embodied in the State statute which would operate under the *Colonial Laws Validity Act*.[81] On the other hand, if a temporal limitation is contained in the State referring Act, and this is adopted in the Commonwealth enacting statute, then it could be that any State legislation repealing the referring Act before the period of time has expired would be invalid as inconsistent with Commonwealth legislation, and therefore inoperative under s 109 of the Constitution. Nevertheless, there are difficulties here: how does one distinguish a referring Act of a State expressed to continue for, say, a hundred year period from an Act purporting to make the reference irrevocable?

This paragraph of the Constitution has not been an effective source of Federal-State co-operation except in a limited area. In 1915 and 1920 attempts were made to refer to the Commonwealth certain war and post-war powers but only a small number of States complied with the scheme. In 1931 powers over the conversion of securities under a Commonwealth-States debt conversion agreement were referred. In 1942 a Commonwealth-States meeting was held and it was decided that legislation should be introduced in each State referring certain enumerated matters to the Commonwealth for a period of five years after the cessation of hostilities. Only a minority of States complied with the draft Bill. The only existing reference legislation still in force is that of Queensland and Tasmania[82] referring power over air navigation to the Commonwealth, and a recent Act of Tasmania referring power over trade practices.[83]

Finally, one may refer to the comment of Professor Anderson to the effect that reference is not the only way of achieving uniformity of legislation throughout the Commonwealth:

The States have naturally enough always been wary of handing over complete control of any matter to the Commonwealth. There is another way of achieving the same result while retaining all control in State hands. Instead of conferring on the Commonwealth the power to make Commonwealth laws on a particular subject, a State may, by legislation, adopt a Commonwealth Act so as to give the Act or regulation the force of State law.[84]

Of course a variant of this is the "mirroring" or joint legislation of the Commonwealth and States on off-shore petroleum resources which involves a co-operative effort on the part of all Australian parliaments.[85] Another example

---

80  See *Uniform Tax Case* (1942) 65 CLR 373 at 416 (Latham CJ).
81  See *Commonwealth Powers Act* 1943 (Qld), s 3.
82  *Commonwealth Powers (Air Transport) Act* 1950 (Qld) and *Commonwealth Powers (Air Transport) Act* 1952 (Tas).
83  *Commonwealth Powers (Trade Practices) Act* 1966.
84  *Essays*, 113.
85  *Petroleum (Submerged Lands) Act* 1967-1968.

is the uniform companies legislation and various other enactments resulting from draft legislation agreed upon by the standing committee of Attorneys-General.[86]

(xxxviii) *The exercise within the Commonwealth, at the request or with the concurrence of the Parliaments of all the States directly concerned, of any power which can at the establishment of this Constitution be exercised only by the Parliament of the United Kingdom or by the Federal Council of Australasia:*[87]

The meaning of this paragraph remains obscure. Both Quick and Garran and Wynes point out that there were three classes or categories of power which, at the time of the establishment of the Constitution, could be exercised by the Imperial Parliament.[88] The three classes were:

(a) the power to amend Imperial legislation extending to the colonies by paramount force (e g, *Merchant Shipping Act* 1894);
(b) the power to enact extra-territorial legislation;
(c) the power to legislate with respect to matters excepted from State control by the Constitution Acts of the colonies (States), or subject to a manner and form procedure laid down in those Constitutions.

It is necessary to examine each category in turn.

As to (a) it was understood at the time when the Constitution Act was passed that the Commonwealth Parliament would continue to be bound by the *Colonial Laws Validity Act,* in particular, by the repugnancy provision, s 2.[89] This would mean that the newly established Commonwealth would still be subject to paramount Imperial control. It is therefore not correct to state that this power was intended to vest in the Commonwealth Parliament a general power to amend or repeal Imperial legislation applying to the States.

(b) The express words "within the Commonwealth" seem to suggest that the power conferred was intended to have an intra-territorial operation, that is to say, to have a territorial connection with the Australian continent and, therefore, would not extend to extra-territorial matters such as navigation and shipping on the high seas. Indeed matters such as these were already covered by certain other Commonwealth powers (see ss 51 (i) and 98) as well as being comprised in Imperial legislation.

(c) Some of the Constitution Acts of the Colonies contained certain classes of matters which were excepted from Colonial, and therefore, later State control e g, duties of customs could not be imposed on goods imported for military purposes. Control over these matters, of course, has now passed to the Commonwealth under various heads of power contained in the Constitution.

There are other classes e g, constitutional amendment Bills which could only be passed in a certain manner and form, for example, with a two-thirds

---

86   For a list of various methods of Commonwealth-State co-operation see *Report of the Senate Select Committee on Off-Shore Petroleum Resources* (1970), Appendix.
87   Quick and Garran, 650-1. Wynes, 162.
88   The addition of the phrase "or by the Federal Council of Australasia" is surplusage, as the subjects over which the Federal Council had legislative power are all conferred on the Commonwealth Parliament under s 51 of the Constitution.
89   Quick and Garran, 351-2.

majority of the colonial legislature or houses thereof, or which required reservation for the royal assent. It might be that s 51 (xxxviii) was intended to permit legislation on these matters to the extent to which they were still embodied in the constitutional legislation of the States which derived its validity from Imperial enactment. However, most of the constitutional legislation of the States has now an indigenous force (i e, is dependent on local enactment).

The passage of the *Statute of Westminster,* which repealed the *Colonial Laws Validity Act* so far as it applied to the Commonwealth Parliament, has led certain writers to speculate that, whatever may have been the position in 1900, the Commonwealth may now legislate in respect of Imperial legislation extending to the States with the consent of the States.[90] Nettheim also considers that the effect of the *Statute of Westminster* on s 51 (xxxviii) is to allow the Commonwealth Parliament to legislate with respect to extra-territorial matters. It is doubted whether these views are correct. In terms of the application of the maxim *contemporanea expositio* the power must be taken as one definable by reference to the constitutional position existing in 1900 and any later extension of Commonwealth power should not be regarded as enabling a legislative power so limited to take on a wider significance. The writers' view is that the interpretation to be given to this head of power is that it is restricted to matters within category (c) outlined above, i e, to that small class of matters excepted from State control or subject to manner and form requirements by force of Imperial legislation.

It is to be noted that s 51 (xxxviii) requires the concurrence of all the State parliaments directly concerned. In so far as these classes of matters would be found in more than one Constitution Act there is some doubt as to whether a request for amendment from one State alone would justify an exercise of legislative power if requests from other States were not forthcoming. In other words, legislative action on the part of the Commonwealth under this section may, in the interests of uniformity, be predicated on the consent of all the States whose Constitutions contain a particular type of provision in respect of which a request for amendment has been made.

(xxxix) *Matters incidental to the execution of any power vested by this Constitution in the Parliament or in either House thereof, or in the Government of the Commonwealth, or in the Federal Judicature, or in any department or officer of the Commonwealth.*[91]

**"Matters incidental to the execution of any power vested by this Constitution in the Parliament"**

In the United States Supreme Court decision, *McCulloch v Maryland*[92] (1819), Marshall CJ pointed out that, in any grant of power, what was necessary to effectuate the purpose of that power was included in the major grant. The absence of a specific clause in the United States Constitution similar to the present clause under study did not prevent the court from holding that in the particular circumstances of that case the establishment of a United

90   See Nettheim, "The Power to Abolish Appeals to the Privy Council", 39 ALJ 39 at 44 et seq.
91   Quick and Garran, 651-6. Wynes, 345-52. Lane, 225-41. Nicholas, 313-6.
92   (1819) 4 Wheat 316 at 408.

States bank with power to issue treasury notes was incidental to the power given to the United States Congress to regulate banking.[93]

At common law the principle of implied or incidental powers has been applied to companies otherwise restricted by the objects clause in their memoranda. In *Small v Smith*[94] Lord Selbourne LC said:

> When you have got a main purpose expressed, and ample authority given to effectuate that main purpose, things which are incidental to it, and which may reasonably and properly be done and against which no expressed prohibition may be found, may and ought, *prima facie*, to follow from the authority for effectuating the main purpose by proper and general means.

Likewise, with a grant of legislative power to the legislature of a political community it might be said that any matters incidental to effectuation of the legislative purposes stated will come within the major grant. In *Crespin and Son v Colac Co-operative Farmers Ltd*[95] Griffith CJ said: "Laws with respect to taxation necessarily include many provisions beside the imposition of taxes, and all such provisions as are reasonably incidental to the exercise of the power of taxation are, irrespective of the express provisions of s 51 (xxxix), authorized by the grant." This seems to suggest that s 51 (xxxix), in relation to its operation on legislative power, was inserted *ex abundanti cautela*. In the same case Barton J said: "Though the incidental power would have been exercisable without this express grant, the sub-section (s 51 (xxxix)) 'makes assurance doubly sure'."[96]

Many of the cases concern the application of the incidental power to the Commonwealth power over arbitration which resulted in a progressive expansion of that power. In *Jumbunna Coal Mine v Victorian Coal Miners' Association*[97] it was held valid for the Parliament to provide for the registration and incorporation of industrial associations of employers or employees. In the *Federal Ironworkers' Association of Australia v Commonwealth*[98] it was held valid for the Federal Parliament to authorise an industrial registrar in certain circumstances to conduct elections of officers of registered unions. Insofar as the unions were, legally speaking, so far as the operations of the Arbitration Commission were concerned, creatures of the Parliament, the Parliament could go further and control the internal affairs of those unions, at least within certain limits. But the incidental power did not enable the Commonwealth Parliament to legislate generally with respect to labour conditions.[99]

There is one case which attaches limits to the operation of s 51 (xxxix), a case which, however, has been subject to much criticism. In the *Royal*

---

93   Cf *Heiner v Scott* 19 CLR 381 at 393 (Griffith CJ), 395 (Barton J), 402 (Powers J).
94   (1884) 10 App Cas 119 at 129.
95   (1916) 21 CLR 205 at 213.
96   Ibid, at 214.
97   (1908) 6 CLR 309.
98   (1951) 84 CLR 268.
99   See *Whybrow's Case* (1910) 11 CLR 311. As Isaacs J said in that case (at 338): "It is not open to the grantee of the power actually bestowed to add to its efficacy, as it is called, by some further means outside the limits of the power conferred, for the purpose of more effectively coping with the evils intended to be met. The authority must be taken as it is created, taken to the full and not exceeded. In other words in the absence of express statements to the contrary, you may complement, but you may not supplement, a granted power".

*Commission: Case*[1] the question was whether the Commonwealth could confer compulsory power on a Royal Commission to call before it witnesses or order the discovery of documents relating to a subject matter which was not within any of the specific powers listed in s 51. The commission had been set up to enquire into matters relating to the sugar industry and had issued a summons to the general manager of the Colonial Sugar Refining Company to attend and to give evidence and produce documents on matters which related to the internal management of the company. The Commonwealth attempted to justify the action on the ground that the incidental power could be used to support the power given by s 1A of the *Royal Commission Acts* 1902-1912 to inquire into and report upon "any matter. ... which relates to or is connected with the peace, order and good government of the Commonwealth, or any public purpose or any power of the Commonwealth." It was said that the matters to be examined and evaluated by the Commission might lead to subsequent action to modify the Constitution by way of referendum under s 128. In that case what was merely a "possible" Commonwealth power would become an actual power.[2]

The High Court was evenly divided on the question, Griffith CJ and Barton J holding that the incidental power did not support legislation requiring a person to given evidence on matters informations as to which was relevant only to the possible amendment of the Constitution under s 128, Isaacs and Higgins JJ holding to the contrary. A certificate under s 74 was granted for the case to be taken to the Privy Council, which accepted the opinion of Griffith CJ and Barton J on the point under discussion: "Until the Commonwealth Parliament has entrusted a Royal Commission with a statutory duty to enquire into a specific subject legislation as to which has been by the Federal Constitution of Australia assigned to the Commonwealth Parliament, that Parliament cannot confer such powers as the Acts in question contain on the footing that they are incidental to enquiries which it may some day direct."[3]

Some doubt exists as to the interpretation to be given to the word "execution" in s 51 (xxxix). It has been suggested that a principal piece of legislation must be in existence before the "incidental" Act can be passed.[4] On this basis the *Royal Commission Acts* could not authorize enquiries into matters within the jurisdiction of the Federal Parliament under s 51 but on which no legislation had actually been passed, i e, on matters of possible future legislation. That does seem to be a narrow view and has been rejected by Fullagar J in *Lockwood v Commonwealth*.[5] If the wider view is adopted, s 1A of the *Royal Commissions Act* 1902-1966 would authorize enquiries on matters relating to specific heads of power of the Commonwealth Parliament but which are not the subject of existing Commonwealth legislation.

It is established that any attempt to justify the exercise of an incidental power as relating to or supporting an attempted exercise of a head of Commonwealth power which has been declared to be invalid will not succeed. This is illustrated by the *Pharmaceutical Benefits Case*.[6] In that case the

---

1   *Attorney-General for the Commonwealth v Colonial Sugar Refining Co Ltd* [1914] AC 237.
2   *Colonial Sugar Refining Co Ltd v Attorney-General for the Commonwealth* (1912) 15 CLR 182.
3   [1914] AC 237 at 257.
4   Wynes, at 347. See also *Ex parte Walsh and Johnson* (1925) 37 CLR 36 at 71 (Knox CJ).
5   (1954) 90 CLR 177 at 182-4.
6   *Attorney-General for Victoria v Commonwealth* (1945) 71 CLR 237.

*Pharmaceutical Benefits Act* of 1944 established an elaborate scheme of free medicine for persons resident in Australia. Constitutional authority for the Act was referred to ss 81 and 51 (xxxix) of the Constitution. But insofar as s 81, the appropriation power, could not justify the application of moneys for such wide purposes (the Act being characterized as a health Bill and not an appropriation Bill), the various sections inserted in the Act to allow the achievement of these Commonwealth purposes were equally invalid.

The importance of the incidental power is seen in terms of legislation purporting to penalize conduct or give powers of seizure to a governmental authority in relation to breaches of legislation. In *Burton v Honan*[7] the forfeiture provisions of the *Customs Act* 1901-1950 were challenged. It was argued that the power to prohibit imports did not carry with it a power to make the prohibition effective by means of seizure and forfeiture after the goods had passed through customs. This argument was, however, rejected by the High Court. Dixon CJ said:

These matters of incidental powers are largely questions of degree, but in considering them we must not lose sight of the fact that once the subject matter is fairly within the province of the federal legislature the justice and wisdom of the provisions which it makes in the exercise of its powers over the subject matter are matters entirely for the legislature and not for the judiciary.[8]

In most of the cases the High Court, in justifying an implemental or ancillary provision of an Act in relation to a valid exercise of a Commonwealth head of power, has not distinguished between the major head of power and s 51 (xxxix). In other words the exercise of power has been justified under either source. In *Australian Coastal Shipping Commission v O'Reilly*[9] Dixon CJ said:

"Section 51 (xxxix) authorises the Parliament to make laws with respect to matters incidental to the execution of any power vested by the Constitution in the Parliament and this has been treated (somewhat unnecessarily or superfluously as I think; see *Le Mesurier v Connor*) as including not only what attends or arises in, the exercise of legislative power, but also what is incidental to the subject matter of each of the powers conferred by the other paragraphs of s 51".[10]

However, in the same case McTiernan J justified a provision in a Commonwealth statute giving exemption to a Commonwealth statutory corporation from State stamp tax on the basis of the incidental power. In his view it was incidental to the exercise of the power deriving from s 51 (i) to establish the commission and to regulate its affairs. The legislative power conferred by s 51 (xxxix) was "not necessarily co-incident with the concomitants of the other specified powers respectively. If the prevention of the application of State laws imposing taxation on the commission is not incidental as far as

---

7 (1952) 86 CLR 169.
8 Ibid, at 179. See also *Australian Coastal Shipping Commission v O'Reilly* (1962) 107 CLR 46, [1962] ALR 502. Compare the *Second Uniform Tax Case* (1957) 99 CLR 575, where it was held that the incidental power could not be relied upon to support a Commonwealth provision (requiring a taxpayer to pay Commonwealth tax in priority to State tax) which interfered with a State constitutional right. See above page 70.
9 (1962) 107 CLR 46.
10 Ibid, at 54. See also *Smith v Oldham* (1912) 15 CLR 355 at 361 (Barton J), *R v Brisbane Licensing Court ex parte Daniell* (1920) 28 CLR 23.

s 51 (i) is concerned, it does not follow that this is not a proper matter of legislative power under s 51 (xxxix)."[11]

Nevertheless, the bulk of judicial opinion favours the proposition that the incidental power has its main operation in relation to the executive and judicial powers and that, so far as the exercise of legislative power is concerned, it affirms in a clear manner what would otherwise be a matter of implication.[12]

### "or in either House thereof"

Each House of Parliament has power to make rules and standing orders relating to their business and privileges (s 50). This part of s 51 (xxxix) affirms the power of Parliament to legislate with respect to matters incidental thereto.

### "or in the Government of the Commonwealth ... or in any department or officer of the Commonwealth"

Under this part of s 51 (xxxix), the Parliament may legislate with respect to matters incidental to the exercise of the executive power (which is derived primarily from s 61 of the Constitution) and with respect to other administrative and departmental matters (e g, the public service). Such a power extends to the enactment of legislation punishing conduct directed against the Commonwealth and its organs of government,[13] and many of the provisions of the *Crimes Act* 1914-1966 have been enacted under it.

One important aspect of the power to legislate with respect to matters incidental to the executive power is the power to legislate with respect to internal security.[14] The opinions of Dixon and Fullagar JJ as to the source of the internal security power are that it is necessarily inherent in the idea of government, and that it is not necessary therefore to invoke an express power in the Constitution to support its exercise. Other judges in the cases relating to internal security derive the power from a combination of s 61 and s 51 (xxxix).

In *Burns' Case* the opinion was expressed that the Federal Parliament could not prohibit purely political criticism of the members of the government,[15] and this seems to reflect one of the basic social values of our system of democracy, the rule of law. But the dividing line between legitimate political criticism and unlawful incitement to disaffection can never be entirely clear, as is well illustrated by the dissenting opinions of Dixon and McTiernan JJ in *Burns' Case*[16] that the words, the uttering of which led to

---

11   107 CLR at 59, [1962] ALR 502 at 507.
12   Note however, that the incidental power may be called in aid to support an "omnibus" section such as s 17 (2) of the *Snowy Mountains Engineering Corporation Act* 1970-1971, which establishes a statutory corporation to perform specified engineering works "in relation to any matter with respect to which the Parliament has power to make laws".
13   *R v Kidman* (1915) 20 CLR 425.
14   On this question see *Burns v Ransley* (1949) 79 CLR 101 especially at 109-10. *R v Sharkey* (1949) 79 CLR 121 especially at 134-8, 148-9. *Communist Party Case* (1951) 83 CLR 1 at 259-61. *R v Hush ex parte Devanny* (1933) 48 CLR 487.
15   79 CLR at 115 (Dixon J).
16   79 CLR at 112 et seq (Dixon J). 79 CLR at 118 et seq (McTiernan J).

the conviction of the defendants, were not expressive of any seditious intention.[17]

The *Communist Party Case*[18] illustrates that the internal security power is complementary to the defence power. The *Communist Party Dissolution Act* made appeals both to the defence power and the internal security power. It was held invalid by the court as an exercise of the internal security power for the same reasons as it was held invalid as an exercise of the defence power.

### "or in the Federal Judicature"

The real force and effect of the incidental power vested in the Parliament is seen in relation to the judicial power. Many of the provisions of the *Judiciary Act* 1903-1969 and the *High Court Procedure Act* 1903-1966 have been enacted pursuant to this power read with sections of the Judicature chapter of the Constitution, e g, ss 76, 77, and 78.[19] The former Act is concerned with the jurisdiction and powers of the High Court, federal courts and State courts exercising federal jurisdiction. The latter Act is concerned mainly with the procedure relating to High Court actions.

The incidental power cannot, however, be called in aid by the Commonwealth to support legislation *reconstituting* a State court exercising federal jurisdiction,[20] nor to support legislation extending the jurisdiction of the High Court beyond the limits laid down in ss 75 and 76.[21]

---

### EXCLUSIVE POWERS OF THE PARLIAMENT

**52.** *The Parliament shall, subject to this Constitution, have exclusive power to make laws for the peace, order, and good government of the Commonwealth with respect to—*

   (i) *The seat of government of the Commonwealth, and all places acquired by the Commonwealth for public purposes:*

   (ii) *Matters relating to any department of the public service the control of which is by this Constitution transferred to the Executive Government of the Commonwealth:*

   (iii) *Other matters declared by this Constitution to be within the exclusive power of the Parliament.*[22]

Unlike s 51 which confers mainly concurrent powers on the Federal Parliament, s 52 contains a grant of exclusive power over three specified

---

17  Latham CJ and Rich J thought otherwise. See also *R v Sharkey* (1949) 79 CLR 121.
18  (1951) 83 CLR 1.
19  See *R v Federal Court of Bankruptcy ex parte Loewenstein* (1938) 59 CLR 556 at 585-9. *Griffin v State of South Australia* (1924) 35 CLR 200. *Ex parte Walsh & Johnson* (1925) 37 CLR 36. *McGlew v New South Wales Malting Co* (1918) 25 CLR 416. *Bayne v Blake* (1908) 5 CLR 497. *Commonwealth v Kreglinger and Fernau Ltd* (1926) 37 CLR 393 at 420-1. *New South Wales v The Commonwealth (No 1)* (1932) 46 CLR 155 at 174 et seq. *Williams v R (No 2)* (1934) 50 CLR 551 at 558-9. *Hume v Higgins* (1949) 78 CLR 116 at 141. See also Comans, "The Jury in Federal Jurisdiction—Constitutional Aspects" (1968) 3 Fed LR 51.
20  *Le Mesurier v Connor* (1929) 42 CLR 481.
21  *In re Judiciary and Navigation Acts* (1921) 29 CLR 257.
22  Quick and Garran, 656-8. Wynes, 89-91.

areas.[23] It also refers to other matters declared by the Constitution to be within exclusive powers. The three areas covered by s 52 are (1) authority over the seat of government of the Commonwealth (2) authority over all places acquired by the Commonwealth for public purposes; (3) authority over matters relating to any department of the public service transferred by the Constitution to the Commonwealth. The interconnection between the heads of power is obvious. For example, not only does the Commonwealth have exclusive power over customs and excise (s 90); it also has exclusive control over the Customs Department and customs buildings whether in Canberra or elsewhere.

### "The seat of government of the Commonwealth"

The location of the seat of government is determined by s 125 of the Constitution. Section 52 (i) gives to the Federal Parliament exclusive authority with respect to the seat of government.[24] Section 122 of the Constitution grants to the Federal Parliament authority over territories, whether surrendered by a State or otherwise acquired by the Commonwealth. The Australian Capital Territory is territory surrendered by the State of New South Wales.

It seems, therefore, that there are two component parts of the Federal Capital Territory. There is the Territory itself, the area delineated by boundaries which were described in the legislation of NSW and that of the Commonwealth dealing with the surrender of the area and its acceptance by the Commonwealth. There is also the seat of government which is located within this territory, i e, in Canberra. The area outside Canberra is primarily rural and agricultural land, and the administrative departments are concentrated in the City, although, of course, it would be quite permissible for Federal Parliament to use any part of the territory for the erection of buildings for the carrying-on of the Federal Governmental administration. The seat of government is a locale or a place (or a collection of locales and places), and from this place not only the national government but also the internal organisation of the Territory is administered. The seat of government, therefore, has a dual function both in respect of the national government of the Commonwealth and in respect of the organisation of what might be called the municipal services of Canberra.

In an article entitled "Where is the Seat of Government?"[25] Mr Ewens, the former Parliamentary Draftsman, has pointed out that nowhere is to be found the exact determination of the limits of the seat of government as distinct from the Federal Capital Territory, nor the precise location of the seat. All that is mentioned is that it shall lie in the district of Yass, Canberra, within the territorial area of the Federal Capital Territory. He points out that the selection of the site was the subject of administrative action which was not even formalized in any proclamation or other administrative act apart from the actual surveying and lay-out of the city, which is set out in a plan of the City of Canberra published under the *Seat of Government (Administration) Act* of 1924. He then explores the question: is legislation for the seat of govern-

---

23  For a comparison with the distribution of power under the United States and Canadian Constitutions see: *Deakin v Webb* (1904) 1 CLR 585 at 605-6 (Griffith CJ), *Nott Brothers v Barkley* (1925) 36 CLR 20 at 29 (Isaacs J), *Roughley v New South Wales* (1928) 42 CLR 162 at 198 (Higgins J).
24  See Quick and Garran, 658-9. Wynes, 108-116. Lane, 758-62.
25  (1951) 25 ALJ 532.

ment legislation supportable under ss 52 or 122 of the Constitution? His view is that the power with regard to the seat of government would enable the Commonwealth to legislate with respect to the seat of government throughout the whole Commonwealth.[26] He uses an example of a law which prohibited the use of the name of the seat of government or required every person between the ages of 25 and 35 to make a visit to the seat of government as being within this power. On the other hand, the power over the Territory itself would have a territorial limitation, and therefore any legislation with regard to the government of the Australian Capital Territory would be legislation supportable under s 122. The power to make laws for the Territory, given by s 12 of the *Seat of Government (Administration) Act*, is a power which must be derived from s 122. This follows from the language of s 122 which refers to the government of a territory. Ordinances made for the Federal Capital Territory would operate not only in the seat of government but in the surrounding area up to the boundaries of the territory. Ewens does admit, however, that various Acts of the Commonwealth relating to territories including the Australian Capital Territory may operate extra-territorially, but considers that such operation does not bring those Acts under s 52 (i).[27]

Despite contrary views expressed by Dixon J in *Laristan's Case*[28] and in the *Australian National Airways' Case*[29] which support the view that laws for the government of the Federal Capital Territory derive their support from s 52 (1) rather than from s 122, the High Court in *Spratt v Hermes* has accepted that the legislative source for such laws is s 122.[30]

Although this distinction may have some effect on the judicial adminis- tration of the Territory,[31] and possibly on the application of certain constitu- tional prohibitions, for our present purposes there is no significance in the distinction. Where, however, legislation is restricted to internal organisation, for example where it applies to buildings, personnel or the administrative structure, then support will be found for that legislation in s 52 (1). A law, for example, regulating the times of employment of Commonwealth public servants in Canberra would be supportable under s 52 (1) and not under s 122. Moreover, as Ewens points out, such laws have full extra-territorial operation (as in the example of the commercial use of seat of government emblems).[32]

### "and all places acquired by the Commonwealth for public purposes"

Under the second paragraph of s 52 (i), the Commonwealth Parliament has exclusive power to make laws for the peace, order and good government

---

26    Ibid, at 535.
27    Ibid, at 536. See also the view of Sawer in *Essays*, 77. See also *Lamshed v Lake* (1958) 99 CLR 132. Cf, *Pioneer Express Pty Ltd v Hotchkiss* (1959) 32 ALJR 256.
28    *Federal Capital Commission v Laristan Building Investment Co Pty Ltd* (1929) 42 CLR 582.
29    (1945) 71 CLR 29 at 83.
30    *Spratt v Hermes* (1965) 114 CLR 226 at 291-2, [1966] ALR 597 at 601 (Barwick CJ); 114 CLR at 257-8, [1966] ALR at 607-8 (Kitto J); 114 CLR at 262-4, [1966] ALR at 615 (Taylor J); 114 CLR at 278, [1966] ALR at 623 (Windeyer J); 114 CLR at 281-2, [1966] ALR at 629 (Owen J).
31    See below, 244-5.
32    25 ALJ at 535. See also *Worthing v Rowell and Muston Pty Ltd* (1970) 44 ALJR 230 at 235, [1970] ALR 769 at 775-6 (Barwick CJ); 44 ALJR at 244, [1970] ALR at 791 (Windeyer J).

of the Commonwealth with respect to all places acquired by the Commonwealth for public purposes.[33]

The question arises as to whether this means that the Commonwealth Parliament has exclusive authority for all purposes over any area of the State which has come under Commonwealth authority or jurisdiction by acquisition or in any other way, e g, post offices and Commonwealth airports are some of the examples which come to mind. The alternative suggestion is that the exclusive power of the Commonwealth relates merely to proprietary control, or at least to political control that is limited to the aspects of places acquired as places, i e, as public property.

In an early case decided by the NSW Supreme Court just after Federation, *R v Bamford*,[34] the question arose as to whether a NSW Act making it an offence to take property of the Postmaster-General, the Act having been passed before Federation, applied after the Postal Department of NSW had been transferred to the Commonwealth under s 69 of the Constitution. It was held by a majority of the Supreme Court[35] that a *Postage Act* of the State continued in force within the area of the Post Office and the accused could be charged under this law. The basis of their decision was s 108 of the Constitution which provided for the continuation of existing laws in force in the State until the Commonwealth legislated otherwise. However, all the members of the court supported the view that the Commonwealth could legislate for its property to the exclusion of the State law and this legislation would be passed by it in its capacity as political sovereign. Although the Post Office and any other Commonwealth property remained within the particular State in which it was to be found, the Commonwealth on this view was given exclusive jurisdiction over that property; therefore it could, for example, make the *Crimes Act* or a law of tort or any other law applicable to the confines of the property or within the boundaries or area of the property which had been acquired. The narrower view is that the power merely applies to the land *sub specie proprietatis*.

In a learned discussion of this matter, Professor Cowen has examined the various alternative opinions on the nature of the power.[36] Cowen refers to the view of Quick and Garran expressed before *R v Bamford* was decided that the power over Commonwealth property was of a wide governmental character. He points out, however, that subsequently, Quick modified this opinion in his 1919 work[37] and adopted the narrower view that the power was a power to enact such special legislation as the peculiar circumstances of Federal land, not acquired as a political territory, might dictate.[38] As against these views there is a dictum in *Commonwealth v NSW*[39] in which Isaacs J states that the grant of exclusive power carries the inevitable inference that the proprietorship and the sovereignty were intended to go together. On the other hand, Wynes seems to agree with the narrower view that the legislation must be

---

33   See Quick and Garran, 659-60. Wynes, 116. Lane, 243-72. Howard, 486-505.
34   (1901) 1 SR (NSW) 337.
35   Owen and Simpson JJ, Stephen J dissenting.
36   *"Alsatias for Jack Sheppards? The Law in Federal Enclaves in Australia"* (1960) 2 MULR 454.
37   *Legislative Powers of the Commonwealth and States of Australia*, 621-2. See also Moore, *The Constitution of the Commonwealth of Australia* (2nd ed 1910) 289.
38   Op cit, at 465.
39   (1923) 33 CLR 1 at 46.

on the subject of places as places.[40] Cowen's conclusion is that the practical merits of the solution of Quick and Wynes are obvious in that it would not give rise to anomalies which would result from the operation of existing State laws of the *R v Bamford* type. It would also provide for the conformity of law throughout the area of the State, "subject always to the power of the Commonwealth to make separate and special provision for its own land and places which will necessarily prevail over State law by operation of s 109."[41]

The matter arose for authoritative determination by the High Court in *Worthing v Rowell*.[42] By a majority of 4-3, the court adopted the wider view of the power. The case concerned the application of building regulations of the State of New South Wales, made under legislation of the State passed subsequent to 1901 (and therefore not within the operation of s 108), to Commonwealth property (an airforce base) within the State. The regulations were made after the land had been acquired by the Commonwealth. The judges forming the majority[43] considered that the type of legislation which s 52 (i) made exclusive to the Commonwealth was not legislation applying *specifically* to Commonwealth places. In their view s 52 (i) constituted the Commonwealth Parliament as the sole authority to exercise legislative power over places acquired by the Commonwealth and consequently the States had no legislative authority over such places. State legislation would be invalid in its application to Commonwealth places even though it was of a general nature.[44] However, one of the majority judges, Walsh J, suggested that the type of law to which s 52 (i) applied must be characterized as a law with respect to places, i e, as "having such a direct and substantial connection with the places therein described that it can be said to be a law made with respect to them."[45] He had no difficulty in holding that the State law regulating building was such a law and therefore outside State power. However in *R v Phillips*,[46] the High Court, again in a majority decision, held that a State criminal law of general application, which was passed *prior* to the date of acquisition, did not apply to a place acquired by the Commonwealth. The effect of this decision is that the characterization question is no longer relevant: all State laws enacted since 1901, whether general or not, and whether enacted prior to or subsequent to the date of the acquisition of the place by the Commonwealth, cannot by their own force operate in Commonwealth places.[47]

---

40    *Legislative Executive and Judicial Powers in Australia*, 195. A typical example would be the *Airports (Surface Traffic) Act* 1960-1966 providing for vehicle and traffic control in Commonwealth airports.

41    Op cit, at 471.

42    (1970) 44 ALJR 230, [1970] ALR 769, discussed by Lane, "The Law in Commonwealth Places", 44 ALJ (1970) 403. See also Ryan and Hiller, "Recent Litigation and Legislation on Commonwealth Places" (1971) 2 ACLR 163.

43    Barwick CJ, Menzies, Windeyer & Walsh JJ, (McTiernan, Kitto & Owen JJ dissenting).

44    One interesting question is as to the scope of the incidental power as it applies to this power. For example, does it permit legislation controlling smoke emission from factories in the vicinity of airports? See Lane, op cit, at 406.

45    (1970) 44 ALJR at 249, [1970] ALR at 800.

46    (1970) 44 ALJR 497; [1971] ALR 161. See Lane, "Law in Commonwealth Places—A Sequel" (1971) 45 ALJ 138.

47    See also *Attorney-General for New South Wales v Stocks and Holdings Pty Ltd* (1971) 45 ALJR 9 (transferee from the Commonwealth not bound by municipal ordinance relating to land which was in the possession of the Commonwealth at the time of the making of the ordinance).

Because of the grave problems raised by these decisions, the Commonwealth Parliament speedily enacted the *Commonwealth Places (Application of Laws) Act*[48] providing that State law was to operate in such places in the absence of Commonwealth legislation.[49] It has thus exercised its power under s 52 (i) by a general law assimilating State law (except to the extent that the State law is inconsistent with Commonwealth legislation).

It must be noted, however, that the source of power over some Commonwealth places (e g, Army property) is also to be found under other heads of power (e g, the defence power).

**"Matters relating to any department of the public service the control of which is by this Constitution transferred to the Executive Government of the Commonwealth."**

This section makes explicit what otherwise would be implicit, i e, the control of the administration and administrative structure of departments of the public service which were transferred from the States to the Commonwealth under s 69 of the Constitution, are subject to the exclusive power of the Commonwealth.[50] As Quick and Garran point out, matters relating to any department would clearly include "all matters relating to the organisation, equipment, working and management of the department, the appointment, classification, and dismissal of officers, and all the general body of law relating to its conduct and administration; it would cover all machinery procedure and regulation, without which a public department would be impotent; but it does not seem to cover the whole of the principal and substantive law dealing with the matters controlled or controllable by the department."[51] Therefore, for example, while substantive matters of defence come within s 51 (vi) the administration of the Defence Department and other service departments comes under s 52 (ii).[52]

The exclusive power conferred by s 52 (ii) is, however, conferred subject to the Constitution and certain limitations on the power are to be found in other sections of the Constitution, e g, s 84.[53]

**"Other matters declared by this Constitution to be within the exclusive power of the Parliament"**

Under this power, the Commonwealth has power to deal exclusively

---

48  No 121 of 1970.
49  For an example of such Commonwealth legislation see *Public Order (Protection of Persons and Property) Act*, No 26 of 1971.
50  See *D'Emden v Pedder* (1904) 1 CLR 96 at 108 (Griffith CJ). (*Audit Act* providing for receipts and vouchers in the administration of a Commonwealth department valid under this head.) As Latham CJ pointed out in *West v Commissioner of Taxation* (NSW) (1937) 56 CLR 657 at 668-9, any legislation of a *State* which dealt *specifically* with Federal salaries or pensions would be invalid as encroaching on this head of power. Cf, Evatt J, ibid, at 685. See also *Wollaston's Case* (1902) 28 VLR 354 at 377 (Madden CJ).
51  *Annotated Constitution*, 660.
52  See *R v Brislan ex parte Williams* (1935) 54 CLR 262 at 274-5. See also *Pirrie v McFarlane* (1925) 36 CLR 170; *Joseph v Colonial Treasurer* (NSW) (1918) 25 CLR 32.
53  *Le Leu v The Commonwealth* (1921) 29 CLR 305. *Cousins v The Commonwealth* (1906) 3 CLR 529. *Pemberton v The Commonwealth* (1933) 49 CLR 382. *Australasian & China Telegraph Co v Federal Commissioner of Taxation* (1923) 33 CLR 426.

with matters declared to be exclusive by various sections of the Constitution.[54] Section 90 gives the Commonwealth exclusive power over Customs, while s 111 gives the Commonwealth Parliament exclusive power over a part of a State surrendered to the Commonwealth. Besides these matters made exclusive, there are other matters which are within exclusive power because of prohibitions included in the Constitution directed against the States, e g, the coining of money is prohibited to the States. The effect of this is that the Commonwealth has exclusive power over coinage. In addition to this, there are other matters which by their nature are exclusive to the Commonwealth as being outside colonial power before Federation and therefore not having been vested in State parliament after Federation, e g, fisheries in Australian waters beyond territorial limits, acquisition of property for Commonwealth purposes, borrowing on the public credit of the Commonwealth, and certain of the railway powers. The remaining powers conferred by s 51 and other sections are, of course, concurrent, but where the Commonwealth legislates under such a head of power it may, by virtue of s 109 of the Constitution, render invalid pre-existing State law.

POWERS OF THE HOUSES IN RESPECT OF LEGISLATION

**53.** *Proposed laws appropriating revenue or moneys, or imposing taxation, shall not originate in the Senate. But a proposed law shall not be taken to appropriate revenue or moneys, or to impose taxation, by reason only of its containing provisions for the imposition or appropriation of fines or other pecuniary penalties, or for the demand or payment or appropriation of fees for licences, or fees for services under the proposed law.*

*The Senate may not amend proposed laws imposing taxation, or proposed laws appropriating revenue or moneys for the ordinary annual services of the Government.*

*The Senate may not amend any proposed law so as to increase any proposed charge or burden on the people.*

*The Senate may at any stage return to the House of Representatives any proposed law which the Senate may not amend, requesting, by message, the omission or amendment of any items or provisions therein. And the House of Representatives may, if it thinks fit, make any of such omissions or amendments, with or without modifications.*

*Except as provided in this section, the Senate shall have equal power with the House of Representatives in respect of all proposed laws.*[55]

This section deals with the relationship between the Upper and Lower Houses in relation to money Bills. It provides that certain classes of Bills, i e, those appropriating revenue or moneys or imposing taxation shall not originate in the Senate. It classifies the types of financial Bills which are not included in the designation of money Bills. As to the amending power of the Senate, it sets out three classes of money Bills which are not subject to amendment, while recognizing, however, the right of the Senate to return such Bills requesting amendment. Finally, it provides that in all other respects the Senate and the House shall have equal powers in relation to proposed laws.

**"Proposed laws"**

The phraseology "proposed laws" is significant. Its use in the first paragraph of s 53 and also in s 54 contrasts with the wording used in other

54   Quick and Garran, 661-2.
55   Ibid, 662-73.

sections, e g, s 55 (laws), and imports a contrast between parliamentary control of Bills which are in the process of passing through Parliament and which are therefore subject to exclusive control by the Houses themselves, and the completed Act of Parliament which may be subject to judicial review if it does not comply with constitutional requirements.

It is, therefore, clear that the controls that will be exercised to ensure that there is compliance with the first paragraph of s 53 are a vigilant president and the body of senators as a whole. If a Bill appropriating revenue or imposing taxation were introduced, it would be the duty of the Senate to reject any consideration of it *ab initio*, but if it happened to pass through the Senate and reach the House of Representatives, and a point of order were taken, it would be the duty of the speaker of the House to uphold the point of order.[56]

If, however, the Bill by some miracle were then passed by the Lower House, it would be beyond the cognizance of the courts to intervene, as those bodies would then be dealing with what is parliamentary procedure cognizable according to traditional view by the Houses of Parliament alone. On the other hand, the effect of s 55 as we shall see later, is to allow judicial review for infringement of the requirements of that section.[57]

Two classes of proposed Bills are prohibited from being introduced in the Senate: Bills imposing taxation or appropriating moneys.

### "appropriating revenue or moneys"

"An appropriation of revenue or moneys is the setting apart, assigning, or applying to a particular use or to a particular person a certain sum of money. It is an application of money already raised or an authority to spend money already available."[58] A distinction is made between revenue in the form of taxation, fees for services and the like which the government receives and which is paid into the Consolidated Revenue Fund, and monies which are raised by way of loan and which under the *Audit Act* are required to be paid into loan funds.[59] Any money received from any of these sources can only be appropriated by Act of Parliament.[60]

### "imposing taxation"

Laws imposing taxation are those by which money is raised by the imposition of financial charges or burdens on the community or part thereof. Such Bills cover a wide range of financial exactions such as income tax, customs and excise duties, and succession or estate duties.[61]

### "shall not originate in the Senate"

The purpose of this part of s 53 is to give recognition to a basic principle of constitutional law which has been adopted from the British parliamentary

---

56  Ibid, 664.
57  See *Osborne v The Commonwealth* (1911) 12 CLR 321 at 336, 351-3, 355-6, 365, 373. *Buchanan v The Commonwealth* (1918) 16 CLR 315 at 329, 335. *Federal Commission of Taxation v Munro* (1926) 38 CLR 153 at 186, 188, 210. *Stephens v Abrahams* (*No 2*) (1903) 29 VLR 229.
58  Quick and Garran, 665.
59  The Audit Act also establishes a trust fund.
60  Under s 83 of the Constitution. See also *Commonwealth v Colonial Ammunition Co Ltd* (1923) 34 CLR 198.
61  See below under s 55. See also *Commonwealth v Colonial Combing, Spinning and Weaving Co Ltd* (1922) 31 CLR 421 at 443 et seq (Isaacs J).

practice on the relationship of the House of Commons and the House of Lords, that Bills dealing with the appropriation of the revenue of the country or imposing taxation on its citizens shall originate only in the Lower House.

However, as Odgers points out,[62] except for the broad principle that the power of initiation of financial matters is vested in the Lower House, the limitations of the "Lords and Commons theory" of financial relationships based on an Upper House which is in no way elective, finds no place in the Australian legislative structure. He continues

In addition to the circumstance that it is fully elected, the Australian Senate has claimed greater powers than those normally accorded Upper Houses because of its special character as the second chamber in a federal system, charged with the responsibility to protect State interests. Nevertheless it must always be remembered that the Senate is not the governing chamber and therefore a proper relationship towards government must always be retained by a responsible Senate.[63]

The formulation of the revenue requirements for the financial year are therefore to be determined by the government of the day, and the Bills piloted through the House of Representatives by the Treasurer, who will inevitably be a member of the Lower House. It is clear, therefore, that it was not to be the task of the Senate to take the initiative in formulating such basic proposals of government.

**"But a proposed law shall not be taken to appropriate revenue or moneys, or to impose taxation, by reason only of its containing provisions for the imposition or appropriation of fines or other pecuniary penalties, or for the demand or payment or appropriation of fees for licences, or fees for services under the proposed law"**

The effect of these words is that certain classes of money Bills are excepted from the prohibition of originating in the Senate: Bills dealing with fines and other penalties and Bills dealing with fees for licences or services. Bills providing for the imposition of fines would include Bills which imposed a monetary penalty for the breach of their provisions. This would be the case of a great number of Acts which regulate a specific subject-matter within Commonwealth power and provide for enforcement of obligations by way of monetary penalty for contravention.

Proposed Bills relating to fees for licences and services are those which require some payment on the part of the citizen for a right conferred by Commonwealth Act or for services performed by a Commonwealth body or instrumentality.[64] Although it was argued in the Convention Debates that the right of the Senate to initiate this type of Bill whittled away the originating power of the House of Representatives, it seems clear that the power of the Senate in relation to initiation of these classes of Bills would not provide an onerous burden on governmental policies. If the Senate's power were restricted in this respect it would automatically follow as we shall see later, that its power of amendment would also be greatly reduced. Many Bills today deal with fees, penalties and the like and, therefore, it would be an unjustified

---

62   *Australian Senate Practice*, 261.
63   Ibid.
64   A good example would be Post and Telegraphs Bills which impose licence fees for the use of wireless or television receiving appliances. See also *Commonwealth v Colonial Combing, Spinning and Weaving Co Ltd* (1922) 31 CLR 421 at 464-5.

increase in the powers of the House of Representatives to include within the prohibition the initiation of revenue Bills of this nature.[65]

It is to be noted that a procedure has been adopted whereby in special circumstances (for example, when the responsible Minister in relation to a particular Bill is a member of the Senate) it is possible for a Bill to be originated in the Senate without an appropriation clause and when it reaches the House of Representatives to be amended by way of including an appropriation clause. This would allow initiation in the Senate without infringing the prohibition in relation to revenue and taxation Bills.[66]

### "The Senate may not amend proposed laws imposing taxation"

Under the second paragraph of s 53, the Senate may not amend Bills imposing taxation or Bills appropriating revenue or moneys for the ordinary annual services of the government. This paragraph, therefore, deals with the power of the Senate in relation to amendment of Bills, and prohibits it from amending two classes of Bills (a) Bills imposing taxation, (b) those appropriating revenue or money for the ordinary annual services of the government. This part of s 53, therefore, gives recognition to the superior authority of the government in relation to the revenue policy to the extent that the second chamber is not authorised to make any amendments to (although it may reject) Bills of the categories specified. However, it is to be pointed out that not all appropriation Bills are excluded from the Senate. A distinction is made between appropriation Bills dealing with the ordinary annual services of the government and those which are not of this nature (which, for example, deal with extraordinary appropriations).

### "or proposed laws appropriating revenue or moneys for the ordinary annual services of the Government"

Quick and Garran point out[67] that public expenditure may be considered under three separate headings—

(1) the costs and expenses of maintaining the ordinary annual services;
(2) fixed charges on permanent appropriations;
(3) extraordinary charges.

The first category comprising recurring expenditure for the ordinary administrative purposes is the basic form of appropriation. Votes in the estimates contain the allocation of expenditure under the headings of various departments of the Commonwealth and statutory authorities. The second category consists of charges of a permanent nature, that is, which extend beyond a particular year. These appropriations are made in some cases by the Constitution,[68] and in other cases by specific Acts of Parliament. As to the third category, Quick and Garran define extraordinary charges as appropriations of revenues or loan money for the construction of public works and buildings, and for the application of revenue or loan money to public purposes of a special character. It is this last class of expenditure to which some difficulty of classification attaches in the light of the increasing involvement of government in establishing public works and services. The traditional viewpoint would demand that all these votes for works and services should be

---

65    Odgers, 265.
66    Ibid, 266-7.
67    *Annotated Constitution,* 669.
68    For example, the salary of the Governor-General.

included in a special appropriation Bill which would be subject to amendment by the Senate. However, taking account of modern governmental policies, there is some merit in the suggestion that the appropriation for public works and buildings might fall within the category of ordinary annual services and therefore be excluded from amendment by the Senate. However, the early practice of the Senate has tended to confirm the view that expenditure Bills of this nature are amendable. In particular parliamentary debates on the issue in 1952 and 1964 show that the Senate has jealously guarded its privileges in this respect. The early stance (in 1952) was taken in the face of an opinion from the Solicitor-General that would allow the Government a wide discretion in determining the nature of the allocation.[69] In 1965 the Leader of the Government in the House of Representatives announced the policy which the Government intended to follow in the future. This statement indicates that the Senate view has prevailed. Henceforth, there would be a separate Bill containing appropriations (a) for the construction of public works and buildings, (b) for the acquisition of sites and buildings, (c) items of plant and equipment which are clearly definable as capital expenditure, (d) grants to the States under s 96 of the Constitution, and (e) new policies not authorised by special legislation. However, subsequent appropriations for such items would be included in the appropriation Bill not subject to amendment by the Senate.[70]

**"The Senate may not amend any proposed law so as to increase any proposed charge or burden on the people"**

In so far as the Senate is prohibited from amending the two classes of money Bills mentioned in the preceding paragraph, and therefore has the power to amend other money Bills, this provision operates to prevent amendments being made to a Bill passed by the House of Representatives in such a way that the appropriation of money needed for fulfilling the purposes of the Bill is increased. Such amendments would have the effect of increasing the burden on the citizens through a higher taxation burden or other measures.[71] However, as Quick and Garran point out, the Senate can still amend such money Bills so as to *reduce* the total amount of expenditure or "to change the method, object and destination of the expenditure, but not to increase the total expenditure originated in the House of Representatives".[72]

**"The Senate may at any stage return to the House of Representatives any proposed law which the Senate may not amend, requesting, by message, the omission or amendment of any items or provisions therein. And the House of Representatives may, if it thinks fit, make any of such omissions or amendments, with or without modifications."**

The power of the Senate to request amendments to any proposed law which it may not amend is a potent weapon of the Upper Chamber in effecting reconsideration by the House of Representatives of provisions for Bills with

---

69    Odgers, 275.
70    Ibid, 279. See also Nicholas, "Appropriation and the Senate" (1952) 26 ALJ 390.
71    See Sawer, *Australian Federal Politics and Law 1901-29*, 30-1; *1929-49*, 65.
72    *Annotated Constitution*, 671. For another way in which this section operates, see Odgers, 294. Odgers mentions the case in which the Senate attempted to amend a bounty Bill to extend retrospectively the period over which the bounty was payable. This, of course, added to the number of growers entitled to the bounty and, therefore, increased the burden on the people.

which the Senate does not agree.[73] The question to be determined is whether the Senate can press its requests and, by doing so, thwart the passage of a Bill already passed by the House, or whether it is limited to one request and on this being rejected by the House, is required to proceed with the passage or rejection of the Bill. One view has been put forward that the words "at any stage" imply the former interpretation of the power, and the Convention debates support this view.[74] On the other hand, if the words "at any stage" are interpreted in a technical parliamentary sense as referring to any stage of the passage of a Bill, (i e, second reading, committee stage etc), it could be said that the words do not authorize a request by the Senate on more than one occasion. Quick and Garran have taken the view that if a request to the Senate is not complied with, the Senate must take the full responsibility for accepting or rejecting the Bill as it stands.[75] On the other hand, on a number of occasions the Senate has taken the view that a request can be pressed.[76] This view, of course, means that the difference between the power of requesting amendments and the power of amendment becomes a purely formal one if the Senate decides to insist on its request. In actual fact, the House of Representatives has accepted the Senate position by receiving and considering reiterated requests on several occasions.[77]

**"Except as provided in this section, the Senate shall have equal power with the House of Representatives in respect of all proposed laws."**

The overall effect of the concluding paragraph of s 53 is admirably summed up by Quick and Garran as follows:

Subject to the exceptions of (1) its inability to originate Bills appropriating revenue or money, or imposing taxation, (2) its inability to amend Bills imposing taxation, and (3) its inability to amend an annual appropriation Bill, and subject also to the limitation that in amending other appropriations it cannot increase the charges or burdens on the people, it is declared by the Constitution that the Senate shall have equal powers with the House of Representatives in respect to all proposed laws. The Senate has co-ordinate power with the House of Representatives to pass all Bills or to reject all Bills. This right of veto is as unqualified as its right of assent. Though the veto power of the Senate, so far as this section is concerned, may be absolute, it is subject to be reviewed by procedure provided for in the deadlock.[78]

APPROPRIATION BILLS

**54.** *The proposed law which appropriates revenue or moneys for the ordinary annual services of the Government shall deal only with such appropriation.*[79]

The purpose of this section is to forbid tacking, that is to say the attachment of matter foreign to ordinary annual services of the Government in the annual appropriation Bill. In so far as the Senate is, under s 53, forbidden to amend ordinary appropriation Bills, this section strengthens the position of the Senate in this regard in that it prevents the Senate from being subjected to a situation whereby a Bill contains not only appropriations for ordinary annual services but certain other types of appropriations.

---

73  For the procedure involved, see Odgers, 292 et seq.
74  Ibid, 294.
75  *Annotated Constitution,* 671.
76  Odgers 298; Sawer, *Australian Federal Politics and Law 1901-29,* 80, 214.
77  Odgers, 300.
78  *Annotated Constitution,* 673.
79  Quick and Garran, 673-4.

Nothing is said in s 54 as to the effect of a proposed law which does contain foreign material or matter. In so far as the phrase "proposed law" is used in this section in the same way as it is used in s 53, it would appear that if the Bill were enacted into law it would not be subject to invalidation by a court. As Quick and Garran point out, the objection must be taken in the Senate before that chamber gives its assent to the proposed law.[80]

Tax Bill

**55.** *Laws imposing taxation shall deal only with the imposition of taxation, and any provision therein dealing with any other matter shall be of no effect.*

*Laws imposing taxation, except laws imposing duties of customs or of excise, shall deal with one subject of taxation only; but laws imposing duties of customs shall deal with duties of customs only, and laws imposing duties of excise shall deal with duties of excise only.*[81]

### "Laws imposing taxation shall deal only with the imposition of taxation"

As with the previous section, so too in relation to this paragraph, the intention of the founders was that the Senate should not be presented with a Bill which included not only the imposition of taxation but other foreign matter. In other words this section was designed to prevent tacking of extraneous provisions to a law imposing taxation.[82] It was the view of the Convention delegates that in so far as the Senate was prevented from amending taxation Bills, it was desirable to prevent the Government of the day from tacking on to a tax Bill other matters in such a way as to prevent the Senate from amending the Bill as a whole.[83]

There has been considerable discussion of the meaning of the phrase "laws imposing taxation". In the early case of *Osborne v Commonwealth,*[84] the question arose as to whether a *Land Tax Assessment Act* which contained provisions for the assessment and collection of tax was such a law. Barton J stated: "It is not every statute dealing with the imposition of taxation that is a taxing law. In terms of the *Assessment Act* it does not purport to be such a law. It certainly is an Act relating to, that is, it deals with the imposition, assessment and collection of a land tax. That does not make it a law imposing taxation".[85] The learned Judge went on to point out that the powers for assessment and collection were proper to an Act *not* imposing taxation.[86]

The opinion that assessment and machinery provisions relating to taxation are properly dealt with together, but separately from the Act imposing taxation without infringing the constitutional requirement has been accepted by

---

80    Ibid, 674. See also *Osborne v The Commonwealth* (1911) 12 CLR 321 at 336, 351-3, 355-6, 365, 373-4; *Buchanan v The Commonwealth* (1913) 16 CLR 315 at 329.

81    Quick and Garran, 674-9. Wynes, 176-80. Lane, 273-85.

82    "The paragraph is clearly to protect the House representing the States from being faced with the alternative of rejecting a tax Bill necessary for the adjustment of finances, or passing it with the addition of some matter of policy independent of taxation, to which they might be emphatically opposed": *Buchanan v The Commonwealth* (1913) 16 CLR 315 at 328 (Barton ACJ).

83    *Annotated Constitution,* 675-7. See generally Jones, "Applicability of s 55 (i) to Non-Revenue Legislation", 7 *Res Judicatae* 415.

84    (1911) 12 CLR 321.

85    Ibid, at 349.

86    Ibid, at 350.

successive Commonwealth Governments. Separate Income Tax and Income Tax Assessment Acts are passed each year.

Cases subsequent to *Osborne's Case* support the view that assessment Acts do not impose taxation. In *Federal Commissioner of Taxation v Munro*[87] Isaacs J said that the provisions of an Assessment Act dealing with the definition of taxable income did not constitute a law imposing taxation. In the course of his judgment he rejected three arguments on the meaning of s 55:

(i) that no known enactment is a law imposing taxation within the meaning of the Constitution unless it directly or by reference completely provides for subject matter, rates or persons liable to tax;

(ii) that a law still deals only with the imposition of taxation when it also enacts provisions regulating assessment, levy, collection and enforcement of the tax . . . ;

(iii) that if an act imposing taxation incorporates an existing Assessment Act, the independent Assessment Act itself thereby becomes a law imposing taxation.[88]

In *Re Dymond*[89] it was stated that "provisions for administration and machinery, the appointment and powers and duties of a Commissioner of Taxation, the making of returns and assessments, the determination of questions of law and fact relating to liability, collection and recovery of tax, and the punishment of offences . . . cannot be said to deal with the imposition of taxation".[90]

**"and any provision therein dealing with any other matter shall be of no effect"**

As contrasted with the language used in ss 53 and 54 (proposed laws), the language of s 55 leaves no doubt as to the effect of non-compliance with the requirements set out in the first paragraph. The offending clause or clauses (providing that they can be severed[91]) are invalid and would be so adjudged by a court. The provisions dealing with the imposition of taxation, however, still stand.[92]

**"Laws imposing taxation, except laws imposing duties of customs or of excise, shall deal with one subject of taxation only"**

The requirement that a Bill deal with one subject of taxation only means that a taxation Act must not impose separate and independent taxes. The

---

87   (1926) 38 CLR 153.
88   Ibid, at 186-187.
89   (1958-59) 101 CLR 11.
90   Ibid, at 21. See also: *Cadbury-Fry-Pascalls Ltd v Federal Commissioner of Taxation* (1946) 70 CLR 362. (*Income Tax Assessment Act* not a law imposing taxation). *Moore v The Commonwealth* (1951) 82 CLR 547. (Legislation characterized as ancillary to levying and collection of income tax and not imposing taxation). *Deputy Commissioner of Taxation v Hankin* (1958-9) 32 ALJR 365. (*Sales Tax Assessment Act* not law imposing taxation). *Federal Commissioner of Taxation v Clyne* (1958) 100 CLR 246 (Provisions of *Income Tax Act* relating to provisional taxation characterized as legislation imposing taxation). *Collector of Customs (NSW) v Southern Shipping Co* (1959) 107 CLR 279 (Provisions of *Excise Act* relating to recovery of excise duty not legislation imposing taxation).
91   See *Barger's Case* (1908) 6 CLR 41 at 77-8.
92   See Quick and Garran 676-7 (examining Convention Debates).

purpose of the paragraph is to preserve the Senate's right to reject specific types of taxes if it so desires without rejecting a tax Bill as a whole.[93] Thus to take an obvious case, a taxing Act cannot combine provisions imposing taxes on both income (income tax) and sales (sales tax).

In a number of cases the High Court has been faced with the question of whether a particular tax Bill dealt with only one subject of taxation. In *Harding's Case*[94] the Act in question provided that the income of any person should, for the purposes of the *Income Tax Act*, include 5 per cent of the capital value of land and improvements used for the purpose of residence by the taxpayer. It was held that this did not deal with a subject of taxation other than income (land): only one subject (income) was dealt with by the Act. Isaacs J said:

The test in my opinion is whether, looking at the subject matter which is dealt with as if it were a unit by Parliament, it can then, in the aspect in which it has been so dealt with, be fairly regarded as a unit or whether it then consists of matters necessarily distinct and separate.[95]

In *Resch's Case*[96] Dixon J said that "the expression 'one subject of taxation' appears to imply that some recognized classification of taxes exists according to subject matter." He continued:

But in fact it was never so. Economists and lawyers have, for their different purposes, referred taxes to categories, the one for their incidences and economic consequences and the other for the legal mechanism employed to secure their collection and for their operation upon the creation, transfer and devolution of rights. But these are not the considerations to which s 55 is directed. It is concerned with political relations and must be taken as contemplating broad distinctions between possible subjects of taxation based on common understanding and general conceptions, rather than on any analytical or logical classifications.[97]

In *Resch's Case* an income tax provision imposing a tax on profits of a capital nature was not regarded as contravening the prohibition of the second paragraph of s 55 as being combined with a tax on profits in the nature of an income.

The effect of these decisions is that an income tax act might select as a criterion for the imposition of taxation the receipt of money, or the possession of land or chattels, and may provide for the calculation of the tax in such a way that it is not restricted to ordinary annual income.[98]

---

93   Ibid, 678.
94   (1917) 23 CLR 119.
95   Ibid, at 135.
96   (1942) 66 CLR 198.
97   Ibid, at 223.
98   See also *Osborne v The Commonwealth* (1911) 12 CLR 321. *Morgan v Deputy Commissioner of Income Tax* (1912) 15 CLR 66. *Nott Brothers v Barkley* (1925) 36 CLR 20. *Moore v The Commonwealth* (1951) 82 CLR 547. *Federal Commissioner of Taxation v Munro* (1926) 38 CLR 153. *Federal Commissioner of Taxation v Hepsleys Ltd* (1926) 38 CLR 219. *National Trustees Executors & Agency Co of Australia v Federal Commissioner of Taxation* (1916) 22 CLR 367.

**"but laws imposing duties of customs shall deal with duties of customs only, and laws imposing duties of excise shall deal with duties of excise only"**

The meaning of this paragraph is obvious. It prevents the combination of duties of excise with duties of customs but it does not prevent any number of tariff items being dealt with in an excise or customs Bill.

It must be pointed out that nothing is said in the second paragraph of s 55 as to the effect of non-compliance with the section. Quick and Garran, therefore, seem to be correct in stating that "where the Constitution intends that one portion of an Act only shall be of no effect and the rest operative it is so expressed. The only conclusion is that an Act embodying a plurality of taxes would be absolutely and completely *ultra vires.*"[99]

### Recommendation of money votes

**56. *A vote, resolution, or proposed law for the appropriation of revenue or moneys shall not be passed unless the purpose of the appropriation has in the same session been recommended by message of the Governor-General to the House in which the proposal originated.*[1]**

This section is designed to strengthen the control by the Executive over the expenditure of moneys by requiring that no action should be taken to pass a Bill, whether in the House or the Senate, unless the purpose of the appropriation has been approved by it. Consequently, a motion from the floor of either House for the appropriation of moneys could not be passed, either as a resolution or as a Bill, unless the Executive had approved the purpose of the appropriation.

It has already been pointed out that, while no appropriation Bill for the ordinary annual services of the Government can originate in the Senate, Bills appropriating moneys derived from fines or penalties may do so and, therefore, this clause is directed against *passage* of any Bill appropriating monies whether it originates in either the House of Representatives or the Senate. The following opinion on s 56 was given by the Solicitor-General, Sir Kenneth Bailey in the 1950s: "The effect of this provision in regard to an appropriation Bill would seem to be that the Governor-General must address a message to the House of Representatives recommending the grant of supply to cover the detailed estimates of expenditure attached to the message. This message must be received by the House before the law which will make the appropriation is passed by the House. These are the only requirements for s 56. Presumably it is politically desirable that the Governor-General's message making known to the House the details of the estimates prepared by the executive government should be received by the House before it proceeds to debate the details of the proposed expenditure".[2]

### Disagreement between the Houses

**57. *If the House of Representatives passes any proposed law, and the Senate rejects or fails to pass it, or passes it with amendments to which the House of Representatives will not agree, and if after an interval of three months***

---

99   *Annotated Constitution*, 679. See also Barton J in *Osborne v The Commonwealth* (1911) 12 CLR 321 at 353. Cf, Higgins J in the same case at 373-4. It is to be noted that s 55 does not apply to legislation passed in relation to a Territory: *Buchanan v The Commonwealth* (1913) 16 CLR 315.

1   Quick and Garran, 679-83.

2   Discussed by Odgers, 280.

*the House of Representatives, in the same or the next session, again passes the proposed law with or without any amendments which have been made, suggested, or agreed to by the Senate, and the Senate rejects or fails to pass it, or passes it with amendments to which the House of Representatives will not agree, the Governor-General may dissolve the Senate and the House of Representatives simultaneously. But such dissolution shall not take place within six months before the date of the expiry of the House of Representatives by effluxion of time.*

*If after such dissolution the House of Representatives again passes the proposed law, with or without any amendments which have been made, suggested, or agreed to by the Senate, and the Senate rejects or fails to pass it, or passes it with amendments to which the House of Representatives will not agree, the Governor-General may convene a joint sitting of the members of the Senate and of the House of Representatives.*

*The members present at the joint sitting may deliberate and shall vote together upon the proposed law as last proposed by the House of Representatives, and upon amendments, if any, which have been made therein by one House and not agreed to by the other, and any such amendments which are affirmed by an absolute majority of the total number of the members of the Senate and House of Representatives shall be taken to have been carried, and if the proposed law, with the amendments, if any, so carried is affirmed by an absolute majority of the total number of the members of the Senate and House of Representatives, it shall be taken to have been duly passed by both Houses of the Parliament, and shall be presented to the Governor-General for the Queen's assent.*[3]

Deadlocks between the two Houses of Parliament may be resolved in the manner prescribed by this section. The section envisages a staggered procedure involving a dissolution of both Houses in the event of a repeated disagreement between the two Houses. If the Bill is re-committed by the Government after the elections for both Houses and disagreement still exists, then a joint sitting of both Houses may be held when voting on the Bill takes place.

**"If the House of Representatives passes any proposed law, and the Senate rejects or fails to pass it, or passes it with amendments to which the House of Representatives will not agree, and if after an interval of three months the House of Representatives, in the same or the next session, again passes the proposed law with or without any amendments which have been made, suggested, or agreed to by the Senate, and the Senate rejects or fails to pass it, or passes it with amendments to which the House of Representatives will not agree, the Governor-General may dissolve the Senate and the House of Representatives simultaneously. But such dissolution shall not take place within six months before the date of the expiry of the House of Representatives by effluxion of time"**

The purpose of s 57 is to allow for the resolution of conflicts between the Houses, which proceed for a certain period of time, by dissolution of both Houses of Parliament. The first paragraph of s 57, therefore, imposes the following requirements for the setting in motion of the dissolution procedure. The Bill must be rejected or amended by, or it must fail to pass the Senate. An interval of three months must elapse and then the House of Representatives must again pass the proposed law with or without the amendments agreed to

---

3   Quick and Garran, 683-8. *Essays,* Ch 2 (Beasley) 63-8.

by the Senate. If the Senate again rejects or fails to pass, or amends the Bill, then at this stage the Governor-General may dissolve both Houses, except that such dissolution cannot take place within six months before the date of expiry of the House of Representatives by effluxion of time (i e, after a period of two and a half years has elapsed since the previous election).

There are two occasions on which the double dissolution procedure has been invoked. In 1914 it was invoked in connection with an industrial relations Bill which, although not a vital issue, became the occasion for the request by the Prime Minister, Mr Joseph Cook, acceded to by the Governor-General, that both Houses should be dissolved.[4] The Senate took a serious view of the Government's action and although some authorities have argued that the deadlock procedure should only be used when the constitutional machine is prevented from properly working, as for example, when the supply Bill has been held up, it seems now to be accepted that the double dissolution procedure can be invoked in the case of any proposed law whether it be the law appropriating revenue or a Bill dealing with a non-financial matter.

The second double dissolution took place in 1951 when dissolution was granted to the Prime Minister, Mr Menzies, on a Commonwealth Bank Bill.[5] This case also led to a discussion of the meaning of the phrase "fails to pass" in the first paragraph of s 57 and also the meaning of the phrase "after an interval of three months". The Senate had not rejected the Bank Bill outright but had referred the Bill to a select committee of the Senate. The Solicitor-General of the time in an opinion stated that the words "fails to pass" involved a suggestion of some breach of duty or some degree of fault, and imported as a minimum that the Senate had avoided a decision on the Bill. This, he said, following the opinion of an earlier Solicitor-General, could occur where the Bill was delayed by being referred to a select committee (as in this case) or being repeatedly adjourned.

As to the meaning of the phrase "after an interval of three months" there was a variety of interpretations on the relevant date. It could be taken from (a) the passing of the Bill by the House of Representatives, (b) its rejection or failure to pass, or amendment by the Senate, or (c) the time at which it was clear that the House of Representatives did not agree to the amendments of the Senate. On this question the Solicitor-General took the view that the relevant date was (b): its rejection, failure to pass or amendment by the Senate. There were substantial considerations, he admitted, in favour of the other alternative dates: the earlier date when the House of Representatives first passed the Bill and the later date when the House made it clear that it would not agree to the Senate's amendments. He continued:

the general structure of s 57 seems to me to lean strongly against the earlier date, and (against the later date) the most natural reading of the section is I think, that in each of the cases specified (rejection, failure to pass or passage with amendments by the Senate) it is conduct by the Senate from which the interval commences. This reading, moreover, explains the use of the rather unusual future tense, 'will not agree'. The section looks to the moment when the Senate passes the Bill with amendments. Only future events will make it clear whether the House will agree to the amendments made by the Senate.[6]

---

4   See Sawer, *Australian Federal Politics and Law 1901-1929*, 121-5. Odgers.
5   See Richardson, "Federal Deadlocks: Origin and Operation of Section 57" (1962) 1 Tasmanian University Law Review, 706 at 713 et seq. Odgers, 22 et seq.
6   See, however, Richardson, op cit, at 714. Richardson's view is that the later date is the correct one, i e, when the House decides that it will not agree to the amendment.

In any case, the 1951 double dissolution precedent indicates that the matter is one which will be evaluated by the Government of the day and advice given to the Governor-General accordingly. The question occurs as to whether the Governor-General may reject that advice. On the two occasions mentioned, the Governor-General accepted the advice of the Prime Minister. In 1956 the Government released the correspondence on the 1951 dissolution and it became clear that the Prime Minister of the day was of the view that, while the Governor-General was not bound to follow his advice in respect of the existence of the conditions of fact set out in s 57, e g, whether there was failure to pass the law, nevertheless once those conditions of fact were accepted there was an obligation on the Governor-General to follow the advice of the Prime Minister.[7] Of course, it would seem that if there was any ambiguity as to the existence of the facts set out in s 57, it would not be the Governor-General's task to resolve the matter against the advice of the Ministers. This would seem to fit in with the view expressed both in the 1914 case and also in the Convention Debates where it was pointed out that the discretion could only be exercised in accordance with advice of Ministers representing the majority in the House of Representatives.[8]

"If after such dissolution the House of Representatives again passes the proposed law, with or without any amendments which have been made, suggested, or agreed to by the Senate, and the Senate rejects or fails to pass it, or passes it with amendments to which the House of Representatives will not agree, the Governor-General may convene a joint sitting of the members of the Senate and of the House of Representatives

"The members present at the joint sitting may deliberate and shall vote together upon the proposed law as last proposed by the House of Representatives, and upon amendments, if any, which have been made therein by one House and not agreed to by the other, and any such amendments which are affirmed by an absolute majority of the total number of the members of the Senate and House of Representatives shall be taken to have been carried, and if the proposed law, with the amendments, if any, so carried is affirmed by an absolute majority of the total number of the members of the Senate and House of Representatives, it shall be taken to have been duly passed by both Houses of the Parliament, and shall be presented to the Governor-General for the Queen's assent"

When the new Parliament meets after such dissolution and the disputed Bill is again passed by the House of Representatives but again suffers its earlier fate at the hands of the Senate, the Governor-General may convene a joint sitting of the members of the Senate and the House of Representatives to resolve the matter. The Bill is then voted upon and it will be taken as being carried if passed by an absolute majority of the number of members of the Senate and the House of Representatives.

In this connection, it has been argued that the joint sitting should take the place of, or be substituted for, the dissolution process as a way of resolving deadlocks.[9] This would, however, weaken the role of the Senate.

---

7    Odgers, op cit, at 17 et seq.
8    Richardson, op cit, at 716.
9    Richardson, op cit, at 735-6. *Report of the Constitution Review Committee* (1959) pars 179-225.

ROYAL ASSENT TO BILLS

**58.** *When a proposed law passed by both Houses of the Parliament is presented to the Governor-General for the Queen's assent, he shall declare, according to his discretion, but subject to this Constitution, that he assents in the Queen's name, or that he withholds assent, or that he reserves the law for the Queen's pleasure.*

RECOMMENDATIONS BY GOVERNOR-GENERAL

*The Governor-General may return to the house in which it originated any proposed law so presented to him, and may transmit therewith any amendments which he may recommend, and the Houses may deal with the recommendation.*[10]

This first paragraph of s 58 is a form of provision common to colonial constitutions at the time of the Federation. In 1900 it was recognised that the Governor-General might, in terms of Imperial interest, withhold assent to a Bill. However, it is clear that later developments, particularly the passage of the *Statute of Westminster,* has brought about the situation where any discretion on the part of the Governor-General in terms of assent to Bills has become a merely formal one. It exists now only in cases covered by s 74 under which the Governor-General is permitted to reserve the Bill affected by that section for the Queen's assent.[11] In all other cases he must act on the advice of his Ministers.[12]

The second paragraph of s 58 refers to a message or statement from the Governor-General returning a Bill and requesting amendments. This would envisage a situation where the Cabinet might, after the passage of a Bill, find some drafting error or discrepancy in it. Instead of the Bill being re-committed in all its stages, the power of recommending amendment might be used to speed up the passage of the Bill, with the amendment being made to the particular clause where the error existed. Or, to put it in the words of Quick and Garran, the power is

of special value towards the end of a session, when Bills have been passed in all their stages in both Houses of Parliament, and when it has been found that inaccuracies or discrepancies have crept into some of them. In such circumstances, Ministers formulate the required amendments, and upon their advice the Governor-General transmits a message to the House in which the Bill or Bills originated requiring rectification. Thereupon, amendments recommended are duly considered and dealt with, and if adopted, are transmitted to the other Chamber for its concurrence.[13]

DISALLOWANCE BY THE QUEEN

**59.** *The Queen may disallow any law within one year from the Governor-General's assent, and such disallowance on being made known by the Governor-General by speech or message to each of the Houses of the Parliament, or by*

---

10    Quick and Garran, 688-92.
11    For an example of royal assent being given at a later stage by the Monarch to a Bill which had by oversight been assented to by the Governor-General personally see *John Sharp Ltd v "Katherine MacCall"* 34 CLR 420 at 429-30.
12    It is possible, however, to imagine a situation where, for example, Parliament and Government were united in infringing the basic provisions of the Constitution: in such circumstances, the reserve power of withholding assent to legislation designed to bring this about might be exercised.
13    Quick and Garran, 692.

*Proclamation, shall annul the law from the day when the disallowance is so made known.*[14]

The power of disallowance, while used in relation to Australian Colonial legislation in the nineteenth century, is now a dead letter and this section must, therefore, take its place with other inoperative sections of the Constitution.

### SIGNIFICATION OF QUEEN'S PLEASURE ON BILLS RESERVED

**60.** *A proposed law reserved for the Queen's pleasure shall not have any force unless and until within two years from the day on which it was presented to the Governor-General for the Queen's assent the Governor-General makes known, by speech or message to each of the Houses of the Parliament, or by Proclamation, that it has received the Queen's assent.*[15]

The only present legal effect of this provision is in relation to Bills reserved for the royal assent under s 74. In respect of these Bills s 60 requires (a) public notification by the Governor-General that it has received the Queen's assent, (b) such notification taking place within two years of the date of reservation.[16]

---

14    Quick and Garran, 692-3.
15    Ibid, 693-8.
16    For an opinion on the possible invalidity of an early Commonwealth Act for non-compliance with this requirement see *John Sharp Ltd v "Katherine MacCall"* (1924) 34 CLR 420 at 430-1 (Isaacs J).

## CHAPTER II

## THE EXECUTIVE GOVERNMENT

EXECUTIVE POWER

**61.** *The executive power of the Commonwealth is vested in the Queen and is exercisable by the Governor-General as the Queen's representative, and extends to the execution and maintenance of this Constitution, and of the laws of the Commonwealth.*[1]

In keeping with the general structure of the Constitution which distributes legal powers between the various organs of government, this section vests the executive power in the Queen but goes on to provide that such power is exercisable by the Governor-General as the Queen's representative.

We have already pointed out[2] that the doctrine of separation of powers so far as it concerns the relationship of executive and legislative power must be viewed in the light of the operation of the doctrine of responsible government—a doctrine which receives at least implicit recognition in succeeding sections of Chapter II. This means the Executive (i e, the Ministry) is not confined to the mere execution and administration of the laws made by Parliament. Its members participate in the legislative power both in the making of direct legislation (as members of Parliament) and in the making of subordinate legislation by delegation of Parliament. The guarantee against abuse of power lies in the fact that by their membership of Parliament the Ministers are subject to its control in terms both of their rule-making functions and in terms of their administrative functions.[3]

Section 61 locates the source of executive power in the Crown. Various other sections confer on the Governor-General or Governor-General in Council[4] specific powers (e g, ss 2, 5, 28, 32, 57, 58, 59, 60, 67, 68, 70 and 72). In all such cases the doctrine of ministerial responsibility requires that these powers be exercised on the advice of the Ministry.

The structure of the Executive government encompasses not only the Queen, Governor-General[5] and Her Majesty's ministers but also the members of the public service and various boards associated with the day to day administration of the affairs of the Commonwealth.[6]

---

1   Quick and Garran, 701-2. Wynes, 362-71. Lane, 287-309. Nicholas, 66-73.
2   See above, pp 14 et seq.
3   See *Victorian Stevedoring and General Contracting Co Pty Ltd v Dignan* (1931) 46 CLR 73. The *Acts Interpretation Act* 1901-1966, s 48, requires regulations to be laid before both Houses of Parliament.
4   See below, under s 63.
5   In *Jerger v Pearce* (1920) 28 CLR 588 at 594 Starke J considered that s 61 was an adequate basis for the exercise by the Governor-General (as distinct from the Queen) of the power to declare the cessation of a state of war.
6   In *R v McFarlane ex parte O'Flanagan and O'Kelly* (1923) 32 CLR 518 at 533 Knox CJ said that it could not be maintained that s 61 prevented any body other than the Governor-General from sharing in the exercise of the

*continues*

The content of the executive power is not exhaustively defined by s 61 and its specific limits have to be determined *aliunde*.[7] Portion of it is to be found in the Constitution itself; another part is derived from the prerogative as elucidated by the courts;[8] while a large part is derived from Commonwealth legislation enacted under the various heads of Commonwealth power. It must be noted in passing that a statute is presumed *not* to bind the Crown unless by express mention or necessary implication in the statute.[9]

In so far as the structure of government is federal, there is a consequential need to allocate the executive functions of government pertaining to the Commonwealth and States' spheres of responsibility. Section 61 (in conjunction with ss 69 and 70) effect in a broad fashion this division. The allocation follows the constitutional division of legislative powers.[10] This is true particularly of the routine matters of administration which fall within the competence of a Commonwealth department.[11] Some of the prerogative powers are by their very nature shared by both Commonwealth and State governments.[12]

The cases in which the Commonwealth executive power has been discussed show certain limitations arising by virtue of the Constitution and by virtue of certain principles of the common law. As to constitutional limitations it is clear that the Commonwealth has no right to enter into a contract (a contract being a common means of exercising executive power) in respect of a matter which falls within State competence or is not conferred on the Commonwealth either expressly or impliedly by the Constitution.[13] In the *Wooltops Case*[14] the facts were that under the *War Precautions (Wool) Regulations* 1916 and the *War Precautions (Sheepskins) Regulations* 1916 the Executive had purported to enter into an agreement with a company under which consent was given to the company to sell wooltops in return for a share in the profits of the transaction (called a "licence fee") or on the basis that the business of manufacturing wooltops would be carried on by the company as agent for the Commonwealth in consideration of the company receiving an annual sum from the Commonwealth. It was accepted that the regulations in question did not confer power on the Commonwealth to enter into such an arrangement. It therefore had to be determined whether the contract was in execution of or in maintenance of any provision in the Constitution. The court gave a negative

---

6   *continued*
     executive power of the Commonwealth. As to the executive power of the Interstate Commission, see *State of New South Wales v The Commonwealth* 20 CLR 54 at 109 (Rich J); *Huddart Parker and Co Ltd v Moorehead* (1909) 8 CLR 330 at 358, 376, 387.

7   See *Le Mesurier v Connor* (1929) 42 CLR 481 at 514 (Isaacs J).

8   *Joseph v Colonial Treasurer* (1918) 25 CLR 32, *Farey v Burvett* (1916) 21 CLR 433 at 452 (war prerogative); *R v Burgess ex parte Henry* (1936) 55 CLR 608 at 644 (power to enter into treaties).

9   On this question see Benjafield and Whitmore, *Principles of Australian Administrative Law* (3rd ed, 1966) 259 et seq. *Cain v Doyle* (1946) 72 CLR 409 (punitive provision does not apply to the Commonwealth Crown). As to the question of how this presumption operates in the federal system see above, pp 73-4.

10  Established by ss 51, 52, 106, 107, 108 and 109.

11  Whether they be departments transferred from the Colonies under s 69 or established under s 64.

12  That is, prerogatives in relation to payment of debts and litigation (most of which have been modified by statute). See *Federal Commissioner of Taxation v E O Farley Ltd* (1940) 63 CLR 278 at 320-321 (Evatt J).

13  See Wynes, at 365.

14  (1922) 31 CLR 421.

answer: no power was to be found in the Constitution to authorize such an arrangement, nor did the subject matter of the contract fall within the area of responsibility of a Commonwealth department under s 64.

In *Commonwealth v Australian Commonwealth Shipping Board*[15] it was held that a contract to sell to a municipal council steam turbo-alternators was not authorized by the executive power. Such a subject matter did not fall within the Commonwealth defence power.

However, it seems that where property has passed under a contract to which the Commonwealth is a party and involving a subject-matter which may fall outside Commonwealth power, the contractor cannot resist a claim for payment for the goods supplied by the Commonwealth under the contract.[16]

Even if the subject matter of a contract is found to lie within a field of Commonwealth power, invalidity may result because the contract has no statutory backing.[17] In the *Wooltops Case* several members of the court considered that the agreements made by the Commonwealth were invalid on this ground. It was pointed out that, under basic principles of constitutional law regulating the relationship between the Legislature and the Executive, the levying of money (taxation) and the disbursement of money (appropriation) required parliamentary authority which was lacking.[18] This suggests that unless a contract involving the payment of or promise of money falls within ordinary administrative business of a Commonwealth department,[19] parliamentary approval must be sought. In any case, no contract is *enforceable* unless the Parliament has appropriated funds to satisfy it (either generally, by virtue of the appropriation to the department for its purposes in the annual appropriation Act, or by virtue of a specific appropriation).[20]

The principle, therefore, seems to be that Parliamentary sanction must be sought for extraordinary Crown contracts involving the grant of moneys or other financial benefits or proprietary rights by the Commonwealth, or for the payment to it by the other contracting party of moneys.[21]

Another specific limitation in the power of the Commonwealth Executive is to be found in the rule that commissions of inquiry which involve compulsive powers (such as the power to summon witnesses or to order the production of documents) must be supported by a valid legislative enactment.[22]

One important aspect of Commonwealth executive power is the protec-

---

15  (1926) 39 CLR 1. Cf, *Attorney-General for Victoria v Attorney-General for the Commonwealth* (1935) 52 CLR 533. See under s 51 (vi). See also *Commonwealth v Colonial Ammunition Co Ltd* (1923) 34 CLR 198.

16  *Re K L Tractors Ltd* (1961) 106 CLR 318, [1961] ALR 410, discussed in Lumb, "Contractual Relations between Government and Citizen", (1962) 35 ALJ 45.

17  See generally Crisp, "Contracts of the Executive Government" 26 ALJ 129, Campbell, "Commonwealth Contracts", (1970) 44 ALJ 14.

18  See, especially, the judgment of Isaacs J, (1922) 31 CLR 421 at 443-51.

19  See *New South Wales v Bardolph* (1934) 52 CLR 455.

20  Ibid.

21  *Wooltops Case* (1922) 31 CLR 421; *Australian Alliance Assurance Co Ltd v Goodwyn* [1916] StRQd 35. *Royal Commission on the Constitution: Minutes of Evidence*, 89, *Report*, 49. See also discussion of ss 81 and 83, below. For a criticism of the rule that absence of parliamentary authority affects the validity of a contract see Campbell, "Commonwealth Contracts" (1970) 44 ALJ 14 at 23, "Federal Contract Law" (1970) 44 ALJ 580.

22  *Clough v Leahy* (1904) 2 CLR 139. *McGuinness v Attorney-General for Victoria* (1940) 63 CLR 73. *Colonial Sugar Refining Co Ltd v Attorney-General (Com)* (1914) 17 CLR 644.

tion of the constitutional organs of government (both the Executive itself as well as the Legislature and Judiciary). A police force, therefore, may be established to carry out this function[23] as well as to enforce the laws of the Commonwealth, either directly, or by coming to the aid of the judicial power.[24]

Consequently, s 61 in conjunction with s 51 (xxxix) is the basis for the legislation of the Commonwealth establishing the Commonwealth police force,[25] the Australian Security Intelligence Organization,[26] and other organs of law enforcement. Such provisions also support various sections in the *Crimes Act* 1914-1966 penalizing conduct directed against the constitutional structure of government of the Commonwealth and its institutions.[27]

## FEDERAL EXECUTIVE COUNCIL

**62.** *There shall be a Federal Executive Council to advise the Governor-General in the government of the Commonwealth, and the members of the Council shall be chosen and summoned by the Governor-General and sworn as Executive Councillors, and shall hold office during his pleasure.*[28]

The powers of the Governor-General are to be exercised on the advice of the federal Executive Council, the members of which are to be chosen by him and hold office during his pleasure. As such, s 62 accords with the nineteenth-century executive pattern under which the Queen's representative was to exercise his powers on the advice of a local Executive Council.

It is not stipulated in this section that the members of the Executive Council are to be chosen from those persons who have the support of the majority of the members of the Lower House, but s 64 provides that the Queen's ministers of state shall be members of the Executive Council and requires that the ministers shall be members of Parliament.[29] Consequently, the doctrine of responsible government receives constitutional recognition. The practical result is, as Quick and Garran point out, that executive power is placed in the hands of a parliamentary committee called the Cabinet, and the real head of the Executive is not the Queen but the Chairman of the Cabinet, or in other words, the Prime Minister.[30]

Basic decisions are, therefore, taken by the Cabinet, and the Executive Council exists mainly to put into an official form, (by way of orders in council, proclamations, notices, etc), decisions which have been arrived at elsewhere. The quorum for the Executive Council is the Governor-General (or vice-President of the Executive Council) and two ministers. Crisp states that, in recent times, there have rarely been more than two or three Commonwealth ministers present at its meetings.[31]

---

23   *Ex parte Walsh and Johnson* (1925) 37 CLR 36 at 122 (Higgins J). Of course, the State authorities also have the duty of enforcing Commonwealth law.
24   *New South Wales v Commonwealth* (1932) 46 CLR 155 at 185 (Starke J).
25   *Commonwealth Police Act* 1957-1966.
26   *Australian Security Intelligence Organization Act* 1956.
27   See the various cases discussed under the "internal security" aspect of the incidental power.
28   Quick and Garran, 703-7.
29   "...No Minister of State shall hold office for a longer period than three months unless he is or becomes a senator or a member of the House of Representatives".
30   *Annotated Constitution,* at 703.
31   *Australian National Government,* at 351. In 1972, for a period of about two weeks, a "two-man Government" (the first Whitlam Administration) was in existence. It would appear that the plural "members" in this section and in s 64 would require a constitutional minimum of two ministers.

The wording of s 62 preserves the archaic form to be found in the constitutional instruments vesting executive power in the vice-regal representatives in the colonies by providing that the Governor-General is "advised" by the Executive Council. In substance, of course, the decisions are those of the Ministry: the word "advice" hides the reality of the situation.

The question arises as to whether there are any circumstances in which the Governor-General may act independently by rejecting the "advice" of the ministers. In other words, does the Governor-General have any "reserve powers"?[32] Reference has already been made to this question in our discussion of requests for a dissolution of the House of Representatives, and for a dissolution of both Houses.[33] Any disputed constitutional question must be resolved either on the advice of the Ministry or by litigation in the courts. One must concede, however, that there are extreme circumstances in which certain reserve powers might be exercised against the advice of ministers; where, for example, the government was acting in clear breach of basic principles of the Constitution.

An affirmation of the duty of the Governor-General to act on the advice of the Ministry was made in 1931 by the Governor-General of the time (Sir Isaac Isaacs). At that time there was a conflict between the House of Representatives and the Senate over delegated legislation. Certain regulations made under a *Transport Workers Act* had been proclaimed by the Governor-General. A motion for their disallowance had been passed by the Senate. They were promulgated again on the advice of the government. The Senate protested that it was illegal for the government to make regulations in the same session of Parliament which were in substance the same as those which had been disallowed. The Governor-General affirmed that constitutional practice (supported by the Balfour Declaration) required that he act on the advice of the Government.[34]

PROVISIONS REFERRING TO GOVERNOR-GENERAL

**63.** *The provisions of this Constitution referring to the Governor-General in Council shall be construed as referring to the Governor-General acting with the advice of the Federal Executive Council.*[35]

It has already been pointed out that the vesting of a power in the Governor-General, as distinct from the Governor-General in Council, is of no constitutional significance.[36] The historical reason for the distinction is that the powers vested in the Governor-General personally are those which were part of the monarch's prerogative at common law, e g, command of the military

---

32    See generally Evatt, *The King and his Dominion Governors* (2nd Ed, Cowen, 1967).

33    See above under ss 5 and 57.

34    Evatt, *The King and his Dominion Governors* 185-189. See also *Victorian Stevedoring and General Contracting Co Pty Ltd v Dignan* (1931) 46 CLR 73, upholding the validity of the promulgation. See above under s 2. It must be noted, however, that the Governor-General satisfied himself that "plain illegality" was not involved. If a minister were to advise such a course of conduct, the Governor-General would be entitled to withhold his approval to the proposed document until the courts had determined the matter.

35    Quick and Garran, 707.

36    See discussion of s 2.

forces (s 68) appointment of ministers (s 64), dissolution of Parliament (s 5), and, therefore, it was considered proper that, in vesting this power in the vice-regal representative, the older form should be recognized. Those powers vested in the Governor-General in Council are the ones which had come under the control of statute law, e g, issue of writs (s 32), the appointment of public servants (s 67), and therefore it was not considered improper to specify that they were exercisable by the Governor-General in Council.[37]

All the powers are controlled by the Constitution and therefore are predicated on the operation of the doctrine of responsible government, although reference may still be made to the common law to determine the scope of some of the prerogative powers.

The distinction between the two categories of powers (viz, those exercisable by the Governor-General and those exercisable by the Governor-General in Council) is one of form. While those exercisable by the Governor-General issue in the form of orders in council, proclamations, notices, etc, as a result of Executive Council acts, those exercisable by the Governor-General may be exercised without the formality of Executive Council ratification.[38]

## MINISTERS OF STATE

**64.** *The Governor-General may appoint officers to administer such departments of State of the Commonwealth as the Governor-General in Council may establish.*

*Such officers shall hold office during the pleasure of the Governor-General. They shall be members of the Federal Executive Council, and shall be the Queen's Ministers of State for the Commonwealth.*

## MINISTERS TO SIT IN PARLIAMENT

*After the first general election no Minister of State shall hold office for a longer period than three months unless he is or becomes a senator or a member of the House of Representatives.*[39]

This section is the cornerstone of the various sections which make up Chapter II. It recognizes the existence of a group of persons called the "Queen's ministers of State for the Commonwealth" who individually will superintend the various government departments subject to their control, and who collectively will administer the affairs of the Commonwealth.

A minister shall not hold office for a longer period than three months unless he becomes a senator or a member of the House of Representatives. This last requirement seems to leave it open for a person to be appointed to a ministerial office who is not a member of Parliament provided he obtains a seat within three months of his appointment; although the practice has been for ministerial appointments to be made from existing members of Parliament. Convention would also require the Prime Minister and the majority of ministers to hold seats in the Lower House.[40] An unusual precedent was

---

37   Quick and Garran, 707.

38   See Moore, *The Constitution of the Commonwealth of Australia* (2nd Ed, 1910) 167.

39   Quick and Garran, 708-711. Crisp, *Australian National Government,* Ch 12. Encol, *Cabinet Government in Australia.*

40   The last paragraph of s 64 recognized that this principle could not have been applied to the first Government of the Commonwealth, i e, the Government which took office at federation. On the events surrounding the choice of the first Ministry see Sawer, *Australian Federal Politics and Law, 1901-1929,* 3-4.

established in 1968 when Senator Gorton was appointed Prime Minister after a "caretaking" period by the Deputy Prime Minister (Mr McEwen). This was after the previous Prime Minister, Mr Holt, had died while in office. Senator Gorton resigned his place in the Senate and was elected to a seat in the House of Representatives.

Section 64, unlike sections in the State Constitution Acts, does not explicitly recognize a central tenet of the doctrine of responsible government, viz, that the Ministry must have the support of the majority of members of the House of Representatives, nor does it recognize the duty of a Ministry defeated at an election to resign. But it is clear that this is the basis for the formation of a government, and therefore the choice of ministers is inextricably bound up with the triennial elections for the House of Representatives. The result of the poll will indicate the return or defeat of the previous Government. If the previous Government is defeated, the Prime Minister will tender the resignation of the Government to the Governor-General who will call upon the leader of the party which has secured the majority of seats in the new House or, if there is a coalition of parties, the leader of the coalition. This person will then be commissioned to form a government. When the members of the new Ministry have been selected, the Governor-General commissions them as the Queen's ministers of state, the portfolios being allocated on the advice of the Prime Minister. If the old government is returned, the Prime Minister will continue in office but may request a new commission from the Governor-General, particularly if he intends to restructure the Ministry.[41]

Vacancies may be filled at any time by the Governor-General on the advice of the Prime Minister who may also relieve a minister of his portfolio by transferring him to another or, in the event of a minister being no longer capable of exercising his duties or being in a state of public dissension with his ministerial colleagues, by dismissing him.[42]

Section 64 provides that the Commonwealth departments are established by the Governor-General in Council. New portfolios may therefore be created at any time, subject to the limitation on the number of ministers (s 65), and duties may be allocated among the portfolios by decision of the Prime Minister. There is, however, no constitutional necessity for a portfolio to be allotted to a minister: since federation there have been instances of the appointment of ministers without portfolio.[43]

The question has arisen as to whether assistant or junior ministers or "parliamentary under-secretaries" may be appointed.[44] This question is of some importance as s 44 prevents a member of Parliament from holding an office of profit under the Crown. This prohibition does not apply to the "Queen's Ministers of State."

In 1952 the Speaker (Cameron) strongly criticised the appointment of parliamentary under-secretaries as being unconstitutional on the ground that

41   There is one situation in which the Governor-General may have some sort of discretion in the choice of the Prime Minister. That would be where a Prime Minister (leading a coalition) dies or resigns his office during the life of a Parliament and no immediate successor is evident. In such a case a "caretaker" Prime Minister may be appointed to hold office until the coalition parties can decide on whom they wish to lead them. This occurred when Mr McEwen was appointed to the Prime Ministership after the death of Mr Holt.
42   Crisp, *Australian National Government*, 355.
43   Ibid, 351.
44   Ibid, 383 et seq.

no minister had power to delegate his authority.[45] This objection does not seem to be firmly based as the responsible minister in such a situation retains overall responsibility for all the matters within his portfolio, and the appointment of another member of Parliament to assist him does not amount to any abdication of his authority.

The more important objection of the Speaker was that if such a member received a salary beyond his ordinary parliamentary salary (s 47), he would be holding an office of profit under the Crown and would, therefore, be disqualified from membership of Parliament under s 44.

It would seem that a salaried parliamentary undersecretary, junior minister, or assistant minister would be regarded as holding an office of profit under the Crown unless he were within the number of ministers specified by legislation passed pursuant to s 65. The method of avoiding this disqualification is to provide merely an expense allowance for these "ministers".[46] Such an allowance would not fall within s 44 or within s 45 (iii) as being a fee for services rendered to the Commonwealth. It would be treated as a parliamentary allowance for services rendered to the Parliament and would therefore be within an appropriation made pursuant to s 47.

Up to the end of 1972 a distinction within the Ministry was made between those who were members of the Cabinet (of about 12 ministers) and those who are outside the Cabinet. There is no constitutional requirement that the Prime Minister call to the Cabinet all the ministers of state to advise him on affairs affecting the Government of the country as a whole as distinct from matters falling within their individual portfolios. Consequently, the size of Cabinet is a matter to be determined by the Prime Minister.

Even in terms of consultation of the Cabinet, the Prime Minister seems to possess some flexibility in terms of the matters which he may bring before it. As Crisp points out, "the traditional absence of a definition of the office, its powers and underpinnings has favoured rather than delimited the development of the office in authority and influence".[47] Clearly the Prime Minister has the constitutional authority to "choose" his ministers (even though in a political sense they may be chosen by the caucus of the party to which he belongs).[48] Once the Ministry has been formed, is it in accordance with constitutional practice for any major executive power to be exercised by the Prime Minister without reference to the Cabinet? On the question of a request for dissolution of the House of Representatives (s 5) Crisp gives this opinion: "Whether a Prime Minister discusses a proposed request for a dissolution with his whole Cabinet or not is, within the limits of the moral authority and ascendancy he enjoys over his colleagues, his own affair."[49] However, those who consider that the essence of responsible government lies in the collective view of the Ministry would not accept this latter statement. Indeed, as Crisp himself points out, "the principle of the corporate unity and solidarity of the Cabinet requires that the Cabinet should have one harmonious policy, both in administration and in legislation, and that the advice tendered by the

---

45   Ibid, 387.

46   Ibid, 389.

47   Ibid, 357.

48   There is, however, no constitutional barrier to the selection of ministers by a vote either of the House of Representatives or of both Houses sitting together: Moore, *The Constitution of the Commonwealth of Australia,* 168.

49   *Australian National Government,* 369. The same would apply to choice of a date for an election.

Cabinet to the Crown should be unanimous and consistent; that the Cabinet should stand and fall together."[50]

### NUMBER OF MINISTERS

**65.** *Until the Parliament otherwise provides, the Ministers of State shall not exceed seven in number, and shall hold such offices as the Parliament prescribes, or, in the absence of provision, as the Governor-General directs.*[51]

Under the *Ministers of State Act* 1952-1971 it is provided that the number of ministers shall not exceed 27.[52]

The allocation of portfolios is made by the Governor-General on the advice of the Prime Minister (see s 64). A minister may be transferred from one portfolio to another, and likewise various duties may be distributed among the various portfolios.

### SALARIES OF MINISTERS

**66.** *There shall be payable to the Queen, out of the Consolidated Revenue Fund of the Commonwealth, for the salaries of the Ministers of State, an annual sum which, until the Parliament otherwise provides, shall not exceed twelve thousand pounds a year.*[53]

Under the *Ministers of State Act* 1952-1973 it is provided that the sum of $302,000 shall be payable for the salaries of ministers out of the Consolidated Revenue Fund.[54] Additional allowances are payable to ministers and special allowances to the Prime Minister and Deputy Prime Minister.

### APPOINTMENT OF CIVIL SERVANTS

**67.** *Until the Parliament otherwise provides, the appointment and removal of all other officers of the Executive Government of the Commonwealth shall be vested in the Governor-General in Council, unless the appointment is delegated by the Governor-General in Council or by a law of the Commonwealth to some other authority.*[55]

The appointment of members of the public service is by this section vested in the Governor-General in Council but it may be delegated to another authority.

The *Public Service Act* 1922-1973 regulates the appointment and conditions of members of the public service. The members of the service are described as those who are members of the departments listed in a schedule to the Act.[56] They are graded by virtue of status into four divisions, the first division consisting of the permanent heads of departments.[57]

The Public Service Board[58] is given the power to appoint persons to the second, third and fourth divisions.[59] Appointment to the first division is

---

50    Ibid, at 354-355.
51    Quick and Garran, 712.
52    Section 4.
53    Quick and Garran, 712.
54    Section 5.
55    Quick and Garran, 712-3.
56    Section 10.
57    Sections 23, 24.
58    Under s 11 the board consists of three persons. They are appointed for a term of years.
59    Section 33.

usually by the Governor-General on the recommendation of the board,[60] but s 54 (2) of the Act permits appointment of these officers by the Governor-General without reference to the board.

Appointment to the armed forces is regulated by the Acts regulating these forces, and appointment to the various Commonwealth instrumentalities is also regulated by specific Acts.

### COMMAND OF NAVAL AND MILITARY FORCES

**68.** *The command in chief of the naval and military forces of the Commonwealth is vested in the Governor-General as the Queen's representative.*[61]

This section, dependant as it is on the operation of the doctrine of responsible Government, places the overall command of the armed forces in the hands of the Executive government (i e, Cabinet).

Under the *Defence Act* 1903-1970, the Governor-General is given power to appoint to commands over or within the military forces.[62] Provision is made for a military board to assist in the administration of the forces.[63] The Governor-General has the power to raise and organize military forces subject to the provisions of the Act.[64]

### TRANSFER OF CERTAIN DEPARTMENTS

**69.** *On a date or dates to be proclaimed by the Governor-General after the establishment of the Commonwealth the following departments of the public service in each State shall become transferred to the Commonwealth:*

> *Posts, telegraphs, and telephones:*
> *Naval and military defence:*
> *Lighthouses, lightships, beacons, and buoys:*
> *Quarantine.*

*But the departments of customs and of excise in each State shall become transferred to the Commonwealth on its establishment.*[65]

This section permits the transfer of certain departments of the public services of the States to the Commonwealth.

The customs and excise departments were transferred on the 1 January 1901.

The proclaimed dates for the transfer of posts, etc, and naval and military defence were the 14 and 25 February 1901, respectively.[66]

No transfer was made of lighthouses, etc, or quarantine. Indeed, these were merely areas of responsibility within larger colonial departments which continued to operate after federation (State marine departments, departments of health).[67] These are areas of concurrent power and are also within the responsibility of Commonwealth departments (shipping and transport, health).

### CERTAIN POWERS OF GOVERNORS TO VEST IN GOVERNOR-GENERAL

**70.** *In respect of matters which, under this Constitution, pass to the Executive Government of the Commonwealth, all powers and functions which*

---

60   Section 54.
61   Quick and Garran, 713-4.
62   Section 8.
63   Section 28.
64   Section 33.
65   Quick and Garran, 714-6.
66   Moore, *The Constitution of the Commonwealth of Australia* (2nd Ed, 1910) 171.
67   See Wynes, at 133.

*at the establishment of the Commonwealth are vested in the Governor of a Colony, or in the Governor of a Colony with the advice of his Executive Council, or in any authority of a Colony, shall vest in the Governor-General, or in the Governor-General in Council, or in the authority exercising similar powers under the Commonwealth, as the case requires.*[68]

This section, in conjunction with ss 64 and 69, operated to provide for the transfer of executive powers from the governments of the Colonies to the Commonwealth government, in relation to those matters within the exclusive power of the Commonwealth (even though the departments which administered them may not have been transferred to the Commonwealth). They comprised both prerogative[69] as well as statutory powers.

---

68   Quick and Garran, 716-8.
69   For example, the war prerogative, ibid, 717.

# CHAPTER III

# THE JUDICATURE

**71.** *The judicial power of the Commonwealth shall be vested in a Federal Supreme Court, to be called the High Court of Australia, and in such other federal courts as the Parliament creates, and in such other courts as it invests with federal jurisdiction. The High Court shall consist of a Chief Justice, and so many other Justices, not less than two, as the Parliament prescribes.*[1]

This section is one of the most important in the Constitution. It has led to the interpretation (discussed below) in *Alexander's Case* and the *Boilermakers' Case* which affirms the paramount and independent position of the courts in the constitutional scheme. The section is tied to the following section, section 72, which prescribes the tenure of High Court and other federal judges.

## "The judicial power of the Commonwealth"

The classic statement of the judicial power, from which nearly all the decisions have proceeded, is that of Griffith CJ in *Huddart Parker v Moorehead*[2]: "The words 'judicial power' as used in s 71 of the Constitution mean the power which every sovereign must of necessity have to decide controversies between its subjects or between itself and its subjects, whether the rights relate to life, liberty or property. The exercise of this power does not begin until some tribunal which has power to give a binding and authoritative decision (whether subject to appeal or not) is called upon to take action."[3] One must, however, heed the warning issued in *R v Davison*[4] that "many attempts have been made to define judicial power, but it has never been found possible to frame a definition that is at once exclusive and exhaustive."[5]

It would seem, therefore, that the controversy would ordinarily be a dispute between parties. However, there are some instances where there is only one direct party to the proceedings and yet the power could be regarded as being judicial. Such is the case of *R v Davison*[6] where the power given to a bankruptcy registrar under the Commonwealth *Bankruptcy Act* to make a

---

1   Quick and Garran, 719-28. Wynes, 386-407. *Essays*, 71-92. Nicholas, 360-2. Lane, 311-54. Howard, 144-90.

2   (1909) 8 CLR 330.

3   Ibid, at 357. The actual decision in the case was that the power of compulsory discovery given to an administrative official, the Comptroller-General of Customs, to interrogate companies was not an exercise of judicial power: it was comparable with the power given to examining justices to decide whether there was a prima facie case against an accused. As such it was tied to the executive side.

4   (1954) 90 CLR 353.

5   Ibid, at 366.

6   Discussed by Sawer in (1954) 28 ALJ 341.

sequestration order upon a debtor's petition was held to be an exercise of the judicial power of the Commonwealth. The background to this case is of interest. In *Le Mesurier v Connor*[7] it had been decided that s 77 (iii) of the Constitution did not allow a Commonwealth officer to act as a functionary of a State court, and that s 51 (xxxix) did not allow a re-constitution of a State court as an incident of the conferment of federal jurisdiction. Subsequent to this decision, the registrar's office had been separated from the court structure and in *Bond v Bond and Co Limited*[8] the High Court upheld the amending legislation as curing the original defect. *Davison's Case* saw a narrower attack not on the status of the official but upon the nature of the acts performed by him.

The decision of the court was based to some extent on examination of the exercise of curial jurisdiction in such matters by English courts. Dixon CJ and McTiernan J pointed out that voluntary sequestration had for a long time been an appropriate subject of judicial power although they accepted that this would not prevent the legislature from devising a different kind of procedure for determining the legal consequences of such an application.[9] A typical example of the exercise of judicial power where only one party was directly involved was the administration of assets or of a trust by a Court of Chancery.[10] In the present case the thing done was the making of an order characteristic of courts. Kitto J pointed out that the controversy need not be a real one: the potentiality of a dispute existed. Since rights and duties were reciprocal, even a voluntary petition created a notional opposition between the persons whose reciprocal positions were affected thereby.[11] The majority of the court therefore held that the power had been invalidly conferred on the registrar.

*Judicial power is a decision on a question in the light of a pre-existing standard.* One discernible characteristic of the judicial approach to the resolution of disputes is that the disputes are conceived of as being resolved in accordance with antecedent legal principles, whether they be embodied in statute, or derived from the general law. This should be contrasted with another method of resolving disputes, viz, by creating a set of rules which ex hypothesi cannot be antecedent to the resolution of the dispute and which are intended to be the basis of the legal relations of the disputants in future, and which themselves may subsequently be the subject of judicial interpretations. The legislative and administrative functions, involving, as they do, the creation of new rights, are therefore not subject to the requirements of s 71. This analysis affects such hybrid powers as industrial arbitration, which involves the making of awards, the fixing of rates of pay and conditions of work. In *Alexander's Case*[12] it was pointed out by Isaacs and Rich JJ that an industrial dispute was a claim by one of the disputants that existing relations should be altered, and by the other, that the claim should not be

---

7  (1929) 42 CLR 481.

8  (1930) 44 CLR 11.

9  (1954) 90 CLR at 365.

10  Ibid, at 368.

11  Ibid, at 383. Cf, *Re Bellis* [1961] ALR 325. See also *Re Moss* (1969) 3 FedLR 101; *Re Watson* 17 ABC 76; *James v Commissioner of Taxation* (1957) 97 CLR 23.

12  (1918) 25 CLR 434.

conceded. Involved, therefore, was a claim for new rights and its settlement by an industrial award was not an exercise of judicial power.[13]

In a number of cases, the High Court has been called upon to determine questions of two types, converse by nature, yet dependent for their resolution upon the same process of reasoning. In the first type of case, the question is whether there has been conferred upon a court capable by virtue of Chapter III of exercising federal jurisdiction, a power which, when characterized, is found to be not judicial and therefore invalidly conferred. The converse situation is where the High Court must decide whether a power which is found to be judicial has been conferred upon a body (whether it be called a court or not) which is precluded by Chapter III from exercising federal jurisdiction. In both situations, the High Court must decide whether the power is judicial or not. In *Alexander's Case* both questions appear. The court found that the enforcement provisions provided for an exercise of judicial power, and it also found that the body exercising the power was not a court, as its members were not appointed for life in accordance with s 72.

The courts may be influenced by the width of the discretion granted to a body although, of course, in certain areas (e g, the Commonwealth *Matrimonial Causes Act*, the State *Companies Acts*) wide discretions have been created.[14] Generally speaking, the wider the discretion the more likely it is that the power conferred upon the body will be treated as a power to create new rights (i e, as constitutive and not interpretative). A comparison in this context may be made between *Silk Brothers Ltd v The State Electricity Commission of Victoria*,[15] and *Queen Victoria Memorial Hospital v Thornton*.[16] In the former case, a power conferred on tribunals called Fair Rents Boards (constituted by stipendiary magistrates) to determine applications by landlords for recovery of premises from their tenants was held to be judicial. The power of ordering ejectment was similar to that conferred upon courts under summary ejectment Acts. It was a controversy between subject and subject in accordance with definite criteria; it involved an assessment of the respective claims of landlord and tenant; and the decision of the board was binding, and could lead to an order that premises be vacated. However, in the same case, it was considered that the power of fixing fair rents was not an exercise of judicial power. Here the circumstances which the board could take into account were not similar to those to be taken into account in determining an action for recovery of premises. They were indeed based on economic and other discretionary factors and therefore the decision was a decision leading to the creation of new rights, e g, the right of the landlord to the higher rent. In *Queen Victoria Memorial Hospital v Thornton* the power in question was given to an inferior State court exercising federal jurisdiction to decide whether

---

13  Ibid, at 462 et seq. The case turned mainly on the argument that the power to enforce an award was not part of the arbitral power but was indeed ancillary to the judicial power. In rejecting this argument Isaacs and Rich JJ said (at 424): "The arbitral function is ancillary to the legislative function and provides the factum upon which the law operates to create the duty or right. The judicial function is an entirely separate branch and first ascertains whether the alleged right or duty exists in law, and, if it finds it, then proceeds, if necessary, to enforce the law".

14  See also *Mikasa (NSW) Pty Ltd v Festival Stores* (1973) 47 ALJR 14 (Discretionary power of Industrial Court to issue injunction under the *Trade Practices Act* 1965-1971 held to be judicial).

15  (1943) 67 CLR 1.

16  (1953) 87 CLR 144.

an employer has refused to engage in employment a person who under rehabilitation legislation was entitled to preference in employment. It was held that this power was non-judicial, there being no issue of facts submitted to the State court for decision. Its function appeared to be entirely administrative and to differ in no respect from the function of the employer himself in considering an application for employment. In other words the decision was a typically administrative decision with the tribunal reviewing the discretion of the employer to decide whether preference was required by the legislation in the circumstances of the particular case. No antecedent rights were to be ascertained, determined or enforced.[17]

No doubt the distinction between a constitutive and an interpretative procedure might appear to be difficult to draw in particular cases. Judicial decisions often contain a certain creative or discretionary element; on the other hand, decisions made by administrative bodies must be made within limits set by the law (although these limits may be set very wide) and this involves interpretation by those administrative authorities of their legal limits. Indeed many administrative tribunals exercise "quasi-judicial" power in areas affecting the rights of the citizens, but these have been held not to exercise power under Chapter III of the Constitution, although federal courts may be invested with jurisdiction to review the decisions of these tribunals on grounds which are justiciable.[18]

A recent case in which the distinction has been discussed by the High Court is *R v Trade Practices Tribunal and Others ex parte Tasmanian Breweries Pty Ltd*.[19] Section 49 of the *Trade Practices Act* provides that if the Trade Practices Tribunal is satisfied that an agreement of a certain kind (examinable agreement) exists, or a practice (examinable practice) is being engaged in, it shall make a determination recording its findings on the matter and also determine whether the relevant restrictions in the agreement are contrary to the public interest. Section 5 of the Act sets out the various matters to be taken into account in determining whether the agreement is contrary to the public interest. It was held by a majority of the High Court that neither the decision as to the existence of the conditions of the Tribunal's jurisdiction nor the decision that an agreement was contrary to the public interest were judicial. In the words of Kitto J, "the Act requires the tribunal in considering the question of the public interest to make a basic assumption and to take certain matters into consideration but the question upon which it has to pronounce is not as to whether the relevant restriction or practice satisfies an ascertained standard but as to whether it satisfies a description the content of which has no fixity—a description which refers the tribunal ultimately to its own idiosyncratic conceptions and modes of thought".[20]

If the decision involves nothing more than interpretation then it may be judicial. As Lord Green pointed out in *Johnson v Minister of Health*,[21] the interpretative element is usually only one step in reaching a decision. The

---

17   Compare *Steele v Defence Forces Retirement Benefits Board* (1955) 29 ALJR 302, *Farbenfabrieken Bayar Aktiengesellschaft v Bayer Pharma Ltd* (1959) 101 CLR 652, *Cominos v Cominos* (1972) 46 ALJR 593.

18   See *Report of the Commonwealth Administrative Review Committee* (1971) Ch 4.

19   (1970) 44 ALJR 126.

20   Ibid, at 129-130. Compare with this case *Cominos v Cominos* (1972) 46 ALJR 593 (discretions under the *Matrimonial Causes Act* 1959-1966 judicial).

21   (1947) 2 All ER 395 at 397 et seq.

relative places occupied in the process of reaching a decision by interpretation and application of legal rules on the one hand and the application of discretionary "policy" on the other hand are likely to change. The greater the element of discretion and the wider that discretion, the more likely it is that a court will say the decision is non-judicial.

Finally, it may be pointed out that many functions may be committed to a court which are not exclusively judicial, that is to say which, considered independently, might belong to an administrator. But that is because they are not independent functions but form incidents of strictly judicial processes or powers.[22] In this respect the incidental power, s 51 (xxxix) allows the conferment of functions incidental to the exercise of judicial power.[23]

*The element of conclusiveness.* At the outset it must be noted that "final" or "binding and authoritative" have occasionally been substituted for the word "conclusive" in this context. A decision may be an interpretative decision, it may be given by a person or tribunal in accordance with pre-existing standards and yet it may lack the finality that attaches to a judicial decision. It may be in effect a mere administrative determination which cannot be enforced by the person or tribunal without a curial decision ordering its execution or enforcement. Or to put it in another way it may be a decision which may be reopened in collateral proceedings, i e, proceedings to enforce the decision or in some other way.

In two cases *British Imperial Oil Company Ltd v Federal Commissioner of Taxation* (the *BIO Case*)[24] and *Shell Company of Australia Ltd v Federal Commissioner of Taxation* (the *Shell Case*)[25] the requirement of conclusiveness was subjected to a very refined analysis. In both cases the plaintiff company was a large oil company challenging assessment of income tax under the *Income Tax Assessment Act.* In the *BIO Case* provisions conferring power on an income tax tribunal were challenged on the ground that they constituted an invalid conferment of judicial power on that body. The body in question was the Taxation Board of Appeal which was given power to review decisions of the income tax commissioner. A taxpayer could request that his case (in so far as the questions raised were not questions of law only) be referred to the High Court, a Supreme Court or the board. The board could make such orders as it thought fit and these were to be final and conclusive on matters of fact. The board was obliged to state a case for the opinion of the High Court (exercising original jurisdiction) on any question, which in the opinion of the board, was a question of law. An appeal could also be taken to the High Court in its appellate jurisdiction from any order of the board, except in relation to one involving a question of fact.

The view of the High Court was that this was a conferment of portion of the judicial power of the Commonwealth on the Taxation Board of Appeal. The board had power to determine questions of law and was associated in terms of the appeal structure with the Supreme Court and the High Court

---

22   In *R v Federal Court of Bankruptcy ex parte Loewenstein* (1938) 59 CLR 556, it was held that the power given to the Bankruptcy Court to prosecute a bankrupt was ancillary to the judicial function. Cf, *Fraser Henleins Pty Ltd v Cody* (1945) 70 CLR 100, *Palling v Corfield* (1971) 45 ALJR 31; [1971] ALR 275.

23   See above p 190.

24   (1925) 35 CLR 422.

25   (1926) 38 CLR 153 (High Court); (1930) 44 CLR 530 (Privy Council).

exercising original jurisdiction. In so far as its members were appointed for a term of years, it was invalidly exercising judicial power.

The legislation was soon altered by the Commonwealth in order to remedy the constitutional defects found by the High Court to exist. The three essential changes were:

(1) The decisions of the Board (which was renamed a Board of *Review*) in reviewing a determination were deemed to be those of the Commissioner (ie, they were to take the place of the commissioner's decision);

(2) The determination of the question whether an issue was a question of law was to be made by the court and not by the board.

(3) The decisions of the board on questions of fact were expressly stipulated not to be final.

The new legislation was challenged before the High Court from which an appeal was taken to the Privy Council. Both courts held that the changes had cured the defects found to exist in the early legislation in the *BIO Case*. The board was now a review tribunal reassessing a taxpayer's return. There were two possible alternatives open to the taxpayer who wanted a commissioner's decision to be reviewed. He could have an administrative reassessment by the board, the decision of which was not conclusive; or he could have the assessment decided or reviewed on a legal point by the High Court in its original jurisdiction. If having chosen the board, he then wished to challenge its determination he could appeal to the High Court in its *original jurisdiction*. This re-assessment would be limited to questions which, in the view of the High Court, were questions of law. It will complete the picture to add that under s 73 of the Constitution an appeal might be taken to the High Court in its appellate jurisdiction from a decision of the High Court in original jurisdiction in such matters.

Lord Sankey speaking for the Judicial Committee said that despite the claim of the Company that the new board was the old board in camouflage, there were real differences. He went on to observe that there were tribunals with many of the trappings of a court which nevertheless were not courts in the strict sense of exercising judicial power. "(1) A tribunal is not necessarily a court in the strict sense because it gives a final decision; (2) nor because it hears witnesses on oath; (3) nor because two or more contending parties appear before it between whom it has to decide; (4) nor because it gives decisions which affect the rights of subjects; (5) nor because there is an appeal to the court; (6) nor because it is a body to which a matter is referred by another body."[26] Of course this comment is a negative one and has the vice of playing down the importance of "trappings" which often surround the judicial decisions. There is no doubt that the different decisions reached in relation to the Board of Review as compared with the Board of Appeal depended to a large extent on the setting of the two bodies within the appeal structure. As we have seen in *Davison's case*, the traditional association of voluntary sequestration petitions with the judicial process was an important factor in the decision in that case. On the other hand, the courts have traditionally distinguished between judicial and quasi-judicial power (which

---

26  [1931] AC at 297. See also *Commonwealth v Melbourne Harbour Trust Commissioners* (1922) 31 CLR 1 at 12: "A law does not usurp judicial power because it regulates the method or burden of proving facts". *R v McFarlane ex parte O'Flanagan and O'Kelly* (1923) 32 CLR 518 at 569 (Higgins J).

has some of the trappings of judicial power). The latter falls outside the requirements of s 71.[27]

Another question which has arisen is whether a power to make a conclusive decision on a question of *fact* is judicial. In the *Shell Case* Isaacs J considered that such a power was not exclusively judicial.[28] The question received detailed examination in the *Rola Case*.[29]

In 1941 the diminution of the male work force due to the war had led to the employment of women in many roles hitherto performed by men. The Commonwealth passed a *Women's Employment Act* in 1942 and this Act, together with statutory rules made under it, made provision for the establishment of a Women's Employment Board to decide whether specific work envisaged was work which could be performed by women. An employer who proposed to employ females was required to make an application to the board for approval of the proposal. The board was given power to decide whether the nature of the employment fell within a certain category, and if so, whether females could be employed in the work. It was also provided that the board's decision should be binding on the employer specified in the decision. Committees of reference were also established to determine whether, in relation to any decision of the board females were employed by an employer in work specified in that decision. A determination made by a committee was declared to be binding both on the employer and females specified in that determination.

The regulation establishing this power was challenged on the ground that it was an invalid conferment of judicial power on a tribunal which was not constituted in accordance with s 72 of the Constitution. It was argued that a committee was given power to determine the precise questions which might in other proceedings have to be determined by the court (e g, in a common law action for wages due) and therefore that the committee was being substituted for the court in the exercise of judicial power. The majority of the High Court (Latham CJ, McTiernan and Starke JJ) held that the function was not a judicial one. Latham CJ made the following points:[30]

(1) The committee had no power to determine jurisdictional facts;

(2) The decision of the committee was part of the decision of the board and they formed a juristic unit. Decisions on a question of fact by the committee bound parties just as the awards of the board bound the parties.

(3) However, it was not the binding quality of the determination which was conclusive as to the presence of judicial power; it was whether or not the decision created an instant liability.

(4) The determination of the committee bound as a matter of evidence, but *of itself* created no instant liability.

Starke J considered that the power given to the committee was essentially one of identification of fact rather than of interpretation. "No one doubts that

---

27    See *Le Mesurier v Connor* 42 CLR 481 at 514-5 (Isaacs J). In *R v Turner ex parte Marine Board of Hobart* (1927) 39 CLR 411, it was held that a Marine Court of Enquiry was not a court within Chapter III of the Constitution. Its functions, according to Isaacs J, were not necessarily judicial and were not infrequently entrusted to quasi-administrative bodies as well as to political bodies (441-442). In *Lockwood v Commonwealth* (1954) 90 CLR 177, the power of enquiry exercised by a Royal Commission was held to fall outside Chapter III.

28    (1926) 38 CLR at 176.

29    *Rola Co (Australia) Pty Ltd v Commonwealth* (1944) 69 CLR 185.

30    Ibid, at 193 et seq.

ascertainment or determination of facts is part of the judicial process, but that function does not belong exclusively to the judicial power."[31] McTiernan J agreed with the judgment of Latham CJ and added that in his opinion the determination was in the nature of an administrative award.[32]

The dissenting judges, Rich and Williams JJ, considered that the power was judicial.[33] They started with the proposition that interpretation and enforcement added up to an exercise of judicial power. The decision of the board created a binding obligation. The committee of reference interpreted the rights so created not as part of the decision of the board but as a step in the enforcement of an existing obligation. The dissenting judges also considered that if the controversy was entirely one of fact, the committee of reference's decision meant that, even if a formal judgment of a court was needed to establish liability, there was nothing left for the court to decide as the decision had already been resolved by the committee's determination.[34]

On the basis of the authorities one may conclude that the power to make conclusive determinations of fact is not ipso facto an exercise of judicial power. A determination of such a nature may occur ancillary to the process of making an administrative decision.[35] It is only when the power of making decisions on questions of law is conclusive that the judicial element will be found to exist, or as Latham CJ put it in the Rola Case, it is only where an instant liability is created that the power will be judicial. This is not to deny that in many cases a judicial determination may involve mixed questions of fact and law.

The word "conclusive" does not necessarily mean final in the sense that no appeal is possible. It means a decision which cannot be reopened with the purpose of trying the issues again in collateral or consequential proceedings. If a tribunal has power to enforce its own decisions by some process of execution, then its decisions must almost inevitably be conclusive as to fact and law and its power would be regarded as judicial.[36] However, the power of imposing penalties or taking some other action in invitos the citizen is not necessarily the exercise of judicial power. Administrators or administrative tribunals may validly exercise such powers as in the case of powers conferred on the Income Tax commissioner and Comptroller-General of Customs.[37]

---

31 Ibid, at 211.
32 Ibid, at 213.
33 Ibid, at 202 et seq (Rich J), 213 et seq (Williams J).
34 See judgment of Williams J at 217. See also Collins v Sobb (1962) 4 FLR 124.
35 See Federal Commissioner of Taxation v Munro (1926) 38 CLR 153 at 176 per Isaacs J.
36 The power of a House of the federal Parliament to imprison for contempt has been held to lie outside the judicature provisions: R v Richards ex parte Fitzpatrick and Brown (1955) 92 CLR 157. Courts-martial, too, have also been held to lie outside these provisions: R v Cox ex parte Smith (1945) 71 CLR 1.
37 Re Dymond (1958) 101 CLR 11, Deputy Commissioner of Taxation v Hankin (1958) 100 CLR 566. See also Roche v Kronheimer (1921) 29 CLR 329 at 337 (power of a minister to vest property in the public trustee under trading with the enemy legislation non-judicial). O'Keefe v Calwell (1949) 77 CLR 261 (power given to minister to deport a prohibited immigrant non-judicial). R v White ex parte Byrnes (1964) 37 ALJR 297; [1964] ALR 365 (power given to public service bodies to discipline members of the public service non-judicial). R v Trade Practices Tribunal (1970) 44 ALJR 126; [1970] ALR 449 (power of tribunal to issue order restraining the enforcement of an
continues

*Combination of Judicial Powers and Non-judicial Powers.* After the decision in *Alexander's Case* in which it was held that the power of enforcing decisions of the Arbitration Court could not be vested in that body as its members were not appointed for life in accordance with s 72,[38] the *Conciliation and Arbitration Act* was amended to provide for life appointment of its members. Thereafter, the court proceeded on the basis that it could not only make awards but it could also give effect to those awards, that is to say, it combined the exercise of judicial power with quasi-legislative power. However in *Attorney General of the Commonwealth v The Queen* (the *Boilermaker's Case*)[39] it was held that a body established with the principal purpose of performing non-judicial functions could not validly have judicial powers conferred upon it even though it might be constituted on the same basis as that of a federal court. Judicial power could not be combined with other types of powers. The consequence of this was that the judicial power conferred on the arbitration court to enforce awards and to punish for contempt was invalid. It was recognised, however, that some administrative power could be conferred so long as it was merely incidental to the exercise of the judicial power. Of course the power of enforcement was pre-eminently judicial. Therefore, its combination with the arbitral powers was not within the constitutional competence of the federal Parliament. It was pointed out that "in a federal form of government a part is necessarily assigned to the judicature which places it in a position unknown in a unitary system or under a flexible constitution where Parliament is supreme .... The conception of independent governments existing in the one area and exercising powers in different fields of action carefully defined by law could not be carried into practical effect unless the ultimate responsibility of deciding upon the limits of respective powers of the governments were placed in the federal judicature."[40] The effect of s 71 was, therefore, to demarcate the judicial power as an independent power which could not be tied to other powers. It was impossible to escape the conviction that "Chapter III does not allow the exercise of a jurisdiction which of its very nature belongs to the judicial power of the Commonwealth by a body established for purposes foreign to the judicial power, notwithstanding that it is organized as a court and in a manner which might otherwise satisfy ss 71 and 72, and that Chapter III does not allow a combination with judicial power of functions which are not incidental to its exercise but are foreign to it."[41]

---

37  *continued*

examinable agreement contrary to the public interest non-judicial). For an article questioning some of the powers of the minister of customs under the *Customs Act* 1901-1971 see Cooper, "Settlement of Cases by the Minister for Customs and Excise—an Exercise of the Judicial Power" (1969) 43 ALJ 133.

38  Reference may also be made to a case decided a few years previously: *New South Wales v Commonwealth*, 20 CLR 54, where the High Court held that the Interstate Commission established under s 101 (the members of which were not appointed for life) could not exercise judicial power.

39  (1957) 95 CLR 529 (Privy Council); (1956) 94 CLR 254 (High Court).

40  94 CLR at 267-8.

41  Ibid, at 296. For a discussion of the case see Thomson, "The Separation of Powers Doctrine in the Commonwealth Constitution" (1958) 2 Sydney Law Review 480. Sawer, "The Separation of Powers in Australian Federalism" (1961) 35 ALJ 177. See also Finnis, "Separation of Powers in the Australian Constitution" (1968) 3 Adelaide LR 159.

Pursuant to this decision, the federal Parliament reorganised the arbitration system. The reorganisation involved the establishment of an *Arbitration Commission* to exercise the arbitral powers of the old Arbitration Court and a new *Industrial Court* to exercise the judicial powers of the old court. In *Seamen's Union v Matthews*[42] it was held that the Industrial Court was a federal court validly established under Chapter III and capable of exercising the judicial power of the Commonwealth.

The allocation of powers (depending on their characterization as judicial or non-judicial) to one or other of these bodies was attacked in subsequent cases. In *R v Spicer ex parte Builders Labourers Federation*[43] the power conferred on the Industrial Court to disallow rules of a trade union on the basis that they were inter alia tyrannical or oppressive to members was held to be invalid. The ratio of this decision was that the grounds on which the court might decide that rules were oppressive were indeterminate, and therefore, that its decision was more in the nature of a restructuring of legal relationships rather than an interpretative decision. Pursuant to this case the Commonwealth Parliament amended the legislation to make provision for the grounds on which the power of this disallowance should be exercised although changes made were more procedural than substantive. The new amendments were upheld in the case of *R v Commonwealth Industrial Court ex parte Amalgamated Engineering Union.*[44] Fullagar J pointed out that the power which was interpreted in the *Builders Labourers Case* was not a power of determination but a general supervisory power which might be exercised by the Industrial Court on its own motion and according to a discretion based on purely industrial or administrative considerations. However, under the new section the court was not entitled to entertain an application of its own motion—it could only act once an application was made to it by a member of an organisation. The fundamental difference in Fullagar J's opinion, between the old provision and the new one, could be expressed by saying that "under the old section the court by its own act—the act of disallowance—nullified the rule whereas under the new section it determined judicially whether the rule was antecedently nullified by virtue of the provision."[45]

The decision suggests that the High Court will not subject Commonwealth legislation conferring judicial power on the Industrial Court to an excessively exacting scrutiny. If the intention of the legislature is to lay down a judicial procedure for the court to observe, and it has sufficiently prescribed steps which the court has to follow, then the conferring of power will not be struck down merely because the considerations which the Industrial Court must take into account are closely related to social policy.[46]

---

42  (1956) 96 CLR 529.
43  (1957) 100 CLR 277.
44  (1960) 103 CLR 368; [1961] ALR 104.
45  103 CLR at 376-7; [1961] ALR at 107-8.
46  See also *Re McSween* (1956) 100 CLR 273 (power to make order directing person to perform rules of organization registered under the Act judicial). *Leary v Australian Builders Labourers Federation* (1961) 2 FLR 342 (power to inquire into alleged irregularities in the election of officers of an organization judicial). As to attacks on the power of the commission, see *R v Gough ex parte Meat and Allied Trades Federation of Australia* (1970) 44 ALJR 48, [1970] ALR 343 (power to order reinstatement in employment judicial and therefore outside the powers of the commission). *R v Austin ex parte Farmers & Graziers Association* (1964) 112 CLR 619, [1965] ALR 599
*continues*

231

"shall be vested in a Federal Supreme Court, to be called the High Court of Australia ... The High Court shall consist of a Chief Justice, and so many other Justices, not less than two, as the President prescribes"

The judicial power vested in the High Court may be either original or appellate.[47] The structure and functions of the High Court are regulated by the *Judiciary Act* 1903-1969 and the *High Court Procedure Act* 1903-1966 (and rules made under those acts). The High Court is a superior court of record and consists of a Chief Justice and six other justices.[48] It is provided that the principal seat of the High Court will be at the Seat of Government on a date fixed by proclamation. Sydney is the present seat by appointment of the Governor-General.[49] Various provisions of the *Judiciary Act* regulate the composition of the court for different types of cases. The minimum composition of a full court is two justices.[50] Appeals from a justice of the High Court exercising original jurisdiction and also from a State court are heard by a full High Court.[51] It is provided that in the case of appeals from a Supreme Court of a State the full High Court shall consist of not less than three judges.[52] In a case where a matter concerns the constitutional powers of the Commonwealth a decision shall not be given unless at least three judges concur in the decision.[53]

In the original jurisdiction of the High Court trials of suits are heard by a judge without a jury,[54] while trials of indictable offences against the laws of the Commonwealth are heard by a Justice with a jury.[55] The content of the original and appellate jurisdiction of the High Court will be discussed later.

"and in such other federal courts as the Parliament creates, and in such other courts as it invests with federal jurisdiction"

It is provided in s 73 that the appellate jurisdiction of the High Court extends to appeals from other federal courts. At the present time there are two federal courts in existence; the Commonwealth Industrial Court and the Commonwealth Bankruptcy Court. It is to be noted that Territory courts are not federal courts, and therefore the members of these courts do not have to be

---

46   *continued*
(power to make orders for the payment of wages due under an award judicial). See also Merralls, "Judicial Power Since the Boilermakers' Case: Statutory Discretion and the Quest for Legal Standards" (1959) 32 ALJ 283, 303. On the question whether federal judges may also occupy non-judicial posts see Sawer 35 ALJ 177 at 180-3.

47   See *R v Court of Conciliation and Arbitration ex parte Whybrow* 11 CLR 1 at 41 (O'Connor J).

48   *Judiciary Act* 1903-1969, s 4.

49   Judiciary Act s 10.

50   *Judiciary Act*, s 19. In practice at least three judges constitute a full court.

51   *Judiciary Act*, s 20.

52   *Judiciary Act*, s 21.

53   *Judiciary Act*, s 23 (1). In a case where there is an equal division of opinion see s 23 (2). See also *Tasmania v Victoria* (1935) 52 CLR 157. *State of Western Australia v Hammersley Iron Pty Ltd (No 2)* (1969) 43 ALJR 399; [1970] ALR 161.

54   *High Court Procedure Act* 1903-1966, s 12.

55   *High Court Procedure Act*, s 15 (a).

appointed in accordance with the provisions of Chapter III of the Constitution.[56]

Under s 77 (iii) of the Constitution, the federal Parliament has power to invest any court of the State with federal jurisdiction. Under s 39 of the *Judiciary Act* the various State courts have been invested with federal jurisdiction in certain matters subject to conditions and restrictions set out in that section. There are also a great number of federal Acts which invest State courts with federal jurisdiction in other matters.[57]

JUDGES' APPOINTMENT, TENURE AND REMUNERATION

**72.** *The Justices of the High Court and of the other courts created by the Parliament—*

    (i) *Shall be appointed by the Governor-General in Council:*

    (ii) *Shall not be removed except by the Governor-General in Council, on an address from both Houses of the Parliament in the same session, praying for such removal on the ground of proved misbehaviour or incapacity:*

    (iii) *Shall receive such remuneration as the Parliament may fix; but the remuneration shall not be diminished during their continuance in office.*[58]

### (i) "Shall be appointed by the Governor-General in Council"

The appointment of federal judges is a Cabinet matter which is formally ratified by the executive council. It is the practice of the Attorney General to recommend to cabinet persons for appointment, though it is the Cabinet which will make the final decision.[59] Appointment of federal judges is for a permanent term. The salary, remuneration and conditions of office of federal judges are set out in the *Judiciary Act.*[60]

### (ii) "Shall not be removed except by the Governor-General in Council, on an address from both Houses of the Parliament in the same session, praying for such removal on the ground of proved misbehaviour or incapacity"

In *Alexander's Case*[61] it was held by a majority of the High Court that judges of federal courts could not be appointed for any term less than life, although it was also accepted that the Constitution did provide for the exercise of federal jurisdiction by judges and magistrates of state courts (holding a tenure less than life) invested pursuant to the provisions of the *Judiciary Act.* One of the arguments against a mandatory life tenure for federal judges in *Alexander's Case* proceeded this way. If the justices of the (old) Arbitration Court were required to have life tenure in order to exercise the judicial power of the Commonwealth, then why should not this requirement apply to the members of State Supreme Courts invested with federal jurisdiction? Such judges, of course, are appointed until a fixed age of retirement. The patent fault in such an argument was the failure to distinguish between the creation of a federal judiciary, and the exercise of federal jurisdiction by courts whose constitution (on the principle of *Le Mesurier v Connor*) could not be affected by federal legislation.

---

56   *Spratt v Hermes* (1965) 114 CLR 226; [1966] ALR 597.
57   See discussion under s 77.
58   Quick & Garran, 728-34. Wynes, 386-95. Howard, 144-54.
59   See *Current Affairs Bulletin,* No 3, 1966.
60   Parts II and VIII.
61   (1918) 25 CLR 434.

In *Alexander's Case* it was held that the appointment of the President of the Arbitration Court for a period of seven years was invalid as being contrary to s 72 (read with s 71).[62] This interpretation means that an Act such as a judges retirement Act (which operates in all of the state legal systems) cannot constitutionally operate in the federal systems.

It was also argued in *Alexander's Case* that this prescription of life tenure for all federal judges caused some inconvenience, for example, if magistrates were to be given life tenure. It is usual for many public service conditions to be applied, at least in the State sphere, to the appointment of magistrates and therefore a tenure which was not determined in any way by a retirement age would, it was said, be excessive. The High Court adopted the view that the inferior courts of the State could be utilised under the provisions allowing federal jurisdiction to be conferred on such courts and that therefore the argument from inconvenience could not be sustained. In any case the "Constitution does not look to the creation of courts which, though subordinate to this court, are of such calibre as to be officered by judges whose tenure is of little importance".[63] Isaacs and Rich JJ pointed out that the independence of a tribunal would be seriously weakened if the Commonwealth Parliament could fix anything less than a life tenure.[64] It must also be noted that magistrates and judges of the courts of the territories, e g, the Northern Territory and the Australian Capital Territory, are not Federal Judges and, therefore, the constitutional requirements of s 72 do not apply to them. (But this does not prevent the government appointing persons to be judges of both the Industrial Court (a federal court) and a Territorial Supreme Court.)

*Method of Removal.* The removal procedure by address from Houses of Parliament is the usual form of removal provided for in the Constitution Acts of the States and has been followed on the federal level.

The question arises as to whether the High Court, if a removal of a judge were challenged before it, would require that a certain burden of proof be satisfied before the judge could be removed, or whether the requirement of proof is a matter which is within the sole jurisdiction of the Houses of Parliament and the Governor-General in Council; in other words, whether the only requirement is that the behaviour must clearly be proved to the satisfaction of the Houses of Parliament and the Governor-General in Council. It is more likely that this latter interpretation would be adopted, and that, apart from the case of a clearly politically motivated removal where there was no evidence of misbehaviour or incapacity, the High Court would not interfere with a proposed removal which had complied with the procedure laid down in s 72.

**(iii) "Shall receive such remuneration as the Parliament may fix; but the remuneration shall not be diminished during their continuance in office"**

The determination of federal judges' salaries is a matter for federal Parliament. The present salary for the Chief Justice of the High Court is

---

62    Higgins J who, together with Gavan Duffy J, dissented, distinguished a tenure for years from a tenure at will: the first was compatible, the second incompatible with s 72: 25 CLR at 474. See also the *Shell Case* 44 CLR 530 at 545, 546.

63    25 CLR at 469, per Isaacs and Rich JJ.

64    Ibid, at 469-470.

$39,000 and for other justices of the High Court $35,300.[65] The requirement that the remuneration of judges should not be reduced during their tenure of office is designed to prevent any parliamentary or executive attempt to reduce salaries in order to undermine judicial independence. This does not prevent salaries from being subjected to higher taxation increases in accordance with the general increases in taxation affecting the community as a whole.

APPELLATE JURISDICTION OF HIGH COURT

73. *The High Court shall have jurisdiction, with such exceptions and subject to such regulations as the Parliament prescribes, to hear and determine appeals from all judgments, decrees, orders, and sentences—*

    (i) *Of any Justice or Justices exercising the original jurisdiction of the High Court:*

    (ii) *Of any other federal court, or court exercising federal jurisdiction; or of the Supreme Court of any State, or of any other court of any State from which at the establishment of the Commonwealth an appeal lies to the Queen in Council:*

    (iii) *Of the Inter-State Commission, but as to questions of law only:*
*and the judgment of the High Court in all such cases shall be final and conclusive.*

*But no exception or regulation prescribed by the Parliament shall prevent the High Court from hearing and determining any appeal from the Supreme Court of a State in any matter in which at the establishment of the Commonwealth an appeal lies from such Supreme Court to the Queen in Council.*

*Until the Parliament otherwise provides, the conditions of and restrictions on appeals to the Queen in Council from the Supreme Courts of the several States shall be applicable to appeals from them to the High Court.*[66]

**"The High Court shall have jurisdiction, with such exceptions and subject to such regulations as the Parliament prescribes, to hear and determine appeals ... But no exception or regulation prescribed by the Parliament shall prevent the High Court from hearing and determining any appeal from the Supreme Court of a State in any matter in which at the establishment of the Commonwealth an appeal lies from such Supreme Court to the Queen in Council"**

This section of the Constitution confers appellate jurisdiction on the High Court from specified types of curial decisions ("judgments, decrees, orders and sentences") (a) of the High Court in its original jurisdiction, (b) of federal courts, (c) of courts exercising federal jurisdiction, (d) of State Supreme Courts, (e) and of the Inter-State Commission, subject to regulations and exceptions prescribed by the Parliament.

At the outset it must be determined whether Parliament may except from the appellate jurisdiction of the High Court whole classes of matters (e g, matters arising under State legislation), or is limited to the prescription of exceptions which depend on some feature of the judgment appealed from (e g, that it is below a prescribed monetary amount).

The former view is supported by a dictum of Isaacs J in the *Tramways*

---

65  *Judiciary Act*, s 47 as amended by the *Remuneration and Allowances Act 1973*, schedule 3. Added to the salary is an allowance of $2250 for the Chief Justice and $1750 for the other justices.
66  Quick & Garran, 734-47. Wynes, 471-85. Nicholas, 362-7. Howard, 199-204. Lane, 405-18.

*Case.*[67] More recently the question has been discussed in *Collins v Charles Marshall Pty Ltd*[68] and *Cockle v Isaksen.*[69] In the former case the majority opinion was that "it would be surprising if [the section] extended to excluding altogether one of the heads specifically mentioned by s 73",[70] thus suggesting that at least one of these broad divisions could not be excluded. However, Taylor J in the same case tended to favour the view that the exceptions must be dependent on some characteristic of the judgment appealed from, that is, they must be concerned with the inherent character of the judgment (e g, the fact that the order was interlocutory or the amount involved was insubstantial).[71] In *Cockle v Isaksen* the High Court was concerned with the validity of s 113 of the *Conciliation and Arbitration Act* which gave to the Commonwealth Industrial Court jurisdiction to hear and determine appeals from magistrates' courts of the States in matters involving offences against the Act, but forbade further appeal from the Industrial Court to the High Court. It was held that this was a valid exercise of the legislative power of the Commonwealth providing exceptions to the appellate jurisdiction of the High Court conferred by s 73. What the Parliament was doing was to except from the appellate jurisdiction of the High Court judgments of an inferior Commonwealth Court to which an appeal had already been taken from State courts. This of course was not a case where a general category of s 73 was excepted (i e, all appeals from the Industrial Court) but merely part of the jurisdiction or class of subject matter dealt with by the Industrial Court.[72]

It appears from the *Privy Council (Limitation of Appeals) Act*[73] which arises under a different section of the Constitution, viz, s 74, that the Commonwealth has acted on the view that under that section certain classes (e g, matters of federal jurisdiction) may be excepted from the appellate jurisdiction of the Privy Council. The wording in s 74 is somewhat different; it allows the Parliament to make laws "limiting the matters in which such leave may be sought" while under s 73 an appellate jurisdiction is conferred on the High Court "subject to such exceptions or regulations Parliament may determine". Nevertheless, there is a similarity between the sections which would enable one to express the opinion that provided all judgments of a particular court were not excepted, but only certain types of matters dealt with by such courts, then such an exception would be regarded as being within the power conferred by s 73.

It is to be noted, however, that the exceptions cannot prevent the High Court from determining appeals from State Supreme Courts in matters in which at the establishment of the Commonwealth an appeal lay to the Privy Council. Therefore these matters are beyond statutory exception.

The general proposition, therefore, is supportable that "it is enough to say that the power does not extend to a wholesale abolition of all the fields. It is equally clear that the power is not limited to exceptions based upon the usual criteria as to an amount, nature of judgment, and the like. In terms,

---

67   (1914) 18 CLR 54 at 76.
68   (1955) 92 CLR 529.
69   (1958) 99 CLR 155.
70   92 CLR at 544.
71   Ibid, at 588.
72   See also *R v Murray and Cormie ex parte the Commonwealth* (1916) 22 CLR 437. *Federated Enginedrivers and Firemen's Association v CSR Ltd* (1916) 22 CLR 103.
73   No 36 of 1968.

[the exception clause in] s 73 would appear to be unlimited but ... this interpretation does not accord with commonsense and the limitations (if any) must be sought in general principles."[74] Conversely, it has been decided that apart from legislation relating to appeals to the High Court from Territory courts which come under s 122,[75] the Parliament cannot extend the appellate jurisdiction of the High Court beyond the terms of s 73.[76]

*Regulation of Appeals.* The Commonwealth Parliament has provided in s 35 of the *Judiciary Act* for the regulation of appeals from the Supreme Courts of the States to the High Court. Appeals as of right may be taken where the matter in issue involves three thousand dollars or property or a civil right of similar amount is involved. There is also an appeal as of right in certain cases dealing with questions of status, e g, bankruptcy (although in matters of divorce an appeal may be taken to the High Court only by special leave). Where, however, the judgment is an interlocutory one (e g, a decision of full Supreme Court of a State remitting back a case to original jurisdiction for further trial) an appeal may be brought only by leave of the High Court.[77] In other cases an appeal lies by *special leave* of the High Court. In *Re Eather v R*[78] the practice of the court was stated as follows. "As we interpret s 35 (1) (b) of the *Judiciary Act* the court has an unfettered discretion to grant or refuse special leave in every case, but we think the term special leave connotes the necessity for making a *prima facie* case showing special circumstances." In *Ross v R*[79] it was said that the High Court was more liberal than the Privy Council (acting under the prerogative) in granting special leave.

### "from all judgments, decrees, orders, and sentences"

Appeals can only be taken to the High Court from courts of the States in matters where the judicial power is involved[80] and which have reached finality.[81] A matter which has not reached finality is not covered by the four types of curial processes mentioned in s 73.

It may also be pointed out that a number of federal Acts allow appeals to the High Court from a number of Commonwealth statutory bodies such as the Taxation Board of Review. However the jurisdiction of the High Court in such cases is original jurisdiction derived from s 75 of the Constitution.[82]

---

74  *Legislative, Executive and Judicial Powers in Australia,* 474.
75  *Capital TV and Appliances Pty Ltd v Falconer* (1971) 45 ALJR 186; [1971] ALR 385. See Comans, "Federal and Territorial Courts" (1971) 4 FedLR 218.
76  *BIO Case* (1925) 35 CLR 422 at 437 (Isaacs J), *Federal Commissioner of Taxation v Munro* (1926) 38 CLR 153 at 174 (Isaacs J). *Consolidated Press Ltd v Australian Journalists' Association* (1947) 73 CLR 549.
77  See *Electricity Commission of New South Wales v Lapthorne* (1971) 45 ALJR 229.
78  (1915) 20 CLR 147.
79  (1922) 30 CLR 246.
80  *Jacka v Lewis* (1944) 68 CLR 455.
81  See *Commonwealth v Mullane* (1961) 106 CLR 166; [1962] ALR 67. *Minister of Works (WA) v Civil and Civic Ltd* (1967) 116 CLR 273; [1967] ALR 514. *Saffron v R* (1953) 88 CLR 523. Cf, *Incorporated Law Institute v Meagher* (1909) 9 CLR 655. *Smith v Mann* (1932) 47 CLR 426. *Commonwealth v Limerick Steamship Co* (1924) 35 CLR 69. *Edie Creek Ltd v Symes* (1929) 43 CLR 53. *Parkin v James* (1905) 2 CLR 315.
82  *R v Commonwealth Court of Conciliation and Arbitration ex parte Whybrow* (1910) 11 CLR 1 at 21-2 (Griffith CJ).

Appeals do not lie directly from a general verdict of a jury or a judgment of a court founded on that verdict although they do lie from a decision of the Supreme Court of a State ordering a new trial.[83] The reason is that the judge and jury below who saw the witnesses and heard the cross-examination are the best judges of the weight of evidence. In the absence of any misdirection, the court will not interfere to set aside a verdict or grant a new trial on the ground that the verdict was against the weight of evidence, unless the verdict was one which no reasonable man could have found. Lord Halsbury put it this way in *Metropolitan Railway Co v Wright*:[84] "If reasonable men might find a verdict which has been found, I think no court has jurisdiction to disturb such a decision of fact which the law has confided to juries, not to judges."[85]

### "Of any Justice or Justices exercising the original jurisdiction of the High Court"

Under s 34 of the *Judiciary Act* it is expressly provided that the High Court, except as provided in that Act, has jurisdiction to hear and determine appeals from all judgments whatsoever of any justice or justices exercising the original jurisdiction of the High Court, whether in court or in chambers. The exception specified in the Act is that an appeal does not lie with respect to decisions on costs, which are at the discretion of the court, except by leave of a justice. Other acts of Parliament also create exceptions.[86] In criminal trials coming before the High Court, appeal is only by special leave of the High Court, apart from the cases of error apparent on the face of the record or by way of case stated.[87]

### "Of any other federal court"

The Commonwealth Parliament has legislated in the *Conciliation and Arbitration Act* and the *Bankruptcy Act* for the regulation of appeals from the Industrial Court[88] and the Bankruptcy Court[89] to the High Court. It has already been mentioned that the Territorial Courts are not treated as federal courts. Therefore, appeals from these courts to the High Court do not come under s 73.[90]

### "or court exercising federal jurisdiction"

The *Judiciary Act*, s 39 (2), invests State courts with federal jurisdiction in all matters in which the High Court has original jurisdiction or in which

---

83    See *Musgrove v McDonald* (1905) 3 CLR 132. *R v Snow* (1915) 20 CLR 315. *Commonwealth v Brisbane Milling Co* (1916) 21 CLR 559. *McDonald and East v McGregor* (1936) 56 CLR 50. Cf, *Buchanan v Byrnes* (1906) 3 CLR 704. In *Brisbane Shipwrights Provident Union v Heggie* (1906) 3 CLR 686 it was held that an appeal would lie to the High Court from the judgment of the State Supreme Court founded on a special verdict of a jury but the verdict itself could not be impeached.
84    (1886) 11 App Cas 152.
85    Ibid, at 156.
86    For example the *Income Tax Assessment Act*. See *Watson v Federal Commissioner of Taxation* (1953) 87 CLR 353.
87    See *Judiciary Act*, ss 76, 77.
88    See *Cockle v Isaksen* (1957) 99 CLR 155. See also discussion of s 77.
89    See *House v R* (1936) 55 CLR 499.
90    See *Mitchell v Barker* (1918) 24 CLR 365. *Porter v R ex parte Yee* (1926) 37 CLR 432.

original jurisdiction may be conferred upon it. It is proposed at a later stage to discuss in greater detail provisions of the *Judiciary Act* which operate to confer such federal jurisdiction. At this stage it is sufficient to point out that the conditions and restrictions attaching to the grant of federal jurisdiction are four in number: (a) every decision of the Supreme Court exercising federal jurisdiction is declared to be final except in so far as an appeal may be taken to the High Court; (b) whenever an appeal lies as of right from an inferior State court or judge to the Supreme Court an appeal may be taken to the High Court (without leave of the High Court) in matters of federal jurisdiction; (c) the High Court may grant special leave to appeal from any State court exercising a federal jurisdiction, e g, a Supreme, District or magistrates court, notwithstanding such an appeal is not available under the law of the particular State;[91] (d) an inferior State court, i e, a magistrates court, exercising federal jurisdiction must be constituted by a magistrate sitting alone.

In *Wishart v Fraser*[92] it was pointed out by Dixon J that an appeal from a State court exercising federal jurisdiction was granted by s 73 (ii) of the Constitution and not by s 39 of the *Judiciary Act* "the operation of which was to distinguish appeals as of right and appeals by special leave."[93] In the case, therefore, of an appeal direct to the *High Court* as of right from an inferior State court, a litigant must be able to show that an appeal of right lay from that inferior court to the *Supreme Court*. Otherwise he must rely on s 39 (2)(c) and seek special leave of the High Court.[94] As will be seen later section 39 (2)(b) and (c) have an ambulatory operation and would apply to grants of federal jurisdiction by legislation passed subsequent to 1901.[95]

**"or of the Supreme Court of any State, or of any other court of any State from which at the establishment of the Commonwealth an appeal lies to the Queen in Council"**

Under this section appeals may be taken from Supreme Courts of the States in both federal and non-federal matters. As far as federal matters are concerned, general restrictions as we have seen are set out in s 39. In relation to non-federal matters s 35 of the *Judiciary Act* provides that apart from cases where the prescribed amount is involved and the other cases already mentioned where an appeal lies as of right, special leave must be sought from the High Court. In *Parkin v James*[96] it was said that the phrase "Supreme Court" as used in this section meant the court which at the time of the establishment of the Commonwealth was known as the Supreme Court in any particular State, which was not necessarily the court of ultimate appeal in the State.[97] An appeal, therefore, lies from a single justice of the Supreme Court to the High Court, by-passing the full Supreme Court.

---

91  See *Prentice v Amalgamated Mining Employees Association of Victoria and Tasmania* (1912) 15 CLR 235. *Troy v Wrigglesworth* (1919) 26 CLR 305. *Hume v Palmer* (1926) 38 CLR 308. *Peterswald v Bartley* (1904) 1 CLR 497. For a discussion of the circumstances under which special leave may be refused see *Kamarooka Gold Mining Co v Keir* (1908) 6 CLR 255.
92  (1941) 64 CLR 470.
93  Ibid, at 480.
94  See *Goward v Commonwealth* (1957) 97 CLR 355; *Grayndler v Cunich* (1939) 62 CLR 573.
95  See below p 264.
96  (1905) 2 CLR 315.
97  It has been decided that an appeal will lie from the Supreme Court sitting as a court of criminal appeal (*Stewart v R* 29 CLR 234) or as a court of Admiralty (*McIlwraith's Case* 70 CLR 175 at 190-1 (Latham CJ)).

One type of question which has arisen for decision is whether an appeal lies from a judge or judges of the Supreme Court exercising a power conferred by State legislation as *persona designata*, that is to say, as a body constituted as a special tribunal for purposes of determining proceedings arising under a particular Act. In *Holmes v Angwin*[98] it was held that a Supreme Court of a State constituted as a Disputed Elections Tribunal was not the Supreme Court within the meaning of s 73, and, therefore, no appeal lay from its decision to the High Court. It is otherwise in cases where an appeal has been taken to a full Supreme Court from such a tribunal and leave is then sought to appeal from the full Supreme Court to the High Court.[99]

Apart from Supreme Courts, the only other court from which an appeal lay to the Privy Council was the Local Court of Appeal of South Australia.

### "Of the Inter-State Commission, but as to questions of law only"

Under this particular provision, an appeal may be taken from the Inter-State Commission, a non-judicial body, on questions of law to the High Court in its appellate jurisdiction. In *New South Wales v Commonwealth*,[1] legislation conferring judicial power on the commission (whose members were not appointed for life) was invalidated. The commission has not functioned since 1920.

### Appeal to Queen in Council

**74.** *No appeal shall be permitted to the Queen in Council from a decision of the High Court upon any question, howsoever arising, as to the limits inter se of the Constitutional powers of the Commonwealth and those of any State or States, or as to the limits inter se of the Constitutional powers of any two or more States, unless the High Court shall certify that the question is one which ought to be determined by Her Majesty in Council.*

*The High Court may so certify if satisfied that for any special reason the certificate should be granted, and thereupon an appeal shall lie to Her Majesty in Council on the question without further leave.*

*Except as provided in this section, this Constitution shall not impair any right which the Queen may be pleased to exercise by virtue of Her Royal prerogative to grant special leave of appeal from the High Court to Her Majesty in Council. The Parliament may make laws limiting the matters in which such leave may be asked, but proposed laws containing any such limitation shall be reserved by the Governor-General for Her Majesty's pleasure.*[2]

Under this section, the High Court is in effect constituted as the final arbiter of two categories of constitutional issues, viz, those involving the relations of Commonwealth and State power and those involving the relations of

---

98   (1906) 4 CLR 297.
99   See also *Webb v Hanlon* (1939) 61 CLR 313. *Medical Board of Victoria v Meyer* (1937) 58 CLR 62. *Kahn v Board of Examiners (Vic)* (1939) 62 CLR 221. *Transport Publishing Co v Literature Board of Review (Qld)* (1956) 187. *McDonald Ltd v South Australian Railways Commissioner* (1911) 12 CLR 221. *Transport Publishing Co v Literature Board of Review* (Qld) (1956) 99 CLR 111.
1   (1915) 20 CLR 54. See discussion of ss 101, 103.
2   Quick and Garran, 747-64. Wynes, 485-98. Nicholas, 367-73. Lane, 419-33. Howard, 197-9.

the powers of two or more States. Appeals may be taken from the High Court to the Privy Council in such matters only by grant of a certificate by the High Court.

In relation to matters which fall outside these categories the prerogative appeal to the Privy Council still continues subject to its being cut down or restricted by federal legislation.

**No appeal shall be permitted to the Queen in Council from a decision of the High Court upon any question, howsoever arising, as to the limits inter se of the Constitutional powers of the Commonwealth and those of any State or States**

The purpose of this section is described in the early case of *Baxter v The Commissioner of Taxation*[3] in this way:

> The intention of the British legislature was to substitute for a distant court, of uncertain composition, imperfectly acquainted with Australian conditions, unlikely to be assisted by counsel familiar with those conditions, and whose decisions would be rendered many months, perhaps years, after its judgment has been invoked, an Australian court, immediately available, constant in its composition, well versed in Australian history and conditions, Australian in its sympathies, and whose judgment, rendered as the occasion arose, would form a working code for the guidance of the Commonwealth.

Dixon J more modestly described its purpose in *Nelungaloo v Commonwealth*:[4]

> "The fact is that the basic purpose of s 74 and of the principles upon which this court has proceeded has been to confine the final decision of the characteristically federal questions described by s 74 to a jurisdiction exercised within the federal system by a court to which the problems and special conceptions of federalism must become very familiar, not without the hope, perhaps, that thus a body of constitutional doctrine might be developed."

Finally in *Pirrie v McFarlane*,[5] Isaacs J described the intention of s 74 as to ensure that "on the purely Australian question of the distribution of the totality of government powers or their content, the High Court of Australia (the highest judicial organ created by the Australian people) was to be the final arbiter unless it voluntarily requested the intervention of the Privy Council."

Throughout the last seventy years, both the High Court and the Privy Council have paid much attention to the characterization question, viz, as to whether a particular constitutional question was an *inter se* question requiring a certificate of the High Court before an appeal to the Privy Council was competent.[6]

The cases, culminating in the decision in *Dennis Hotels Pty Ltd v Victoria*,[7] establish these propositions:

---

3  (1907) 4 CLR 1087 at 1118. In this case the High Court rejected an interpretation of the Constitution adopted by the Privy Council in *Webb v Outrim*. In later cases it was shown why the matter litigated in *Webb v Outrim* should never have reached the Privy Council. See discussion of s 77.

4  (1952) 85 CLR 545 at 573.

5  (1925) 36 CLR 170 at 196.

6  See Wynes at 488 et seq.

7  (1960) 104 CLR 529 (HC); (1961) 104 CLR 621 (PC); [1960] ALR 129 (HC); [1961] ALR 904 (PC). The case is discussed by Cowen, "Inter se questions and Exclusive Powers" (1961) 35 ALJ 239.

(1) The essential feature of an *inter se* question is the mutuality in the relation between the powers belonging to the Commonwealth and the States.[8]

(2) The question of the scope of an exclusive power of the Commonwealth which involves such mutuality is an *inter se* question. Thus whether a particular tax is an excise under s 90 is clearly of this nature as it affects the interaction of Commonwealth and State power: the power of the Commonwealth to tax and the power of the States to tax or to impose licence fees. But other types of exclusive powers, such as the power of the Commonwealth to make laws for the Commonwealth public service (s 52),[9] do not involve mutuality and therefore do not give rise to *inter se* questions.

(3) Concurrent powers may be classified similarly. Those which involve the stated relationship are of an *inter se* nature; those which involve Commonwealth interests alone are not.[10]

(4) Section 92 does not give rise to an *inter se* question. It is predicated on the basis of a denial of power to both the Commonwealth[11] and the States. It does not affect the relationship between Commonwealth and State power.[12]

(5) Questions arising under s 109 of the Constitution (inconsistency) are not *inter se* questions. Here the issue concerns relationship between laws, i e, a factual issue. It does not depend on the power of the Commonwealth or the State to make the law.[13] Of course, if such a question is *also* raised, then under the preceding rules an *inter se* question may arise.

(6) In cases where the decision of the High Court raised several constitutional issues at least one of which was an *inter se* question, then a certificate was necessary where the appeal to the Privy Council could not be upheld or dismissed without the decision of the *inter se* question.[14]

With the passage of the *Privy Council (Limitation of Appeals) Act* of 1968, the characterization question is no longer important in this area (except in relation to a certificate application to the High Court) as the effect of the Act is to exclude constitutional questions from the appellate jurisdiction of the Privy Council. Consequently the present significance of an *inter se* question is to be seen when a constitutional matter arises in a State Supreme Court.

Under s 38A of the Judiciary Act, a Supreme Court is forbidden to hear or determine an *inter se* question.[15]

**"or as to the limits inter se of the Constitutional powers of any two or more States"**

There has been no example of a dispute between the States involving their constitutional powers which has been taken to the Privy Council under a certificate granted by the High Court. An example of such a case would be a dispute by two or more States as to their exercise of power over a

---

8   *Ex parte Nelson (No 2)* (1929) 42 CLR 258 at 270-1 (Dixon J).

9   Or the question of the doctrine of separation of powers which the Privy Council examined in the *Boilermakers Case* (1957) 95 CLR 529.

10   See *Nelungaloo Pty Ltd v Commonwealth* (1952) 85 CLR 545 at 564 (Dixon J).

11   Although this was not decided until *James v Commonwealth*. See discussion of s 92.

12   *James v Cowan* (1932) 47 CLR 386.

13   *O'Sullivan v Noarlunga Meat Ltd* (1956) 95 CLR 177.

14   *Nelungaloo Pty Ltd v Commonwealth* (1952) 85 CLR 545 at 596 (Kitto J).

15   See below under s 77.

subject matter which was subjected to two or more sets of laws, or a dispute over boundaries involving questions of constitutional power.[16]

**"The High Court may so certify if satisfied that for any special reason the certificate should be granted, and thereupon an appeal shall lie to Her Majesty in Council on the question without further leave"**

Only one certificate has been granted and this in a case where the High Court was evenly divided on an *inter se* question.[17] It is unlikely in the light of the recent decision of the High Court in *The State of Western Australia v Hammersley Ltd (Certificate Appeal)*[18] involving an application for a certificate to appeal from an evenly-divided court, which application was rejected, that the High Court in future would grant such a certificate, as it has taken the view that it should be the final arbiter on all constitutional questions. If, however, a certificate were granted the applicant would not have to seek further special leave from the Privy Council.

**"Except as provided in this section, this Constitution shall not impair any right which the Queen may be pleased to exercise by virtue of Her Royal prerogative to grant special leave of appeal from the High Court to Her Majesty in Council"**

**"The Parliament make make laws limiting the matters in which such leave may be asked, but proposed laws containing any such limitation shall be reserved by the Governor-General for Her Majesty's pleasure"**

In cases outside the category of *inter se* matters the prerogative appeal from the High Court to the Privy Council (i e, by special leave of the Privy Council) is preserved subject, however, to its limitation by federal Parliament.

The federal Parliament has legislated to cut off the right of appeal to the Privy Council in all cases involving the interpretation of the Constitution or federal legislation.[19] As we have said, this has led to the result that it is of little importance now at the High Court level to characterize a question as coming within the *inter se* category. In so far as all other federal constitutional matters or matters arising under federal legislation cannot be taken on appeal to the Privy Council, this means that only those matters arising under State legislation or the common law may be taken on appeal from the High Court.

*Reservation of Bills for Her Majesty's pleasure.* Bills limiting appeals to the Privy Council cannot be assented to by the Governor-General but must be sent to London for formal assent by the Queen. This assent, however, is merely a formality; in the case of the *Privy Council (Limitations of Appeals) Bill* it was given within a short period.

ORIGINAL JURISDICTION OF HIGH COURT

75. *In all matters—*

(i) *Arising under any treaty:*

---

16  As distinct from the location of the boundary, on which matter see *South Australia v Victoria* [1914] AC 283.
17  *Colonial Sugar Refining Co v Commonwealth* 15 CLR 182.
18  (1969) 43 ALJR 398, [1970] ALR 161.
19  *Privy Council (Limitations of Appeals) Act* 1968. It also prohibits appeals being taken from decisions of the High Court given on appeal from State Supreme Courts exercising federal jurisdiction, or on appeal from Territory Courts. See discussion by Mason in (1968) 3 FedLR 1.

(ii) *Affecting consuls or other representatives of other countries:*
(iii) *In which the Commonwealth, or a person suing or being sued on behalf of the Commonwealth, is a party:*
(iv) *Between States, or between residents of different States, or between a State and a resident of another State:*
(v) *In which a writ of Mandamus or prohibition or an injunction is sought against an officer of the Commonwealth:*
*the High Court shall have original jurisdiction.*[20]

Section 75 specifies five categories of matters in which the High Court has original jurisdiction, while the following section, s 76, specifies four additional categories in respect of which original jurisdiction may be conferred on the High Court by federal Parliament. In the one case, therefore, the jurisdiction is entrenched by the Constitution while in the other case it is conferred by legislative enactment which may be repealed.

It must be noted that the jurisdiction conferred by ss 75 and 76 is not necessarily exclusive of that of the State courts: in other words it may be a concurrent jurisdiction. However, legislation may be passed under s 77 making any of the categories mentioned in ss 75 and 76 exclusive to the High Court. Certain categories have, in fact, been made exclusive by the *Judiciary Act 1903-1969.*

### "In all matters"

Under both ss 75 and 76 jurisdiction only exists or may be conferred in respect of "matters".

Originally the *Judiciary Act* contained a provision which permitted the Governor-General to refer to the High Court for an advisory opinion any question of law as to the validity of an Act of Parliament. In *Re Judiciary and Navigation Acts,*[21] it fell to the High Court to determine whether the Governor-General could refer to the High Court questions as to the validity of certain sections of the Commonwealth *Navigation Act.* It was argued that the term "matter" meant a legal proceeding which the legislation in question had created, and, therefore, it was appropriately a matter with respect to which the High Court could exercise jurisdiction under s 76 (i). The court rejected the argument holding that there could be no matter within the meaning of s 76 unless "there was some immediate right, duty or liability to be established by the determination of the court."[22] The court could not make a declaration of law separate from the adjudication of a legal question. The power to hand down an advisory opinion was a "power to determine abstract questions of law without the right or duty of any body or person being involved." It was thus not a matter in which the court had jurisdiction.[23]

One question which has been before the High Court is whether the court has original jurisdiction in respect of acts occurring in the Territories

---

20  Quick and Garran, 764-88. Wynes, 417-66. Nicholas, 373 et seq. Howard, 206 et seq. Lane, 465-526. Cowen, *Federal Jurisdiction in Australia* Chs 1, 2.
21  (1921) 29 CLR 257.
22  Ibid, at 264-6. See also *South Australia v Victoria* (1911) 12 CLR 667.
23  The effect of the decision has to some extent been whittled away by the extension of the remedy of the declaration in the constitutional arena. See the *Pharmaceutical Benefits Case* (1945) 71 CLR 231. *Attorney-General for Victoria v Attorney-General for Commonwealth* (1935) 52 CLR 533. See also Foster, "The Declaratory Judgment and Injunction in Australia and the United States", 1 MULR 207, 347.

under this or the following section (s 76). In *Waters v Commonwealth*[24] Fullagar J held that Chapter III of the Constitution did not apply to the Territories which were governed by the power conferred by s 122. However, in the more recent case of *Spratt v Hermes*[25] several judges rejected this restriction on the jurisdiction of the High Court holding that the jurisdiction existed wherever the acts or omissions giving rise to its exercise occurred, whether in a Territory or a State[26] (although under s 122 courts could be created without observing the requirements of s 72).

The word "matter" includes every issue or aspect of the controversy before the court, not only the constitutional issue or aspect. In *Pirrie v McFarlane*[27] Isaacs J said:

... Looking at s 75, the "matter" would not necessarily be simply that part of the controversy depending on the construction or effect of a treaty, or that part of the controversy relating to a consul or the Commonwealth. There might be other necessary parties and other essential questions, all of which would be factors constituting the matter. The controversy is not intended to be decided piecemeal by different tribunals, State and federal.[28]

### (i) "Arising under any treaty"

The purpose of this paragraph is to confer on the High Court jurisdiction in matters arising under treaties or "inter-nation" agreements (i e, agreements between the Commonwealth and other countries). It was considered appropriate that, in this politically sensitive area, the national court should have original jurisdiction.

It is to be noted that s 38 (a) of the *Judiciary Act* makes exclusive to the jurisdiction of the High Court matters arising directly under treaty, thereby implying that matters arising *indirectly* under a treaty shall be within the concurrent jurisdiction of State courts as well as the High Court. Wynes comments that "it is not easy to envisage a matter arising under a treaty which would not at the same time arise under a Commonwealth or State law."[29] He goes on to point out that, in English law, treaties do not of their own force apply to, or affect, private rights. Under American law (in contrast), certain treaties are regarded as self-executing, i e, of their own force they apply within the internal legal structure of the United States and do not need to be incorporated by legislation. In Australia the rule is that *customary* international law, to the extent to which it is not inconsistent with legislation or with common law is applied by the courts. A *treaty* (conventional international law) on the other hand which affects legal rights or duties of Australian citizens or requires the appropriation of money must in accordance with the general principle stated above be incorporated in the legal structure by legislation. In this sense there is no such thing as a self-executing treaty.

In *Bluett v Fadden*[30] the Supreme Court of New South Wales was called

---

24  (1951) 82 CLR 188.
25  (1965) 114 CLR 226; [1966] ALR 597.
26  See Barwick CJ 114 CLR at 241-245, [1966] ALR at 599-603; Taylor J 114 CLR at 264, [1966] ALR at 616; Menzies J 114 CLR at 266, [1966] ALR at 618. See also *Federal Capital Commission v Lariston Building Society Pty Ltd*, (1929) 42 CLR 582.
27  (1925) 36 CLR 170.
28  Ibid, at 198. See also *R v Turner ex parte Marine Board of Hobart* (1927) 39 CLR 411 at 427 (per Isaacs J).
29  *Legislative, Executive and Judicial Powers in Australia*, 422.
30  (1956) 56 SR (NSW) 254, discussed by Cowen, *Federal Jurisdiction in Australia* 29 et seq.

upon to interpret the meaning of s 75 (i) of the Constitution and s 38 of the *Judiciary Act*. This case concerned an action brought against the Commonwealth Treasurer in relation to the vesting in a Treasury official (the Controller of Enemy Property) of certain shares that were alleged to come under the operation of enemy property legislation (i e, to be "enemy-tainted"). Under the Act and regulations made pursuant to it the Governor-General could make orders for the purpose of giving effect to an international agreement on reparation payments which allowed enemy property to be confiscated. In the present case he had made an order affecting shares which were claimed to be "enemy-tainted". McLelland J said that s 75 referred to cases where the decision of the case depended on the interpretation of the treaty. On the other hand where rights had been conferred by legislation implementing a treaty the matter could not be said to arise *directly* under the treaty. When the pleadings in the case were amended pursuant to this expression of opinion to bring out the fact that the basis of the dispute was a question of whether the shares were "enemy-tainted" in the light of various provisions of the agreement on reparations, McClelland J held that it was a matter which arose *directly* under the treaty and therefore was a matter falling within the exclusive jurisdiction of the High Court.[31]

It is suggested that, where the terms of a treaty are incorporated into a statute, the matter will be regarded as arising *indirectly* under the treaty and, therefore, within the concurrent jurisdiction of both the High Court and State courts. Where, however, the statute itself does not give immediate operative effect to the terms of the treaty but empowers the Executive to take action in accordance with those terms (as in *Bluett v Fadden*) the view may be taken that the question arises *directly* under the treaty where it is a matter of interpreting the treaty. Likewise, where an Act of Parliament merely approves or ratifies a treaty without transforming the words of the treaty into the terms of the actual legislation and a question of interpretation of the treaty arises, the matter could be regarded as arising directly under the treaty. For example, the *Petroleum (Submerged Lands) Act*[32] in providing for the exercise of jurisdiction by the Commonwealth and States over petroleum resources of the continental shelf does not incorporate the terms of the Convention on the Continental Shelf into the legislation, but merely sets out the convention in a schedule to the Act. Any question as to the nature of the rights conferred by that convention (as distinct from rights conferred by the Act) would seem to be a question arising *directly* under treaty and therefore within the exclusive jurisdiction of the High Court.[33]

The policy lying behind s 38 of the *Judiciary Act* is quite clear. It is appropriate that the High Court should have sole jurisdiction to deal with a political agreement, convention or treaty which has been entered into by the Commonwealth Executive and which may affect the fundamental international relations of Australia. If, however, the Commonwealth Parliament has actually transformed the terms of the treaty into a statute so that the direct operative effect of the duties created by the treaty is derived from the provisions of the statute, then there is no reason why a State court, as well as the High Court, should not be enabled to interpret that statute in the same way as it has jurisdiction to interpret any other statute.

---

31  Ibid, at 29.
32  No 118 of 1967.
33  Cf s 19 of the *Civil Aviation (Carriers' Liability) Act* 1959-1970. See also s 7 of the *Diplomatic Privileges and Immunities Act* 1967.

### (ii) "Affecting consuls or other representatives of other countries"

At the time of federation, Australia's diplomatic relations with other countries were under the control of the Imperial government. It was not envisaged at the time that Australia would have its own Foreign Affairs Department conducting on behalf of the Commonwealth diplomatic relations with other countries. As Cowen states, "At the date of federation, Australia's independent external relations were conceived of as primarily commercial in character."[34] It was natural, therefore, that consuls who were agents conducting commercial and various other relations (of a notarial nature) with foreign countries would receive primary recognition in the category to be set out in s 75 (ii). Nevertheless it is clear that ambassadors and diplomatic representatives would be regarded as falling within the phrase "other representatives of other countries". Therefore, matters affecting these representatives would be within the jurisdiction of the High Court. The word "affecting" means touching or concerning a consul or diplomatic representative in respect of his status or actions. It may be a matter that affects him in terms of the operation of the criminal law of a State or Territory, or it may be a matter affecting him in terms of the civil law.

The question arises as to whether the effect of s 75 (ii) is to give the High Court original jurisdiction in any matter affecting consuls, or only when the consul or other diplomatic representative is involved in his official capacity as plaintiff or defendant.[35] The view of Quick and Garran that the clause applies only to consuls and other representatives in their official capacity[36] seems to be a correct one and, therefore, when any litigation concerns one of these representatives and no claim is made that the action of the representative giving rise to liability has occurred in the performance of or in relation to the official duties or that he is entitled to diplomatic immunity, then it would seem that the High Court would not have original jurisdiction.

The jurisdiction of the High Court under s 75 (ii) is not exclusive of the jurisdiction of the State courts unless the matter is one which also directly arises under a treaty.

### (iii) "In which the Commonwealth, or a person suing or being sued on behalf of the Commonwealth, is a party"

It was natural that the founders would wish to confer on a High Court original jurisdiction in matters involving the new juristic entity created by the Constitution—the Commonwealth of Australia.[37] Indeed, it appears that the State courts may not have had jurisdiction over the Commonwealth as a defendant to an action without some positive grant of jurisdiction by the Constitution.

In the *Bank Nationalization Case*[38] Dixon J affirmed that "the purpose of s 75 (iii) obviously was to ensure that the political organization called into existence under the name of the Commonwealth and armed with enumerated

---

34   *Federal Jurisdiction in Australia*, 31.
35   It must be kept in mind that a claim of diplomatic immunity may be made at any time during proceedings in which a diplomatic representative is involved.
36   *Annotated Constitution of the Commonwealth*, 772. However, as Cowen points out (at 32) the matter is still unresolved.
37   See Cowen, *Federal Jurisdiction in Australia*, 33 et seq.
38   (1948) 76 CLR 1.

powers and authorities, limited by definition, fell in every way within a jurisdiction in which it could be impleaded and which it could invoke."[39]

However, it is necessary to determine whether s 75 (iii) operates merely as a grant of jurisdiction in cases in which the Commonwealth is a party and which must be complemented by legislation giving rights to proceed against the Commonwealth under s 78 of the Constitution, or whether it also operates so as to expose the Commonwealth to liability by creating a jurisdiction in which the Commonwealth may be impleaded without the need for support from legislation passed under s 78. The latter view is supported by the decision of the majority of the High Court in *Commonwealth v New South Wales*.[40] However, in *Werrin v Commonwealth*[41] there is an expression of opinion on the part of Dixon J that the liability of the Commonwealth to suit does not arise from s 75 (iii) but from various sections of the Judiciary Act.[42] Section 75 (iii) does not, therefore, preclude the Commonwealth from controlling its liability by legislation passed pursuant to s 78.[43] This would mean that until the Commonwealth subjected itself to suit under the provisions of the *Judiciary Act*, it could not be sued in the High Court. More recently Windeyer J has supported the view of Dixon J.[44]

Opinions expressed in the *Asiatic Steamship Case*[45] suggest that the liability of the Commonwealth arises from a combination of ss 75 (iii) and 78 of the Constitution together with ss 56 and 64 of the *Judiciary Act*.

It would seem clear that the Commonwealth could preclude actions against itself arising within the limits of the judicial power if it is accepted that it also can make provisions for such actions to be commenced. If, however, liability to suit is created by force of the Constitution then it might be impossible to extinguish a general right of action against the Commonwealth vested in either a State or a private individual.

The question may be related to a determination of the source of Commonwealth liability. If Commonwealth liability is created by a Commonwealth statute then clearly it is possible for that liability to be terminated by a repeal or modification of the statute. If, however, it is claimed that Commonwealth liability exists under the Common Law or under a State statute, the issue is clearly joined. Sections 79 and 80 of the *Judiciary Act* make provision for the application of both the common law and State statutes (in the absence of Commonwealth legislation) where proceedings are taken against the Commonwealth. This is a statutory application of "choice of law" rules to suits in which the Commonwealth is a party.[46] In the absence of these provisions of the *Judiciary Act*, would State law and common law be applied? The

---

39   Ibid, at 363.
40   (1923) 32 CLR 200. This case dealt with the liability of a *State* to suit under s 75, the majority holding that s 75 (iii) operated to confer jurisdiction on the High Court in a suit by the Commonwealth against a State without the consent of the State. It would seem to follow that, where the Commonwealth was a defendant, a similar liability would follow from s 75 (iii).
41   (1937) 59 CLR 150.
42   Ibid, at 166.
43   See also *Musgrave v Commonwealth* (1937) 57 CLR 514.
44   *Suehle v Commonwealth* (1967) 116 CLR 353; [1967] ALR 572. See also Hogg, "Suits against the Commonwealth in Federal Jurisdiction" (1970) 44 ALJ 425 and articles cited in Wynes, 432 n 72.
45   *Asiatic Steam Navigation Co Ltd v Commonwealth* (1956) 96 CLR 397 at 419-420.
46   See below under s 78.

question here is a basic constitutional one and it is associated with the question whether legislation of the State can bind the Commonwealth. It is discussed at a later stage in this work.[47]

It is to be noted that it is not only where the Commonwealth is named as a direct party to an action that the original jurisdiction can be invoked. It may also be invoked where a Commonwealth official is a party and is being sued in his representative capacity. It has been held that original jurisdiction is conferred by s 75 (iii) where the Commonwealth commences *ex parte* proceedings in *mandamus*[48] and also where the Commonwealth is acting as a prosecutor in respect of offences against the laws of the Commonwealth.[49] There is also the case where a Commonwealth agency or instrumentality is being sued; in the *Bank Nationalization Case* it was pointed out that an agency such as the Commonwealth Bank would fall within this category. In the view of a number of judges the test applied in determining whether a body is within the shield of the Crown could be applied in this area, and an examination of the powers of the Commonwealth Banking Corporation showed that it was an agency of the Commonwealth. However, Dixon and Starke JJ considered that the authority did not have to be within the shield of the Crown in the strict sense in order to be sued under section 75 (iii) of the Constitution. More recently, in *Inglis v Commonwealth Trading Bank of Australia*[50] it has been held that the Commonwealth Trading Bank can be sued under s 75 (iii), Kitto and Windeyer JJ taking the view that it was being "sued on behalf of the Commonwealth", while Barwick CJ favoured the view that the Commonwealth was a direct party, therefore accepting the fact that the bank was within the shield of the Crown.

The *Bank Nationalization Case* decided also that the original jurisdiction of the High Court could not be shut out by Commonwealth legislation conferring exclusive jurisdiction to determine matters arising under that legislation on another court (viz, a Court of Claims which had jurisdiction to determine the value of shares and property of the private banks which were to be compulsorily acquired under the nationalizing legislation).[51]

Under s 38 (c) of the *Judiciary Act*, suits by the Commonwealth against a State, or a State against the Commonwealth, or persons suing or being sued on their behalf, are exclusive to the High Court.

(iv) "Between States, or between residents of different States, or between a State and a resident of another State"

*Between States.* It is fitting that the High Court should be invested with original jurisdiction where two or more States of the Commonwealth are

---

47   See below under s 106.
48   *R v Registrar of Titles for Victoria ex parte the Commonwealth* (1915) 20 CLR 379.
49   *R v Kidman* (1915) 20 CLR 425. However, in *R v Murray and Cormie ex parte the Commonwealth* (1916) 22 CLR 437, the High Court by a slender majority of 4-3 held that it did not have jurisdiction in proceedings where the Commonwealth had applied for a writ of prohibition against a district court judge exercising federal jurisdiction. Three of the majority judges held that the Commonwealth was not a party to the proceedings for the prohibition while the fourth held that, although the Commonwealth was a party, it had no suitor's interest in the matter of excess of jurisdiction.
50   (1969) 43 ALJR 330. See also *Commonwealth v Rhind* (1966) 119 CLR 584. [1967] ALR 483 (Barwick CJ).
51   See also *Shaw Savill and Albion Co Ltd v Commonwealth* (1940) 66 CLR 344.

involved in litigation. Paragraph four of s 75 affords a forum where a determination of such an inter-State dispute can take place without regard to particular State interests which otherwise might carry undue weight if the Supreme Court of a particular State had jurisdiction in such matters. The number of cases in which actions between States (as distinct from actions between the State and the Commonwealth or vice versa) have occurred in the original jurisdiction of the High Court are few. An early case dealing with the question of the determination of the boundaries of South Australia and Victoria is an example. In that case[52] it was held that the High Court would have jurisdiction over such inter-State disputes if they were justiciable, i e, subject to resolution by legal as distinct from political criteria.

*Between residents of different States.* This has been described as diversity jurisdiction. An example of this jurisdiction would be where a New South Wales resident sued a Queensland resident for an injury incurred in either New South Wales or Queensland. In such a case the plaintiff has the option of suing in the High Court in its original jurisdiction or in the Supreme Court of one of the States.[53] It must be established, however, that the parties at the time of the bringing of the action were residents of different States.[54]

It is to be noted, however, that a company is not treated as a resident for the purposes of s 75 (iv).[55] A natural person, of course, has a residence in one or other State of the Commonwealth, and this residence would be determined on the basis of location of dwelling house, occupation, period of time spent in the area and the like. A juristic person, such as a company, cannot dwell in or inhabit a particular place or State although for the purposes of particular legislation, e g, taxation, such residence may be attributed to it.

*Between a State and a resident of another State.* In *Daly v State of Victoria*[56] and *State of New South Wales v Bardolph*[57] actions were brought in the High Court under this head. The specific provision of the *Judiciary Act* providing for the enforcement of a right of a private person against a State (in matters where the High Court has original jurisdiction) is s 58.[58]

Under s 38 (b) of the *Judiciary Act,* suits between States, or between persons suing or being sued on behalf of different States, or between a State and a person suing or being sued on behalf of another State, are exclusive to the High Court.

(v) **"In which a writ of Mandamus or prohibition or an injunction is sought against an officer of the Commonwealth"**

This paragraph gives jurisdiction in cases where specific types of remedies are sought against a Commonwealth officer. It is, therefore, to be compared

---

52   *South Australia v Victoria,* 12 CLR 667.
53   As to whether the High Court may refuse to exercise jurisdiction on the basis of *forum non conveniens* see Cowen, *Federal Jurisdiction in Australia,* 69-73, Barwick, "The Australian Judicial System: Proposed New Superior Court", (1964-5), 1 FedLR 1 at 9 et seq. See also *Gleeson v Williamson* (1972) 46 ALJR 677.
54   *Dahms v Brandsch* (1911) 13 CLR 336. See also *R v Macdonald* (1953) 88 CLR 197; *R v Oregan* (1957) 97 CLR 323; *R v Langdon* (1953) 88 CLR 158.
55   See *Australian Temperance and General Mutual Life Assurance Society Ltd v Howe* (1922) 31 CLR 290. *Cox v Journeaux* (1934) 52 CLR 282.
56   (1920) 28 CLR 395.
57   (1935) 52 CLR 455.
58   As to the rights which apply in suits where the Commonwealth or a State is involved see below under s 78.

with the previous grants of jurisdiction which depend either on *subject matter* or on the classification of the *parties to an action*. The paragraph, which lists three types of remedies, gives rise to the query whether there is any need for specification of these as falling within the High Court's original jurisdiction when on more general principles, they would seem to fall within the ordinary jurisdiction of the High Court either under its inherent jurisdiction or jurisdiction derived from sections of the *Judiciary Act*[59] to grant remedies in respect of any matters falling within the limits of the judicial powers (which are delimited by ss 75 and 76).

In the case of mandamus and prohibition, the Crown is always named as a party to the proceedings, and the private citizen who wishes to seek such a remedy sues *ex parte*. However, it is also a fact that a writ of prohibition or an injunction may be brought against a named person performing some function under Commonwealth law who, although a Commonwealth officer, could not be shown to be a person who is being sued on behalf of the Commonwealth. It would seem therefore that the ground covered by s 75 (iii) is much narrower than the ground covered by s 75 (v) and that, therefore, there is a need for the extension of jurisdiction with respect to the grant of remedies against an officer of the Commonwealth, which is the purpose of s 75 (v).

In the *Tramways Case*[60] it was held, affirming *Whybrow's Case*,[61] that the term "officer of the Commonwealth" was not restricted to non-judicial officers, i e, to members of the Commonwealth public service.[62] It included members of a "judicial" body such as the Arbitration Court, but not a judge of the State court exercising federal jurisdiction.[63] It also was not restricted to specific individuals but could comprise corporations whether sole or aggregate.

The writ of prohibition is the normal method of challenging excesses of jurisdiction by the Commonwealth Arbitration Commission (which since the *Boilermakers Case* is not a court within s 71). The writ would also be available against other quasi-judicial bodies. It is not available against bodies which merely fulfil an administrative function, e g, of advising a minister, without having any power of enforcing an obligation.[64]

It has been held that prohibition is available not only to prevent a body acting in excess of jurisdiction at a stage before final judgment, but even after final judgment is reached, provided that the judgment of that body has a continuing effect upon the rights and duties of the persons affected by its order. In *R v Hibble ex parte BHP Ltd*[65] it was said: "So long . . . as a judgment or order made without jurisdiction remains in force so as to impose

---

59 That is ss 32, 33 discussed in *Whybrow's Case* (1910) 11 CLR 1 and *Ah Yick v Lehmert* (1905) 2 CLR 593 at 608-9 (Barton J). The effect of the provision is that the High Court can control inferior federal courts irrespective of the existence of a statutory right of appeal.
60 (1914) 18 CLR 54.
61 (1910) 11 CLR 1.
62 In *R v Registrar of Companies* (*ACT*) *ex parte Ganke* (1960) 1 FLR 109 it was held that a Registrar of Companies in the Capital Territory was an officer of the Commonwealth.
63 *R v Murray and Cormie* (1916) 22 CLR 439. But note if the Commonwealth is a *party* to the proceedings under s 75 (iii) of the Constitution review could be achieved by writ of prohibition.
64 *R v Macfarlane ex parte O'Flanagan and O'Kelly* (1923) 32 CLR 518. Cf, *R v Cox ex parte Smith* (1945) 71 CLR 1. (Prohibition lies to a Court-martial.) See also *R v Governor of South Australia* (1907) 4 CLR 1497.
65 (1920) 28 CLR 456 at 463.

liabilities upon an individual, prohibition will lie to correct the excess of jurisdiction."

The writ of mandamus has two uses. Its primary use is to enforce the carrying out of a duty by a public official where that public official has neglected to do so.[66] The secondary use depends on the thesis that an improper exercise of jurisdiction is wholly ineffective and, therefore, mandamus should lie to compel the *correct* exercise of that jurisdiction. Mandamus is available against purely administrative officials as well as against inferior judicial bodies.

Injunctions are available under s 75 (v) against federal officers to prevent them from acting contrary to statute or in an unconstitutional manner.

It must be noted that s 75 (v) does not exhaust the remedies that are available to the High Court which otherwise arise from its inherent or statutory jurisdiction.[67] Some doubts exist as to the availability of the writ of certiorari (which is not mentioned in s 75 (v)) to challenge a decision of a lower tribunal which is alleged to have acted contrary to statutory provisions.[68] But in any case, any inconvenience which the absence of certiorari in s 75 (v) may have caused has been avoided by peculiarily Australian extension of prohibition exemplified in *R v Hickman*.[69]

Other remedies which a superior Court of Record has in the exercise of its jurisdiction are, of course, available in the High Court, e g, the right to hand down a declaratory judgment.

It has been held that the jurisdiction exercisable by the High Court under s 75 (v) is original jurisdiction and cannot be taken away by a federal Parliament.[70] A so-called privative clause (a clause purporting to exclude judicial review) cannot, therefore, deprive the High Court of jurisdiction to entertain an action against an officer of the Commonwealth if that officer has acted in excess of constitutional powers.[71] As has already been mentioned, the usual case where a writ of prohibition is sought is to prevent the Arbitration Commission from deciding a matter which is not covered by the grant of power in s 51 (xxxv) of the Constitution (e g, because it is not an industrial dispute). However, s 75 is not limited to a grant of prohibition on *constitutional* grounds: it also is available where a Commonwealth officer on whom has been imposed the duty of acting in a judicial manner[72] has exceeded the jurisdiction conferred upon him by the empowering statute: *R v Hickman*.[73] In *Hickman's Case* it was held that prohibition would issue to a local reference board which had acted outside its jurisdiction in making a settlement of a dispute. There

---

66    See for example *R v Police Magistrate of Cairns ex parte Nanook* [1913] StR Qd 176.
67    See *Judiciary Act*, s 33, for other remedies (including *habeas corpus*) which may be granted.
68    See *R v District Court of Queensland ex parte Thompson* (1968) 42 ALJR 173, [1968] ALR 509, where Barwick CJ and McTiernan J differed on this question.
69    (1945) 70 CLR 598.
70    For a discussion of the cases see Wynes, 443 et seq. See also Anderson, "The Application of Privative Clauses to Proceedings of Commonwealth Tribunals" (1956) 3 U of QLJ 35.
71    *Australasian Coal and Shale Employees' Federation v Aberfield Coal Mining Co* (1942) 66 CLR 161. *R v Commonwealth Court of Conciliation and Arbitration ex parte Ozone Theatres Ltd* (1949) 78 CLR 389.
72    Or quasi-judicially: see *Waterside Workers' Federation v Gilchrist* (1924) 34 CLR 482 at 553 et seq (Starke J).
73    (1945) 70 CLR 598 at 606-7 (Latham CJ).

was a privative clause in the regulations establishing the board's jurisdiction those being based on the power to make laws in regard to defence. The regulations permitted the reference board to make determinations in respect of the coal mining industry. The board had purported to apply a determination to persons engaged in the carrying of coal from collieries and it was argued that these persons were not engaged in the coal mining industry. Despite the privative clause, the High Court decided that prohibition should issue against a body which was an "officer of the Commonwealth" on the ground that it had exceeded its statutory authority. This means that a privative clause will only exclude the writ of prohibition for excess of statutory authority "so long as the powers of the judicial authority are exercised bona fide for the purpose for which they were conferred."[74] In *Hickman's Case* the order was a clear excess of authority and was not, therefore, to be regarded as validated by the privative clause.[75]

Under s 38 (e) of the *Judiciary Act* the High Court has exclusive jurisdiction in matters in which a writ of mandamus or prohibition is sought against an officer of the Commonwealth or a federal court.

ADDITIONAL ORIGINAL JURISDICTION

**76.** *The Parliament may make laws conferring original jurisdiction on the High Court in any matter—*

    (i) *Arising under this Constitution, or involving its interpretation:*
    (ii) *Arising under any laws made by the Parliament:*
    (iii) *Of Admiralty and maritime jurisdiction:*
    (iv) *Relating to the same subject-matter claimed under the laws of different States.*[76]

**"Arising under this Constitution, or involving its interpretation"**

Section 76 (i) refers to jurisdiction in any matter arising under the Constitution or involving its interpretation, while s 76 (ii) refers to jurisdiction arising under any laws made by the Parliament.

The differences between the two sections were discussed by Latham CJ in *R v Commonwealth Court of Conciliation and Arbitration ex parte Barrett.*[77] "The terms of paragraph (i) show that a matter may arise under the Constitution without involving its interpretation, and that a case may involve the interpretation of the Constitution without arising under the Constitution. Paragraph (ii) is limited to matters arising under federal statutes, and does *not* extend to matters involving interpretation of such statutes if they do not arise thereunder."[78] *Barrett's Case* was one of a number of actions consolidated under an application for a writ of prohibition to the Commonwealth Arbitration Court in respect of a decision by an Arbitration Court judge concerning elections to a union. It was argued for the prosecutors that since all that was in issue was a disputed union election, there was no law made by the Parliament under which the matter could be said to arise, and therefore s 58 (a)[79]

---

74   *Baxter v New South Wales Clickers' Association* (1909) 10 CLR 114 at 162 (Isaacs J).
75   See also *R v Connell ex parte Hetton Bellbird Collieries Ltd* (1944) 69 CLR 407.
76   Quick and Garran, 789-801. Wynes, 446-55. Lane, 527-48. Cowen, *Federal Jurisdiction in Australia* Ch 1.
77   (1945) 70 CLR 141.
78   Ibid, at 154.
79   which purported to confer the jurisdiction.

of the *Arbitration Act* was not a valid conferment of original federal jurisdiction. The court rejected this argument and held that the matter arose under a federal law and was therefore within s 76 (ii).

Section 30 of the *Judiciary Act* confers jurisdiction on the High Court in matters covered by s 76 (i). It is quite clear that section 76 is designed to allow the federal Parliament to invest the High Court with a jurisdiction in constitutional matters, whether these matters arise in a specific suit claiming relief by virtue of a constitutional provision or in some other suit which on its facts or pleadings does not depend for relief on a constitutional provision but which will involve the interpretation of one or other section of the Constitution.[80] Equally, in both cases the matter would be covered by s 76 (i). In *Hooper v Egg and Egg Pulp Marketing Board*[81] questions arose as to whether a particular fee imposed by a Victorian Marketing Board under State legislation constituted an excise duty and therefore was contrary to s 90 of the Constitution. The question was argued that, once the constitutional issue had been disposed of, the case could no longer proceed in federal jurisdiction but would have to be remitted to a State court for a decision on the non-constitutional issues. The court rejected the argument. Latham CJ said that the fact that the constitutional objection had failed did not deprive the court of jurisdiction provided that the facts relied upon were raised *bona fide* and were such as to raise a constitutional question.[82] Starke J, who dissented, considered that the mere allegation of some contravention of the Constitution was not sufficient to invoke the original jurisdiction of the High Court under s 30 of the *Judiciary Act*. In his view the allegations in the pleadings in the case being colourable, the matter was not one properly to be dealt with by a federal court.[83]

Once the federal matter is disposed of, the High Court can settle the whole case even though it involves merely the interpretation of a State statute or the principles of common law.

### "Arising under any laws made by the Parliament"

A matter may be said to arise under federal law "when the right or duty in question owes its existence to federal law or depends upon federal law for its enforcement, whether or not the determination of the controversy involves the interpretation (or validity) of the law."[84] The High Court has had occasion to examine s 76 (ii) in a number of cases where the validity of Commonwealth legislation defining the jurisdiction of federal courts other than the High Court (under s 77 (i)) has been in issue. The legislative power conferred by

---

80    For example, as in *Troy v Wrigglesworth* 26 CLR 305 where an officer of the defence forces was prosecuted under State legislation for dangerous driving, an issue being whether the Constitution had any effect on the application of the Act to him. See also *James v South Australia* 40 CLR 1. Cf, *Hogan v Ochiltree*, 10 CLR 535, *Heimman v Commonwealth* 54 CLR 126.

81    (1939) 61 CLR 665.

82    Ibid, at 673-674.

83    Ibid, at 677. See also his judgments in *Commonwealth v Limerick Steamship Co Ltd* (1924) 35 CLR 69 at 118, *Carter v Egg & Egg Pulp Marketing Board* (1942) 66 CLR 557 at 587. In *R v Bevan ex parte Elias and Gordon* (1942) 66 CLR 452 at 465-6 the same judge found that, although the point had not been raised by counsel, interpretation of the Constitution was involved in respect of a question as to the status and jurisdiction of courts-martial.

84    *Barrett's Case* 70 CLR 141 at 154, per Latham CJ.

s 77 is limited to matters mentioned in the previous two sections, viz, ss 75 and 76. This means that the Parliament cannot confer on any inferior federal court jurisdiction wider than that permitted by ss 75 and 76. In *Collins v Charles Marshall Pty Ltd*[85] the matter involved was the validity of the section of the *Conciliation and Arbitration Act* which conferred on the Arbitration Court an *appellate* jurisdiction in proceedings arising under the Act or involving the interpretation of the Act, as well as in proceedings arising under an award or order of the court or involving the interpretation of that order or award. The initial proceedings in this case involved a prosecution under a State Industrial Act and the defence to this prosecution was that the State Act was inconsistent with an award made by the Arbitration Court. The matter did not arise under a Commonwealth Act even although the interpretation of the Act and the award was in issue. The High Court, therefore, held that the conferment of jurisdiction on the Arbitration Court under s 77 (i) could not be upheld as a conferment of jurisdiction in a matter arising under federal legislation.[86] In *Barrett's Case* (referred to previously) it was argued for the prosecutors that, since all that was in issue was a disputed union election, there was no specific law made by the Parliament under which the matter could be said to arise, and, therefore, that s 58 (a) of the *Conciliation and Arbitration Act* was not a valid conferment of original federal jurisdiction in terms of s 77. However, the High Court considered that s 58 (a) vested in the Arbitration Court a jurisdiction in respect of matters arising under the Act in respect of the enforcement of union rules—a matter which was incidental to the prevention and settlement of industrial disputes. It was therefore a matter arising under a law made by Parliament.[87]

There is a specific provision in the *Judiciary Act* conferring jurisdiction in the High Court in trials of indictable offences against Commonwealth laws.[88] The federal Parliament has also, in numerous Acts, conferred jurisdiction on the High Court in matters arising under these Acts.[89]

### "Of Admiralty and maritime jurisdiction"

The legislative basis of Admiralty jurisdiction in Australia is partially derived from an Imperial Act, *The Colonial Courts of Admiralty Act* of 1890.

Section 2 (1) of that Act provides:

Every court of law in a British possession which is for the time being declared in pursuance of this Act to be a Court of Admiralty, or which, if no such declaration is in force in the possession, has therein original unlimited civil jurisdiction, shall

85  (1955) 92 CLR 529.
86  See Cowen, *Federal Jurisdiction in Australia*, 53-54.
87  See also *Felton v Mulligan* (1971) 45 ALJR 525. *Waterside Workers Federation v Gilchrist* (1924) 34 CLR 482. *Hooper v Hooper* (1955) 91 CLR 529. *McGlew v NSW Malting Co Ltd* (1918) 25 CLR 416. *Commonwealth v Cole* (1923) 32 CLR 602. In *Cole's Case* a judgment creditor sought to garnishee money owed by the Commonwealth to a debtor under the Commonwealth *Public Service Act*, 1922-1973. This could be done only if the debtor was an employee of the Commonwealth. A Tasmanian court had erroneously held that the debtor was such an employee. Nevertheless, an appeal was held to lie to the High Court on the basis that the claim was one arising under a federal statute.
88  Section 30, discussed in *R v Kidman* (1915) 20 CLR 425.
89  For a list of legislation see Byers & Toose, "The Necessity for a New Federal Court" (1963) 36 ALJ 308 at 311.

be a Court of Admiralty, with the jurisdiction in this Act mentioned, and may for the purpose of that jurisdiction exercise all the powers which it possesses for the purpose of its other civil jurisdiction, and such court in reference to the jurisdiction conferred by this Act is in this Act referred to as a Colonial Court of Admiralty.

Section 2 (2) sets out the nature of the jurisdiction:

The jurisdiction of a Colonial Court of Admiralty shall, subject to the provisions of this Act, be over the like places, persons, matters, and things, as the Admiralty jurisdiction of the High Court in England, whether existing by virtue of any statute or otherwise, and the Colonial Court of Admiralty may exercise such jurisdiction in like manner and to as full an extent as the High Court in England, and shall have the same regard as that court to international law and the comity of nations.

Section 3 deals with the powers of a colonial legislature in relation to Admiralty jurisdiction:

"The Legislature of a British possession may by any Colonial law—(a) declare any court of unlimited civil jurisdiction, whether original or appellate, in that possession to be a Colonial Court of Admiralty, and provide for the exercise by such court of its jurisdiction under this Act, and limit territorially, or otherwise, the extent of such jurisdiction; and (b) confer upon any inferior or subordinate court in that possession such partial or limited admiralty jurisdiction under such regulations and with such appeal (if any) as may seem fit: Provided that any such Colonial law shall not confer any jurisdiction which is not by this Act conferred upon a Colonial Court of Admiralty."

The legislatures of the States (which are treated as legislatures of a British possession)[90] have taken no steps to declare their Supreme Courts to be Colonial Courts of Admiralty. Therefore, in the absence of such a declaration those courts having unlimited civil jurisdiction within the territorial limits of a State are Colonial Courts of Admiralty under the Act.[91] There is no doubt, however, that the High Court, having unlimited civil jurisdiction within the Commonwealth, is also a Colonial Court of Admiralty.[92] Moreover, under the *Colonial Courts of Admiralty Act*, appeal may be taken from the Supreme Court to the High Court, and therefore the High Court is also an appellate tribunal under this Act.[93]

Section 39 of the *Judiciary Act* invests State Supreme Courts with jurisdiction in matters covered by s 76 (iii), i e, matters of admiralty and maritime jurisdiction. It therefore appears that the Supreme Courts may have a dual admiralty jurisdiction, one derived from the Commonwealth Parliament and the other derived from the Imperial Parliament.[94] There are some suggestions[95] that the jurisdiction derived from the *Colonial Courts of Admiralty Act* may not be co-extensive with that derived from s 76 (iii) of the Constitution in

---

90   *McArthur v Williams* (1936) 55 CLR 324.
91   *McIlwraith McEacharn Ltd v Shell Co of Australia Ltd* (1945) 70 CLR 175. But see McGrath, "Admiralty Jurisdiction and the Statute of Westminster" (1932) 6 ALJ 215.
92   *John Sharp & Sons v "Kathryn Mackall"* (1924) 34 CLR 420.
93   See *McIlwraith McEacharn Ltd v Shell Co of Australia Ltd* (1945) 70 CLR 175 at 192 per Latham CJ.
94   At one time, the High Court had also been invested with jurisdiction under s 76 (iii) of the Constitution but this investment was withdrawn in 1939.
95   See *McIlwraith's Case* 70 CLR at 208 per Dixon J, citing the *Yuri Maru and the Woron* (1927) AC 906.

respect of applicable law. According to this view the jurisdiction derived from the *Colonial Courts of Admiralty Act* may be frozen as at 1890, the date of the enactment of the Act.[96] It may well be, therefore that State courts exercising their federal jurisdiction under s 39 of the *Judiciary Act* would have a wider jurisdiction on admiralty matters than the High Court.

It remains to point out that admiralty jurisdiction covers, inter alia, any damage done by a ship. [97] This means damage done by the operations of the ship or its gear. It does not cover any type of injury occurring to a person on board ship.

It has been suggested that the Commonwealth cannot, by legislation passed incidental to s 76 (iii), impose controls on ships engaged in intra-State as distinct from inter-State and overseas trade.[98]

### "Relating to the same subject-matter claimed under the laws of different States"

There is great uncertainty as to the meaning of this paragraph. It is clear that in disputes between States, the High Court has jurisdiction under s 75 (iv). Consequently, it might well be that the section is intended to cover a jurisdiction where private parties are involved in a dispute in which the *res* or subject matter may fall under two different systems of State law. Such could be the case of succession to property where the deceased died in one State, and the property has its *locus* in another State and the question arises as to which State has the right to impose estate duties. Wynes seems to support this proposition when he says that the section would enable the High Court to be invested with jurisdiction in matters of private international law in relation to the Australian States.[99]

As against this view it could be said that State and federal courts are entitled to apply such rules (being rules of common law) in any suit in which they have jurisdiction. A number of such cases have been dealt with by the High Court on *appeal* from State courts. Where the parties are residents of different States *original* jurisdiction is conferred by virtue of s 75 (iv).

It would seem, therefore, that more practical political reasons lay behind the inclusion of s 76 (iv) than solicitude for the rules of private international law. An analysis of the convention debates seems to indicate that the thought uppermost in the minds of the founders was the possibility of a conflict between Victoria and New South Wales over the River Murray waters. On this view the subject matter referred to in s 76 (iv) could be water or land which might be the subject of a boundary dispute between States. But it is difficult to imagine a case where a dispute would arise over such a matter which did not involve States or residents of different States. Therefore, the operative effect of s 76 (iv) is negligible in the light of the existing jurisdiction of the High Court under s 75. The federal Parliament has taken no steps to legislate pursuant to s 76 (iv).

---

96   See also *Nagrint v The Ship "Regis"* (1939) 61 CLR 688. Cowen, *Federal Jurisdiction in Australia,* 62-65.

97   See *Union Steamship Co of New Zealand v Ferguson* (1969) 43 ALJR 108; [1969] ALR 409. The jurisdiction is set out in the *Admiralty Courts Act* (Imp), 1861.

98   *Owners of SS "Kalibia" v Wilson* (1910) 11 CLR 689.

99   "The Judicial Power of the Commonwealth" (1938) 12 ALJ 8 at 9-10.

POWER TO DEFINE JURISDICTION

**77.** *With respect to any of the matters mentioned in the last two sections the Parliament may make laws—*

(i) *Defining the jurisdiction of any federal court other than the High Court:*

(ii) *Defining the extent to which the jurisdiction of any federal court shall be exclusive of that which belongs to or is invested in the courts of the States:*

(iii) *Investing any court of a State with federal jurisdiction.*[1]

**"With respect to any of the matters mentioned in the last two sections the Parliament may make laws—**

**(i) Defining the jurisdiction of any federal court other than the High Court"**

The effect of this paragraph is to empower the federal Parliament to confer jurisdiction on federal courts (including the High Court)[2] in respect of matters listed in ss 75 and 76. The power extends to the conferment of both original and appellate jurisdiction on such courts.[3] The word "jurisdiction" means power to adjudicate. It implies that a federal court would be seized of the right to inquire into and offer relief in respect of any matter that is contained in the previous two sections. The qualifications to be noted, however, are that it is not possible under this section for the federal Parliament to confer on an inferior federal court an appellate jurisdiction from decisions of State courts exercising their ordinary *State* jurisdiction,[4] nor is it possible for the Commonwealth Parliament to create any appellate tribunal over a State Supreme Court.[5]

At the present time there are two federal courts in existence, the Industrial Court the jurisdiction of which is defined by the *Conciliation and Arbitration Act,* and the Bankruptcy Court the jurisdiction of which is defined by the *Bankruptcy Act.* Proposals have been put forward to establish a Commonwealth superior court which would deal with many of the matters contained in ss 75 and 76. However, despite intensive study of the possible jurisdiction of such a court by academic and practising lawyers, the federal Parliament has not yet legislated on the matter.

In *Collins v Charles Marshall Pty Ltd*[6] the High Court was concerned with the interpretation of a provision of the Commonwealth *Conciliation and Arbitration Act* which, it will be remembered, conferred appellate jurisdiction on a federal court in relation to proceedings arising under or involving the interpretation of the Act, or arising under or involving the interpretation of an award made by the Arbitration Court. The court considered that "proceed-

---

1    Quick and Garran, 801-4. Wynes, 407-13. Lane, 379-91, 549-68. Howard, 230-49. Cowen, *Federal Jurisdiction in Australia* Chs 3, 5.

2    *Pirrie v McFarlane*, 36 CLR 170 at 176 (Knox CJ).

3    See *Ah Yick v Lehmert* (1905) 2 CLR 593 at 603-9. (Griffith CJ). *New South Wales v Commonwealth* (1915) 20 CLR 54 at 90 (Isaacs J). *George Hudson Ltd v Australian Timber Workers' Union* (1922-3) 32 CLR 413 at 429 (Isaacs J). *Cockle v Isaksen* (1957) 99 CLR 155.

4    *Collins v Charles Marshall Pty Ltd* (1955) 92 CLR 529, Cowen, *Federal Jurisdiction in Australia,* 114.

5    See *R v Spicer ex parte Truth and Sportsman Ltd* (1957) 98 CLR 48 at 61 (Kitto J).

6    (1955) 92 CLR 529.

ings" were not necessarily synonymous with "matters".[7] It also pointed out that it was the appeal and not the original proceeding which must contain a matter arising under the federal law. One reason for this was that in "a 'proceeding under the Act' in the primary court the whole matter so far as it rests on the Act may be confessed and reliance may be placed wholly on matters in avoidance which have nothing to do with the Act or an order or award and to that alone the appeal may be addressed."[8] Such a matter would not be within federal jurisdiction. Moreover, it was only part of the particular section under discussion in *Collin's Case* which could be said to encompass matters within federal jurisdiction, i e, matters *arising* under the Arbitration Act. The other types of proceedings[9] were not covered by s 76 (ii) (although it was true that some matters arising under award might sometimes be considered as arising under the Act). The High Court, therefore, held that this was an invalid attempt to define the jurisdiction of the federal court under s 77 (i).[10]

**(ii) "Defining the extent to which the jurisdiction of any federal court shall be exclusive of that which belongs to or is invested in the courts of the States"**

Insofar as s 75 does not confer an *exclusive* original jurisdiction on the High Court, it was necessary to give power to the federal Parliament to define those matters within the jurisdiction of the High Court and other federal courts which were exclusive to those bodies and therefore withdrawn from the jurisdiction of State tribunals.[11] Pursuant to the power conferred by s 77 (ii), the Commonwealth Parliament has enacted provisions in the *Judiciary Act* which define the matters which are exclusive to the High Court and matters which while still within the jurisdiction of State courts are nevertheless in the *federal* jurisdiction of those courts. The three major sections are ss 38, 38A and 39 of the *Judiciary Act*.

Section 38 of the *Judiciary Act* lists the following matters as within the exclusive jurisdiction of the High Court: (a) matters arising directly under any treaty, (b) suits between States or between persons suing or being sued on behalf of different States, or between a State and a person suing or being sued on behalf of another State, (c) suits by the Commonwealth, or any person suing on behalf of the Commonwealth, against a State, or any person being sued on behalf of a State, (d) suits by a State, or any person suing on behalf of a State against the Commonwealth, or any persons being sued on behalf of the Commonwealth, (e) matters in which a writ of mandamus or prohibition is sought against an officer of the Commonwealth or a federal court.

---

7  See *In re Judiciary Act* (1921) 29 CLR 257.

8  92 CLR at 541.

9  Matters involving the interpretation of the Act or an award or arising under an award.

10  Cf, *Cockle v Isaksen* (1957-58) 99 CLR 155 where a section of the *Conciliation and Arbitration Act* conferring appellate jurisdiction on the Commonwealth Industrial Court from judgments of State courts (other than Supreme Courts) in respect of any matter arising under the Act was upheld as a valid exercise of s 77 (i). On the relationship between the jurisdiction of the Industrial Court and a State Supreme Court in certain matters see *Williams v Hursey* (1959) 103 CLR 30.

11  On the jurisdiction of State courts before the enactment of the *Judiciary Act* see *Lorenzo v Carey* (1921) 29 CLR 243 at 251.

It can be seen, therefore, that what one might call the more federal or national jurisdictional matters covered by s 75 are vested in the High Court in its *exclusive* original jurisdiction. While matters arising directly under the treaty are within the federal jurisdiction, matters that only incidentally arise under treaty are left to concurrent jurisdiction. However, matters affecting consuls or other representatives of other countries remain within concurrent jurisdiction. Commonwealth-State or State-State disputes are within the exclusive jurisdiction of the High Court, while suits in which the Commonwealth and a private individual are parties are within the concurrent jurisdiction of federal and State courts. Finally, jurisdiction in respect of the writs of mandamus or prohibition against an officer of the Commonwealth are exclusively vested in the High Court while injunctions remain within concurrent jurisdiction.

Section 38A was inserted in the *Judiciary Act* in 1907 pursuant to the decision of the Privy Council in *Webb v Outrim*.[12] In this case the Privy Council, dealing with a case taken directly on appeal from the Victorian Supreme Court, took a different view of the law to that later adopted by the High Court. This case involving as it did the doctrine of intergovernmental immunities involved an *inter se* question and the purpose of s 74 of the Constitution was to prevent such a matter getting to the Privy Council without a certificate from the High Court. In order to prevent *inter se* matters arising before the Supreme Court and thus the possibility of such cases being taken on appeal direct to the Privy Council under the *Judicial Committee Acts* of 1833 and 1844, s 38A was inserted in the *Judiciary Act*. It provides that whenever in any matter, other than trials of indictable offences against the laws of the Commonwealth, a question arises as to the limits *inter se* of the constitutional powers of the Commonwealth and those of any State or States or as to the limits *inter se* of constitutional powers of any two or more States, then the jurisdiction of the High Court is to be exclusive of the jurisdiction of the Supreme Courts of the States. To this end section 40A provides that when in any cause pending in the Supreme Court of a State there arises any question as to the limits *inter se* of the constitutional powers of the Commonwealth and those of any State or States, or as to the limits *inter se* of the Constitutional powers of any two or more States, the cause is to be removed automatically into the High Court.[13] It is also necessary to refer to s 40 of the *Judiciary Act* which provides that any cause or part of a cause arising under the Constitution or involving its interpretation, pending in a court of a State, may be removed to the High Court upon an order of the High Court.[14] As we have

---

12   [1907] AC 81.

13   "... Section 40A of the *Judiciary Act* passed under the power vested in the Commonwealth by the second sub-section of s 77 of the Constitution ... has made the jurisdiction of this court entirely exclusive of that of the State Supreme Courts with respect to questions as to the limits *inter se* of the constitutional powers of the Commonwealth and of the States": *Joseph v Colonial Treasurer* (NSW) (1918) 25 CLR 32 at 49 (Isaacs, Powers and Rich JJ). See also *Commonwealth v Rhind* (1966) 119 CLR 584; [1967] ALR 483. Once before the High Court, that court can dispose of the whole cause. See also *Lansell v Lansell* (1864) 110 CLR 353 at 358, [1965] ALR 153 at 155-156 (Kitto J).

14   Made by the High Court as of course upon the application of the Attorney-General of the Commonwealth or a State, or for sufficient cause on the application of other parties.

seen such matters which are covered by s 76 (i) of the Constitution have by virtue of s 30 of the *Judiciary Act,* been vested in the High Court. Such matters, of course, still remain within the concurrent jurisdiction of the State courts but provision is made by s 40 for the cause to be removed to the High Court so that a decision by the highest court in the country can be given on any constitutional matter without it having to go through the appeal structure of the State system. These particular sections of the *Judiciary Act* have been upheld by the High Court as an exercise of jurisdiction under s 77 (ii) of the Constitution.[15]

Section 39 of the *Judiciary Act* is a most complex section involving an exercise of power by the federal Parliament under both ss 77 (ii) and (iii). The first paragraph of s 39 provides that the jurisdiction of the High Court, so far as it is not exclusive of the jurisdiction of any court of a State by virtue of ss 38 and 38A, is deemed to be exclusive "except as provided in the section." Paragraph two of the section provides that the several courts of the States are invested with federal jurisdiction in all matters in which the High Court has original jurisdiction *or* in which original jurisdiction may be conferred on the High Court, subject to the following conditions:

(a) Every decision of the Supreme Court of a State is deemed to be final except insofar as an appeal may be brought to the High Court.

(b) Whenever an appeal lies from a decision of an inferior State court to the Supreme Court it may be brought directly to the High Court without any leave.

(c) The High Court may grant special leave to appeal from any decision of the State court notwithstanding that the state law may prohibit such appeal.

(d) The federal jurisdiction of the magistrates' court shall be exercisable only by a stipendiary, police or special magistrate or a magistrate of the State who is specially authorized by the Governor-General to exercise such jurisdiction.

The effect of these conditions is as follows. Firstly, appeals from State courts exercising federal jurisdiction may not be taken to the Judicial Committee but must go directly to the High Court, and they cannot go beyond the High Court.[16] Secondly, appeals may be taken directly to the High Court from a subordinate State court exercising federal jurisdiction bypassing the Supreme Court. The High Court may grant special leave even in the face of a prohibition of a State law against such an appeal. Thirdly, courts of inferior jurisdiction cannot be composed of justices of the peace sitting alone; they must be composed of magistrates.

Portion of s 39 of the *Judiciary Act* was challenged in *Lorenzo v Carey*[17] on the ground that it was not competent for the federal Parliament under s 77 (ii) to attach conditions to a grant of federal jurisdiction.[18] This argument was rejected by the High Court on the ground that a conferment of jurisdiction could be absolute or subject to conditions (although no final opinion was expressed on the validity of s 39 (2) (a) controlling the right of appeal to the Privy Council).

---

15  *Ex parte Walsh and Johnson* (1925) 37 CLR 36. *Pirrie v McFarlane* (1925) 36 CLR 170.

16  The doubt that s 39 in its original form might not be sufficient to exclude the prerogative appeal was resolved with the passage of the *Judiciary Act,* No 134 of 1968, which in terms specifically abolished any appeal by special leave.

17  (1921) 29 CLR 243.

18  The question in this case was the validity of s 39 (2)(b) of the *Judiciary Act* providing for an appeal to the High Court from an *inferior* State court in federal jurisdiction.

It was also pointed out in that case that even without a grant of federal jurisdiction by investment, State courts had, before the enactment of the *Judiciary Act* (in 1903), power under their own Constitutions and laws in respect of a number of matters listed in ss 75 and 76 of the Constitution. In other words, they had a pre-existing State jurisdiction. Section 39 of the *Judiciary Act* was intended to divest them of this State jurisdiction in a number of matters and to replace this jurisdiction with a federal jurisdiction subject to the conditions already mentioned. In the view of the High Court "the phrase 'federal jurisdiction' means jurisdiction derived from the Federal Commonwealth. It does not denote a power to adjudicate in certain matters, though it may connote such a power." It denoted "the power to act as the judicial agent of the Commonwealth, which must act through agents if it acts at all."[19] Consequently, in respect of the matters within pre-existing State jurisdiction and in respect of additional matters covered by ss 75 and 76, the State courts had become judicial agents of the Commonwealth.

However, it is to be noted that s 39, after stating that the jurisdiction of the High Court shall be exclusive of that of the State courts subject to the conditions outlined, purports to confer jurisdiction on those courts in all matters in which the High Court has original jurisdiction under s 75 or under s 76 (by virtue of investing legislation) or may have a jurisdiction conferred upon it by a future legislative enactment of the federal Parliament (so-called potential jurisdiction); there is a certain lack of conformity, then, between the *divesting* and *investing* paragraphs of s 39. The High Court has original jurisdiction under all five paragraphs of s 75 by the force of the Constitution. The federal Parliament has conferred federal jurisdiction on the High Court in matters arising under the Constitution or involving its interpretation (see *Judiciary Act* s 30). However, in respect of the great bulk of matters covered by s 76 (ii), there has been no conferment of jurisdiction on the High Court. That is to say, mere interpretation of Commonwealth statutes remains a matter for the State courts. Moreover, no conferment exists in respect of matters covered by s 76 (iii) and (iv). The effect of s 39 appears to be that with respect to all the matters of s 75 and those matters in s 76 that are already within the original jurisdiction of the High Court by federal legislative enactment, the State courts are divested of their State jurisdiction and invested with federal jurisdiction alone, (although this was doubted by Hodges J of the Victorian Supreme Court in *Webb v Outrim*).[20] With respect to matters falling within s 76 (ii) which have not been vested in the High Court and also with respect to matters covered in ss 76 (iii) and (iv), the State courts are invested with federal jurisdiction. But it remains uncertain whether they also retain their pre-existing State jurisdiction. In other words, insofar as the High Court has not been invested with original jurisdiction in these matters there is lack of symmetry between the investing and divesting paragraphs of s 39, which may have the effect of continuing pre-existing State jurisdiction, that is, there may well be a *dual* jurisdiction. According to this view, the divesting paragraph does not operate in respect of matters not vested in the High Court by existing legislation under s 76 (ii) or matters covered by s 76 (iii) and (iv). The effect of this view would be that in respect of these matters the State courts could exercise *both* State and federal jurisdiction. In *Lorenzo v Carey* it was stated: "When federal jurisdiction is given to a State court and the jurisdiction which belongs to it is not taken away, we see no

---

19    29 CLR at 251-252.
20    [1905] VLR 433 at 464 et seq. See also *Lorenzo v Carey* 29 CLR at 251-252.

difficulty in that court exercising either jurisdiction at the instance of a litigant."[21]

The opposite view has been expressed by Dixon J in *Ffrost v Stevenson*[22]: "It has always appeared to me that, once the conclusion was reached that the federal jurisdiction was validly conferred, then under s 109 of the Constitution it was impossible to hold valid a State law conferring jurisdiction to do the same thing, whether subject to no appeal or subject to appeal in a different manner or to a different tribunal or tribunals, or otherwise producing different consequences". On this view State jurisdiction is rendered inoperative by a paramount exercise of authority by the Commonwealth, and, therefore, federal jurisdiction alone exists.[23]

One particular condition imposed by s 39 of the Judiciary Act (that limiting appeals to the Privy Council embodied in s 39 (2)(a)) was called into question by the Judicial Committee in *Webb v Outrim*.[24] This was a case involving taxation under State legislation of a Commonwealth public servant's salary. The Supreme Court of Victoria (Hodges J) decided in favour of the State, upholding the legislation. An appeal was taken direct to the Privy Council from the Supreme Court, bypassing the High Court. It was argued before the Judicial Committee that s 39 (2)(a) required that an appeal in federal jurisdiction be taken to the High Court. However, the Judicial Committee considered that the Commonwealth Parliament did not have power to take away the right of appeal from State Supreme Courts to the Privy Council, a right which was conferred by Imperial Legislation, the *Judicial Committee Acts*, in the nineteenth century. On this view, therefore, s. 39 (2)(a) was to that extent invalid.

However, in two cases decided at a later stage by the High Court, the *Limerick Case*[25] and the *Kreglinger Case*[26] the validity of s 39 (2)(a) was upheld. In the *Limerick Case*, which involved an action against the Commonwealth (and therefore arose in federal jurisdiction as it was a matter covered by s 75 (iii) of the Constitution), the majority of the High Court held that s 77 was a sufficient basis for imposing restrictions on the exercise of a litigant's right of appeal from a state court invested with federal jurisdiction. The Federal Constitution being an Act later in time than the *Judicial Committee Acts*, insofar as it dealt with matters which were covered by the earlier Acts, prevailed over them. There was an inconsistency between those Acts which allowed appeals direct from the Supreme Court to the Privy Council and the later Constitution Act which permitted federal Parliament to impose restrictions on that right of appeal. The restrictions were wide enough to encompass the condition that the appellant must choose the High Court and not the Privy

21 29 CLR at 252. See also Cowen, *Federal Jurisdiction in Australia*, 193 et seq; *Booth v Shelmerdine* [1924] VLR 76. Cf, *Troy v Wrigglesworth* (1919) 26 CLR 305 at 310.
22 (1937) 58 CLR 528 at 573.
23 See *Felton v Mulligan* (1971) 45 ALJR 525. Cowen, *Federal Jurisdiction in Australia*, 195
24 [1907] AC 81. In *Baxter v Commissioner of Taxation* (NSW) (1907) 4 CLR 1087 the High Court rejected the constitutional doctrine espoused by the Privy Council in *Webb v Outrim*. For a discussion of the history of this conflict between the two courts see Mason, "The Limitation of Appeals to the Privy Council" (1968) 3 FedLR 1 at 7 et seq.
25 *Commonwealth v Limerick Steamship Co and Kidman* (1924) 35 CLR 69.
26 *Commonwealth v Kregliner and Fernau Ltd and Bardsley* (1926) 37 CLR 393.

Council if he decided to appeal from the Supreme Court's decision. But of course it was possible for the federal Parliament to impose this restriction only in matters of federal jurisdiction. *Webb v Outrim* was interpreted as an authority only in relation to the exercise of purely *State* jurisdiction and not of federal jurisdiction.[27]

In *Kreglinger's Case,* involving an appeal from the New South Wales full court[28] which had granted leave to appeal to the Privy Council in a matter in which the Commonwealth was a party, the question was precisely put by Isaacs J in this way: "Has the Commonwealth Parliament power under the Constitution so to regulate the exercise of federal jurisdiction by a State Supreme Court that appeals from that court, exercising that jurisdiction, shall be brought only to the High Court on appeal?"[29] An affirmative answer was given to the question. In the *Kreglinger Case* it was also pointed out that the validity of s 39 (2) (a) involved an *inter se* question and therefore it was the duty of the Full Court of New South Wales to proceed no further with the action when the matter was raised, as s 38A and 40A required the matter to be remitted to the High Court. Consequently, the Full Court of New South Wales had erred in entertaining the matter and in granting leave to appeal to the Privy Council.[30]

We are faced, therefore, with an inconsistency between the reasoning of the High Court in the cases just mentioned and that of the Privy Council in *Webb v Outrim*. Dixon J has expressed the opinion that *Webb v Outrim* is not binding on the High Court on the ground that it raised an *inter se* question which could not be determined by the Privy Council without a certificate from the High Court.[31]

Until 1969 there was some doubt as to whether s 39 (2) (a) operated to cut off the prerogative appeal as well as the appeal under the *Judicial Committee Acts*. An amendment to the Judiciary Act in that year made it clear that the prerogative appeal was excluded.[32]

The federal jurisdiction conferred on State courts by s 39 is given subject to limits as to subject-matter and locality of those courts, unless these are changed by specific Commonwealth legislation. Section 39 is an ambulatory provision, that is to say, it applies to the jurisdiction of the State courts as it exists from time to time and is not restricted to the jurisdiction existing in 1903 (the date of the passing of the *Judiciary Act*). Consequently, any amendments to State jurisdiction by legislation passed subsequently will extend the corresponding limits of federal jurisdiction.[33] This does not mean

---

27    35 CLR at 94, 95, 118.
28    Of course an "internal" appeal may be taken from a single judge of the Supreme Court to a full Supreme Court in matters of federal jurisdiction: *Minister of Army v Parbury Henty and Co Ltd* (1945) 70 CLR 459 at 505-6 (Dixon J).
29    37 CLR at 403.
30    See Cowen, *Federal Jurisdiction in Australia,* 176.
31    *McIlwraith McEacharn Ltd v Shell Co of Australia Ltd* (1945) 70 CLR 175 at 209.
32    Act No 134 of 1968.
33    On this question see *Minister for the Army v Parbury Henty and Co Ltd* (1945) 70 CLR 459 at 505. *Commonwealth v District Court of the Metropolitan District* (1954) 90 CLR 13 at 22-23. *Goward v Commonwealth* (1957) 97 CLR 355 at 360-66.

that the federal Parliament cannot by special enactment confer a jurisdiction on State courts otherwise than under s 39.[34]

### (iii) "Investing any court of a State with federal jurisdiction"

Unlike the American situation, where a hierarchy of federal courts including original and appellate tribunals have been established, the Australian tradition has been to endow State courts with federal jurisdiction. The phrase "autochthonous expedient" has been coined to describe this experiment.[35] Cowen considers that while "economy alone does not explain departure from the American precedent, the desire for economy linked to a more willing acceptance of a unified federal system furnishes an adequate explanation for the Australian choice".[36]

Federal jurisdiction granted by this section is either original or appellate jurisdiction.[37] But such investment must be with respect to matters listed in ss 75 and 76.[38] Consequently any conferment of jurisdiction in respect of non-judicial power is beyond the jurisdiction of the federal Parliament.[39] Section 77 (iii) constitutes an exclusive source for investment of State courts with federal jurisdiction.[40] There is some difference of opinion on the question whether State courts exercising federal jurisdiction remain State courts or for this purpose are treated as part of the federal judicature.[41]

It is clear that in conferring federal jurisdiction on State courts the federal Parliament cannot alter the structure of the State courts. This is illustrated by *Le Mesurier v Connor*.[42] Section 12 (5) of the *Bankruptcy Act 1924-1928* not only provided for the appointment of registrars in bankruptcy, but purported to make them officers of the State courts which the Act invested with bankruptcy jurisdiction, thereby altering (by addition) the existing structure of the State court. In holding the section invalid the majority of the Court (Knox CJ, Rich and Dixon JJ) said:

The power is to confer additional judicial authority upon a court fully established by another legislature. Such a power is exercised and its purposes achieved when

---

34  *Seagg v R* (1932) 48 CLR 252, *Australian Red Cross Society v Beaver Trading Co Ltd* (1947) 75 CLR 320. Cf, *Adams v Cleeve* (1935) 53 CLR 185 especially at 190-1.
35  *Boilermakers' Case* (1956) 94 CLR 254 at 268.
36  *Federal Jurisdiction in Australia*, 150.
37  *Ah Yick v Lehmert* (1905) 2 CLR 593.
38  A wide discretion may be given to a court invested with federal jurisdiction to define the substantive law affecting an action or transaction governed by federal statute. See *Hooper v Hooper* (1955) 91 CLR 529 at 535 discussed by Cowen, *Federal Jurisdiction in Australia*, 108; *Connolly v Connolly* 115 CLR 166; *Commonwealth v Anderson* (1957) 97 CLR 345 at 352.
39  *Queen Victoria Memorial Hospital v Thornton* (1953) 87 CLR 144. Cf, *Cominos v Cominos* (1972) 46 ALJR 593.
40  *Peacock v Newton Marrickville and General Co-operative Building Society* (1943) 67 CLR 25.
41  See Cowen, *Federal Jurisdiction in Australia*, 153-4. As to whether Parliament can authorize the investment of federal jurisdiction by subordinate legislation see *Minister for the Army v Parbury Henty Ltd* (1945) 70 CLR 459. *Peacock v Newton, Marrickville and General Co-operative Building Society* (1943) 67 CLR 25. *Le Mesurier v Connor* (1929) 42 CLR 481. *Willocks v Anderson* (1971) 45 ALJR 375, [1971] ALR 703 (investment under s 76). Cowen, *Federal Jurisdiction in Australia*, 156-8.
42  (1929) 42 CLR 481.

the Parliament has chosen an existing court and has bestowed upon it part of the judicial power belonging to the Commonwealth. To affect or alter the constitution of the court itself or the organization through which its jurisdiction and powers are exercised is to go outside the limits of the power conferred and to seek to achieve a further object, namely, the regulation or establishment of the instrument or organ of government in which federal power is vested, an objective for which the Constitution provides another means, the creation of federal courts.[43]

It is clear, therefore, that s 77 (iii) does not enable the Parliament of the Commonwealth to make a Commonwealth officer a functionary of a State court and authorize him to act on its behalf and administer part of its jurisdiction. The incidental power could not be regarded as a basis for authorising this conferment either.

After the decision in *Le Mesurier v Connor*, the provisions of the *Bankruptcy Act* were amended. A main change was that, under the amended section, the registrar, while being at the courts' disposal, was not part of the curial structure. It was held that these amendments had cured the previous defects: *Bond v George Bond and Company*.[44] As Rich and Dixon JJ put it:

Instead of forming part of its official system and exercising the authority of an officer of the court, the registrar is now to be estranged to the court and its organisation. But the registrar is nevertheless to be amenable to the court orders and directions, if it chooses to give him any.[45]

Section 39 of the *Judiciary Act* refers to the exercise of federal jurisdiction by a State court within the limits imposed as to locality, subject matter or otherwise. This means that, unless the Commonwealth Parliament has otherwise provided, the locality and other restrictions will continue to exist. However, this does not prevent the federal Parliament from modifying such incidents of curial structure. It is well recognised that the federal Parliament has power to determine the nature and limits of the jurisdiction which it confers on State courts and therefore, federal jurisdiction may differ from that exercised by the State court exercising its own State jurisdiction. This principle is illustrated by the case of *Adams v Watson*[46] where the jurisdiction conferred by a federal taxation Act to institute proceedings of a criminal nature at any time was upheld even though, under State law, prosecutions had to be instituted within a particular time limit. There is also no objection to federal Parliament modifying the area over which a particular court has jurisdiction (e g, a Melbourne magistrates' court might be given jurisdiction over an offence occurring in a country area of Victoria). Likewise, there would seem to be no reason why the federal legislature could not extend or modify the monetary limits of particular State courts.

It must be borne in mind, however, that the judicial power of the Commonwealth can only be exercised by "courts". It has been decided that masters or registrars of the Supreme Court of a State are not part of the State court structure for the purposes of the exercise of federal jurisdiction.[47]

---

43   Ibid, at 496.
44   (1930) 44 CLR 11.
45   Ibid, at 20. See also *Peacock's Case* 67 CLR 25 at 37 (per Latham CJ).
46   (1938) 60 CLR 545.
47   See *Kotsis v Kotsis* (1971) 45 ALJR 62; [1971] ALR 333. *Knight v Knight* (1971) 45 ALJR 315; [1971] ALR 644.

PROCEEDINGS AGAINST COMMONWEALTH OR STATE

**78.** *The Parliament may make laws conferring rights to proceed against the Commonwealth or a State in respect of matters within the limits of the judicial power.*[48]

The effect of this section is to allow the Commonwealth Parliament to legislate with respect to suits against the Commonwealth or a State in matters of federal jurisdiction including matters covered by ss 75 and 76. It has done so in Part IX of the *Judiciary Act.*[49]

A person may sue the Commonwealth in contract or tort in the High Court, the Supreme Court of the State or Territory in which the claim arose, or in any other court of competent jurisdiction in the State or Territory in which the claim arose.[50] Where, however, a State makes any claim against the Commonwealth in contract or tort, the suit may be brought in the High Court.[51] A person making any claim against a State whether in contract or tort in respect of a matter covered by ss 75 or 76 of the Constitution may institute the proceeding in the State Supreme Court or the High Court (if the High Court has original jurisdiction).[52] A State making a claim against another State may bring the suit in the High Court.[53] Later sections of the *Judiciary Act* make provision for certain rules to be observed in such proceedings. Section 64 of the Act provides that in any suit to which the Commonwealth or a State is a party, the rights of the parties shall "as nearly as possible be the same, and judgment may be given and costs awarded on either side as in a suit between subject and subject."[54] There has been discussion of the question whether s 64 is directed to procedural matters or operates so as to confer substantive rights on the parties.[55] The better opinion appears to be that its effect is procedural. Reference has already been made to the question whether s 75 (iii) is a sufficient basis for making the Commonwealth liable

---

48   Quick and Garran, 804-7. Wynes, 424-34. Lane, 391-404.
49   In particular, in sections 56, 57, 58, 59 and 64. See *Commonwealth v Baume* (1905) 2 CLR 405 at 412, 417; *R v Registrar of Titles (Vic) ex parte the Commonwealth* (1915) 20 CLR 379 at 388 (Isaacs J); *New South Wales v Commonwealth (No 1)* (1932) 46 CLR 155 at 174 (Rich and Dixon JJ). See also Phillips, "Choice of Law in Federal Jurisdiction" (1961) 3 MULR 170, 348. Hogg, "Suits against the Commonwealth or States in the Federal Jurisdiction" (1970) 44 ALJ 425. Renard, "Australian Interstate Common Law" (1970) 4 Federal Law Review 87. Campbell, "Federal Contract Law" (1970) 44 ALJ 580.
50   Section 56.
51   Section 57. The jurisdiction of the High Court is exclusive under s 38.
52   Section 58.
53   Section 59. Again, the jurisdiction of the High Court is exclusive under s 38.
54   For an example of the operation of this section see *Griffin v South Australia* (1924) 35 CLR 200.
55   See *Commonwealth v New South Wales* (1923) 32 CLR 200 at 215 (Isaacs, Rich and Starke JJ). *Asiatic Steam Navigation Co Ltd v Commonwealth* (1955-56) 96 CLR 397. *Commonwealth v Anderson* (1960) 105 CLR 303, discussed by Wynes 429 et seq. Wynes agrees with the view of Windeyer J in *Anderson's Case* that "s 64 operates primarily to remove the common law privileges of the Crown—in right of the Commonwealth or a State—in proceedings with subjects, leaving the substantive law to operate according to its tenor so that, if a State Act expressly exempts the Crown from liability either in contract or tort, s 64 would not operate to remove the exemption— in the case of a Commonwealth Act similar considerations would apply". (*Legislative, Executive and Judicial Powers in Australia*, 431.)

to suit or whether there must be further support for such liability by legislative provisions such as are contained in Part IX of the *Judiciary Act*.[56]

A particular matter which arises for discussion is the nature of the law to be applied in suits falling within Part IX of the *Judiciary Act*. The *Judiciary Act* contains two sections (79, 80), the effect of which is to provide that the laws of a State (statute and common law) to the extent to which they are not inconsistent with the Commonwealth Constitution or Commonwealth statutes shall apply to suits in federal jurisdiction.

Under these provisions, the law to be applied by a federal court (including the High Court) or a State court exercising federal jurisdiction, will be the law in force from time to time[57] in the State in which the matter is heard.[58] This of course is subject to any contrary constitutional provision or federal statute.[59]

It includes not only substantive but also procedural law,[60] provided that if a State statute is in question it must appear from its terms that it is intended to apply to the matter before the court.

Also included are the forum's conflict of law rules including the rules as to the choice of law where there is an inter-State element.[61]

NUMBER OF JUDGES

**79.** *The federal jurisdiction of any court may be exercised by such number of judges as the Parliament prescribes.*[62]

Under this section the Commonwealth Parliament may control the number of judges sitting in a State court exercising federal jurisdiction as well as the number of judges in a federal court. Reference may be made to s 22 of the *Judiciary Act* which provides that applications for leave to appeal to the Judicial Committee on *inter se* matters must be heard by a full court consisting of not less than three judges, and s 23 which provides that at least three judges must concur in a decision affecting the constitutional powers of the Commonwealth, as examples of legislation valid under this section and also the incidental power (s 51 (xxxix)).[63]

---

56   See discussion under s 75 (iii).

57   The view expressed in *Washington v Commonwealth* (1939) 39 SR (NSW) 133, that the date at which liability was to be determined (and therefore the applicable law) was 1903, the date when the *Judiciary Act* came into operation, but the better view is that the liability is to be determined in accordance with the law in force at the time when the proceedings occur. See Windeyer J in *Suehle v Commonwealth* (1967) 116 CLR 353 at 356-375; [1967] ALR 572 at 574; Hogg, op cit, at 435.

58   *R v Oregan* (1957) 97 CLR 323. *Pedersen v Young* (1964) 110 CLR 162 at 165, 167; [1964] ALR 798 at 799, 800-1. *Parker v The Commonwealth* (1965) 112 CLR 295 at 306, [1965] ALR 1094 at 1100.

59   Such as may found in the *Judiciary Act* or *High Court Procedure Act*. See *Musgrave v The Commonwealth* 57 CLR at 547-548. *Suehle v The Commonwealth* 116 CLR 353 at 356; [1967] ALR 572 at 573-4.

60   Although differing views were expressed on this question in *Pedersen v Young*, it would appear that the better view is that procedural law is included. See Nygh, *Conflict of Laws in Australia* (2nd ed, 1971) 782-3.

61   See *Parker v Commonwealth* (1965) 112 CLR 295; [1965] ALR 1094. *Musgrave v Commonwealth* (1937) 57 CLR 514. *Suehle v Commonwealth* (1967) 116 CLR 353 at 355-6; [1967] ALR 572 at 573-4. See also Hogg, op cit, at 426 et seq. Lane, "State Courts Exercising Federal Jurisdiction", (1966) 40 ALJ at 52-55. See also below under s 118.

62   Quick and Garran, 807. Wynes, 414.

63   See above p 190.

Section 39 (2) (d) of the *Judiciary Act* provides that a court of summary jurisdiction shall be constituted by a magistrate. In *Queen Victoria Memorial Hospital v Thornton*[64] the High Court upheld the validity of this section and pointed to its source of validity in either s 79 or s 51 (xxxix). Section 79 of the Constitution refers to the *number* of judges while s 39 (2) (d) of the *Judiciary Act* seems to be more a provision dealing with the *qualifications* of judicial officers or the *composition* of a court and therefore dependent for its source of validity on the incidental power.[65]

TRIAL BY JURY

**80.** *The trial on indictment of any offence against any law of the Commonwealth shall be by jury, and every such trial shall be held in the State where the offence was committed, and if the offence was not committed within any State the trial shall be held at such place or places as the Parliament prescribes.*[66]

This section prescribes that indictable offences must be heard before a jury and cannot be dealt with summarily.[67] The Commonwealth *Crimes Act*, which contains many indictable offences, makes provision for jury trial in accordance with this section. On the other hand, there are a number of provisions in the Act for summary trial, and to these provisions s 80 is not applicable.

In *R v Archdall*[68] it was held that the federal Parliament was not required to lay down an indictment procedure for an offence which carried one year's imprisonment; such an offence could be dealt with summarily. Indeed there are some provisions in Commonwealth legislation requiring offences carrying more than one year's imprisonment to be tried summarily.[69] The position, therefore, is, in the words of Higgins J in *Archdall's Case*, that "if there be an indictment, there must be a jury; but there is nothing to compel procedure by indictment".[70] The supposed constitutional guarantee of trial by jury in criminal cases is therefore rather ineffective.[71] Finally, it has been held that s 80 has no application to the Territories.[72]

---

64  (1953) 87 CLR 144 at 152.
65  See *R v Ray ex parte Smith* [1948] SASR 216. Cf, *Ex parte Coorey* (1945) SR (NSW) 287 at 305 (Jordan CJ). See also *New South Wales v The Commonwealth (No 1)* (1932) 46 CLR 155 at 179 (Rich and Dixon JJ). Cowen, *Federal Jurisdiction in Australia*, 160-164. See also Isaacs J in *Le Mesurier v Connor* (1929) 42 CLR 481 at 511-512: "While s 79 enables the Parliament to prescribe the number of judges to exercise the jurisdiction, nothing is said about bailiffs, ushers and doorkeepers. Apparently, they would all have to form part of the tribunal. But, in truth, the official staff of the courts are no more part of the court than the parliamentary official staff are part of Parliament".
66  Quick and Garran, 807-10. Wynes, 415-6. Nicholas, 385.
67  See generally, Comans, "The Jury in Federal Jurisdiction—Constitutional Aspects" (1968) 3 FedLR 51.
68  (1928) 41 CLR 128.
69  For example, *National Service Act* 1951-1971, s 51. See *Zarb v Kennedy* (1968) 43 ALJR 1; [1969] ALR 292.
70  41 CLR at 139-140. See also *R v Federal Court of Bankruptcy ex parte Lowenstein* (1938) 59 CLR 556 at 570 (Latham CJ). *Sachter v Attorney-General for the Commonwealth* (1954) 94 CLR 86. *R v Snow* 20 CLR 315 at 323, 328, 358, 365, 374-5.
71  See *Spratt v Hermes* 114 CLR 226 at 244, [1966] ALR 597 at 602-3 (Barwick CJ).
72  *R v Bernasconi* (1915) 19 CLR 629.

## CHAPTER IV

## FINANCE AND TRADE

CONSOLIDATED REVENUE FUND

81. *All revenues or moneys raised or received by the Executive Government of the Commonwealth shall form one Consolidated Revenue Fund, to be appropriated for the purposes of the Commonwealth in the manner and subject to the charges and liabilities imposed by this Constitution.*[1]

The purpose of this section is to establish the Consolidated Revenue Fund and make provision for the appropriation of moneys from it by the Commonwealth.

**"All revenues or moneys raised or received by the Executive Government of the Commonwealth shall form one Consolidated Revenue Fund"**

This paragraph incorporates the British statutory requirement, derived originally from 27 Geo III, c 13 (1787), that revenue received by the Executive government shall form one single fund. It is clear that ease of financial administration as well as public scrutiny is promoted by a requirement that the receipt of Government revenue be organized in this manner, as contrasted with a system whereby moneys can be paid into a multitude of different funds.

The question has arisen as to whether loan moneys and moneys received on trust for specific purposes are required by this section to be paid into the Consolidated Revenue Fund. Quick and Garran consider that the word "moneys" is controlled (according to the maxim *noscitur a sociis*) by the word "revenue" and is limited to government income in the nature of revenue, and that the Constitution does not prevent the payment of moneys received by way of loan into a separate fund.[2] This would mean that there is no constitutional barrier to the creation of a loan fund (or a trust fund) in addition to the Consolidated Revenue Fund.

In actual fact, the *Audit Act* 1901-1969 makes provision for the establishment of two additional funds (Loan Fund and Trust Fund) in addition to the Consolidated Revenue Fund. It is provided in this Act that moneys received by the Commonwealth shall be paid to the Commonwealth Public Account which shall be kept in such banks and under such subdivisions as the Treasurer may direct.[3] Under s 55, "a separate account shall be kept in the Treasury of all moneys which shall be raised by way of loan upon the public credit of the Commonwealth and which shall have been placed to the credit of the Commonwealth Public Account". This account is called the Loan Fund and is organized in the way required by the *Loan Acts*.

Section 60 deals with the Trust Fund and provides that "a separate account shall be kept in the Treasury to be called the Trust Fund of all moneys which shall be placed to the credit of that fund under such separate heads

---

1 Quick and Garran, 811-2. Wynes, 334-8.
2 *Annotated Constitution of the Commonwealth*, 811.
3 Section 21 (i).

as may be directed by the Treasurer." Succeeding sections deal with the power of the Treasurer to establish specific Trust Accounts.[4]

### "to be appropriated for the purposes of the Commonwealth in the manner and subject to the charges and liabilities imposed by this Constitution"

A central question relating to the interpretation of this paragraph is whether the phrase "for the purposes of the Commonwealth" limits the Commonwealth spending power to purposes associated with the areas of Commonwealth power (legislative, executive, and judicial), or whether it permits a much wider appropriation of moneys for Australian purposes without regard to the division of powers between the Commonwealth and States. This question received the consideration of the court in the *Pharmaceutical Benefits Case*.[5]

The *Pharmaceutical Benefits Act* (Com) of 1945 provided for the supply by chemists without charge to the public of certain medicines prescribed by medical practitioners, appropriated money to be paid to chemists for the medicine supplied, and imposed duties on medical practitioners and chemists in relation to the prescription and supply of the medicine. It was held by a majority (Latham CJ, Rich, Starke, Dixon and Williams JJ, McTiernan J, dissenting) that the Act was neither authorized by s 81 nor by s 51 (xxxix). It was in effect an Act relating to public health which was not (apart from quarantine aspects), an area of Commonwealth power.

On the particular question as to the nature of the appropriation power, Latham CJ[6] and McTiernan J[7] considered that s 81 extended to the appropriation of moneys for Australian purposes. McTiernan J emphatically stated that "any purpose for which the elected representatives of the people of the Commonwealth determine to appropriate the revenue is a purpose of the Commonwealth."[8] The opposite view was expressed by Williams J[9] (with whom Starke J in substance agreed on this question):

The phrase ("purposes of the Commonwealth") must have been inserted to have some effect, and if it is to have any effect it must place some constitutional limitation upon the purposes for which the Commonwealth Parliament can pass an appropriation Act. The object of the Constitution was to superimpose on the existing body politics consisting of the States a wider over-riding body politic for certain specific purposes. It was for these particular purposes and these alone that the body politics consisting of the States agreed to create the body politic known as the Commonwealth of Australia. These purposes must all be found within the four corners of the Constitution.[10]

Dixon J (with whom Rich J[11] agreed) took what could be described as a *via media*:

"It was said that s 81 of the Constitution, in referring to appropriation for the purposes of the Commonwealth, empowers the Parliament to expend money for any purpose that is for the benefit of the people of the Commonwealth, or for the

---

4 Sections 62A, 62B.
5 *Attorney-General for Victoria ex rel Dale v Commonwealth* (1945) 71 CLR 237.
6 Ibid, at 256.
7 Ibid, at 273 et seq.
8 Ibid, at 279.
9 Ibid, at 265-266. See also his judgment in *Attorney-General (Vic) v Commonwealth* (1935) 52 CLR 533 at 567-8.
10 (1945) 71 CLR at 282.
11 Ibid, at 264.

advancement of their interest and that, for the rest, s 51 (xxxix) warranted an amplification or extension of the area of legislation once the description of the benefit or advancement had been determined on. This is not the view which in the past I have entertained of the power of appropriation given by s 81 and of the requirement expressed by s 83 that the appropriation must be "by law". No-one, I think, suggests, and I certainly do not, that any narrow interpretation or application should be given to these provisions. Even upon the footing that the power of expenditure is limited to matters to which the federal legislative power may be addressed, it necessarily includes whatever is incidental to the existence of the Commonwealth as a state and to the exercise of the functions of a national government. These are things which, whether in reference to the external or internal concerns of government, should be interpreted widely and applied according to no narrow conception of the functions of the central government of a country in the world of to-day."[12]

The consensus (such as it is) which emerges from the *Pharmaceutical Benefits Case* supports the view that there is some limitation, deriving from the nature of the federal system, on the appropriation of moneys by the Commonwealth although the power is not limited to the specific legislative heads granted to the Commonwealth. It was this decision which, as Sawer says, appeared to establish the narrow view of the spending power,[13] that led the Commonwealth government to support in 1946 the constitutional amendment which incorporated s 51 (xxiiiA) as a head of Commonwealth power.

On the other hand, we have to remember that an individual must establish *locus standi* before challenging an appropriation Act or, for that matter, any other Act. We have already pointed out that a general taxpayer's action is not available under the principles as to locus standi adopted by the High Court.[14] Consequently, in the absence of a State Attorney-General's *fiat*, an individual or group would not be able to challenge Commonwealth appropriation legislation unless the necessary interest on his or their part was established. In any case, it will often be found that an appropriation made to an organization will encompass purposes some of which are within, and some outside, Commonwealth heads of power. It would be impossible for a Court to separate the items of expenditure of the organization which are within from those outside power.[15]

In recent years, the Commonwealth has enacted legislation establishing various bodies and appropriating money for their operating expenses. Examples are the *Snowy Mountains Engineering Corporation Act*,[16] the *Criminology Research Act*,[17] the *Australian Film Development Corporation Act*,[18] and the *National Regional and Urban Development Authority Act*.[19] The purposes for which these organizations have been established are mainly within the area of State legislative power—design works for irrigation purposes, research into the causes of crime, film production, investigation of urban and regional development—but in some aspects touch upon various Commonwealth powers. The current *Appropriation Acts* also contain grants to various public bodies

---

12    Ibid, at 269.
13    *Cases on the Constitution of the Commonwealth*, (3rd ed), 550.
14    See Introduction, above p 21.
15    Sawer, op cit, n 13, at 551.
16    No 39 of 1970.
17    No 15 of 1971.
18    No 21 of 1970.
19    No 117 of 1972. Renamed the Cities Commission by the *Cities Commission Act* of 1973.

engaged in promoting recreational and cultural activities within the States (e g, National Fitness Council, Australian Elizabethan Theatre Trust). In so far as this financial assistance benefits the community generally, it is unlikely that a State Attorney-General would grant his *fiat* to a taxpayer or group who wished to challenge the constitutionality of the legislation.[20]

The final words of s 81 are of little importance. They require that, before Parliament proceeds to appropriate revenue during a financial year, it must ensure that any appropriation provided for in the Constitution must be satisfied. The following section (s 82) establishes the costs of collecting revenue as a first charge on the Consolidated Revenue Fund. Other sections provide for the payment of salaries to various Commonwealth officials either directly (e g, s 3: salary of Governor-General), or indirectly (e g, s 72: salaries of judges).

### EXPENDITURE CHARGED THEREON

**82.** *The costs, charges, and expenses incident to the collection, management, and receipt of the Consolidated Revenue Fund shall form the first charge thereon; and the revenue of the Commonwealth shall in the first instance be applied to the payment of the expenditure of the Commonwealth.*[21]

The effect of this section is clear. It is recognized that the first charges on the Consolidated Revenue Fund are the various departmental outlays necessary for the collection, receipt and management of the Fund. This would cover primarily expenses relating to the Treasury and the Auditor-General. It would also cover all other departments (e g, the PMG's department) which received revenue.

The section does not constitute an appropriation of an undefined sum for these purposes. It is necessary for the government to include in the annual appropriation Acts the required amounts. These amounts will form part of the estimates for the various departments.

The final part of the section requires that initial provision be made in the appropriation legislation for the funds directed to Commonwealth expenditure (e g, the public service). As Quick and Garran point out, this in effect includes expenses of collection associated with the Consolidated Revenue Fund.[22]

### MONEY TO BE APPROPRIATED BY LAW

**83.** *No money shall be drawn from the Treasury of the Commonwealth except under appropriation made by law.*

*But until the expiration of one month after the first meeting of the Parliament the Governor-General in Council may draw from the Treasury and expend such moneys as may be necessary for the maintenance of any department transferred to the Commonwealth and for the holding of the first elections for the Parliament.*[23]

---

20  Perhaps the most adventurous piece of legislation is the *Child Care Act*, No 121 of 1972, which appropriates money for the construction and recurrent costs of child minding centres. It is difficult to fit these purposes within those covered by s 51 (xxiiiA) unless they could be described as "family allowances."
21  Quick and Garran, 812-3.
22  Ibid, at 813.
23  Quick and Garran, 813-5.

As the effect of the second paragraph was exhausted in the early period of federation, we are concerned with the requirements of the first paragraph.

The basic constitutional requirement for the spending of public revenue is parliamentary sanction. Accordingly, s 83 prohibits the disbursement of money from the Treasury except pursuant to the authorization of an Act of Parliament.

This prohibition applies to a unilateral act of payment by a Commonwealth officer as well as to a bilateral transaction (e g, a contract) in which the Commonwealth is involved. We have already seen[24] in our discussion of the executive power that the courts have recognized that a contract to pay money is unenforceable unless Parliament has appropriated money to satisfy it (either under a general or specific appropriation).[25]

Appropriation legislation may be either annual or special (operating for a period beyond the financial year). Certain special appropriations are contained in the Constitution itself (e g, the salary of the Governor-General, s 3). Others (e g, salaries of federal judges, ministers) are provided for in the Acts of Parliament establishing the salaries.

The major appropriations (i e, for the public service, social services) are made annually in the budget session of Parliament. The most important of these acts is the *Appropriation Act No 1*, which is introduced with the estimates of expenditure, these estimates being dealt with at the Bill's committee stage in the House of Representatives.[26] In the Senate special estimates committees deal with areas of expenditure, grouped under certain headings.[27] *Supply Acts* are passed near the end of a session to validate expenditure for the initial period of the ensuing financial year until the next appropriation Act is passed.

It remains for us to recall that under s 56 no Bill appropriating revenue can be passed unless the purpose of the appropriation has been recommended by the Governor-General (i e, by Cabinet). Consequently, the Executive has full control over appropriation legislation.

### TRANSFER OF OFFICERS

**84.** *When any department of the public service of a State becomes transferred to the Commonwealth, all officers of the department shall become subject to the control of the Executive Government of the Commonwealth.*

*Any such officer who is not retained in the service of the Commonwealth shall, unless he is appointed to some other office of equal emolument in the public service of the State, be entitled to receive from the State any pension, gratuity, or other compensation, payable under the law of the State on the abolition of his office.*

*Any such officer who is retained in the service of the Commonwealth shall preserve all his existing and accruing rights, and shall be entitled to retire from office at the time, and on the pension or retiring allowance, which would be*

---

24　See under s 61.

25　It has been usual in recent years to include in one of the main appropriation Acts appropriation of a sum described as an advance to the Treasurer which allows the Cabinet to meet unforeseen expenditure in excess of a specific appropriation. Note also *Audit Act* 1901-1969, s 37. Hanks and Fajgenbaum, *Australian Constitutional Law* (1972) 150.

26　Under the system prevailing until 1963, the Budget was introduced in the House of Representatives sitting as the Committee of Supply. See Crisp, *Australian National Government*, 306-7.

27　See Crisp, at 349.

*permitted by the law of the State if his service with the Commonwealth were
a continuation of his service with the State. Such pension or retiring allowance
shall be paid to him by the Commonwealth; but the State shall pay to the
Commonwealth a part thereof, to be calculated on the proportion which his
term of service with the State bears to his whole term of service, and for the
purpose of the calculation his salary shall be taken to be that paid to him by
the State at the time of the transfer.*

*Any officer who is, at the establishment of the Commonwealth, in the
public service of a State, and who is, by consent of the Governor of the State
with the advice of the Executive Council thereof, transferred to the public
service of the Commonwealth, shall have the same rights as if he had been an
officer of a department transferred to the Commonwealth and were retained in
the service of the Commonwealth.*[28]

The purpose of this section was to provide for the continuance of certain
rights of officers of the various State public services who were retained by the
Commonwealth when their departments were transferred to the Commonwealth
under the provisions of s 69.[29] If an officer were not retained and did not
receive a similar appointment in another State department, then he was entitled
to receive a pension or other compensation under the provisions of State law
(e g, a State *Public Service Act*) on the abolition of the office.

The pension rights of the "retained" officer were preserved with a duty
cast on the State to contribute a *pro rata* amount calculated on the length of
service with the State.

The final paragraph of s 84 relates to State officers who by arrangement
between the State and Commonwealth transferred to the Commonwealth public
service. The rights of such officers were to be the same as those who were
members of transferred departments.

There is some slight doubt as to whether s 84 applies to departments
transferred to the Commonwealth otherwise than under s 69. In *Trower v
Commonwealth*[30] Isaacs J said that s 84 applied to "the transfer of departments, which are by the Constitution destined to be transferred to the Commonwealth as soon as they conveniently can be." In *Cosway v Commonwealth*[31]
the question was referred to briefly by McTiernan J. In that case, the issue
was raised by the plaintiff who had worked in dockyards under the control of
the Victorian Government, and who had subsequently resigned to join the
Commonwealth public service when the Commonwealth, by purchase, acquired
the dockyards from the State. McTiernan J referred to the dictum of Isaacs J
without comment. He went on to say that s 84 did not apply, as the dockyard
was not a department of the public service which had been transferred, but
"an aggregate of State property which passed to the Commonwealth by
purchase."[32]

The view of Isaacs J seems sound. If any department of the public service
of a State is transferred to the Commonwealth, it is a matter for arrangement
between the Commonwealth and States as to the protection of rights of existing
officers. No doubt the minimum conditions recognized by s 84 (which are
based on equity) would be observed but they would not apply as a matter of
constitutional obligation.

---

28  Quick and Garran, 815-9.
29  As to the transfer of these departments, see above under s 69.
30  (1923) 32 CLR 585 at 589.
31  (1942) 65 CLR 628.
32  Ibid, at 637.

It may be mentioned that when the Commonwealth introduced the uniform tax scheme, provision was made under the *Income Tax (War-time Arrangements) Act*[33] for the Commonwealth Treasurer to make such arrangements for the (temporary) transfer of officers of the States connected with the assessment and collection of income tax. Various sections of the Act made provision for the continuance of certain rights of the transferred officers.[34]

### TRANSFER OF PROPERTY OF STATE

**85.** *When any department of the public service of a State is transferred to the Commonwealth—*

(i) *All property of the State of any kind, used exclusively in connexion with the department, shall become vested in the Commonwealth; but, in the case of the departments controlling customs and excise and bounties, for such time only as the Governor-General in Council may declare to be necessary:*

(ii) *The Commonwealth may acquire any property of the State, of any kind used, but not exclusively used in connexion with the department; the value thereof shall, if no agreement can be made, be ascertained in, as nearly as may be, the manner in which the value of land, or of an interest in land, taken by the State for public purposes is ascertained under the law of the State in force at the establishment of the Commonwealth:*

(iii) *The Commonwealth shall compensate the State for the value of any property passing to the Commonwealth under this section; if no agreement can be made as to the mode of compensation, it shall be determined under laws to be made by the Parliament:*

(iv) *The Commonwealth shall, at the date of the transfer, assume the current obligations of the State in respect of the department transferred.*[35]

This section may be read in conjunction with the previous section which, as we have said, applies to departments transferred under s 69. It provides that, on the transfer of a department of the public service of a State, the property of the State used exclusively in connection with the department is vested in the Commonwealth, with the right to acquire other property used partially in connection with the department. There was a duty to compensate the State in the manner laid down, and the Commonwealth was obliged to assume current obligations of the State in respect of the transferred department.

Under the provisions of the *Income Tax (War-time Arrangements) Act* 1942, provision was made for the Commonwealth to take (temporary) possession of office accommodation, furniture and equipment of a State used in respect of the assessment and collection of income tax. It was provided that compensation to the State was to be determined by arrangement between the Commonwealth and States but, failing agreement, by an arbitrator appointed by the Governor-General.[36] There was also a provision for the transfer of records (with a right of access on the part of the State after transfer).[37]

---

33    No 21 of 1942.
34    See ss 6, 7, 8, 9, 10.
35    Quick and Garran, 819-22.
36    See s 11 of the Act.
37    Section 13.

In relation to compulsory acquisition of property of a State, s 51 (xxxi) requires that just terms be observed by the Commonwealth. In the *Uniform Tax Case*[38] the majority of the court sustained the *Income Tax (War-time Arrangements) Act* as an exercise of the defence power. They did not pass judgment on the validity of the compensation procedure under s 51 (xxxi) as the question was not argued.[39] It would seem, however, that a provision that compensation is to be determined by an arbitrator appointed by the acquiring party would not fulfil the requirement of just terms.

**86.** *On the establishment of the Commonwealth, the collection and control of duties of customs and of excise, and the control of the payment of bounties, shall pass to the Executive Government of the Commonwealth.*[40]

This section, read in conjunction with ss 69 and 90, gives full power to the Commonwealth over the collection and control of the revenue from customs and excise, and the disbursement of moneys in the form of bounties.

**87.** *During a period of ten years after the establishment of the Commonwealth and thereafter until the Parliament otherwise provides, of the net revenue of the Commonwealth from duties of customs and of excise not more than one-fourth shall be applied annually by the Commonwealth towards its expenditure.*

*The balance shall, in accordance with this Constitution, be paid to the several States, or applied towards the payment of interest on debts of the several States taken over by the Commonwealth.*[41]

This clause has become known as the Braddon Clause. It was named after Braddon, the Premier of Tasmania at the time of the Second Convention, who moved its adoption (in its original form).[42]

The purpose of the clause was to ensure a guaranteed return of the major source of governmental revenue of the time (customs and excise duties) to the States, or towards the payment of State debts if these were taken over by the Commonwealth.

In its initial form no time limit was imposed on the operation of the clause. New South Wales, however, was firmly opposed to any fixed arrangement which might operate in perpetuity to the detriment of its interests; and the distribution clause conferring on all the States such a proportion of customs and excise revenue was viewed in this light. A last moment compromise was reached by the Premiers of the Colonies on the matter which included the time limit of 10 years with future arrangements to be left in the hands of the federal Parliament.[43]

When the time limit expired in 1910, it became clear that the Commonwealth was not prepared to continue the arrangement. Instead a State grants scheme of 25 shillings per head of population per annum was instituted.[44] This scheme continued until the Financial Agreement of 1927, when the grants to the States were replaced by Commonwealth contributions to the interest payable by the States on their debts.[45]

---

38   *South Australia v The Commonwealth* (1942) 65 CLR 373.
39   See comments of Latham CJ at 430, Rich J at 438, Williams J at 467.
40   Quick and Garran, 823-4.
41   Ibid, 824-9.
42   Ibid, at 825.
43   Ibid.
44   By the *Surplus Revenue Act* of 1910. See *Essays* (Hannan) at 252.
45   Ibid, at 254.

UNIFORM DUTIES OF CUSTOMS

**88.** *Uniform duties of customs shall be imposed within two years after the establishment of the Commonwealth.*[46]

In order to allow sufficient time for the phasing out of colonial duties and for arriving at a decision on the first uniform tariff, a period of up to two years was allowed by the founders for the framing of the tariff.

PAYMENT TO STATES BEFORE UNIFORM DUTIES

**89.** *Until the imposition of uniform duties of customs—*

    (i) *The Commonwealth shall credit to each State the revenues collected therein by the Commonwealth.*

    (ii) *The Commonwealth shall debit to each State—*

        (a) *The expenditure therein of the Commonwealth incurred solely for the maintenance or continuance, as at the time of transfer, of any department transferred from the State to the Commonwealth;*

        (b) *The proportion of the State, according to the number of its people, in the other expenditure of the Commonwealth.*

    (iii) *The Commonwealth shall pay to each State month by month the balance (if any) in favour of the State.*[47]

This section is, in the words of Quick and Garran, one of a series of three (ss 93 and 94 being the others) which provided for the distribution of the federal surplus among the States during three periods: (1) Before the uniform tariff, (2) During the transition period immediately following the imposition of the uniform tariff, (3) after that period.[48]

In accordance with the overall scheme of providing for a distribution of surplus revenue to the States during these periods, this section deals with the first period, i e, the two year period before the imposition of the uniform tariff.

The control of customs had passed to the Commonwealth immediately on federation, but until the imposition of the uniform tariff, duties were to be collected on inter-state trade under the tariff in force in the particular State.

This section provided for a book-keeping procedure whereby the States were credited with the revenue collected within their respective boundaries but debited with Commonwealth departmental expenditure (relating to the maintenance of the transferred departments) as well as general Commonwealth expenditure in each State, which was worked out on a per capita basis. Any surplus was to be paid to the State in monthly instalments.

EXCLUSIVE POWER OVER CUSTOMS, EXCISE, AND BOUNTIES

**90.** *On the imposition of uniform duties of customs the power of the Parliament to impose duties of customs and of excise, and to grant bounties on the production or export of goods, shall become exclusive.*

*On the imposition of uniform duties of customs all laws of the several States imposing duties of customs or of excise, or offering bounties on the production or export of goods, shall cease to have effect, but any grant of or*

---

46    Quick and Garran, 829-30.
47    Ibid, 831-5.
48    Ibid, at 832.

*agreement for any such bounty lawfully made by or under the authority of the Government of any State shall be taken to be good if made before the thirtieth day of June, one thousand eight hundred and ninety-eight, and not otherwise.*[49]

**"On the imposition of uniform duties of customs the power of the Parliament to impose duties of customs and of excise, and to grant bounties on the production or export of goods, shall become exclusive"**

Section 88 of the Constitution required the imposition of uniform duties of customs within two years after the establishment of the Commonwealth. The imposition of uniform duties of customs was made the occasion for (a) making the power of the Commonwealth Parliament to impose duties of customs and excise, and to grant bounties on the production or export of goods, exclusive;[50] (b) terminating the effect of State laws on those matters; and (c) bringing into operation s 92 of the Constitution.[51]

The power of the Commonwealth Parliament to impose duties of customs and excise is derived from s 51 (ii) of the Constitution—the taxation power. The duties must be uniform (s 88). The power to make laws with respect to bounties is contained in s 51 (iii); such bounties must be uniform throughout the Commonwealth.

Section 69 of the Constitution provided for the departments of customs and of excise in each State to become transferred to the Commonwealth on its establishment. Section 52 (ii) gives the Commonwealth Parliament exclusive power to make laws with respect to any matters relating to such departments.

*Duties of Customs and of Excise.* There is no difficulty about the meaning of the term "duties of customs". They are duties levied upon the importation or exportation of commodities into and out of the Commonwealth.[52] But the interpretation of the expression "duties of excise" has given rise to much litigation.

The starting point is the decision in *Peterswald v Bartley.*[53] The question was whether a State licence fee for carrying on the business of a brewer was a duty of excise and hence outside the power of the State to impose. In English revenue legislation, the term was used to cover such imposts.[54] However, it was held that it had a more restricted meaning in Australian usage and in the context of the Constitution. "Bearing in mind that . . . when used in the Constitution it is used in connection with the words 'on goods produced or manufactured in the States', the conclusion is almost inevitable that, whenever it is used, it is intended to mean a duty analogous to a customs duty imposed upon goods either in relation to quantity or value when produced or manufactured, and not in the sense of a direct tax or personal tax."[55]

This definition was applied in *Commonwealth Oil Refineries Ltd v South*

---

49  Quick and Garran, 835-40. Wynes, 354-61. Howard, 373-90. Lane, pp 569-95.
50  Section 91 contains an exception for bounties on mining for metals, and for bounties on production or export with the consent of both Houses of the Parliament of the Commonwealth.
51  As Higgins J commented in *Duncan v Queensland* (1916) 22 CLR 556 at p 636, there was no need of s 92 for the mere purpose of ending State customs duties. This was effected by s 90.
52  *Commonwealth Oil Refineries Ltd v South Australia* (1926) 38 CLR 408, at p 438 (per Starke J).
53  (1904) 1 CLR 497.
54  See the passage from Quick and Garran, cited by Griffith CJ at 508.
55  1 CLR at 509 (per Griffith CJ).

*Australia*[56] to hold invalid a State tax of threepence per gallon on petrol sold and delivered in the State to persons within that State for the first time after entry into the State, or on production or refining in the State. Higgins and Starke JJ considered that so far as the legislation imposed a burden on imported goods, it amounted to a customs duty, and so far as it imposed a burden on domestically produced goods, it was a duty of excise. In *John Fairfax and Sons Ltd v New South Wales*[57] a tax of one halfpenny upon each copy of a newspaper issued for sale and actually sold in the State was held to be duty of excise. So also in *Attorney-General (NSW) v Homebush Flour Mills Ltd*, was a tax paid in respect of flour produced or manufactured in the State.

The test as stated in *Peterswald v Bartley*[58] received an extension in *Matthews v Chicory Marketing Board*[59] where a levy imposed in respect of areas planted with chicory was held (Latham CJ and McTiernan J dissenting) to be a duty of excise. The dissenting judgments emphasised that it was impossible to establish any relation between the levy and the quantity or value of the article produced. Rich and Starke JJ considered on the contrary that the tax was in respect of the production of chicory. The other member of the majority, Dixon J, agreed that it was a tax upon production; but at the same time he expressed disagreement with the notion that duties of excise were restricted to duties calculated directly on the quantity or value of the goods, or duties on goods of domestic manufacture or production.

The question whether a duty imposed in relation to the sale or distribution of goods, as distinct from their production or manufacture, was a duty of excise came before the Court in *Parton v Milk Board*.[60] Latham CJ and McTiernan J reaffirmed their view that only a tax upon the production or manufacture of goods was a duty of excise. A tax imposed on the producer of goods when he sold the goods would be a tax upon production; but a tax imposed after the producer had disposed of the goods was a tax merely upon sale and not upon production. Rich and Williams JJ accepted that to be a duty of excise a levy must be imposed so as to be a method of taxing the production or manufacture of goods, but they considered that "the production or manufacture of an article will be taxed whenever a tax is imposed in respect of some dealing with the article by way of sale or distribution at any stage of its existence, provided that it is expected and intended that the taxpayer will not bear the ultimate incidence of the tax himself but will indemnify himself by passing it on to the purchaser or consumer.[61] Dixon J considered that a tax upon a commodity at any point in the course of distribution before it reached the consumer was a duty of excise.

A sharp divergence of views on this matter was evident also in *Dennis Hotels Pty Ltd v Victoria*.[62] A Victorian Act imposed a charge of six per cent on the wholesale selling price of liquor as a condition for a grant of a victualler's licence. For a temporary licence, the charge was one pound for each day the licence was in force, in addition to the six per cent charge. The levies in respect to both the victualler's and temporary licences were held not to impose a duty

---

56    (1926) 38 CLR 408.
57    (1926) 39 CLR 139.
58    (1904) 1 CLR 497.
59    (1938) 60 CLR 263.
60    (1949) 80 CLR 229.
61    80 CLR at 252.
62    (1960) 104 CLR 529; [1960] ALR 129; see also *Whitehouse v Queensland* (1960) 104 CLR 609; [1960] ALR 178.

of excise by Fullagar, Kitto and Taylor JJ, while Dixon CJ, McTiernan and Windeyer JJ held that they did. Menzies J held that a duty of excise was not imposed in respect to the victualler's licence, but that it was imposed in respect to the temporary licence.

Those members of the Court who held that the charges amounted to a duty of excise emphasised that it was a tax directly affecting the goods, and that it was the kind of tax which tended to be recovered by the person paying it in the price he charged for the goods which bore the imposition. It was not necessary for the tax to be imposed on the production of the goods to qualify as a duty of excise.[63]

The views of those who held that no duty of excise was imposed were more varied. Fullagar J accepted as correct the definition of a duty of excise given in *Peterswald v Bartley*,[64] and considered that the fact that the fee did not fall upon a producer or manufacturer was decisive. Kitto and Taylor JJ considered that the fees were imposed not on goods, but on licences; they were imposed in respect of the acquisition of a right to engage in a business, and not by reference to the liquor sold during the currency of the licence.

Menzies J agreed that the victualler's licence fee was a tax upon a person as the price for his franchise to carry on a business, and hence was not a duty of excise. However, he considered that the temporary licence fee was a tax upon each purchase of liquor for sale under the licence and hence imposed a duty of excise.[65]

The central issue in the *Dennis Hotels Case*[66] was thus whether the tax imposed was "upon" the goods, or whether it was a fee payable as a condition of a right to carry on a business. In *Browns Transport Pty Ltd v Kropp*,[67] it had been held that the imposition of licensing fees in relation to a licence for the carriage of goods was not a tax "upon" goods, or "in respect of" goods, or "in relation to" goods, but was a fee payable for the right to carry goods and hence was not a duty of excise.

In *Bolton v Madsen*,[68] the Court unanimously accepted a re-definition of a duty of excise. It stated:

It is now established that for constitutional purposes duties of excise are taxes directly related to goods imposed at some step in their production or distribution before they reach the hands of consumers ... The tax is a duty of excise only when it is imposed directly upon goods or, to put the same thing in another way, when it directly affects goods, and to establish no more than that its imposition has increased the cost of putting goods upon the market by a calculable amount falls short of establishing the directness of relation between the tax and the goods that is the essential characteristic of a duty of excise.[69]

---

63  McTiernan J accepted that *Parton v Milk Board* (1949) 80 CLR 229 had established that duties of excise included duties imposed subsequently to production or manufacture.

64  (1904) 1 CLR 497. Fullagar J however was "not satisfied that it is an essential element of a duty of excise that it should be measured by quantity or value of goods": 104 CLR at 556; [1960] ALR at 141.

65  A matter referred to in several judgments but not decided is whether a duty of excise can be levied only on domestically produced goods. This matter is also considered in *Anderson's Pty Ltd v Victoria* (1964) 111 CLR 353; [1965] ALR 828.

66  (1960) 104 CLR 529; [1960] ALR 129.

67  (1958) 100 CLR 117.

68  (1963) 110 CLR 264; [1963] ALR 518.

69  110 CLR at 271; [1963] ALR at pp 520-1.

Applying this principle, it was held in *Andersen's Pty Ltd v Victoria*[70] that a State law imposing stamp duty upon hire-purchase agreements calculated upon the amount to be paid thereunder by instalments for goods did not impose a duty of excise.

However, the court divided again in *Western Australia v Hammersley Iron Pty Ltd (No 1)*.[71] A State Act required a person who had supplied goods in the State to issue an acknowledgment to be duly stamped as if it were a receipt for any payment for such goods made outside the State. Barwick CJ, Windeyer and Owen JJ held that it imposed a duty of excise. Owen J stated that "to impose a tax upon the receipt of the price for which a commodity is sold by its producer is, in my opinion, to tax a dealing with the commodity and such a tax is in reality a sales tax notwithstanding the fact that it takes the form of a duty upon an instrument which the recipient of the price of the commodity is required to bring into existence."[72] McTiernan, Kitto and Menzies JJ dissented. Kitto J emphasised that the liability of the supplier to stamp duty was not a consequence of his having supplied the goods; it arose because payment for the goods had been made outside the State. The tax bore no close relation to the production or manufacture or distribution of goods, affecting them as the subjects of manufacture or production or as articles of commerce.

It would appear from the statement quoted above from *Bolton v Madsen*[73] that taxes imposed on the consumer are not duties of excise. In *Parton v Milk Board*[74] Dixon J changed the opinion he had expressed in *Matthews v Chicory Marketing Board*[75] that a tax on commodities might be an excise although it was levied upon consumption.

**"On the imposition of uniform duties of customs all laws of the several States imposing duties of customs or of excise, or offering bounties on the production or export of goods, shall cease to have effect, but any grant of or agreement for any such bounty lawfully made by or under the authority of the Government of any State shall be taken to be good if made before the thirtieth day of June, one thousand eight hundred and ninety-eight, and not otherwise"**

Uniform customs duties came into effect throughout Australia with the introduction of the first Commonwealth customs tariff on 8 October 1901. State legislation imposing duties of customs or of excise or offering bounties on the production or export of goods thereupon ceased to have effect.

*Legislation.* The *Customs Act* 1901-1972 is concerned mainly with the administration and control of the customs throughout the Commonwealth. It specifies such matters as the goods which are subject to the control of the customs, the control which may be exercised over the importation, warehousing and exportation of goods,[76] the payment or computation of duties, the powers

---

70  (1964) 111 CLR 353; [1965] ALR 828; Lane: "Economic Federalism, Excise Duty and Receipt Duty" (1969) 43 ALJ 614.
71  (1969) 120 CLR 42; [1969] ALR 817.
72  120 CLR at 71; [1969] ALR at 834.
73  (1963) 110 CLR 264; [1963] ALR 518.
74  (1949) 80 CLR 229, at 261.
75  (1938) 80 CLR at 300. The change was made in consequence of the decision in *Atlantic Smoke Shops Ltd v Condon* [1943] AC 550.
76  The provisions relating to control over importation and exportation of goods are noted in the commentary on s 51 (i).

of customs officers, the licensing of customs agents, and penalties for customs offences.

Duties of customs are imposed by the *Customs Tariff* 1966-1972. It provides for general and preferential rates of duty. Preferential rates apply to certain goods the procedure or manufacture of a number of Commonwealth countries and declared preference countries. General rates of duty apply to imports which do not qualify for preferential rates. Some imported goods are also charged with primage duties, which are duties of customs imposed under s 27 of the customs tariff. Goods may be admitted free of duty or at rates lower than those normally applicable under customs by-laws and ministerial determinations made by the Minister for Customs and Excise under the *Customs Act*.

The customs tariff is designed to protect economic and efficient Australian industries. The Tariff Board, constituted under the *Tariff Board Act* 1921-1972 is the authority responsible for recommending protection. Temporary protection may be recommended by a Special Advisory Authority.

The *Customs Tariff (Dumping and Subsidies) Act* 1961-1965 provides for the imposition of dumping duty and countervailing duty in specified circumstances where unfair trading would cause or threaten injury to a competitive Australian industry.

The *Excise Act* 1901-1972 is, like the *Customs Act,* primarily concerned with the administration and control of excise throughout the Commonwealth. Duties of excise are imposed by the *Excise Tariff* 1921-1972 on goods dutiable under the schedule to the Act, and manufactured or produced in Australia.

EXCEPTIONS AS TO BOUNTIES

**91.** *Nothing in this Constitution prohibits a State from granting any aid to or bounty on mining for gold, silver, or other metals, nor from granting, with the consent of both Houses of the Parliament of the Commonwealth expressed by resolution, any aid to or bounty on the production or export of goods.*[77]

This section constitutes a qualification on the exclusive power conferred on the Commonwealth Parliament by s 90 to grant bounties on the production or export of goods. It operates in two different ways. In the first place, it enables a State, without approval from the Commonwealth, to grant bounties for the mining of metals (non-metallic minerals such as coal are therefore not included). However bounties may be granted on all goods (including non-metallic minerals) by a State with the approval of both Houses of the Federal Parliament expressed by resolution.

The exception of metals from the exclusive power to grant bounties was intended to assist the mining development of the States. In the words of Quick and Garran [78] "The convention was . . . not satisfied with the absolute prohibition of bounties, any more than with the absolute prohibition of preferences; they wished to protect purely developmental bounties, while forbidding unfederal bounties. The difficulty was, however, to frame a definition. Bounties on mining metals were, without much dispute, accepted as developmental; but as regards other bounties, no definition was possible, and therefore the matter was left to the decision of the federal Parliament in much the same way as the question of unfederal rates is left to the Inter-State Commission."

---

77   Quick and Garran, 840-3.
78   Ibid, at 841.

Trade within the Commonwealth to be free

**92.** *On the imposition of uniform duties of customs, trade, commerce, and intercourse among the States, whether by means of internal carriage or ocean navigation, shall be absolutely free.*

*But notwithstanding anything in this Constitution, goods imported before the imposition of uniform duties of customs into any State, or into any Colony which, whilst the goods remain therein, becomes a State, shall, on thence passing into another State within two years after the imposition of such duties, be liable to any duty chargeable on the importation of such goods into the Commonwealth, less any duty paid in respect of the goods on their importation.*[79]

**"On the imposition of uniform duties of customs, trade, commerce, and intercourse among the States, whether by means of internal carriage or ocean navigation, shall be absolutely free"**

The lengthy series of judicial decisions on the meaning and scope of the immunity afforded by s 92 is ample testimony to the difficulty involved in giving some precise meaning to a provision which in reality expresses a political slogan rather than a legal precept. Rich J once pithily described the lot of the High Court in relation to s 92 as being "to explain the elliptical and expound the unexpressed",[80] and he emphasised that the practical necessity of determining precisely what impediments were no longer to obstruct inter-State trade "obliged the court to attempt the impossible task of supplying an exclusive and inclusive definition of a conception to be discovered only in the silences of the Constitution".

Barton J recalled in the first decision given on the operation of s 92 that "one of the chief objects of the struggle for federation was to secure that which s 92 ordains, free trade among the States".[81] It is a matter for debate and to some extent for conjecture what effect the participants in the federal conventions ascribed to s 92.[82] The course of judicial decision has however been marked not by speculation as to what objects the framers of the Constitution may have intended to attain by the insertion of that section, but by an attempt to re-express it in terms of a meaningful legal rule, and to apply it to situations which probably were never envisaged at the foundation of the Commonwealth.

One conceivable view of s 92 has always been rejected by the High Court,

---

79   Quick and Garran, 844-60. Wynes, 237-81. Howard, 210-98. *Essays* 275-92. Lane, 597-675. Anderson: "Main Frustrations of the Economic Functions of Government Caused by s 92 and Possible Escapes Therefrom" (1953) 26 ALJ 518, 566. Freedom of Interstate Trade: Essence, Incidence and Device under s 92 of the Constitution (1959) 33 ALJ 276; Lane: "The Present Test for Invalidity under s 92 of the Constitution" (1958) 31 ALJ 715, "Approaches to and Principles of s 92 of the Constitution" (1959) 32 ALJ 335, "Section 92: Inconsistency, Shibboleths and Uncertainty" (1960) 33 ALJ 399; Morris: "Section 92 of the Commonwealth Constitution" (1964) 4 UQLJ 369; Nygh: "The Concept of Freedom in Interstate Trade" (1967) 5 UQLJ 317; Stone: "A Government of Laws and Yet of Men" (1950) 25 NYULR 462.

80   *James v Cowan* (1930) 43 CLR 386 at 422.

81   *Fox v Robbins* (1909) 8 CLR 115 at 123.

82   For a discussion of the drafting history of s 92, see Beasley: "Commonwealth Constitution: Section 92, Its History in the Federal Conventions", Annual Law Review (University of WA) 97, 273, 433; Sharwood: "Section 92 in the Federal Conventions—A Fresh Appraisal" 1 MULR 331.

namely that inter-State trade and commerce is free from all laws of every description. Griffith CJ stated in 1916 that "the word 'free' does not mean *extra legem*, any more than freedom means anarchy. We boast of being an absolutely free people, but that does not mean that we are not subject to law."[83] His words have frequently been repeated with approval by the courts, and are incontestably correct. But if the expression "absolutely free" does not mean free from all laws, from what is inter-State trade, commerce and intercourse to be absolutely free?

An answer to that question which in many respects is still tentative has only emerged in the course of the prolonged litigation to which s 92 has given rise, in which several formulations were attempted and eventually discarded. It is convenient to consider the development of the present doctrine over three periods: from the foundation of the Commonwealth to *McArthur's Case* in 1920; from *McArthur's Case* to *James v The Commonwealth* in 1936; and from *James v The Commonwealth* to the *Bank Nationalisation Case* in 1949. An examination will then be made of some of the principal issues which have come before the Courts where the operation of s 92 has been considered.

THE PERIOD TO MCARTHUR'S CASE. Two decisions were given by the High Court prior to the First World War on s 92 which raised rather simple issues. In the first case, *Fox v Robbins*,[84] a State law which prescribed a higher licence fee for a wine licence authorising the sale of wine made from fruit grown in any other State than the fee for the licence authorising the sale of its own wine was held to infringe s 92. The enactment, said Barton J, was inter-State protection, not inter-State free trade.[85] In *R v Smithers*,[86] a State law which made it an offence for a person to enter the State within three years of his conviction of an offence in another State was held invalid.[87]

Three war-time decisions involved more complex issues. In *NSW v The Commonwealth* (the *Wheat Case*),[88] the High Court held that the *Wheat Acquisition Act* 1914 of New South Wales did not infringe s 92. That Act empowered the Crown to expropriate wheat in the State whereupon the proprietary rights of persons in the wheat were to be converted into claims for compensation. Existing contracts relating to the sale of wheat were declared void unless they had been completed by delivery. The judgment of Griffith CJ in particular stressed that s 92 had nothing to say about questions of title. If a person ceased to be the owner of goods, because they had been acquired compulsorily by the Crown, s 92 would cease to have any operation in relation to his right to dispose of those goods. The legislation did not affect the owner's power of disposition; it simply changed the ownership of the wheat. Hence it did not contravene s 92.

In *Foggit Jones and Co v NSW*[89] the court held that a New South Wales Act which declared that stock and meat in any place in the State were to be held and kept for the disposal of the Imperial Government for the use of the army was invalid so far as it could be considered as authorising the State to

---

83   *Duncan v Queensland* (1916) 82 CLR 556 at 573.
84   (1909) 8 CLR 115. See also under s 113.
85   8 CLR at 123.
86   (1912) 16 CLR 99.
87   Griffith CJ and Barton J reached this conclusion without reference to s 92, while Isaacs and Higgins JJ considered the enactment an interference with freedom on "intercourse" within the meaning of s 92. See also under s 117.
88   (1915) 20 CLR 54.
89   (1916) 21 CLR 357.

prevent the owner of stock from removing it into another State. Griffith CJ stressed that in this case there had been no expropriation of property, and that an interference with the right of removal across the border was prohibited by s 92. However, he changed his mind on this point shortly afterwards in *Duncan v Queensland*[90] holding in relation to identical legislation that the declaration that the stock and meat were to be kept for the disposal of the Imperial Government operated as a dedication of the stock and meat to public purposes, and hence created a special proprietary interest in the Crown. The principle he had enunciated in the *Wheat Case* was therefore applicable. Gavan Duffy and Rich JJ, in coming to the same conclusion, emphasised that the prohibition against removal of the stock was not directed against inter-State trade, commerce or intercourse, but against any dealing that might prejudice the option of the Crown to take what was needed for the army.[91] Barton and Isaacs JJ dissented.

The issue in *McArthur v Queensland*[92] was whether a State could, consistently with s 92, impose a maximum price for the sale in the State of goods which under the contract of sale were to come from another State. The court[93] held that it could not. It was argued for the State that s 92 did not forbid all State legislation affecting inter-State trade, but only restrictions or impediments placed upon it by reason of its inter-State character. The judgment of Knox CJ, Isaacs and Starke JJ rejected this argument. In their opinion the words "absolutely free" in s 92 meant "absolutely free from every sort of impediment or control by the States with respect to trade, commerce and intercourse between them, considered as trade, commerce and intercourse". In their view, the prohibition by a State Legislature of inter-State sales of commodities either absolutely or subject to conditions imposed by State law was a direct contravention of s 92.[94]

The only legislation under consideration in *McArthur's Case* was a State Act, and it was strictly unnecessary for the Court to pronounce upon an argument that s 92 bound both Commonwealth and States. Nevertheless it did so, and declared that the Commonwealth was not bound by s. 92. The major consideration in reaching this conclusion was that to hold the contrary would practically nullify s 51 (i) of the Constitution.

McArthur's Case to James v The Commonwealth. The formula laid down in 1920 in *McArthur's Case* in relation to the immunity afforded by s 92 was that inter-State trade, commerce and intercourse were to be absolutely free from impediment or control by the States. The formula proved to be simple to apply in some situations which came before the High Court over the succeeding sixteen years, but ambiguous in its application in other situations. It is convenient to divide the cases into the following categories.

---

90   (1916) 222 CLR 556.
91   Higgins and Powers JJ also held the legislation valid.
92   (1920) 28 CLR 530.
93   Knox CJ, Isaacs, Higgins, Rich and Starke JJ, Gavan Duffy J dissenting.
94   In dealing with an argument that *Duncan v Queensland* (1916) 22 CLR 556 was authority for saying that a State might legislate so as to affect inter-State trade without there being an interference with inter-State trade, they observed: "If the goods themselves can be prohibited, if commercial dealings between the States can be restricted to dealings on the basis of such prices as the State fixes to suit its own special conditions, then there is no practical freedom even from border duties and bounties. It is the old inter-colonial trade war perpetuated in an outwardly different form". 28 CLR at 545. *Duncan v Queensland* was accordingly overruled.

(a) THE MARKETING CASES. In *James v South Australia*,[95] the Court held that a provision in a State Act authorising a determination by a marketing board of the quantity of dried fruits produced in the State which might be marketed within the Commonwealth was obnoxious to s 92. In the words of Isaacs ACJ and Powers J, s 92 operated "to shut off all forms of State obstruction and to confer upon the individual a right to be protected against all forms of State action amounting to, or authorising anyone to commit, such obstruction."[96]

A further provision in the same Act was considered by the Privy Council in *James v Cowan*.[97] This authorised the relevant Minister to acquire compulsorily any dried fruits in the State; the Minister's powers were however made subject to s 92. The provision was obviously drawn in the hope that action taken under it would fall within the principle expressed by Griffith CJ in the *Wheat Case,* namely that s 92 would not avail a person whose property had been compulsorily acquired by the State. But, without overruling that case, their Lordships stated that they would not be prepared to assent to the proposition in the simple form in which it had been expressed by Griffith CJ. They added that "if the real object of arming the minister with the power of acquisition is to enable him to place restrictions on inter-State commerce, as opposed to a real object of taking preventive measures against famine or disease and the like, the legislation is as invalid as if the Legislature itself had imposed the commercial restrictions".[98] As it appeared that in this case the direct object of the exercise of the powers was to interfere with inter-State trade, the exercise of those powers was invalid.

In *Peanut Board v Rockhampton Harbour Board*[99] the High Court (with Evatt J dissenting) applied *James v Cowan* to render ineffective an Order in Council made under a Queensland Act in relation to inter-State sales of peanuts. The Act declared all peanuts grown in Queensland produced or to be produced for sale for a period of ten years to be a commodity, it divested the commodity from the growers, and vested it in a statutory board. There was an infringement of s 92 because the State "acquired the property in the peanuts as and when they came into existence in order to insure that the grower producing them for sale should not exercise his former freedom of selling them by an ordinary transaction of commerce whether intra-State or inter-State".[1]

The ambiguity inherent in the formula propounded in *McArthur's Case* became manifest in *Ex parte Nelson (No 1)*.[2] The States must not interfere with acts of inter-State trade; but what were "acts of inter-State trade"? The issue in *Ex parte Nelson* was the validity of a section of a New South Wales *Stock Act* which authorised the Governor by proclamation to restrict, or absolutely prohibit, for any specified time, the importation or introduction of any stock from any other State in which there was reason to believe any infectious or contagious disease in stock existed. The Court split evenly on this issue. Knox CJ, Gavan Duffy and Starke JJ upheld the validity of the Act. In

---

95   (1927) 40 CLR 1.
96   40 CLR at 32.
97   (1932) 47 CLR 386.
98   47 CLR at 396.
99   (1933) 48 CLR 266.
 1   48 CLR at 288 (per Dixon J). In *Crothers v Sheil* (1933) 49 CLR 399 a scheme of compulsory acquisition of milk was held not to contravene s 92 on the ground that no element of inter-State trading was affected.
 2   (1928) 42 CLR 209.

their view, the Act was not to be characterised as one to regulate inter-State trade; rather, its object was to protect the large flocks and herds of New South Wales against contagious and infectious diseases. The validity of legislation was thus to be ascertained by looking at its object, at its "pith and substance". If this was to restrain acts of inter-State commerce, it would be invalid. If, on the other hand, the real object was otherwise, the legislation would be valid although it had an incidental effect on the conduct and liability of those engaged in inter-State commerce. Isaacs, Higgins and Powers JJ dissented. Isaacs J pointed out that the section struck at the most characteristic element of inter-State trade and commerce, the passing of goods from one State to another; it purported therefore to regulate the very act of inter-State trade, contrary to the doctrine laid down in *McArthur's Case*.

The "pith and substance" test amounted in effect to a qualification of the *McArthur* test, in that freedom was guaranteed only from State laws which could be characterised as laws with respect to inter-State trade. It received support in a number of subsequent cases[3] but was strongly criticised by Dixon J in *Tasmania v Victoria*.[4] In that case the High Court held (with Starke J dissenting) that a proclamation by the Governor in Council of Victoria reciting that in his opinion the introduction of potatoes from Tasmania was likely to introduce disease into Victoria and thereupon prohibiting the importation into Victoria of potatoes from Tasmania was invalid. Dixon J emphasised that s 92 was not concerned with a classification of subjects of legislative power, and that whatever purpose might be disclosed by State legislation, it might not restrict the absolute freedom of trade, commerce and intercourse between the States guaranteed by s 92.

(b) THE TRANSPORT CASES. Over the period from 1933 to *James v Commonwealth* in 1936, five cases came before the High Court in which the validity of State legislation was questioned in relation to inter-State transport operations. In the first of these, *Willard v Rawson*,[5] the High Court (with Dixon J dissenting) upheld a conviction under a Victorian Act of a carrier resident in New South Wales whose vehicle was registered in that State but not in Victoria. The carrier at the relevant time was using the truck to carry goods from New South Wales to Victoria. Rich J supported the legislation on the ground that "what is forbidden by s 92 is State legislation in respect of trade and commerce when it operates to restrict, regulate, fetter or control it and to do this immediately or directly as distinct from giving rise to some consequential impediment".[6] In the view of Rich J, the burden in this case was consequential, mediate or indirect. Starke J also supported it by applying the "pith and substance" test, holding that the character of the legislation was to regulate motor cars. Evatt J adopted the principle expressed by Higgins J in *Roughley v New South Wales*[7] that to invalidate the State Act, it had to be shown that it was legislation pointed directly at the act of entry, in course of commerce, into the second State. McTiernan J agreed substantially with Rich J. Dixon J on the other hand held that the imposition of a licence fee as

---

3   See in particular the judgments of Starke J in *Willard v Rawson* (1933) 48 CLR 316 and *Peanut Board v Rockhampton Harbour Board* (1933) 48 CLR 266.
4   (1935) 52 CLR 157.
5   (1933) 48 CLR 316.
6   48 CLR at 322. This formula was first enunciated by Rich J in *James v Cowan* (1930) 43 CLR at 425.
7   (1929) 42 CLR at 199.

a condition of carrying out an operation of inter-State commerce was in opposition to s 92.

The succeeding cases are of interest primarily for the development of the opinions of Evatt J on the one side and Dixon J on the other. The judgment of Evatt J in *R v Vizzard*[8] was noteworthy in particular since it rejected explicitly the conception of trade and commerce and the immunity accorded by s 92 as expounded in *McArthur's Case*. In that conception, the protection of s 92 extended to the individual trader in respect of the whole of the acts and transactions which together constituted inter-State trade and commerce. Evatt J on the other hand stated that s 92 postulated the free flow of goods inter-State, so that goods produced in any State might be freely marketed in every other State, and so that nothing could lawfully be done to obstruct or prevent such marketing. The real object of s 92 was to secure the free flow and passage and marketing of commodities among the States and to secure the right of passage of persons from State to State. Moreover, he pointed out that absolute freedom was ascribed to trade, to commerce and to intercourse, and was not ascribed to traders or to travellers considered merely as individuals. Section 92 did not guarantee that, in each and every part of a transaction which included the inter-State carriage of commodities, the owner of the commodities had the right to ignore State transport or marketing regulations and to choose how, when and where to transport and market the commodities.

The judgment of Dixon J in *O Gilpin Ltd v Commissioner of Road Transport*[9] reveals a completely antithetical understanding of the protection accorded by s 92. As against the "aggregative" notion of trade and commerce expressed by Evatt J, he emphasised that any act or transaction for which protection is claimed under s 92 must be a part of trade, commerce or inter-course among the States, that is to say, it must be something done as preparatory to, in the course of, or as a result of inter-State movement of persons and things or inter-State communication.[10] The freedom guaranteed by s 92 was from any restriction or burden placed upon an act because it was commerce, or trade, or intercourse, or because it involved movement into or out of the State. Moreover he stated that

Trade, commerce and intercourse among the States is an expression which describes the activities of individuals. The object of s 92 is to enable individuals to conduct their commercial dealings and their personal intercourse with one another independently of State boundaries. The Constitutional provision is not based on mere economic considerations. I am unable to agree with the view that trade, commerce and intercourse should, in applying s 92, be regarded as a whole and not distributively. The Constitution is dealing with a governmental power. It is not easy to appreciate the meaning of a guarantee of freedom of trade and inter-course unless it gives protection to the individual against interference in his commercial relations and movements.[11]

(c) THE STATE TAXATION CASES. In *Commonwealth and Commonwealth Oil Refineries v South Australia*,[12] a South Australian Act imposing a tax

8   (1933) 50 CLR 30.
9   (1935) 52 CLR 189.
10  52 CLR at 204.
11  52 CLR at 211. Other "transport cases" of this period are *Bessell v Dayman* (1935) 52 CLR 215 and *Duncan and Green Star Trading Co v Vizzard* (1935) 53 CLR 493.
12  (1926) 38 CLR 408.

on motor spirit, including motor spirit brought into South Australia from other States, was held to be a burden on inter-State sales and obnoxious to the provisions of s 92. In *Vacuum Oil Co Pty Ltd v Queensland*,[13] it was held that a Queensland Act which required the first person who, after petrol reached the State, held it for sale or sold it, to buy a prescribed proportion of power alcohol, was invalid. Dixon J pointed out that the legislation imposed a burden upon the importer of petrol from another State in his character of importer, and thereby selected as a ground of liability an essential quality of inter-State trade. An important point established by these cases is that taxing or otherwise burdening the first sale of a commodity subsequent to its introduction from one State into another may in some circumstances amount to an infringement of s 92.

*James v The Commonwealth* to the *Bank Nationalisation Case*. In the course of the fifteen years subsequent to *McArthur's Case*, the two central notions expressed in that decision had come increasingly under attack. The first of these was that s 92 bound the States only. This was repeated in 1928 in *James v The Commonwealth*.[14] It was disapproved in 1933 by Gavan Duffy CJ, Evatt and McTiernan JJ in *Vizzard's Case*[15] and by Dixon J in *Gilpin's Case*.[16] This disapproval was repeated by Dixon, Evatt and McTiernan JJ in 1935 in *James v The Commonwealth*.[17] The second notion related to the nature of the freedom accorded by s 92. This was expressed in the formula that all the commercial dealings by which trade was effectuated were "free from every sort of impediment or control by the States with respect to trade, commerce and intercourse between them, considered as trade commerce and intercourse.[18] As has been stated, this formula was analysed in inconsistent ways by various members of the High Court and was explicitly rejected by Evatt J in *Vizzard's Case*.[19]

The inability of the States to control the marketing of dried fruits within Australia led to Commonwealth intervention. The *Dried Fruits Act* 1928-1935 (Comm) had the effect that the owner of dried fruit was prevented from marketing any dried fruit inter-State except upon the terms and conditions prescribed, which included conditions as to the export of dried fruit from Australia. Control was imposed by the fixing of a quota of fruit to be marketed outside Australia. Owners of dried fruits were unable to market the fruit in other States without a licence, and a licence could be obtained only on condition that they agreed to a determination as to the quantity of fruit to be marketed overseas. Essentially the same means were employed as in the South Australian legislation which was held to contravene s 92 in *James v Cowan*.[20] The High Court upheld its validity in *James v The Commonwealth*[21] but only because of its previous decisions that s 92 did not bind the Commonwealth.

The subsequent appeal to the Privy Council raised the two issues, viz, whether s 92 bound the Commonwealth, and what was the nature of the freedom predicated by s 92. The answer given by the Privy Council to the

13   (1934) 51 CLR 108.
14   (1928) 40 CLR 442.
15   (1933) 50 CLR 30 at 47, 88 and 98.
16   (1935) 52 CLR 189 at 212.
17   (1935) 52 CLR 570 at 593 and 602.
18   (1920) 28 CLR at 554.
19   (1933) 50 CLR 30.
20   [1932] AC 342; 47 CLR 386.
21   (1935) 52 CLR 570.

first of these questions was unambiguous: the Commonwealth is bound by s 92. The objection that if s 92 applied to the Commonwealth, s 51 (i) of the Constitution would be bereft of any practical effect was answered by stating that "though trade and commerce mean the same thing in s 92 as in s 51 (i), they do not cover the same area, because s 92 is limited to a narrower context by the word 'free'."[22]

The answer to the second question was summed up in the phrase "freedom as at the frontier". The basic conception was that "the people of Australia were to be free to trade with each other and to pass to and fro among the States without any burden hindrance or restriction based merely on the fact that they were not members of the same State".[23] This would seem to imply that legislation which was non-discriminatory would not infringe s 92; but their Lordships admitted that an Act might contravene s 92 though it operated in restriction both of intra-State and of inter-State trade. To state that the freedom guaranteed was at the crucial point in inter-State trade, that is at the barrier, and at the same time to concede that the actual restraint or burden might operate while the goods were still in the State of origin or after they had arrived in the other State, was to erect a guide which could provide little assistance in solving problems of any complexity. The formula was dutifully repeated in a number of High Court judgments, but it did little if anything to resolve the conflict within the High Court on the scope of the immunity afforded by s 92.

It is convenient to divide the cases in the period under discussion into cases concerned with marketing, transport, lotteries, the right of personal movement, and nationalisation.

(a) MARKETING. In *Hartley v Walsh*[24] it was held (Dixon J dissenting) that a regulation under a Victorian Act which made it an offence to sell or buy dried fruits unless they had been packed in a packing shed registered under the Act did not infringe s 92. It was argued that the regulation prevented growers selling dried fruits to packing sheds in other States. The argument was rejected by Latham CJ on the ground that "where the marketing legislation controls and directs and regulates inter-State trade and, as in the present case, insists upon proper standards being preserved, such a law is not a mere restriction of 'freedom at the frontier' and is therefore not rendered invalid by s 92."[25]

*Milk Board (NSW) v Metropolitan Cream Pty Ltd*[26] applied *Crothers v Sheil*[27] though a substantial inter-State trade in milk existed. The case is interesting for the formulation of the prohibition-regulation test by Latham CJ, which subsequently was approved by the Privy Council in the *Bank Nationalisation Case*. He stated:

One proposition which I regard as established is that simple legislative prohibition (federal or State) as distinct from regulation of inter-State trade and commerce is invalid. Further, a law which is "directed against" inter-State trade and commerce is invalid. Such a law does not regulate such trade, it merely prevents it. But a law prescribing rules as to the manner in which trade (including transport) is to be

---

22   55 CLR at p 60.
23   55 CLR at p 58.
24   (1937) 57 CLR 372.
25   57 CLR at 382.
26   (1939) 62 CLR 116.
27   (1933) 49 CLR 399. See footnote 22 above.

conducted is not a mere prohibition and may be valid in its application to inter-State trade notwithstanding s 92.[28]

(b) TRANSPORT. In *Riverina Transport Pty Ltd v Victoria*[29] the Court (including Dixon J) upheld the validity of the Victorian *Transport Regulation Act* on the basis that the legislation was substantially the same as that considered in the previous transport cases. Latham CJ, Rich and Evatt JJ considered that the matter was settled by the approval given in *James v Commonwealth*[30] to *Vizzard's Case*.[31] The main attack in this case was based on an allegation that the Victorian transport board refused all licences for vehicles carrying goods inter-State for the reason that they were carrying goods inter-State. The attack failed because, in the words of Evatt J[32] "the applications were refused, not because the vehicles were carrying, or intended to carry, goods inter-State but because, in the board's opinion, the carriage of goods inter-State was being provided for already and in a more efficient manner by co-ordinating the services of the railway systems of the two States with local motor transport from all points in the Riverina to appropriate railway terminals".

(c) LOTTERIES. In three cases, *R v Connare*,[33] *Home Benefits Pty Ltd v Crafter*[34] and *R v Martin*[35] State Acts making sales of tickets in lotteries (including lotteries conducted in other States) an offence were upheld on various grounds as not being obnoxious to s 92.

(d) INTERCOURSE. In *Gratwick v Johnson*[36] an order which provided that no person should without a permit travel by rail or commercial passenger vehicle from any State in the Commonwealth to any other State, and that a Commonwealth official might grant or refuse any application for a permit was held to be invalid as a direct interference with the freedom of intercourse among the States accorded by s 92. The language of the order showed "an indifference to, if not a disdain of, the terms of s 92."[37] An argument that the real purpose of the Order was to effectuate the defence of the Commonwealth was rejected both because the defence power is made subject to s 92, and because the terms of the legislation directly prohibited personal movement between the States; it did not merely regulate it for defence purposes.

---

28    62 CLR 127. In *Andrews v Howell* (1941) 65 CLR 255, the *National Security (Apple and Pear Acquisition) Regulations* were held not to contravene s 92 by Rich ACJ and McTiernan on the basis of the decision in *Milk Board NSW v Metropolitan Cream Pty Ltd* (1939) 62 CLR 116 and by Dixon J on the basis of the decision in *Crothers v Sheil* (1933) 49 CLR 399. In *Field Peas Marketing Board (Tasmania) v Clements and Marshall Pty Ltd* (1948) 76 CLR 414, a proclamation purporting to vest all the field peas the subject matter of contracts of sale by growers to the respondents in the appellant board, and therefore to prevent their redelivery by the respondent to purchasers to whom it had resold the field peas in other States, was held to infringe s 92; the decision in *Peanut Board v Rockhampton Harbour Board* (1933) 48 CLR 266 was applied.

29    (1937) 57 CLR 327.
30    (1936) 55 CLR 1.
31    (1933) 50 CLR 30.
32    57 CLR at 369.
33    (1939) 61 CLR 596.
34    (1939) 61 CLR 701.
35    (1939) 62 CLR 457.
36    (1945) 70 CLR 1.
37    Per Dixon J, at 19.

(e) NATIONALISATION. It was on the subject of the power of the Commonwealth to create a monopoly in favour of its agencies in certain fields of trade and commerce that the major constitutional cases involving s 92 in the post-war period turned, and it was in these cases that the main lines of the current interpretation of s 92 were settled.

In the *Airlines Case*,[38] the High Court had to consider whether provisions in a Commonwealth Act that a Commonwealth instrumentality would have a monopoly in inter-State airline services on routes adequately served by the government service infringed s 92. The Court held unanimously that they did. Latham CJ described the provisions as amounting to a prohibition of inter-State air services, and not merely a system of regulation of such services. Starke J said that an Act which was entirely restrictive of any freedom of action on the part of traders and which operated to prevent them from engaging their commodities in any trade was necessarily obnoxious to s 92. Dixon J commented that if the test of freedom at the frontier was applied, it was plain that it was because the business involved crossing the frontier that it was eliminated.

The point which had emerged most clearly from the cases subsequent to *James v Commonwealth*[39] was that legislation or executive acts which constituted a direct prohibition on inter-State trade infringed s 92. Despite this, the Commonwealth attempted in the *Banking Act* 1947 to prohibit private banks from carrying on business in Australia. The attempt was held to infringe s 92 by the High Court, and on appeal by the Privy Council. The Commonwealth argued, in the first place, that banking was only a facility that might be used by commerce, but was not itself trade or commerce. Latham CJ and McTiernan J accepted this argument, but it was rejected by the other members, who held that the conception of commerce covered intangibles as well as the movement of goods and persons. The majority opinion was affirmed by the Privy Council. Secondly, it was argued that s 92 safeguarded trade among the States, not the trade exercised by an individual. The rejection of this proposition by the Privy Council was explicit: s 92 gave the citizen of State or Commonwealth "the right to ignore, and if necessary, to call upon the judicial power to help him to resist, legislative or executive action which offends against the section."[40] If s 92 did not safeguard the right of an individual trader, the decisions in favour of Mr James in the *James Cases* were inexplicable. A cognate argument that s 92 was not infringed if a law prohibiting inter-State business had no purpose or tendency to reduce the volume of flow of business also failed, as being inconsistent with the *James Cases*, and as being unreal and unpractical in application.

The Privy Council accepted two propositions as to the qualifications to be made to the freedom guaranteed by s 92: These were: "(1) that regulation of trade commerce and intercourse among the States is compatible with its absolute freedom, and (2) that s 92 is violated only when a legislative or executive act operates to restrict such trade commerce and intercourse directly and immediately as distinct from creating some indirect or consequential impediment which may fairly be regarded as remote."

In the subsequent history of the constitutional interpretation of s 92, one of the main tasks faced by the Courts has been the clarification of the scope of those two propositions and their application to the legislative or executive acts which have been challenged. The initial battleground was the field of

---

38   *Australian National Airways Pty Ltd v Commonwealth* (1945) 71 CLR 29.
39   (1935) 52 CLR 570.
40   79 CLR at 635.

control of transport. Concurrently and subsequently, the impact of the Privy Council's interpretation of s 92 on the control of other aspects of economic life, including production quotas, price fixing, and marketing, has presented, and continues to present, problems for the Courts.

A further problem for which the *Bank Nationalisation Case* provides little guidance is that of the inter-State character of an activity. The problem has presented itself in two forms. First, there is the question of border-hopping, that is crossing a State border so as to attract the operation of s 92. Secondly, there is the question whether an intra-State activity may come within the protection of s 92 because in the context it is really part of a protected inter-State activity.

The remaining sections of this commentary on s 92 will deal therefore with three matters—(a) the regulation of road transport; (b) the regulation of other aspects of the economy; and (c) the inter-State character of activities.

*The Regulation of Road Transport.* The impact of the *Bank Nationalisation* decision on the legislation which had been upheld in the *Riverina Case*[41] arose for consideration by the High Court in 1950 in *McCarter v Brodie*.[42] The central issue was whether the *Transport Regulation Act* of Victoria was regulatory or prohibitive. A majority of the High Court[43] held that they did not contravene s 92. The same conclusion was reached by a majority in *Hughes and Vale Pty Ltd v NSW*[44] as to the validity of the NSW *State Transport (Co-ordination) Act*.[45] In this case Dixon CJ, formed one of the majority, since he considered that he should act on the authority of *McCarter v Brodie*, of which he disapproved, on the ground that the transport cases offered a pragmatic solution to the particular problem of the control by the States of the use of roads provided and maintained by the States and were confined to that issue.

An appeal to the Privy Council was successful.[46] Their Lordships agreed with and reproduced the analysis in *McCarter v Brodie* by Dixon CJ who pointed out that three of the grounds upon which the *Transport Cases* were based had been destroyed by the judgment of the Privy Council in the *Bank Nationalisation Case*. These were:

(a) that s 92 does not guarantee the freedom of individuals;

(b) that if the same volume of trade flowed from State to State before as after the interference with the individual trader, the freedom of trade among the States remained unimpaired;

(c) that because a law applies alike to inter-State commerce and to the domestic commerce of a State, it may escape objection notwithstanding that it prohibits, restricts or burdens intra-State commerce.

In addition, two further principles were settled by that case which were relevant to the basis upon which the *Transport Cases* rested.

One is that the object or purpose of an Act challenged as contrary to s 92 is to be ascertained from what is enacted and consists in the necessary legal effect of the

41   (1937) 57 CLR 327.
42   (1950) 80 CLR 432.
43   Latham CJ, McTiernan, Williams and Webb JJ, Dixon and Fullagar JJ dissenting.
44   (1953) 87 CLR 49.
45   Dixon CJ, McTiernan, Williams and Webb JJ, with Fullagar, Kitto and Taylor JJ dissenting.
46   *Hughes and Vale Pty Ltd v NSW* (1954) 93 CLR 1.

law itself and not in its ulterior effect socially or economically. The other is that the question what is the pith and substance of the impugned law, though possibly of help in considering whether it is nothing but a regulation of a class of trans- actions forming part of trade and commerce, is beside the point when the law amounts to a prohibition or the question of regulation cannot fairly arise.[47]

A sixth ground was also rejected by Dixon J, namely that based upon the distinction between motor vehicles as integers of traffic, and the trade of carrying by motor vehicle as part of commerce.[48]

The only ground which could be relied upon therefore to support the legislation was that it was merely regulatory of the commercial carriage of goods by road, and not prohibitive of freedom of inter-State trade and commerce. But the legislation forbade carriage of goods inter-State unless an executive body in the exercise of an uncontrollable discretion saw fit to grant a licence to do so. Of this, Fullagar J said in words approved by the Privy Council[49]

As to what is *not* regulatory in the relevant sense, one thing at least is clear. Prohibition is not regulation . . .
It is quite impossible, in my opinion, to distinguish the present case from the case of a simple prohibition. If I cannot lawfully prohibit altogether, I cannot lawfully prohibit subject to an absolute discretion on my part to exempt from the prohibition.

The result was that the majority views in *Vizzard's Case*[50] were rejected, and a declaration was made that the provisions of the Act requiring application to be made for a licence were inapplicable to the appellant while operating its vehicles in the course and for the purposes of inter-State trade or to the vehicles while so operated. The approach to s 92 which had been taken by Dixon J, expressed above all in his judgment in *Gilpin's Case*[51] received the express approval of the Privy Council.

The reversal of the decision in *Vizzard's Case* made it imperative for the States to recast their transport legislation. The form it took in relation to inter- State trade was to make it an offence for a person to operate a motor vehicle unless it was licensed, but also to make the exercise of the power to refuse a licence subject to limitations and controls. However, these were expressed in such wide terms that the result of the amending legislation in New South Wales was described as being

"to forbid the use of motor vehicles for the carriage of goods in the course of trade between New South Wales and another State except by the licence of an administrative agency of New South Wales whose only duty to allow it is in practical effect unenforceable and in any case does not arise unless the agency does not regard only a number of very wide indefinite and sometimes intangible objections as existing and if and when it arises it is not a duty to licence the use of the vehicle as asked but only subject to any conditions (falling within certain very wide descriptions) which the agency may choose to impose, conditions which may not be consistent with the inter-State trade or transaction in view.[52]

The legislation was held to be inconsistent with s 92 in *Hughes and Vale*

---

47  80 CLR at 466.
48  See for example the judgment of Rich J in *Vizzard's Case* 50 CLR at 51.
49  93 CLR at 26.
50  50 CLR 30.
51  (1935) 52 CLR 189.
52  *Hughes and Vale Pty Ltd v NSW (No 2)* (1955) 93 CLR 127 at 159.

*Pty Ltd v NSW (No 2)*.[53] Fullagar J observed that a law does not "regulate" in any relevant sense if it leaves the conditions on which trade or commerce may be carried on to be determined ad hoc by some person or body nominated for the purpose.

The Parliament of New South Wales may be said to be permitted by s 92 to make "regulatory" laws, but it does not make a regulatory law if it leaves to "some individual or individuals" a discretion to impose conditions on any relaxation of a prohibition.[54]

The impugned legislation provided not only for a licensing system in respect to motor vehicles engaged in inter-State trade, but also for a pecuniary levy upon inter-State road transportation. All member of the High Court agreed in *Hughes and Vale Pty Ltd (No 2)* that these provisions in the legislation were invalid, but they differed as to the right of a State to make a charge for the use made of roads by vehicles engaged in inter-State trade. Kitto J considered that the States were unable to make any charge for the use made of roads by such vehicles. "The relevant freedom is given, once and for all, and is not made available for purchase. The section is uncompromising in its decree, and its severe demand is not open to mitigation by reference to the just and equitable."[55] Taylor J also considered that any charge which was made payable as a condition of engaging in a carrying on inter-State trade must offend against s 92; but he thought that it was competent for a State to exclude from its roads those vehicles which, by reason of their weight or construction were calculated to work such destruction to the roads that they ought not to be there at all, and to relax that prohibition on payment of a stipulated charge.[56] But the other members[57] held that the States were entitled to impose a fair and reasonable charge for the use made of roads by vehicles engaged in inter-State trade. The joint judgment of Dixon CJ, McTiernan and Webb JJ referred to

grounds which make it possible to reconcile with the freedom postulated by s 92 the exaction from commerce using the roads, whether the journey be inter-State or not, of some special contribution to their maintenance and upkeep in relief of the general revenues of the State drawn from the public at large. The American phrase is that inter-State commerce must pay its way. It is but a constitutional aphorism, but it serves to bring home the point that in a modern community the exercise of any trade and the conduct of any business must involve all sorts of fiscal liabilities from which, in reason, inter-State trade or business should have no immunity. Those who pay them are not unfree, they merely pay the price of freedom.[58]

Once again the States were compelled to amend their legislation. This

---

53    (1955) 93 CLR 127. See Derham: "Second Hughes and Vale Case" 29 ALJ 476. Fullagar J described the legislation as "glaringly inconsistent" with s 92. See the report, at p 204.

54    93 CLR at 206. The principles established in *Hughes and Vale Pty Ltd (No. 2)* were applied to strike down Queensland legislation in *Hughes and Vale Pty Ltd v Queensland* (1955) 93 CLR 247, Victorian legislation in *Armstrong v Victoria* (1955) 93 CLR 264, and South Australian legislation in *Nilson v South Australia* (1955) 93 CLR 292 and *Pioneer Tourist Coaches Pty Ltd v South Australia* (1955) 93 CLR 307.

55    93 CLR at 224.

56    93 CLR at 239-40.

57    Dixon CJ, McTiernan, Williams, Webb and Fullagar JJ.

58    93 CLR at 172.

time their efforts proved successful.[59] The State legislation the validity of which was sustained imposed upon owners of commercial goods vehicles a road charge at a rate per mile of public roads travelled in the State towards compensation for wear and tear to public roads caused by such travel. In *Armstrong's Case (No 2)*[60] the State of Victoria gave evidence to establish that the charge was a proper tonnage rate per mile to compensate for the wear and tear of the highway used. The court concluded that although the information supplied was unsatisfactory in several respects, the charge imposed complied with the requirements laid down in *Hughes and Vale Pty Ltd (No 2)* so as not to be inconsistent with s 92. Subsequently it ruled that evidence was not admissible to establish that a charge imposed by an Act bore no relation to wear and tear upon the roads or to the costs of road maintenance.[61]

It is convenient at this point to refer to two cases in which attempts were made by the States to defeat claims which were available against them in consequence of the invalidation of legislation by the *Hughes and Vale Cases*. In *Antill Ranger and Co Pty Ltd v Commissioner for Motor Transport*[62] the High Court held that an Act purporting to extinguish and bar any action against the State and its officials for recovery of charges collected under the invalidated legislation or for acts done under its authority infringed s 92. In *Barton v Commissioner for Motor Transport*[63] legislation which purported to bar a remedy after twelve months had elapsed from the time when the money was paid or collected was also held by a majority of the High Court to be invalid in its application to causes of action actually existing more than twelve months before the enactment of the legislation, since it attempted to bar absolutely the legal remedy to recover money already exacted in violation of the freedom assured by s 92.[64]

*Economic Regulation.* (a) MARKETING. In *Wilcox Mofflin Ltd v NSW*[65] an attack was made on provisions in a New South Wales statute requiring all hides to be submitted for appraisement within twenty-eight days of coming into the possession of a licensed dealer and acquiring compulsorily all such hides, other than those intended or required for interstate trade. The court by majority held that s 92 was not infringed. The joint judgment of Dixon, McTiernan and Fullagar JJ made explicit the different context in which the hides scheme operated from the dried fruits schemes of the *James Cases*.

The marketing plan in question in *James v South Australia*,[66] *James v Cowan*[67] and

---

59   *Armstrong v Victoria (No 2)* (1957) 99 CLR 28; *Commonwealth Freighters Pty Ltd v Sneddon* (1959) 102 CLR 280; *Boardman v Duddington* (1959) 104 CLR 456.
60   (1957) 99 CLR 28.
61   *Breen v Sneddon* (1961) 106 CLR 406. [1962] ALR 340. In that case, Windeyer J gave a wide operation to the notion of upkeep or maintenance of roads, so as to include certain capital improvements (see at p 424). Compare the view of Dixon CJ that capital expenditure could not be included in the costs taken as the basis for computation of a charge: *Hughes and Vale Pty Ltd (No 2)* 93 CLR at 176.
62   (1955) 93 CLR 83. Affd by the Privy Council: 94 CLR 177.
63   (1957) 97 CLR 633.
64   97 CLR at 641 (per Dixon CJ). See also *Mason v New South Wales* (1959) 102 CLR 108.
65   (1952) 85 CLR 488.
66   (1927) 40 CLR 1.
67   (1930) 43 CLR 386.

*James v The Commonwealth*[68] was one for restricting the amount of the commodity to be sold in Australia and, by its quotas and by the use against James of the power to acquire dried fruits, the plan sought to prevent the sale in any State of dried fruit lying in South Australia, or in the last case the sale of dried fruit anywhere, across any State boundary. In the present case, the purpose and effect of the statutory plan is not to restrict but to increase the amount of the commodity available for sale in Australia.[69]

The *James Cases* were concerned with legislation which imposed restrictions upon sales within Australia so as to force the surplus onto the export market. Marketing legislation which involves such restrictions will almost inevitably call s 92 into play, whereas legislation which is not directed to imposing such restrictions does not face the same difficulty. However, could it not be said that every expropriation of a vendible commodity was invalid, because it deprived the owner of property which otherwsie he might sell from one State into another? The court answered this objection in the following passage:

It is pressing s 92 far beyond its meaning and purpose if the immunity it confers is extended to the preservation of movable property against compulsory acquisition, although no overt act has been done with reference to such property which will, or upon a contingency may, result in a dealing or movement inter-State. We cannot assent to the view that because ownership may be considered as a prerequisite of the sale of goods, therefore no trader to whom inter-State trade in the goods would otherwise be open can be deprived of ownership consistently with s 92. There may be many situations where to take a trader's goods is inconsistent with s 92. But that depends on some closer connection with inter-State trade than the two facts that to engage in inter-State trade is open to him if he chooses and that the goods are his property.

Such a view would mean that all vendible commodities would be outside the effective reach of the powers of compulsory acquisition of States and Commonwealth in peace and war. The reason why such a view cannot be sustained may be stated in a variety of ways. One simple reason is that s 92 has provided for the freedom of inter-State trade, commerce and intercourse and has not extended the immunity to antecedent conditions. Another way of stating it is that the notion that what is ancillary to an immunity is covered by the immunity is a confusion between doctrines applicable to legislative powers and the principles which should govern the interpretation and operation of constitutional restraints upon power. Still another is that, unless by reason of circumstances, an acquisition of property does not directly or immediately interfere with the acts, transactions or movement constituting trade commerce and intercourse among the States, but can at most effect them consequentially.[70]

(b) QUOTAS ON PRODUCTION. The passage quoted in the preceding paragraph is particularly relevant to the consideration of the conformity with s 92 of quotas upon the production of goods. The leading case on this subject is *Grannall v Marrickville Margarine Pty Ltd*.[71] A New South Wales statute prohibited the manufacture of table margarine unless the manufacturer obtained a licence, which could be given or refused at the discretion of the

---

68   (1936) 55 CLR 1.
69   85 CLR at 516-7.
70   85 CLR at 519. A law which expropriates a chattel when there is no present intention to commit it to inter-State trade does not infringe s 92: *Carter v Potato Marketing Board* (1951) 84 CLR 460. Compare *R v Wilkinson, Ex parte Brazell Garlick and Co* (1952) 85 CLR 407.
71   (1955) 93 CLR 55.

relevant Minister, and which if granted must contain a condition limiting the quantity which might be manufactured. A claim that the Act infringed s 92 failed. As the court pointed out:

It is of course obvious that without goods there can be no inter-State or any other trade in goods. In that sense manufacture or production within, or importation into, the Commonwealth is an essential preliminary condition to trade and commerce between the States in merchandise. But that does not make manufacture production or importation trade and commerce among the States. It is no reason for extending the freedom which s 92 confers upon trade and commerce among the States to something which precedes it and is outside the freedom conferred.[72]

It is convenient at this point to refer to *R v Anderson, ex parte Ipec Air Pty Ltd*.[73] Despite the clear rejection by the High Court in the *Margarine Case* of the proposition that there could be no effective prohibition of the importation of goods into Australia if they were merchandise intended to be bought and sold in inter-State trade,[74] it was argued that the refusal by the Director General of Civil Aviation to grant permission to import aircraft, so as to prevent them when imported from being used in inter-State trade, was contrary to s 92. The High Court treated the matter as settled against the prosecution by its decision in *Grannall v Marrickville Margarine Pty Ltd*.[75]

(c) PRICE FIXING. In *McArthur's Case*[76] the validity of legislation fixing the maximum prices at which certain goods could be sold in Queensland was the central question for determination. The precise issue in that case was accurately expressed by the Privy Council in *James v Commonwealth*[77] as being whether agents for the plaintiffs, a Sydney firm, were committing a breach by selling in the State at prices higher than the prescribed prices, goods of the plaintiffs to be despatched from Sydney and delivered to the purchasers in the State. It was held that they were not, on the ground that the prohibition by a State law of inter-State sales contravened s 92. However, the Privy Council added the comment that the decision deprived Queensland of its sovereign right to regulate its internal prices.

If this comment could be understood to imply that *McArthur's Case* was authority for saying that s 92 prohibited a State from fixing prices which might be charged in that State for goods imported from another State, it was shown to be misleading in *Wragg v State of New South Wales*.[78] The judgment of Taylor J, with which Dixon CJ, Williams, Fullagar and Kitto JJ agreed, emphasised that in *McArthur's Case* the only transaction which was held to be an inter-State transaction was one under which agents for the plaintiff agreed in Queensland to sell goods to persons in Queensland, the goods to be despatched from the plaintiff's warehouse in Sydney and to be delivered by the plaintiff to purchasers in Queensland.

In *Wragg's Case*, a declaration was sought that orders made fixing the

---

72   93 CLR at 71-2. Manufacture to fulfil a contract requiring delivery in another state is not protected by s 92: *Beal v Marrickville Margarine Pty Ltd* (1966) 114 CLR 283; [1967] ALR 76. See also *Damjanovic and Sons Pty Ltd v Commonwealth* (1968) 117 CLR 390; [1969] ALR 653.
73   (1965) 113 CLR 177; [1965] ALR 1067.
74   93 CLR at 79.
75   (1955) 93 CLR 55.
76   (1920) 28 CLR 530.
77   (1936) 55 CLR 1 at 48-9.
78   (1953) 80 CLR 353.

maximum prices at which potatoes might be sold by wholesalers and retailers, including wholesalers who had imported the potatoes from another State, were invalid as infringing s 92. The plaintiffs argued that the fixing of maximum prices at any stage in the marketing of potatoes imported from another State directly burdened inter-State trade as such. The answer given to this by Taylor J was that "any effect which the prescription of a general price for intra-State sales may have on the business of importing potatoes from Tasmania is not a direct effect but an economic consequence too remote to constitute an impairment of the freedom which s 92 assures."[79]

(d) CONTROL OF SALES. A number of cases have raised the issue of the power of State legislatures to control sales of products imported from another State.[80]

It is convenient to refer in the first place to a marketing case, *Fish Board v Paradiso*.[81] A Queensland Act provided that no person should in any district sell or purchase any fish unless such fish had first been brought to a market in that district and there sold at a sale conducted by the Fish Board. A fish was brought to Queensland and delivered to the defendant pursuant to a contract between him and a New South Wales company and resold to an inspector of the Fish Board. The plaintiff's contention was that the re-sale was an intra-State sale and as such outside the protection of s 92. The High Court concluded however that the prohibition against re-selling goods purchased for re-sale had as its object the compulsion of the purchaser to place his property in the disposition of the Board, and was as much a direct restriction on inter-State trade as a provision that all fish, whether in the course of inter-State trade or not, should be delivered to the Board for sale.[82]

Barwick CJ (with whom Owen J agreed) regarded the decision in *Fish Board v Paradiso* as determinative of the case in *SOS (Mowbray) Pty Ltd v Mead*.[83] A Tasmanian Act prohibited the sale of cooking margarine to which there had been added any prohibited colouring substance or prohibited flavouring substance. The appellant ordered from a company based in Sydney a quantity of cooking margarine, and on its arrival in his store he displayed it for sale and sold it to a retail purchaser. The margarine contained the prohibited additives. Barwick CJ and Owen J considered that the appellant's sale was part of his inter-State trade in the margarine, and that the effect which a prohibition of that sale would bring about would be the direct and immediate operation of the Act. Walsh J also considered that the law was one imposing an absolute prohibition on sale and as such it was incompatible with s 92. The majority opinion however was that the sales were not part of the appellant's inter-State trade, or that the Act operated merely so as to create a remote impediment to inter-State trade.

A similar division of opinion is to be found in a number of other cases relating to power to control sales, including *Harper v Victoria*,[84] *O'Sullivan v*

---

79   88 CLR at 398. See also the judgment of Dixon CJ at p 387.
80   Agreements which require delivery of goods to another State are governed by the same principles as are applicable to agreements for the delivery of goods from another State: *Chapman v Suttie* (1963) 110 CLR 321 at 338; [1963] ALR 321.
81   (1956) 95 CLR 443.
82   See *Cam & Sons Pty Ltd v Chief Secretary of New South Wales* (1951) 84 CLR 442.
83   (1972) 46 ALJR 192; [1972] ALR 417.
84   (1966) 114 CLR 361; [1966] ALR 731.

*Miracle Foods (SA) Pty Ltd*,[85] and *Samuels v Readers Digest Association Pty. Ltd.*[86] The division reflects two fundamentally different conceptions of the scope of the immunity afforded by s 92, and in particular of the notion of a direct burden on inter-State trade. The majority view echoes the conception expressed by Dixon J in *Gilpin's Case*,[87] and reformulated by him in *Hospital Provident Fund Pty Ltd v Victoria*[88] in the following terms:

If a law takes a fact or an event or a thing itself forming part of trade, commerce or intercourse, or forming an essential attribute of that conception, essential in the sense that without it you cannot bring into being that particular example of trade, commerce or intercourse among the States, and the law proceeds by reference thereto or in consequence thereof, to impose a restriction, a burden or a liability, then that appears to me to be direct or immediate in its operation or application to inter-State trade, commerce and intercourse, and, if it creates a real prejudice or impediment to inter-State transactions, it will accordingly be a law impairing the freedom which s 92 says shall exist. But if the fact or event or thing with reference to which or in consequence of which the law imposes its restriction or burden or liability is in itself no part of inter-State trade and commerce and supplies no element or attribute essential to the conception, then the fact that some secondary effect or consequence upon trade or commerce is produced is not enough for the purposes of s 92.

The opposing view is expressed most clearly in the dissenting judgment of Barwick CJ in *Samuels v Readers Digest Association Pty Ltd*:[89]

I find myself unable to accept the view that their Lordships affirmed the proposition that only laws which fastened upon a characteristic which a transaction of inter-State trade, commerce or intercourse as the criterion upon which the law's operation depends can be obnoxious to s 92. Nor can I accept the view that such a conclusion logically follows from a consideration of the terms of the constitutional guarantee ... To my mind, the first question always is whether the direct as distinct from the merely consequential and remote effect of the operation of the law whatever its topic constitutes in a practical sense a burden upon trade, commerce or intercourse amongst the States or any part or aspect of it. The second is whether, if so, the law can be said, none the less, not to impair the freedom of that trade and commerce because the burden or hindrance is compatible with it. It will be so if the law is regulatory in character in relation to the impact upon that trade and commerce which results directly and not remotely from its operation.

On either view, a law which is merely regulatory of inter-State trade in the sense that it forms part of the legal framework within which s 92 contemplates inter-State trade, commerce and intercourse as being freely carried on[90] is not obnoxious to s 92. It was on that ground that the High Court held in *Mikasa (NSW) Pty Ltd v Festival Stores*[91] that the provisions in the Trade Practices Act 1965-1971 making the practice of resale price maintenance unlawful and providing for the granting of injunctions to restrain such practices were compatible with s 92.

---

85  (1966) 115 CLR 177; [1966] ALR 1184.
86  (1969) 120 CLR 1.
87  (1934) 52 CLR 189 at 206.
88  (1953) 87 CLR 1 at 17-18.
89  (1969) 120 CLR 1 at 17.
90  For an analysis of the concept of regulation of inter-State trade, see the judgment of Kitto J in *Hughes & Vale Pty Ltd (No 2)* (1955) 93 CLR 127 at 218; and in *Greutner v Everard* (1960) 103 CLR 177 at 188. [1960] ALR 550.
91  (1973) 47 ALJR 14.

(e) LOTTERIES. In *Mansell v Beck*[92] the High Court affirmed (Kitto J dissenting) its decisions in *R v Connare*[93] and *R v Martin*,[94] but for varied reasons. One was that the conduct of a lottery was not trade, commerce or intercourse. Another was that the relevant section was concerned only with intra-State trade, and that any impediment to inter-State trade was merely indirect and consequential. A third ground was that the law did not select any element or attribute of inter-State trade as the basis of its operation.

*The Inter-State Character of Activities.* In *Hospital Provident Fund Pty Ltd v Victoria*,[95] Fullagar J observed that carrying on business in more than one State is not the same as carrying on inter-State business. The appellant's business involved making contracts involving the receipt of money and the payment of money on the occurrence of certain contingencies. But

for a company to contract with a man that, in consideration of the latter making payments to it at any given place, the company will in a specified contingency make a payment to him at some other place is not to engage in inter-State commerce. Neither the making of the contract nor the performance of the contract by either side involves any step or dealing which of itself forms part of inter-State commerce even if a State line runs between the two places.[96]

The question whether an act was of an inter-State character has arisen mainly[97] in two contexts.

(a) INTRA-STATE PARTS OF INTER-STATE JOURNEYS. A series of cases beginning with *Hughes v Tasmania*[98] has raised the question of the circumstances in which the protection of s 92 will be available to a trader in respect to an intra-State carriage of goods when this forms part of an inter-State movement of those goods.

The first point which emerges from these cases is that s 92 is infringed only if the imposition of a burden upon the carrier interferes with the inter-State trade of the person for whom the goods are being carried. It was held that it did so in *Russell v Walters*[99] where the carrier was the servant of the person engaged in inter-State trade, and in *Simms v West*[1] where he was his agent.[2] On the other hand, in *Hughes v Tasmania*[3] it was decided that an independent contractor engaged to carry goods intra-State was unable to invoke s 92, on the ground that those who engaged him were using his services as part of their inter-State transportation of goods, since there was in that case no burden upon the customer whose goods were being carried.

Secondly, the carriage of goods from one place in a State to another place in the same State is protected by s 92 if that carriage is part of the inter-State

---

92   (1956) 95 CLR 550.
93   (1939) 61 CLR 596.
94   (1939) 62 CLR 457.
95   (1953) 87 CLR 1 at 8.
96   87 CLR at 14 (per Dixon CJ).
97   For other instances of cases where the issue has arisen, see *Carter v The Potato Marketing Board* (1951) 84 CLR 460 and *R v Wilkinson; ex parte Brazell, Garlick and Coy* (1952) 85 CLR 467.
98   (1955) 93 CLR 113.
99   (1957) 96 CLR 177.
 1   (1961) 107 CLR 157; [1962] ALR 211.
 2   See also *Britton Bros Pty Ltd v Atkins* (1963) 108 CLR 529, [1963] ALR 338 and *Bell Bros Pty Ltd v Rathbone* (1963) 109 CLR 225; [1963] ALR 433.
 3   (1955) 93 CLR 113.

movement of goods.[4] But there must be a continuous journey of an inter-State character if a carriage of goods within a State is to be regarded as part of their inter-State movement. If a journey is merely a preliminary step in the process of initiating an inter-State transaction, it will not be protected by s 92 for the reasons expounded in the *Margarine Cases*.[5]

(b) BORDER-HOPPING. In *Naracoorte Transport Pty Ltd v Butler*[6] it was held that the protection of s 92 was available to a carrier who transported wool from a place in South Australia to a place in Victoria, though the wool was grown in Victoria and transported therefrom by a separate carrier to South Australia. The motives of the consignors in using this method for having the wool transported were treated as irrelevant.[7]

Several cases have raised the question whether s 92 could be applicable where the point of departure of a carrier and the point of destination were in the same State, but in the course of the journey a State border was crossed. Fullagar J said in *Golden v Hotchkiss*[8] that he had "no hesitation in saying that, if you have a single continuous journey which involves the crossing of a border between two States, then prima facie that journey is an inter-State journey, even though the point of departure and the point of destination are in the same state." But the principle merely creates a presumption, and the circumstances may rebut its application. In *Golden v Hotchkiss* itself, in *Beach v Wagner*,[9] in *Roadair Pty Ltd v Williams*[10] and in *J & J Ward Pty Ltd v Williams*[11] the principle was held to be applicable. It was otherwise in *Harris v Wagner*,[12] in *Western Interstate Pty Ltd v Madsen*[13] and in *Winton Transport Pty Ltd v Horne*,[14] where the crossing and recrossing of the border were not regarded as "steps taken in furtherance of the object of getting the goods to their predetermined final destination".[15]

**"But notwithstanding anything in this Constitution, goods imported before the imposition of uniform duties of customs into any State, or into any Colony which, whilst the goods remain therein, becomes a State, shall, on thence passing into another State within two years after the imposition of such duties,**

---

4   *Deacon v Mitchell* (1965) 112 CLR 353 at 364 (per Menzies J); [1965] ALR 961.
5   *Grannall v Marrickville Margarine Pty Ltd* (1955) 93 CLR 55 and *Beal v Marrickville Margarine Pty Ltd* (1966) 114 CLR 283; [1967] ALR 76. See *Tamar Timber Trading Co Pty Ltd v Pilkington* (1968) 117 CLR 353, [1968] ALR 285. See also *Webb v Stagg* (1965) 112 CLR 374; [1965] ALR 976.
6   (1956) 95 CLR 455.
7   See also *Jackson v Horne* (1965) 114 CLR 82; [1966] ALR 368, and *Barry v Stewart* (1965) 114 CLR 341; [1966] ALR 697.
8   (1959) 101 CLR 568 at 590.
9   (1959) 101 CLR 604.
10  (1968) 118 CLR 644.
11  (1969) 119 CLR 318.
12  (1959) 103 CLR 452.
13  (1961) 107 CLR 102; [1962] ALR 528.
14  (1966) 115 CLR 322.
15  *Harris v Wagner* (1959) 103 CLR 452 at 466 (per Fullagar J). McTiernan J (at p 461) observed that if the only purpose of crossing the border was to attempt to obtain immunity under s 92, the purpose was not one pertaining to trade, commerce or intercourse among the States. See also *Egg Marketing Board v Bonnie Doone Trading Co (NSW) Pty Ltd* (1962) 107 CLR 27; [1962] ALR 561.

be liable to any duty chargeable on the importation of such goods into the Commonwealth, less any duty paid in respect of the goods on their importation"

The operation of this provision has long been exhausted, since uniform customs duties came into effect in October 1901.

PAYMENT TO STATES FOR FIVE YEARS AFTER UNIFORM TARIFFS

**93.** *During the first five years after the imposition of uniform duties of customs, and thereafter until the Parliament otherwise provides—*

(i) *The duties of customs chargeable on goods imported into a State and afterwards passing into another State for consumption, and the duties of excise paid on goods produced or manufactured in a State and afterwards passing into another State for consumption, shall be taken to have been collected not in the former but in the latter State:*

(ii) *Subject to the last subsection, the Commonwealth shall credit revenue, debit expenditure, and pay balances to the several States as prescribed for the period preceding the imposition of uniform duties of customs.*[16]

This section embodies the second stage of the distribution structure provided for in the Constitution. It was to operate for five years from the imposition of the uniform tariff (i e, from 1901) and thereafter until the Parliament otherwise provided. The bookkeeping procedure laid down in s 89 was to apply to this period subject to the modifications prescribed in sub-section (i). The effect of this sub-section was described by Moore as follows:

... The interest of those States whose import trade was largely not direct from foreign countries but through some distributing centre, such as Sydney or Melbourne, within the Commonwealth, was protected by a provision that, where imported goods passed into other states for consumption, the duty should be taken to have been collected in and therefore be credited to the consuming State.[17]

It is clear that the distribution sections (ss 89, 93) operating for the first seven years of federation, while conferring on the States a legal right to surplus revenue,[18] did not guarantee to the States a fixed return as the Commonwealth could determine the amount which was to be expended for its own purposes. It was for this reason that s 87 was inserted in the Constitution.

DISTRIBUTION OF SURPLUS

**94.** *After five years from the imposition of uniform duties of customs, the Parliament may provide, on such basis as it deems fair, for the monthly payment to the several states of all surplus revenue of the Commonwealth.*[19]

With the expiration of the fixed periods for distribution, the federal Parliament was to have power to make provision for the distribution of surplus revenue to the States. Such generosity was not forthcoming. Instead, it enacted the *Surplus Revenue Act* in 1908 which provided that payments made to trust funds, established under the *Audit Act* 1901-1906, of moneys appropriated for the purposes of the Commonwealth, should be deemed to be expenditure.

---

16   Quick and Garran, 860-3.
17   *The Constitution of the Commonwealth of Australia* (2nd ed, 1910) 532.
18   Ibid at 533.
19   Quick and Garran, 863-5.

In the same year the *Old Age Pensions Appropriation Act* and the *Coast Defence Appropriation Act* were passed. These Acts directed that certain sums in excess of Commonwealth requirements for the financial year should be paid into trust funds to be used for defraying the costs of these services in succeeding years. The effect of this legislation was to eliminate any surplus revenue.

This action was challenged but the High Court in *New South Wales v Commonwealth*[20] held that money so appropriated was expenditure within the meaning of s 89 and could not therefore form part of the surplus revenue distributable under s 94.[21]

## CUSTOMS DUTIES OF WESTERN AUSTRALIA

**95.** *Notwithstanding anything in this Constitution, the Parliament of the State of Western Australia, if that State be an Original State, may, during the first five years after the imposition of uniform duties of customs, impose duties of customs on goods passing into that State and not originally imported from beyond the limits of the Commonwealth; and such duties shall be collected by the Commonwealth.*

*But any duty so imposed on any goods shall not exceed during the first of such years the duty chargeable on the goods under the law of Western Australia in force at the imposition of uniform duties, and shall not exceed during the second, third, fourth, and fifth of such years respectively, four-fifths, three-fifths, two-fifths, and one-fifth of such latter duty, and all duties imposed under this section shall cease at the expiration of the fifth year after the imposition of uniform duties.*

*If at any time during the five years the duty on any goods under this section is higher than the duty imposed by the Commonwealth on the importation of the like goods, then such higher duty shall be collected on the goods when imported into Western Australia from beyond the limits of the Commonwealth.*[22]

This section was designed to alleviate the special difficulties of Western Australia which relied more than any other state on customs duties on goods imported from other parts of the Australian continent.

Accordingly, this section introduced a special provision for the State that during the period of five years after the introduction of the uniform tariff, the Parliament of that State could impose duties (to be collected by the Commonwealth) on goods passing into the State from another State, and which had not been originally imported from abroad.

The rate was to be determined according to the method laid down in the section. It was a reducing rate and was to cease at the end of the fifth year after the imposition of the uniform tariff by the federal Parliament.

## FINANCIAL ASSISTANCE TO STATES

**96.** *During a period of ten years after the establishment of the Commonwealth and thereafter until the Parliament otherwise provides, the Parliament may grant financial assistance to any State on such terms and conditions as the Parliament thinks fit.*[23]

---

20  (1908) 7 CLR 179.
21  See *Essays*, 251-2.
22  Quick and Garran, 865-8.
23  Quick and Garran, 868-71. Wynes, 338-41. Howard, 75-86. Lane, 677-89. Nicholas, 170-7. *Essays*, (Ch IX: Hannan).

This clause was inserted in the Constitution to provide some flexibility in Commonwealth-State financial relations, which were rigidly controlled in the early period of federation by the distribution clauses (ss 87, 89, 93), and to assist the smaller States which stood to lose most by the last-minute compromise at the Premiers Conference in 1899 restricting the operation of the Braddon Clause (s 87) to an initial period of ten years.[24] Its historical rationale, however, belies the fundamental importance which it now has in the sphere of Commonwealth-State financial relations.[25]

When the Braddon Clause expired, the Commonwealth enacted the *Surplus Revenue Act* and "otherwise provided" by abolishing the obligation to return 75 per cent of customs and excise duties to the States. In its place a system of *per capita* grants was introduced under which each State received an annual grant computed on the basis of 25 shillings per head of population. This system continued until 1927 (without any increase in the rate to take account of inflation). It was replaced at that time by an annual contribution to the interest on debts of the States which had been taken over by the Commonwealth pursuant to the Financial Agreement.[26]

From an early date the Commonwealth had also made grants to the "necessitous" or, as they later became known, the "claimant", states, to compensate them for financial disabilities arising from their geographical position and paucity of resources. These grants were placed on a more scientific basis with the establishment of the Commonwealth Grants Commission in 1933 to advise the Commonwealth on the amounts which should be provided.[27] Tasmania, Western Australia, South Australia and Queensland have all, at one time or other, been "claimant" States.

But these grants are small in comparison with the other two major forms of grants provided by the Commonwealth: the tied or special purpose grants, and the general revenue grants made by the Commonwealth since 1942 to "compensate" the States for their loss of income tax[28] which resulted from the *Uniform Tax Case.*[29]

As to the former, the question arose in 1926 in *Victoria v Commonwealth*[30] whether the Commonwealth could attach conditions to a grant which in effect determined the purposes to which the grant was to be applied and the manner in which those purposes would be effectuated. The legislation in question, the *Federal Aid Roads Act* of 1926, authorized the execution of a road aid agreement between the Commonwealth and States under which money was made available to the States for road construction and re-construction purposes. The agreement, *inter alia,* prescribed the types of roads which could be built and

---

24    Quick and Garran, 869.
25    For recent discussions of s 96 see Campbell, "The Commonwealth Grants Power", (1969) 3 Federal Law Review 221. Myers, "The Grants Power—Key to Commonwealth-State Financial Relations" (1970) 7 MelbULR 549.
26    *Essays,* 252 et seq.
27    See *Commonwealth Grants Commission Act* 1933-1966.
28    However, since 1959, the Commonwealth has in its general revenue grants legislation omitted the "taxation re-imbursement" reference. The present formula is set out in the *States Grants Act* No 109 of 1970, s 10.
29    *South Australia v Commonwealth* (1942) 65 CLR 373. It is to be noted that in 1970 the Commonwealth introduced a type of grant which is intermediate between the special purpose and general revenue grant. See the *States Grants (Capital Assistance) Act* 1970-1972. This provides revenue to the States for expenditure of a capital nature and provides that the money to be used for the purposes is to be raised by Commonwealth loan.
30    (1926) 38 CLR 399.

provided that future payments were dependent on the Commonwealth being satisfied that the roads were properly maintained by the States. This legislation was upheld by the High Court.

The effect of the case was summed up by Dixon CJ in a later case[31] in this way:

This means that the power conferred by [s 96] is well exercised although (1) the state is bound to apply the money specifically to an object that has been defined, (2) the object is outside the powers of the Commonwealth, (3) the payments are left to the discretion of the Commonwealth minister, (4) the money is provided as the Commonwealth's contribution to an object for which the State is also to contribute funds.[32]

But the full significance of s 96 was not to be realized until the *Uniform Tax Case*[33] in 1942. That case established the right of the Commonwealth to attach conditions to grant to the States which reached into the very heart of State governmental power. Section 4 of the *Grants Act* which was the central act in the overall scheme provided:

In every financial year during which this Act is in operation in respect of which the Treasurer is satisfied that a State has not imposed a tax upon incomes, there shall be payable by way of financial assistance to that State the amount set forth in the schedule to this Act against the name of that State, less an amount equal to any arrears of tax collected by or on behalf of that State during that financial year.

In other words, the grant was conditional on the abstention of the States from operating their income tax legislation.

It was argued for the States which challenged the legislation that this was an attempt by the Commonwealth to use its powers in order to weaken the constitutional position of the States. But the majority of the court (with Starke J dissenting) upheld the validity of the legislation. In their judgments, the vital distinction was to be made between a coercive law (which would be unconstitutional) and a law which merely provided on inducement to a State by the offer of financial assistance not to exercise its powers in a particular way.[34] The *Grants Act* fell within this latter category.

In the *Second Uniform Tax Case*[35] Dixon CJ who had not been in the bench in the first case, indicated that, if the matter had been before the court afresh, support existed for the proposition that s 96 could not be applied in this way. He said:

It may well be that s 96 was conceived by the framers as (1) a transitional power, (2) confined to supplementing the resources of the Treasury of a State by particular subventions when some special or particular need or occasion arose, and (3) imposing terms or conditions relevant to a situation which called for special relief or assistance from the Commonwealth.[36]

However, he added, "the course of judicial decision has put any such limited interpretation of s 96 out of consideration."[37] In so far as the *Grants Act* did

---

31  *Victoria and New South Wales v Commonwealth* (*Second Uniform Tax Case*) (1957) 99 CLR 575.
32  Ibid at 606.
33  (1942) 65 CLR 373.
34  See, for example, the judgment of Latham CJ, ibid at 417. Campbell, op cit, n 25 at 228.
35  (1957) 99 CLR 575.
36  Ibid at 609.
37  Ibid.

not amount to a coercive law, it could not be impugned. But it is recognised that it would be incompetent for the Commonwealth Parliament to attach to a State grant a condition that the State should *abdicate* a field of constitutional power. This would also infringe the principle that a State Parliament cannot bind a future Parliament as to matters of substance.[38]

It is clear, therefore, that the Commonwealth has power to impose a wide range of conditions in its State grants legislation which will have an important effect on the manner in which the concurrent or residuary powers of the States are exercised. A survey of recent legislation indicates the number of areas in which "special purpose" grants have been made to the States on conditions which involve considerable control by the Commonwealth over the execution of State policies. For example, grants have been made to benefit Aboriginals,[39] independent schools,[40] universities,[41] nursing homes,[42] rural reconstruction,[43] housing,[44] beef roads.[45] In a number of cases the conditions attached to Commonwealth approval involve Commonwealth determination of standards not only in terms of capital works but of the manner in which a body or instrumentality will determine its priorities.[46] The consequence is that what legally is a "fiscal incentive" has become a means whereby the Commonwealth has assumed at least a general policy control over many areas falling within State residuary power.

As compared with the taxation and bounties provisions of the constitution which forbid discrimination, there is no requirement that grants made under s 96 should not discriminate between States. This was decided in *Moran's Case*.[47] Pursuant to a Commonwealth-States agreement to introduce a wheat stabilization scheme to assist wheatgrowers, legislation was passed by the Commonwealth to impose an excise tax on flour. The proceeds from this tax were placed in a special fund to be returned to the States which would use the money to assist the growers, but in the case of Tasmania no such conditions were attached to the grant. The reason was that Tasmania was not a wheat-growing State. It was recognized, therefore, that Tasmania would use the money to relieve the persons who had paid the flour tax in that State. This was done in the *Flour Tax Relief Act* (Tasmania). The scheme was challenged on the ground that it amounted to an unconstitutional discrimination between the States. By a majority (with Evatt J dissenting) the High Court held that there was nothing to prevent the power conferred by s 96 from being exercised in this manner. The High Court judgment was upheld by the Privy Council on appeal, although there is a dictum in the latter judgment to the effect that "under the guise or pretence of assisting a State with money, the real substance and purpose of the Act might simply be to effect discrimination in regard to

38   *South Australia v Commonwealth* (1942) 65 CLR 373 at 416 (Latham CJ).

39   *States Grants (Aboriginal Advancement) Act*, 1968-1973.

40   *States Grants (Independent Schools) Act*, 1969-1972.

41   *States Grants (Universities) Act*, 1957-1973.

42   *States Grants (Nursing Homes) Act*, 1969-1972.

43   *States Grants (Rural Construction) Act*, 1971-1972.

44   *States Grants (Housing) Act*, 1971-1972.

45   *States Grants (Beef Roads) Act*, 1968.

46   See, for example, the *States Grants (Advanced Education) Act*, 1965-1972, s 3.

47   *Deputy Federal Commissioner of Taxation (NSW) v W R Moran Pty Ltd* (1939) 61 CLR 735 (High Court); (1940) 63 CLR 338 (Privy Council). Discussed by Singh, "Legislative Schemes in Australia" (1964) 4 MelbULR 355 at 355-61.

taxation. Such an act might well be ultra vires of the Commonwealth Parliament."[48]

Reference may also be made to *Magennis' Case*[49] where the High Court invalidated federal legislation giving effect to a Commonwealth-States Agreement on the settlement of ex-servicemen on land. The legislation in question purported to approve the agreement whereby, *inter alia*, the Commonwealth agreed to grant financial assistance to the States for the acquisition of land by the States after the end of the Second World War but on pre-1942 prices. The basis of compensation did not comply with the "just terms" requirement of s 51 (xxxi). It was held by a majority that the legislation was in substance legislation with respect to the acquisition, and therefore invalid as not providing "just terms".

It is possible therefore that the characterization question will be relevant in determining the validity of grants legislation which also regulates a subject-matter outside Commonwealth power or to which some constitutional impediment is directed. In actual fact the problem raised in *Magennis Case* can often be overcome if the Commonwealth-States Agreement is not ratified by legislation but is merely left to operate on the administrative level. The actual grant therefore would be isolated from the subject-matter to be regulated under State legislation. It was in this way that the land settlement scheme was successfully operated after the *Magennis* decision.[50]

Under the *Commonwealth Grants Commission Act* 1973, provision is made for the re-constitution of the Commonwealth Grants Commission. A major change is that local government bodies grouped on a regional basis may make application to the Commission for assistance and the Commission is empowered to make recommendations to the Commonwealth government on what grants should be made to the States for local government purposes.

AUDIT

**97.** *Until the Parliament otherwise provides, the laws in force in any Colony which has become or becomes a State with respect to the receipt of revenue and the expenditure of money on account of the Government of the Colony, and the review and audit of such receipt and expenditure, shall apply to the receipt of revenue and the expenditure of money on account of the Commonwealth in the State in the same manner as if the Commonwealth, or the Government or an officer of the Commonwealth, were mentioned whenever the Colony, or the Government or an officer of the Colony, is mentioned.*[51]

Under this section the Commonwealth Parliament has power to make laws with respect to auditing of the receipt and expenditure of moneys on account of the Commonwealth. Until the enactment of the legislation (which occurred in 1901) State laws were to apply, *mutatis mutandis*, to the auditing of Commonwealth moneys within each State.

As we have seen, the *Audit Act* 1901-1969 makes provision for the establishment of two funds (the Loan Fund and the Trust Fund) besides the Consolidated Revenue Fund which is established by s 81 of the Constitution.[52]

---

48  63 CLR at 350. Cf, *South Australia v Commonwealth* (1942) 65 CLR 373 at 428 (Latham CJ).
49  *P J Magennis Pty Ltd v Commonwealth* (1949) 80 CLR 382.
50  See *Pye v Renshaw* (1951) 84 CLR 58.
51  Quick and Garran, 872.
52  See above under s 81.

Moneys received by the Commonwealth are paid into the Commonwealth public account which is kept in such banks and under such subdivisions as the Treasurer directs. A separate fund called the Loan Fund is created in that account and all moneys raised by loan upon the public credit of the Commonwealth are paid into that fund. Section 60 of the Act makes provision for the Trust Fund: moneys received on trust are placed to the credit of that fund under such separate heads as the Treasurer directs.[53]

The following matters which are dealt with in the divisions of the Act indicate the nature of the subject-matter covered by the term "audit": the status and powers of the Auditor General and accounting officers, collection and payment of moneys, audit and inspection of public accounts, and the establishment of special funds.

One particular matter to which special reference may be made is the procedure to be followed in relation to payment of moneys out of the Consolidated Revenue and Loan Funds. This procedure is set out in ss 32 and 33 of the Act. It involves the following steps.

(1) The Treasurer must notify the Auditor-General that an amount of money lawfully available for expenditure by virtue of an appropriation is required to be drawn from the Commonwealth public account in respect of the services or purposes for which the appropriation is made.

(2) The Auditor-General after satisfying himself that the amount is lawfully available is required to give a certificate to this end.

(3) If not satisfied, he shall set out in writing the amount considered not lawfully available and the grounds on which he bases his opinion.

(4) When the Auditor-General has given a certificate, the Governor-General[54] is empowered to issue a warrant to the Treasurer authorizing the drawing of the amount from the Commonwealth public account.

(5) On the issue of the warrant, the Treasurer may make the payment out of any bank account in which the Commonwealth public account is kept in respect of the services or purposes referred to in the warrant.

TRADE AND COMMERCE INCLUDES NAVIGATION AND STATE RAILWAYS

**98.** *The power of the Parliament to make laws with respect to trade and commerce extends to navigation and shipping, and to railways the property of any State.*[55]

As early as the *Kalibia Case*[56] it was decided that s 98 of the Constitution merely explained the meaning of the words "trade and commerce" as applied to matters within the ambit of the trade and commerce power (s 51 (i)). It was therefore held that it was not within the power of the Commonwealth Parliament to legislate with respect to the relation of employer and employee on ships trading entirely within the limits of one State. In *Newcastle and Hunter River Steamship Co Ltd v Attorney-General for the Commonwealth*,[57] it was held that the Commonwealth Parliament was not at liberty to regulate the manning of ships not engaged in inter-State or foreign trade or commerce

---

53    There is also a special trust fund created by the *National Debt Sinking Fund Act* 1966. See discussion of s 105A.
54    It is provided that the Governor-General may act without obtaining the advice of the Executive Council.
55    Quick and Garran, 872-5.
56    (1910) 11 CLR 689.
57    (1921) 29 CLR 357; 27 ALR 373.

merely because they went on the high seas or in waters used by ships engaged in such trade or commerce. Similarly it was held in *R v Turner ex parte Marine Board of Hobart*[58] that Parliament was not at liberty to direct a Court of Marine Inquiry established under the *Navigation Act* 1912 to deal with a collision between two vessels not engaged in inter-State or foreign trade or commerce merely because the collision occurred in a navigable river in a State, at a short distance outside the course ordinarily used by ships engaged in such trade or commerce, and shortly after the colliding vessels had traversed part of such course.

In *Australian Steamships Ltd v Malcolm,*[59] s 98 was paraphrased as saying in effect that the power to make laws with respect to trade and commerce shall include a power to make laws with respect to navigation and shipping as ancillary to such trade and commerce. It was decided in that case that the *Seamen's Compensation Act* 1911 was a valid exercise of the legislative power of the Commonwealth Parliament, since s 98 "authorised Parliament to make laws with respect to shipping and the conduct and management of ships as instrumentalities of trade and commerce, and to regulate the relations and reciprocal rights and obligations of those conducting the navigation of ships in the course of such commerce both among themselves and in relation to their employers on whose behalf the navigation was conducted."[60]

More generally, it was held in *Morgan v Commonwealth*[61] that ss 98 to 102 inclusive of the Constitution should be read as applying only to laws which could be made under the power conferred by s 51 (i).

In *Australian Coastal Shipping Commission v O'Reilly*[62] Dixon CJ treated it as beyond doubt that the combination of s 51 (i) with s 98 gave the widest power to deal with the whole subject matter of navigation and shipping in relation to trade and commerce with other countries and among the States. That necessarily included complete power to establish a government shipping line for the purpose of such trade and commerce.

That case was concerned with the validity of a provision in the *Australian Coastal Shipping Commission Act* 1956-1969.[63] The Act established the Australian Coastal Shipping Commission as a body corporate, with the function of establishing, maintaining and operating shipping services for the carriage of passengers or mails or making provision for doing so. The services are limited to inter-state and overseas carriage and carriage to Territories.

The *Navigation Act* 1912-1972 contains comprehensive provisions dealing with masters and seamen, including the establishment of a complement of officers for a ship, supplying seamen to be entered on board ships, the rating of seamen, the approval of engagements of seamen, their wages, discharge, discipline, and protection. It deals also with the condition of ships—with surveys and survey certificates, with safety convention certificates, with unseaworthy ships, safety and other equipment, and with collisions. It includes also

---

58   (1927) 39 CLR 411.
59   (1914) 19 CLR 298 at 335.
60   19 CLR at 335.
61   (1947) 74 CLR 421.
62   (1962) 107 CLR 46 at 54; [1962] ALR 502 at 504.
63   The section provided that the commission was not subject to taxation under a law of a State to which the Commonwealth was not subject. The validity of the provision was sustained by the court.

provisions on such matters as wrecks[64] and salvage, and courts of marine inquiry.[65]

In *Union Steamship Co of New Zealand Ltd v Commonwealth*,[66] provisions in the *Navigation Act* with respect to engagements and discharges of seamen were held to be within the powers of the Commonwealth under ss 51 (i) and 98 of the Constitution, but it was also held that the provisions were void and inoperative as being repugnant to the Imperial provisions contained in the *Merchant Shipping Acts* of 1894 and 1906.

Section 735 of the *Merchant Shipping Act*, 1894 authorises the Legislature of any British possession by an Act or Ordinance, confirmed by Her Majesty in Council, to repeal provisions of that Act relating to ships registered in that possession. The *Navigation Act* 1912 was so confirmed. It appears that s 735 operated on the condition stated to remove a limitation on the power of the Commonwealth Parliament to make laws with respect to navigation, but that it did not confer power, which had to be sought in s 98 together with s 51 (i) or in other relevant heads of power conferred by the Constitution. However, ss 2 and 5 of the *Statute of Westminster* have removed the limitations on the Commonwealth Parliament arising from s 735 of the *Merchant Shipping Act*.

The reference in s 98 to "railways the property of any State" was included to remove any doubt on the question whether s 51 (i) would be construed to extend the authority of the Commonwealth to the Government railways of the States.[67]

COMMONWEALTH NOT TO GIVE PREFERENCE

**99.** *The Commonwealth shall not, by any law or regulation of trade, commerce, or revenue, give preference to one State or any part thereof over another State or any part thereof.*[68]

Section 99 is a prohibition directed to the Commonwealth—not merely to the Legislature, but also to the Executive.[69] To establish that s 99 has been contravened, three things must be established:

(a) The impugned Commonwealth law or regulation is one of trade, commerce or revenue. In *Morgan v Commonwealth*,[70] an attack was made on the validity of regulations and orders made under the *National Security Act* 1939 in relation to the rationing of goods which were not applicable generally throughout Australia. The first question was whether the regulations came within the description "any law or regulation of trade, commerce, or revenue" within the meaning of s 99. It was held that they did not, and that

---

64 Quaere whether s 308 of the *Navigation Act* providing that the Commonwealth is entitled to all unclaimed wreck found in Australia is justified by the Commonwealth Constitution. Compare s 523 of the *Merchant Shipping Act* 1894.

65 See further the commentary on s 51 (i) (trade and commerce power) and on s 76 (iii) (Admiralty and maritime jurisdiction).

66 (1925) 36 CLR 130.

67 Quick and Garran, 875.

68 Quick and Garran, 875-9. Wynes, 233-7. Lane, 60-6. Howard, 358-65. Essays, 106-8, 290-2.

69 *Elliott v Commonwealth* (1936) 54 CLR 657 at 682.

70 (1947) 74 CLR 428.

the description included, so far as trade and commerce was concerned, only laws made under s 51 (i) of the Constitution.[71]

(b) A preference has been given. The "preference" prohibited by s 99 was defined by Dixon J in *Crowe v Commonwealth*[72] in the following terms:

In relation to trade and commerce, as distinguished from revenue, the preference referred to by s 99 is evidently some tangible advantage obtainable in the course of trading or commercial operations, or, at least, some material or sensible benefit of a commercial or trading character.

In that case it was held that no tangible or material advantage was given to the trade and commerce of one State over another by a provision providing for inequality in the number of representatives of growers from different States on a Dried Fruits Control Board. The position was different in *James v Commonwealth*.[73] Commonwealth regulations provided that licences permitting inter-State carriage of dried fruits could only be obtained from the prescribed authority of the State in which the dried fruits were delivered for carriage. No authority was prescribed for the State of Queensland or the State of Tasmania. It was held that the regulations gave preference to one State over another State.

The fullest description of the concept of a preference is to be found in *Elliott v The Commonwealth*.[74] The *Transport Workers (Seamen) Regulations* 1935 provided a system for licensing seamen, but the system applied only at ports in the Commonwealth specified by the Minister as ports in respect of which licensing officers should be appointed. Unlicensed persons were not permitted to engage or be engaged as seamen at ports so specified. The minister specified ports in four States, but not in the other two States. Latham CJ stated that s 99 should not be construed as prohibiting any differentiation or discrimination; it came into operation only if a tangible commercial advantage was given to a State or a part of a State over another State or part thereof. In the instant case, where there was difficulty in specifying the nature and the recipients of the preference, he held that no preference had been given. Dixon J agreed that not every discrimination between States amounted to a preference of one over the other. But he considered that "the section does not call upon the court to estimate the total amount of economic or commercial advantage which does or will actually ensue from the law or regulation of trade or commerce. It is enough that the law or regulation is designed to produce some tangible advantage obtainable in the course of trading or commercial operations, or some material or sensible benefit of a commercial or trading character".[75]

(c) The preference must be given to one State or any part thereof over another State or any part thereof. In *Elliott's Case*[76] the court was divided on the question whether the prohibited preference must be in relation to local situation in any part of the six States, or in relation to States or parts of States.

---

71   The law or regulation made under s 51 (i) may be in respect of inter-state or foreign trade. For example, export controls which gave a preference to one State or any part thereof over another State or any part thereof would infringe s 99.
72   (1935) 54 CLR 69.
73   (1928) 41 CLR 442.
74   (1936) 54 CLR 65.
75   54 CLR at 683.
76   (1936) 54 CLR 657.

Latham CJ held that "the *discrimen* which s 99 forbids the Commonwealth to select is not merely locality as such, but localities which for the purpose of applying the *discrimen* are taken as States or parts of States".[77] On the other hand, Evatt J summarised his views on the question in the following propositions:

(1) Section 99 forbids laws or regulations which accord preferential treatment to persons or things as a consequence of local situation in any part of the six States, regardless of all other circumstances.[78]

(2) The section is not infringed if the preferential treatment is a consequence of a number of circumstances, including the circumstance of locality.

(3) Section 99 may apply although the legislation or regulations contain no mention of a State *eo nomine*, e g, the section may be infringed if preference is given to part of a State (e g, that part of New South Wales which is represented by the port of Sydney) over another State (e g, Western Australia) or any part of another State (e g, Fremantle or Brisbane).

Dixon CJ adverted briefly to the question in *FCT v Clyne*[79] where he confessed that he had "the greatest difficulty in grasping what exactly is the requirement that the selection of an area shall be as part of the State" . . . and that he was "unable to appreciate the distinction between the selection by an enactment of an area in fact forming part of a State for the bestowal of a preference upon the area and the selection of the same area for the same purpose 'as part of the State'."

It should be observed that while every discrimination does not amount to a preference, there can be no preference without discrimination. The cases decided on the meaning of the expression in s 51 (ii) of the Constitution, "but so as not to discriminate between States or parts of State", are therefore relevant in determining whether a preference has been given. Moreover, there is no clear distinction in meaning between the terms "between States or parts of States" in s 51 (ii), and, "to one State or any part thereof over another State or any part thereof" in s 99.

NOR ABRIDGE RIGHT TO USE WATER

**100.** *The Commonwealth shall not, by any law or regulation of trade or commerce, abridge the right of a State or of the residents therein to the reasonable use of the waters of rivers for conservation or irrigation.*[80]

We have seen that the Commonwealth may under s 98 regulate matters pertaining to navigation on inter-State rivers.

Section 100 imposes a restriction on this power by providing that the Commonwealth shall not abridge the right of a State or its residents to the reasonable use of such rivers for conservation and irrigation. These matters fall within the residuary powers of the States.

A major question is whether s 100 guarantees to riparian States and their

---

77   54 CLR at 675. Substantially this is the view expressed by Isaacs J in *Barger's Case* (1908) 6 CLR at 107, that "the treatment that is forbidden, discrimination or preference, is in relation to the localities considered as parts of States, and not as mere Australian localities, or parts of the Commonwealth considered as a single country".

78   *R v Barger* (1908) CLR at 78-81, per Griffith CJ, Barton and O'Connor JJ.

79   (1958) 100 CLR 246.

80   Quick and Garran, 879-94.

residents access to the use of waters for irrigation and conservation or whether it merely imposes a restriction on the power of the Commonwealth when legislating under ss 51 (i) and 98.[81] The question occupied an important place in discussions in the earlier years of federation on the use of the River Murray waters by New South Wales, Victoria and South Australia. Legal opinions given at the time were conflicting but it would seem that the better view is that s 100 does not confer riparian rights on those States but merely obliges the Commonwealth to recognize such rights when legislating under the navigation power.[82] The basic conflict in relation to the River Murray was settled in 1914 with the signing of the River Murray Waters Agreement by the Commonwealth and the three States which contained various provisions with regard to protection of navigation and the building of conservation and irrigation works.[83]

The question whether apart from s 100 there was any pre-existing law protecting the riparian rights of States which share a river or catchment system is more difficult to answer[84] but it would appear that the view of Quick and Garran on this matter is the correct one:

Before Federation, it is clear that the legal rights of each colony—or of the residents of that colony, as against residents of another colony—to the use of the waters or rivers flowing through the colony were absolute. There is no such thing as a riparian law between independent States; and consequently each colony had, as part of its law, the riparian common law of England. But that law became the law of each colony separately, and not law between the colonies, nor the general law of all the colonies.[85]

Any challenge by one State directed against another's diversion of the waters of a shared river would in the absence of an inter-State common law be met with the plea that the matter was not justiciable,[86] i e, was a matter which could only be determined by political negotiations. The River Murray Waters Agreement and various ancillary agreements[87] are the result of such negotiations.[88]

## INTER-STATE COMMISSION

**101.** *There shall be an Inter-State Commission, with such powers of adjudication and administration as the Parliament deems necessary for the execution and maintenance, within the Commonwealth, of the provisions of this Constitution relating to trade and commerce, and of all laws made thereunder.*[89]

---

81  See *Morgan v Commonwealth* (1947) 74 CLR 421 at 455.
82  See Clark, "The River Murray Question" 8 MULR (1971) 215, esp 217-20.
83  See *River Murray Waters Act*, 1915-1970.
84  See Clark, op cit, n 3.
85  Quick and Garran at 887. On the nature of the riparian doctrine see Clark and Renard, "The Riparian Doctrine and Australian Legislation" 7 MULR (1970) 475.
86  Cf, Renard, "Australian Inter-State Common Law" 4 Federal Law Review (1970) 87 at 111-3.
87  One of the latest was the Dartmouth Dam Agreement. See *Dartmouth Reservoir Agreement Act*, No 7 of 1970.
88  See also the New South Wales-Queensland Border Rivers Agreement of 1946 (on the use of the waters of the Dumaresq and MacIntyre Rivers forming a common border between the two States).
89  Quick and Garran, 895-901.

By the *Inter-State Commission Act* 1912, the federal Parliament established an inter-State commission consisting of three members. Section 24 of the Act conferred upon the commission jurisdiction to hear and determine any complaint, dispute, or question, and to adjudicate upon any matter arising as to—

(a) Any preference, advantage, prejudice, disadvantage, or discrimination given or made by any State or any State authority or by any common carrier in contravention of this Aact, or of the provisions of the Constitution relating to trade or commerce or any law made thereunder;

(b) the justice or reasonableness of any rate in respect of inter-State commerce, or affecting such commerce;

(c) anything done on or omitted to be done by any State or by any State authority or by any common carrier or by any person in contravention of this Act or of the provisions of the Constitution relating to trade or commerce or any law made thereunder.

Following sections of the Act granted the Commission certain enforcement powers including the power to grant injunctions against future contraventions of the law.

In *New South Wales v Commonwealth*,[90] the High Court by a majority of 4-2[91] held that s 101 of the Constitution did not authorize the Parliament to constitute the inter-State commission as a court and therefore the judicial powers, including the power to issue an injunction, were invalidly conferred on the commission.

It was argued that the tribunals established under Chapter III of the Constitution were not intended to be the sole repositories of judicial power. In particular the phrase "powers of adjudication", it was said, showed that the commission was intended to exercise a limited form of judicial power. This argument was rejected by the majority which considered that the phrase "powers of adjudication" imported powers of an administrative or quasi-judicial nature. The provisions of the Constitution relating to the Interstate Commission were described by Isaacs J as follows:

The Constitution provided for the possible establishment of a novel administrative and consultative organ with incidental quasi-judicial functions, very much as a Commissioner of Patents has to exercise quasi-judicial functions before exercising the executive act of issuing a patent, or a Collector of Customs has sometimes in a quasi-judicial way to examine and come to a conclusion on the dutiability of goods, and the conclusion is sometimes made a binding one. The usefulness of the commission was not necessarily to stop at s 102. It might be seen that the commerce provisions of the Constitution or the Commonwealth laws would be greatly aided if the same body were to have its authority extended, and the ordinary administrative departments might be materially assisted by such an extension.[92]

The result of the decision in *New South Wales v The Commonwealth* meant that the powers of the commission were greatly reduced and it became defunct in 1920.[93] If the body were re-established it could only exercise administrative and quasi-judicial functions of executing and maintaining the provisions of the Constitution relating to trade and commerce (e g, s 92) and

---

90    (1915) 20 CLR 54.
91    Griffith CJ, Isaacs, Powers and Rich JJ (Barton and Gavan Duffy JJ dissenting).
92    (1915) 20 CLR 54 at 92.
93    See Sawer, *Australian Federal Politics and Law, 1901-1929*, 193 n 81, 204.

the laws made thereunder.[94] Its value would be its position of independence because of the tenure of its numbers prescribed by s 103. The Joint Committee on Constitutional Review in 1959 recommended the reconstitution of the commission.[95]

## PARLIAMENT MAY FORBID PREFERENCES BY STATE

**102.** *The Parliament may by any law with respect to trade or commerce forbid, as to railways, any preference or discrimination by any State, or by any authority constituted under a State, if such preference or discrimination is undue and unreasonable, or unjust to any State; due regard being had to the financial responsibilities incurred by any State in connexion with the construction and maintenance of its railways. But no preference or discrimination shall, within the meaning of this section, be taken to be undue and unreasonable, or unjust to any State, unless so adjudged by the Inter-State Commission.*[96]

Under ss. 51 (i) and 98 the Commonwealth Parliament has power inter alia, to legislate with respect to inter-State trade carried on by State railways. This section spells out that the power extends to the prohibition of railway preferences or discriminations practiced by States. The limitations on this power are described by Latham CJ in *Riverina Transport Pty Ltd v State of Victoria*[97] as follows:

(1) The preference or discrimination must be undue and unreasonable, or unjust to some State.

(2) Due regard must be had to the financial responsibilities incurred by the discriminating or preferring State in connexion with the construction and maintenance of its railways.

(3) It is for the inter-State commission, and not for the Parliament itself, to determine, in the case of State railways, whether any preference or discrimination is, within the meaning of the section, undue and unreasonable, or unjust to any State.[98]

The case just cited is one of the *Transport Cases,* involving a limited interpretation of the protection afforded by s 92, which were overruled in *Hughes and Vale Pty Ltd v State of New South Wales.*[99] However, there has been no dissent from the elucidation of s 102 given by Latham CJ.

## COMMISSIONERS' APPOINTMENT, TENURE, AND REMUNERATION

**103.** *The members of the Inter-State Commission—*

(i) *Shall be appointed by the Governor-General in Council:*

(ii) *Shall hold office for seven years, but may be removed within that time by the Governor-General in Council, on an address from both Houses of the Parliament in the same session praying for such removal on the ground of proved misbehaviour or incapacity:*

---

94  That is, laws made under s 51 (i). See *Riverina Transport Pty Ltd v State of Victoria* (1937) 57 CLR 327 at 352 (Latham CJ).
95  *Report* at 119.
96  Quick and Garran, 901-18.
97  (1937) 57 CLR 327 at 350 et seq.
98  Ibid at 354-5.
99  (1954) 93 CLR 1. See under s 92.

   (iii) *Shall receive such remuneration as the Parliament may fix; but such remuneration shall not be diminished during their continuance in office.*[1]

The tenure of the members of the commission is set out in this section. It is to be noted that the conditions are similar to those of federal judges with the exception that their appointment is for an initial period of seven years.

## SAVING OF CERTAIN RATES

   **104.** *Nothing in this Constitution shall render unlawful any rate for the carriage of goods upon a railway, the property of a State, if the rate is deemed by the Inter-State Commission to be necessary for the development of the territory of the State, and if the rate applies equally to goods within the State and to goods passing into the State from other States.*[2]

As we have seen in our discussion of s 102 the Commonwealth Parliament could under its trade and commerce power fix rates for the inter-state carriage of goods upon a State railway. Section 104 constitutes a limitation on this power. It operates "to prevent the Commonwealth Parliament from making certain goods rates unlawful either by direct declaration that they are unlawful or by fixing a different rate as the rate to be applied. The rates which are so protected are such as the inter-State commission deems to be necessary for the development of the territory of a State".[3]

## TAKING OVER PUBLIC DEBTS OF STATES

   **105.** *The Parliament may take over from the States their public debts, or a proportion thereof according to the respective numbers of their people as shown by the latest statistics of the Commonwealth, and may convert, renew, or consolidate such debts, or any part thereof; and the States shall indemnify the Commonwealth in respect of the debts taken over, and thereafter the interest payable in respect of the debts shall be deducted and retained from the portions of the surplus revenue of the Commonwealth payable to the several States, or if such surplus is insufficient, or if there is no surplus, then the deficiency or the whole amount shall be paid by the several States.*[4]

This section was, in the words of Quick and Garran, designed to permit the transfer of State public debts to the Commonwealth in order to "substitute the credit of the Commonwealth for the credit of the States—to make the Commonwealth the debtor to whom the bondholders will have to look, and to release the States from any obligation to the bondholders, imposing on them instead an obligation to indemnify the Commonwealth for the amount of principal and interest."[5]

It encompassed two alternatives: the taking over the whole of the state debts existing at federation (although the words "existing at the establishment of the Commonwealth" were deleted pursuant to a constitutional amendment in 1910) or to take over part of these debts on a *per capita* basis.

---

1   Quick and Garran, 918-9.
2   Quick and Garran, 920-2.
3   *Riverina Transport Pty Ltd v State of Victoria* (1937) 57 CLR 327 at 356 (Latham CJ).
4   Quick and Garran, 922-6.
5   Ibid at 924.

The weakness of s 105 was that it provided no basis for co-ordinating future borrowing. Moreover, the Commonwealth's duty to contribute to the interest payments on debts taken over was out of the "surplus revenue" of the Commonwealth. In so far as the events of 1908 showed that the Commonwealth could, by a "bookkeeping" operation, abolish surplus revenue,[6] the States could not have relied on s 105 for any permanent, guaranteed assistance from the Commonwealth. It was for this reason that a new system was agreed upon by the States and the Commonwealth in 1927 and became s 105A of the Constitution.

## AGREEMENTS WITH RESPECT TO STATE DEBTS

**105A.** (1) *The Commonwealth may make agreements with the States with respect to the public debts of the States, including—*

(a) *the taking over of such debts by the Commonwealth;*

(b) *the management of such debts;*

(c) *the payment of interest and the provision and management of sinking funds in respect of such debts;*

(d) *the consolidation, renewal, conversion, and redemption of such debts;*

(e) *the indemnification of the Commonwealth by the States in respect of debts taken over by the Commonwealth; and*

(f) *the borrowing of money by the States or by the Commonwealth, or by the Commonwealth for the States.*

(2) *The Parliament may make laws for validating any such agreement made before the commencement of this section.*

(3) *The Parliament may make laws for the carrying out by the parties thereto of any such agreement.*

(4) *Any such agreement may be varied or rescinded by the parties thereto.*

(5) *Every such agreement and any such variation thereof shall be binding upon the Commonwealth and the States parties thereto notwithstanding anything contained in this Constitution or the Constitutions of the several States or in any law of the Parliament of the Commonwealth or of any State.*

(6) *The powers conferred by this section shall not be construed as being limited in any way by the provisions of section one hundred and five of this Constitution.*[7]

This section, probably the major constitutional amendment since federation, gives effect to the financial agreement between the Commonwealth and the States which was entered into in 1927, enacted by the federal Parliament in 1928[8] and approved at a referendum in the same year, and inserted as s 105A in the Constitution in 1929.[9] Between the years 1927 and 1929, the agreement continued in existence on a voluntary basis.

An excellent description of the agreement is to be found in the judgment of Rich and Dixon JJ in *New South Wales v Commonwealth (No 1)*.[10]

---

6  See above under s 94.

7  *Essays,* 115-7, 252-6. Nicholas, 164-70.

8  *Financial Agreement Act,* No 5 of 1928.

9  *Constitutional Alteration (State Debts) Act,* No 1 of 1929. See also *Financial Agreement Validation Act,* No 4 of 1929.

10  (1931) 46 CLR 155.

By that agreement the Commonwealth agreed to take over the balance unpaid of the gross public debt of each State, and, in respect of the debts taken over, to assume as between the Commonwealth and the States the liabilities of the States to bondholders. The Commonwealth agreed to pay to bondholders from time to time interest payable on the public debts of the States taken over. Towards the interest payable by the States in each year it agreed to provide certain amounts, and each of the States agreed to pay to the Commonwealth the excess over the amounts so provided necessary to make up the interest charges on its public debt taken over by the Commonwealth. The Commonwealth and the States agreed to establish a sinking fund to answer the public debts taken over, and agreed that the contributions which they each undertook to make should be debts payable to the National Debt Commission. Each State agreed with the Commonwealth that it would by the faithful performance of its obligations under the agreement indemnify the Commonwealth against all liabilities whatsoever in respect of the public debt of that State taken over by the Commonwealth. The agreement further contained provisions for the control of future borrowing by the States and the Commonwealth, and of the conversion, renewal, redemption and consolidation of the public debts of the Commonwealth and of the States. As a consequence of these provisions any new securities required, whether upon a conversion or renewal of an existing loan or because of further borrowing, would be issued upon the credit of the Commonwealth.[11]

Under the agreement (which has been amended in minor ways several times)[12] the Commonwealth agreed to contribute towards the payment of interest on the public debts of the States a sum which approximated to the 25 shillings per capita payments which had been made to the States from the time when the *Surplus Revenue Act* was passed in 1910 to make up for the loss of revenue by the States when the temporary ten year period of sharing in Commonwealth revenue expired. The contribution period was 58 years from 1 July 1927. Each State agreed to pay the excess over the amount provided by the Commonwealth in respect of the interest payable on its own debt.[13]

In addition a sinking fund was established for the redemption of the net public debts of the States with the Commonwealth and States agreeing to contribute according to specified proportions. The period of contribution is also 58 years. These sinking funds are controlled by the National Debt Commission established by the agreement.[14]

The Loan Council was established to regulate borrowing by both the Commonwealth and the States. It consists of the Prime Minister (or his deputy) and the Premiers of the States (or their deputies). Each State has one vote, while the Commonwealth has two votes and a casting vote.[15]

Each Government submits its annual borrowing programme to the Council. Excluded from the programme are amounts required for the conversion

---

11   Ibid at 175. Under the *Financial Agreements (Commonwealth Liability)* Act 1932 No 2, the Commonwealth acknowledged its liability to pay the bondholders interest on the public debts taken over from the States.

12   The latest in 1966. See *Financial Agreement Act* of that year. See also Nicholas, at 184.

13   Agreement, cl 11.

14   Agreement, cl 12. Different sinking funds contributions were payable according as to whether the debt has been incurred before or after 30 June 1927. Special provision was also made for loans for the conversion, renewal or redemption of state debts.

15   Agreement, cl 3. For an account of the Loan Council see Davis, "A Unique Federal Institution", 2 Univ WA Law Review, 350 et seq. See also Menzies, *Central Power in the Australian Commonwealth*, Ch 7.

of existing loans, for temporary purposes, and (on the part of the Commonwealth) for defence purposes. Borrowing on behalf of semi-government instrumentalities and municipal authorities in excess of $400,000 is included.[16]

The Council decides the amount of the loan programme for the particular financial year. However allocation of the amount between each borrower is to be decided by unanimous resolution; failing unanimity it is decided according to a formula whereby, the Commonwealth, if it wishes, is entitled to one fifth of the amount and the remainder is divided among the States on the basis of the borrowing by each State during the preceding five years.[17]

As we have seen, the supervision of payments into and out of the sinking fund is vested in the National Debt Commission, the powers of which are set out in the *National Debt Sinking Fund Act*.[18] Under s 7 of the Act a fund known as the National Debt Sinking Fund is established within the Trust Fund. Separate accounts are required to be maintained in the sinking fund in relation to Commonwealth and individual State payments. By s 9 the Treasurer is required to place certain amounts in the Sinking Fund each year. Moneys standing to the credit of the Commonwealth Sinking Fund may be applied to the reduction of the public debt of the Commonwealth by the repurchase or redemption of securities of the Commonwealth.[19] Provision is also made for investment of moneys standing to the credit of the Commonwealth Sinking Fund.[20]

Between 1950 and 1970, new money raisings were insufficient (in all but two years) to finance the total borrowing programme approved by the council. The Commonwealth had in these circumstances made arrangements for lending to the States moneys from its own funds to meet the shortfall. Because the debt burden on these loans had adversely affected the States which had to find the interest from general revenue funds, the Commonwealth in 1970, 1971 and 1972 made grants to assist the States with capital expenditure on their housing and works programmes.[21] Also in 1970 the *States Grants (Debt Charges Assistance) Act*[22] was passed. Under this Act the Commonwealth has undertaken (for a period of five years) to provide assistance by way of grants to the States in respect of interest and sinking fund charges on particular parcels of State debts in addition to that required under the financial agreement.

*Enforcement of the Agreement.* At the time of the depression, the Lang Government in New South Wales defaulted on the payments which it was obliged to make under the agreement. The *Financial Agreements Enforcement Act* was passed by the Commonwealth Parliament in 1932 to operate for a period of two years. It provided, *inter alia,* for the recoupment by the Commonwealth of interest not paid by a State out of that State's revenue. The legislation was challenged involving as it did an interference with the State's constitutional power over the appropriation of its revenue. In *New South Wales v Commonwealth (No 1)*[23] the High Court by a majority of 4-2[24]

16   See Nicholas, at 182. This was by way of a "gentlemen's agreement" reached in 1936 and subsequently varied.
17   Agreement, cl 3 (10).
18   No 65 of 1966.
19   Section 15.
20   Section 16.
21   *States Grants (Capital Assistance) Act* 1970-1972.
22   No 110 of 1970.
23   (1931) 46 CLR 155.
24   Rich, Starke, Dixon and McTiernan JJ, Gavan Duffy CJ and Evatt J dissenting.

upheld the legislation. The main question was whether the legislation, constituting as it did, unilateral enforcement of the provisions of the Agreement could be regarded as legislation for the "carrying out by the parties thereto of any such agreement" under s 105A (iii) of the Constitution. Rich and Dixon JJ, two of the majority judges, considered that it was of this nature:

A law which provides the alternative to voluntary performance by the parties and compels involuntary satisfaction appears to us to be properly described as a law for the carrying out by the parties thereto of the agreement.[25]

The majority interpretation was further aided by the words "binding nature" to be found in s 105A (iv).

This exegesis of s 105A meant that it constituted an exception to the general principle of intergovernmental immunity recognized in the *Australian Railways Union Case*[26] that the Commonwealth could not interfere with the power of a State to control the appropriation of its revenue.

In *New South Wales v Commonwealth (No 3)*[27] a further challenge to the *Financial Agreements Enforcement Act* was directed against s 15 of that Act which required the chief executive officer of a bank to furnish a return of the amount of the balance standing to the credit of a State, and to pay the amount of the balance to a person authorized by the Commonwealth. This section was upheld on the same grounds as were accepted in the earlier case.

---

25   46 CLR at 178. The views of Starke J and McTiernan JJ were of similar import. Gavan Duffy CJ and Evatt J, however, considered that s 105A did not enable the Commonwealth to coerce a State into payment.
26   (1930) 44 CLR 319. See above under s 51.
27   (1931) 46 CLR 246.

## CHAPTER V

## THE STATES

SAVING OF CONSTITUTIONS

**106.** *The Constitution of each State of the Commonwealth shall, subject to this Constitution, continue as at the establishment of the Commonwealth, or as at the admission or establishment of the State, as the case may be, until altered in accordance with the Constitution of the State.*[1]

This section makes it clear that the Constitution of each State, as amended from time to time in accordance with the State's constitutional procedures, will remain unimpaired by the federal Constitution except to the extent to which the latter otherwise provides or gives to the Commonwealth Parliament power to deal with matters previously falling within State constitutional power.

Consequently, it is clear that those provisions of the State Constitutions dealing with the structure of the legislature, executive and judiciary remain intact, although a number of the powers which were exercised by these organs in pre-federation times have been withdrawn from the States by being made exclusive to the Commonwealth (see ss 52, 61, 69, 70, 77, 107). Furthermore, those powers of the State Parliaments which are concurrent powers are subject to the paramount authority of the Commonwealth (ss 107, 108, 109). It can be seen, therefore, that the federal Constitution has had a considerable impact on the power of a State Parliament to make laws for the "peace, order and good government" of a State, on the powers of the executive governments of the States, and the jurisdiction of State courts to deal with federal constitutional matters.

The *structure* of the State Constitutions has, however, in the main remained unimpaired. Consequently, the federal Parliament cannot legislate with respect to the composition of the Houses of a State Parliament or the method of election of the members of these Houses and their privileges.[2]

The same is true of the State executive government headed by the Governor: the federal Parliament and Government cannot control the exercise of the powers of a State Governor or State ministers except in relation to certain matters affecting the federal Constitution. The 1891 draft Bill had made provision for all communications between the Governor and the Colonial Office to go through the Governor-General but this provision was dropped because of the opposition of a number of the delegates.[3]

As to the courts the federal Parliament has no power to alter the structure of these bodies although it has certain incidental powers over them relating to the conferment of federal jurisdiction.[4]

---

1  Quick and Garran, 929-32. Lumb, *The Constitutions of the Australian States* (3rd ed, 1972).
2  However, incidental aspects may be affected by a law falling within a certain head of Commonwealth power. *Stuart Robertson v Lloyd* (1932) 47 CLR 482 at 491-2 (Allowance payable to a member under the NSW Constitution held to be subject to Commonwealth bankruptcy provisions).
3  Quick and Garran at 932.
4  See previously under Ch III, particularly s 77.

In *Australian Railways Union v Victorian Railways Commissioners*[5] Dixon J drew attention to the importance of s 106 as providing a check on the legislative power of the Commonwealth to enforce as against a State financial obligations arising under a Commonwealth arbitration award affecting State as well as private employers, without a State parliamentary appropriation of moneys necessary to satisfy the award.[6] It is clear that a basic constitutional power of a State is the appropriation of moneys out of the (State) Consolidated Revenue Fund for State purposes. While the *Engineers Case*[7] had of course established the authority of the federal Parliament to affect the activities of the States, enforcement of financial obligations against a State revenue was a different matter.[8] However, the power of enforcement can be conferred by virtue of a specific section such as 105A.[9]

*State laws binding the Commonwealth.* The Constitutions of each of the States grant to the State Parliaments a general legislative power described as a power to make laws "for the peace, order (or welfare) and good government" of the State. The question which arises is in what way the power may be exercised to affect the Commonwealth, its instrumentalities, or personnel.[10]

It will be recalled that this was one of the first questions to come before the High Court—in *D'Emden v Pedder*[11]—and that the doctrine of immunity of instrumentalities was applied to exempt a Commonwealth official from payment of State stamp duty on a receipt given for his salary. The *Engineers Case*[12] rejected the doctrine but nevertheless upheld the decision in *D'Emden v Pedder* on the basis of inconsistency between the Commonwealth and State legislation.

However it is clear that the Commonwealth enjoys an immunity from the operation of State laws which is far greater than the limited immunity held by the States from Commonwealth legislation.

In the first place the Commonwealth may by virtue of s 109 exempt itself and its instrumentalities from the operation of State laws.[13]

Secondly, State legislation cannot impinge on an exclusive power of the Commonwealth (e g, the customs power).[14]

But it is equally clear that in the absence of Commonwealth legislation regulating the status and powers of a Commonwealth servant, such a person is subject to the civil and criminal law in force in the State in which he is resident

---

5   (1930) 44 CLR 319.
6   Ibid at 391-2.
7   *Amalgamated Society of Engineers v Adelaide Steamship Co Ltd* (1920) 28 CLR 129.
8   See also *NSW v Bardolph* (1934) 52 CLR 455 at 459-60 (Evatt J).
9   *NSW v Commonwealth (No 1) (The Garnishee Case)* (1931) 46 CLR 155. For a discussion of the relationship between Commonwealth and State power, particularly in relation to the doctrine of immunity of instrumentalities see above pp 68 et seq.
10   See Howard, Ch 2, 102-133. Sawer, "State Statutes and the Commonwealth", (1961) 1 Tas ULR 580. Howard, "Some Problems of Commonwealth Immunity and Exclusive Legislative Powers", (1972) 5 Federal Law Review. Evans, "Rethinking Commonwealth Immunity", (1972) 8 MULR 521.
11   (1904) 1 CLR 91.
12   (1920) 28 CLR 129 at 156.
13   Provided that the exemption is incidental to a Commonwealth head of powers: *Australian Coastal Shipping Commission v O'Reilly* (1962) 107 CLR 46; [1962] ALR 502. *Commonwealth v State of Queensland* (1920) 29 CLR 1. Although *D'Emden v Pedder* was "explained away" on the basis of s 109 it is difficult to see that any real inconsistency existed in that case.
14   *Steel Rails Case* (1908) 5 CLR 818.

and carries out his duties.[15] Among other laws, his salary or pension may be subject to State taxing laws. This is the basis of the decision of the High Court in *West v Commissioner of Taxation (NSW)*[16] where a retired Commonwealth public servant's pension was held to be subject to a general non-discriminatory State tax.[17]

Furthermore, it seems equally clear that the States cannot tax the Commonwealth Government. The *Pay-roll Tax* principle does not, as it were, apply in reverse. In *Essendon Corporation v Criterion Theatres Ltd*[18] Dixon J said:

To my mind the incapacity of the States directly to tax the Commonwealth in respect of something done in the exercise of its power or functions is a necessary consequence of the system of government established by the Constitution. It is hardly necessary at this stage of our constitutional development to go over the considerations which make it impossible to suppose that the Constitution intended that the States should levy taxes upon the Commonwealth—the nature of the Federal Government, its supremacy, the exclusiveness or paramountcy of its legislative powers, the independence of its fiscal system and the elaborate provisions of the Constitution governing the financial relations of the central government and the constituent States. To describe the establishment of the Commonwealth as the birth of a nation has been a commonplace. It was anything but the birth of a taxpayer.[19]

A further question is to what extent a State can affect a prerogative right of the Commonwealth. In *Uther's Case*[20] Dixon J found himself among the minority on this question:

Like the goddess of wisdom the Commonwealth *uno ictu* sprang from the brain of its begetters armed and of full stature. At the same instant the colonies became States; but whence did the States obtain the power to regulate the legal relations of the new polity with its subjects? It formed no part of the old Colonial power. The Federal Constitution does not give it.[21]

In 1961 in the *Cigamatic Case*[22] *Uther's Case* was overruled and Dixon CJ found himself in the majority. But the reasoning in the *Cigamatic Case* is rather compressed. The facts were similar to those in *Uther's Case*: could the State Parliament under the winding up provision of its *Companies Act* affect the prerogative right of the Commonwealth to payment of certain debts due to it? It was held that it was beyond the constitutional power of a State to affect the prerogative of the Commonwealth. Dixon CJ indicated that he preferred the use of the phrase "fiscal right" to that of "the prerogative".

---

15   *Pirrie v McFarlane* (1925) 36 CLR 170. (Commonwealth soldier held subject to licensing provisions of *Motor Car Act* 1915 (Vic). It should be noted that Regulations made under the *Defence Act* now provide otherwise, and therefore State legislation would not apply.)

16   *West v Commissioner of Taxation* (NSW) (1936-37) 56 CLR 657.

17   Evatt J went further and held that the Commonwealth could not grant to its employees immunity from State taxation (at 709-10).

18   (1947) 74 CLR 1.

19   Ibid at 22. On the question whether the immunity extends to Commonwealth instrumentalities see Zines, "Sir Owen Dixon's Theory of Federalism", (1965) 1 Federal Law Review, 221 at 229-30. See also *Pay-roll Tax (State Taxation of Commonwealth Authorities) Act* (Com), No 104 of 1971.

20   *Uther v Federal Commissioner of Taxation* (1947) 74 CLR 508.

21   Ibid at 530.

22   *Commonwealth of Australia v Cigamatic Pty Ltd* (1962) 108 CLR 372; [1963] ALR 304.

Such fiscal rights of the Commonwealth Government could not in any way be modified by state legislation.[23]

The widest formulation of the doctrine of Commonwealth immunity from State legislation is to be found in the judgment of Fullagar J in *The Commonwealth v Bogle*:[24]

The Commonwealth—or the Crown in right of the Commonwealth, or whatever you choose to call it—is, to all intents and purposes a juristic person, but it is not a juristic person which is subjected either by any State Constitution or the Commonwealth Constitution to the legislative power of a State Parliament.[25]

Under this formulation, the immunity of the Commonwealth could extend beyond the area of the prerogative and fiscal rights to all situations in which the Commonwealth is involved with its citizens. And yet neither Dixon CJ nor Fullagar J consider that the immunity extends this far. In *Farley's Case*,[26] Dixon CJ considered that the law of contract might regulate the formation performance and discharge of the contracts which the Commonwealth found it necessary to make in the course of the ordinary administration of government: "Where there is no federal statute affecting the matter, an exercise of the legislative power of the State over the general law of contract might incidentally apply in the case of the Commonwealth alike with the citizen."[27]

If the Commonwealth as a juristic entity is exempt from the operation of State law, how does it find itself subjected to the rules of contract and other "civil" rules? The answer given by Dixon J is as follows:

In the practical administration of the law, the decision of questions of that sort depends less upon constitutional analysis than on s 80 and perhaps s 79 of the *Judiciary Act*. There is, however, a clear distinction between the general law, the content or condition of which, although a matter for the legislature of the State, may incidentally affect Commonwealth administrative action, and, on the other hand, governmental rights and powers belonging to the federal executive as such.[28]

This dictum holds the key to the answer to the question. It suggests a distinction between the federal government acting as a "citizen" within the territorial boundaries of a State and therefore impliedly accepting the general code of law in force in the State, and on the other hand, acting as the national government in the performance of the functions appropriate to that status. Consequently in relation to the activities of its servants it may become subject to the general law of contract or of tort (although not in respect of its occupation of land acquired by it).[29] Where, however, governmental rights (not just fiscal rights) as distinct from rights which are common to ordinary citizens are involved, its immunity from the operation of State law comes into operation. The effect of ss 79 and 80 of the *Judiciary Act*[30] is to make it clear that where

---

23   108 CLR at 377, 378; [1963] ALR at 305-306.
24   (1953) 89 CLR 229.
25   Ibid at 259. The actual decision in the case was that the body involved—*Commonwealth Hostels Ltd*—was not an agent of the Crown and, therefore, not entitled to Crown immunities. Fullagar J also considered that a reference to the Crown in a State Act must be construed as a reference to the Crown in right of the State alone. On this question see above under s 51. See also *Essendon Corporation v Criterion Theatres Ltd* (1947) 74 CLR 1.
26   (1940) 63 CLR 278.
27   Ibid at 308.
28   Ibid at 308.
29   See discussion of s 52 of the Constitution.
30   And also of s 56 of that Act.

the Commonwealth is involved in litigation in respect of "ordinary" matters, then the rules of State law will be applied in the absence of any Commonwealth legislation regulating the matter.

## SAVING OF POWER OF STATE PARLIAMENTS

**107.** *Every power of the Parliament of a Colony which has become or becomes a State, shall, unless it is by this Constitution exclusively vested in the Parliament of the Commonwealth or withdrawn from the Parliament of the State, continue as at the establishment of the Commonwealth, or as at the admission or establishment of the State, as the case may be.*[31]

The effect of this section is summarized by Windeyer J in the case of *R v Phillips*:[32]

Section 107 preserves the legislative competence of State Parliaments in respect of any topic that is not exclusively vested in the Parliament of the Commonwealth or withdrawn from the Parliament of the State. This is simply an expression of an element that is implicit in any federal system in which defined powers are granted to the central authority and the undefined residue remains with the constituent parts. Section 107 confirms that as the underlying principle of Australian federalism.[33]

The residuary legislative power of the States does not cover those matters (a) which are made exclusive by virtue of s 52 or other sections conferring exclusive power, (b) which are withdrawn from the States by prohibition directed to the States, (c) which by their nature are exclusive to the Commonwealth. The positive effect of s 107 is therefore to preserve State legislative competence with respect to matters within concurrent power (subject to the operation of s 109) and within State residuary power.

*Exclusive powers of the Commonwealth.* The exclusive powers of the Commonwealth falling within category (a) are:

(1) The power to make laws with respect to the seat of Government and all places acquired by the Commonwealth for public purposes (s 52 (i)).

(2) The power to make laws with respect to the departments of the public service of the Commonwealth (s 52 (ii)).

(3) The power to make laws imposing duties of custom and excise and granting bounties (s 90).

(4) The power to make laws with respect to Commonwealth territories (ss 111, 122).

The exclusive powers of the Commonwealth falling within category (b) are:

(5) The power with respect to coinage (s 115).

(6) The power to raise and maintain military forces for the defence of the Commonwealth (s 114).

The exclusive powers of the Commonwealth falling within category (c) are:

(7) Borrowing money on the public credit of the Commonwealth (s 51 (iv)).

(8) Naturalization (s 51 (xix)).

(9) Service and execution throughout the Commonwealth of the process and judgments of state courts (s 51 (xxiv)).

---

31  Quick and Garran, 933-7.
32  (1970) 44 ALJR 497.
33  Ibid at 505.

(10) Recognition throughout the Commonwealth of State laws and records (s 51 (xxv)).

(11) Relations of the Commonwealth with islands of the Pacific (s 51 (xxx)).

(12) Acquisition of State railways with the consent of the State (s 51 (xxxiii)).

(13) Matters in respect of which the Constitution makes provision until the Parliament otherwise provides (s 51 (xxvi)). These include the various powers[34] relating to the federal parliamentary and executive structure.

(14) Exercise of any power not exercisable by the States at the establishment of the Constitution (s 51 (xxxviii)).[35]

(15) Matters incidental to the exercise of any power vested in the *Houses* of the Parliament, federal government (and officers), and federal courts.

*Concurrent powers.* This leaves a large group of powers under s 51 which can be described as concurrent powers. They are:

(1) Trade and commerce with other countries and among the States (s 51 (i)).
(1A) Taxation (apart from customs and excise).
(2) Postal and other services (s 51 (v)).
(3) Defence (s 51 (vi)).[36]
(4) Light houses etc (s 51 (vii)).
(5) Astronomical and meteorological observations (s 51 (viii)).
(6) Quarantine (s 51 (ix)).
(7) Fisheries in Australian waters beyond territorial limits (s 51 (x)).[37]
(8) Census and Statistics (s 51 (xi)).
(9) Banking (s 51 (xiii)).
(10) Insurance (s 51 (xiv)).
(11) Weights and measures (s 51 (xv)).
(12) Bills of exchange etc (s 51 (xvi)).
(13) Bankruptcy (s 51 (xvii)).
(14) Copyrights etc (s 51 (xviii)).
(15) Aliens (s 51 (xix)).
(16) Corporations (s 51 (xx)).
(17) Marriage (s 51 (xxi)).
(18) Divorce and matrimonial causes (s 51 (xxii)).
(19) Invalid and old age pensions (s 51 (xxiii)).
(20) Various social services (s 51 (xxiiiA)).
(21) People of any race (s 51 (xxvi)).
(22) Immigration and emigration (s 51 (xxvii)).[38]
(23) Influx of criminals (s 51 (xxviii)).
(24) External affairs (s 51 (xxix)).[39]
(25) Acquisition of property (s 51 (xxxi)).
(26) Control of railways with respect to defence purposes (s 51 (xxxii)).
(27) Railway construction and extension (s 51 (xxxiv)).
(28) Conciliation and arbitration (s 51 (xxxv)).
(29) Matters referred to the Commonwealth (s 51 (xxxvii)).

---

34 Contained in Chapter I of the Constitution.
35 Although this is not exclusive in relation to the Imperial Parliament. See above pp 184-5.
36 As to the argument that the whole of the defence power is exclusive, see under s 51 (vi).
37 As to the power of the States to legislate with respect to fisheries outside territorial limits see *Bonser v La Macchia* [1969] ALR 741 at 747 (Barwick CJ), 773-774 (Windeyer J).
38 As to the exclusive power of the Commonwealth to regulate the *act* of immigrating (ie, entering the Australian community) see under s 51 (xxvii).
39 As to the relationship between Commonwealth and State legislative power over the subject-matter of a treaty see under s 51 (xxix).

(29) Matters incidental to the execution of any power vested in the *Parliament of the Commonwealth* (s 51 (xxxix)).[40]

With respect to these powers, the Commonwealth Parliament has paramount power over the States. It has exercised the power in many of the areas excluding the operation of State legislation. In other areas only part of the field has been covered.[41]

*State residuary power.* There remains finally the area of residuary power of the States. Quick and Garran describe this as embracing "a large mass of constitutional, territorial, municipal and social powers."[42]

Among the areas within this power are:

| | |
|---|---|
| Agriculture | Land |
| Charities | Licenses |
| Constitutions of the States | Mining |
| Courts | Municipal institutions |
| Departments of State Governments | Police |
| Factories and shops | Prisons |
| Fisheries | Trade and commerce (including |
| Game | transport) within a state |
| Health | State works |

However, in the light of the increasing use by the Commonwealth of the grants-in-aid power (s 96),[43] its appropriation power (s 83) and its incidental power (s 51 (xxxix)) which affect many of these areas, it is difficult to say to-day that any area is within *exclusive* State competence. Indeed, there are some Commonwealth ministers, the titles of whose portfolios are similar to those of State ministers, e g, Ministers of Education, Health, although these general areas (as distinct from specific areas such as quarantine) are not heads of Commonwealth power. Nevertheless the list is a useful one as it indicates those areas which fall within the general power of the States under their Constitutions to make laws for the peace, order and good government of their territorial areas.

Apart from its utilization in the pre-*Engineers Case* decisions as a ground for supporting a reduced area of operation of Commonwealth power (an interpretation which was rejected in the *Engineers Case*), s 107 has been referred to by the High Court to support the proposition that a State Parliament still retains a concurrent power (in relation to its territorial jurisdiction) with respect to the matters listed in s 51 which are not exclusive to the Commonwealth.[44]

## SAVING OF STATE LAWS

**108.** *Every law in force in a Colony which has become or becomes a State, and relating to any matter within the powers of the Parliament of the Commonwealth, shall, subject to this Constitution, continue in force in the State; and, until provision is made in that behalf by the Parliament of the Commonwealth, the Parliament of the State shall have such powers of alteration and of repeal*

---

40  To the extent to which the subject-matter of the power is not exclusive.
41  See under s 109.
42  *Annotated Constitution of the Commonwealth* at 935.
43  See above, p 308.
44  See *Roughley v New South Wales* (1928) 42 CLR 162 at 193 (power over trade and commerce). *Clyde Engineering Co v Cowburn* (1926) 37 CLR 466 at 488 (industrial matters). *Ex parte Nelson (No 1)* (1928) 42 CLR 209 (quarantine).

*in respect of any such law as the Parliament of the Colony had until the Colony became a State.*[45]

There has been some dispute as to the effect of s 108 in the light of the decisions relating to s 52 (i). In *R v Bamford*[46] Owen J described its effect as follows:

These rules seem to me to enact that the existing laws of the State are to continue in force, even though they relate to matters within the exclusive power of the Parliament of the Commonwealth, until that Parliament enacts laws relating to such matters; provided that such State laws are not inconsistent with a law of the Commonwealth. But that the power of the State Parliament to make future laws shall cease where the power is exclusively vested in the Parliament of the Commonwealth, except for the purpose of altering or repealing such laws.[47]

In *Bamford's Case*[48] a conviction was upheld for an offence (occurring on post office premises) against a pre-federation New South Wales *Postage Act*. The offence had occurred after the department of posts and telegraphs in New South Wales had been transferred to the Commonwealth and, therefore, had become subject to the exclusive power of the Commonwealth to make laws for places acquired by it.

The first portion of the section is therefore clear and needs little elucidation. It was intended to ensure that, as Isaacs J put it in *Commonwealth v New South Wales*,[49] a state of anarchy did not exist after federation in relation to matters within exclusive Commonwealth power before federal legislation covering these matters had been passed. Thus in *Ex parte Shuck*,[50] it was held that a section of a New South Wales *Customs Act* applied to an event occurring on 2 October 1901—a few days before the first Commonwealth *Customs Act* was passed (under s. 90).

The first part of s 108 also applied to continue in operation colonial laws falling within a concurrent head of power (although in this respect it is superfluous) as well as Imperial laws affecting a matter within s 51.[51]

As we have seen the nature of the exclusive power referred by s 52 (i) came before the High Court in the series of cases: *Worthing v Rowell* & *Muston Pty. Ltd.*,[52] *R v Phillips* and *Attorney-General (NSW) v Stock Holdings.*[53] In *R v Phillips*[54] there were references to the relationship between s 52 (i) and s 108 (although the case did not directly raise s 108 as the State law in that case had been passed after 1900). The difficulty surrounds the second part of s 108 which provides:

And until provision is made in that behalf by the Parliament of the Commonwealth, the Parliament of the State shall have such powers of alteration and of repeal in respect of any such law as the Parliament of the colony had until the colony became a State.

---

45    Quick and Garran, 937-8.
46    (1901) 1 SR (NSW) 337.
47    Ibid at 352.
48    (1901) 1 SR (NSW) 337.
49    (1923) 33 CLR 1 at 43.
50    (1902) 2 SR (NSW) 420.
51    *McKelvey v Meagher* (1906) 4 CLR 265. (*Fugitive Offenders Act* held to be in operation under this section).
52    (1970) 44 ALJR 230.
53    (1971) 45 ALJR 9.
54    (1970) 44 ALJR 497.

The question is whether the power of alteration and repeal of a pre-federation colonial law applies to matters within exclusive power or only to matters within concurrent power. Quick and Garran's opinion is that the power of alteration and repeal could only extend to matters within concurrent power. To extend the States right of alteration any further would encroach on Commonwealth exclusive power affirmed by s 52.[55] This view was also supported by Harrison Moore.[56] In *R v Phillips*[57] Windeyer J was of the opinion that the second part of s 108 applied only to matters within the concurrent power. Indeed he considered that s 108 was the "statutory sponsor" of the theory of concurrent powers in the Australian Constitution.[58] Gibbs J also thought that the power of alteration and repeal did not apply to matters within exclusive power.[59] On the other hand, Menzies J took the opposite view, viz, that the second part of s 108 applied *only* to matters within exclusive power:

Section 108 . . . continues the operation of colonial laws in the territory which ceases to be a colony and becomes a State, and confers a limited legislative power upon the Parliament of the State: viz, to alter or repeal colonial laws upon matters falling within the exclusive legislative power of the Commonwealth until provision is made in that behalf, by the Parliament of the Commonwealth.[60]

The difference between the two approaches has little practical operation today in the light of the passage of the *Commonwealth Places (Application of Laws) Act 1970*[61] by which the Commonwealth has "otherwise provided" in relation to places acquired by it. Legislation in respect of other matters of exclusive power has been in existence many years.

As to the power of alteration or repeal of pre-federation colonial legislation within matters of concurrent power, s 109, as Menzies J pointed out,[62] would seem to provide an ample basis for resolving any question of inconsistency.[63]

## INCONSISTENCY OF LAWS

**109.** *When a law of a State is inconsistent with a law of the Commonwealth, the latter shall prevail, and the former shall, to the extent of the inconsistency, be invalid.*[64]

The distribution of legisative powers between Commonwealth and States is based, as we have seen, on a distinction between concurrent and exclusive powers. As Windeyer J said in *R v Phillips*,[65] "it is on the combined effect of ss 107, 108 and 109 that the theory of concurrent power and the nature of Australian federalism firmly rests." In so far as the States retained the power to legislate with respect to many areas covered by s 51, it was necessary to provide for the resolution of any conflict between an exercise of Commonwealth and State power: s 109 attributes paramountcy to the Commonwealth exercise

---

55   *Annotated Constitution* at 938.
56   *The Constitution of the Commonwealth of Australia* (2nd ed, 1910) 412.
57   (1970) 44 ALJR 497.
58   Ibid at 506.
59   Ibid at 512-3.
60   Ibid at 502.
61   See previously under s 52 (i).
62   (1970) 44 ALJR 497 at 502.
63   See further Lane, *The Law in Commonwealth Places—A Sequel* (1971) 45 ALJ 138.
64   Quick and Garran, 938-39. Howard, 27-45. Wynes, 91-102. *Essays*, 44-5, 99-100. Lane, 691-719. Nicholas, 303-9.
65   (1970) 44 ALJR 497 at 506; [1971] ALR 161 at 176.

of power. Such a conflict, however, may arise not only in the area of concurrent power but also where a law has been made under a Commonwealth exclusive power which may affect the area covered by a State Act passed under State residuary power. Of course, it is only a valid Commonwealth law which prevails over a State law. If the Commonwealth statute is held to be outside the constitutional limits of the Commonwealth Parliament, no question of inconsistency can arise.[66]

A law of the Commonwealth includes not only a statute applying generally throughout the Commonwealth but also a law made in relation to a specific Territory.[67] Reference must also be made to the number of inconsistency cases dealing with conflicts between State statutes and awards made by the Commonwealth Arbitration Commission. In so far as the *Conciliation and Arbitration Act* is a valid law of the Commonwealth, provisions of that Act giving awards the force of law enable such awards to displace inconsistent State legislation, provided that the award is made pursuant to the Act and is within the constitutional limits laid down by s 51 (xxxv).[68]

Inconsistency may arise in different ways, and it will be convenient to summarize these under the headings of "direct inconsistency" and "covering the field".

*Direct inconsistency.* A Commonwealth law imposing a duty on an official or a citizen may conflict with a State law imposing such a duty. This is the clearest case of inconsistency and is illustrated by the case of *R v Brisbane Licensing Court*.[69] A section of the *Commonwealth Electoral Act* provided that on a polling day fixed for a federal election, a referendum or vote of the electors of a State or part thereof, should not be taken. A local option poll had been taken on such a day under Queensland legislation. It was held that a direct inconsistency existed, and that the local option poll was therefore invalid.

In other cases, while there is no direct conflict of *duties*, inconsistency may arise because a State law destroys or modifies a right, power or privilege conferred by the Commonwealth, or conversely, because a State law confers a right, power or privilege which a Commonwealth law destroys or modifies. In such a case, the inconsistency does not arise out of the impossibility of obeying both laws—both laws may be obeyed simply by refraining from exercising the right, power or privilege created by one of the laws. But clearly there is an inconsistency to the extent that the State law seeks to restrain some activity which is authorized by the Commonwealth law, or to authorize some activity which is forbidden by the Commonwealth law.

Such a case is *Colvin v Bradley Bros Pty Ltd*.[70] An order made pursuant

---

66   See *Airlines of New South Wales v State of New South Wales (No 2)* (1965) 113 CLR 54; [1965] ALR 984. *R v Railways Appeals Board (NSW) ex parte Davis* (1957) 96 CLR 429.

67   *Lamshed v Lake* (1958) 99 CLR 132.

68   As Dixon J said in *Ex parte McLean*, (1930) 43 CLR (at 484-5), "if the Act means not only to give the determination of the arbitrator binding force between the disputants but also to enable him to prescribe completely or exhaustively what, upon any subject in dispute, shall be their industrial relations, then s 109 would operate to give paramountcy to these provisions of the Statute, unless they were ultra vires, and they in turn would give to the award an exclusive operation which might appear equivalent almost to paramountcy".

69   (1920) 28 CLR 23.

70   (1943) 68 CLR 151.

to a section of a NSW *Factories and Shops Act* prohibited the employment of women on a milling machine. An award had been made by the Commonwealth Arbitration Court under the *Conciliation and Arbitration Act* which permitted the employment of females on work, which included work on a milling machine, unless the work was declared to be unsuitable for women by a Board of Reference. No such declaration had been made. It was held that the order was inconsistent with the award by virtue of s 109 in that it directly prohibited something which the Commonwealth award permitted.

In *Clyde Engineering Co v Cowburn*,[71] a Commonwealth arbitration award fixed rates of pay and overtime on the basis of a 48 hour working week while a State Act purported to deal with the same matter on the basis of a 44 hour working week. An employee claimed the award rates of pay but on the basis of a 44 hour working week. It was argued that there was no inconsistency between the award and the Act because the employer, it was said, could obey both laws by observing the State 44 hour working week but on the basis that the pay scale determined by the award applied to the 44 hour working week. The High Court rejected this argument and found that an inconsistency existed, as the State law operated to vary the adjustment of industrial relations established by the award.[72]

*Covering the field.* In *Cowburn's case*[73] Isaacs J gave the first clear formulation of this test:

If a competent legislature expressly or impliedly evinces its intention to cover the whole field, that is a conclusive test of inconsistency where another legislature assumes to enter to any extent upon the same field.

The test was adopted by Dixon J in *Ex parte McLean*:[74]

When the Parliament of the Commonwealth and the Parliament of a State each legislate upon the same subject and prescribe what the rule of conduct should be, they make laws which are inconsistent notwithstanding that the rule of conduct is identical, which each prescribes, and s 109 applies . . . . But the reason is that, by prescribing the rule to be observed, the federal Statute shows an intention to cover the subject matter and provide what the law upon it should be. If it appeared that the federal law was intended to be supplementary to or cumulative upon the State law, then no inconsistency would be exhibited in imposing the same duties or in inflicting different penalties. The inconsistency does not lie in the mere co-existence of two laws which are susceptible of simultaneous obedience. It depends upon the intention of the paramount legislature to express by its enactment, completely, exhaustively, or exclusively, what shall be the law governing the particular conduct or matter to which its attention is directed. When a federal statute declares such an intention, it is inconsistent with it for the law of a State to govern the same conduct or matter.

It must be noted that several of the cases mentioned under the preceding section can also be treated as cases illustrating the "covering the field" test.[75]

This is a difficult test to apply and yet, in the light of the more recent cases, the most important. It depends on ascertaining whether the Common-

---

71    (1926) 37 CLR 466.
72    See especially the judgment of Isaacs J at 489 et seq. See also *Ex parte Maclean* 1930) 43 CLR 472. *Hume v Palmer* (1926) 38 CLR 441 (Identical regulations but different penalties—state law displaced).
73    (1926) 37 CLR 466 at 489.
74    (1930) 43 CLR 472 at 483. See also *The Kakariki* (1937) 58 CLR 618 at 630.
75    See *Clyde Engineering Co v Cowburn* (1926) 37 CLR 466 at 490.

wealth in legislating on a particular topic has intended to provide an exhaustive code to the exclusion of State legislation. The difficulty usually is to determine whether the intention of the Commonwealth (which of course can only be ascertained from the provisions of the legislation in question) is to cover the whole field regulated by a State enactment or only portion of it. In some cases the Commonwealth Act makes clear its intention to cover the whole field,[76] but in many cases there is no such clear statement of intention in the Act (or subordinate legislation or award), and then it is necessary to examine the Commonwealth Act as a whole in order to ascertain its true intent.

A good illustration is *Stock Motor Ploughs Ltd v Forsyth*.[77] It will be recalled that the alleged inconsistency was between a NSW *Moratorium Act* restricting the enforcement of contractual relations and a Commonwealth *Bills of Exchange Act* prescribing formalities for the execution and regulation of various instruments including promissory notes. The majority of the court rejected the argument that the NSW Act could not validly affect the enforcement of a note given as a collateral security for a debt. There was no inconsistency between the NSW and Commonwealth legislation. The fields were different: that covered by the NSW Act was the area of contractual relations, while the Commonwealth Act dealt with negotiable instruments. There was no evidence to be derived from the latter Act that it intended to displace the general contract law (as modified by state legislation).[78]

On the other hand, in *Wenn v Attorney-General (Vic)*,[79] a Commonwealth Act was held to cover a particular field to the exclusion of State legislation. The Commonwealth legislation—the *Re-establishment and Employment Act*—dealt with the obligations of employers to give preference to ex-servicemen in employment (but included no provision as to the duty to give preference in *promotion* to ex-servicemen already employed). The State Act dealt with the same matter, but also included a provision requiring employers to give preference in promotion. Was the Commonwealth field the whole area of preference in employer-employee relations (which made no provision for preference in promotion), or did it allow for the operation of supplemental state legislation in the area of promotion? The court held that the Commonwealth legislation was an exhaustive code allowing no room for the operation of State legislation in relation to matters not covered by the Commonwealth Act: the Victorian rule giving preference in promotion was therefore displaced.[80]

A case of some difficulty is *O'Sullivan v Noarlunga Meat Co Ltd*[81] where the question was whether a South Australian Act, prohibiting the slaughter of stock for export without a State licence, was inconsistent with Commonwealth export regulations prohibiting export of meat from stock which had not been slaughtered on premises registered under the regulations. In an evenly-divided court, the opinion of the Chief Justice prevailed. It was held that the

---

76    *Marriage Act* 1961, s 94. *Life Insurance Act* 1945, s 8.
77    (1932) 48 CLR 128. See also under s 51 (xvi).
78    Ibid at 141 et seq. See also *Y Z Finance Co Ltd v Cummings* (1964) 109 CLR 395; [1964] ALR 667.
79    (1948) 77 CLR 84.
80    A particular provision of the Commonwealth Act indicated that it was to apply to the exclusion of any provisions (providing for preference in any matter relating to the employment of discharged members of the Forces) of any law of a State.
81    (1954) 92 CLR 565.

Commonwealth regulations were detailed enough to show that they covered the whole field of "slaughter for export", and, therefore, the State licensing requirement did not apply. The minority of the court considered that the regulations were designed to establish conditions for the export of meat and did not prevent State slaughtering laws from supplementing these requirements.[82]

The tendency in some of the later cases on inconsistency has been to limit the scope of the doctrine of "covering the field". This is so particularly in cases where it is alleged that a Commonwealth arbitration award displaces a State industrial act. Thus in *Collins v Charles Marshall Ltd*[83] it was held that a Victorian Act giving long service leave to employees in the State applied to workers covered by a Commonwealth award. Although the Commonwealth award dealt comprehensively with conditions of employment (including annual leave), it was held that the Victorian Act provided an "extra" benefit and could operate supplementary to the other conditions covered by the award.[84]

In *Airlines of New South Wales Pty Ltd v State of New South Wales (No 2)*[85] the question concerned the relationship between a State *Air Transport Act* (applying *inter alia* to air transport) and the Commonwealth *Air Navigation Act* together with regulations made under that Act. Under the Commonwealth Act a licence was required to operate aircraft within the territorial boundaries of New South Wales (and other States). A licence was also required under the New South Wales Act. It was held by the majority that the Commonwealth legislation (the constitutional validity of which was founded on either the trade and commerce or external affairs power, or on a combination of both, and which was designed to promote safety and efficiency in air navigation) could not validly exclude the operation of State legislation which covered a different area, viz, the licensing of air transport operations within State territorial boundaries.[86] This case is an example of the proposition that the Commonwealth cannot give its legislation an operation outside the limits of its power by "manufacturing" an inconsistency with legislation enacted by a State under its residuary power (in this case, power over transport within State boundaries).

*Effect of s 109.* The final words of s 109 provide that the State Act "shall to the extent of the inconsistency be invalid." If the invalid portion of the statute can be read down or severed from the valid portion, the remaining part will have a valid operation.[87]

In so far as the State Act is not outside the constitutional power of the

---

82 Cf, *Swift Australian Co Pty Ltd v Boyd Parkinson* (1962) 108 CLR 189; [1963] ALR 724. A state law (which did not refer specifically to slaughtering for export) held not inconsistent with Commonwealth export regulations. Here the chickens slaughtered for export amounted to no more than 5 per cent of the total number of birds slaughtered. It was held that the State act applied to such premises.

83 (1955) 92 CLR 529.

84 See also *Robinson & Sons Pty Ltd v Haylor* (1957) 97 CLR 177; *Clarke v Keir* (1956) 94 CLR 489 (State law fixing hours for opening and closing of shops not inconsistent with an award dealing with hours of work). Cf, *Blackley v Devondale Cream Co Pty Ltd* (1968) 117 CLR 253; [1968] ALR 307.

85 (1965) 113 CLR 54; [1965] ALR 984.

86 See also *Johnston v Krakowski* (1965) 113 CLR 552; [1966] ALR 357. *Forsyth v Commissioner of Stamp Duties (NSW)* (1966) 114 CLR 194; [1966] ALR 809. *Victoria v Commonwealth* (1937) 58 CLR 618.

87 See Introduction, above pp 21-2.

State, it will be revived when the Commonwealth law which gives rise to the inconsistency is repealed or becomes inoperative.[88]

## PROVISIONS REFERRING TO GOVERNOR

**110.** *The provisions of this Constitution relating to the Governor of a State extend and apply to the Governor for the time being of the State, or other chief executive officer or administrator of the government of the State.*[89]

The section is self-explanatory. The powers conferred by the Constitution on the State Governor, including the power to issue writs for the elections of Senators (s 12) and to fill casual vacancies in the Senate (s 15), are during his absence or incapacity exercisable by the Lieutenant-Governor or Administrator of the State.[90]

## STATES MAY SURRENDER TERRITORY

**111.** *The Parliament of a State may surrender any part of the State to the Commonwealth; and upon such surrender, and the acceptance thereof by the Commonwealth, such part of the State shall become subject to the exclusive jurisdiction of the Commonwealth.*[91]

Under this section a State may surrender part of its territory to the Commonwealth. On its acceptance by the Commonwealth, that area becomes a Commonwealth territory subject to the exclusive jurisdiction of the Commonwealth under s 122. Two areas have been established as federal Territories in this way: the Australian Capital Territory[92] and the Northern Territory,[93] although there is additional support for the acquisition of the Australian Capital Territory in s 125 of the Constitution.

In *Kean v Commonwealth*,[94] it was argued that the legislation ratifying

---

88   *Butler v Attorney-General for Victoria* (1961) 106 CLR 268; [1961] ALR 650. For further discussions of the inconsistency doctrine, see Tammelo, "The Test of Inconsistency between Commonwealth and State Laws" (1957) 30 ALJ 496. Zelling "Inconsistency between Commonwealth and State Laws", (1948) 22 ALJ 45.

89   Quick and Garran, 939-40.

90   See also ss 7, 21, 84.

91   Quick and Garran, 941-2. Wynes, 108. Nicholas, 92-4.

92   In 1908, the federal Parliament determined that the seat of government should be in the Goulburn-Yass region of New South Wales. Pursuant to this determination, the NSW and Commonwealth governments entered into an agreement, the former to surrender, the latter to accept, the territory. See *Seat of Government Surrender Act* 1909 (NSW), *Seat of Government Acceptance Act* 1909 (Com). Subsequently, the federal Parliament provided for its administration in the *Seat of Government (Administration) Act*. In 1915 Jervis Bay, an area on the NSW Coast, was surrendered by the State and accepted by the Commonwealth pursuant to a similar agreement, and Jervis Bay became part of the ACT. See *Commonwealth v Woodhill* (1917) 23 CLR 482 at 486-7. The ACT is under the direct control of the Commonwealth.

93   Surrendered by South Australia pursuant to the *Northern Territory Surrender Act* 1907 (SA) and accepted by the Commonwealth under the *Northern Territory Acceptance Act* 1910. Legislative power over this territory is vested in a Territorial legislature (consisting of one House) subject to overall control by the Commonwealth Parliament.

94   (1963) 5 FLR 432.

the agreement for the surrender of the Northern Territory constituted a "fundamental law" for future legislation over the Territory, so that a subsequent ordinance of the Territory which departed from provisions in the original legislation confirming existing land rights was outside power. This argument was rejected by the Northern Territory Supreme Court which held that the grant of exclusive power to legislate over a surrendered area which had become a Territory carried with it a power to vary pre-existing rights and obligations arising under the original agreement between the Commonwealth and the State concerned.[95]

The section must be read in conjunction with s 122 which has a wider operation in conferring power on the commonwealth not only to legislate with respect to Territories acquired from the States but also with respect to Territories acquired in other ways.

STATES MAY LEVY CHARGES FOR INSPECTION LAWS

**112.** *After uniform duties of customs have been imposed, a State may levy on imports or exports, or on goods passing into or out of the State, such charges as may be necessary for executing the inspection laws of the State; but the net produce of all charges so levied shall be for the use of the Commonwealth; and any such inspection laws may be annulled by the Parliament of the Commonwealth.*[96]

This section constitutes an exception to s 92 in that it enables inspection charges to be made by a State in relation to goods passing into one State from another State. It also enables such charges to be made on goods imported from or exported to a foreign country. (In this respect the power is a concurrent one with the Commonwealth which can legislate under s 51 (i)). Such inspection charges would buttress the quarantine powers to the States and Commonwealth directed to the maintenance of standards of hygiene for the transport of goods.[97] The charges may be made at the point of exit or entry (i e, at a State border) or at any other locality in the State.

This exception to s 92 is, however, subject to stringent safeguards. It permits only such charges[98] as may be necessary for executing the State's inspection laws; the net produce of the charges is for the use of the Commonwealth; and the inspection laws imposing the charges may be annulled by the federal Parliament.

In *Ex parte Nelson*[99] it was accepted that s 112 could not be used to grant to a State any wider immunity from s 92 than that set out: in particular a State could not enact inspection laws under which discrimination was exercised against goods or animals passing into that State from another State.[1]

INTOXICATING LIQUIDS

**113.** *All fermented, distilled, or other intoxicating liquids passing into any State or remaining therein for use, consumption, sale, or storage, shall be subject to the laws of the State as if such liquids had been produced in the State.*[2]

---

95    Ibid at 437.
96    Quick and Garran, 942-4. Wynes, 352.
97    See above under s 51 (ix).
98    Described as "compensation for services rendered" and not "taxes" by Barton J in *Duncan v State of Queensland* (1916) 22 CLR 556 at 588.
99    (1928) 42 CLR 209 at 240 (Isaacs J).
1    See also *Tasmania v Victoria* (1935) 52 CLR 157 at 186 (Dixon J).
2    Quick and Garran, 944-8. Wynes, 353-4.

Section 113 constitutes another exception to s 92 but, again, of a limited nature. It subjects intoxicating liquor which is brought into one State from another State to the same restrictions as may be applied to locally-produced liquor. The section is based on a United States statute (the *Wilson Act* of 1890). Its effect is explained by Quick and Garran as follows:

...It is not intended to authorize the States to prohibit the introduction of intoxicating liquids; once introduced they cannot be prevented from reaching their destination—the consignee. What the section provides is that intoxicating liquids, upon passing into any State for use, consumption, sale or storage, shall become subject to the laws of the State as if they had been produced in the State. They are liable to the same licensing laws as locally produced intoxicants; they are liable to the same restrictive and regulating laws; they are liable to the same prohibitive laws. Their sale may be restricted to certain limited purposes; or to certain defined localities; it may be allowed to be conducted by certain qualified persons only; or it may be forbidden altogether. The only condition to the legality of the liquor laws of a State is that they must apply without discrimination to intoxicants locally produced as well as to those imported.[3]

An example of this latter qualification is to be found in *Fox v Robbins*[4] where Isaacs J stated that s 113 could not be used to support a State law which required a larger fee for a license to sell wine produced in another State as compared with the fee required for wine produced in the licensing State.[5]

---

STATES MAY NOT RAISE FORCES. TAXATION OF PROPERTY OF COMMONWEALTH OR STATE

**114.** *A State shall not, without the consent of the Parliament of the Commonwealth, raise or maintain any naval or military force, or impose any tax on property of any kind belonging to the Commonwealth, nor shall the Commonwealth impose any tax on property of any kind belonging to a State.*[6]

**"A State shall not, without the consent of the Parliament of the Commonwealth, raise or maintain any naval or military force"**

The first part of this section must be read in conjunction with s 51 (vi). It invests the Commonwealth Parliament with exclusive power over that part of the defence power which relates to the armed forces. It implicitly recognizes, however, that the Parliament may delegate to a State power to raise or maintain a naval or military force (e g, a State militia).

**"or impose any tax on property of any kind belonging to the Commonwealth, nor shall the Commonwealth impose any tax on property of any kind belonging to a State"**

This section is one of the few sections in the Constitution defining the nature of inter-governmental immunities. It prohibits both the Commonwealth and States from imposing a tax on the other's property. The prohibition encom-

---

3    *Annotated Constitution* at 947.

4    (1908) 8 CLR 115 at 128.

5    See also *Duncan v State of Queensland* (1916) 22 CLR 556 at 589-98 (Barton J).

6    Quick and Garran, 948-50.

passes taxation by subordinate authorities.[7] Thus the Commonwealth is exempt from municipal rates.[8]

The section only prevents taxation of property (whether real or personal, corporeal or incorporeal). It does not prevent levies being imposed on the importation of goods by a State.[9] Nor does it prevent a tax being imposed on a person who holds a leasehold estate from the Crown.[10]

Section 114 does not exhaust the area of intergovernmental immunities. It has already been suggested that, under a general doctrine based on federal implications, a State cannot tax the Commonwealth[11] although the *Payroll Tax Case*[12] indicates that the States do not have a similar immunity from Commonwealth legislation.

STATES NOT TO COIN MONEY

**115.** *A State shall not coin money, nor make anything but gold and silver coin a legal tender in payment of debts.*[13]

This section read with s 51 (xii) would seem to have the effect not only of making the power over coinage exclusive to the Commonwealth but also of vesting in the Commonwealth sole power over the monetary exchange system (viz, currency, legal tender).

Although the words appearing in the second part of the section seem to permit a State to make gold and silver coin legal tender, the Commonwealth Parliament has the exclusive authority to convert these metals into coinage which will be necessary before these metals become legal tender.[14]

COMMONWEALTH NOT TO LEGISLATE IN RESPECT OF RELIGION

**116.** *The Commonwealth shall not make any law for establishing any religion, or for imposing any religious observance, or for prohibiting the free exercise of any religion, and no religious test shall be required as a qualification for any office or public trust under the Commonwealth.*[15]

This section contains one of the few guarantees of individual rights to be found in the Constitution. It does not, however, apply to the States but only to the Commonwealth.[16] Since religion as such falls under the residuary

---

7  *Municipal Council of Sydney v Commonwealth* (1904) 1 CLR 208 at 230 (Griffith CJ).
8  Ibid. The exemption applies even though the municipal rate does not create a charge on the land but only imposes a personal liability on the owner or occupier. See also *Essendon Corporation v Criterion Theatres Ltd* (1947) 74 CLR 1 at 13.
9  *Attorney-General of New South Wales v Collector of Customs for New South Wales* (1908) 5 CLR 818.
10  *Attorney-General for Queensland v Attorney-General for the Commonwealth* (1915) 20 CLR 148.
11  See above under s 106.
12  (1971) 122 CLR 353; [1971] ALR 449.
13  Quick and Garran, 950. Wynes, 140-1. Nicholas, 187-90.
14  Quick and Garran at 950. But see Wynes at 90, n 3.
15  Quick and Garran, 951-3. Wynes, 126-30.
16  It would seem that the prohibition also applies to the Commonwealth Territories: *Lamshed v Lake* (1958) 99 CLR 132 at 143. See also Pannam, "Section 116 and the Federal Territories," (1961) 35 ALJ 209. Cumbrae-Stewart, "Section 116 of the Constitution," (1946) 20 ALJ 207. Contrast, Gibbs, "Section 116 and the Territories of the Commonwealth" (1946) 20 ALJ 375.

power of the States and not within a specific head of Commonwealth power, the effect of s 116 is limited. Nevertheless, it is clear that the restraint may operate to invalidate laws passed by the Commonwealth under a specific head of power if their effect is to breach the prohibition contained in s 116 either by establishing any religion or by prohibiting the free exercise thereof.[17] As will be seen, portion of the section is directed at preventing Commonwealth involvement with religion which amounts to "establishment", while the other parts of the section protect the freedom of an individual to practice a religion.

**"The Commonwealth shall not make any law for establishing any religion, or for imposing any religious observance"**

It is instructive to compare this section with the establishment clause in the United States Constitution. Under the First Amendment, Congress "shall not make any law respecting an establishment of religion". The difference in terminology is significant. Section 116 refers to the establishment of *any* religion while the American clause prohibits the establishment of religion. This suggests that what s 116 is aimed at is any type of assistance tending to promote the interests of one Church or religious community as against others.[18] A non-discriminatory law which is directed towards assisting religion generally may fall foul of the American provision[19] but may not be invalid under s 116. Before federation, there were in existence endowment Acts appropriating part of the colonial revenue for assisting the Christian religion.[20] It is possible that such endowment legislation, if passed by the Commonwealth, would not be invalidated by s 116, although it is clear that it was not envisaged that the Commonwealth would pass such legislation. In any case, the need for financial assistance to religious groups as such reflected the sparsely-settled nature of the Australian continent and the inability of country groups to maintain their communities without State assistance.

The main thrust of this part of s 116 is directed towards preventing Commonwealth promotion of religious observances. In Quick and Garran's words, "by the establishment of religion is meant the erection and recognition of a State church, or the concession of special favours, titles and advantages to one Church which are denied to others. It is not intended to prohibit the federal government from recognizing religion or religious worship."[21] Indeed, the preamble to the Constitution which uses the words "humbly relying on Almighty God" imports a reliance on the religious spirit. The reading of a prayer by the presiding officers of the federal House at the beginning of the daily sessions is also indicative of the proposition that s 116 does not prevent the Commonwealth from recognizing, as distinct from imposing, religious practices.[22]

---

17　*Jehovah's Witnesses Case* (1943) 67 CLR 116 at 123.
18　See Cumbrae-Stewart, op cit as 207-8. Contrast Pannam, "Travelling s 116 with a US Road Map" (1964) 4 MULR 41 at 61.
19　See Wynes at 126.
20　See, for example, the *Victorian Constitution Act*, 18 & 19 Vict, c 55, s 53.
21　At 951.
22　The adoption of the clause at the convention debates was supported by Higgins who pointed out that in the United States a Sunday observance-type law had been passed by Congress to prevent an exhibition from being held on a Sunday. There should, he said, be a clear statement in the Australian Constitution prohibiting the passing of such a law by the Commonwealth: Quick and Garran, at 952. However, Sunday observance laws were part of the Imperial legal inheritance applying in the colonies.

A question which has arisen recently is whether financial assistance to denominational schools (in addition to State schools) violates s 116.[23] In so far as the financial assistance is made under s 96 as grants to the States and, therefore, depend on State co-operation, it cannot be characterized as coercive or as in any way compelling a State to give recognition to religious practices.[24] The legislation does not "single out" any group of church schools for special treatment (and the educational practice of these schools must conform to certain standards). More important, however, is the fact that its primary effect is not to aid religion but education in schools and their pupils. In the light of the *Jehovah's Witnesses Case*[25] to be discussed later, this characterization would suggest that such grants do not involve an establishment of religion.

**"or for prohibiting the free exercise of any religion, and no religious test shall be required as a qualification for any office or public trust under the Commonwealth"**

This part of s 116 emphasizes the principle of religious freedom. No person shall be subject to penalties or any form of discrimination based on his religious beliefs. Whether a religious believer or a non-believer, he is immune from laws which discriminate against or burden his beliefs or practices.

The judgment of Latham CJ in the *Jehovah's Witnesses Case*[26] makes it clear, however, that religious beliefs are not a ground for exempting the believer from compliance with the ordinary civil or criminal law. In that case, the *National Security (Subversive Associations) Regulations* which depended for their constitutional support on the defence power were challenged by a religious denomination, the Jehovah's Witnesses. The regulations prohibited, *inter alia*, the advocacy of doctrines which were prejudicial to the prosecution of the war in which the Commonwealth was engaged, provided for the dissolution of associations propogating such doctrines, and vested their property in the Commonwealth. We have seen that a portion of these regulations was invalidated on the ground that they were outside s 51 (vi).[27] The argument was also canvassed that they were in contravention of s 116. In his judgment[28] Latham CJ examined the nature and scope of the religious freedom protected by s 116. The following is a summary of his views.

1. Section 116 protects all religions. A definition of religion which satisfies the adherents of all religions would be difficult, if not impossible. Religion could be regarded as a system of beliefs or a code of conduct or ritual observance. Section 116 mut be regarded as operating in relation to all these aspects of religion, irrespective of varying opinions in the community as to the truth of particular religious doctrines, as to the goodness of conduct prescribed by a particular religion, or as to the propriety of any particular religious observance.

2. Section 116 protects the religion (or absence of religion) of minorities, although it is true that in determining what is religious and what is not religious, the current application of the word "religion" must necessarily be taken into account.

---

23  This assistance has been provided under the *States Grants (Science Laboratories) Act* 1967-1971, the *States Grants (Secondary School Libraries) Act* 1968-1971, the *States Grants (Schools) Act* 1972.
24  See Lane, "Commonwealth Reimbursements for Fees at State Schools" (1964) 38 ALJ 130. See also under s 51 (xxiiiA).
25  (1943) 67 CLR 116.
26  Ibid at 122 et seq.
27  See previously under s 51 (vi).
28  (1943) 67 CLR 116 at 122-48.

3. Section 116 protects practices as well as beliefs.[29]

4. As to the free exercise of religion: the word "free" does not mean licence. The concept of freedom can only be evaluated in a particular context. For example, free speech does not mean the right to create a panic by calling out "fire" in a crowded theatre.[30] Likewise, as various American cases show, the free exercise of religion does not empower individuals because of their religious beliefs to break the law of the country.[31]

5. The High Court is the arbiter of the occasions when a legislative provision unduly infringes religious freedom. This makes it possible to accord a real measure of practical protection to religion without involving the community in anarchy.

Applying these principles to the facts of the case Latham CJ considered that the doctrine expressed by the Jehovah's Witnesses as to non-co-operation with the Commonwealth in terms of military obligation was prejudicial to the defence of the community and s 116 did not give immunity to it.[32]

The only other decision of the High Court directly on s 116 is the early case of *Krygier v Williams*[33] where it was held that a *Commonwealth Defence Act* which imposed obligations on all male inhabitants of the Commonwealth to perform military service applied to a person whose religious beliefs were opposed to military service.[34] As in the *Jehovah's Witnesses Case*, the decision was based on the ground that a law imposing civic duties could not be characterized as a law infringing religious freedom.

It is also clear that s 116 does not prevent a court exercising jurisdiction under Commonwealth legislation (e g, matrimonial causes legislation) from adjudicating on the conduct of parties based on religious beliefs and practices, when this is necessary for the effective exercise of its jurisdiction.[35]

## RIGHTS OF RESIDENTS IN STATES

**117.** *A subject of the Queen, resident in any State, shall not be subject in any other State to any disability or discrimination which would not be equally applicable to him if he were a subject of the Queen resident in such other State.*[36]

---

29   On this matter see Pannam, "Travelling s 116 with a US Road Map", op cit at 65.
30   67 CLR at 127, referring to *Schenck v United States* (1919) 249 US 47 at 52.
31   (1943) 67 CLR 116 at 129-31.
32   Ibid at 146. However, on the question of the validity of the regulations under the defence power see earlier under s 51 (vi).
33   (1912) 15 CLR 366.
34   Under the *National Service Act*, s 18, provision is now made for conscientious objection. In *Judd v McKeon* (1926) 38 CLR 380 at 387 Higgins J suggested that abstention from voting on religious grounds might be a valid reason for failure to vote at a federal election. It would seem, however, that this dictum is incorrect. See Wynes at 130.
35   See *Kiorgaard v Kioorgaard and Lange* [1967] StRQd 162. An order was made by a judge under the *Matrimonial Causes Act* (Com) awarding custody of a child to one parent and imposing conditions on the access of the other parent which prohibited the latter from educating the child in the tenets of a particular sect, (until the trial of the action). It was held that this order, directed as it was to the welfare of the child, was a matter to be determined by the judge under the Act and did not contravene s 116. Cf, *Evers v Evers* (1972) 19 FLR 296.
36   Quick and Garran, 953-61. Wynes, 102-6.

The intention of this section is to preserve a certain equality in treatment of certain classes of persons but it falls far short of the equality preserved by a similar clause in the US Constitution.[37]

A person, to assume the protection afforded by the section, must be a "subject of the Queen". This means that only Australian citizens and British subjects are protected. By its very nature, therefore, it excludes aliens or migrants who have not taken out citizenship.[38]

Secondly, the persons must be resident in a State. As Isaacs J put it in *Howe's Case*[39] "every Australian is when all the facts are known residentially identifiable pre-eminently with some one State. Indicia of residence include place of permanent home, and place of employment and other factors.[40]

If a person falls within these two categories then he is protected in *another* State from any disability or discrimination which does not equally apply to residents of that State.

The cases decided by the High Court indicate that the protection afforded by s 117 against discrimination is rather weak. In *Davies and Jones v State of Western Australia*[41] the question at issue was the validity of a provision in a Western Australian *Administration Act* 1903 which allowed a reduction in estate duty in relation to beneficial interests passing to persons who were "bona fide residents of and domiciled in Western Australia". The plaintiff in the case, who was a beneficiary under a will relating to Western Australian property, was a resident of Queensland. He claimed that the provision was contrary to s 117. It was held by the High Court that, in so far as the discrimination embodied in the Act was based on an element additional to residence, viz, domicile, s 117 had not been infringed.

The members of the court were agreed that the word "domiciled" must be interpreted in its technical legal sense, and not as a mere descriptive word accompanying the word "resident". In the words of O'Connor J, "We must take it that the legislature was well aware that there were many thousands of persons who were in fact permanent residents of Western Australia, but who yet maintained homes for their families in the Eastern States, and who in law would still be regarded as having their domicile in one or other of those States".[42] It was true, however, as Barton J pointed out,[43] that residence in the place of domicile was the normal condition, and residence away from it "is in the view of law not permanent until it becomes of such a kind as to merge in its turn into a domicile of choice." In so far as the discrimination affected by the Western Australian Act worked, not in favour of its residents, but in favour of persons who were both resident *and* domiciled in the State, the Queensland plaintiff in *Davies Case* could not show a discrimination against himself based on residence. The basis of the distinction is clearly quite technical

37 See generally Pannam, "Discrimination on the Basis of Residence in Australia and the United States," (1967) 6 MULR 105.

38 As to the choice of the phrase "subject of the Queen" as against "citizen", see Quick and Garran, 957.

39 (1922) 31 CLR 290 at 308. Corporations are not "residents" for the purpose of s 117.

40 See Lane, *Some Principles and Sources of Australian Constitutional Law* at 154.

41 (1904) 2 CLR 29.

42 Ibid at 51.

43 Ibid at 47.

and it would seem to allow a State to effectuate what in substance amounts to discrimination against non-residents by superadding a domicile requirement.[44]

With this case should be compared *Commissioner of Taxes v Parks*[45] which concerned the validity of provisions of a Queensland *Income Tax Act* which exempted from tax persons earning less than £150 per year, but went on to provide that, in the case of persons who did not ordinarily reside in Queensland, the exemption allowance should be "such part of the sum of £150 or part thereof as the part of the year during which the person earned or derived such income in Queensland bears to the whole year." The effect of this provision was to cut down the benefit for "other-State" residents by relating it to earnings in Queensland or from Queensland sources. The plaintiff tax-payer, who argued that this contravened s 117, was a person whose home was in New South Wales, but who piloted ships down the Queensland coast, and who had been allowed an exemption of part of the £150 proportionate to the fraction of the year during which he earned income in Queensland territorial waters. It was held by Henchman J that the plaintiff was a resident of New South Wales, even though he spent a major portion of the year (because of his work) outside the State. As to whether the provision in the Act offended s 117, Henchman J was of the opinion that the discrimination resulting from the system of tax exemptions relating to locally-acquired income of "other-State" residents was a discrimination against them which was clearly based on residence.[46]

In the light of *Lee Fay v Vincent*[47] it is clear that the section only applies to protect the rights of a resident of a State who alleges discrimination arising from the laws of another State. Consequently if he has taken up residence in that other State he cannot claim the protection of s 117. In other words, past residence in some other State is no ground for invoking s 117.[48]

It follows, therefore, that if a State law prescribes a period of residence as requisite for the attainment of a particular qualification or right (e g, to be admitted to a profession), s 117 does not operate, as the "other-State" resident must enter the State in which such qualifications are prescribed as an initial step towards attaining the qualification. Having done so and remaining there, he then becomes a resident of that State and subject to its laws which apply to all residents alike (irrespective of origin).

RECOGNITION OF LAWS, ETC OF STATES

**118.** *Full faith and credit shall be given, throughout the Commonwealth, to the laws, the public Acts and records, and the judicial proceedings of every State.*[49]

This broad constitutional direction is to be read together with s 18 of the *State and Territorial Laws Recognition Act* 1901-1964, enacted under the

---

44　See the criticism of Pannam, op cit at 133.
45　[1933] StRQd 306.
46　Ibid at 322-3.
47　(1908) 7 CLR 389.
48　Ibid at 392. See also the opinion of Griffith CJ in *R v Smithers ex parte Benson* (1912) 16 CLR 99. Cf, Pannam, op cit at 143 et seq.
49　Quick and Garran, 961-4. Wynes, 163-5. *Essays*, 293-326 (Cowen). Lane, 721-9. Nicholas, 384-5. Nygh, Conflict of Laws in Australia, (1968) Ch 32. Sykes, Australian Conflict of Laws (1972) 239-42.

power conferred on the Commonwealth Parliament by s 51 (xxv) of the Constitution. Section 18 provides:

All public acts, records and judicial proceedings of any State or Territory, if proved or authenticated as required by the Act, shall have such full faith and credit given to them in every court and public office as they have by law or usage in the courts and public offices of the State or Territory from whence they are taken.

There are slight differences in terminology between the constitutional provision and s 18 but these are minor ones. For example, the constitutional provision includes, but s 18 omits, the word "laws". This word would seem to refer to the common law. The common law operates in all the States and the Territories, and because of the position of the High Court and Privy Council in the judicial system, any variations in interpretation of that law by State or Territorial courts would ultimately be resolved by the appellate courts: the unity of the common law throughout Australia is therefore to be presumed.[50]

In *Harris v Harris*[51] Fullagar J considered that there was a substantive difference between the statutory and constitutional provisions, the former requiring absolute recognition to be given to the decisions of sister States in the State in which the mandate is invoked, the latter being subject to qualification based on legitimate State policies. It is doubtful, however, whether this distinction can be maintained and it is preferable to regard the statutory provision as "backing up" the constitutional mandate.

Credit is to be given to four basic types of legal "acts" using that word in its widest sense: the common law, statutory enactments (including subordinate legislation) judicial proceedings (including judgments, decrees and other types of court orders) and public records such as certificates of Registrars of Births, Deaths and Marriages, and of various administrative boards.

It is quite clear that s 118 has an important evidentiary effect. It requires public officers (judges and administrators), whether federal or State, to give recognition to these public documents providing they are properly authenticated. That means, for example, that a court must take judicial notice of them. As such, the requirement preserves a unity between the States which assists in the administration of the laws in relation to persons or subject-matter where an inter-State element is involved.

The difficult question is, however, to determine whether the constitutional and statutory requirements have also a substantive operation as requiring the laws and judgments of one State to be given effect to in another State in resolving a legal dispute arising in the latter state.

As to judgments, the decision of Fullagar J in *Harris v Harris*[52] supports the view that s 18 of the *State and Territorial Laws and Records Recognition Act* has a substantive operation. In that case, a divorce decree had been pronounced in New South Wales on the basis of the petitioner's domicile within that State. Subsequently, in Victoria, this person had petitioned for a dissolution of a later marriage. It transpired that the petitioner had never lost his domicile of origin in Victoria. According to the rules of private international law of the time (1947) the decree of the New South Wales court was not entitled to recognition as domicile in that State was a necessary foundation for the exercise

---

50   As compared with the position in the United States. See Nygh, op cit at 662.
51   [1947] VLR 44 at 59.
52   [1947] VLR 44.

of the jurisdiction. However, Fullagar J held that he was compelled to recognize the decree by virtue of s 18.

As to the recognition of statutes, there are dicta in the case of *Merwin Pastoral Co Ltd v Moolpa Pastoral Co Ltd*[53] which favour the view that substantive effect is also to be given to statutes of a sister State. In this case, a mortgage agreement had been made in Victoria relating to land situated in New South Wales. In proceedings in Victoria to enforce this contract, a New South Wales Act (which made agreements of this nature unenforceable) was pleaded by the defendant company as preventing such enforcement. The plaintiff company argued that the enforcement of the NSW statute would be contrary to Victorian public policy. As the contract affected immovables in New South Wales, the proper law was that of New South Wales, and the Act was held to validly affect the contractual relations of the parties. Views were expressed that s 118 of the Constitution did not allow one State to refuse recognition to the Statutes of a sister State on the ground of public policy.[54]

However, recent cases of the High Court tend to support the proposition that s 118 does not have a substantive operation. In *Anderson v Eric Anderson Radio and TV Pty Ltd*[55] the plaintiff had been injured by the negligence of the defendant's servant in the ACT. Being a resident of New South Wales he brought an action in the NSW Supreme Court to recover damages. Under New South Wales law (at that time) contributory negligence was a complete defence and the defendant relied on this. There was, however, an ACT ordinance which displaced the rule as to contributory negligence being a complete defence and provided for apportionment of damages. It was argued by the plaintiff that s 18 of the *State and Territorial Laws and Records Recognition Act* compelled the NSW Court to give effect to the ACT Ordinance as being the law applicable as the *lex loci delicti*. It was held that the Ordinance could not be relied upon as it only applied to actions tried in the ACT and neither s 18 nor s 118 of the Constitution operated to extend the territorial ambit of the Ordinance. To like effect is the decision of the High Court in *Finlayson v Permanent Trustee Co (Canberra) Ltd*.[56]

It is true that neither case is inconsistent with the *Merwin Pastoral Case*[57] as the sister State statute in both cases was construed as having an intra-territorial operation. One judge, however, expressed the view that s 18 did not have a substantive operation.[58] On this basis it would appear that if the Statutes under consideration in these cases were expressed to have extra-territorial effect, s 118 would not support them if, under the constitutional powers of the States which enacted them, they could not have such an operation.

It would therefore be appropriate to sum up as follows: the High Court

---

53   (1933) 48 CLR 565.
54   Ibid at 577 (Rich & Dixon JJ) 587-8 (Evatt J). See also *Re E & B Chemicals & Wool Treatment Pty Ltd* [1939] SASR 441 at 443-4.
55   (1965) 114 CLR 20; [1966] ALR 423.
56   (1969) 43 ALJR 42 at 44. See also *Estate of Hancock* [1962] NSWR 1171; *Pederson v Young* (1964) 110 CLR 162; [1964] ALR 798. Cf, *Estate of Searle* (1963) 5 FLR 137.
57   (1933) 48 CLR 565.
58   *Anderson v Eric Anderson Radio and TV Pty Ltd* (1965) 114 CLR 20 at 46 (Windeyer J); [1966] ALR at 440. See also *Varawa v Howard Smith Co Ltd* (1911) 13 CLR 35 at 69 (O'Connor J). See also Pryles, "The Applicability of Statutes to Multistate Transactions" (1972) 46 ALJ 629.

seems quite prepared to allow the ordinary common law rules of private international law to operate, subject to any statutory exclusion effected by the
*lex fori* (due regard being paid to the doctrine of extra-territoriality so far as
it affects the legislative competence of a sister State), and that the requirements of s 118 (and s 18 of the *State and Territorial Laws and Records
Recognition Act*) are evidentiary in nature.

## PROTECTION OF STATES FROM INVASION AND VIOLENCE

**119.** *The Commonwealth shall protect every State against invasion and,
on the application of the Executive Government of the State, against domestic
violence.*[59]

The first part of this section is an explicit assertion of the duties cast upon
the Commonwealth in the exercise of its executive power over defence against
external enemies and needs no further elucidation.[60]

The second part of the section relates to domestic violence. In so far as
the State governments, through their police forces, are primarily responsible
for law and order, Commonwealth military or police action can only be taken
on matters affecting the "peace order and good government" of a State at the
request of the State Government. However, where the violence is directed
against Commonwealth institutions (e g, barracks, post offices) or affects
matters falling within Commonwealth power (e g, diplomatic personnel,
election activities),[61] then the Commonwealth can intervene without a request
from the State in which the violence occurs or is imminent.[62]

## CUSTODY OF OFFENDERS AGAINST LAWS OF THE COMMONWEALTH

**120.** *Every State shall make provision for the detention in its prisons of
persons accused or convicted of offences against the laws of the Commonwealth,
and for the punishment of persons convicted of such offences, and the Parliament of the Commonwealth may make laws to give effect to this provision.*[63]

To relieve the Commonwealth from the burden of erecting Commonwealth
prisons to house persons accused of, or convicted of, offences against Commonwealth laws,[64] this constitutional provision directs the States to receive such
persons. It goes further, however, in empowering the Commonwealth to make
laws to give effect to this obligation, and therefore affects a matter lying within
State residuary power (viz, control of prisons).

Under the *Removal of Prisons (Territories) Act* 1923-1968 provision is
made for the Governor-General to recommend to the Governor of a State that
a prisoner be removed from a Territory to undergo sentence in that State.

---

59  Quick and Garran, 964-5.
60  See earlier under ss 51 (vi) and 61.
61  See *Commonwealth Places (Application of Laws) Act* 1970. *Public Order
    (Protection of Persons and Property) Act* 1971.
62  Quick and Garran, 964. As to the immunity of Commonwealth officers from
    State law when acting pursuant to this section see the (dissenting) judgment
    of Isaacs J in *Pirrie v McFarlane* (1925) 36 CLR 170 at 206. On the procedure
    to be followed in relation to Commonwealth action on an application from a
    State government for protection see the *Defence Act*, s 51.
63  Quick and Garran, 965-6.
64  Including offences against the laws of a Territory. *Lamshed v Lake* (1958) 99
    CLR 132.

However, it is provided that the concurrence of the Governor of the State is necessary before such removal can take place. The Act provides for the cost of the removal to be borne by the Commonwealth or the Territory Administration.[65]

Section 120 received the elucidation of the Court in *R v Turnbull ex parte Taylor*[66] where it was pointed out[67] that (i) the section did not impose a duty on the State to receive federal prisoners; (ii) of its own force it did not empower any federal official to remove a prisoner; (iii) such a power must be derived from Commonwealth legislation which the section contemplates; (iv) in a proper case the section could give rise to judicial proceedings at the instance of the Commonwealth to enforce the obligations which it creates.[68]

---

65   As to the ACT see *Removal of Prisoners (Australian Capital Territory) Act* 1968.
66   (1968) 43 ALJR 45.
67   Ibid at 49.
68   The actual decision in the case was that the *Removal of Prisoners (Territories) Act* 1923-1962 had not been complied with in removing a prisoner from ACT to NSW. See now *Removal of Prisoners (Australian Capital Territory) Act* 1968, amending previous legislation.

# CHAPTER VI

# NEW STATES

NEW STATES MAY BE ADMITTED OR ESTABLISHED

**121.** *The Parliament may admit to the Commonwealth or establish new States, and may upon such admission or establishment make or impose such terms and conditions, including the extent of representation in either House of the Parliament, as it thinks fit.*[1]

### "The Parliament may admit to the Commonwealth or establish new States"

The two methods by which new States of the Commonwealth may be created are by admission or establishment. The words "admit to the Commonwealth" were intended to refer to the admission of political communities outside the Commonwealth which were British colonies or dependencies (e g, Fiji and other colonies in the Pacific area).[2] However, the wording of s 121 is not restricted to such communities and there does not seem to be anything in the Constitution which prevents the admission of foreign States which desire to become States of the Commonwealth.

The word "establishment" would cover the situation whereby a Territory of the Commonwealth is granted statehood, or a new State is created from an existing State or States whether by partition, union of the whole or parts of two or more States, or by the junction of contiguous parts of two or more States.[3] In such cases the restrictions imposed by ss 123 and 124 will have to be considered.

### "and may upon such admission or establishment make or impose such terms and conditions, including the extent of representaion in either House of the Parliament, as it thinks fit"

The Commonwealth before passing legislation to admit a new State, may impose certain terms or conditions before such admission is approved. For example, it may require that the Constitution of the new State provide for a certain type of suffrage; it may provide that the population of the State reach a certain level; or it may impose either economic or political conditions before granting the application for admission. In particular it may deal with the question of representation and in this respect it is to be noted that the rule of equal representation in the Senate may be departed from, as this requirement only applies to the original States. Quick and Garran state that even the principle of proportional State representation in the House of Representatives, though expressed without qualification in s 24, might, under the words of this section "including the extent of representation in either House", be varied in the case of new States.[4] However, no terms or conditions could be imposed which are inconsistent with the provisions of the Constitution, e g, nothing

---

1   Quick and Garran, 967-70. Wynes, 106-8. Nicholas, 95-8.
2   Moore, *The Constitution of the Commonwealth of Australia*, 593.
3   Quick and Garran, 969.
4   Ibid at 970.

could be done to prevent the judicature chapter of the Constitution from applying to the new State.

GOVERNMENT OF TERRITORIES

**122.** *The Parliament may make laws for the government of any territory surrendered by any State to and accepted by the Commonwealth, or of any territory placed by the Queen under the authority of and accepted by the Commonwealth, or otherwise acquired by the Commonwealth, and may allow the representation of such territory in either House of the Parliament to the extent and on the terms which it thinks fit.*[5]

### "The Parliament may make laws for the government of any territory"

Under this head of power, the Commonwealth has a general power of legislating for a Territory. It may do so by means of paramount legislation passed by the Commonwealth Parliament or by setting up a Territorial legislature with its own legislative powers, although these will always be subject to the overriding authority of the Commonwealth Parliament.

The power is a plenary one[6] which may be exercised extra-territorially,[7] and is not subject to the limitations which restrain the Commonwealth in legislating under the various paragraphs of s 51. Thus in *Tau v Commonwealth*[8] it was held that the Commonwealth may legislate under s 122 to acquire property without being under an obligation to provide "just terms". In *Buchanan v Commonwealth*[9] it was held that the limitations imposed by s 55 upon the making of laws imposing taxation did not apply to taxation legislation enacted in relation to a Territory. It appears, however, that certain constitutional limitations deriving from other sections of the Constitution (e g, s 116) might control legislation relating to a Territory.[10] And it is clear that the Territories power cannot be used to override basic constitutional provisions protecting the States (e g, s 123).

One difficulty has been the extent to which s 122 is affected by Chapter III of the Constitution. *R v Bernasconi*[11] supports the proposition that s 80 does not apply to the Territories.[12] Moreover, the status of the courts of the

---

5   Quick and Garran, 971-4. Wynes, 108-16. Nicholas, 86-94. Lane, 731-62. Howard, 461-86. *Essays,* 327-42.
6   *Australian National Airways Pty Ltd v Commonwealth* (1945) 71 CLR 29 at 61 (Latham CJ).
7   *Lamshed v Lake* (1958) 99 CLR 132. (Legislation in relation to Northern Territory held to affect activities within the State of South Australia).
8   *Tau v The Commonwealth* (1970) 44 ALJR 25. Commented upon in 44 ALJ 49.
9   (1913) 16 CLR 315.
10   See *Lamshed v Lake* 99 CLR at 142 (Dixon CJ). Pannam, "Section 116 and the Federal Territories" (1961) 35 ALJ 209. Gibbs, "Section 116 of the Constitution and the Territories of the Commonwealth" (1947) 20 ALJ 375.
11   (1915) 19 CLR 629.
12   Of course the practical reasons underlying the decision are obvious: at the time of federation it would have been difficult to envisage the empanelling of jurors for indictable offences in all the areas of the Territory (See Isaacs J 19 CLR at 638). See also *Porter v R, ex parte Yee* (1926) 37 CLR 432. (Appellate jurisdiction cannot be conferred on the High Court from decisions of the Supreme Courts of the Territories under s 73 but may be conferred under s 122)

Territories is not determined by ss 71 and 72: consequently judges of Territorial courts need not have life tenure.[13] However, the dictum of the Privy Council in the *Boilermakers' Case*[14] that the legislative power in respect of the Territories is a "disparate and non-federal matter", does not accord with certain views expressed in *Spratt v Hermes*[15] nor with the tenor of the judgment of Dixon CJ in *Lamshed v Lake*.[16] Indeed in *Spratt v Hermes* Menzies J rejected the argument that the Territories were not part of the Commonwealth or to put it in the words of Isaacs J in *Buchanan's Case* were not "fused with it."[17] The result of this view would be, as pointed out in *Lamshed v Lake*, that general legislation enacted under s 51 would apply not only to the States but also to the Territories forming part of the Commonwealth[18] (unless a contrary intention were expressed).

In summing up, it would seem preferable to steer a middle course between the view that the legislative power over the Territories is a "disparate non-federal matter" as though it was completely disjoined from the rest of the Constitution and the "absorption" view, that the Territories are in every respect in a similar position to the States so far as the operation of general constitutional provisions are concerned. The middle course is the "modified integration" theory as one writer has called it:[19] to proceed in an empirical way, determining where and when the occasion arises as to the application or otherwise of the particular provision in question to the Territories. This seems to accord with the approach adopted by the High Court in *Tau v Commonwealth*.[20]

### "surrendered by any State to and accepted by the Commonwealth, or of any territory placed by the Queen under the authority of and accepted by the Commonwealth, or otherwise acquired by the Commonwealth"

The various ways in which the Commonwealth may acquire territory are mentioned in s 122. The first method is by surrender, that is, by a State Parliament passing an Act surrendering part of its territory to the Commonwealth which must afterwards be accepted by the Commonwealth Parliament. Indeed, s 111 authorizes the State to surrender parts of its territory to the Commonwealth. This has occurred in the case of the Northern Territory

---

13   *Spratt v Hermes* (1965) 114 CLR 226; [1966] ALR 597.

14   (1957) 95 CLR 529 at 549.

15   (1965) 114 CLR 226 at 243; [1966] ALR 597 at 601-602 (Barwick CJ); 114 CLR at 269-271; [1966] ALR at 620-622 (Menzies J). Cf, Kitto J 114 CLR at 257 et seq; [1966] ALR at 611 et seq. See also Zines, "Laws for the Government of any Territory" (1966) 2 Federal Law Review 72; Finlay, "The Dual Nature of the Territories Power of the Commonwealth" (1969) 43 ALJ 256.

16   99 CLR 132 at 145.

17   114 CLR at 270; [1966] ALR at 621. Indeed, at the time of federation the Northern Territory and the ACT were parts of States. See *Lamshed v Lake*, 99 CLR at 151.

18   99 CLR at 143 (Dixon CJ) 151 (Menzies J). It does seem necessary to make a distinction between Territories forming part of the Commonwealth (eg, Northern Territory) and the external territories, as this distinction is recognized in many Commonwealth Acts. Cf, Menzies J 114 CLR at 270; [1966] ALR at 621.

19   Zines, op cit, 2 FedLR at 74.

20   (1970) 44 ALJR 25.

surrendered by South Australia, and in the case of the Federal Capital Territory which was surrendered by New South Wales.

The second method is by a Territory being placed by the Queen under the authority of the Commonwealth and subsequently being accepted by the Commonwealth. This happened with Papua[21] and Norfolk Island,[22] which were placed under the authority of the Commonwealth by the Queen in the early part of this century and became Commonwealth territories. The third method is by acquisition "otherwise" by the Commonwealth. This would apply to any other method of acquiring territory, whether by cession, transfer from some other government, or by the acquisition of an original title whether on the basis of possession or in some other way which would be recognised by international law.[23] In the 1950s, the Cocos Islands and Christmas Island in the Indian Ocean were placed under the authority of Australia by the Queen pursuant to enabling legislation passed by the United Kingdom as well as by the federal Parliament[24] in accordance with the *Statute of Westminster*.

Questions have arisen as to the acquisition of the Trust Territory of New Guinea. Originally, this Territory was acquired under the old League of Nations' mandate system. After the Second World War it was brought under the trusteeship system and joined with Papua in an "administrative union" with the sanction of the United Nations. In various cases decided by the High Court it has been held that New Guinea is subject to the legislative power conferred by s 122 either in terms of being a "territory placed by the Queen under the authority of and accepted by the Commonwealth" or being "otherwise acquired by the Commonwealth",[25] despite a vigorous dissent of Evatt J who refused to accept that a mandated Territory, in the light of its international status, could be "acquired" by the mandatory power.[26]

**"and may allow the representation of such territory in either House of the Parliament to the extent and on the terms which it thinks fit"**

The Commonwealth is not required to give representation to either its internal or external territories in the federal Parliament. In the case of New Guinea and Papua which are now ruled jointly under the terms of legislation passed in 1949,[27] there is no representation in the federal Parliament and the policy of the federal Government is to allow the Territory to evolve towards independence. In the case of the Australian Capital Territory and the Northern Territory, there are representatives from both these territories who have full voting rights in the House of Representatives. The smaller island territories do not have representation in the federal Parliament and are ruled by administrators under the authority of the Commonwealth and advised by local officials and councils.

---

21   See *Strachan v Commonwealth* (1906) 4 CLR 455.
22   See *Newberry v R* (1965) 7 FLR 34.
23   See *Ffrost v Stevenson* (1937) 58 CLR 528 at 555 (Latham CJ).
24   *Cocos (Keeling) Islands (Request and Consent) Act* No 76 of 1954. *Christmas Island (Request and Consent) Act* No 102 of 1957.
25   See *Mainka v Custodian of Expropriated Property* (1924) 34 CLR 297. *Jolley v Mainka* (1933) 49 CLR 242. *Ffrost v Stevenson* (1937) 58 CLR 528. *Fishwick v Cleland* (1960) 106 CLR 193; [1961] ALR 147.
26   See in particular his judgment in *Ffrost v Stevenson* (1937) 58 CLR at 586 et seq. *Jolley v Mainka* (1933) 49 CLR 242 at 277 et seq. Evatt J considered that the source of the legislative power was to be found in s 51 (xxix)—the external affairs power.
27   *Papua and New Guinea Act* 1949-1972.

The representation of the Territories in the Senate does raise certain constitutional difficulties. In so far as s 7 restricts membership of the Senate to persons chosen by the people of the States, it would seem that a representative of a Territory would not be a Senator but merely a representative of that Territory and therefore his rights would be restricted to voting on matters affecting the particular Territory represented.

The opinion expressed in the preceding paragraph is inconsistent with the provisions of a Bill introduced in the federal Parliament in 1973, under which the Northern Territory and the Australian Capital Territory are to be represented in the Senate by two "senators" for each Territory with no restrictions on voting rights. The Bill was passed by the House of Representatives but rejected by the Senate in June.

## ALTERATION OF LIMITS OF STATES

**123.** *The Parliament of the Commonwealth may, with the consent of the Parliament of a State, and the approval of the majority of the electors of the State voting upon the question, increase, diminish, or otherwise alter the limits of the State, upon such terms and conditions as may be agreed on, and may, with the like consent, make provision respecting the effect and operation of any increase or diminution or alteration of territory in relation to any State affected.*[28]

As Quick and Garran point out, the limits of a State can be increased by the addition of part of another State, or by the annexation of a federal Territory, while the limits of a State can be diminished by taking from it territory along its border and giving it to another State or transferring it to the Commonwealth.[29] The section requires that any boundary alteration of this nature be approved by the Parliament of the Commonwealth, the Parliaments of the States affected as well as the electors of the States affected voting at a referendum.

One question of difficulty is whether the admission of a new State formed under the procedure laid down in s 124, also comes under s 123, i e, in cases where there is a boundary alteration, or whether s 124 is a separate grant of power subject only to the conditions laid down in that section. This question will be considered under the next section.[30]

The question of the determination of a State boundary which was imperfectly defined has led to litigation on one occasion since federation.[31] The decision in that case rested on the principle that the executive governments of the affected colonies had been given an implied authority to mark out by agreement the lines defined in the legislative or executive acts as constituting the borders of their colonies, and that this power had been exercised before federation. Consequently any error which may have occurred could not be corrected by any judicial authority. Where the boundary has not been marked out, it may be that the powers conferred by the Imperial Act 24 & 25 Vict c 44 allow the executive governments of the affected States to perform this task.[32]

---

28  Quick and Garran, 974-6. Wynes, 106-8.
29  *Annotated Constitution,* 975.
30  See below under s 124.
31  *South Australia v Victoria* (1911) 12 CLR 667 (High Court); [1914] AC 283 (Privy Council).
32  See Moore, *The Constitution of the Commonwealth of Australia,* 596.

At the beginning of 1973 a dispute erupted between the Commonwealth and the State of Queensland over a proposal to transfer to Papua New Guinea certain islands in the Torres Strait which were within the boundaries of the State. The Queensland Premier in stating that such a boundary alteration would fall under s 123 was probably correct. The Territories power (s 122) while empowering the Commonwealth to modify a territorial boundary of Papua New Guinea would not enable the limits of the State of Queensland to be modified. The same restriction would also apply to the use of *Colonial Boundaries Act* of 1895 if such Act is still in operation.[33]

## FORMATION OF NEW STATES

**124.** *A new State may be formed by separation of territory from a State, but only with the consent of the Parliament thereof, and a new State may be formed by the union of two or more States or parts of States, but only with the consent of the Parliaments of the States affected.*[34]

The ways in which a new State may be created are set out in this section although they are not exhaustive of the methods of creation. We have seen that a new State may be formed by admission to the Commonwealth or establishment by the Commonwealth as in the case of a federal Territory raised to statehood. However, where a new State is formed by separation or union, there must be consent of the Parliaments of the States affected.

Quick and Garran consider that s 123 does not apply to establishment or creation of States under ss 124 or 121, or to surrender of territory under s 111, even when such creations involve boundary alterations, as for example when parts of two States join together—an event which would naturally affect the boundaries of both States. The mischief designed to be prevented by s 123 in their opinion was in terms of adjustments to boundaries, for example, if the Riverina District were to be added to Victoria or the Northern Rivers District to Queensland.[35] In such a case, s 123 would guarantee a vote to the electors of the adjacent States affected on this question. However, to take another example, if North Queensland were to be created a new State, this would come under s 124 and while it would incidentally affect the boundaries of the present State of Queensland it would not in the view of Quick and Garran be a boundary alteration under s 123.[36] In such a case, of course, the federal Parliament would still have the power of "establishing" the new State under s 121.

---

33   See above under Covering Clause VIII.
34   Quick and Garran, 976-7. Wynes, 106-8.
35   *Annotated Constitution*, 975.
36   See also Lumb, "Territorial Changes in the States and Territories of the Commonwealth" (1963) 37 ALJ 172.

# CHAPTER VII

## MISCELLANEOUS

Seat of Government

**125.** *The seat of Government of the Commonwealth shall be determined by the Parliament, and shall be within territory which shall have been granted to or acquired by the Commonwealth, and shall be vested in and belong to the Commonwealth, and shall be in the State of New South Wales, and be distant not less than one hundred miles from Sydney.*

*Such territory shall contain an area of not less than one hundred square miles, and such portion thereof as shall consist of Crown lands shall be granted to the Commonwealth without any payment therefor.*

*The Parliament shall sit at Melbourne until it meet at the seat of Government.*[1]

The requirements of this section were complied with when the State of New South Wales transferred to the Commonwealth, under s 111, the area which is now known as the Australian Capital Territory. The seat of government, as we have seen, is in Canberra which is the capital city of the Federal Capital Territory. The various provisions relating to this grant of territory are to be found in the legislation of 1909 and 1910[2] which led to its transfer by New South Wales and the acceptance and the setting up of the seat of government by the Commonwealth.

The meaning of the phrase "Crown land shall be granted to the Commonwealth without any payment therefor" means that the Commonwealth became owner of Crown lands belonging to the State of New South Wales without any payment of compensation to New South Wales under s 51 (xxxi).[3]

The words in the first paragraph "or acquired by the Commonwealth" suggest that in the event of the State of New South Wales failing to surrender territory under s 111, the Commonwealth could compulsorily acquire it. The relevance of this power to-day can be seen as enabling the Commonwealth to exercise a "reserve" power of acquisition of additional territory from New South Wales in the light of population requirements in the ACT, if negotiations with the State of New South Wales towards that end were not successful.

Power to Her Majesty to authorise Governor-General to appoint deputies

**126.** *The Queen may authorise the Governor-General to appoint any person, or any persons jointly or severally, to be his deputy or deputies within any part of the Commonwealth, and in that capacity to exercise during the*

---

1 Quick and Garran, 975-82.
2 *Seat of Government Acceptance Act,* No 23 of 1909; *Seat of Government (Administration) Act,* No 25 of 1910.
3 It would also seem in the light of *Tau v Commonwealth* (1970) 44 ALJR 25; [1971] ALR 190, that the acquisition of land held by private individuals would not be subject to the requirements of just terms.

*pleasure of the Governor-General such powers and functions of the Governor-General as he thinks fit to assign to such deputy or deputies, subject to any limitations expressed or directions given by the Queen; but the appointment of such deputy or deputies shall not affect the exercise by the Governor-General himself of any power or function.*[4]

This section allows deputies within various parts of the Commonwealth to be appointed, i e, it is possible for the Governor-General to appoint deputies within each State. This power must be distinguished from the power to appoint an administrator or acting Governor-General during the Governor-General's incapacity or absence from the Commonwealth. It merely allows the delegation of functions to deputies within parts of the Commonwealth while the Governor-General continues in full exercise of his powers. Up until the present time no appointment has been made of deputies and the Governor-General (or an administrator during his absence or incapacity) has exercised his functions throughout the Commonwealth.

**127.** [Repealed by Act No 55, 1967, s 3.]

---

4   Quick and Garran, 983.

# CHAPTER VIII

## ALTERATION OF THE CONSTITUTION

MODE OF ALTERING THE CONSTITUTION

**128.** *This Constitution shall not be altered except in the following manner:*

*The proposed law for the alteration thereof must be passed by an absolute majority of each House of the Parliament, and not less than two nor more than six months after its passage through both Houses the proposed law shall be submitted in each State to the electors qualified to vote for the election of members of the House of Representatives.*

*But if either House passes any such proposed law by an absolute majority, and the other House rejects or fails to pass it, or passes it with any amendment to which the first-mentioned House will not agree, and if after an interval of three months the first-mentioned House in the same or the next session again passes the proposed law by an absolute majority with or without any amendment which has been made or agreed to by the other House, and such other House rejects or fails to pass it or passes it with any amendment to which the first-mentioned House will not agree, the Governor-General may submit the proposed law as last proposed by the first-mentioned House, and either with or without any amendments subsequently agreed to by both Houses, to the electors in each State qualified to vote for the election of the House of Representatives.*

*When a proposed law is submitted to the electors the vote shall be taken in such manner as the Parliament prescribes. But until the qualification of electors of members of the House of Representatives becomes uniform throughout the Commonwealth, only one-half the electors voting for and against the proposed law shall be counted in any State in which adult suffrage prevails.*

*And if in a majority of the States a majority of the electors voting approve the proposed law, and if a majority of all the electors voting also approve the proposed law, it shall be presented to the Governor-General for the Queen's assent.*

*No alteration diminishing the proportionate representation of any State in either House of the Parliament, or the minimum number of representatives of a State in the House of Representatives, or increasing, diminishing, or otherwise altering the limits of the State, or in any manner affecting the provisions of the Constitution in relation thereto, shall become law unless the majority of the electors voting in that State approved the proposed law.*[1]

Any alteration which affects in any way, whether it be verbally or substantially, any part of the Constitution[2] must be subjected to the constitutional alteration procedure prescribed by s 128.[3] Constitutional amendments are

---

1  Quick and Garran, 985-95. Wynes, 504-7. Nicholas, 387-91. Howard, 505-12.
2  The power would extend, subject to the possible qualifications noted below, to alteration of the covering clauses.
3  The following literature on s 128 should be referred to: Latham, "Changing the Constitution", 1 Sydney Law Review, 14. Evatt, "Amending the Constitution", 1 Res Judicatae, 264. Canaway, "The Safety Valve of the Constitution",

*continues*

357

therefore initiated in the Parliament. Ordinarily, the Bill will be passed by both Houses and within the time prescribed (not less than two nor more than six months after passage) will be submitted to the electorate. It is provided however, that if one House amends, rejects or fails to pass a proposed law which the other House has passed and if, after an interval of three months, the first-mentioned House again passes the proposed law with a similar reaction from the other House, i e, if a state of deadlock exists, then the Governor-General may submit the proposed law to the electors (qualified to vote for House of Representatives elections).[4]

The question arises as to whether the Governor-General would in all cases act on the advice of the Cabinet in making a decision whether to submit the proposed law to the electorate. In 1914 the Senate had passed a number of constitutional alteration Bills twice. They were not passed by the House of Representatives on the first occasion but had only been before the House for a short period on the second occasion. There had been no "rejection" or "amendment" of these Bills and the only question therefore was whether there had been a failure to pass the Bills under s 128. The Senate requested the Governor-General that the Bills be submitted to the electorate. Acting on the advice of the Cabinet, he rejected this request.[5]

It would seem clear that there had been no "failure to pass" by the House of Representatives and that therefore the condition precedent for the holding of a referendum had not been fulfilled. Nevertheless the precedent has been interpreted by some as suggesting that passage through the Senate alone would not be sufficient to oblige the Governor-General to submit the proposed law to a referendum if the Cabinet advice was to the contrary.[6]

The absolute majority required for the passage of the proposed law in the Houses would be at the last stage of its progress through the House. This would usually be the third reading stage.[7]

A majority vote is required for approval in four out of the six States, in addition to an overall majority of the electors throughout the Commonwealth (not including the Territories). However, in cases where the proportionate representation of any State in either House of the Parliament is diminished (ss 7, 24) or the minimum number of representatives of a State in the House of Representatives is diminished (s 24) or the limits of a State are affected (s 123), a majority of electors must cast their vote in favour of the proposed law in the State or States affected by the proposed amendments.[8] Thus where it would be a case of a legislative proposal which affected the basic structure of representation throughout Australia, then a favourable vote in all six States would be necessary before the Bill became law. It would appear that the amendment of s 128 itself is a matter which would require the approval of a majority of the electors in all the States.[9]

---

3   *continued*
     (1938) 12 ALJ 108, "The By-Pass to Constitutional Reform", (1940) 13 ALJ 394, "The Evolution of s 128", (1940) 14 ALJ 274. Sawer, "Some Legal Assumptions of Constitutional Changes" (1957) 4 West Aust Ann Law Review, 1.
4   The method of voting is provided for in the *Referendum (Constitutional Alteration) Act* 1906-1966.
5   See Sawer, *Australian Federal Politics and Law 1901-1929*, 124-125.
6   Evatt, op cit, n 3 at 264.
7   See Sawer, *Australian Federal Politics and Law 1901-1929*, 54.
8   The abolition of the Senate would also be caught by the requirement of all-States approval.
9   See Latham, op cit, n 3 at 19.

Because of the rigidity of the amendment requirements, only a small number of amendments have been accepted by the electorate, the most important being the social services and financial agreement referenda.[10] Where a matter is affected by party politics, especially on questions involving the widening of the legislative powers of the Commonwealth, the electorate has been disinclined to give its assent to the proposed amendments.[11]

It finally remains to consider the question whether there are any limits on the power of amendment. In this connection, it is necessary to refer to the phrase "indissoluble federal Commonwealth" which appears in the preamble. Does this phrase, taken in conjunction with the title, the covering clauses of the *Constitution Act,* and various sections of the Constitution itself, amount to a declaration that the federal principle can never be abolished by conversion of the Constitution to a unitary form or by the deletion of one of its component units?

Sawer has expressed the opinion that references to an "indissoluble federal Commonwealth" are merely historical and do not impose restrictions on the subsequent power of amendment.[12] The question is basically a jurisprudential one: whether the federal principle as expressed in the Preamble and the Covering Clauses as well as the Constitution itself is a *grundnorm* of the Constitution prevailing over any attempts at amendment, even those which comply with the amendment process prescribed by s 128. The answer to it depends, to some extent, on a conception of a hierarchy of norms including s 128 which are interrelated in terms of criteria of greater or lesser status. In conceptual terms there is no doubt that a revised Constitution which abolished the distribution of power between the Commonwealth and the States would be quite a different Constitution, but if one views s 128 as a paramount provision allowing the Constitution to be so radically changed, then such a revision would be regarded as valid.[13] On the other hand, if one sees s 128 as occupying a status subordinate to the federal structure derived from the preamble, covering clauses and the Constitution itself, then the conversion of the federal system into a unitary one would not be regarded as valid.[14]

---

10  *Constitutional Alteration (Social Services) Act* 1946 (adding new paragraph (xxiiiA) to s 51). *Constitutional Alteration (State Debts) Act* 1928 (adding new s 105A). The other successful referenda were the *Constitutional Alteration (Senate Elections) Bill* 1906 (to amend s 13 of the Constitution to enable Senators to take office on the 1st July following an election); the *Constitutional Alteration (State Debts) Bill* 1909 (amending s 105); the *Constitutional Alteration (Aboriginals) Bill* 1967 (altering s 51 (xxvi) to omit certain words relating to the aboriginal race, and repealing s 127).

11  This was the fate, inter alia, of the *Constitutional Alteration (Legislative Powers) Bill* of 1910, a series of Bills in 1913, the *Constitutional Alteration (Legislative Powers) Bill* of 1919, and the *Constitutional Alteration (Post-War Reconstruction and Democratic Rights) Bill* of 1944. The most recent proposed alterations which failed were the *Constitutional Alteration (Powers to deal with Communists and Communism) Bill* 1951, and the *Constitutional Alteration (Parliament) Bill* 1967 (designed to break the "nexus" between the House of Representatives and Senate prescribed by s 24).

12  *Australia: The British Commonwealth—The Development of its Laws and Constitution* (ed Paton), 46. Cf, Marshall, *Parliamentary Sovereignty and the Commonwealth,* 115.

13  This is the view of Latham, op cit, n 3 at 18; Canaway, "The Safety Valve of the Constitution", op cit, n 3 at 109.

14  See the discussion in Wynes, at 504-10.

Although the preamble to the Constitution refers to an indissoluble federal Commonwealth "under the Crown of the United Kingdom of Great Britain and Ireland", it is tenable that the conversion of the Commonwealth from a monarchial to a republican system of government would be valid under s 128.[15]

As to secession of one or more States from the federation, the petition of Western Australia to secede from the Commonwealth in 1933 was studied by British law officers who took the view that to enact secession legislation was within the power of the Imperial Parliament alone, but that such legislation would not, in accordance with constitutional convention, be enacted without the request and consent of the Dominion concerned. They also pointed out that, on the adoption of the Statute of Westminster, it would be necessary for the Imperial Parliament to obtain the concurrence of the Commonwealth Parliament.[16] However, as Marshall points out,[17] the request and consent of the Commonwealth of Australia must be expressed in terms of the structure established by the Constitution and s 128 sets out the requisite manner and form for such an amendment. Therefore, for all practical purposes today, there is no other alternative method of amending the Constitution other than that provided in the Constitution itself. This brings us back to the question whether an "indigenous" amendment permitting secession of one or more of the original States is permissible. The same considerations outlined above in relation to the abolition of the federal structure would also be applicable in this context.

---

15   See, however, Canaway, "The Evolution of Section 128", op cit, n 3, at 277.
16   See O'Connell and Riordan, *Opinions on Imperial Constitutional Law* (1971), 416.
17   *Parliamentary Sovereignty and the Commonwealth*, 116.

# RECENT ACTS AND BILLS

### *Pipeline Authority Act 1973

This Act establishes a Commonwealth Pipeline Authority to "(a) construct pipelines for the conveyance of petroleum recovered from Australian petroleum pools to centres of population and points of export with a view to the establishment of a national integrated system of such pinelines, and to maintain and operate those piplines; (b) to convey, through the pipes operated by the Authority, petroleum belonging to the Authority or other persons; and (c) to buy and sell petroleum, whether in Australia or elsewhere" (s 13 (1)).

It is interesting to note that s 31 (2) refers to a number of legislative powers of the Commonwealth on which the validity of the Act might depend. They comprise (a) the corporations power (s 51 (xx)), the Territories power (s 122) the trade and commerce power (s 51 (i)), the defence power (s 51 (vi)), and the incidental power (s 51 (xxxix)).

### Commonwealth Electoral Bill (No. 2) 1973

Under this Bill the quota variation is reduced from 20 per cent to 10 per cent. (See discussion under s 24 of the Constitution.)

It is also provided that the following matters shall be taken account of by Distribution Commissioners in making a distribution of a State into divisions:

(a) Community of interests within the division, including economic, social and regional interests;

(b) means of communication and travel within the division;

(c) the trend of population changes within the State;

(d) the physical features of the division; and

(e) existing boundaries of divisions and subdivisions.

At the time of writing the Bill has been passed by the House of Representatives but rejected by the Senate.

### Australian Citizenship Bill 1973

This Bill proposes certain amendments to the *Citizenship Act* 1948-1969. (See discussion under s 51 (xix) of the Constitution.)

The most significant changes are that the procedures whereby a citizen of a Commonwealth country can become an Australian citizen by registration or notification have been abolished.

A certificate of citizenship may be granted where a number of conditions are satisfied, including a period of residence, amounting in all to 3 years, with a continuous period of one year prior to the grant of a certificate. (However, there is provision for citizens of Commonwealth countries to be granted a certificate after one year of residence under certain conditions.)

A new oath of allegiance is provided for in the 2nd Schedule: "I swear by Almighty God that I will faithfully uphold the Constitution of Australia and observe the laws of Australia."

---

* No 4, date of assent 7 June 1973, date of commencement 15 June 1973.

The Bill has been passed by the House of Representatives but amended by the Senate to restore the oath of allegiance to Queen Elizabeth as Queen of Australia. The Bill as amended by the Senate has now been passed by the House of Representatives.

### Conciliation and Arbitration Bill 1973

Under this Bill major changes have been proposed to the *Conciliation and Arbitration Act*. (See discussion under s 51 (xxxv) of the Constitution.) Among the changes are the following:

1. The designation of Commissioners as Conciliation or Arbitration Commissioners has been abolished: henceforth they will be known simply as Commissioners (s 6).

2. The powers of the Commission, except as provided for in the Act, may be exercised by a single member of the Commission (whether presidential member or commissioner). Where a member of the Commission has exercised the powers of the Commission with respect to the conciliation in relation to an industrial dispute, he cannot take part in arbitration proceedings in that dispute if a party to the dispute objects (s 22).

3. Arbitration proceedings may be commenced only after conciliation proceedings in relation to a dispute have been completed (s 30).

4. Bans clauses forbidding strikers may no longer be inserted in awards (s 46A).

5. The penal powers of the Court are consequentially amended (s 119) and the offence of inciting a "boycott" of an award is abolished (s 138).

6. Members and officers of an organisation are given immunity from actions in tort arising under State law for inducing breach of contract (s 146A).

7. The power of the Court to cancel the registration of a union for a course of conduct amounting to a continued breach of an award is abolished (s 143).

At the time of writing the Bill has been passed by the House of Representatives but rejected by the Senate. A new Bill omitting some of the provisions has since been passed by the House of Representatives.

### Seas and Submerged Lands Bill

This Bill, introduced in the Federal Parliament in 1973, declares Commonwealth sovereignty over the territorial sea (including the sea-bed and superjacent airspace) and the continental shelf. Provision is made for the Governor-General to determine the baselines from which the territorial sea is to be measured as well as its breadth. The Bill also contains a mining code to be applied to the mining of minerals other than petroleum (which is regulated by the *Petroleum (Submerged Lands) Acts*).

The Bill would seem to be designed to put to the test the opinions of Barwick CJ and Windeyer J expressed in *Bonser* v *La Macchia* (see discussion under s 51 (x)) and also the opinions of Evatt and McTiernan JJ on the scope of the external affairs expressed in *Burgess' Case* (see discussion under s 51 (xxix)).

It was passed by the House of Representatives in May but delayed by the Senate in order to give the State Premiers the opportunity of petitioning the Judicial Committee for an advisory opinion (under the *Judicial Committee Act 1833*, s 3) on the nature of State power over the territorial sea.

### Privy Council Appeals Abolition Bill

This Bill which has been introduced into, but at the time of writing not considered by, the House of Representatives, is designed to abolish appeals from State Courts (in State jurisdiction) which now lie to the Judicial Committee under the Judicial Committee Acts of 1833 and 1844. Its structure is twofold. Clauses 4-6 provide for the abolition of such appeals by the power of the Commonwealth Parliament alone. In this respect the constitutional head of power on which such a power depends seems to be lacking. It is not to be found in Chapter III of the Constitution. It is arguable that the external affairs power (s 51 (xxix)) might provide the basis, although it would be extremely difficult to accept such a view. It would appear that the appeal from State Courts exercising State jurisdiction to the Judicial Committee is a matter affecting the States' constitutional structure and therefore is not an "external affair" under s 51 (xxix).

Section 2 of the *Statute of Westminster* which permits the Commonwealth Parliament to repeal United Kingdom legislation operating as part of the law of the Dominion does not take one any further, as this refers to legislation forming part of the law of the Commonwealth (as distinct from the constituent States).

Clause 8 of the Bill provides for an alternative method of abolition ie it is a "request and consent" provision (in the form set out in a Schedule) directed to the United Kingdom Parliament under s 4 of the *Statute of Westminster*. However, the power conferred by s 4 would not seem to encompass matters which fall within the areas of State power, and s 9 of the Statute gives recognition to this understanding.

All in all, it would seem that the available methods of abolishing appeals to the Judicial Committee from State Courts (in matters of State jurisdiction) are two in number—

(a) by amendment of the *Statute of Westminster* by the United Kingdom Parliament acting with the advice and consent of the Commonwealth and at least a majority of the States;

(b) by constitutional amendment under s 128.

**Privy Council (Appeals from the High Court) Bill 1973**

This Bill which, like the previous one, has at the time of writing not yet been considered by the House of Representatives, is designed to eliminate the residue of appeals available from the High Court to the Privy Council after the passage of the *Privy Council (Limitation of Appeals) Act* 1968. It would therefore apply to matters of common law or State legislation.

The Bill raises the question whether it can be characterised as a law "limiting the matters in which such leave [from the Judicial Committee] may be asked". (See discussion under the third paragraph of s 74.)

**\*Acts Interpretation Act 1973**

This Act is designed to provide for the use of the word "Australia" interchangeably with the word "Commonwealth" in references to the Federal Government and Federal acts and regulations. (It is to be noted, however, that it cannot, and in fact does not, provide for such substitution in relation to the official designations embodied in the Constitution itself.)

**Constitutional Convention**

The Convention (in which Commonwealth, State and local government representatives participated) was held between 3 and 7 September 1973.

---

\* No 79, date of assent 7 June 1973, date of commencement 7 June 1973 except s 17(M) which commenced 1 July 1973.

After discussion of agenda matters, which were arranged under thirteen separate heads, it was decided to establish four committees, each with a group of subjects to consider. These committees will report beack to a further meeting of the Convention in 1974.

**Referendum on prices and incomes**

Under the Constitutional Alteration (Prices) Bill and The Constitutional Alteration (Incomes) Bill, the questions of adding to the list of Commonwealth powers in s 51 powers over (a) prices and (b) incomes are to be presented to the electorate in December, 1973.

# COMMONWEALTH OF AUSTRALIA CONSTITUTION ACT

---

## (63 & 64 VICTORIA, CHAPTER 12)

## An Act to constitute the Commonwealth of Australia

[9th July 1900]

Whereas the people of New South Wales, Victoria, South Australia, Queensland, and Tasmania, humbly relying on the blessing of Almighty God, have agreed to unite in one indissoluble Federal Commonwealth under the Crown of the United Kingdom of Great Britain and Ireland, and under the Constitution hereby established:

And whereas it is expedient to provide for the admission into the Commonwealth of other Australasian Colonies and possessions of the Queen:

Be it therefore enacted by the Queen's most Excellent Majesty, by and with the advice and consent of the Lords Spiritual and Temporal, and Commons, in this present Parliament assembled, and by the authority of the same, as follows:—

**1. Short title.**—This Act may be cited as the Commonwealth of Australia Constitution Act.

**2. Act to extend to the Queen's successors.**—The provisions of this Act referring to the Queen shall extend to Her Majesty's heirs and successors in the sovereignty of the United Kingdom.

**3. Proclamation of Commonwealth.**—It shall be lawful for the Queen, with the advice of the Privy Council, to declare by proclamation that, on and after a day therein appointed, not being later than one year after the passing of this Act, the people of New South Wales, Victoria, South Australia, Queensland, and Tasmania, and also, if Her Majesty is satisfied that the people of Western Australia have agreed thereto, of Western Australia, shall be united in a Federal Commonwealth under the name of the Commonwealth of Australia. But the Queen may, at any time after the proclamation, appoint a Governor-General for the Commonwealth.

**4. Commencement of Act.**—The Commonwealth shall be established, and the Constitution of the Commonwealth shall take effect, on and after the day so appointed. But the Parliaments of the several colonies may at any time after the passing of this Act make any such laws, to come into operation on the day so appointed, as they might have made if the Constitution had taken effect at the passing of this Act.

**5. Operation of the constitution and laws.**—This Act, and all laws made by the Parliament of the Commonwealth under the Constitution, shall be binding on the courts, judges, and people of every State and of every part of the Commonwealth, notwithstanding anything in the laws of any State; and the laws of the Commonwealth shall be in force on all British ships, the Queen's ships of war excepted, whose first port of clearance and whose port of destination are in the Commonwealth.

**6. Definitions.**—"The Commonwealth" shall mean the Commonwealth of Australia as established under this Act.

"The States" shall mean such of the colonies of New South Wales, New Zealand, Queensland, Tasmania, Victoria, Western Australia, and South Australia, including the northern territory of South Australia, as for the time being are parts of the Commonwealth, and such colonies or territories as may be admitted into or established by the Commonwealth as States; and each of such parts of the Commonwealth shall be called "a State."

"Original States" shall mean such States as are parts of the Commonwealth at its establishment.

**7. Repeal of Federal Council Act.**—The Federal Council of Australasia Act, 1885, is hereby repealed, but so as not to affect any laws passed by the Federal Council of Australasia and in force at the establishment of the Commonwealth.

Any such law may be repealed as to any State by the Parliament of the Commonwealth, or as to any colony not being a State by the Parliament thereof.

[48 & 49 Vict. c. 60.]

**8. Application of Colonial Boundaries Act.**—After the passing of this Act the Colonial Boundaries Act, 1895, shall not apply to any colony which becomes a State of the Commonwealth; but the Commonwealth shall be taken to be a self-governing colony for the purposes of that Act.

[58 & 59 Vict. c. 34.]

**9. Constitution.**—The Constitution of the Commonwealth shall be as follows:—

---

## THE CONSTITUTION.

This Constitution is divided as follows:—

# CHAPTER I.

## The Parliament.

### Part I.—General.

**1. Legislative power.**—The legislative power of the Commonwealth shall be vested in a Federal Parliament, which shall consist of the Queen, a Senate, and a House of Representatives, and which is herein-after called "The Parliament," or "The Parliament of the Commonwealth."

**2. Governor-General.**—A Governor-General appointed by the Queen shall be Her Majesty's representative in the Commonwealth, and shall have and may exercise in the Commonwealth during the Queen's pleasure, but subject to this Constitution, such powers and functions of the Queen as Her Majesty may be pleased to assign to him.

**3. Salary of Governor-General.**—There shall be payable to the Queen out of the Consolidated Revenue fund of the Commonwealth, for the salary of the Governor-General, an annual sum which, until the Parliament otherwise provides, shall be ten thousand pounds.

The salary of a Governor-General shall not be altered during his continuance in office.

**4. Provisions relating to Governor-General.**—The provisions of this Constitution relating to the Governor-General extend and apply to the Governor-General for the time being, or such person as the Queen may appoint to administer the Government of the Commonwealth; but no such person shall be entitled to receive any salary from the Commonwealth in respect of any other office during his administration of the Government of the Commonwealth.

**5. Sessions of Parliament, Prorogation and dissolution.**—The Governor-General may appoint such times for holding the sessions of the Parliament as he thinks fit, and may also from time to time, by Proclamation or otherwise, prorogue the Parliament, and may in like manner dissolve the House of Representatives.

**Summoning Parliament.**—After any general election the Parliament shall be summoned to meet not later than thirty days after the day appointed for the return of the writs.

**First session.**—The Parliament shall be summoned to meet not later than six months after the establishment of the Commonwealth.

**6. Yearly session of Parliament.**—There shall be a session of the Parliament once at least in every year, so that twelve months shall not intervene between the last sitting of the Parliament in one session and its first sitting in the next session.

### Part II.—The Senate.

**7. The Senate.**—The Senate shall be composed of senators for each State, directly chosen by the people of the State, voting, until the Parliament otherwise provides, as one electorate.

But until the Parliament of the Commonwealth otherwise provides, the Parliament of the State of Queensland, if that State be an Original State, may make laws dividing the State into divisions and determining the number of senators to be chosen for each division, and in the absence of such provision the State shall be one electorate.

Until the Parliament otherwise provides there shall be six senators for each Original State. The Parliament may make laws increasing or diminishing the number of senators for each State, but so that equal representation of the several Original States shall be maintained and that no Original State shall have less than six senators.

The senators shall be chosen for a term of six years, and the names of the senators chosen for each State shall be certified by the Governor to the Governor-General.

**8. Qualification of electors.**—The qualification of electors of senators shall be in each State that which is prescribed by this Constitution, or by the Parliament, as the qualification for electors of members of the House of Representatives; but in the choosing of senators each elector shall vote only once.

**9. Method of election of senators.**—The Parliament of the Commonwealth may make laws prescribing the method of choosing senators, but so that the method shall be uniform for all the States. Subject to any such law, the Parliament of each State may make laws prescribing the method of choosing the senators for that State.

**Times and places.**—The Parliament of a State may make laws for determining the times and places of elections of senators for the State.

**10. Application of State laws.**—Until the Parliament otherwise provides, but subject to this Constitution, the laws in force in each State, for the time being, relating to elections for the more numerous House of the Parliament of the State shall, as nearly as practicable, apply to elections of senators for the State.

**11. Failure to choose senators.**—The Senate may proceed to the despatch of business, notwithstanding the failure of any State to provide for its representation in the Senate.

**12. Issue of writs.**—The Governor of any State may cause writs to be issued for elections of senators for the State. In case of the dissolution of the Senate the writs shall be issued within ten days from the proclamation of such dissolution.

**13. Rotation of senators.**—As soon as may be after the Senate first meets, and after each first meeting of the Senate following a dissolution thereof, the Senate shall divide the senators chosen for each State into two classes, as nearly equal in number as practicable; and the places of the senators of the first class shall become vacant at the expiration of three years, and the places of those of the second class at the expiration of six years, from the beginning of their term of service; and afterwards the places of senators shall become vacant at the expiration of six years from the beginning of their term of service.

The election to fill vacant places shall be made within one year before the places are to become vacant.

For the purposes of this section the term of service of a senator shall be taken to begin on the first day of July following the day of his election, except in the cases of the first election and of the election next after any dissolution of the Senate, when it shall be taken to begin on the first day of July preceding the day of his election.

[S 13 *altered, Act No. 1, 1907 s 2.*]

**14. Further provision for rotation.**—Whenever the number of senators for a State is increased or diminished, the Parliament of the Commonwealth may

368

make such provision for the vacating of the places of senators for the State as it deems necessary to maintain regularity in the rotation.

**15. Casual vacancies.**—If the place of a senator becomes vacant before the expiration of his term of service, the Houses of Parliament of the State for which he was chosen shall, sitting and voting together, choose a person to hold the place until the expiration of the term, or until the election of a successor as herein-after provided, whichever first happens. But if the Houses of Parliament of the State are not in session at the time when the vacancy is notified, the Governor of the State, with the advice of the Executive Council thereof, may appoint a person to hold the place until the expiration of fourteen days after the beginning of the next session of the Parliament of the State, or until the election of a successor, whichever first happens.

At the next general election of members of the House of Representatives, or at the next election of senators for the State, whichever first happens, a successor shall, if the term has not then expired, be chosen to hold the place from the date of his election until the expiration of the term.

The name of any senator so chosen or appointed shall be certified by the Governor of the State to the Governor-General.

**16. Qualifications of senator.**—The qualifications of a senator shall be the same as those of a member of the House of Representatives.

**17. Election of President.**—The Senate shall, before proceeding to the despatch of any other business, choose a senator to be the President of the Senate; and as often as the office of President becomes vacant the Senate shall again choose a senator to be the President.

The President shall cease to hold his office if he ceases to be a senator. He may be removed from office by a vote of the Senate, or he may resign his office or his seat by writing addressed to the Governor-General.

**18. Absence of President.**—Before or during any absence of the President, the Senate may choose a senator to perform his duties in his absence.

**19. Resignation of senator.**—A senator may, by writing addressed to the President, or to the Governor-General if there is no President or if the President is absent from the Commonwealth, resign his place, which thereupon shall become vacant.

**20. Vacancy by absence.**—The place of a senator shall become vacant if for two consecutive months of any session of the Parliament he, without the permission of the Senate, fails to attend the Senate.

**21. Vacancy to be notified.**—Whenever a vacancy happens in the Senate, the President, or if there is no President or if the President is absent from the Commonwealth the Governor-General, shall notify the same to the Governor of the State in the representation of which the vacancy has happened.

**22. Quorum.**—Until the Parliament otherwise provides, the presence of at least one-third of the whole number of the senators shall be necessary to constitute a meeting of the Senate for the exercise of its powers.

**23. Voting in Senate.**—Questions arising in the Senate shall be determined by a majority of votes, and each senator shall have one vote. The President shall in all cases be entitled to a vote; and when the votes are equal the question shall pass in the negative.

PART III.—THE HOUSE OF REPRESENTATIVES.

**24. Constitution of House of Representatives.**—The House of Representatives shall be composed of members directly chosen by the people of the Commonwealth, and the number of such members shall be, as nearly as practicable, twice the number of the senators.

The number of members chosen in the several States shall be in proportion to the respective numbers of their people, and shall, until the Parliament otherwise provides, be determined, whenever necessary, in the following manner:—

(i) A quota shall be ascertained by dividing the number of the people of the Commonwealth, as shown by the latest statistics of the Commonwealth, by twice the number of the senators:

(ii) The number of members to be chosen in each State shall be determined by dividing the number of the people of the State, as shown by the latest statistics of the Commonwealth, by the quota; and if on such division there is a remainder greater than one-half of the quota, one more member shall be chosen in the State.

But notwithstanding anything in this section, five members at least shall be chosen in each Original State.

**25. Provision as to races disqualified from voting.**—For the purposes of the last section, if by the law of any State all persons of any race are disqualified from voting at elections for the more numerous House of the Parliament of the State, then, in reckoning the number of the people of the State or of the Commonwealth, persons of that race resident in that State shall not be counted.

**26. Representatives in first Parliament.**—Notwithstanding anything in section twenty-four, the number of members to be chosen in each State at the first election shall be as follows:—

| | | | | | |
|---|---|---|---|---|---|
| New South Wales | .. | .. | .. | .. | twenty-three; |
| Victoria | .. | .. | .. | .. | twenty; |
| Queensland | .. | .. | .. | .. | eight; |
| South Australia | .. | .. | .. | .. | six; |
| Tasmania | .. | .. | .. | .. | five; |

Provided that if Western Australia is an Original State, the numbers shall be as follows:—

| | | | | | |
|---|---|---|---|---|---|
| New South Wales | .. | .. | .. | .. | twenty-six; |
| Victoria | .. | .. | .. | .. | twenty-three; |
| Queensland | .. | .. | .. | .. | nine; |
| South Australia | .. | .. | .. | .. | seven; |
| Western Australia | .. | .. | .. | .. | five; |
| Tasmania | .. | .. | .. | .. | five. |

**27. Alteration of number of members.**—Subject to this Constitution, the Parliament may make laws for increasing or diminishing the number of the members of the House of Representatives.

**28. Duration of House of Representatives.**—Every House of Representatives shall continue for three years from the first meeting of the House, and no longer, but may be sooner dissolved by the Governor-General.

**29. Electoral divisions.**—Until the Parliament of the Commonwealth otherwise provides, the Parliament of any State may make laws for determining the divisions in each State for which members of the House of Representatives may be chosen, and the number of members to be chosen for each division. A division shall not be formed out of parts of different States.

In the absence of other provision, each State shall be one electorate.

**30. Qualification of electors.**—Until the Parliament otherwise provides, the qualification of electors of members of the House of Representatives shall be in each State that which is prescribed by the law of the State as the qualification of electors of the more numerous House of Parliament of the State; but in the choosing of members each elector shall vote only once.

**31. Application of State laws.**—Until the Parliament otherwise provides, but subject to this Constitution, the laws in force in each State for the time being relating to elections for the more numerous House of the Parliament of the State shall, as nearly as practicable, apply to elections in the State of members of the House of Representatives.

**32. Writs for general election.**—The Governor-General in Council may cause writs to be issued for general elections of members of the House of Representatives.

After the first general election, the writs shall be issued within ten days from the expiry of a House of Representatives or from the proclamation of a dissolution thereof.

**33. Writs for vacancies.**—Whenever a vacancy happens in the House of Representatives, the Speaker shall issue his writ for the election of a new member, or if there is no Speaker or if he is absent from the Commonwealth the Governor-General in Council may issue the writ.

**34. Qualifications of members.**—Until the Parliament otherwise provides, the qualifications of a member of the House of Representatives shall be as follows:—

(i) He must be of the full age of twenty-one years, and must be an elector entitled to vote at the election of members of the House of Representatives, or a person qualified to become such elector, and must have been for three years at the least a resident within the limits of the Commonwealth as existing at the time when he is chosen:

(ii) He must be a subject of the Queen, either natural-born or for at least five years naturalized under a law of the United Kingdom, or of a Colony which has become or becomes a State, or of the Commonwealth, or of a State.

**35. Election of Speaker.**—The House of Representatives shall, before proceeding to the despatch of any other business, choose a member to be the Speaker of the House, and as often as the office of Speaker becomes vacant the House shall again choose a member to be the Speaker.

The Speaker shall cease to hold his office is he ceases to be a member. He may be removed from office by a vote of the House, or he may resign his office or his seat by writing addressed to the Governor-General.

**36. Absence of Speaker.**—Before or during any absence of the Speaker, the House of Representatives may choose a member to perform his duties in his absence.

**37. Resignation of member.**—A member may by writing addressed to the Speaker, or to the Governor-General if there is no Speaker or if the Speaker is absent from the Commonwealth, resign his place, which thereupon shall become vacant.

**38. Vacancy by absence.**—The place of a member shall become vacant if for two consecutive months of any session of the Parliament he, without the permission of the House, fails to attend the House.

**39. Quorum.**—Until the Parliament otherwise provides, the presence of at least one-third of the whole number of the members of the House of Representatives shall be necessary to constitute a meeting of the House for the exercise of its powers.

**40. Voting in House of Representatives.**—Questions arising in the House of Representatives shall be determined by a majority of votes other than that of the Speaker. The Speaker shall not vote unless the numbers are equal, and then he shall have a casting vote.

## PART IV.—BOTH HOUSES OF THE PARLIAMENT.

**41. Right of electors of States.**—No adult person who has or acquires a right to vote at elections for the more numerous House of the Parliament of a State shall, while the right continues, be prevented by any law of the Commonwealth from voting at elections for either House of the Parliament of the Commonwealth.

**42. Oath or affirmation of allegiance.**—Every senator and every member of the House of Representatives shall before taking his seat make and subscribe before the Governor-General, or some person authorised by him, an oath or affirmation of allegiance in the form set forth in the schedule to this Constitution.

**43. Member of one House ineligible for other.**—A member of either House of the Parliament shall be incapable of being chosen or of sitting as a member of the other House.

**44. Disqualification.**—Any person who—

(i) Is under any acknowledgment of allegiance, obedience, or adherence to a foreign power, or is a subject or a citizen or entitled to the rights or privileges of a subject or a citizen of a foreign power: or

(ii) Is attainted of treason, or has been convicted and is under sentence, or subject to be sentenced, for any offence punishable under the law of the Commonwealth or of a State by imprisonment for one year or longer: or

(iii) Is an undischarged bankrupt or insolvent: or

(iv) Holds any office of profit under the Crown, or any pension payable during the pleasure of the Crown out of any of the revenues of the Commonwealth: or

(v) Has any direct or indirect pecuniary interest in any agreement with the Public Service of the Commonwealth otherwise than as a member and in common with the other members of an incorporated company consisting of more than twenty-five persons:

shall be incapable of being chosen or of sitting as a senator or a member of the House of Representatives.

But sub-section iv does not apply to the office of any of the Queen's Ministers of State for the Commonwealth, or of any of the Queen's Ministers for a State, or to the receipt of pay, half pay, or a pension, by any person as an officer or member of the Queen's navy or army, or to the receipt of pay as an officer or member of the naval or military forces of the Commonwealth by any person whose services are not wholly employed by the Commonwealth.

**45. Vacancy on happening of disqualification.**—If a senator or member of the House of Representatives—

(i) Becomes subject to any of the disabilities mentioned in the last preceding section: or
(ii) Takes the benefit, whether by assignment, composition, or otherwise, of any law relating to bankrupt or insolvent debtors: or
(iii) Directly or indirectly takes or agrees to take any fee or honorarium for services rendered to the Commonwealth, or for services rendered in the Parliament to any person or State:

his place shall thereupon become vacant.

**46. Penalty for sitting when disqualified.**—Until the Parliament otherwise provides, any person declared by this Constitution to be incapable of sitting as a senator or as a member of the House of Representatives shall, for every day on which he so sits, be liable to pay the sum of one hundred pounds to any person who sues for it in any court of competent jurisdiction.

**47. Disputed elections.**—Until the Parliament otherwise provides, any question respecting the qualification of a senator or of a member of the House of Representatives, or respecting a vacancy in either House of the Parliament, and any question of a disputed election to either House, shall be determined by the House in which the question arises.

**48. Allowance members.**—Until the Parliament otherwise provides, each senator and each member of the House of Representatives shall receive an allowance of four hundred pounds a year, to be reckoned from the day on which he takes his seat.

**49. Privileges, etc., of Houses.**—The powers, privileges, and immunities of the Senate and of the House of Representatives, and of the members and the committees of each House, shall be such as are declared by the Parliament, and until declared shall be those of the Commons House of Parliament of the United Kingdom, and of its members and committees, at the establishment of the Commonwealth.

**50. Rules and orders.**—Each House of the Parliament may make rules and orders with respect to—

(i) The mode in which its powers, privileges, and immunities may be exercised and upheld:
(ii) The order and conduct of its business and proceedings either separately or jointly with the other House.

## PART V.—POWERS OF THE PARLIAMENT.

**51. Legislative powers of the Parliament.**—The Parliament shall, subject to this Constitution, have power to make laws for the peace, order, and good government of the Commonwealth with respect to:—

(i) Trade and commerce with other countries, and among the States:
(ii) Taxation; but so as not to discriminate between States or parts of States:
(iii) Bounties on the production or export of goods, but so that such bounties shall be uniform throughout the Commonwealth:
(iv) Borrowing money on the public credit of the Commonwealth:

(v) Postal, telegraphic, telephonic, and other like services:

(vi) The naval and military defence of the Commonwealth and of the several States, and the control of the forces to execute and maintain the laws of the Commonwealth:

(vii) Lighthouses, lightships, beacons and buoys:

(viii) Astronomical and meteorological observations:

(ix) Quarantine:

(x) Fisheries in Australian waters beyond territorial limits:

(xi) Census and statistics:

(xii) Currency, coinage, and legal tender:

(xiii) Banking, other than State banking; also State banking extending beyond the limits of the State concerned, the incorporation of banks, and the issue of paper money:

(xiv) Insurance, other than State insurance; also State insurance extending beyond the limits of the State concerned:

(xv) Weights and measures:

(xvi) Bills of exchange and promissory notes:

(xvii) Bankruptcy and insolvency:

(xviii) Copyrights, patents of inventions and designs, and trade marks:

(xix) Naturalization and aliens:

(xx) Foreign corporations, and trading or financial corporations formed within the limits of the Commonwealth:

(xxi) Marriage:

(xxii) Divorce and matrimonial causes; and in relation thereto, parental rights, and the custody and guardianship of infants:

(xxiii) Invalid and old-age pensions:

(xxiiiA) The provision of maternity allowances, widows' pensions, child endowment, unemployment, pharmaceutical, sickness and hospital benefits, medical and dental services (but not so as to authorize any form of civil conscription), benefits to students and family allowances:

[*Placitum* (xxiiiA) *inserted, Act No* 81, 1946 *s* 2.]

(xxiv) The service and execution throughout the Commonwealth of the civil and criminal process and the judgments of the courts of the States:

(xxv) The recognition throughout the Commonwealth of the laws, the public Acts and records, and the judicial proceedings of the States:

(xxvi) The people of any race for whom it is deemed necessary to make special laws:

[*Placitum* (xxvi) *altered, Act No.* 55, 1967 *s* 2.]

(xxvii) Immigration and emigration:

(xxviii) The influx of criminals:

(xxix) External affairs:

(xxx) The relations of the Commonwealth with the islands of the Pacific:

(xxxi) The acquisition of property on just terms from any State or person for any purpose in respect of which the Parliament has power to make laws:

(xxxii) The control of railways with respect to transport for the naval and military purposes of the Commonwealth:

(xxxiii) The acquisition, with the consent of a State, of any railways of the State on terms arranged between the Commonwealth and the State:

(xxxiv) Railway construction and extension in any State with the consent of that State:

(xxxv) Conciliation and arbitration for the prevention and settlement of industrial disputes extending beyond the limits of any one State:

(xxxvi) Matters in respect of which this Constitution makes provision until the Parliament otherwise provides:

(xxxvii) Matters referred to the Parliament of the Commonwealth by the Parliament or Parliaments of any State or States, but so that the law shall extend only to States by whose Parliaments the matter is referred, or which afterwards adopt the law:

(xxxviii) The exercise within the Commonwealth, at the request or with the concurrence of the Parliaments of all the States directly concerned, of any power which can at the establishment of this Constitution be exercised only by the Parliament of the United Kingdom or by the Federal Council of Australasia:

(xxxix) Matters incidental to the execution of any power vested by this Constitution in the Parliament or in either House thereof, or in the Government of the Commonwealth, or in the Federal Judicature, or in any department or officer of the Commonwealth.

**52. Exclusive powers of the Parliament.**—The Parliament shall, subject to this Constitution, have exclusive power to make laws for the peace, order, and good government of the Commonwealth with respect to—

(i) The seat of government of the Commonwealth, and all places acquired by the Commonwealth for public purposes:

(ii) Matters relating to any department of the public service the control of which is by this Constitution transferred to the Executive Government of the Commonwealth:

(iii) Other matters declared by this Constitution to be within the exclusive power of the Parliament.

**53. Powers of the Houses in respect of legislation.**—Proposed laws appropriating revenue or moneys, or imposing taxation, shall not originate in the Senate. But a proposed law shall not be taken to appropriate revenue or moneys, or to impose taxation, by reason only of its containing provisions for the imposition or appropriation of fines or other pecuniary penalties, or for the demand or payment or appropriation of fees for licences, or fees for services under the proposed law.

The Senate may not amend proposed laws imposing taxation, or proposed laws appropriating revenue or moneys for the ordinary annual services of the Government.

The Senate may not amend any proposed law so as to increase any proposed charge or burden on the people.

The Senate may at any stage return to the House of Representatives any proposed law which the Senate may not amend, requesting, by message, the omission or amendment of any items or provisions therein. And the House of Representatives may, if it thinks fit, make any of such omissions or amendments, with or without modifications.

Except as provided in this section, the Senate shall have equal power with the House of Representatives in respect of all proposed laws.

**54. Appropriation Bills.**—The proposed law which appropriates revenue or moneys for the ordinary annual services of the Government shall deal only with such appropriation.

**55. Tax Bill.**—Laws imposing taxation shall deal only with the imposition of taxation, and any provision therein dealing with any other matter shall be of no effect.

Laws imposing taxation, except laws imposing duties of customs or of excise, shall deal with one subject of taxation only; but laws imposing duties of customs shall deal with duties of customs only, and laws imposing duties of excise shall deal with duties of excise only.

**56. Recommendation of money votes.**—A vote, resolution, or proposed law for the appropriation of revenue or moneys shall not be passed unless the purpose of the appropriation has in the same session been recommended by message of the Governor-General to the House in which the proposal originated.

**57. Disagreement between the Houses.**—If the House of Representatives passes any proposed law, and the Senate rejects or fails to pass it, or passes it with amendments to which the House of Representatives will not agree, and if after an interval of three months the House of Representatives, in the same or the next session, again passes the proposed law with or without any amendments which have been made, suggested, or agreed to by the Senate, and the Senate rejects or fails to pass it, or passes it with amendments to which the House of Representatives will not agree, the Governor-General may dissolve the Senate and the House of Representatives simultaneously. But such dissolution shall not take place within six months before the date of the expiry of the House of Representatives by effluxion of time.

If after such dissolution the House of Representatives again passes the proposed law, with or without any amendments which have been made, suggested, or agreed to by the Senate, and the Senate rejects or fails to pass it, or passes it with amendments to which the House of Representatives will not agree, the Governor-General may convene a joint sitting of the members of the Senate and of the House of Representatives.

The members present at the joint sitting may deliberate and shall vote together upon the proposed law as last proposed by the House of Representatives, and upon amendments, if any, which have been made therein by one House and not agreed to by the other, and any such amendments which are affirmed by an absolute majority of the total number of the members of the Senate and House of Representatives shall be taken to have been carried, and if the proposed law, with the amendments, if any, so carried is affirmed by an absolute majority of the total number of the members of the Senate and House of Representatives, it shall be taken to have been duly passed by both Houses of the Parliament, and shall be presented to the Governor-General for the Queen's assent.

**58. Royal assent to Bills.**—When a proposed law passed by both Houses of the Parliament is presented to the Governor-General for the Queen's assent, he shall declare, according to his discretion, but subject to this Constitution, that he assents in the Queen's name, or that he withholds assent, or that he reserves the law for the Queen's pleasure.

**Recommendations by Governor-General.**—The Governor-General may return to the house in which it originated any proposed law so presented to him, and may transmit therewith any amendments which he may recommend, and the Houses may deal with the recommendation.

**59. Disallowance by the Queen.**—The Queen may disallow any law within one year from the Governor-General's assent, and such disallowance on being made known by the Governor-General by speech or message to each of the Houses of the Parliament, or by Proclamation, shall annul the law from the day when the disallowance is so made known.

**60. Signification of Queen's pleasure on Bills reserved.**—A proposed law reserved for the Queen's pleasure shall not have any force unless and until within two years from the day on which it was presented to the Governor-General for the Queen's assent the Governor-General makes known, by speech or message to each of the Houses of the Parliament, or by Proclamation, that it has received the Queen's assent.

---

## CHAPTER II.

### The Executive Government.

**61. Executive power.**—The executive power of the Commonwealth is vested in the Queen and is exerciseable by the Governor-General as the Queen's representative, and extends to the execution and maintenance of this Constitution, and of the laws of the Commonwealth.

**62. Federal Executive Council.**—There shall be a Federal Executive Council to advise the Governor-General in the government of the Commonwealth, and the members of the Council shall be chosen and summoned by the Governor-General and sworn as Executive Councillors, and shall hold office during his pleasure.

**63. Provisions referring to Governor-General.**—The provisions of this Constitution referring to the Governor-General in Council shall be construed as referring to the Governor-General acting with the advice of the Federal Executive Council.

**64. Ministers of State.**—The Governor-General may appoint officers to administer such departments of State of the Commonwealth as the Governor-General in Council may establish.

Such officers shall hold office during the pleasure of the Governor-General. They shall be members of the Federal Executive Council, and shall be the Queen's Ministers of State for the Commonwealth.

**Ministers to sit in Parliament.**—After the first general election no Minister of State shall hold office for a longer period than three months unless he is or becomes a senator or a member of the House of Representatives.

**65. Number of Ministers.**—Until the Parliament otherwise provides, the Ministers of State shall not exceed seven in number, and shall hold such offices as the Parliament prescribes, or, in the absence of provision, as the Governor-General directs.

**66. Salaries of Ministers.**—There shall be payable to the Queen, out of the Consolidated Revenue Fund of the Commonwealth, for the salaries of the Ministers of State, an annual sum which, until the Parliament otherwise provides, shall not exceed twelve thousand pounds a year.

**67. Appointment of civil servants.**—Until the Parliament otherwise provides, the appointment and removal of all other officers of the Executive Government of the Commonwealth shall be vested in the Governor-General in Council, unless the appointment is delegated by the Governor-General in Council or by a law of the Commonwealth to some other authority.

**68. Command of naval and military forces.**—The command in chief of the naval and military forces of the Commonwealth is vested in the Governor-General as the Queen's representative.

**69. Transfer of certain departments.**—On a date or dates to be proclaimed by the Governor-General after the establishment of the Commonwealth the following departments of the public service in each State shall become transferred to the Commonwealth:—

Posts, telegraphs, and telephones:
Naval and military defence:
Lighthouses, lightships, beacons, and buoys:
Quarantine.

But the departments of customs and of excise in each State shall become transferred to the Commonwealth on its establishment.

**70. Certain powers of Governors to vest in Governor-General.**—In respect of matters which, under this Constitution, pass to the Executive Government of the Commonwealth, all powers and functions which at the establishment of the Commonwealth are vested in the Governor of a Colony, or in the Governor of a Colony with the advice of his Executive Council, or in any authority of a Colony, shall vest in the Governor-General, or in the Governor-General in Council, or in the authority exercising similar powers under the Commonwealth, as the case requires.

---

## CHAPTER III.

### THE JUDICATURE.

**71. Judicial power and Courts.**—The judicial power of the Commonwealth shall be vested in a Federal Supreme Court, to be called the High Court of Australia, and in such other federal courts as the Parliament creates, and in such other courts as it invests with federal jurisdiction. The High Court shall consist of a Chief Justice, and so many other Justices, not less than two, as the Parliament prescribes.

**72. Judges' appointment tenure, and remuneration.**—The Justices of the High Court and of the other courts created by the Parliament—

(i) Shall be appointed by the Governor-General in Council:

(ii) Shall not be removed except by the Governor-General in Council, on an address from both Houses of the Parliament in the same session, praying for such removal on the ground of proved misbehaviour or incapacity:

(iii) Shall receive such remuneration as the Parliament may fix; but the remuneration shall not be diminished during their continuance in office.

**73. Appellate jurisdiction of High Court.**—The High Court shall have jurisdiction, with such exceptions and subject to such regulations as the Parliament prescribes, to hear and determine appeals from all judgments, decrees, orders, and sentences—

(i) Of any Justice or Justices exercising the original jurisdiction of the High Court:

(ii) Of any other federal court, or court exercising federal jurisdiction; or of the Supreme Court of any State, or of any other court of any State from which at the establishment of the Commonwealth an appeal lies to the Queen in Council:

(iii) Of the Inter-State Commission, but as to questions of law only:

and the judgment of the High Court in all such cases shall be final and conclusive.

378

But no exception or regulation prescribed by the Parliament shall prevent the High Court from hearing and determining any appeal from the Supreme Court of a State in any matter in which at the establishment of the Commonwealth an appeal lies from such Supreme Court to the Queen in Council.

Until the Parliament otherwise provides, the conditions of and restrictions on appeals to the Queen in Council from the Supreme Courts of the several States shall be applicable to appeals from them to the High Court.

**74. Appeal to Queen in Council.**—No appeal shall be permitted to the Queen in Council from a decision of the High Court upon any question, howsoever arising, as to the limits inter se of the Constitutional powers of the Commonwealth and those of any State or States, or as to the limits inter se of the Constitutional powers of any two or more States, unless the High Court shall certify that the question is one which ought to be determined by Her Majesty in Council.

The High Court may so certify if satisfied that for any special reason the certificate should be granted, and thereupon an appeal shall lie to Her Majesty in Council on the question without further leave.

Except as provided in this section, this Constitution shall not impair any right which the Queen may be pleased to exercise by virtue of Her Royal prerogative to grant special leave of appeal from the High Court to Her Majesty in Council. The Parliament may make laws limiting the matters in which such leave may be asked, but proposed laws containing any such limitation shall be reserved by the Governor-General for Her Majesty's pleasure.

**75. Original jurisdiction of High Court.**—In all matters—

(i) Arising under any treaty:

(ii) Affecting consuls or other representatives of other countries:

(iii) In which the Commonwealth, or a person suing or being sued on behalf of the Commonwealth, is a party:

(iv) Between States, or between residents of different States, or between a State and a resident of another State:

(v) In which a writ of mandamus or prohibition or an injunction is sought against an officer of the Commonwealth:

the High Court shall have original jurisdiction.

**76. Additional original jurisdiction.**—The Parliament may make laws conferring original jurisdiction on the High Court in any matter—

(i) Arising under this Constitution, or involving its interpretation:

(ii) Arising under any laws made by the Parliament:

(iii) Of Admiralty and maritime jurisdiction:

(iv) Relating to the same subject-matter claimed under the laws of different States.

**77. Power to define jurisdiction.**—With respect to any of the matters mentioned in the last two sections the Parliament may make laws—

(i) Defining the jurisdiction of any federal court other than the High Court:

(ii) Defining the extent to which the jurisdiction of any federal court shall be exclusive of that which belongs to or is invested in the courts of the States:

(iii) Investing any court of a State with federal jurisdiction.

**78. Proceedings against Commonwealth or State.**—The Parliament may make laws conferring rights to proceed against the Commonwealth or a State in respect of matters within the limits of the judicial power.

**79. Number of judges.**—The federal jurisdiction of any court may be exercised by such number of judges as the Parliament prescribes.

**80. Trial by jury.**—The trial on indictment of any offence against any law of the Commonwealth shall be by jury, and every such trial shall be held in the State where the offence was committed, and if the offence was not committed within any State the trial shall be held at such place or places as the Parliament prescribes.

---

## CHAPTER IV.

### FINANCE AND TRADE.

**81. Consolidated Revenue Fund.**—All revenues or moneys raised or received by the Executive Government of the Commonwealth shall form one Consolidated Revenue Fund, to be appropriated for the purposes of the Commonwealth in the manner and subject to the charges and liabilities imposed by this Constitution.

**82. Expenditure charged thereon.**—The costs, charges, and expenses incident to the collection, management, and receipt of the Consolidated Revenue Fund shall form the first charge thereon; and the revenue of the Commonwealth shall in the first instance be applied to the payment of the expenditure of the Commonwealth.

**83. Money to be appropriated by law.**—No money shall be drawn from the Treasury of the Commonwealth except under appropriation made by law.

But until the expiration of one month after the first meeting of the Parliament the Governor-General in Council may draw from the Treasury and expend such moneys as may be necessary for the maintenance of any department transferred to the Commonwealth and for the holding of the first elections for the Parliament.

**84. Transfer of officers.**—When any department of the public service of a State becomes transferred to the Commonwealth, all officers of the department shall become subject to the control of the Executive Government of the Commonwealth.

Any such officer who is not retained in the service of the Commonwealth shall, unless he is appointed to some other office of equal emolument in the public service of the State, be entitled to receive from the State any pension, gratuity, or other compensation, payable under the law of the State on the abolition of his office.

Any such officer who is retained in the service of the Commonwealth shall preserve all his existing and accruing rights, and shall be entitled to retire from office at the time, and on the pension or retiring allowance, which would be permitted by the law of the State if his service with the Commonwealth were a continuation of his service with the State. Such pension or retiring allowance shall be paid to him by the Commonwealth; but the State shall pay to the Commonwealth a part thereof, to be calculated on the proportion which his term of service with the State bears to his whole term of service, and for the purpose of the calculation his salary shall be taken to be that paid to him by the State at the time of the transfer.

Any officer who is, at the establishment of the Commonwealth, in the public service of a State, and who is, by consent of the Governor of the State with the advice of the Executive Council thereof, transferred to the public service of the Commonwealth, shall have the same rights as if he had been an officer of a department transferred to the Commonwealth and were retained in the service of the Commonwealth.

**85. Transfer of property of State.**—When any department of the public service of a State is transferred to the Commonwealth—

(i) All property of the State of any kind, used exclusively in connexion with the department, shall become vested in the Commonwealth; but, in the case of the departments controlling customs and excise and bounties, for such time only as the Governor-General in Council may declare to be necessary:

(ii) The Commonwealth may acquire any property of the State, of any kind used, but not exclusively used in connexion with the department; the value thereof shall, if no agreement can be made, be ascertained in, as nearly as may be, the manner in which the value of land, or of an interest in land, taken by the State for public purposes is ascertained under the law of the State in force at the establishment of the Commonwealth:

(iii) The Commonwealth shall compensate the State for the value of any property passing to the Commonwealth under this section; if no agreement can be made as to the mode of compensation, it shall be determined under laws to be made by the Parliament:

(iv) The Commonwealth shall, at the date of the transfer, assume the current obligations of the State in respect of the department transferred.

**86.**—On the establishment of the Commonwealth, the collection and control of duties of customs and of excise, and the control of the payment of bounties, shall pass to the Executive Government of the Commonwealth.

**87.**—During a period of ten years after the establishment of the Commonwealth and thereafter until the Parliament otherwise provides, of the net revenue of the Commonwealth from duties of customs and of excise not more than one-fourth shall be applied annually by the Commonwealth towards its expenditure.

The balance shall, in accordance with this Constitution, be paid to the several States, or applied towards the payment of interest on debts of the several States taken over by the Commonwealth.

**88. Uniform duties of customs.**—Uniform duties of customs shall be imposed within two years after the establishment of the Commonwealth.

**89. Payment to States before uniform duties.**—Until the imposition of uniform duties of customs—

(i) The Commonwealth shall credit to each State the revenues collected therein by the Commonwealth.

(ii) The Commonwealth shall debit to each State—

(a) The expenditure therein of the Commonwealth incurred solely for the maintenance or continuance, as at the time of transfer, of any department transferred from the State to the Commonwealth;

(b) The proportion of the State, according to the number of its people, in the other expenditure of the Commonwealth.

(iii) The Commonwealth shall pay to each State month by month the balance (if any) in favour of the State.

**90. Exclusive power over customs, excise, and bounties.**—On the imposition of uniform duties of customs the power of the Parliament to impose duties of customs and of excise, and to grant bounties on the production or export of goods, shall become exclusive.

On the imposition of uniform duties of customs all laws of the several States imposing duties of customs or of excise, or offering bounties on the production or export of goods, shall cease to have effect, but any grant of or agreement for any such bounty lawfully made by or under the authority of the Government of any State shall be taken to be good if made before the thirtieth day of June, one thousand eight hundred and ninety-eight, and not otherwise.

**91. Exceptions as to bounties.**—Nothing in this Constitution prohibits a State from granting any aid to or bounty on mining for gold, silver, or other metals, nor from granting, with the consent of both Houses of the Parliament of the Commonwealth expressed by resolution, any aid to or bounty on the production or export of goods.

**92. Trade within the Commonwealth to be free.**—On the imposition of uniform duties of customs, trade, commerce, and intercourse among the States, whether by means of internal carriage or ocean navigation, shall be absolutely free.

But notwithstanding anything in this Constitution, goods imported before the imposition of uniform duties of customs into any State, or into any Colony which, whilst the goods remain therein, becomes a State, shall, on thence passing into another State within two years after the imposition of such duties, be liable to any duty chargeable on the importation of such goods into the Commonwealth, less any duty paid in respect of the goods on their importation.

**93. Payment to States for five years after uniform tariffs.**—During the first five years after the imposition of uniform duties of customs, and thereafter until the Parliament otherwise provides—

(i) The duties of customs chargeable on goods imported into a State and afterwards passing into another State for consumption, and the duties of excise paid on goods produced or manufactured in a State and afterwards passing into another State for consumption, shall be taken to have been collected not in the former but in the latter State:

(ii) Subject to the last subsection, the Commonwealth shall credit revenue, debit expenditure, and pay balances to the several States as prescribed for the period preceding the imposition of uniform duties of customs.

**94. Distribution of surplus.**—After five years from the imposition of uniform duties of customs, the Parliament may provide, on such basis as it deems fair, for the monthly payment to the several States of all surplus revenue of the Commonwealth.

**95. Customs duties of Western Australia.**—Notwithstanding anything in this Constitution, the Parliament of the State of Western Australia, if that State be an Original State, may, during the first five years after the imposition of uniform duties of customs, impose duties of customs on goods passing into that State and not originally imported from beyond the limits of the Commonwealth; and such duties shall be collected by the Commonwealth.

But any duty so imposed on any goods shall not exceed during the first of such years the duty chargeable on the goods under the law of Western

Australia in force at the imposition of uniform duties, and shall not exceed during the second, third, fourth, and fifth of such years respectively, four-fifths, three-fifths, two-fifths, and one-fifth of such latter duty, and all duties imposed under this section shall cease at the expiration of the fifth year after the imposition of uniform duties.

If at any time during the five years the duty on any goods under this section is higher than the duty imposed by the Commonwealth on the importation of the like goods, then such higher duty shall be collected on the goods when imported into Western Australia from beyond the limits of the Commonwealth.

**96. Financial assistance to States.**—During a period of ten years after the establishment of the Commonwealth and thereafter until the Parliament otherwise provides, the Parliament may grant financial assistance to any State on such terms and conditions as the Parliament thinks fit.

**97. Audit.**—Until the Parliament otherwise provides, the laws in force in any Colony which has become or becomes a State with respect to the receipt of revenue and the expenditure of money on account of the Government of the Colony, and the review and audit of such receipt and expenditure, shall apply to the receipt of revenue and the expenditure of money on account of the Commonwealth in the State in the same manner as if the Commonwealth, or the Government or an officer of the Commonwealth, were mentioned whenever the Colony, or the Government or an officer of the Colony, is mentioned.

**98. Trade and commerce includes navigation and State railways.**—The power of the Parliament to make laws with respect to trade and commerce extends to navigation and shipping, and to railways the property of any State.

**99. Commonwealth not to give preference.**—The Commonwealth shall not, by any law or regulation of trade, commerce, or revenue, give preference to one State or any part thereof over another State or any part thereof.

**100. Not abridge right to use water.**—The Commonwealth shall not, by any law or regulation of trade or commerce, abridge the right of a State or of the residents therein to the reasonable use of the waters of rivers for conservation or irrigation.

**101. Inter-State Commission.**—There shall be an Inter-State Commission, with such powers of adjudication and administration as the Parliament deems necessary for the execution and maintenance, within the Commonwealth, of the provisions of this Constitution relating to trade and commerce, and of all laws made thereunder.

**102. Parliament may forbid preferences by State.**—The Parliament may by any law with respect to trade or commerce forbid, as to railways, any preference or discrimination by any State, or by any authority constituted under a State, if such preference or discrimination is undue and unreasonable, or unjust to any State; due regard being had to the financial responsibilities incurred by any State in connexion with the construction and maintenance of its railways. But no preference or discrimination shall, within the meaning of this section, be taken to be undue and unreasonable, or unjust to any State, unless so adjudged by the Inter-State Commission.

**103. Commissioners' appointment, tenure, and remuneration.**—The members of the Inter-State Commission—

383

(i) Shall be appointed by the Governor-General in Council:

(ii) Shall hold office for seven years, but may be removed within that time by the Governor-General in Council, on an address from both Houses of the Parliament in the same session praying for such removal on the ground of proved misbehaviour or incapacity:

(iii) Shall receive such remuneration as the Parliament may fix; but such remuneration shall not be diminished during their continuance in office.

**104. Saving of certain rates.**—Nothing in this Constitution shall render unlawful any rate for the carriage of goods upon a railway, the property of a State, if the rate is deemed by the Inter-State Commission to be necessary for the development of the territory of the State, and if the rate applies equally to goods within the State and to goods passing into the State from other States.

**105. Taking over public debts of States.**—The Parliament may take over from the States their public debts or a proportion thereof according to the respective numbers of their people as shown by the latest statistics of the Commonwealth, and may convert, renew, or consolidate such debts, or any part thereof; and the States shall indemnify the Commonwealth in respect of the debts taken over, and thereafter the interest payable in respect of the debts shall be deducted and retained from the portions of the surplus revenue of the Commonwealth payable to the several States, or if such surplus is insufficient, or if there is no surplus, then the deficiency or the whole amount shall be paid by the several States.

[S 105 *altered, Act No. 3, 1910 s 2.*]

**105A. Agreements with respect to State debts.**—(1) The Commonwealth may make agreements with the States with respect to the public debts of the States, including—

(a) the taking over of such debts by the Commonwealth;

(b) the management of such debts;

(c) the payment of interest and the provision and management of sinking funds in respect of such debts;

(d) the consolidation, renewal, conversion, and redemption of such debts;

(e) the indemnification of the Commonwealth by the States in respect of debts taken over by the Commonwealth; and

(f) the borrowing of money by the States or by the Commonwealth, or by the Commonwealth for the States.

(2) The Parliament may make laws for validating any such agreement made before the commencement of this section.

(3) The Parliament may make laws for the carrying out by the parties thereto of any such agreement.

(4) Any such agreement may be varied or rescinded by the parties thereto.

(5) Every such agreement and any such variation thereof shall be binding upon the Commonwealth and the States parties thereto notwithstanding anything contained in this Constitution or the Constitution of the several States or in any law of the Parliament of the Commonwealth or of any State.

(6) The powers conferred by this section shall not be construed as being limited in any way by the provisions of section one hundred and five of this Constitution.

[S 105A *inserted, Act No. 1, 1929 s 2.*]

## CHAPTER V.

### THE STATES.

**106. Saving of Constitutions.**—The Constitution of each State of the Commonwealth shall, subject to this Constitution, continue as at the establishment of the Commonwealth, or as at the admission or establishment of the State, as the case may be, until altered in accordance with the Constitution of the State.

**107. Saving of Power of State Parliaments.**—Every power of the Parliament of a Colony which has become or becomes a State, shall, unless it is by this Constitution exclusively vested in the Parliament of the Commonwealth or withdrawn from the Parliament of the State, continue as at the establishment of the Commonwealth, or as at the admission or establishment of the State, as the case may be.

**108. Saving of State laws.**—Every law in force in a Colony which has become or becomes a State, and relating to any matter within the powers of the Parliament of the Commonwealth, shall, subject to this Constitution, continue in force in the State; and, until provision is made in that behalf by the Parliament of the Commonwealth, the Parliament of the State shall have such powers of alteration and of repeal in respect of any such law as the Parliament of the Colony had until the Colony became a State.

**109. Inconsistency of laws.**—When a law of a State is inconsistent with a law of the Commonwealth, the latter shall prevail, and the former shall, to the extent of the inconsistency, be invalid.

**110. Provisions referring to Governor.**—The provisions of this Constitution relating to the Governor of a State extend and apply to the Governor for the time being of the State, or other chief executive officer or administrator of the government of the State.

**111. States may surrender territory.**—The Parliament of a State may surrender any part of the State to the Commonwealth; and upon such surrender, and the acceptance thereof by the Commonwealth, such part of the State shall become subject to the exclusive jurisdiction of the Commonwealth.

**112. States may levy charges for inspection laws.**—After uniform duties of customs have been imposed, a State may levy on imports or exports, or on goods passing into or out of the State, such charges as may be necessary for executing the inspection laws of the State; but the net produce of all charges so levied shall be for the use of the Commonwealth; and any such inspection laws may be annulled by the Parliament of the Commonwealth.

**113. Intoxicating liquids.**—All fermented, distilled, or other intoxicating liquids passing into any State or remaining therein for use, consumption, sale, or storage, shall be subject to the laws of the State as if such liquids had been produced in the State.

**114. States may not raise forces. Taxation of property of Commonwealth or State.**—A State shall not, without the consent of the Parliament of the Commonwealth, raise or maintain any naval or military force, or impose any tax on property of any kind belonging to the Commonwealth, nor shall the Commonwealth impose any tax on property of any kind belonging to a State.

**115. States not to coin money.**—A State shall not coin money, nor make anything but gold and silver coin a legal tender in payment of debts.

**116. Commonwealth not to legislate in respect of religion.**—The Commonwealth shall not make any law for establishing any religion, or for imposing any religious observance, or for prohibiting the free exercise of any religion, and no religious test shall be required as a qualification for any office or public trust under the Commonwealth.

**117. Rights of residents in States.**—A subject of the Queen, resident in any State, shall not be subject in any other State to any disability or discrimination which would not be equally applicable to him if he were a subject of the Queen resident in such other State.

**118. Recognition of laws, etc., of States.**—Full faith and credit shall be given, throughout the Commonwealth to the laws, the public Acts and records, and the judicial proceedings of every State.

**119. Protection of States from invasion and violence.**—The Commonwealth shall protect every State against invasion and, on the application of the Executive Government of the State, against domestic violence.

**120. Custody of offenders against laws of the Commonwealth.**—Every State shall make provision for the detention in its prisons of persons accused or convicted of offences against the laws of the Commonwealth, and for the punishment of persons convicted of such offences, and the Parliament of the Commonwealth may make laws to give effect to this provision.

---

## CHAPTER VI.

### New States.

**121. New States may be admitted or established.**—The Parliament may admit to the Commonwealth or establish new States, and may upon such admission or establishment make or impose such terms and conditions, including the extent of representation in either House of the Parliament, as it thinks fit.

**122. Government of territories.**—The Parliament may make laws for the government of any territory surrendered by any State to and accepted by the Commonwealth, or of any territory placed by the Queen under the authority of and accepted by the Commonwealth, or otherwise acquired by the Commonwealth, and may allow the representation of such territory in either House of the Parliament to the extent and on the terms which it thinks fit.

**123. Alteration of limits of States.**—The Parliament of the Commonwealth may, with the consent of the Parliament of a State, and the approval of the majority of the electors of the State voting upon the question, increase, diminish, or otherwise alter the limits of the State, upon such terms and conditions as may be agreed on, and may, with the like consent, make provision respecting the effect and operation of any increase or diminution or alteration of territory in relation to any State affected.

**124. Formation of new States.**—A new State may be formed by separation of territory from a State, but only with the consent of the Parliament thereof, and a new State may be formed by the union of two or more States or parts of States, but only with the consent of the Parliaments of the States affected.

## CHAPTER VII.

### Miscellaneous.

**125. Seat of Government.**—The seat of Government of the Commonwealth shall be determined by the Parliament, and shall be within territory which shall have been granted to or acquired by the Commonwealth, and shall be vested in and belong to the Commonwealth, and shall be in the State of New South Wales, and be distant not less than one hundred miles from Sydney.

Such territory shall contain an area of not less than one hundred square miles, and such portion thereof as shall consist of Crown lands shall be granted to the Commonwealth without any payment therefor.

The Parliament shall sit at Melbourne until it meet at the seat of Government.

**126. Power to Her Majesty to authorise Governor-General to appoint deputies.**—The Queen may authorise the Governor-General to appoint any person, or any persons jointly or severally, to be his deputy or deputies within any part of the Commonwealth, and in that capacity to exercise during the pleasure of the Governor-General such powers and functions of the Governor-General as he thinks fit to assign to such deputy or deputies, subject to any limitations expressed or directions given by the Queen; but the appointment of such deputy or deputies shall not affect the exercise by the Governor-General himself of any power or function.

[S 127 *repealed, Act No.* 55, 1967 *s* 3.]

---

## CHAPTER   VIII.

### Alteration of the Constitution.

**128. Mode of altering the Constitution.**—This Constitution shall not be altered except in the following manner:—

The proposed law for the alteration thereof must be passed by an absolute majority of each House of the Parliament, and not less than two nor more than six months after its passage through both Houses the proposed law shall be submitted in each State to the electors qualified to vote for the election of members of the House of Representatives.

But if either House passes any such proposed law by an absolute majority, and the other House rejects or fails to pass it, or passes it with any amendment to which the first-mentioned House will not agree, and if after an interval of three months the first-mentioned House in the same or the next session again passes the proposed law by an absolute majority with or without any amendment which has been made or agreed to by the other House, and such other House rejects or fails to pass it or passes it with any amendment to which the first-mentioned House will not agree, the Governor-General may submit the proposed law as last proposed by the first-mentioned House, and either with or without any amendments subsequently agreed to by both Houses, to the electors in each State qualified to vote for the election of the House of Representatives.

When a proposed law is submitted to the electors the vote shall be taken in such manner as the Parliament prescribes. But until the qualification of electors of members of the House of Representatives becomes uniform throughout the Commonwealth, only one-half the electors voting for and against the proposed law shall be counted in any State in which adult suffrage prevails.

And if in a majority of the States a majority of the electors voting approve the proposed law, and if a majority of all the electors voting also approve the proposed law, it shall be presented to the Governor-General for the Queen's assent.

No alteration diminishing the proportionate representation of any State in either House of the Parliament, or the minimum number of representatives of a State in the House of Representatives, of increasing, diminishing, or otherwise altering the limits of the State, or in any manner affecting the provisions of the Constitution in relation thereto, shall become law unless the majority of the electors voting in that State approve the proposed law.

---

## SCHEDULE.

---

### OATH.

I, A.B., do swear that I will be faithful and bear true allegiance to Her Majesty Queen Victoria, Her heirs and successors according to law. So HELP ME GOD!

### AFFIRMATION.

I, A.B., do solemnly and sincerely affirm and declare that I will be faithful and bear true allegiance to Her Majesty Queen Victoria, Her heirs and successors according to law.

(NOTE.—*The name of the King or Queen of the United Kingdom of Great Britain and Ireland for the time being is to be substituted from time to time.*)

# INDEX

389

395

**National Service,** see **Defence**

**Nationality,** see **Naturalization**

**Nationalization,** see **Freedom of Interstate Trade**

**Naturalization**
generally, 122
citizenship, loss of, 123
Parliament, membership of, effect on, 44, 57
residence and, 123, 343
   see also **Aliens; Elections; Immigration; Parliament**

**Naval Forces,** see **Armed Forces; Defence**

**Navigation**
air, 148
British ships, and, 27
on high seas, 184
trade and commerce, and, 49
   see also **Lighthouses**

**New States**
borders of, 353, 354
establishment of, 349, 354
representation of, 37, 49, 349

**Nexus,** see **House of Representatives; Senate**

**Northern Territory**
surrender to Commonwealth, 336
   see also **Territories**

**Oath,** 361
   see also **Naturalization; Parliament**

**Office of Profit**
anomaly, 59
disqualification for holding, 59, 217, 218
exception, 59
ministry, and, 217, 218
   see also **Ministry; Parliament**

**Orders-in-Council,** see **Governor-General**-in-Council

**Original States**
representation of, 37, 46, 49

**"Otherwise Provides"**
generally, 181
continuance of colonial laws, 329-331
   see also **Parliament**

**Pacific Islands**
protectorate status, 153
relations with Commonwealth, 153
   see also **Inconsistency; Racial Distinctions**

**Paramountcy**
Commonwealth legislation, of, 331
Imperial legislation, of, 184
   see also **Imperial Legislation; Inconsistency**

**Pardons,** see **Prerogative**

**Parliament, Commonwealth**
actions against Commonwealth or States, and, 267-268
affirmation, 57
bicameral, 31
broadcasting of, 63
committees, 37, 63
common informers action and, 58, 61
composition of, 31
concurrent powers, 67, 327, 329
contempt of, 64
court, as, 61, 62 et seq.
Court of Disputed Returns and, 43, 61
delegation of powers, 31, 67, 211
disqualification from membership of, 57 et seq., 60
dissolution of, 32, 34, 206 et seq., 218
electorates, 50
exclusive powers, 67, 190 et seq., 327, 329
federal courts, and, 258 et seq.
immunities of, 65-66

interchangeability, 57
joint sittings of Houses of, 206, 208
limitation on powers of, 67
members of
  allowances of, 60, 62
  control of, 61, 63
  penalty if disqualified, 61
  qualification of, 44, 52, 61
oath, 57
papers of, 63
"peace, order and good government", 67
powers of
  generally, 62 et seq., 74 et seq.
  to confer original jurisdiction on High Court, 253 et seq.
powers of Governor-General in relation to, 34
privileges, 63
prorogation of, 35
responsible government, 31
retrospective laws, 68, 143
sanction for appropriation, 213
Senate elections, provisions for, 39, 43
sessions, 35, 36
sittings, 33
standing orders, 63, 66, 189
State borders, and, 353-354
term, 35, 49, 50
vote in referenda, 46
   see also **Bankruptcy; Concurrent Powers; Elections; Electors; Exclusive Powers; Executive; House of Representatives; Ministry; Prime Minister; Queen; Senate; Separation of Powers; Ultra Vires**

**Parliament, States,** see **States**

**Patents**
generally, 121
definition, 121
   see also **Copyright; Parliament; Trademarks;**

**Payroll Tax,** see **Taxation**

**"Peace, Order and Good Government",** see **Parliament**

**Pensions**
generally, 132
powers in relation to, concurrent, 132
types of, 132
   see also **Parliament; Social Services**

**Petroleum**
Federal-State co-operation, and, 183
offshore, 246
   see also **Continental Shelf**

**Pharmaceutical Benefits,** see **Social Services**

**Places**
acquired by Commonwealth, exclusive power over, 190

**Plural Voting,** see **House of Representatives; Senate**

**Police, Commonwealth**
protection of constitutional laws and organs, 214
   see also **Executive Power; Parliament**

**Polling,** see **Elections**

**Pooling,** see **Acquisition**

**Posts and Telegraphs**
Australian Broadcasting Commission, 93
licence, 93
"pirate broadcasting", 94
services generally, 93
"tapping", 95
telecommunications, 95
television and, 93
transfer from States, 93
   see also **Parliament**

400